FISCAL LEADERSHIP *for* SCHOOLS

CONCEPTS *and* PRACTICES

DAVID C. THOMPSON
Kansas State University

R. CRAIG WOOD
University of Florida

DAVID S. HONEYMAN
University of Florida

Longman
New York & London

Fiscal Leadership for Schools: Concepts and Practices

Longman, 10 Bank Street, White Plains, N.Y. 10606

Associated companies:
Longman Group Ltd., London
Longman Cheshire Pty., Melbourne
Longman Paul Pty., Auckland
Copp Clark Pitman, Toronto

To Our Wives

Acquisitions editor: Stuart B. Miller
Sponsoring editor: Raymond T. O'Connell
Development editor: Virginia L. Blanford
Production editor: Ann P. Kearns
Cover design: Kevin C. Kall
Text art: Fine Line, Inc.
Production supervisor: Anne P. Armeny

Library of Congress Cataloging-in-Publication Data

Thompson, David C.
    Fiscal leadership for schools : concepts and practices / David C.
Thompson, R. Craig Wood, David S. Honeyman.
        p.   cm.
    Includes bibliographical references (p.).
    ISBN 0-8013-0809-7
    1. Education—United States—Finance. 2. Public schools—United
States—Business management. 3. Education and state—United States.
4. Education—United States—Finance—Planning. I. Wood, R. Craig.
II. Honeyman, David Smith. III. Title.
LB2825.T53 1992
371.2′06′0973—dc20   93-19860
                                                    CIP

1 2 3 4 5 6 7 8 9 10-MA-9796959493

Contents

Preface

WHY THIS BOOK?

This book arose from the perceived need for a different textbook for courses in school finance and school business management—a text that would bridge the conceptual division that we have encountered in our own teaching in major universities across the country. We wanted to develop a textbook that reflects *how we teach* and how we think many other professors teach—namely, our focused approach begins with the foundations of education finance theory and culminates with a vigorous introduction into how theory is translated into practice. The idea arose that this text needed to be a *principles-to-policy-to-practice* book that would

- ground students of education finance in the principles of sound finance, and then
- facilitate the transmission of those principles into the concept of how fiscal activities are actually set in motion (and with what consequences) in the real word of school fiscal administration.

Fiscal Leadership for Schools: Concepts and Practices introduces the elements and concepts of sound education finance theory, extends those concepts to the practice of education finance and fiscal management in a practical way, and dispels many of the old attitudes about education finance and fiscal management that no longer hold in today's complex sociopolitical environment. If administrators are to meet the needs of children in the competitive intellectual and resource-driven environment of the twenty-first century, they must become knowledgeable and trained *fiscal leaders*. Hence this book is aimed at everyone in the school business and is driven by our belief that money makes a difference. Children will suffer if educators at all levels do not understand and appreciate the critical value of adequate and equitable resources, and this task weighs most heavily on those charged with the overall leadership of schools.

WHO IS THIS BOOK FOR?

We have just said that this book is for *everyone* who is involved in the business of schools. Education finance is complex and vital because it exists on multiple planes: conceptual/theoretical; economic/political; operational/managerial. To address the nature of this complexity, we first aim at students who are being introduced to the exciting discipline of education finance for the first time. For these students, the text begins at the roots of today's issues and builds toward progressively higher conceptual levels. We hope that professors of education finance and fiscal management will find here a challenging primary text for their students, as well as a valuable resource for themselves. We also aim at practicing administrators who, for whatever reason, find themselves seeking further knowledge about school fiscal affairs. For these administrators, the text provides an excellent review of concepts and perhaps casts new and different light on issues, given the freshness of its data and its intense focus on political environments. Finally we hope this book will prove useful to a larger audience of policymakers in the area of school finance and of classroom teachers, because we believe that enlightenment about education finance ought not to be reserved for the anointed or the appointed but should be accessible to all those involved in education.

HOW IS THIS BOOK ORGANIZED?

Fiscal Leadership for Schools comprises fourteen chapters, divided into two groups. The topics in these parts represent the vehicle through which fiscal leaders in school settings may carry out sound education finance theory. In other words, we argue throughout this book that *education finance theory and fiscal operations cannot be, and ought not to be, disconnected,* but should instead be linked into a vibrant, interactive mode that will assist both new students and practicing administrators in perceiving the interconnectedness (and the consequences of the *failure* to interconnect) of this exciting discipline.

Part I, "Principles and Foundations of School Finance," includes chapters on the social and economic context of public school finance; the origins of modern public schools including their financing; sources of revenue for public schools; specific and detailed exploration of how schools are funded; and the role that the courts have played in shaping modern education. These topics provide a strong basis for understanding the sociopolitical and technolegal structure of education finance.

In Part II, "Primary Functions of School Fiscal Leadership," we explore the actual tasks performed by fiscal administrators in schools. Although we recognize that these chapters might be ordered in a variety of ways, we have chosen to present them according to the broad theme of fiscal *planning.* We therefore consider in some depth the concepts and practices of effective planning in a number of crucial areas: budgeting; accounting, auditing, and reporting; fiscal aspects of personnel administration; purchasing, inventory, distribution, and control; risk management; transportation and food management; capital outlay, maintenance, and operations; and technology in educational decision making.

Finally, the Conclusion, "School Fiscal Leadership and the Future," reviews in a single chapter the themes of the book and prognosticates about the future.

Our intent to write a principles-to-policy-to-practice text is evidenced in the structure of both the text and its individual chapters: each begins with theory and ends with observations and applications to practice. Each chapter comprises an academic essay laced with applications, accompanied by a list of additional readings from "great books" in the discipline. The chapter proper ends with Review Points, followed by a *case study* with its guided discussion questions. The case studies are not contrived—*each case study is a real life scenario* experienced by one of the authors, a problem that had to be resolved by that person within the context of school, community, board, legal, and political environments. Our goal throughout this text has been to integrate sound theory, wise practice, and current data in the context of real life experiences.

The structure of this book, then, reflects a policy perspective for diversely experienced audiences. Its goal is understanding and enlightenment, which we hope to achieve by offering current data and by presenting alternative perspectives, in an attempt to avoid inappropriate advocacy for any single position. Our only bias—one that we happily and proudly admit—is an unabashed concern for children. We are, however, cognizant of a fundamentally imperfect world in which human needs will inevitably outstrip available resources. We do not, therefore, reach for the impossible; rather, we try to confine ourselves to the best, but not the perfect, solution. This approach should not be mistaken for compromise. We continue to make harsh and strident demands for constant vigilance to assure that children are the focus of all educational activity. They represent the best—the *only*—hope for the future. We stand firm in averring that the future depends heavily on *fiscal leadership for schools* and the intelligent interaction of *concepts and practices,* which must be common to the core of effective schools.

ACKNOWLEDGMENTS

Given all the foregoing, we are obviously deeply indebted to our reviewers who labored long over this text. Without their assistance the quality would be less, and our pride in this book is increased by the stature of our reviewers. Although the list is long, such an extensive review stands as a commendation to the text and to us. Clearly a book that withstands the tremendous knowledge held by these reviewers has real promise to make a valuable contribution to the literature of education finance. Accordingly, we extend a debt of gratitude and admiration to the following professors, among whom we find many old friends:

Robert Arnold, Illinois State University

Patricia Anthony, University of Massachusetts, Amherst

John Brown, Auburn University

George Corrick, University of North Florida

Jess House, University of Toledo

Gary Johnson, Mississippi State University

George Kavina, University of Nevada, Las Vegas

Philip Kearney, University of Michigan, Ann Arbor

Bettye MacPhail-Wilcox, North Carolina State University

Kenneth Matthews, University of Georgia

Maureen McClure, University of Pittsburgh

William Poston, Iowa State University

Richard Salmon, Virginia Polytechnic and State University

William Sparkman, Texas Tech University

Neil Theobald, Indiana University

Deborah Verstegen, University of Virginia

Dean Webb, Arizona State University

Ward Weldon, University of Illinois, Chicago

We extend an especially warm appreciation to our friends and respected colleagues who bravely bore up to the tremendous task of final review of the entire manuscript, consisting of more than one thousand pages:

Richard V. Hatley, University of Missouri, Columbia

Hal J. Jester, Ball State University

Eugene McLoone, University of Maryland

Kenneth R. Stevenson, University of South Carolina

Thomas C. Valesky, Memphis State University

Even yet, there will be shortcomings—for these no blame can be laid except on the authors, which we humbly accept.

We also express our appreciation for the valuable assistance provided by certain persons at Longman who patiently and expertly saw this project to completion: Laura McKenna, senior acquisitions editor in education, and Stuart Miller, acquisitions editor; development editor Ginny Blanford; and production editor Ann Kearns.

PART I

Principles and Foundations of Public School Finance

CHAPTER 1

Introduction: The Social and Economic Context of Public School Finance

CHAPTER THEME

- The fear of economic and social decline is so great that education reform has become a national agenda wherein critics link America's preeminence in world markets, gainful employment, and the survival and stability of democracy to the education system. As administrators, it is important to understand that school finance is at the heart of schooling, because it requires much money to pay for *either* the successes or failures of education. Because reform demands are occurring in the midst of great social and economic change, good administrators must understand the scope and nature of education's social and economic context in financial terms.

CHAPTER OUTLINE

- The scope of the educational enterprise as seen by the size of the fiscal support base required to operate the schools
- A starkly realistic view of education's emerging clientele in regard to the changing demographics of the nation and schools
- The economic and social benefits of a good educational system, including the relationship between achievement and money
- The need to assure adequate and equitable fiscal resources to schools to enhance equal educational opportunity in a society that demands both economic growth and social equity
- The complexity of these issues as seen by the uneasy relationship inherent to a capitalist democracy where the goals of liberty, equality, and efficiency in schooling are often in conflict. The chapter sets the stage for examination of historic and current issues that have shaped American education.

CHAPTER OBJECTIVE

- A wider view of the social and economic problems of education and its complex mission in society

History is not kind to idlers. The time is long past when America's destiny was assured simply by an abundance of natural resources and inexhaustible human enthusiasm, and by our relative isolation from the malignant problems of older civilizations. The world is indeed one global village. We live among determined, well-educated, and strongly motivated competitors. We compete with them for international standing and markets, not only with products but also with ideas of our laboratories and neighborhood workshops. America's position in the world may once have been reasonably secure with only a few exceptionally well-trained men and women. It is no longer. . . . Knowledge, learning, information, and skilled intelligence are the new raw materials of international commerce and are today spreading throughout the world as vigorously as miracle drugs, synthetic fertilizers, and blue jeans did earlier. If only to keep and improve on the slim competitive edge we still retain in world markets, we must dedicate ourselves to the reform of the educational system for the benefit of all—old and young alike, affluent and poor, majority and minority. Learning is the indispensible investment required for success in the "information age" we are entering.

National Commission on Education, A Nation at Risk

If these words from the report of the National Commission on Excellence in Education in *Nation at Risk*[1] are any indicator of how Americans view education, there is every reason to believe that the fate of the nation hangs in a precarious balance. The very title of the report implies that our preeminence as a world power and our economic survival are in unparalleled jeopardy unless we dramatically reform education.

In the nearly 10 years following publication of *Nation at Risk,* the fear of economic and social decline has been so great that education reform has become a national agenda. More than 30 major reports by various organizations have been issued calling for fundamental reform of the nation's schools (see Table 1.1). The reports, almost without exception, have sought to link America's preeminence in world markets, gainful employment, and the survival and stability of democracy to the education system. For example, the 1986 report of the Carnegie Forum on Education and the Economy declared: "America's ability to compete in world markets is eroding. As jobs requiring little skill are automated or go offshore and demand increases for the highly skilled, the pool of educated and skilled people grows smaller and the backwater of the unemployable rises . . . Large numbers of American children are in limbo—ignorant of the past and unprepared for the future."[2] These reports have further concluded that the nation's education system is failing to keep pace with education in other industrialized nations in an increasingly global marketplace. The crisis mentality was best captured in *Nation at Risk* in the Commission's statement, "If an unfriendly foreign power had attempted to impose on America the mediocre educational performance that exists today, we might well have viewed it as an act of war."[3]

As if these reports alone were not enough to discourage optimism and hope, they have emerged in a period of national economic downturn. Although the United States has experienced periods of prosperity and recession throughout history, there has generally been an overall growth pattern as the nation moved from its agrarian roots through stages of industrialization into the present age in which knowledge is power. The American people have endured hardship, but each generation has held forth hope for a better life for its children. However, many now believe that the reward structure that has long driven the United States is in decline—a decline many persons attribute to a corresponding lack of productivity in the educational engine that is believed to fuel national prosperity. While many have suggested that ingratitude fol-

TABLE 1.1   Selected reports on education in America

Early

Commission on Reorganization of Secondary Education, *Cardinal Principles of Secondary Education,* Washington, D.C., Bureau of Education (1918).

Educational Policies Commission, *Education for All American Youth in American Democracy,* Washington, D.C., The Commission (1938).

National Association of Secondary School Principals, *Planning for American Youth,* Washington, D.C., The Association (1951).

Commission on Life Adjustment Education, *Vitalizing Secondary Education,* Washington, D.C., U.S. Office of Education Bulletin No. 3 (1951).

Second Commission on Life Adjustment Education and Youth, *A Look Ahead in Secondary Education,* Washington, D.C., U.S. Office of Education Bulletin No. 4 (1954).

Committee for the White House Conference on Education, *A Report to the President,* Washington, D.C., U.S. Government Printing Office (1956).

Recent

A Nation at Risk, National Commission on Excellence in Education (1983).

"Report of the Task Force on Federal Elementary and Secondary Education Policy," Twentieth Century Fund (1983).

"Academic Preparation for College: What Students Need to Know and Be Able to Do," The College Board (1983).

"America's Competitive Challenge: The Need for a National Response," Business-Higher Education Forum (1983)

"Action for Excellence: A Comprehensive Plan to Improve Our Nation's Schools," Task Force on Education for Economic Growth of the Education Commission of the States (1983).

"Educating Americans for the 21st Century," National Science Board's Commission on Precollege Education in Mathematics, Science, and Technology (1983).

High School: A Report on Secondary Education in America, Carnegie Foundation for the Advancement of Teaching (1983).

A Place Called School: Prospects for the Future, John Goodlad (1984).

Horace's Compromise: The Dilemma of the American High School, Theodore Sizer (1984).

"High Schools and the Changing Workplace: The Employer's View," National Academy of Sciences (1984).

"Beyond the Commission Reports: The Coming Crisis in Teaching," RAND Corporation (1984).

"Changed Lives: The Effects of the Perry Preschool Program on Youths Through Age 19," High/Scope Educational Research Foundation (1984).

"The Unfinished Agenda: The Role of Vocational Education in the High School," National Commission on Secondary Vocational Education (1984).

"Make Something Happen: Hispanics and Urban High School Reform," National Commission on Secondary Schooling for Hispanics (1984).

"Barriers to Excellence: Our Children at Risk," National Coalition of Advocates for Students (1985).

"The Shopping Mall High School," Arthur Powell et al. (1985).

"A Call for Change in Teacher Education," National Commission for Excellence in Teacher Education (1985).

"Becoming a Nation of Readers," National Academy of Education (1985).

"The Governors' Report on U.S. Education: 1991," National Governors' Association (1985).

"Reconnecting Youth: The Next Stage of Reform," Business Advisory Commission of Education Commission of the States (1985).

"Investing in Our Children," Committee for Economic Development (1985).

The Last Little Citadel, Robert Hampel (1986).

"Tomorrow's Teachers," Holmes Group (1986).

"A Nation Prepared: Teachers for the 21st Century," Carnegie Task Force on Teaching as a Profession (1986).

"First Lessons," U.S. Education Department (1986).

"Time for Results," National Governors' Association (1986).

"School Boards: Strengthening Grass Roots Leadership," Institute for Educational Leadership (1986).

"Dropouts in America: Enough Is Known for Action," Andrew Hahn et al., Institute for Educational Leadership (1987).

"Public and Private High Schools: The Impact of Communities," James Coleman and Thomas Hoffer (1987).

"Bringing Down the Barriers," National Governors' Association (1987).

"Children in Need," Committee for Economic Development (1987).

"James Madison High School: A Curriculum for American Students," William Bennett (1987).

"New Voices: Immigrant Students in U.S. Public Schools," National Coalition of Advocates for Students (1988).

SOURCE: Reprinted with permission from "Reports on U.S. Reform Since 'A Nation at Risk,' " *Education Week* 7:31 (April 27, 1988): 21.

lows closely in generations that have enjoyed continual prosperity, there is no doubt that concern over the decline in education and economic productivity has contributed to a national pessimism and even anger directed at education for its inability to reverse this trend.

With such powerful emotions sweeping the nation, American schools have come under attack and the calls for reform have been persistent. At its most fundamental level, reform is inextricably tied to funding. Logic reasons that economic adversity requires retrenchment, and a fundamental principle of management demands scrutiny of the costs of any enterprise in light of its productivity. Logic then reasons that what works well is what gets funded, and what gets funded has the best opportunity to work well; therefore, investing in a poor product is a poor investment. In light of the high costs of education and doubts about productivity, a fundamental question emerges as to whether education works well any longer, raising the equally fundamental question of whether education will continue to be funded well, if at all. Critics of education claim its failure on both economic and social planes. Inasmuch as proposals to restructure education through the use of family choice plans such as vouchers and tuition tax credits have survived for many years and are enjoying renewed popularity, a reasonable person can appreciate the critical juncture at which education now stands. Given the barely restrained utilitarian impatience of Americans, education is currently facing a test of its practical value.

Although the arguments of critics are prudent, worthy counter-arguments must also be considered. While no reasonable person would argue against increased productivity and improved standards of living, few people seem to understand that the scope of education's costs in America is related to the ever-changing face of the nation. Neither is there overt comprehension of the likely results of abandoning traditional education models in favor of a competitive merit system. While failure to account for the consequences of not attempting to educate all people is partially explained by naïveté, another portion can be attributed to lack of understanding of the problems facing education, which gives critics' arguments a warm welcome because there is so much resentment over declining life-styles and high-cost populations. Although there is abundant research on the problems of education, their complexity and breadth are seldom appreciated except in a very small circle of scholars. Even educators in the public schools lack sufficient knowledge of the problems' tremendous scope. A major failure of education resides in its inability to communicate problems and consequences in an articulate and calm discourse to a public comprising both politicians and citizens. If the public were better convinced of the value of education rather than focused on its failure and more cognizant of the consequences of neglecting egalitarian education, the growing anger over education costs could be reexamined in a less emotional light.

This chapter is designed to provide prospective and practicing school administrators with a reflective introduction to the social and economic problems of education as seen through the lens of education finance. The central point of the chapter is that economic growth and prosperity are desirable goals, but that the current criticism of education is counterproductive because it often proposes withdrawing support for public schools at a time when prosperity is declining *because* the mission of schools has changed drastically. In diametrical opposition to the historic narrow view of education productivity for economic advancement, public schools have become vast social agencies with a clientele almost completely unprepared to compete in the economic model on which schools have historically been structured. Because schools are now expected to both provide social services *and* perpetuate an economic model, costs have risen dramatically but the results have been unsatisfactory. The chapter therefore views education's costs in the context of its present and emerging clientele, its contribution to social fairness in a democratic society, and the implications of not understanding education's contribution to individual, social, and national well-being. The outcome of this chapter should be a wider view of the social and economic problems of education and its complex mission in society. The chapter thus lays an information base on which future chapters build by exploring the complex nature of an appropriate system for funding schools which, in turn, has an obvious impact on the philosophical bases from which administrators attempt to influence policymakers and citizens to provide good schools.

To achieve these goals, the chapter first sets the stage for the scope of the educational enterprise by looking at the size of the fiscal support base required to operate the schools. The chapter then offers a starkly realistic view of education's emerging clientele by considering the changing demographics of the nation and schools. The chapter next focuses on the economic and social benefits of a good educational system, and expands the discussion to include the relationship between achievement and money. The chapter then considers the need to assure adequate and equitable fiscal resources to schools to enhance equal educational opportunity in a society that increasingly demands simultaneous economic growth and social equity. Finally, the chapter concludes with discussion of the complexity of these issues by noting the uneasy relationship inherent to a capitalist democracy where the goals of liberty, equality, and efficiency in schooling are often in conflict. In sum, the chapter sets the stage for later examination of historic and current issues that have shaped American education and for eventual consideration of whether solutions to education's problems can be found—conditions that clearly demand strong fiscal leadership for America's schools.

THE SCOPE OF EDUCATION FINANCE IN AMERICA

Nearly every textbook on education finance written in the last 50 years has begun with the observation that education is big business. This text is no exception. The enormity of education's demands on human and fiscal resources is staggering even in an era when the national debt exceeded $2.6 trillion in 1990, a sum almost beyond human comprehension.[4] To repay just the interest on the nation's debt, the federal government requires approximately $24.4 million every hour of the day, 365 days a year. At the same time that the United States is incurring mounting deficits, the nation is also spending a vast amount of money for public K–12 education—over $200 billion in 1992. In contrast to the ever-increasing national debt, however, expenditures for schools are generally funded on an *annualized current basis,* which requires that revenues at least equal expenditures. Under these conditions, the level of fiscal sacrifice for education in the United States is truly extraordinary.[5]

Fiscal Growth and Expenditures

Growth in expenditures for education has been phenomenal in historical perspective, even during the earlier periods of the nation when educational needs were much simpler. Although needs were less complex and costly, education expenditures have exhibited a steady upward pattern despite periods of economic downturn. Although financial records were generally not kept in the fledgling nation and were certainly not kept in any system allowing for direct comparison,[6] expenditures across the period from 1900 to 1992 have exhibited upward growth over time that has reflected the increasing importance of education to the nation (see Table 1.2). In 1900, total expenditures for K–12 education were $215 million, or 1% of the gross national product (GNP). By 1910, expenditures nearly doubled, and by 1920, they reached a record $1.036 billion. By 1930, expenditures increased again to $2.3 billion, or 2.2% of GNP. An interesting observation is that despite the enormous resources required to fight World War I, education's expenditures rose steadily, due in part to the need for training a fighting force and to the prosperity that followed the war.

The pattern of increasing educational expenditures has paused only briefly over the years. Although the first 30 years of the twentieth century saw rapid increases in expenditures, only the Great Depression caused major slackening in expenditure growth. Expenditures continued to grow from 1930 to 1940, despite severe economic depression caused by the stock market crash in 1929. Between 1930 and 1940, expenditures rose 1.3%—a remarkable increase, as the GNP slipped −3.4% during the same period. This indicates that education expenditures have been steady, if not elastic, even in periods of national economic distress.[7]

The rapid upward spiral in education expenditures resumed with the economic recovery spurred by World War II (see Figure 1.1, p. 10). In the decade from 1940 to 1950, spending rose to $5.8 billion (+148%), consuming 2% of the GNP. A similar pattern continued in the postwar decade from 1950 to 1960, aided by the space race following the launching of the Soviet satellite Sputnik, which gave strong impetus to a national education agenda under the National Defense Education Act (NDEA, 1958). With enactment of the NDEA, educational expenditures received unprecedented increases as Congress responded to fears of Soviet world domination. The NDEA resulted in massive federal funding targeted at math and science education, fueling an era in which information would be recognized as the replacement for a fading industrial economy.

The new global awareness created by Sputnik was accompanied by rapid change in the social structure of the United States, especially in the 20-year period from 1950 to 1970. As the nation's population moved out of rural America into cities and suburbs to become an economic and political world power toughened by depression and two world wars, internal social problems were also dramatically reshaping the nation and its education system. Two events in particular changed both education and its expenditure patterns during this period. The first of these events was the *Brown v. Board of Education*[8] decision (1954), when the U.S. Supreme Court ruled that the racial segregation practice of "separate but equal" was inherently unequal under the Constitution. The second event was the social revolution of the 1960s, exemplified by the War on Poverty under President Lyndon Johnson. *Brown* dramatically reshaped the structure of education by requiring aggressive desegregation, which resulted in massive costs to taxpayers, while the War on Poverty marked the beginning of a vast list of federal entitlements to education for disadvantaged populations. While the federal government had long taken an interest in aiding education,[9] these two events sparked a revolution that irreversibly altered the countenance of education in America. Although these events alone did not account for all increases in education expenditures during this period, the era from 1950 to 1970 stands unequaled as expenditures increased to $15.61 billion (+169%) by 1960, rising again by 1970 to $40.68

TABLE 1.2 Historical summary of public elementary and secondary school total revenues, 1869–1990 (amounts in current millions of dollars)

Finance	1869–1870	1879–1880	1889–1890	1899–1900	1909–1910	1919–1920	1929–1930	1939–1940	1949–1950	1959–1960	1969–1970	1979–1980	1987–1988	1988–1989	1990
Total revenue receipts from	—	—	$143	$220	$433	$970	$2,089	$2,261	$5,437	$14,747	$40,267	$96,881	$169,562	$191,210	—
Federal government	—	—	—	—	—	2	7	40	156	652	3,220	9,504	10,717	11,872	—
State governments	—	—	—	—	—	160	354	684	2,166	5,768	16,063	45,349	84,004	91,158	—
Local sources, including intermediate	—	—	—	—	—	808	1,728	1,536	3,116	8,327	20,985	42,029	74,841	88,180	—
Percentage of revenue receipts from															
Federal government	—	—	—	—	—	0.3	0.4	1.8	2.9	4.4	8.0	9.8	6.3	6.2	—
State governments	—	—	—	—	—	16.5	16.9	30.3	39.8	39.1	39.9	46.8	49.5	47.7	—
Local sources, including intermediate	—	—	—	—	—	83.2	82.7	68.0	57.3	56.5	52.1	43.4	44.1	46.1	—
Total expenditures for public schools	$63	$78	$141	$215	$426	$1,036	$2,317	$2,344	$5,838	$15,613	$40,683	$95,962	$172,400	$189,800	$198,864
Current expenditures	—	—	114	180	356	861	1,844	1,942	4,687	12,329	34,218	86,984	157,098	172,932	—
Capital outlay	—	—	26	35	70	154	371	258	1,014	2,662	4,659	6,506	—	—	—
Interest on school debt	—	—	—	—	—	18	93	131	101	490	1,171	1,874	—	—	—
Other expenditures	—	—	—	—	—	3	10	13	36	133	636	598	—	—	—
Percentage of total expenditures devoted to															
Current expenditures	—	—	81.3	83.5	83.6	83.1	79.6	82.8	80.3	79.0	84.1	90.6	—	—	—
Capital outlay	—	—	18.7	16.5	16.4	14.8	16.0	11.0	17.4	17.0	11.5	6.8	—	—	—
Interest on school debt	—	—	—	—	—	1.8	4.0	5.6	1.7	3.1	2.9	2.0	—	—	—
Other expenditures	—	—	—	—	—	0.3	0.4	0.6	0.6	0.8	1.6	0.6	—	—	—

SOURCE: U.S. Department of Education, National Center for Education Statistics, *Digest of Education Statistics, 1991* (Washington, D.C.: National Center for Education Statistics, 1991), 47.

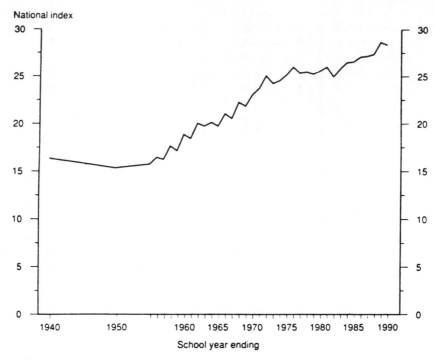

National index

FIGURE 1.1 Trends in the national index of public school revenues per pupil in relation to per capita income for selected school years ending 1940–1990

SOURCE: U.S. Department of Education, National Center for Education Statistics, *The Condition of Education 1992* (Washington, D.C.: National Center for Education Statistics, 1992), 131.

billion (+160%). Although inflation accounted for some increase, growth was a confirmed reality as expenditures more than doubled in relation to the GNP, jumping to 4.7% of the nation's $1.015 trillion GNP in 1970.

The depression years had proved that education expenditures can respond to economic conditions. Yet short of global war or total economic devastation, education expenditures have exhibited resilience with only minor fluctuations. Expenditures from 1970 to 1990 illustrate the point. The period from 1970 to 1980 was heavily marked by both continued social reform and inflation, as many states had their systems for financing education ruled unconstitutional[10] and as education's costs continued to rise as the result of high inflation. By 1980, expenditures had risen to $95.96 billion, up 136%. Although public education's share of the GNP dropped to 4.1% in 1980, public perception of ever-increasing expenditures was an accurate reflection of reality because massive redistribution of wealth and expenditure increases occurred through continued restructuring of education systems by the courts. Additionally, education's share of the GNP is misleading, as inflation had slowed and expenditure increases began to stabilize by 1980. Although education's share of the GNP declined, the resiliency of education expenditures has been evident during the period of economic downturn in the 1980s and 1990s. Although the nation has languished in economic recession since the 1980s, expenditures have continued to increase, more than doubling to $198.9 billion in 1990. While a considerable increase can be attributed to reform by states following publication of *Nation at Risk,* the fact remains that periodic events have heightened consciousness about education's importance and served to provide real fiscal gains throughout most of the twentieth century.

The foregoing data seem to suggest that education has little to complain about, and perhaps even faces an embarrassment of riches. Although many have drawn such a conclusion, there is another side to the argument. While it is true that expenditures have risen, and while it is equally true that education has held its own in a society that increasingly depends on a skilled and literate work force, there are at least two factors that may have limited education's fiscal ability to serve its clients at the same or increasing levels of service. First, the data speak only to averages in the nation. As will be seen, experience among individual states is unique to each state's abilities and preferences in educational consumption. Just as individual states have been differently affected by economic conditions, so have educational revenues been individually affected. Second and more importantly, there is evidence suggesting that education's ability to serve its clients may have diminished despite massive fiscal resources. Education is said to be in such decline that despite vastly increased expenditures, productivity is in a downward spiral as evidenced by achievement test scores. Educators, on the other hand, argue that decline may actually mask increased productivity because schools are undergoing unprecedented demographic changes in student population—a population that must be served if (to return to a venerable American argument) the nation is to preserve and increase prosperity and world preeminence. Thus an embarrassment of riches, if ever existent, would seem to be most contentious.

The data on both sides appear strong, making resolution a formidable task. From these arguments, however, three points emerge that are critical to viewing the social and economic context of education through the lens of finance. First, Americans have consistently perceived education to be the key to economic prosperity and social mobility. Second, Americans have historically placed vast resources behind public schools. Third, Americans have tended to believe that investment in education has led to an unequaled standard of living. But as *Nation at Risk* noted, America is at a crossroads of increasing costs and declining productivity. Under these conditions, it is entirely reasonable to ask whether a disenchanted public will continue to approve the placement of vast resources behind a system that seems to be losing its grip. Given the American proclivity to fund well only that which works well, it is imperative to next examine why the system may no longer work as well as it once did—reasons that many claim are tied to the changed mission of schools given the new demographics of the nation.

DEMOGRAPHICS OF A CHANGING AMERICA[11]

The United States has always been a land of prosperity and high promise. Inscribed on the Statue of Liberty are the famous words "Give me your tired, your poor, your huddled masses," a beckoning call for millions seeking a better life. While the nation has for centuries welcomed the world's refugees fleeing brutal oppression, economic stress in a postindustrial society and a rapidly expanding population with attendant social costs have caused some Americans to begin questioning the eventual impact of such policy on the nation's future.

The Demographic Mix

For centuries, the United States has been an eclectic collection of the world's peoples. Persons of every nationality, religion, and political origin have helped lead the nation into the future, particularly as the nation sought to populate itself and to complete a vigorous westward expansion. Yet while waves of immigrants have inexorably changed the nation's population, it has only been in the latter part of the twentieth century, with economic woes coupled with rapid increases in nonwhite populations and dramatic restructuring of family units, that signs of internal stress have become especially noticeable.

The contributions of immigrant populations to establishment of the nation are well documented. Early settlers seeking religious sanctuary, refugees from political and economic oppression, and others simply pursuing a distant call of freedom contributed to the birth of a nation whose roots lay in willingness to risk lives and fortunes on an opportunity to experience liberty and self-destiny—a willingness that led to pain and bloodshed in the pursuit of freedom from restrictive patronage of the English Crown. The anguish and price of freedom was likewise paid in the Civil War as the nation strove to examine its identity by being forced to confront the meaning and limits of freedom, democracy, and the human condition. Similarly, the westward expansion of the United States is well documented, telling of the sacrifice of other European and Asian immigrants to thrust the nation into the forefront of world power, building railroads and great cities and taming a hostile frontier. Waves of other immigrants have answered the call, lured by the promise of freedom and awed by the apparent riches of America. But while the promise has usually been greater than the reward, in recent years the countenance of America has begun to take on even more shapes and colors, with attendant consequences for economic and social prosperity and especially for funding and productivity of schooling.

While it is true that the United States has always been a colorful assemblage of world diversity, it has at the same time been a nation of class domination, both social and economic. Although similar observation could be made about most nations, it is appropriate to note that for the first time in American history, the nation is experiencing demographic changes that have profound implications for change in America's fundamental social and economic structures. No one has captured the impact of change so succinctly as Hodgkinson when he observed that the combination of age, births, and family status is the future.[12] For a nation built on the sacrifices of immigrants, the United States is currently undergoing a new wave of change that will alter the nation based on age, birthrates, and family status—a wave unequaled in any previous generation.

In the United States, the combination of age, births, and family status coupled with immigration foreshadows the evolving complexion of the nation with great clarity. Birthrates, for example, demonstrate the declining dominance of the white majority that has characterized the nation for more than 200 years. Given current population growth requiring 2.1 children per female to stabilize population groups, white births (at 1.7 children per female) are slipping rapidly, while black births (at 2.4 children per female) are nearly 50% higher, and Hispanic births (at 2.9 children per female) are more than 70% higher. Current data sharply contrast with those of previous generations, when immigration characteristics and birthrates among the traditional white majority kept pace with repopulation. Recent immigration by non-Europeans has had an enormous impact, as total immigration in the three major racial groups has experienced great shifts. From 1820 to 1990, about 65% of all immigrants were European, 22.9% were Hispanic, 10.6% were Asian, and only 0.6% were African (see Table 1.3). By 1961, however, the European flow had shrunk to only 33.8%, while Hispanics increased to 51.7%, Asians to 12.9%, and Africans to 0.9%. From 1971 to 1980, European immigration fell again to only 17.8%, while Asians rose to 35.2%, Hispanics to 44.3%, and Africans to 1.8% of the total. The impact of these shifts is apparent in the 1990 census, showing that whites account for only 31% of total population, while the largest minority groups—African-Americans and Hispanics—comprise nearly 50%. The fastest growing group, African-Americans, now represent 25%, and Hispanics 22% of U.S. residents. Population projections suggest greater change, as white population is expected to shrink rapidly. By A.D. 2000, the nation's blacks are expected to nearly double to 44 million; Hispanics are expected to triple to 47 million, many young and unskilled (see Table 1.4, p. 16). When these trends are coupled with immigration waves by other groups, such as Asians whose entry into the United States increased by 116% from 1976 to 1986, it is safe to predict that by the turn of the century, America's minorities will have become the new majority. As seen in Figure 1.2 (p. 17), these trends have powerful social and fiscal implications for schools.

The changing makeup of the family is also having dramatic impacts on the nation and its schools. More than any other institution, the United States has long believed in the traditional nuclear family, drawing sustenance and stability from traditional values. But as Hodgkinson notes, out-of-wedlock births have reached epidemic levels, with 50% of all illegitimate children born to teenage mothers. Every day some 40 teenage girls bear their third child, many of whom are malnourished infants born to child mothers who are themselves ill-fed.[13] The grim statistics on family disintegration are familiar but shocking, as the data show that of each 100 infants born in the United States, 20 are illegitimate, 12 have parents who will divorce before the child reaches 18, some 5 have parents who will separate, 6 will lose a parent in death, 40 will live in a female-headed household, 13 are born to teen mothers, 15 are born to homes where no parent is employed, 15 are born to homes with poverty wages, and 25 will eventually receive welfare.[14] These data suggest that few children will live in a traditional nuclear home, leading some to argue that an entire generation is at risk.[15]

The notion of a generation at risk is supported by additional data indicating that poverty is growing (see Table 1.5), especially in single-parent households headed by minority females. In 1990, fully 50% of all such households were below federal poverty guidelines, compared to 12% of households headed by males. Similarly, in 1990 almost half of all children could be designated below the federal poverty definition, an increase of 10% over 1983 when 14 million children (40%) were in poverty. As Hodgkinson has noted, a child under age 6 has a 600% greater chance of living in poverty than a person over age 65, in part because federal spending for children's programs has steadily declined while federal spending for aging populations has increased.[16] While poverty was reduced throughout the first three-quarters of the twentieth century, by 1979 that trend had markedly reversed—a condition accompanied by additional data suggesting that 86% of all poor children are also of minority background.

The risks attached to minority status, family disintegration, and poverty appear enormous and have a particularly powerful impact on children. These problems, however, are by no means the full measure of demographic realities facing public schools. The extent of change cannot be adequately appreciated without recognition that one in every five children suffers from developmental delays, learning disabilities, or emotional problems, leading critics to observe on the "new morbidity of child-

TABLE 1.3 Immigration by country of last residence, 1820–1990

Country	Total 1820–1990 (thousands)	Total 1961–1970 (thousands)	Total 1971–1980 (thousands)	Total 1981–1990 (thousands)	1985 (thousands)	1986[10] (thousands)	1989[11] (thousands)	1990 (thousands)	1820–1990 (percent)	1961–1970 (percent)	1971–1980 (percent)	1981–1990 (percent)
All countries*	56,994	3,321.7	4,493.3	7,338.0	570.0	643.0	1,090.9	1,536.5	100.0	100.0	100.0	100.0
Europe	37,101	1,123.5	800.4	761.5	69.5	71.8	94.3	124.0	65.1	33.8	17.8	10.4
Austria[1]	4,343	20.6	9.5	18.9	1.9	2.5	2.8	3.8	7.8	0.6	0.2	0.3
Hungary	211	5.4	6.6	5.9	0.6	0.7	0.7	1.0	0.4	0.2	0.1	0.1
Belgium	146	9.2	5.3	6.6	0.8	0.7	0.7	0.8	0.3	0.3	0.1	0.1
Czechoslovakia	371	3.3	6.0	5.4	0.7	0.7	0.5	0.6	0.7	0.1	0.1	0.1
Denmark	372	9.2	4.4	5.4	0.5	0.6	0.6	0.7	0.7	0.3	0.1	0.1
Finland	37	4.2	2.9	2.8	0.2	0.3	0.3	0.3	0.1	0.1	0.1	0.1
France	787	45.2	25.1	32.3	3.5	3.6	4.1	4.3	1.4	1.4	0.6	0.4
Germany[1]	7,083	190.8	74.4	92.1	10.2	9.7	10.4	12.1	12.4	5.7	1.7	1.3
Great Britain[2]	5,119	214.5	137.4	159.0	15.6	14.7	17.0	19.0	8.9	6.5	3.1	2.2
Greece	704	86.0	92.4	38.5	3.5	4.7	4.6	3.9	1.2	2.6	2.1	0.5
Ireland	4,723	33.0	11.5	31.9	1.3	5.1	7.0	9.7	8.3	1.0	0.3	0.4
Italy	5,373	214.1	129.4	67.2	6.4	5.3	11.1	16.2	9.4	6.4	2.9	0.9
Netherlands	375	30.6	10.5	12.3	1.2	1.2	1.2	1.5	0.7	0.9	0.2	0.2
Norway[9]	754	15.5	3.9	4.2	0.4	0.4	0.6	0.6	1.3	0.5	0.1	0.1
Poland[1]	606	53.5	37.2	83.2	7.4	7.3	13.3	18.4	1.1	1.6	0.8	1.1
Portugal	501	76.1	101.7	40.3	3.8	3.3	3.9	4.0	0.9	2.3	2.3	0.5
Spain	285	44.7	39.1	20.5	2.3	2.0	2.2	2.7	0.5	1.3	0.9	0.3
Sweden[9]	1,246	17.1	6.5	11.1	1.2	1.2	1.2	1.4	2.2	0.5	0.1	0.2
Switzerland	359	18.5	8.2	8.0	1.0	0.9	1.1	1.3	0.6	0.6	0.2	0.1
USSR[1,3]	3,444	2.5	39.0	57.6	1.5	1.4	4.6	14.8	6.0	0.1	0.9	0.8
Yugoslavia	136	20.4	30.5	18.7	1.5	2.0	2.5	2.8	0.2	0.6	0.7	0.3
Other Europe	294	9.1	18.9	37.3	4.0	3.4	4.0	4.1	0.5	0.2	0.2	0.5
Asia	6,019	427.6	1,588.2	2,738.1	255.2	254.7	296.4	321.9	10.6	12.9	35.2	37.3
China[4]	897	34.8	124.3	298.9	33.1	34.3	39.3	22.7	1.6	1.0	2.8	4.1
Hong Kong[6]	302	75.0	113.5	98.2	10.8	11.8	15.2	14.4	0.5	2.3	2.5	1.3
India	456	27.2	164.1	250.7	24.5	25.3	28.6	28.8	0.8	0.8	3.7	3.4
Iran	177[4]	10.3	45.1	116.0	12.3	9.8	13.0	14.9	0.3	0.3	1.0	1.6
Israel	138[4]	29.6	37.7	44.2	4.3	4.4	5.5	5.9	0.2	0.9	0.8	0.6
Japan	462[4]	40.0	49.8	47.0	4.6	5.1	5.4	6.4	0.8	1.2	1.1	0.6
Jordan	74	11.7	27.5	31.1	2.7	3.1	3.8	4.3	0.1	0.4	0.6	0.4
Korea	642[4,5]	34.5	267.6	333.8	34.8	34.2	33.0	31.0	1.1	1.0	6.0	4.5
Lebanon	95[8]	15.2	41.3	33.2	2.5	3.5	3.8	4.0	0.2	0.5	0.9	0.5
Philippines	1,026	98.4	355.0	548.7	53.1	61.0	66.1	71.3	1.8	3.0	7.9	7.5
Turkey	412	10.1	13.4	23.4	1.7	2.2	2.5	3.2	0.7	0.3	0.3	0.3
Vietnam	459[6]	4.3	172.8	281.0	20.4	12.8	13.3	14.8	0.8	1.1	3.8	3.8
Other Asia	879	36.5	176.1	631.4	50.4	47.1	66.7	100.0	1.5	1.1	3.8	8.6

TABLE 1.3 (*Continued*)

America	13,068	1,716.4	1,982.5	3,615.6	225.5	294.9	672.6	1,051.0	22.9	51.7	44.3	49.3
Argentina	131[7]	49.7	29.9	27.3	1.9	2.6	3.8	6.0	0.2	1.5	0.7	0.4
Brazil	98[7]	29.3	17.8	26.1	2.6	3.0	3.7	4.6	0.2	0.9	0.4	0.4
Canada	4,296[7]	413.3	169.9	158.0	16.4	15.8	18.3	24.6	7.5	12.4	3.8	2.2
Colombia	296	72.0	77.3	122.9	11.8	10.2	14.9	23.8	0.5	2.2	1.7	1.7
Cuba	748[8]	208.5	264.9	144.6	17.1	16.6	9.5	9.4	1.3	6.3	5.9	2.0
Dominican Rep.	510[7]	93.3	148.1	252.0	23.9	27.2	26.7	42.1	0.9	2.8	3.3	3.4
Ecuador	155[7]	36.8	50.1	56.2	4.6	4.7	7.6	12.5	0.3	1.1	1.1	0.8
El Salvador	296[7]	15.0	34.4	213.5	10.1	12.0	57.6	79.6	0.5	0.5	0.8	2.9
Guatemala	137[7]	15.9	25.9	89.0	4.4	5.8	19.2	32.9	0.2	0.5	0.6	1.2
Haiti	235[8]	34.5	56.3	138.4	9.9	34.8	13.3	19.9	0.4	1.0	1.3	1.9
Honduras	91[7]	15.7	17.4	49.6	3.7	4.3	7.6	12.0	0.2	0.5	0.4	0.7
Mexico	3,888[7]	453.9	640.3	1,655.7	61.3	95.2	405.6	680.2	6.8	13.7	14.3	22.6
Panama	94[7]	19.4	23.5	33.5	3.2	3.0	3.9	3.9	0.2	0.6	0.5	0.5
Peru	121	19.1	29.2	63.5	4.1	5.8	10.0	15.4	0.2	0.6	0.6	0.9
West Indies	1,209	133.9	271.8	336.8	28.5	32.3	38.0	41.0	2.1	4.0	6.1	4.9
Other America	796	106.1	125.7	263.7	22.0	21.5	32.7	58.0	1.4	3.1	2.8	3.6
Africa	334	29.0	80.8	176.8	15.2	17.1	22.5	32.8	0.6	0.9	1.3	2.4
Australia and New Zealand	147	19.6	23.8	24.1	2.5	2.5	2.9	3.4	0.3	0.6	0.5	0.3
Other Oceania	57	5.6	17.6	20.5	2.1	1.8	2.0	3.0	0.1	0.1	0.4	0.3
Unknown or not reported	267	—	—	0.8	—	—	—	0.5	0.5	—	—	0.1

*Figures may not add to total due to rounding.

[1]1938–1945, Austria included with Germany; 1899–1919, Poland included with Austria-Hungary, Germany, and USSR.

[2]Beginning 1952, includes data for United Kingdom not specified, formerly included with "Other Europe."

[3]Europe and Asia.

[4]Prior to 1951, included with "Other Asia."

[5]Prior to 1961, Philippines included with "All other."

[6]Prior to 1953, data for Vietnam not available.

[7]Prior to 1951, included with "Other America."

[8]Prior to 1951, included with "West Indies."

[9]Norway and Sweden were combined from 1820 to 1868.

[10]First full year with Immigration Reform and Control Act of 1986 in effect.

[11]Data include 476,814 previously illegal aliens who were granted permanent resident status under section 245A of the Immigration Reform and Control Act of 1966. These aliens are not new residents of the United States.

SOURCE: *The World Almanac and Book of Facts*, 1992 ed. (New York: Pharos Books, 1991), 137.

TABLE 1.4 Population projections of young people, aged 0–24, by race/ethnicity and age, 1990–2010

Race/Ethnicity and Age	Population, in Millions				Percentage Change			
	1990	1995	2000	2010	1985–1990	1990–1995	1995–2000	2000–2010
Total, all ages*	249.7	259.6	268.0	283.2	4.6	4.0	3.2	5.7
All races	90.1	90.8	92.0	92.5	−1.6	0.8	1.3	0.6
Under 5	19.2	18.6	17.6	18.0	4.0	−3.0	−5.3	2.0
5–13	32.2	34.4	34.4	31.9	8.5	7.0	−0.2	−7.3
14–17	13.0	14.1	15.4	15.0	−12.1	8.7	9.2	−2.6
18–24	25.8	23.7	24.6	27.7	−10.2	−8.1	3.8	12.4
White, non-Hispanic	64.1	63.1	62.5	59.9	−4.1	−1.6	−1.0	−4.1
Under 5	13.2	12.5	11.5	11.2	2.4	−5.4	−8.2	−2.7
5–13	22.7	23.8	23.2	20.3	6.1	4.6	−2.2	−12.6
14–17	9.3	10.0	10.6	9.9	−15.3	7.5	6.4	−6.9
18–24	18.9	16.9	17.2	18.6	−12.4	−10.7	1.8	8.0
Hispanic	9.5	10.5	11.5	13.3	10.0	10.4	9.5	16.0
Under 5	2.3	2.4	2.5	2.9	14.2	5.7	3.5	14.3
5–13	3.5	4.0	4.4	4.8	15.8	16.6	8.3	9.0
14–17	1.4	1.5	1.8	2.1	5.5	11.5	21.0	13.5
18–24	2.4	2.5	2.8	3.6	1.6	5.2	10.2	30.1
Black[1]	14.1	14.6	15.2	16.1	1.9	3.7	4.1	6.1
Under 5	3.2	3.2	3.1	3.3	5.2	−1.6	−2.7	7.2
5–13	5.1	5.7	5.8	5.6	14.6	12.1	1.1	−2.2
14–17	1.9	2.2	2.5	2.5	−9.5	11.0	17.9	−0.0
18–24	3.8	3.5	3.8	4.6	−8.2	−6.7	6.5	21.9
Other[1]	3.0	3.3	3.5	4.0	7.6	8.6	7.7	13.7
Under 5	0.6	0.7	0.7	0.8	1.7	10.1	7.8	14.5
5–13	1.1	1.2	1.3	1.4	13.2	4.4	7.7	15.6
14–17	0.5	0.5	0.5	0.6	7.0	18.0	−3.5	20.0
18–24	0.8	0.9	1.0	1.1	5.4	8.0	14.6	7.5

*Details may not add to totals because of rounding. Percentages are computed on unrounded data.
[1]Includes small numbers of Hispanics.
SOURCE: U.S. Department of Education, National Center for Education Statistics, *Youth Indications 1991* (Washington, D.C.: National Center for Education Statistics, 1991), 12.

hood."[17] Not only is humanity an imperfect species, but the problems of social and economic class often combine to create multiple disadvantages for children. Of the 47.6 million children in school in 1992, more than 2 million faced severe language barriers, with some of the nation's larger school systems already approaching a majority of minorities. For example, Los Angeles's Limited English Proficient (LEP) students have increased from 15% of total school population in 1980 to nearly 50% in 1992. New York and Chicago also have huge language minorities speaking more than 100 languages, including Apache, Tagalog, Urdu, Cherokee, Greek, and Russian.[18] Border states such as Texas have been especially affected, as in Brownsville where LEP enrollment in elementary grades reached 51% in 1989. LEP growth cannot be accurately estimated because the numbers are so large, but officials speculate that as many as 50% of school districts in some states may not be able to comply with bilingual mandates.[19] For these and other children, the barriers are at least multiple, if not multiplicative. Migrant children, for example, are among the most affected in that they are

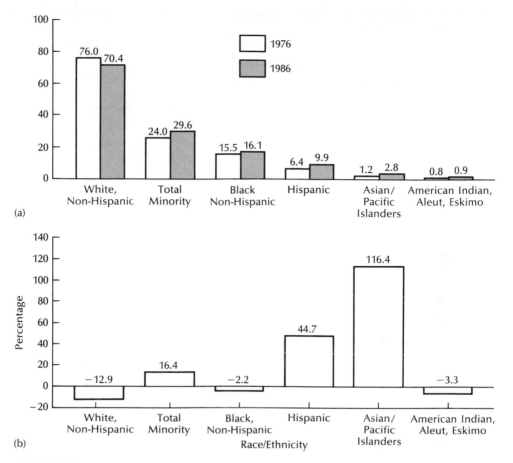

FIGURE 1.2   Enrollment in public elementary and secondary education by race/ethnicity, 1976 and 1986. (a) Percentage of total enrollment. (b) Percentage change within race/ethnicity group, 1976–1986.

SOURCE: U.S. Department of Education, National Center for Education Statistics, *The Condition of Education 1991* (Washington, D.C.: National Center for Education Statistics, 1991).

not only transient, but are also often members of poor and/or language minority groups. Of about 300,000 migrant children in 1990, the dropout rate approached 90%—a conservative estimate because of complications in census-taking among the urban homeless and because alien children were underground before the Immigration Control and Reform Act of 1986 (P.L. 99-603). Many such children start school behind their peers and combine with traditional special education populations to make a vast pool of persons whose needs must be met if they are to support democratic government.

The phenomenal growth in special education has exacerbated the social and economic condition of education by requiring vast amounts of human and fiscal resources to serve the needs of unique children. In its thirteeth annual report to Congress, the Department of Education's Office of Special Education Programs (OSEP)

TABLE 1.5 Federal Aid to Families with Dependent Children (AFDC) and federal income tax exemptions per dependent, 1950–1990

Year	Number of Recipients of AFDC[1] Payments, in Thousands		Percentage of Children under 18 Receiving AFDC Payments	Average Monthly Payment				Federal Income Tax Exemption per Dependent	
				Current Dollars		Constant 1990 Dollars			
	Total[2]	Children under 18		Per Family	Per Recipient	Per Family	Per Recipient	Current Dollars	Constant 1990 Dollars
1950	2,233	1,661	3.9	$71	$21	$385	$114	$600	$3,254
1955	2,192	1,661	3.0	85	23	415	112	600	2,926
1960	3,073	2,370	3.7	108	28	477	124	600	2,649
1965	4,396	3,316	5.0	137	33	568	137	600	2,490
1970	9,659	7,033	10.5	190	50	640	168	625	2,105
1975	11,404	8,106	12.9	229	72	556	175	750	1,822
1980	11,101	7,599	13.2	288	100	457	159	1,000	1,586
1981	10,613	7,125	12.1	302	103	434	148	1,000	1,438
1982	10,504	6,972	12.0	310	106	420	144	1,000	1,354
1983	10,865	7,130	12.4	321	110	421	144	1,000	1,312
1984	10,740	7,114	12.4	335	115	421	145	1,000	1,258
1985	10,924	7,247	12.6	341	118	414	143	1,040	1,263
1986	11,065	7,374	12.7	358	122	427	145	1,080	1,288
1987	10,862	7,296	12.6	358	123	412	142	1,900	2,186
1988	10,920	7,325	12.7	369	126	408	139	1,950	2,154
1989	10,934	7,370	12.5	378	130	398	137	2,000	2,108
1990	11,464	7,761	13.2	379	131	379	131	2,050	2,050

[1]The Aid to Families with Dependent Children (AFDC) program provides cash support for low-income families with dependent children who have been deprived of parental support due to death, disability, continued absence of a parent, or unemployment.
[2]Includes the children and one or both parents or one caretaker other than a parent in families where the needs of such adults were considered in determining the amount of assistance.
SOURCE: U.S. Department of Education, National Center for Education Statistics, *Youth Indicators 1991* (Washington, D.C.: National Center for Education Statistics, 1991), 40.

reported that nearly 4.7 million disabled children were served in special education and early intervention programs in 1989–1990, an increase of 2.2% over the prior year—the largest single-year increase of the decade. Of equal note, OSEP reported that the number of students served by traditional special education has increased 26.4% since the 1976 inception of the Education for All Handicapped Children Act (now Individuals with Disabilities Education Act—IDEA). Special education populations have grown rapidly and now represent nearly 12% of all public school enrollments in the age group 0–21 (see Table 1.6, pp. 20–21).

Although growth in special education is a combination of legal rulings and heightened social consciousness, it also has deep roots in the nation's fundamental demographic changes. Beginning in the early 1980s and accelerating rapidly since the 1986 implementation of Part H of the Early Childhood Handicapped Act under Public Law 99-457 mandating programs for children with disabilities between ages 3 and 5, growth in special populations has soared dramatically. Most growth has been in the four categories of Specific Learning Disabilities (SLD), Speech/Language (S/L), Mental

Retardation (MR), and Seriously Emotionally Disturbed (SED), accounting for 94% of all identified students with disabilities. Yet at the same time, growth in services has not always matched the needs of children, as it is estimated that less than half of all students who could qualify for SED services are currently served—a reality leading advocacy groups to currently press Congress to enact a new definition of Emotional and Behavior Disorders (EBD) classification and to create a new Attention Deficit Disorders (ADD) classification distinct from LD and SED.[20]

While no one would argue that these children should not receive services, it is important to realize that a sizable portion of growth is related to demographic changes in race, familial disintegration, and other social stresses. While some groups appear to be at risk for misidentification based on race and language,[21] others are equally at risk for failure to receive services soon enough. For example, the first children to be prenatally damaged by crack/cocaine and those suffering from fetal alcohol syndrome have begun to arrive at schools across the nation. While no firm data on the effect of these social problems are yet in place, preliminary estimates suggest enormous social and educational problems, including physical disabilities, developmental delays, emotional disturbance, extreme irritability, antisocial behavior, distractability, and violence. Based on estimates of 158,400 cocaine births annually since the 1990s,[22] many of the nation's cocaine-exposed infants have required extensive hospitalization for cerebral bleeding, heart and liver defects, blindness, and death, at an annual cost of $504 million exclusive of doctors' fees, delayed medical bills, and therapy.[23] The impact on schools is enormous. For example, a Los Angeles pilot preschool project for mildly impaired prenatally exposed children estimated educational costs at $17,000 per year per child, while the Florida Department of Health and Rehabilitative Services estimated costs to age 18 as high as $750,000 per child.[24] When these children are burdened by other disadvantage relating to discrimination and family disintegration, the difficulty of providing appropriate services to a new generation is sobering.

Educational Implications of the New Demography

Hodgkinson's observation that the future is the combination of age, births, and family status combines with immigration to create profound implications for schools in terms of mission, pedagogy, productivity, and of course, funding. Granted, Americans have long been of color, have faced family disintegration, and have survived personal and economic perils associated with establishing a new nation on a rugged and vast continent. Much of the nation was built on the hope of oppressed peoples who accepted an invitation to become part of a new land of promise. Yet never before has the nation faced such formidable challenges; equally important, never before has any generation had reason to expect less from the future than its parents could expect. For many Americans, however, a declining life-style looms because the new demography does not contain a majority equipped to prosper in a postindustrial economy. For schools, the implications are obvious: education has not eradicated social and economic differences among peoples, and its clientele is increasingly made up of those whose social history leaves them at a disadvantage.

The data examined thus far presents two apparently opposing views. The first argument is that while growth in revenues and expenditures has been dramatic and education has managed to maintain and/or improve its financial position in relation to the economy, productivity has declined, thus questioning the wisdom of contin-

TABLE 1.6 Children aged 0–21 served in federally supported special programs, by type of handicap, 1976–1989

Type of Disability	1976–1977	1978–1979	1979–1980	1980–1981	1981–1982	1982–1983	1983–1984	1984–1985	1985–1986	1986–1987	1987–1988	1988–1989	1989–1990
All Disabilities (number served[1] in thousands)	3,692	3,889	4,005	4,142	4,198	4,255	4,298	4,315	4,317	4,374	4,447	4,544	4,641
Specific learning disabilities	796	1,130	1,276	1,462	1,622	1,741	1,806	1,832	1,862	1,914	1,928	1,987	2,050
Speech or language impairments	1,302	1,214	1,186	1,168	1,135	1,131	1,128	1,126	1,125	1,136	953	967	973
Mental retardation	959	901	869	829	786	757	727	694	660	643	582	564	548
Serious emotional disturbance	283	300	329	346	339	352	361	372	375	383	373	376	381
Hearing impairments	87	85	80	79	75	73	72	69	66	65	56	56	57
Orthopedic impairments	87	70	66	58	58	57	56	56	57	57	47	47	48
Other health impairments	141	105	106	98	79	50	53	68	57	52	45	43	52
Visual impairments	38	32	31	31	29	28	29	28	27	26	22	23	22
Multiple disabilities	—	50	60	68	71	63	65	69	86	97	77	85	86
Deaf-blindness	—	2	2	3	2	2	2	2	2	2	1	2	2
Preschool disabled[2]	(³)	(³)	(³)	(³)	(³)	(³)	(³)	(³)	(³)	(³)	363	394	422
All Disabilities (percentage distribution of children served)	100.0	100.0	100.0	100.0	100.0	100.0	100.0	100.0	100.0	100.0	100.0	100.0	100.0
Specific learning disabilities	21.6	29.1	31.9	35.3	38.6	40.9	42.0	42.4	43.1	43.8	43.4	43.6	44.2
Speech or language impairments	35.3	31.2	29.6	28.2	27.0	26.6	26.2	26.1	26.1	26.0	21.4	21.1	21.0
Mental retardation	26.0	23.2	21.7	20.0	18.7	17.8	16.9	16.1	15.3	14.7	13.1	12.7	11.8
Serious emotional disturbance	7.7	7.7	8.2	8.4	8.1	8.3	8.4	8.6	8.7	8.8	8.4	8.3	8.2
Hearing impairments	2.4	2.2	2.0	1.9	1.8	1.7	1.7	1.6	1.5	1.5	1.3	1.3	1.2
Orthopedic impairments	2.4	1.8	1.6	1.4	1.4	1.3	1.3	1.3	1.3	1.3	1.1	1.1	1.0
Other health impairments	3.8	2.7	2.6	2.4	1.9	1.2	1.2	1.6	1.3	1.2	1.0	1.0	1.1

TABLE 1.6 (Continued)

Visual impairments	1.0	0.8	0.8	0.7	0.7	0.7	0.7	0.7	0.6	0.6	0.5	0.5	0.5
Multiple disabilities	—	1.3	1.5	1.6	1.7	1.5	1.5	1.6	2.0	2.2	1.7	1.8	1.9
Deaf-blindness	0.1	0.1	[4]	0.1	[4]	[4]	0.1	[4]	[4]	[4]	[4]	[4]	[4]
Preschool disabled[2]	[3]	[3]	[3]	[3]	[3]	[3]	[3]	[3]	[3]	[3]	8.2	8.7	9.1
All Disabilities (number served as a percentage of total enrollment[5])	8.33	9.14	9.62	10.13	10.47	10.75	10.95	11.00	10.95	11.00	11.11	11.30	11.44
Specific learning disabilities	1.80	2.66	3.06	3.58	4.05	4.40	4.60	4.67	4.72	4.81	4.82	4.94	5.06
Speech or language impairments	2.94	2.85	2.85	2.86	2.83	2.86	2.87	2.87	2.85	2.86	2.38	2.41	2.40
Mental retardation	2.16	2.12	2.09	2.03	1.96	1.91	1.85	1.77	1.68	1.62	1.45	1.40	1.35
Serious emotional disturbance	0.64	0.71	0.79	0.85	0.85	0.89	0.92	0.95	0.95	0.96	0.93	0.94	0.94
Hearing impairments	0.20	0.20	0.19	0.19	0.19	0.18	0.18	0.18	0.17	0.16	0.14	0.14	0.14
Orthopedic impairments	0.20	0.16	0.16	0.14	0.14	0.14	0.14	0.14	0.14	0.14	0.12	0.12	0.12
Other health impairments	0.32	0.25	0.25	0.24	0.20	0.13	0.13	0.17	0.14	0.13	0.11	0.11	0.13
Visual impairments	0.09	0.08	0.08	0.08	0.07	0.07	0.07	0.07	0.07	0.07	0.05	0.06	0.06
Multiple disabilities	—	0.12	0.14	0.17	0.18	0.16	0.17	0.17	0.22	0.24	0.19	0.21	0.21
Deaf-blindness	—	0.01	0.01	0.01	[6]	0.01	0.01	[6]	0.01	[6]	[6]	[6]	[6]
Preschool disabled[2]	[3]	[3]	[3]	[3]	[3]	[3]	[3]	[3]	[3]	[3]	0.91	0.98	1.04

[1]Includes students served under Chapter 1 and individuals with Disabilities Education Act (IDEA), formerly the Education of the Handicapped Act.

[2]Includes preschool children aged 3–5 years and 0–5 years served under Chapter 1 and IDEA, respectively.

[3]Prior to 1987–1988, these students were included in the counts by handicapping condition. Beginning in 1987–1988, states are no longer required to report preschool handicapped students (0–5 years) by handicapping condition.

[4]Less than 0.05.

[5]Based on the enrollment in public schools, kindergarten through 12th grade, including a relatively small number of prekindergarten students.

[6]Less than 0.005.

SOURCE: U.S. Department of Education, National Center for Education Statistics, *Digest of Education Statistics 1992* (Washington, D.C.: National Center for Education Statistics, 1992), 64.

uing to fund the traditional education model. The second argument is that the old model is outdated and growth in education's social and economic responsibilities has overwhelmed revenues and expenditures. This view warns that society is losing sight of the future in a nation that in 1992 spent an average of $30,000 per year per child to incarcerate increasing numbers of juveniles[25] but only $5,261 per child for an education[26] (see Figure 1.3). The argument concludes that the mission of schools has changed, and that the new mission must become widely accepted because the clientele no longer fit the historic model of education; and that a concerted effort must be made to bring the schools' clients into the mainstream of social and economic prosperity if for no other reason than that these persons will comprise the bulk of the nation's labor force for the foreseeable future. The debate has raged without resolution; the only point of agreement is that something must be done soon.

Whether productivity has suffered too much, or has simply been temporarily slowed until schools and society can come to grips with the new realities of change, is an unanswered issue that begs the question of the best approach to educational and economic productivity. But to argue whether to reduce resources to schools for performance failure seems diametrically opposed to the long-standing American view of education's role in producing the individual and collective socioeconomic rewards that have shaped the nation. Under these conditions, we turn next to the state of knowledge about whether spending for education is, in fact, an investment or an expense.

FIGURE 1.3   Arrest rates for youths: Number of arrests per 1,000 persons, by age, 1950–1988

SOURCE: U.S. Department of Education, National Center for Education Statistics, *Youth Indicators 1991* (Washington, D.C.: National Center for Education Statistics, 1991), 129.

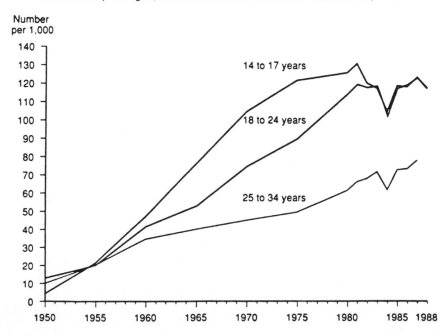

EDUCATION AS AN ECONOMIC AND SOCIAL GOOD

The national debate over the condition of education, coupled with the size of education's costs and changing demographics, has sparked renewed interest in education's contribution to the economy and society. Although education and economics have not always enjoyed a close relationship or even mutual interests, there has long been an underlying assumption about the positive contribution of education to economic and social welfare. In the present century, the alliance of education with economics and social conditions has enjoyed increased attention and investigation. While beyond the scope of this text, it is useful to note several key concepts, especially since there is substantial argument about whether education is an investment or an expense. These concepts, which include defining economics, exploring education's effect on the economy, and the social and financial returns on investment in education, provide a basis for later consideration of the importance of an adequate and equitable system of funding public education.

Economics Defined

While economists might argue against reducing a complex field into a brief discussion and its vast implications into a simple definition, it is helpful for the purposes of this text to define economics as the study of the production, allocation, and consumption of goods and services for the satisfaction of human needs and wants. As such, economics is concerned with both material and nonmaterial products, typically thought of as goods and services, particularly in goods and services in relation to supply and demand. Rogers and Ruchlin described it best when they stated that "economics is concerned with two primary phenomena, desires and resources. . . . Because desires are psychological and physical, economics deals with man; because resources are constructed from matter, economics deals with nature. . . . The confrontation is brought into being primarily because desires are infinite, whereas resources are finite."[27] Economics in a capitalist society, then, requires that some goods and services will be scarce or unequally available, while others will be plentiful and less valued.

This definition creates an interesting dilemma for a capitalist democracy, particularly when the commodity is education. Capitalism demands a market; democracy demands egalitarian distribution of essential commodities that promote basic freedoms. The issue becomes complicated, however, when it is recognized that education in a democracy is a purchased commodity that has a positive relationship to economic productivity and social mobility, and benefits both individuals and society. These realizations raise difficult questions about how to fund and distribute educational services.

Education as an Economic and Social Good

Because economics is concerned with both goods and services and the supply of commodities to individuals and society, economics has an obvious relationship to education which in turn has as its primary function the supply of goods (knowledge) and services (teaching) to its client base. While these linkages are obvious, others are thought to be equally evident or at least imputed. Among the most important are that education produces human capital, contributes to national economic health, and in large part determines the economic and social welfare of nations. These same benefits can be said to accrue at individual and societal levels as well. As such, they are critical to considerations about whether education is an investment or an expense.

Education and Human Capital.   The series of national reports issued in the 1980s on the status of education was a clear reminder of long-standing beliefs that education produces human capital. Economists have also frequently investigated the relationship between economic prosperity and education and have generally come to the conclusion that while relationships are not fully explained, education and economics engage in constant interdependency. Leading economists, including John Kenneth Galbraith, Milton Friedman, and Theodore Schultz, have declared a positive relationship, and conclude that the historic elements of land, capital, and labor must embrace the notion of human capital. Schultz captured the concept best when he stated:

> Human capital has the fundamental attributes of the basic economic concept of capital; namely, it is a source of future satisfactions, or of future earnings, or both of them. What makes it human capital is the fact that it becomes an integral part of the person.[28]

Under these conditions, the national importance of education takes on substantive meaning. Whereas previously ownership of land, accumulation of capital assets, and costs of unskilled labor were the bases of economic thought, the concept of human capital permits viewing the costs of unskilled labor as true cost and the expense of creating more productive skilled workers as an investment with tangible returns. As capital begets capital, the concept of human capital represents a first step in assessing whether education is an expense or an investment, which increases organizational gain rather than reducing its profits.

Education and National Economic Health.   The philosophical justification for a capitalist society is the accumulation of private wealth through economic competition in a free marketplace. The philosophical justification for a democratic society is in part the abuses that occur naturally in a survival-of-the-fittest economy where wealth is permitted to grow unchecked. Thus a free capitalist market in a democratic society requires some modification to prevent extreme centralization of wealth. Applied to education, schooling in a free marketplace would accrue only to those best able to purchase its benefits. The ultimate test of the concept of education as human capital has occurred in the United States, where one of the most powerful modifications has been to distribute education widely so that more persons can accumulate a greater store of private wealth (i.e., education), in that they are able to sell their skills in an open marketplace at a higher competitive price. This modification reflects a strong belief that education results in economic benefit. Rather than the deleterious effect of competition feared by some,[29] and rather than the high cost of labor shutting down production as feared by others favoring a totally free market,[30] distributing education has been assumed to yield a healthier economy.

Belief in the relationship between economic productivity and education has historically been strong, particularly in the twentieth century. In 1918, the Commission on Reorganization of Secondary Education declared as one of its Seven Cardinal Principles the need for schools to prepare students for vocational success. In 1938, the

Educational Policies Commission promoted four responsibilities for schools, among which economic efficiency was prominent. In 1951, the Ten Imperative Needs of Youth issued by the National Association of Secondary School Principals also emphasized vocational education. In 1955, the White House Conference on Education promoted 14 goals for education, among which effective work habits was prominent. Also in 1955, the Chamber of Commerce of the United States declared: "People who have a good education produce more goods, earn more money, buy and consume more goods, read more magazines and newspapers, are more active in civic and national affairs, enjoy a higher standard of living, and in general, contribute more to the economy than those who are not as well educated."[31] In 1960, Downey, Seager, and Slagle[32] synthesized the various pronouncements on the benefits of education into four categories—intellectual, social, personal, and productive—and placed strong emphasis on vocational preparation. More recently, the various national reports of the 1980s (see Table 1.1) reaffirmed belief in the relationship between productivity and education. From these data, it appears that some prosperity of the United States has flowed from beliefs creating a self-fulfilling prophecy.

Whether there is irrefutable proof of a positive relationship between education and national economic health seems less critical when comparing the obvious differences among developed and underdeveloped nations. Few would argue that educational benefits widely dispersed across the population do not enhance economic and social progress. As the World Bank has noted repeatedly: "The emphasis in low income countries is on the development of low-cost basic education. . . . In middle income countries, where first-level education is already widely available, educational quality is emphasized and with it the expansion of facilities to meet the needs of an increasingly sophisticated economy. . . . As the absorptive capacity of an economy grows, the priority tends to shift toward providing higher level technical skills, as well as developing skills in science, technology, information processing, and research."[33] Little amplification is needed for such a concept, as Americans have observed that education feeds itself as an industry by creating its jobs, and feeds the total job market and consumption industry by providing the technology to create more and better products and the desire to acquire those products and services among consumers. If human capital is a first step, the concept of positive linkages between education and national economic health represents a second step in assessing whether education is an expense or an investment, because the economy would falter without the demand education creates for itself.

Education and Individual Benefits.   Because recipients of education are individuals, it follows that education has individual benefits. This important concept provides a third step in assessing the investment-expense issue.

The *benefit* and *exclusion* principles are refinements of economic concepts relating to the impact of expenditures on population subgroups. The benefit principle is straightforward by asking who benefits by an expenditure or receipt of a good or service. In education, it is clear that individuals receive the goods (knowledge) and the services (teaching), leading to the conclusion that the initial impact of education falls in the private sector.[34] While a broader impact will be discussed later, the benefit principle clearly applies to the commodity of education. The meaning of the exclusion principle is less clear, but it is equally applicable. The exclusion principle asks whether benefits are automatically applicable *beyond* the individual beneficiary. The concept is clearer when another commodity is substituted. A purchaser of gasoline, for example, is the obvious sole recipient of the benefit principle, and the purchase of gasoline has no automatic benefit to any other person. True, the purchaser can choose to offer a ride to another person, but unless that choice is made, the benefit of the purchase automatically excludes all other persons. In contrast, the benefit from the tax paid on gasoline is more nebulous because such taxes are often earmarked for highway construction and maintenance. In that case, society at large benefits from the purchase because the individual is neither able nor desirous to exclude others from road use. In fact, purchasing gasoline would be pointless if drivers were required to provide private roads. Applying these principles to schools, it is clear that education does benefit individuals. But it is also clear that there is a spillover benefit to society.

The individual benefits of education have been extensively documented. Clearly, individuals are the prime beneficiaries of their educations, and others are excluded from direct and equal use of each person's unique education storehouse. In the broader sense, individuals benefit because they have personal access to greater social mobility, better pay and higher socioeconomic status, and more cultural opportunities. As seen earlier, because salaries are returned to the economy through consumerism, higher salaries result in more active consumer markets and lead to better individual life-styles. These events are self-enhancing, as better educated people have been shown to be less susceptible to illness,[35] have less unemployment,[36] are more receptive to new ideas and knowledge,[37] provide higher quality goods and services,[38] and work at greater levels of efficiency.[39] Weisbrod's identification of seven areas of economic benefit is helpful in understanding the impact of education on individuals:

1. *Direct financial returns.* Given job markets, this benefit is indisputable as individuals will be the prime beneficiaries of any relationship between level of education and increased earnings.
2. *Financial options.* Given salary increments for progressively higher skills, this benefit is likewise indisputable.
3. *Hedging options.* As the individual's skills increase, there is a commensurate increase in retraining capacity, minimizing technological obsoleteness.
4. *Non-market returns.* As education increases, so does the ability to "make-do," such as filing an income tax return without assistance.
5. *Residence-related benefits.* Both the individual and neighbors benefit from higher economic status (overlaps with external benefits).
6. *Employment-related benefits.* An individual's productivity may have a stimulative effect on organizations and coworkers.
7. *Societal benefits.* Literacy diminishes dependency, results in more intelligent government, and spurs economic activity.[40]

Weisbrod's list illustrates that not all benefits can be isolated to individuals under the exclusion principle, as there are spillover (external) benefits to the larger society that spark economic productivity and social mobility. Yet at the same time, such benefits ultimately accrue to individuals because the motivation for quality performance comes back to each person—a basic tenet of capitalism. Individual benefits of education can therefore be seen as the most fundamental concept governing the investment-expense argument for education.

The benefits of education to individuals are best seen in data on life employment based on education. Although other data will be discussed later on rate-of-return studies to individuals and external social benefits from investing in education, the individual benefits of education can be summarized convincingly as seen in Table 1.7. A person with more years of schooling can expect more and better employment. Conversely a person with fewer years of schooling can expect a lifetime of low employment. The difference is large, as four or more years of college results in an unemployment rate of only 3% in this population, while dropping out of high school results in 14.8% unemployment in that specific population. While total earnings do not reflect the same linear relationship due to a variety of factors, including career selection and the principle of diminishing returns,[41] it is accurate to say that education has a powerful effect on both employment prospects and lifetime earnings for individuals.

Education and External Benefits.   As pointed out previously, the exclusion principle does not apply perfectly to education because education does produce several important spillover benefits reaching beyond the individual. In contrast to the benefit and exclusion principles, these broader linkages are often termed *externalities* and provide a fourth step in determining whether education is an investment or an expense.

The exclusion principle held that one person could be found to be the sole beneficiary of an expenditure or a good or service. Implicit was the concept that exclusion is hopefully at least neutral to others and, importantly, economically efficient. In other words, for exclusion to operate properly, depriving others of a benefit should not result in unconscionable harm and the expenditure for the benefit should be economically feasible for the beneficiary. The earlier example of highway taxes illustrates the point. It might be argued that failure to provide the benefit of roads does not result in unconscionable harm to others. But attempting to apply the exclusion principle to roads would not result in economic efficiency because individuals could not supply their own roads due to the costs of construction and obtaining rights-of-way. Many goods and services are therefore more efficiently produced in the public sector with wide benefit at a small cost to each person. In fact, the basis for most governmental services is public economic efficiency, so that small sacrifices by many make up a collective benefit. It is important to note that under such a concept each individual need not benefit equally, or indeed benefit at all in a direct sense, because the value to society outweighs individual loss—particularly since each person does benefit at least indirectly (for example, people who do not own cars or drive but who buy food transported on highways). Such externalities provide wide economic and utilitarian benefits to society.

Externalities are thus generally characterized in at least two ways. First, spillover benefits occur in regard to a product or service because exclusion is unfeasible. Second, efficiency makes privatization undesirable or impossible. Like many other government services, education is characterized by externalities. Although there is argument about privatizing schooling to force improved performance, it is clear that education does not neatly fit the exclusion principle, despite individual benefits. It is impossible to declare that the student is the sole beneficiary because spillovers follow in social mobility, higher pay, socioeconomic status, increased consumption that aids the economy, lower unemployment and greater productivity, enjoyment of cultural opportunities, and many other by-products. Likewise, it is clear that on a wide scale people cannot privately provide educational services because of economic inefficiency. Not only would it be impossible for many, if not most, persons to contract for education, the level and consumption of services would be highly varied, negating

TABLE 1.7 Unemployment rate of persons 16 years old and over, by age, sex, race/ethnicity, and years of schooling completed

Sex, Race/Ethnicity, and Years of School Completed	Percentage Unemployed[1]							
	Total, 16 Years and Over	16–19 Years	20–24 Years	25–34 Years	35–44 Years	45–54 Years	55–64 Years	65 Years and Over
All Persons								
All education levels	6.8	18.8	10.9	6.8	5.1	4.5	4.1	3.3
8 years or less	11.7	36.5	15.8	13.5	12.0	10.7	7.0	4.1
1 to 3 years of high school	14.8	21.6	22.7	16.1	11.2	7.3	5.5	3.7
4 years of high school	7.0	15.7	11.4	7.6	5.7	4.5	3.9	3.0
1 to 3 years of college	5.4	9.1	7.9	5.2	4.8	4.1	4.3	3.9
4 or more years of college	3.0	—	6.9	3.3	2.6	2.4	2.5	2.6
Men								
All education levels	7.1	19.9	11.7	7.0	5.4	4.8	4.6	3.3
8 years or less	11.5	36.0	13.8	12.5	12.1	10.3	7.3	4.6
1 to 3 years of high school	14.9	22.3	21.8	15.2	11.7	8.0	6.4	2.8
4 years of high school	7.5	16.2	11.8	7.7	6.5	5.0	4.5	3.1
1 to 3 years of college	5.5	9.9	8.5	5.0	5.0	4.3	4.9	4.1
4 or more years of college	3.0	—	7.6	3.4	2.3	2.7	2.6	2.6
Women								
All education levels	6.4	17.5	10.0	6.7	4.8	4.2	3.5	3.3
8 years or less	12.1	37.6	21.5	15.9	11.8	11.4	6.2	3.4
1 to 3 years of high school	14.5	20.8	24.3	17.7	10.6	6.3	4.2	4.7
4 years of high school	6.4	15.2	10.8	7.4	4.9	4.2	3.3	3.0
1 to 3 years of college	5.3	8.5	7.3	5.5	4.5	4.0	3.5	3.8
4 or more years of college	3.1	—	6.3	3.3	2.9	2.1	2.1	2.6
White[2]								
All education levels	6.0	16.5	9.2	6.0	4.7	4.2	4.1	3.1
8 years or less	11.4	33.1	14.3	13.0	11.6	10.6	7.3	3.8
1 to 3 years of high school	13.3	19.3	19.3	13.9	10.3	6.9	5.1	3.1
4 years of high school	6.1	13.3	9.5	6.7	5.3	4.1	3.9	2.9
1 to 3 years of college	4.8	8.3	6.8	4.4	4.2	3.8	4.2	3.9
4 or more years of college	2.9	—	6.5	3.1	2.4	2.4	2.5	2.4
Black[2]								
All education levels	12.5	36.4	22.0	12.8	8.7	7.3	4.4	5.2
8 years or less	14.1	58.4	45.8	24.6	17.6	12.3	4.8	5.1
1 to 3 years of high school	22.5	39.4	40.2	27.6	15.5	8.0	6.2	7.9
4 years of high school	12.6	33.5	21.2	13.1	8.3	7.8	4.0	4.9
1 to 3 years of college	10.0	16.2	15.9	9.9	8.7	7.2	4.8	6.1
4 or more years of college	4.5	—	12.2	5.7	3.9	2.2	1.3	—

TABLE 1.7 (*Continued*)

Sex, Race/Ethnicity, and Years of School Completed	Percentage Unemployed[1]							
	Total, 16 Years and Over	16–19 Years	20–24 Years	25–34 Years	35–44 Years	45–54 Years	55–64 Years	65 Years and Over
Hispanic Origin[3]								
All education levels	9.9	23.1	11.5	9.3	8.2	8.0	6.8	6.8
8 years or less	12.6	25.5	12.6	12.5	12.3	13.1	9.2	8.4
1 to 3 years of high school	16.2	28.1	16.3	13.5	12.6	11.4	8.4	4.3
4 years of high school	8.3	16.1	10.3	8.8	6.7	5.0	4.5	5.5
1 to 3 years of college	5.7	10.0	8.5	5.1	4.9	3.8	5.2	7.9
4 or more years of college	4.3	—	8.5	4.6	3.7	3.7	4.2	1.9

[1]The unemployment rate is the percent of individuals in the labor force who are not working and who made specific efforts to find employment sometime during the prior 4 weeks. The labor force includes both employed and unemployed persons.
[2]Includes persons of Hispanic origin.
[3]Persons of Hispanic origin may be of any race
— = Data not available.
SOURCE: U.S. Department of Education, National Center for Education Statistics, *Digest of Education Statistics 1992* (Washington, D.C.: National Center for Education Statistics, 1992), 389.

many of the efficiencies of a public sector enterprise and souring democratic ideals of self-governance. Thus, the externalities of education cannot be efficiently substituted by any other mechanism.[42]

The Ability Principle.   The externalities of education introduce another fundamental concept on which many government services, including education, have come to be based. It requires little explanation to understand that, if a major goal of education is socioeconomic mobility, those least able to pay for the benefits of education are in many instances the same persons in the greatest need of services. In other words, poor people need the social and economic rewards of education more than persons who are already advantaged by social and economic status. This logic has resulted in the *ability principle,* which declares that given the social value of externalities, the benefits of a government service should be provided without regard to the person's ability to pay. Applied to education, it is obvious that a poor family with many children has great need for educational services, but their access to education should in no way be conditioned on their financial support. The ability principle has been widely applied to government services and forms the basis of the federal tax system.[43]

Application of the exclusion principle, the benefit principle, and the externalities of education forms a strong support base for paying for education according to the ability principle. In fact, historic assumptions about the value of investing in education are tied to all these concepts, arguing that the cost of education is outweighed by its rewards. Beliefs and practices are not always in perfect alignment, however, and argument continues over the "cost" of education relative to productivity as imperfect educational funding systems continue to operate throughout the country. Although all states provide a system of "free" public schools, and although many states have made a clear attempt to provide educational services without regard to financial status or in inverse relationship to ability to pay, significant evidence remains that education's support structure is tied to differences in local wealth and results in differing quantity and quality of education among schools, communities, and states[44]—and of course, the argument still rages over whether education's productivity is worth the price.

Returns on Educational Investment

There is little question that this chapter has proposed that Americans have historically expected a return on investment in education. It was suggested early in the chapter that what works well gets funded well, with significant questions about the viability of continuing to fund an enterprise with dubious productivity. Numerous scholarly studies, alluded to in the discussion on individual benefits and representing a fifth step in assessing the investment-expense debate, have attempted to assess the return on educational investment to answer practical questions about the effect of increasing or reducing expenditures for education, and indeed, to assist in the debate.

Studies of returns on educational investment can be grouped into at least two separate areas, the first of which looks in depth at studies exploring education and economic growth, the second of which more closely examines the return on investment that accrues at two levels of individual and public benefit. These may be jointly classed into a general category of rate-of-return studies.

Education and Economic Growth.   Earlier discussion indicated that there is strong interest and belief in the contribution of education to economic growth. While the literature suggests difficulty in isolating effects, particularly of a broadly dispersed and highly variable commodity like education, a few studies have attempted to determine the nature and extent of the contribution of educational expenditures to economic growth. These studies generally examine changes in the GNP and attempt to estimate the contribution of education to observed change (i.e., human capital).

Questioning the return on educational investment in a society that spent approximately $200 billion in 1992 for public K–12 education is indeed sensible. Answering the question of quality purchased in the same concrete numerical analysis, however, is more difficult. Although economists like to work with discrete variables and produce specific results, they are sometimes forced to settle for less finite estimates of contribution of variables in an econometric equation. Because no way has been found by which to precisely measure the productivity output of educational investment relative to the input variable of fiscal resources, economists often rely on estimation of "residual" effects in the economy.

A *residual* effect may be understood by the analogy of a sum and its parts. While a series of values can be added accurately into a sum, in less concrete sciences, the more common phrase is that "the whole is greater than the sum of its parts." While application of the analogy to the field of economics is perhaps not precisely correct, that analogy helps to understand the approach taken by some economists to understanding the dynamic contribution of education to the economy. Traditionally, economics has considered growth in the economy to be a function of changes in land inputs, the labor force, and the volume of physical capital. If one of these variables is altered, production is expected to change.

$$\frac{\Delta Q}{Q} = \infty \frac{\Delta A}{A} + \beta \frac{\Delta K}{K} + y \frac{\Delta L}{L}$$

where:
 Δ = changes
 ∞, β, and y are constants
 Q = GNP
 A = land inputs
 K = physical capital
 L = labor inputs

The equation states that changes in GNP are dependent on changes in land, capital, and labor. Where the equation is incomplete, of course, is in relation to changes in the "educational stock" of employees discussed earlier as "human capital," because labor has not traditionally included a value for different levels of educational qualifications. The failure of the equation to account for human capital has resulted in an unexplained residual effect. In other words, calculation of the equation results in the reverse of the analogy of the sum and its parts, (i.e., the sum of traditional land, labor, and capital amounts to *less* than 100% of the dynamic increase in GNP). The difference between the full amount of growth and the sum of the parts is referred to as the residual, and the lack of explanation for the difference is generally thought to be caused by increases in the value of worker productivity (i.e., human capital), which is in turn logically associated with level of educational preparation.[45]

Studies have generally supported the concept of residual effects of human capital development on economic productivity. Schultz,[46] for example, argued that an individual's acquired stock of knowledge and skills is useless until put to work. As the individual's stock of knowledge grows, the economy reaps the benefits because productivity also increases. Schultz examined data on the labor force, looking at distribution of education by years of schooling and the cost of education at each level represented after adjusting for increases in the length of the school year. Schultz found that the "stock of education" measured by the costs of producing that same education had increased from $180 billion (price-adjusted to 1956 levels) in 1929 to $535 billion in 1957 for an increase of $355 billion. Schultz also determined that only $69 billion could be attributed to the 38% growth in the size of the labor force. From this, he imputed that the remaining $286 billion represented a net increase in the stock of education. At the same time, labor income increased by $71 billion beyond where he estimated it would have gone, keeping earnings constant at 1929 levels. The $71 billion was then termed the residual attributable to education. After several additional calculations annualizing rates of return to individuals, Schultz declared that the increase in education per person that occurred from 1929 to 1957 explained 36%–70% of residual growth in the economy. In sum, Schultz argued that the economy was 36%–70% better off as a consequence of investment in education.

A second approach to economic growth analysis is seen in Denison's commonly cited work.[47] Denison examined the contribution of twenty variables to economic growth in the United States in the period 1909–1957, including shifts in worker age, sex, hours, and other variables. He calculated increases in labor productivity, holding wages constant to a base year, and determined that there was an unexplained residual of 0.93% for the period, with 0.67% of that amount accounted for by education's contribution to the change. Although the numbers appear small, these changes actually find 23% of increased economic productivity attributable to education. In a later study,[48] Denison continued to affirm his findings by showing that increases in education explained a residual of one-third of growth in GNP from 1973 to 1981. A third Denison study[49] is even more broadly implicative of the economic importance of education, as he examined the relative contribution of education to the economies of nine western nations. Denison concluded that the contribution of education is higher for the United States than in any other country. The unexplained portion, while always leaving room for the effect of other unknown variables, is generally attributed to growth in human capital stock (i.e., education). Although precise quantification of investment-expense is elusive, education and economic growth seem closely and consistently tied together.

Rate-of-Return Studies.   As noted earlier, individuals benefit greatly from education. Obviously, individuals benefit by greater social mobility, higher socioeconomic status, and better pay. Weisbrod's[50] identification of direct financial returns in the job market, financial options due to higher skills, hedging options, and nonmarket returns are clear examples of individual benefit from private investment in education. Similarly, the individual impact on employment based on education seen earlier in Table 1.7 is clear indication of the value of investing in education. Research on private investment has gone beyond general observation, however, by calculating in sophisticated studies the estimated value of education at elementary, secondary, and postsecondary levels. This research can be categorized into two groups: (1) research calculating the present discounted value of education, and (2) research calculating an individual rate-of-return on additional years of education.[51] Both methods and their variations are designed to estimate the value of education at some point in time, with the implication that consumer decisions about how much education to buy has a relationship to individual incomes.

The present discounted value (PDV) method of determining education's worth is found by taking the actual present value and multiplying by a discount rate to estimate its value in the future. The PDV method is much like a price deflator used to hold dollars constant at some level for multiyear comparisons. In other research, price deflators are often used with the Consumer Price Index (CPI) to determine relative purchasing power over time. For example, the average teacher salary in the Midwest in the early 1970s was about $6,000. By 1992, the figure had risen to about $30,000. Although numerous factors such as seniority in the profession could account for some increase, a large part can be attributed to the rapid inflation of the 1970s. A price deflator properly applied by holding prices constant at 1969 levels and deflating teachers' salaries to the same year would permit comparison of real gains or losses in purchasing power, which would reveal whether salaries had actually increased by the apparent 500%. The analogy is helpful in understanding the present discounted value method of assessing the worth of education to an individual at some point in the future.

The individual rate-of-return method, sometimes called internal rate of return (IRR), has been the most popular means of assessing the value of education to individuals. Part of the reason for its popularity is that it avoids the difficult task of selecting a discount rate, an imprecise task central to other methods of estimation.[52] The IRR avoids the problem by using a zero interest rate: what is education worth in *today's* marketplace. The value is assessed by looking at the cost of each level of education, compared to the benefit gained from each level of education. The basic rationale is that the higher the expected income and the lower the cost, the higher the rate of return. Table 1.8 dramatically illustrates general data on lifetime earnings based on dropping out, finishing high school, and completing several levels of college. The data illustrate that for a white male, 16 years of schooling results in almost half again the income of a high school graduate, and nearly twice the annual earnings of a high school dropout. From these data, the positive rate-of-return to individuals on additional units of schooling is strikingly apparent.

Data on the value of elementary, secondary, and postsecondary investment in education are even more revealing. Of particular importance is realization that some levels of education are more costly than others, while at the same time additional units of education may not result in exactly proportional earnings gains. Several studies illustrate these important points.

It is obvious that different levels of education are more costly than others. For example, it is reasonable to believe that elementary schooling costs the least, if for no other reason than educational facilities need not be as sophisticated as those required

TABLE 1.8   Annual earnings of young adults, 1970–1990

	9–11 Years of School				16 or More Years of School			
	Male		Female		Male		Female	
Year	White	Black	White	Black	White	Black	White	Black
1970	0.87	0.78	0.60	0.52	1.21	(*)	1.81	2.08
1971	0.86	0.78	0.64	0.64	1.20	1.45	1.84	2.13
1972	0.85	0.75	0.56	0.79	1.16	1.43	1.74	2.03
1973	0.88	0.76	0.69	0.70	1.14	1.25	1.80	1.84
1974	0.85	0.75	0.60	0.62	1.14	1.11	1.77	1.69
1975	0.82	0.67	0.64	0.60	1.15	1.24	1.75	1.69
1976	0.80	0.80	0.57	0.58	1.16	1.47	1.61	1.59
1977	0.80	0.77	0.59	0.63	1.13	1.39	1.53	1.63
1978	0.79	0.74	0.56	0.48	1.13	1.46	1.58	1.39
1979	0.79	0.78	0.71	0.65	1.11	1.34	1.57	1.50
1980	0.77	0.76	0.61	0.72	1.16	1.35	1.50	1.64
1981	0.75	0.69	0.60	0.56	1.26	1.40	1.55	1.57
1982	0.72	0.77	0.64	0.69	1.30	1.51	1.63	1.65
1983	0.73	0.65	0.65	0.65	1.30	1.48	1.68	1.59
1984	0.62	0.65	0.57	0.53	1.30	1.64	1.61	1.69
1985	0.72	0.69	0.60	0.65	1.41	1.75	1.66	1.78
1986	0.69	0.87	0.62	0.78	1.43	1.69	1.75	1.96
1987	0.74	0.86	0.72	0.55	1.43	1.49	1.74	1.92
1988	0.73	0.56	0.51	0.62	1.42	1.37	1.78	1.93
1989	0.74	0.61	0.64	0.50	1.44	1.41	1.89	2.05
1990	0.73	0.72	0.56	0.44	1.42	1.66	1.89	2.09

NOTE: The ratio is most usefully compared to 1.0. For example, the ratio of 1.42 in 1990 for white males with 16 or more years of school means that they earned 42% more than white males with 12 years of school. The ratio of 0.72 in 1990 for black males with 9–11 years of school means that they earned 28% less than black males with 12 years of school.
* = incomplete data.
SOURCE: U.S. Department of Education, National Center for Education Statistics, *The Condition of Education 1992* (Washington, D.C.: National Center for Education Statistics, 1992), 84.

for secondary pursuits such as vocational education and extensive physical education programs. But there are other costs associated with different levels of education that dramatically shape profitability of additional units of schooling. For example, in more advanced nations, child labor is nonexistent. Yet as children grow older, the costs of education should include the loss of earnings resulting from being in school rather than in the labor force. Similarly, at the postsecondary level, costs of education are compounded by payments for tuition, room and board, and the like. Additionally, perpetually increasing units of education do not result in unlimited earnings potential since career choice has a dramatic impact on income. For example, a teacher with a doctorate degree has never approached the earnings of a medical doctor, even though the contribution to society may be equal or greater. In other words, elementary, secondary, and postsecondary education have different traits that impact on rates-of-return to individuals, necessitating scrutiny of these differences both academically and pragmatically.[53]

Relatively few studies have examined the returns of elementary schooling. At least in more advanced nations, the logic has likely been that there is a moral imperative to such schooling regardless of cost. Such societies recognize that some minimum functional competency is required of every person, particularly to prevent unemployment and to increase prosperity. The few studies that exist have calculated a high rate of return, primarily because the opportunity costs (e.g., forgone earnings) and actual costs (when set off against making a person gainfully employable) are close to zero. Hansen's early study[54] found infinite private returns, and Hanoch's study[55] calculated a 100% rate of return. Other estimates have varied widely. Schultz's work,[56] departing from the high rate of return in most studies, concluded that return on elementary schooling was about 35%. Although lower than other estimates, Schultz maintained that the rate of return on elementary schooling is high, particularly since the rates of return for education continue to exceed rates of return for investment in physical capital.[57]

Far more studies have explored the return rates on secondary schooling. Generally, rates of return have been lower than for elementary education, primarily because of factors associated with opportunity costs. Becker longitudinally estimated the returns on secondary schooling in the twentieth century, noting a private rate of return to high school graduates of 16% in 1939, 20% in 1949, 25% in 1956, and 28% in 1958.[58] These estimates, which show continual increase, are remarkably close to work by Schultz, who estimated the rate of return for high school education at approximately 25%.[59] Still other studies have shown similar results, with the noteworthy observation that human capital investment has increased while the share of income due to property investment has declined,[60] indicating that investment in both elementary and secondary education has visibly productive results.

The expectation of increased private rates of return for postsecondary education is less supported for several reasons. As noted earlier, career choice has a strong bearing on earnings. Further, the principle of diminishing returns appears to influence progressively higher levels of education. Additionally, there is some argument that the United States is overinvested in higher education,[61] resulting in a market glut of overqualified persons because the nation's progress toward a professional economy has not kept pace with the production of college graduates. Ironically, societal expectations may have produced an oversupply, as greater expectations result in greater job entry demands. Rate-of-return studies for postsecondary education show private returns for undergraduate education ranging from 13%[62] to 17.5%,[63] with estimates varying by career field. Graduate education produces much lower returns, averaging about 7%.[64] Yet, despite varying returns and other factors that effectively introduce unstable elements into the investment equation, the data seem relatively clear that private returns on educational investment are sizable. When the alternatives to investment in education are weighed, there seems to be no reason to disparage private investment because history has illustrated a steadily escalating minimum standard of education for social and economic reasons.

Education and Socioeconomic Investment

It was noted earlier that some goods and services can be better provided by collective investment than by private initiative. Examples include roads, hospitals, police and fire protection, and in many people's minds, education. While private schools, independent security guards, and the like suggest that some of these goods and services could be provided privately, most people assume that greater efficiency follows public investment and that a far larger segment of society can consequently access these important services. Efficiency is therefore a primary basis for public investment. Other benefits, however, are equally important: democracy, reduced crime, less need for other public assistance programs, and encouragement of socioeconomic mobility. These and other benefits have led scholars to claim that society supports many public costs that basically attempt to stem an adverse tide, while the cost of education actually helps reverse the tide and pays long-term investment dividends.

At the most fundamental level, the greatest return on education is survival of democracy. Democracy has been described as government by consent, with the freedom to decide to be led and to decide for oneself the leaders to be followed. As an intelligent form of government, democracy carries prerequisites. A certain level of thinking skills and literacy is required to prevent class-based opportunism and to encourage informed voters. This view has been held by conservative and liberal alike, as Adam Smith noted long ago in *The Wealth of Nations* that education was necessary to prevent people from becoming "not only incapable of relishing or bearing a part in any rational conversation, but of conceiving any generous, noble, or tender sentiment, and consequently forming any just judgement concerning many even of the ordinary duties of private life."[65] The great champion of education Thomas Jefferson also exhorted the nation toward literacy, noting that consent to government required an intelligent people who could discern political corruption, observe government vigilantly, and choose leaders wisely.[66] Nowhere is the benefit of education to democracy more evident than in the Declaration of Independence:

> We hold these truths to be self-evident, that all men are created equal, that they are endowed by their Creator with certain unalienable Rights, that among these are Life, Liberty, and the pursuit of Happiness. That to secure these rights, Governments are instituted among Men, deriving their just powers from the consent of the governed. That, whenever any Form of Government becomes destructive of these ends, it is the Right of the People to alter or to abolish it, and to institute new Government, laying its foundation on such principles and organizing its powers in such form, as to them shall seem most likely to effect their Safety and Happiness.

From democracy, then, flows freedom, since the ability to discern wise leadership is rooted in self-determination. But from these roots also flow other benefits, as people responsibly manage their destinies. Much data, for example, point to reduced crime resulting from education.[67] If the cost of education is high, the cost of crime is higher because such money could be put to other use. Prison data are alarming, as in 1988, nearly 604,000 people were jailed in the United States, an increase of 90% over 1980. In recent years, the rate of incarceration has required 800 new prison beds per week to contain the growing number of criminals. Many of these persons are prime candidates for education—for example, in 1988, almost 8 million juveniles were arrested for violent crimes. When the cost of education is compared to the cost of incarcerating a juvenile, the loss to the economy—and freedom—through inadequate education is overwhelmingly apparent.

In addition to reduced crime, less need for other public assistance follows closely from educational investment. Low income is linked to education, and it is clear that low income is linked to welfare, food stamps, unemployment, Aid for Families with Dependent Children (AFDC), and the like. In 1989, federal and state government spent $13.2 billion for unemployment, $1.2 billion for welfare, $12.7 billion for food stamps, and $16.6 billion for AFDC. While most citizens endorse these programs, nearly everyone would concede that such money invested in the front end through education and job training would greatly reduce the number of persons temporarily or chronically dependent on public subsidy. Yet despite massive social rehabilitation expenditures, educational programs with a successful record of moving people into the mainstream have often been poorly funded. For example, Head Start, which has been shown to have a return of $8:1 on investment, has never been able to serve more than 20% of eligible children, and programs such as Chapter 1 services for poor children have experienced fiscal reductions resulting in increased pupil-teacher ratios of nearly 13%.[68] While it may be true that the poor will always exist, it is equally true that the choices are to allow the effects of poverty and understanding to proliferate, or to reduce those effects by investing in appropriate educational services.

Although some argue that social problems are endemic and irremediable,[69] education's success in reducing crime, public dependency, and despotism seems historically secure. But if that record of success is to be preserved, effective educational services must be provided to the children who will make up the next generation of leaders. As never before, that task is challenged by the investment-expense debate. Yet despite education's cost, the social and economic returns on education foster literacy, reduced dependency, intelligent self-government, and healthy economic activity.[70] Perhaps the greatest accolade to private and public investment in education was stated by Marshall, as he concluded:

> We may then conclude that the wisdom of expending public and private funds on education is not to be measured by its direct fruits alone. It will be profitable as a mere investment, to give the masses of the people much greater opportunities than they can generally avail themselves of . . . for one new idea, such as Bessemer's chief invention, adds as much to England's productive power as the labour of a hundred thousand men. . . . All this spent during many years in opening the means of . . . education to the masses would be well paid for if it called out one more Newton or Darwin, Shakespeare or Beethoven.[71]

While the world cannot settle for only one more great leader, education is indeed an *investment* and a *moral imperative*. But given the expectations of education and given the precarious realities and changes facing America, the importance of investing in education stands unequaled in the history of the world. Yet in all fairness to the vast sums of money that flow to schools, we must next turn to examining the topic of direct relationships between fiscal resources and educational achievement—a topic that speaks to both efficiency and direction.

EDUCATIONAL ACHIEVEMENT AND RESOURCES

The data in this chapter, and indeed much of the entire body of research literature,[72] suggest that the relationship between educational achievement and resources is positive. In the face of data on declining productivity and increasing socioeconomic disadvantage, particularly in relation to charges of school failure, it is easy to blame the educational system for every social and economic ill facing the nation. Two potential responses generally follow. One response was suggested earlier in which critics advocate abandonment of a failing system. The other response is to claim that these ills would dissipate if education were better funded. In both these views, a linear relationship between fiscal input and system output is assumed. While it is advocated here that there is some relationship between achievement and money, it would be inaccurate not to question such causality.[73]

The literature is far too vast to discuss in depth or even summarize in an introductory textbook. But it is important to recognize that quite apart from the economist's view of investment in education, the topic of educational productivity has been a constant area of research across several disciplines for many years. As discussed earlier, much effort has been devoted to documenting the economic and social effects of education under the broad heading of cost-benefit analysis,[74] and these efforts have often been characterized by a macroperspective in an attempt to generalize to the largest possible population. At the same time, much effort has also been directed toward understanding the relationship between resources and achievement at a micro level, often under the heading of *production-function* research. While much has been learned by cost-benefit analysis and econometric models, the unique value of production-function studies has been to reduce educational achievement to a more controlled environment wherein the effect of manipulating input variables can be more readily observed.

Production-function research is a relatively new phenomenon, responding to both social agenda concerns and a new sophistication in examining the complex puzzle of student achievement. The Coleman Report[75] is credited with beginning a flurry of activity in this arena, in part sparked by negative reaction to its findings. The Coleman study, noted for its pessimistic view of the ability of schools to alter the effects of heredity and environment, used 93 input variables grouped into four areas of home, teacher characteristics, student characteristics, and school facility and curriculum. Output was assessed by examining student scores on standardized achievement tests in a large sample in over 3,000 schools. Of the large number of variables examined, Coleman found that home-related factors together with native student characteristics were the strongest predictors of academic achievement, and that the major contributing influence by schools was found in teacher verbal ability. For educators, the results were extremely discouraging because only a very small number of truly effective influencers on achievement were seen as amenable to deliberate manipulation. For education finance, the implications were clear: throwing more money at education would likely change very little in the achievement puzzle.

The Coleman study drew outrage from educational reformers who charged that bias, noninclusiveness, and methodological error severely distorted the study's credibility. Many studies followed, including the widely cited Summers and Wolfe study[76] which used data on 29 independent variables for 627 sixth graders in Philadelphia. Findings of that study were encouraging to reformers, in that the study found that school inputs (specifically teacher academic preparation, class size, and so forth) and student inputs (specifically racial makeup, presence of high achievers, and so forth) had a positive influence. For reformers, the Summers and Wolfe data supported the potential to increase performance of low achievers by integrating classrooms to contain students of varied backgrounds and abilities. Such techniques, reformers argued, would pull up low achievers by association with high achievers and without significant harm to anyone. For education finance, the implications were profound: with sufficient resources, change could follow by manipulating the purchased educational environment.

The Coleman study also sparked other research intent on "disproving" what was widely construed as a fatalistic interpretation of what must ultimately be viewed as a socioeconomic reform agenda.[77] Among the larger efforts was a body of literature known as the Effective Schools Research.[78] While research on effective schools, like the Coleman and Summers and Wolfe reports, has not accounted for fiscal resource impacts in a traditional sense, the findings have had a broad impact on schooling, including how resource allocation issues affect student achievement.[79] A basic premise of effective schools research has been the notion that educational outcomes can be altered by emulating the traits of effective schools. Generally the effective schools research has indicated that positive change can follow when schools reflect organizational and process variables designed to alter student performance. These variables have been drawn from field research contrasting the characteristics of effective and ineffective schools. According to this research, effective schools exhibit the following characteristics, with implications for financial resources:

Organizational Variables

1. *Effective schools emphasize school site management with considerable autonomy given to the school's leadership and staff.* This reasonably implies that new structures for resource determinations and allocation will follow, especially on the level at which such decisions have the greatest impact. Logically, targeting fiscal resources becomes a critically important activity.

2. *Effective schools enjoy strong instructional leadership by principals and teachers.* In contrast to the view of loose coupling,[80] effective schools are tightly knit communities that have accepted the view that they can no longer afford to engage in acts not efficiently related to productivity. This implies broadly dispersed leadership in a professional model, requiring investment in training leaders and decision makers about resource effects, available resources and, of course, empowerment to tap those resources.

3. *Effective schools structure stability and continuity into the system, allowing for cohesion and agreement.* For long-term school improvement to occur, conventional authority relationships must be replaced. This would imply that such a process demands large amounts of purchased time to design structures for stability and continuity and engaging in consensus building on difficult issues such as resource allocation, and, of course, the

purchase of highly skilled staff, rather than traditional fiscal profiles of teaching staffs.

4. *Effective schools engage in curriculum articulation involving agreement and coordination across grade levels.* The perspective of resources and achievement demands that the school must focus on its principal task: maximizing production in the context of resource investment relationships. This implies that school effectiveness and production-function are direct correlates to investment in in-service staff training and other curriculum improvement activities, including the purchase of release time for group meetings and cross-disciplinary curriculum articulation and coordination.

5. *Effective schools recognize academic success.* A simple but powerful concept, the effective schools perspective demands that schools create student and faculty achievement. This implies resources devoted to academic support, instructional innovation, and improvement activities, including funds to purchase awards, field trips, and support for faculty development.

6. *Effective schools use time effectively with fewer disruptions in academic activities.* A serious flaw of schools noted in most of the national reports on the condition of education is the small amount of time spent on learning activities in a normal school day. Much criticism focuses on time-on-task and organizational impediments to quality teacher-student interaction. This would imply that there must be a commitment to let teachers teach, to purchase instruction assistance, to provide aides to free teachers from noninstructional duties, and to deliberately employ only those teachers who possess critical attributes linked to effective instruction.

7. *Effective schools have support from the district.* Effective schools are located in districts that subordinate the traditional hierarchy of centralized administration by initiating and modeling achievement-based support for buildings, classrooms, teachers, and students. This would imply that school site leadership is required and fiscally supported, including block grants and resource allocation decision structures tied to instructional expertise.

8. *Effective schools involve parents in school goals and inform them of student responsibilities.* Schools have either a tremendous barrier or an enormous resource resulting from the home environment. This would imply that effective schools invest time and money in nurturing communication by purchasing time and tools to convey information to parents, engaging parents in dialogue about the school and student responsibilities, involving them in active support of the instructional program including workshops and techniques to help students learn, and involving parents in school-based decisions, including decisions about resource allocations.

9. *Effective schools engage in ongoing staff development.* Virtually every correlate of effective schools depends on the attributes of staff and the organizational structures and processes that support them. This implies total commitment to improving staff on the basis of known resource effects.

Process Variables

1. *Collaborative planning and collegiality are among the critical hallmarks of effective schools.* Closely intertwined with the foregoing organizational variables, this implies that management decisions, including resource

allocation, are cooperative activities that must be nurtured at some expense.

2. *Effective schools reduce alienation.* Even a casual observer is struck by the literature on organizations noting the similarity between schools and hostile environments such as prisons.[81] This implies that schools must carefully structure their environments for staff and students, with implications for investment in resources to achieve this goal.

3. *Effective schools provide high goals and expectations.* As inferred in the Summers and Wolfe study,[82] the effective schools research bases increased achievement on a self-fulfilling prophecy and on gains by association. This implies that all students can learn, that students learn better if expectations are high, and that these characteristics depend on purchased resources.

4. *Effective schools operate from clear rules.* Effective schools demand and receive performance based on stated expectations. This implies no loss of rigor from decentralization, but it follows that the traits of effective schools demand performance based on accountable resource decisions.

The effective schools research thus lays out an action plan for enhancing achievement in schools. The plan is rational in that it deliberately expects and designs outcomes, and it is quasi-empirically based in that it seeks to emulate schools that have managed to achieve despite the pessimistic predictions of the Coleman study.[83] As Peter Coleman[84] states, effective schools are those which are able to intentionally alter their structures along the organizational variables to facilitate the process variables. A good school uses resources effectively at the teacher level, taking into account under conditions of district and building ethos both process and structural variables in a continuous cycle to aid the production function—a process that could reasonably be expected to occur at no small expense.

Criticism of the effective schools literature has abounded. Among the more serious attacks has been the issue of objectivity given that the effective schools movement was principally founded on negative reaction to and interpretation of the original Coleman report. Additionally, the effective schools literature is more zealous in its conclusions than other studies might support. While several studies could be discussed to secure this point, two summarize the achievement-resource debate.

The literature has become so vast that researchers have begun to attempt to collect the smaller pieces to the achievement-resource puzzle into a research technique known as meta-analysis. Cognizant of the uncertainty and alleged bias of the literature, meta-analyses have sought to coalesce the knowledge about achievement and fiscal resources into a series of generalizations. Unfortunately, the results of meta-analyses have also been vague, but they have served two very important purposes. First, these studies summarize a complex picture in a highly useful way. Second, they do so in the language of school finance, thus making the issues relevant and helpful to interested administrators.

The uncertainty of fiscal production-function research in education was underscored by Childs and Shakeshaft[85] in a meta-analysis of nearly 500 dissertations and other publications examining the relationship between student achievement and expenditures. The research was framed in three basic questions. First, what is the relationship between expenditures and achievement? Second, under what conditions does increased spending lead to higher achievement? Third, does the effect of expenditures on achievement interact with grade level? The findings alone were not particularly instructive to policy-making at any level. Results on the first question showed that only 1%–5% of variance in achievement was correlated to expenditures, and the data also showed that this relationship has declined over time. Results of the second question were likewise unimpressive, as very few conditions were found in which expenditures accounted for more than 4% of variance in achievement, with the greatest gains derived from increased expenditures in math and science. Results of the third question found no evidence of interaction of grade level with expenditures, and no consistent pattern of correlation of grade levels with expenditures could be found. From these results, it would be difficult to confidently state that increased expenditures would lead to increased achievement—a most unimpressive argument for increasing inputs, particularly since so many studies apparently found little meaningful relationship between resources and achievement.

Yet despite failing to find significant and/or causal relationships between resources and achievement, the Childs and Shakeshaft study is an important and fairly accurate reflection of the policy implications stemming from state-of-the-art production-function research in the education finance discipline. The contribution of their work was largely in their evaluation of the outcomes of the investigation. The authors were critical of the nature of such research, and argued that a lack of sophistication in research design is a potentially fatal flaw in accounting for the lack of support in the data. Childs and Shakeshaft speculated that: (1) since no schools with unlimited funds exist, no control group comparisons can be made and are unlikely to ever be made,[86] (2) *how* money is spent has been almost totally unaccounted for in most studies which have merely examined *how much* is spent, (3) approximately two-thirds of all studies were not sophisticated enough to distinguish whether money was spent for noninstructional items such as gymnasiums, or for core curriculum activities, and (4) virtually none of the studies made a consistent effort to control for the impact of extraneous variables such as the home, news media, differences in culture, or differences in student aptitude, making confidence of variable effects or interstudy comparisons extremely tenuous. Yet despite the lack of powerful data either supporting or rejecting a relationship between resources and achievement, Childs and Shakeshaft maintained that a positive relationship exists when money is used for instructional purposes[87] and argued for more sophisticated research, especially since there is little hope of ever receiving unlimited funds to facilitate experimental research.

A somewhat more optimistic picture was painted by MacPhail-Wilcox and King,[88] in their analysis of production-function research. MacPhail-Wilcox and King analyzed studies conducted across a 30-year period in various disciplines, reaching cautious but helpful conclusions from a morass of conflicting data. MacPhail-Wilcox and King concluded that, while the issue is extremely complex and frustrated by confounding variables in an endless set of entangled interaction, at least seven statements can be made based on production functions. First, characteristics of students combine with parental, peer, and community attributes to lend more to learning than is contributed by any purchased resource. Second, teachers' socioeconomic status, salary, experience, and verbal skills are related to achievement. Third, academic preparation of teachers is not necessarily linked to student achievement. Fourth, there are many indications of relationship of class size to achievement. Fifth, teacher preparation load has an impact on achievement by reducing preparation time and by preventing expertise in staff with multiple academic subject area responsibilities. Sixth, heterogeneous student grouping does not detract from high achievers' opportunities. Seventh, expenditure levels are closely related to achievement because, after other variables are controlled, achievement in districts with more money is higher than in less wealthy districts. MacPhail-Wilcox and King thus argued that few inputs have striking impact, but those few are probably powerful in consequence. Notably, they found that teacher characteristics and policy and administrative structures for distributing resources influence achievement, especially through decisions affecting teacher-student interactions, such as resource flows and class size. While a discerning eye might find some discrepancies, their broad generalizations seem supportable.[89]

Production-function research thus largely supports contentions about the importance of resources suggested by the larger body of cost-benefit analysis and economic research. Yet unfortunately there are several major stumbling blocks to this line of research.[90] First, there is no limit to the depth at which production functions can be posited. Second, while it may always be possible to postulate the existence of a production function at a more disaggregated level, there are several good reasons for not doing so. For example, consider the possibly adverse effects of policy-making that focuses on the smallest elements while neglecting the larger spectrum. Additionally, such research begins to look more like psychological, sociological, or even anthropological research—as Monk notes, this may entail looking at neurological and other physiological phenomena.[91] Finally, consider how much uncertainty in prediction is inherent to social science methods. Monk cites the Summers and Wolfe study,[92] which never rose above 27% explanation for the observed variation in achievement, and notes how unimpressive this is by most standards, despite its impressiveness in our discipline.[93] Notwithstanding methodological criticism of the original Coleman report, it is easy to see how its findings were reached and equally easy to see how it might be misinterpreted. In fact, none of the production-function research has ventured far from Coleman's findings—rather, it simply tends to interpret them differently in a sociopolitical context that seeks to find a more aggressive set of intervention strategies.

For reasonable people, four observations about achievement and resource interaction appear sound. First, the data are not conclusive, but the findings are sufficiently persuasive to at least presume *a deleterious effect* of insufficient resources on achievement. Second, in the absence of absolute covariance, there is sufficient data to compel reasonable people to err in favor of the lesser evil. In other words, if one must err by investing too much in a marginally productive equation as opposed to doubting the wisdom of further expenditure, the choice should be clear: it is far wiser to spend millions of dollars on an imprecise relationship than to spend hundreds of millions in a vain attempt to clean up the social consequences of failing to educate well. Third, all lines of research form a plea for increased investigation into the factors that make a difference in achievement. Fourth, to at least some degree the outcome appears to point the clear path toward discovering more about *how* resources are distributed, rather than on *how much* is available. These four elements, then, understandably form the basis of the next two sections of this chapter, which explore the importance of adequate resource levels and equitable distribution schemes. In light of the data, nothing less than adequate and equitable resources will provide quality education.

FINANCING SCHOOLS ADEQUATELY

The importance of financing elementary and secondary education in the United States in the last decade of the twentieth century is brought into sharp focus by the enormous scope and costs of education, the demographics of an ever-increasing disadvantaged population, and the relationship of education to economic and social progress. Even though research has not granted unquestioned faith in the relationship between achievement and expenditures, the assumption has remained that until dispositive proof can be found, simple prudence dictates guarding against underinvestment as a destructive economic and social policy. Within this context, policymakers have been challenged to maintain educational services at some minimum level of fiscal support.

Maintaining—or even determining—an adequate support level for education has grown increasingly difficult over the course of the present century. As shown earlier, costs have steadily risen, rising from $215 million in 1900 to more than $200 billion in 1992. Taxpayer burden has also risen while other social services have proliferated. The years from 1920 to 1970 were the most vigorous years for progressive government services, beginning in 1921 with implementation of the first national budget law, followed by initiation of federal income tax, social security, welfare and other assistance programs, state income taxes, steadily rising sales and use taxes, and a myriad of government programs that reached their peak during the War on Poverty. These events were not without heavy costs, creating competition for finite resources and forcing difficult choices between forgoing social services and overburdening taxpayers. While it was indicated earlier that education's revenues have remained fairly constant, there has been considerable resentment over the high cost of education.

At the same time that educational costs have risen fairly uniformly across the nation, population and revenues have not. Immigration and migratory patterns have accounted for some changes, while other social and educational programs such as special education have accounted for others. These events have resulted in crises in some parts of the nation brought on in part by uncontrollable factors and, in some instances, aided by unwillingness on the part of citizens and elected representatives to accept the inevitability of change. Some state legislatures have tried to meet the challenges, but have not been able to keep pace with the climate of change that permeates education in the late twentieth century. These concepts can be illustrated by using national and state data on enrollment trends, expenditure and revenue patterns, and one state's projections to the year A.D. 2000, in funding extensive mandated education reforms.

Increasing enrollment has been a major characteristic of schools for more than a hundred years (see Table 1.9). In raw numbers alone, public school enrollment has increased from about 6.9 million students in 1869 to nearly 42 million in 1992 (see Table 1.10, pp. 45–46). Much growth is attributable to westward expansion and immigration; an additional share, however, is due to students staying in school longer. In 1869, approximately 57% of all children aged 5–17 were in school. In contrast, 88.5% of all such children were still in school in 1989. It is important to note that these numbers have increased *despite* a 36% decline in the proportion of school-age children to the total population. These events, among others, have brought about the need for longer school years, which increased more than 36% from 1869 to 1989. Money has been required to pay for increased enrollments and longer school years, as well as for responding to a very different clientele with expensive needs.

While it is true that population, revenues, and expenditures have regularly increased throughout the nation, it is equally true to point out that growth has not been uniform. As seen in Table 1.10 and in Figure 1.4 (p. 47), the nation has seen dramatic shifts in population that promise to continue. Figure 1.4(a) illustrates a growing movement away from the central portions of the nation in the period 1986–1991 and an increase in the coastal areas of the south, southwest, and west. Figure 1.4(b) illustrates the increasing acceleration of these changes, indicating

TABLE 1.9 Enrollment growth in public elementary and secondary schools, 1869–1870 to 1988–1989 (in millions of current dollars)

Item	1869–1870	1879–1880	1889–1890	1899–1900	1909–1910	1919–1920	1929–1930	1939–1940	1949–1950	1959–1960	1969–1970	1979–1980	1987–1988	1988–1989
Population, Pupils, and Instructional Staff														
Total population, in thousands	39,818	50,156	62,948	75,995	90,492	104,512	121,770	130,880	148,665	179,323	201,385	224,567	243,419	245,807
Population aged 5–17 years, in thousands	12,055	15,066	18,543	21,573	24,009	27,556	31,417	30,150	30,168	43,881	52,386	48,041	45,291	45,388
Percentage of total population 5–17	30.3	30.0	29.5	28.4	26.5	26.4	25.8	23.0	20.3	24.5	25.8	21.4	18.6	18.5
Total enrollment in elementary and secondary schools, in thousands	6,872	9,867	12,723	15,503	17,814	21,578	25,678	25,434	25,112	36,087	45,619	41,645	40,008	40,189
Kindergarten and grades 1–8, in thousands	6,792	9,757	12,520	14,984	16,899	19,378	21,279	18,833	19,387	27,602	32,597	27,931	27,932	28,503
Grades 9–12, in thousands	80	110	203	519	915	2,200	4,399	6,601	5,725	8,485	13,022	13,714	12,076	11,686
Enrollment as a percentage of total population	17.3	19.7	20.2	20.4	19.7	20.6	21.1	19.4	16.9	20.1	22.4	18.5	16.4	16.3
Percentage of population aged 5–17 enrolled	57.0	65.5	68.6	71.9	74.2	78.3	81.7	84.4	83.2	82.2	86.9	86.7	88.3	88.5
Percentage of total enrollment in high schools (grades 9–12 and postgraduate)	1.2	1.1	1.6	3.3	5.1	10.2	17.1	26.0	22.7	23.5	28.5	32.9	30.2	29.1
High school graduates, in thousands	—	—	22	62	111	231	592	1,143	1,063	1,627	2,589	2,748	2,500	2,401
Average daily attendance, in thousands	4,077	6,144	8,154	10,633	12,827	16,150	21,265	22,042	22,284	32,477	41,934	38,289	37,051	37,282
Total number of days attended by pupils enrolled, in millions	539	801	1,098	1,535	2,011	2,615	3,673	3,858	3,964	5,782	7,501	6,835	—	—
Percentage of enrolled pupils attending daily	59.3	62.3	64.1	68.6	72.1	74.8	82.8	86.7	88.7	90.0	90.4	90.1	—	—
Average length of school term, in days	132.2	130.3	134.7	144.3	157.5	161.9	172.7	175.0	177.9	178.0	178.9	178.5	—	—
Average number of days attended per pupil	78.4	81.1	86.3	99.0	113	121.2	143	151.7	157.9	160.2	161.7	160.8	—	—
Total instructional staff, in thousands	—	—	—	—	—	678	880	912	962	1,464	2,253	2,441	—	—
Supervisors, in thousands	—	—	—	—	—	7	7	5	9	14	32	35	—	—
Principals, in thousands	—	—	—	—	—	14	31	32	39	64	91	106	—	—
Teachers, librarians, and other nonsupervisory instructional staff, in thousands	201	287	364	423	523	657	843	875	914	1,387	2,131	2,300	2,398	2,447
Men, in thousands	78	123	126	127	110	93	140	195	195	402	691	782	—	—
Women, in thousands	123	164	238	296	413	585	703	681	719	985	1,440	1,518	—	—
Percentage men	38.7	42.8	34.5	29.9	21.1	14.1	16.6	22.2	21.3	29.0	32.4	34.0	—	—

SOURCE: U.S. Department of Education, National Center for Education Statistics, *Digest of Education Statistics 1991* (Washington, D.C.: National Center for Education Statistics, 1991), 47.

TABLE 1.10 Enrollment in educational institutions, by level and by control of institution, 1869–1870 to fall 2000 (in thousands)

Year	Total Enrollment, All Levels	Elementary and Secondary, Total	Public Elementary and Secondary Schools			Private Elementary and Secondary Schools			Higher Education		
			Total	Kindergarten–Grade 8	Grades 9–12	Total	Kindergarten–Grade 8	Grades 9–12	Total	Public	Private
1869–1870	—	—	6,872	6,792	80	—	—	—	52	—	—
1879–1880	—	—	9,868	9,757	110	—	—	—	116	—	—
1889–1890	14,491	14,334	12,723	12,520	203	1,611	1,516	95	157	—	—
1899–1900	17,092	16,855	15,503	14,984	519	1,352	1,241	111	238	—	—
1909–1910	19,728	19,372	17,814	16,899	915	1,558	1,441	117	355	—	—
1919–1920	23,876	23,278	21,578	19,378	2,200	1,699	1,486	214	598	—	—
1929–1930	29,430	28,328	25,678	21,279	4,399	2,651	2,310	341	1,101	—	—
1939–1940	29,539	28,045	25,434	18,832	6,601	2,611	2,153	458	1,494	797	698
1949–1950	31,151	28,492	25,111	19,387	5,725	3,380	2,708	672	2,659	1,355	1,304
Fall 1959	44,497	40,857	35,182	26,911	8,271	5,675	4,640	1,035	3,640	2,181	1,459
Fall 1964	52,996	47,716	41,416	30,025	11,391	6,300	5,000	1,300	5,280	3,468	1,812
Fall 1965	54,394	48,473	42,173	30,563	11,610	6,300	4,900	1,400	5,921	3,970	1,951
Fall 1966	55,629	49,239	43,039	31,145	11,894	6,200	4,800	1,400	6,390	4,349	2,041
Fall 1967	56,803	49,891	43,891	31,641	12,250	6,000	4,600	1,400	6,912	4,816	2,096
Fall 1968	58,257	50,744	44,944	32,226	12,718	5,800	4,400	1,400	7,513	5,431	2,082
Fall 1969	59,124	51,119	45,619	32,597	13,022	5,500	4,200	1,300	8,005	5,897	2,108
Fall 1970	59,853	51,272	45,909	32,577	13,332	5,363	4,052	1,311	8,581	6,428	2,153
Fall 1971	60,230	51,281	46,081	32,265	13,816	5,200	3,900	1,300	8,949	6,804	2,144
Fall 1972	59,959	50,744	45,744	31,831	13,913	5,000	3,700	1,300	9,215	7,071	2,144
Fall 1973	60,031	50,429	45,429	31,353	14,077	5,000	3,700	1,300	9,602	7,420	2,183
Fall 1974	60,277	50,053	45,053	30,921	14,132	5,000	3,700	1,300	10,224	7,989	2,235
Fall 1975	60,976	49,791	44,791	30,487	14,304	5,000	3,700	1,300	11,185	8,835	2,350
Fall 1976	60,496	49,484	44,317	30,006	14,311	5,167	3,825	1,342	11,012	8,653	2,359
Fall 1977	60,003	48,717	43,577	29,336	14,240	5,140	3,797	1,343	11,286	8,847	2,439
Fall 1978	58,896	47,636	42,550	28,328	14,223	5,086	3,732	1,353	11,260	8,786	2,474

(Continued)

TABLE 1.10 (*Continued*)

Year	Total Enrollment, All Levels	Elementary and Secondary, Total	Public Elementary and Secondary Schools			Private Elementary and Secondary Schools			Higher Education		
			Total	Kindergarten–Grade 8	Grades 9–12	Total	Kindergarten–Grade 8	Grades 9–12	Total	Public	Private
Fall 1979	58,215	46,645	41,645	27,931	13,714	5,000	3,700	1,300	11,570	9,037	2,533
Fall 1980	58,414	46,318	40,987	27,674	13,313	5,331	3,992	1,339	12,097	9,457	2,640
Fall 1981	57,971	45,599	40,099	27,267	12,833	5,500	4,100	1,400	12,372	9,647	2,725
Fall 1982	57,678	45,252	39,652	27,156	12,496	5,600	4,200	1,400	12,426	9,696	2,730
Fall 1983	57,532	45,067	39,352	26,997	12,355	5,715	4,315	1,400	12,465	9,683	2,782
Fall 1984	57,237	44,995	39,295	26,918	12,377	5,700	4,300	1,400	12,242	9,477	2,765
Fall 1985	57,313	45,066	39,509	27,049	12,460	5,557	4,195	1,362	12,247	9,479	2,768
Fall 1986	57,794	45,289	39,837	27,404	12,434	5,452	4,116	1,336	12,505	9,715	2,790
Fall 1987	58,140	45,371	40,024	27,886	12,138	5,347	4,118	1,229	12,768	9,975	2,793
Fall 1988	58,286	45,437	40,196	28,390	11,806	5,241	4,036	1,206	12,849	10,045	2,804
Fall 1989	58,682	45,595	40,323	28,818	11,505	5,272	4,097	1,175	13,087	10,188	2,899
Fall 1990	59,325	46,112	40,772	29,373	11,399	5,340	4,176	1,164	13,213	10,291	2,922
Fall 1991	59,951	46,718	41,306	29,803	11,503	5,412	4,237	1,175	13,233	10,308	2,925
Fall 1992	60,495	47,369	41,883	30,189	11,694	5,486	4,292	1,194	13,126	10,228	2,898
Fall 1993	61,037	48,011	42,455	30,473	11,982	5,556	4,332	1,224	13,026	10,154	2,872
Fall 1994	61,599	48,644	43,023	30,642	12,381	5,621	4,356	1,265	12,955	10,102	2,853
Fall 1995	62,057	49,122	43,453	30,751	12,702	5,669	4,372	1,297	12,935	10,090	2,845
Fall 1996	62,466	49,493	43,788	30,785	13,003	5,705	4,376	1,329	12,973	10,121	2,852
Fall 1997	62,745	49,697	43,974	30,767	13,207	5,723	4,374	1,349	13,048	10,178	2,870
Fall 1998	62,884	49,722	43,997	30,763	13,234	5,725	4,373	1,352	13,162	10,264	2,898
Fall 1999	62,950	49,668	43,954	30,603	13,351	5,714	4,351	1,363	13,282	10,356	2,926
Fall 2000	62,908	49,530	43,835	30,417	13,418	5,695	4,324	1,371	13,378	10,427	2,951

SOURCE: U.S. Department of Education, National Center for Education Statistics, *Digest of Education Statistics* (Washington, D.C.: National Center for Education Statistics, 1992), 12.

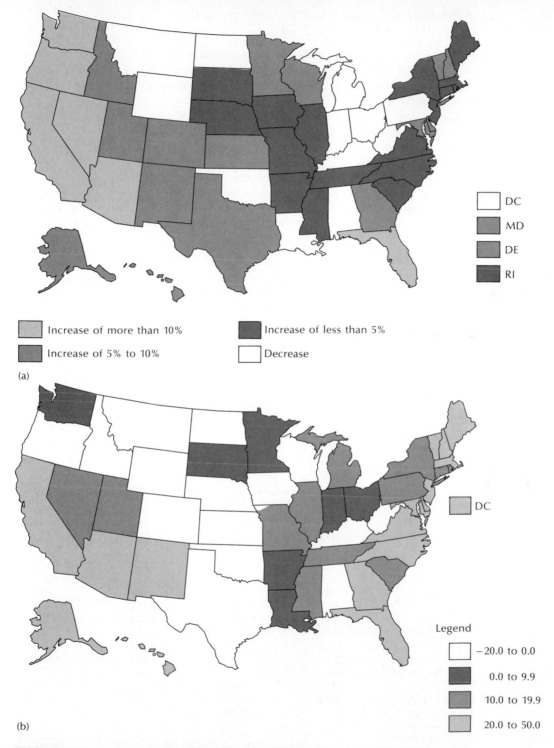

Legend (a):
- Increase of more than 10%
- Increase of 5% to 10%
- Increase of less than 5%
- Decrease

- DC
- MD
- DE
- RI

(a)

Legend (b):
- −20.0 to 0.0
- 0.0 to 9.9
- 10.0 to 19.9
- 20.0 to 50.0

- DC

(b)

FIGURE 1.4 Enrollment Shifts, 1983–2002. (a) Percentage change in public elementary and secondary enrollment, by state, fall 1986 to fall 1991. (b) Percentage change in grades K–12 enrollment in public schools, by state, fall 1990 to fall 2002.

SOURCE: U.S. Department of Education, National Center for Education Statistics, *Projections of Education Statistics to 2002* (Washington, D.C.: National Center for Education Statistics, 1991), p. 98.

that the plains region will continue to lose enrollments rapidly, while the east and west coasts will experience large increases. Not surprisingly, these increases relate to minority populations, as immigration centers continue to receive a heavy influx into the United States.

The impact of increased populations and attendant educational needs is reflected in data on historic and projected expenditures. Rising from $63 million in 1869 to approximately $211 billion in 1992, the steady growth in costs can be seen in Table 1.11. The line of increase is quite sharp, as expenditures per pupil increased almost four times over the 40-year period 1950–1989, a trend that will continue as government projections indicate that expenditures will reach more than $272 billion by A.D. 2002. Much of the increase will result from changing

TABLE 1.11 Total and per-pupil expenditures in constant 1989–1990 dollars and in current dollars, in fall enrollment in public elementary and secondary schools, 50 states and D.C., 1976–1977 to 2001–2002

| | | Current Expenditures | | | |
| | | Constant 1989–1990 Dollars | | Current Dollars | |
Year Ending	Fall Enrollment (in Thousands)	Total (in Billions)	Per Pupil in Fall Enrollment	Total (in Billions)	Per Pupil in Fall Enrollment
1977	44,317	$ 144.7	$ 3,265	$ 66.9	$ 1,509
1978	43,577	148.2	3,401	73.1	1,677
1979	42,550	146.4	3,441	79.0	1,855
1980	41,645	142.4	3,419	87.0	2,089
1981	40,918	138.3	3,380	94.3	2,305
1982	40,022	136.4	3,409	101.1	2,526
1983	39,566	140.1	3,541	108.3	2,736
1984	39,252	144.0	3,669	115.4	2,940
1985	39,208	151.7	3,869	126.3	3,222
1986	39,422	160.0	4,059	137.2	3,479
1987	39,753	167.2	4,207	146.6	3,687
1988	40,008	172.2	4,303	157.1	3,927
1989	40,189	181.2	4,508	172.9	4,303
1990	40,526	185.2	4,571	185.2	4,571
1991	41,026	188.1	4,584	199.0	4,850
1992	41,575	193.4	4,653	211.0	5,074
1993	42,250	201.3	4,764	227.5	5,386
1994	42,971	210.6	4,902	248.5	5,784
1995	43,749	221.3	5,058	273.4	6,249
1996	44,442	231.1	5,201	298.8	6,723
1997	45,074	240.1	5,328	—	—
1998	45,585	247.0	5,418	—	—
1999	45,955	252.6	5,497	—	—
2000	46,276	258.9	5,596	—	—
2001	46,539	265.0	5,695	—	—
2002	46,782	272.1	5,817	—	—

SOURCE: U.S. Department of Education, National Center for Education Statistics, *Projections of Education Statistics to 2002* (Washington, D.C.: National Center for Education Statistics, 1991), 88–89.

demographics, including disadvantage on multiple fronts such as language, economic and racial discrimination, and system overload due to complex factors such as immigration patterns. These are serious barriers to adequate funding for schools because the numbers are enormous and because the public simply sees ever-increasing tax demands. This point comes home summatively in Table 1.12 where education expenditures by individual states are contrasted between 1959 and 1991 levels. These data suggest that educational expenditures have increased more than

TABLE 1.12   Current expenditures for public elementary and secondary education, by state, 1959–1960 to 1991–1992 (in thousands of dollars)[1]

State or Other Area	1959–1960	Estimated 1991–1992[2]	State or Other Area	1959–1960	Estimated 1991–1992[2]
United States	$12,329,389	[3]$213,237,595	Nevada	23,770	946,871
Alabama	171,130	2,456,000	New Hampshire	33,185	[4]987,735
Alaska	20,641	931,010	New Jersey	459,413	[4]9,757,153
Arizona	104,054	[4]2,976,126	New Mexico	73,396	[4]1,215,910
Arkansas	83,896	[4]1,677,378	New York	1,383,706	20,200,000
California	[5]1,481,908	23,707,000	North Carolina	238,059	5,113,851
Colorado	136,760	[4]3,066,963	North Dakota	46,254	491,388
Connecticut	185,336	3,740,000	Ohio	632,932	10,500,000
Delaware	33,425	[4]630,606	Oklahoma	151,181	2,172,000
District of Columbia	45,617	[4]723,102	Oregon	154,691	2,571,000
Florida	276,506	9,283,503	Pennsylvania	732,486	10,580,365
Georgia	208,096	5,187,205	Rhode Island	48,686	905,395
Hawaii	42,499	831,573	South Carolina	116,939	2,476,685
Idaho	42,719	762,931	South Dakota	47,899	533,854
Illinois	663,849	9,006,771	Tennessee	175,152	2,868,269
Indiana	318,073	4,300,000	Texas	605,577	14,456,735
Iowa	197,768	2,168,329	Utah	69,755	1,284,111
Kansas	153,346	2,037,568	Vermont	24,132	[4]663,029
Kentucky	132,068	2,561,345	Virginia	207,399	4,871,257
Louisiana	230,402	[4]2,954,528	Washington	239,069	4,403,126
Maine	51,465	1,218,909	West Virginia	108,673	1,582,429
Maryland	209,606	4,248,763	Wisconsin	254,626	4,688,678
Massachusetts	324,408	5,015,486	Wyoming	32,175	590,649
Michigan	605,048	8,972,228	Outlying areas		
Minnesota	267,376	4,000,000	American Samoa	308	[4]30,843
Mississippi	100,020	1,582,426	Guam	3,020	[4]143,280
Missouri	242,447	3,361,000	Northern Marianas	—	[4]13,916
Montana	54,079	747,000	Puerto Rico	54,375	[4]1,296,562
Nebraska	87,692	1,229,354	Virgin Islands	1,662	147,427

[1]Data revised from previously published figures.
[2]Data estimated by state education agencies.
[3]U.S. total includes National Center for Education Statistics imputations for nonreporting states.
[4]Estimated by the National Center for Education Statistics.
[5]Includes an estimated $144,942,000 for summer schools, adult education, and community colleges.
SOURCE: U.S. Department of Education, National Center for Education Statistics, *Digest of Education Statistics 1992* (Washington, D.C.: National Center for Education Statistics, 1992), 151.

TABLE 1.13 School districts—selected financial data, enrollment, and certificated employees 1972–1973 to (est.) 1991–1992 (in thousands of dollars)

	1972–1973	Estimated 1991–1992	Increase, 1972–1973 to 1991–1992 Amount	Increase, 1972–1973 to 1991–1992 Percentage
School district equalization				
General state aid	98,562	526,977	428,415	434.7
Income tax rebate	0	204,267	204,267	0.0
Subtotal	98,562	731,244	632,682	641.9
Transportation aid	6,000	44,550	38,550	642.5
Total	104,562	775,794	671,232	641.9
Increase over prior year	0	(9,300)		
Budgets				
General Fund	386,217	1,718,671	1,332,454	345.0
Increase over prior year	0	72,193		
Budget controls	0	.75–2.25		
General state aid and income				
Tax rebate percent of Unified School District General Fund budgets	25.5	42.5		
Tax levies—General Fund				
Property tax—General Fund and levies now part of General Fund	257,902	851,212	593,310	230.1
Motor vehicle dealers' stamp tax	0	0	0	0.0
Motor vehicle tax	0	125,000	125,000	0.0
Total	257,902	976,212	718,310	278.5
Increase over prior year	0	119,547		
Other state aids				
Retirement—school	14,937	48,307	33,370	223.4
Special education	4,183	121,275	117,092	2,799.2
Deaf/blind and severely handicapped	39	99	60	153.8
Driver education	900	1,344	444	49.3
Vocational education	255	0	(255)	(100.0)
Special district	510	1,608	1,098	215.3
Food assistance	0	2,340	2,340	0.0
Adult basic education	0	187	187	0.0
Bilingual education	0	545	545	0.0
Motorcycle safety	0	51	51	0.0
Mineral production tax	0	3,168	3,168	0.0
In-service education	0	990	990	0.0
Asbestos aid	0	0	0	0.0
Human sexuality/aids	0	0	0	0.0
Building-based education	0	0	0	0.0
At-risk pupil/innovative	0	2,386	2,386	0.0
Parent education program	0	990	990	0.0
Rent/lease vehicle sales tax	0	0	0	
Local ad valorem tax reduction	10,700	0	(10,700)	(100.0)
Total	31,524	183,290	151,766	481.4
Increase over prior year	0	(4,194)		
Total state aid				
State general fund	135,186	953,521	818,335	605.3
Increase over prior year	0	(13,414)		
State safety fund	900	1,344	444	49.3
Motorcycle safety fund	0	51	51	0.0
At-risk pupil/innovative	0	1,000	1,000	

TABLE 1.13 (*Continued*)

	1972–1973	Estimated 1991–1992	Increase, 1972–1973 to 1991–1992	
			Amount	*Percentage*
Mineral production tax	0	3,168	3,168	0.0
Rent/lease vehicle sales tax	0	0	0	
Total	136,086	959,084	822,998	604.8
Increase over prior year	0	(13,494)		
Enrollment, K–12				
Full-time equivalency, September 20	474,747	423,968	(50,779)	(10.7)
Change from prior year	0	9,375		
Certified employees	29,542	34,500	4,958	16.8
Change from prior year	0	292		

SOURCE: Kansas State Department of Education, *School Districts—Selected Data 1972–1992* (Topeka: Kansas State Department of Education, 1992).

17-fold in a 30-year period, straining a tax system already burdened by other soaring requirements.

The impact of demographics and other issues pressuring an adequate level of educational funding has been highly differential among the states. Because there is no national education system in the United States, it is correct to observe that states fund education differently and have different experiences based on their individual populations and individual economies. This wide variety is troublesome because it may be assumed that children receive different levels of education based on available resources that are state-dependent and based on how widely those resources must be spread across needy populations. These differences may be sizable even among states that have not experienced the recent tremendous demographic changes found in some states, simply because the various states are not equal in their abilities and preferences to fund education.

The variations among states in adequately funding education can be illustrated by data from two midwestern states. These states are exemplary for several reasons. First, they have classic populations without the dramatic surges and declines experienced in some other states. Second, both states have experienced recent court challenges over the method of financing education. Third, both have exhibited interest in educational reform in recent years, with one of the two states passing legislation dramatically increasing requirements on local school districts and providing additional appropriations to assist in meeting the costs of "improved" educational quality. The data on these two states are thus useful in illustrating changes in revenue and expenditure patterns and in estimating the adequacy of revenues to meet costs in the foreseeable future.

Table 1.13 illustrates revenue growth for one state in the context of adequate funding levels for education. In addition to assessing revenue growth over a 20-year period, the time span allows observation of other important changes that have occurred in service, levels of support, and public attitudes over a volatile period of national and state history.

Three important observations stand out strikingly from the data. First, revenues increased dramatically over the period 1972–1992, with general fund budgets increasing 345% to more than $1.33 billion. Second, state aid also increased, to more than $428 million (+434.7%), an increase much greater than expenditure growth. Third, this state, like many others, did not limit increased state participation to traditional expenditure areas; that is, the state also assumed a more active role in other areas, such as transportation, where expenditures went up $38.55 million (642.5%). A fourth observation regarding new roles for the state is equally important to the growing complexity of school funding schemes. Column 1 reflects the increasing state role, showing that many new state aids were introduced in the 20-year period. Areas receiving increased state aid included aid to special education, which increased by 2,799%. A final observation notes that in total, state aid to general fund expenditures increased 605.3% over the period, while the sum of total general fund budgets in the state increased a significant, although smaller, 345%. At the same time, however, it is important to note that K–12 enrollment decreased –10.7%, while the number of certified employees increased 16.8%.

These data reflect dramatically increased state involvement in education funding and an unprecedented expansion of educational services, accompanied by decline in the number of students served by an increasing number of staff. The reasons are apparent to most educators: staff growth is largely attributable to special education, and other growth derives from inflation and new programs and services. The growth in state participation is also apparent, as the state's share of budgets increased from an average 25.5% in 1972–1973 to 42.5% in 1991–1992. Under these conditions, education appears to have increased in importance to the state, making it difficult for administrators to argue a lack of adequate support for schools. Not every state, however, has fared as well, and the future is in many instances highly uncertain.

The uncertainty of adequate revenues for education can be illustrated by looking at a second midwestern state's experience. With increased national concern over the cost-benefit debate, state legislatures have begun to look beyond counting course offerings and auditing school days in session to determine the quality of education. Some legislatures have become more aggressive in their attempts to increase student achievement by tying funding to test data. Data on our second state fall within that category because, in exchange for continuing to qualify for state aid, schools must meet newly enacted reform standards calling for districts to standardize curricula using outcomes standards for core subjects. Additionally, the state required every kindergarten teacher to become certified in early childhood education, required every district to provide early childhood services, demanded that all students in grades 3, 5, 7, 9, and 11 must pass a competency test before moving to the next grade, and ordered that every senior must pass a criterion-referenced test with a score sufficiently high to permit entry into the state's higher education system without remediation. Additionally, the legislature ordered the state board of education to close or annex any school failing to meet standards and mandated that class sizes shall not exceed 20 students in grades K–6 or more than 120 students in a six-hour day in grades 7–12. Finally, districts were ordered to provide parent education, to raise teacher salaries by 29% over five years, and to provide staff development that would collectively amount to millions of dollars in new expenditures.

As expected, a coalition of school districts filed a lawsuit alleging that the reforms could not be met because revenue had been historically inadequate to provide a quality education and that newly promised appropriations would not be sufficient to meet the added costs. As seen in columns 5 and 6 of Table 1.14, meeting class size mandates

TABLE 1.14 Plaintiff costs

District Name	Percentage State Aid	Percentage in Local Dollars	Percentage Federal Aid	Teachers Class Size	Teachers Content	Salary Cost 5 Years	All Dollars 5 Years
District A	68.38	27.89	3.71	264	8	$ 2,873,000	$ 11,184,600
District B	58.27	39.48	2.24	56	6	2,243,000	52,671,940
District C	75.65	20.54	3.8	59	23	1,477,100	5,910,099
District D	74.11	15.2	10.68	11	5	721,008	2,205,122
District E	59.07	19.88	21.04	30	0	10,380,064	11,165,332
District F	71.6	23.49	89	3	0	790,600	1,215,144
District G	76.2	20.99	2.8	0	2	908,338	1,069,528
District H	78.01	17.81	4.16	1	1	132,130	261,694
District I	72.07	23.2	4.71	14	2	546,000	2,821,000
District J	74.17	22.58	3.24	0	1	199,093	222,647
District K	66.6	28.66	4.72	0	0	109,000	141,800
District L	74.52	19.14	6.33	11	4	415,981	857,075
District M	81.68	13.95	4.36	0	1	227,955	257,215
District N	71.97	24.09	3.93	3	0	697,825	876,450
District O	70.51	25.18	4.3	0	2	220,800	1,052,702
District P	67.22	24.23	8.53	2	0	823,500	918,500
District Q	66.51	27.49	5.98	0	0	547,200	617,200
District R	74.51	21.37	4.1	0	0	0	0
District S	62.48	30.65	6.85	0	1	132,000	314,500
District T	56.84	40.72	2.42	68	6	8,747,771	10,447,630
District U	72.59	22.46	4.94	10	13	15,410,935	6,168,212
District V	61.52	36.3	2.16	360	15	4,470,752	13,498,752

(*Continued*)

TABLE 1.14 (*Continued*)

District Name	Percentage State Aid	Percentage in Local Dollars	Percentage Federal Aid	Teachers Class Size	Teachers Content	Salary Cost 5 Years	All Dollars 5 Years
District W	57.88	39.98	3.13	5	13	385,162	9,954,093
District X	70.85	23.46	5.67	2	1	396,792	471,456
District Y	59.88	25.21	14.89	0	1	299,000	380,000
District Z	71.36	25.38	3.25	1	1	119,400	287,216
District AA	75.75	15.95	8.29	3	3	200,000	1,445,620
District BB	71.82	25.05	3.11	0	5	584,168	2,481,566
District CC	75.57	19.72	4.69	1	1	415,676	499,376
District DD	86.04	11.38	2.56	1	1	36,500	100,030
District EE	48.57	45.75	5.67	222	18	47,479,000	55,701,915
District FF	73.42	21.97	4.59	13	3	2,933,928	3,543,166
District GG	71.37	26.15	2.47	197	0	16,906,000	53,862,000
District HH	67.45	29.68	2.85	8	10	1,984,500	5,422,500
District II	72.56	22.64	4.78	1	3	765,600	2,252,074
District JJ	74.7	17.08	8.21	12	30	1,110,000	2,000,079
District KK	68.04	27.76	4.19	3	0	345,600	597,676
District LL	78.02	15.22	6.75	2	4	1,616,767	1,795,641
District MM	60.18	36.08	3.72	0	13	3,000,000	11,588,751
Total				1363	197	$130,652,145	$276,260,301

source: David C. Thompson, David Honeyman, and R. Craig Wood, *Adequacy of Educational Revenues in Oklahoma School Districts: Expert Analysis on Behalf of Plaintiff in Fair School Finance Council, Inc., v. State of Oklahoma* (Manhattan, Kans.: Wood, Thompson & Associates, 1992), 80.

and comprehensive new curriculum content was forbidding, requiring a total of 1,363 new teachers to reduce class size in plaintiff districts alone, and with another 197 new teachers needed in those same districts to deliver increased subject requirements. Reform costs were formidable, as columns 7 and 8 put the price of simply meeting salary enhancements in all plaintiff districts at more than $130 million and with the total cost of reform topping $276 million in plaintiff districts alone. Much of the cost was for catching up by rectifying deficiencies flagged by the state. Among the commonly flagged violations were insufficient library and guidance staff, high dropout rates, low test scores, low performing school sites, and new subject areas including language arts, mathematics, social studies, health, physical education, fine arts, computers, foreign languages, technical education, and practical arts. Under these conditions, plaintiffs alleged inadequate funding, with severe impact on instructional programs.

Although the legislature had promised enhanced appropriations, revenues were estimated to fall short of both current costs and the costs of reform. A task force had concluded earlier that reforms alone would require approximately $214 million in the first year, and that the total cost of reform would require an additional $721 million *per year* to sustain the initiative. Additionally, the task force noted that approximately $82 million would be required annually to shore up existing unfunded mandates, and that only $232 million in state monies would be available from expected growth in tax collections from current sources. The problem of adequate funding is strikingly illustrated in Table 1.15, which reveals data on projected revenues. The data show that the costs of reform are expected to increase annually at about 40% per year in this state throughout the first five years of reform, as the most costly mandates, such as reducing class size, are achieved. In contrast, revenue growth averaging 2% falls far short of costs, resulting in a shortfall of about −$122 million per year. As seen in Figure 1.5, revenue adequacy in this state is in serious question despite hundreds of millions of school dollars assessed annually to taxpayers.

TABLE 1.15   Budget estimates fiscal year 1991–1995 of property tax projections for the common schools (in thousands of dollars)

	1990–1991	1991–1992	1992–1993	1993–1994	1994–1995
Costs					
Unfunded mandates/cost increases	$ 68,200	$ 71,000	$ 88,900	$ 88,900	$ 88,900
Other legislative funds	802	1,255	1,340	1,380	1,380
Projected costs	214,430	326,035	455,515	684,957	721,268
Total program costs	$283,432	$398,290	$545,755	$775,237	$811,548
Increase percentage		40.52%	37.02%	42.05%	4.68%
Revenues (including cost savings)					
With 4% ad valorem increase	$455,840	$517,330	$585,962	$655,313	$728,093
Ad valorem increase	120,000	124,800	129,792	134,983	140,383
Rev. net ad valorem increase		392,530	456,170	520,330	587,710
Increase (percentage)		2.04%	2.00%	1.96%	2.03%
Surplus (shortage)	$172,408	$119,040	$40,207	($119,924)	($83,455)

SOURCE: David C. Thompson, David Honeyman, and R. Craig Wood, *Adequacy of Educational Revenues in Oklahoma School Districts: Expert Analysis on Behalf of Plaintiff in Fair School Finance Council, Inc., v. State of Oklahoma* (Manhattan, Kans.: Wood, Thompson & Associates, 1992), 91.

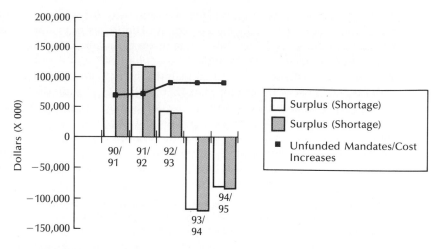

FIGURE 1.5   Change in revenue surplus from all sources compared to growth in unfunded program costs, 1990–1991 through 1994–1995

SOURCE: David C. Thompson, David Honeyman, and R. Craig Wood, *Adequacy of Educational Revenues in Oklahoma School Districts: Expert Analysis on Behalf of Plaintiff in Fair School Finance Council, Inc., v. State of Oklahoma* (Manhattan, Kans.: Wood, Thompson & Associates, 1992), 92.

The scenario of dramatically increased revenues and shortfalls has become commonplace in the last decade, and data on adequate revenue for education are a confusing morass of desires, resentments, mandates, and frustrations. On one hand, the numbers are so enormous it is hard to imagine that revenues are not enough, and to ask for more must stretch the limits of reason, particularly since it must be recognized that education is only one of the many functions of government. On the other hand, data from the second illustration show the depth of needs and reflect the ever-increasing demand on schools from all quarters of society.[94] Thus it is far easier to consider the concept of adequate funding than it is to quantify a dividing line between adequate and inadequate revenues. There are no easy answers. All that remains certain is that education and socioeconomic status are linked, that needs will continue to increase while public debate rages, and that the controlling principle of economics, which pits unlimited needs against finite resources, is both simple and profoundly enduring.

FINANCING SCHOOLS EQUITABLY

In contrast to the difficult task of defining adequacy in education finance, equity has been easier both to define and to measure. Yet not all facets of an equitable system of financing education have been discovered, nor has any state achieved equity for students or taxpayers because our understanding of equity continues to expand. In the absence of hard data on the critical point for determining whether revenue is adequate to produce satisfactory educational opportunities, however, researchers have been more successful in defining equitable resource distribution.

If *adequacy* is the concept of having *enough* resources to provide for children's educational needs, *equity* is the concept of a *fair and just method of distributing resources* among those same children. But *equity is not blind equality*—indeed, scholars have noted that equality may be a very great vice if practiced rigidly or naïvely. Nearly 20 years ago, Benson succinctly summarized the depth of the issue of equity versus equality:

> Obviously, providing equal dollar inputs for unequal students produces un-equal results. Equal spending does not make education the "great equalizer of the conditions of men" as Horace Mann suggested in the last century. If education is to facilitate the movement of the poor and disadvantaged into the mainstream of American social and economic life, if it is to afford every-one equal probability of success (however one defines it), then equal facili-ties, teaching skills, and curriculums are not the answer. Additional re-sources must be made available to students who enter and pass through the educational system with handicaps such as language barriers for which they are not responsible.[95]

While many people continue to believe that equality requires all persons to be treated the same or fail to go beyond Benson's reference to a limited special popula-tion, equity has taken on a progressively more sophisticated meaning. Equality and equity have become widely different concepts resulting in a myriad of rules, regula-tions, and court decisions in an attempt to change attitudes and practices surrounding these difficult issues. A classic example is the vast amount of resources channeled toward special education since the 1976 enactment of special education laws in the United States.[96] Other examples include special entitlement programs, such as Chap-ter 1 reading and math for low income children and Head Start that grew out of the dramatic social reforms of the 1960s, and the sweeping changes affecting general education expenditures that resulted from a series of school finance lawsuits starting in the late 1960s and continuing today. Yet while equity and equality differ, their interrelationship is vitally important. In a summative sense, *equity may be seen as the precondition of equality where the hope for equal opportunities requires unequal inputs.*

Concern for equity raises questions of how sensitive society should be about equitable treatment of individuals or groups. These are not easy questions because resources are limited, and policymakers have had to settle for less than fully satisfac-tory solutions. While no one questions that children must be the object of equity, the search for solutions has been confused. For example, when courts are forced to choose under limited resource scenarios, their solutions are often perceived as less concerned about taxpayer equity than with child equity issues. But can a distribution scheme treat children equitably without concomitant concern for taxpayer burden since taxpayers ultimately pay for all governmental services, including education? Clearly, it would be an easier task to focus on *either* children or taxpayers, but the interrelatedness of these groups complicates the issue, particularly as every taxpayer has a different level of financial ability to support education—a complex problem since all states except Hawaii have many school districts, all with varying tax base capacity. Further, questions of groups versus individuals are unresolved. For example, is it prerequisite of an equitable finance plan to microscopically examine the impact of an aid formula on each child, or is it enough to provide roughly equal money to similar children? In the first instance, equity might require that finance systems be evaluated by research methods similar to the model criticized earlier in which the grasp of school finance experts is quickly exceeded by moving into microlevel and psychological dimensions of education. In the second instance, equity might propose that children be exactly equal in funding within a state, with some limited recognition of other needs such as handicap, low enrollment, geographic isolation, or similar circumstance. But under such a plan, perfect equity and equality are conceptually abandoned because children are not treated individually. The problems are enormous because history has shown great imprecision in establishing categories into which children are placed without firm confidence of their accuracy. Yet, no method assures equal outcomes—the focus remains on front loading in hopes of a better product—an assumption flawed by its very nature.

This brief glimpse of the complexity of child-taxpayer equity issues can be confirmed using actual 1991 data from lawsuits in one state that has recently experienced litigation over the state aid distribution scheme. Table 1.16 suggests that unless some other explanation justifies differences, children in this state are unequal on the front end of the distribution and expenditure plan. Using average (mean) general fund expenditures as the basis of comparison between districts, plaintiffs spent a mean $2,036.65 per pupil compared to a mean $2,232.05 for all nonplaintiff districts. The 10 wealthiest districts, in contrast, spent a mean $3,944.01. This pattern holds true for each expenditure category. If actual expenditures had been used instead of averages, differences would have been far greater, since the highest-spending district spent more than $10,000 per pupil, while the lowest-spending district spent less than $1,300 per pupil. If one were to judge solely on these data, it would be concluded that, absent other explanation, equity is unacceptably violated because children are so unequally funded.

Table 1.17 offers additional insight by considering whether there are any justifia-

TABLE 1.16 Selected per-pupil expenditure patterns for plaintiff districts compared to other districts (1991)

Category	Plaintiff Mean	Percentage of General Fund	Non-plaintiff Mean	Percentage of General Fund	10 Wealthy Districts— Mean	Percentage of General Fund
General Fund						
Total general fund expend.	$2,036.65	100.00	$2,232.05	100.00	$3,944.01	100.00
Administration	91.03	4.47	127.52	5.71	255.16	6.47
Instruction	1,296.83	63.67	1,359.29	60.90	2,031.20	51.50
Transportation	81.57	4.01	114.30	5.12	280.56	7.11
Food services	34.61	1.70	59.82	2.68	137.07	3.48
Student body activities	6.58	0.32	11.70	0.52	23.17	0.59
Capital outlay	34.08	1.67	83.83	3.76	361.86	9.17
Non general fund categories						
Constant building fund	$ 57.47		$ 91.68		$ 472.30	
Debt service sinking	36.76		32.54		25.74	

SOURCE: David C. Thompson, David Honeyman, and R. Craig Wood, *Adequacy of Educational Revenues in Oklahoma School Districts: Expert Analysis on Behalf of Plaintiff in Fair School Finance Council, Inc., v. State of Oklahoma* (Manhattan, Kans.: Wood, Thompson & Associates, 1992), 33.

TABLE 1.17 Percentage differences of selected expenditures per pupil, plaintiffs compared to all others (1991)

Category	Plaintiff Mean	Percentage Difference Nonplaintiff	Percentage Difference 10 Wealthy
General fund			
Tot. general fund expend.	$ 2,036.65	8.75	48.36
Administration	91.03	28.62	64.32
Instruction	1,296.83	4.60	36.15
Transportation	81.57	28.64	70.93
Food services	34.61	42.14	74.75
Student body activities	6.58	43.76	71.60
Capital outlay	34.08	59.35	90.58
Non general fund categories			
Constant building fund	$ 57.47	37.31	87.83
Debt service sinking	36.76	−12.97	−42.81

SOURCE: David C. Thompson, David Honeyman, and R. Craig Wood, *Adequacy of Educational Revenues in Oklahoma School Districts: Expert Analysis on Behalf of Plaintiff in Fair School Finance Council, Inc., v. State of Oklahoma* (Manhattan, Kans.: Wood, Thompson & Associates, 1992), 36.

ble reasons for expenditure differences, and extends the discussion to the concept of taxpayer equity. While determining whether a formula satisfies equity is complex, Table 1.17 suggests that while legitimate expenditure differences may exist in this state, there are also highly illegitimate differences. The issue of improper difference is seen in the consistently lower expenditures in plaintiff districts compared to all districts and compared to the state's 10 wealthiest districts, confirming unfavorable relationships between tax base and expenditure. In every budget category, plaintiff expenditures are below the equivalent categories in all nonplaintiff districts and below equivalent categories in the 10 wealthiest districts. Differences are particularly striking in individual line items. For example, the wealthiest districts spend 36.15% more for instruction, 71.6% more for student activities, 90.58% more for capital outlay, and 87.83% more for the building fund. Considered in tandem with other data, the table suggests the higher a district's tax base, the more revenue is available to actually be spent, leaving a prima facie assumption of inequity. Because students in poorer districts receive less, pupil equity is suspect. Because taxpayers cannot support educational programs equal to their wealthier counterparts under equal tax effort, tax equity is also suspect. Equity is thus extraordinarily complex—but nonetheless more obvious than what constitutes an adequate level of revenues and expenditures.

The data in Tables 1.16 and 1.17 are not anomalies to the various states. In fact, the differences shown are not great by comparison to some states (see Table 1.12). Disparity in revenue and expenditure is common, despite a lengthy history of litigation seeking more equitable systems of school finance. Part of the issue is protectiveness, as persons in wealthy districts enjoy higher resource levels. But still another part is that equity is deceptively simple: it is easier to define but deeper than it appears, and painfully complex to achieve.

One of the most important questions is whether equity should be considered only horizontally (equal treatment of equals) or also vertically (unequal treatment of unequals). A second question is whether to be concerned only for students or to include taxpayers—an issue that may also be horizontal or vertical: shall tax equity be a function of neutral property assessment without consideration for income level or percentage of property ownership, or shall taxpayer equity also include the owner's equity in a property and income's relationship to the tax burden?[97] As noted previously, can taxpayer equity accurately be separated from pupil equity? Critically important is the basic question of how equitable should the system be. Equity is so profoundly broad in its potential definition that nothing less than absolute income equality might be required if socioeconomic opportunity in an egalitarian society is ever to be fully achieved—an issue highly problematic for capitalist society.[98] These and many other problems continue to plague the search for fiscal equity, even when all parties agree that children are the primary focus. The current sophistication of research is such that inequity is easily identified, but solutions are technically difficult and politically improbable. The best scenario yet to be devised has been compromise, calling for continued sensitivity and vigilance to the critical value of education, and seeking to apply justice to education on the broadest acceptable scale.[99]

ECONOMICS, EQUALITY, PRODUCTIVITY, AND LIBERTY IN A CAPITALIST DEMOCRACY

The status of education in society is a direct reflection on the level of civilization a nation has achieved. As civilizations progress, education becomes more important in creating and sustaining economic and social patterns—so much so that the nation itself becomes dependent on its ability to produce a continually improved educational product. When a break occurs in the cycle, the security and prosperity of the nation and its people are threatened.

As the United States prepares to enter a new millennium, few would argue that the nation is secure against such a breach. Few would further deny that the productivity of the American educational system has slipped during the last half of the twentieth century. Most would also agree that a part of that slippage is attributable to problems in the larger society that are now beginning to confront education on a large scale. Society's problems have created enormous tensions among the forces of economics, equality, productivity, liberty, and capitalist democracy. While it cannot be said that a perfect society is one in which no such tensions exist, the security of the future depends on finding an acceptable middle ground if current negative trends are to be reversed. Changing the course of a nation requires strong social policies which, as Guthrie notes, are themselves influenced by technical, cultural, and political considerations.[100] The difficulty is that these tensions may be fundamentally irreconcilable within our present form of government since equality and productivity are antithetical, and there is likewise cognitive dissonance between equality and liberty. These structural incompatibilities will likely be enhanced, given recent population changes in the nation, unless solutions appear that reflect technical mechanisms, cultural sensitivity, and political redefinition of traditional capitalist democracy.

Technical, cultural, and political solutions are currently in short supply. Economic survival must be addressed, and solutions created that address economics in the context of the changing demographics of the nation. Cultural barriers must be recognized, as waves of poorly educated immigrants and growth in disadvantaged populations have raised questions and resentment about how socioeconomic mobility and prosperity will be transmitted among generations in the future—a very difficult question given Hodgkinson's observation that the combination of age, birthrate, and family status *is* the future. Political solutions promise to be difficult as well, as the United States was built on a history of fierce individualism, basically ignoring the incompatibility of the diverse goals of equality, productivity, liberty, capitalism, and democracy. Yet solutions must be found, because as one critic in *Nation at Risk* noted, "For the first time in the history of our country, the educational skills of one generation will not surpass, will not equal, will not even approach, those of their parents." If this statement is permitted to become reality, then the nation indeed *is* in a state of decline.

The remaining chapters in Part 1 of this text seek to explore many of these difficult problems by discussing historic and current thinking on technical, cultural, and political issues. We now turn in Chapter 2 to examining the history of school finance in America by tracing the development of federal, state, and local governments' role in funding education. From that discussion, we can gather a better appreciation of how such complex problems have developed, achieve a clearer sense of why government has become more responsible for education, and gain a fuller understanding of the incompleteness of responsibility for education that still exists today.

Review Points

THE SCOPE OF EDUCATION FINANCE IN AMERICA

Growth in K-12 education revenues and expenditures has been phenomenal, increasing from $215 million in 1900 to more than $200 billion in 1992. Fiscal growth in education has been remarkable, increasing even in cataclysmic events such as the Great Depression.

Growth has been hastened by crises. These have included world wars, the space race, and social confrontations such as civil rights, social reform, and school finance litigation to better equalize educational opportunity.

Americans have been willing to fund massive increases principally because of a national psychology that links education to social and economic prosperity.

DEMOGRAPHICS OF A CHANGING AMERICA

The United States has always been a nation of diverse population as evidenced by its assemblage of nationalities that made up settlement of the new land.

Recent changes in the demographic mix, however, have begun to reshape the nation. Of particular import have been new immigration patterns in nonwhite populations; dramatic redefinition of the family; tremendous growth in special education populations; rapid growth in poverty; and social disintegration such as severe drug problems and crime.

Educational implications of the new demography include continued growth in special needs populations; emphasis on new and broadened special needs categories; increased identification and placement of special needs children; a need to change instructional methods based on a variety of socioeconomic needs relating to cultural differences and social problems that affect a child's environment; a need to acknowledge and approve the changed mission of schools in meeting clientele needs; and the need to recognize that the options are education or national decline.

EDUCATION AS AN ECONOMIC AND SOCIAL GOOD

Economics and education are partners in that schools prepare children to become productive citizens; education also stimulates the economy by creating a demand for itself.

Education develops human capital by improving the worth of workers.

Education has both private and public benefits, wherein individuals profit by investment in education, with spillovers that benefit all of society.

The externalities of education are a prime driver behind paying for schools according to the ability-to-pay principle.

Returns on educational investment include significant residuals attributable to human capital.

While the rate-of-return on investment is not exactly proportional to investment, it is clear that more education has more benefits than less education.

Research on achievement and resources indicate that some critical influencers of achievement can be purchased, making these decisions critically important.

FINANCING SCHOOLS ADEQUATELY

Despite massive investment, an adequate level of funding is difficult to achieve given the persistent context of limited resources and unlimited needs.

State reform efforts are laudable, but they may force worse problems if inadequately funded.

FINANCING SCHOOLS EQUITABLY

Equity has been sought more fervently since it is more easily defined, more measurable, and more achievable.

Equity is deceptive because it is not achieved by mere equality—that is, equity must consider multiple dimensions relating to students and taxpayers, and inherent inequalities among them.

ECONOMICS, EQUALITY, PRODUCTIVITY, AND LIBERTY IN A CAPITALIST DEMOCRACY

Education faces major challenges related to diverse and antithetical goals.

Some major tensions are irresoluble—for example, liberty seeks individual freedom, while equity seeks class-based justice—similarly, equality seeks a degree of uniformity that may conflict with the competitiveness of productivity.

It can be argued that these tensions, in balance, are necessary because any alternative would be antidemocratic.

Solutions must be sought, but perfect equilibrium is doubtful since complex technical, cultural, and political variables will compete for superiority.

Case Study

You have recently taken a new position as assistant to the superintendent in a school district that has a history of taxpayer militancy on government's budget proposals. In this state, no public referendum on the annually adopted budget is required, but the state's open meetings law provides for both public hearing on the budget and a recorded vote by board of education members on the proposed budget. You know that community members through a highly vocal organization calling itself the Home Owners Trust (HOT) have been pressuring board members to reduce property taxes. HOT's logic is as follows: First, the school district's legal spending limit has permitted an increase in the general fund budget of approximately 640% over the last 20 years, and the board has chosen to tax to its permissible maximum authority. Second, property taxes in the district have gone up by about 400% in the same period, with the largest increases in the last four years as a result of closure of two major industries in the community, sharp tax increases due to property reappraisal under court order to bring assessments into constitutional requirements, severe agricultural depression, special education mandates, and increased tax delinquency—all of which have forced the district's tax rate upward. Third, the state has reduced aid to the district because it is losing enrollment, which affects its budget through an enrollment decline penalty designed to require districts to be fiscally efficient. These and other problems have led HOT to demand property tax relief. Specifically, they are proposing a mandatory 30% expenditure cut with targeted actual line item reductions. They want to cut 7 administrators (−$285,700), 158 teachers (−$3.5 million), 86 other personnel (−$1.3 million), computer program products (−$66,200), supplies and textbooks (−$426,300), furniture and computer purchases (−$28,500), athletics (−$192,800), and student projects (−$16,000). Additionally, they have recommended reducing specific program budgets, including vocational education (−3.37%), capital projects (−20.7%), bilingual education (−4.41%), food services (−1.26%), and in-service education (−50%). The business office estimates total net proposed reductions at $7.2 million, or approximately 4% of the total budget. To make matters worse, HOT has the sympathy of several influential business people, including your board president.

As assistant to the superintendent, you have been told to prepare a response to these requests. The superintendent's office will provide help in preparing the report, and the two of you will schedule meetings with every organization you can persuade to give you time. Fortunately, it is now September and the current year's budget is already in place, but HOT has informed the board that it wants quick action so next year's budget can reflect significant economies. The superintendent's goal is to make 100 presentations over the next eight months. Using the following sets of information and questions to help guide your deliberations and class discussion, what do you anticipate your approach to be? Why? Defend your view through logic, data, and use of appropriate theory.

Case Study Directed Discussion

1. As you prepare your presentation, you have gathered other information about the district. Specifically, you have learned that many of the district's 45,000 students have serious problems. For example, nearly 50% of all junior high students are in active at-risk support programs (defined by the district as students having attendance problems, low test scores, low grades, frequent disciplinary action, free/reduced lunches, broken family, a substance abuse history, or are victims of abuse). Statistics show 980 drug users receiving homebound instruction; a 400% increase in reported physical or sexual abuse to 700 cases in only three years; nearly 1,000 children receiving English as a Second Language (ESL) instruction in 52 languages; 550 teen births last year representing 7% of all county births; and a 26% dropout rate. Last year, expenditures for Chapter 1 services were $5 million, but 8,000 eligible students were not served. Nearly 12% of all children were in special education, ranging in *excess* cost from a low $3,500 (gifted) to a high $16,100 (Severely Mentally Handicapped—SMH). You also calculated that at-risk spending alone is an additional $1,100 per child, totalling nearly $17 million (almost 10% of the district's budget). How will such data add to your presentation?

2. In recent years, protest to government has become extremely common. Disaffected groups continually raise their concerns, often in opposingly strident voices. For example, groups commonly seek to ban books and purge courses or materials of objectionable content. Alternatively, there is a powerful movement to force the teaching of forms of tolerance that may contradict belief systems. The common mode on both sides is to attempt enlistment of government's help in putting forward a particular philosophy. As you read this case study, do you speculate that there are any motives beyond the desire to reduce spending? If not, why not? If so, how might these be manifested in the data? As you read the case study and available data, do you think the critics have any valid points? What are they, and how will they factor into your presentation?

3. It may be suggested that protest behavior against government is an acceptable outlet for resentments that have become submerged in a culture that many say severely censures political incorrectness. How do you think this might factor into HOT's attitude—or alternatively, is speculating about such a motive simply a knee-jerk mirror image to an overstated perception of "in-your-face" politics? In other words, should political overtones be removed, leaving only the question of whether it is unreasonable to reduce a budget by 4%—that is, how much of the budget is devoted to "nonessential" services in light of the proposed cuts? If it is true that another agenda is operating here, how should you respond? If it is not true, what response is most appropriate?

4. What short-term and long-term impacts would you envision if these cuts are carried out? Additionally, remember that HOT has actually served notice that it eventually expects the cuts to be much deeper—4% now in specific targeted items, and 26% later, either targeted or left to district discretion. Can

this be done realistically? Is there a reasonable response to these demands, that is, are the demands themselves reasonable leading to reasonable reply; and alternatively, can a reasoned reply be effective if demands are not reasonable? If these demands are not met, what is the anticipated outcome? If they are met, what behavior can be expected of HOT in the future? How will this factor into your presentation?

5. How does this brief case study compare with reality in your state? Have there been similar instances, either greater or lesser? What is the general tenor of school budget politics and social awareness where you live? Could this happen to you? Do you think this represents a passing phase, or will administrators be expected to live with such crisis demands for the foreseeable future? Do you think that such intense scrutiny of schools is healthy in the long-term by forcing overdue efficiencies, or is it the mark of political fractiousness and internal social decay? What should be the posture of educational leaders toward either reality?

6. As this case study was based on a real event, you should know the outcome. In response to the short-term demands, the board proposed a budget for the following year that would cut 200 teachers and 24 central administrators and 141 other nonteaching staff; cut $190,000 from athletics; allow a $2.9 million shortfall in special education; a $1.5 million shortfall in vocational education, and a $300,000 shortfall in in-service; eliminate 32 area directors; cut 10 social service/special education coordinators; cut 2 high school principals and 20 assistant high school principals; eliminate all 21 assistant middle school principals; and eliminate 13 elementary principals and all 18 elementary assistant principals. As you view these proposals, do you think the board responded appropriately, both politically and within the law? Why or why not? If cuts were forced, would you make these same cuts?

NOTES

1. National Commission on Excellence in Education, *A Nation at Risk: The Imperative for Educational Reform* (Washington, D.C.: National Commission on Excellence in Education, 1983), p. i.

2. Carnegie Task Force on Teaching as a Profession, *A Nation Prepared: Teachers for the 21st Century* (Washington, D.C.: Carnegie Task Force on Teaching as a Profession, 1986).

3. NCEE, *Nation at Risk,* 5.

4. Growth in the national debt has been phenomenal. Debt in 1870 was $2.4 billion or $61 per capita. The national debt actually declined from 1870 to 1930, with the exception of 1920 when the debt jumped to $24.2 billion from $1.1 billion in 1910. In contrast, the 1988 national debt amounted to $10,534 per capita, with $214.1 billion in interest charges, and totaling 20.1% of all federal outlays.

5. Some knowledgeable persons could take exception to the statement of annualized expenditures because a few states do permit deficit spending within current operational budgets. General practice in most states, however, is to require balanced operating budgets with only bonded indebtedness as the common obligation against districts' future revenues.

6. More detailed discussion of earlier periods in education's history in the United States appears in Chapter 2.

7. Growth in revenues and expenditures is a complex topic that cannot be developed fully in a text of this nature. Economists and school finance experts are often quick to warn readers against simple interpretations of raw numbers because of other extraneous variables, such as inflation, which tend to draw down the real net increases in monetary value. The authors concur with that view, but note that in the context of introducing educational practitioners to school finance, it is accurate to say that both current and net revenues and expenditures for schools have increased dramatically over the current century because of education's increasing share of the GNP and because even after adjusting for net growth, the smaller adjusted net increases over a substantial period of time still result in substantial real revenue and expenditure growth. Both economists and school finance experts likely err by virtue of the nature of their disciplines.

8. 347 U.S. 483, 74 S.Ct. 686 (1954). A fuller discussion of the impact of this landmark U.S. Supreme Court case appears in Chapter 5.

9. The reader should not assume a tight federal partnership for education from this statement. As will be seen in later chapters, the federal role has indeed been omnipresent, but in a limited interest based on current social, economic, or security concerns as in the National Defense Education Act (1958), the Elementary and Secondary Education Act (ESEA, 1965), later retitled the Education Consolidation and Improvement Act (ECIA, 1981), and other legislation demonstrating limited federal intent.

10. Chapter 5 discusses the breadth and implications of court rulings on federal and state participation in school finance.

11. This section borrows heavily from David C. Thompson, "State Education Finance Policies and Special Student Populations," in *Who Pays for Student Diversity? Population Changes and Educational Policy,* ed. James G. Ward and Patricia Anthony. 1991 American Education Finance Association Yearbook (Beverly Hills: Sage, 1991). The section also draws significantly from David C. Thompson, "Funding Rural Special Populations," in *Helping At-Risk Students,* 1992 American Education Finance Association Yearbook, ed. Patricia Anthony and Stephen Jacobson (Beverly Hills: Sage, 1992).

12. Harold Hodgkinson, *All One System: Demographics of Education, Kindergarten Through Graduate School* (Washington, D.C.: Institute for Educational Leadership, 1985).

13. Hodgkinson, *All One System,* 3.

14. Children's Defense Fund, *A Vision for America's Future: An Agenda for the 1990's: A Children's Defense Budget* (Washington, D.C.: Children's Defense Fund, 1989).

15. See, for example, Thompson, "State Education Finance Policies," 97–124.

16. Hodgkinson, *All One System,* 5.

17. Nicholas Zill, *Developmental, Learning, and Emotional Problems: Health of Our Nation's Children* (Washington, D.C.: Child Trends, 1990).

18. Reynaldo Macias, "Bilingual Teacher Supply and Demand in the United States," in *Staffing the Multilingually Impacted Schools of the 1990s,* National Forum on Personnel Needs for Districts with Changing Demographics (Washington, D.C.: U.S. Department of Education, Office of Bilingual Education and Minority Languages Affairs, 1989).

19. Macias, "Bilingual Teacher Supply and Demand."

20. More difficult than providing services under budget constraints is recognition of new needs. The process is so slow and uncertain that even advocacy groups cannot agree on the need and level of services to be provided. For example, the proposed ADD classification is the subject of much controversy. A letter dated August 28, 1991, forwarded to members of the Education and Labor Committee in Washington and jointly prepared and signed by 17 national and/or state education associations, urged deletion of the ADD classification from redefinitions of disability under the Education of the Handicapped Act (EHA).

21. The National Alliance of Black Educators has charged that black students are too frequently misidentified and directed into special education programs. Similarly, estimates suggest

that nearly two-thirds of LEP students in Texas may be incorrectly identified as learning disabled (LD) due to reading comprehension problems. *EHA Newsletter* (January 1991).

22. Estimates of cocaine births differ markedly by authoring organization. The Government Accounting Office has estimated 375,000 such births annually. The government believes that if testing were uniform across public assistance and privately insured populations, higher incidence would be found. The government cites as reason for distrust that its own study found hospitals varied widely in tests for drugs and some hospitals did not test infants or mothers at all unless the mother identified herself as a user or unless the baby's condition signaled drug exposure. The main reason cited for the difference was that the National Hospital Discharge Survey is reluctant to ask paying (as opposed to Medicaid) patients to submit to drug tests. David C. Thompson, "Special Needs Students: A Generation At-Risk," in *Who Pays for Student Diversity? Population Changes and Educational Policy,* ed. James G. Ward and Patricia Anthony (Beverly Hills: Sage, 1992), 107.

23. National Association for Perinatal Addiction Research and Education (1991).

24. *Counterpoint* (1990).

25. National Center for Education Statistics, *Youth Indicators, 1991,* (Washington, D.C.: National Center for Education Statistics, 1991); Regents' Task Force on Education, *Building Hope for Tomorrow: Creating Education in Tomorrow,* A Special Report to the Governor and Citizens of Kansas (Topeka: 1992), 3.

26. National Education Association, *Rankings of the States, 1991* (Washington, D.C.: National Education Association, 1991), 59.

27. Daniel C. Rogers and Hirsch S. Ruchlin, *Economics and Education* (New York: Free Press, 1971), 5.

28. Theodore Schultz, "The Human Capital Approach to Education," in *Economic Factors Affecting the Financing of Education,* ed. Roe L. Johns et al., (Gainesville, Fla.: National Educational Finance Project, 1970), 31.

29. See, for example, the writings of Karl Marx, whose communist philosophy greatly influenced many nations of the world. Marx argued that government must have total control of all aspects of the economy and society to rescue the helpless victims of capitalist societies. Much of Marx's work was reaction to exploitation of workers in the Industrial Revolution.

30. In contrast, see Adam Smith (n. 65) whose capitalist philosophy sprang from bitter opposition to British oppression at the time of the American Revolution. Smith argued that economies must be governed by natural forces and that government must be restricted to preserving law and order, defending the nation, and enforcing justice.

31. U.S. Chamber of Commerce, *Education: An Investment in People* (Washington, D.C.: Chamber of Commerce of the United States, Education Department, 1955), 3.

32. Lawrence W. Downey, Roger C. Seager, and Allen T. Slagle, *The Task of Public Education* (Chicago: Midwest Administration Center, University of Chicago, 1960), 24.

33. Habte Aklilu, *Education and Development: Views from the World Bank* (Washington, D.C.: World Bank, 1983), 8.

34. The term "private" is not used here to mean the same thing as a private school education. The private sector refers to private individuals as recipients of the benefits of educational experiences.

35. Howard Bowen, *Investment in Learning* (San Francisco: Jossey-Bass, 1977).

36. U.S. Bureau of the Census, *Statistical Abstract of the United States* (Washington, D.C.: U.S. Bureau of the Census, 1992).

37. Ronnie Davis, "The Social and Economic Externalities of Education" in *Economic Factors Affecting Financing,* ed. Johns et al.

38. Bowen, *Investment in Learning.*

39. Ibid.

40. Rogers and Ruchlin, *Economics and Education,* 3–4.

41. This concept states that additional units of education may not result in exactly incremental increases in earnings. For example, later discussion under rate-of-return studies will show that elementary and secondary schooling have the highest return rates, while multiple college degrees may not equal gains in earnings achieved from K–12 education. Likewise, some professions (e.g., medicine and law) are more profitable than other professions (e.g., the professoriate and social work).

42. This is not to imply that the arguments supporting private schools or proposals to increase parental choice in schooling are invalid, as some competition for efficiency's sake is desirable. However, abandonment of the foundations of public education is likely unwise, as one need only read the history of public schooling in America to understand the dismal result of basing social and economic mobility on class privilege.

43. The ability principle in taxation is generally described as a progressive system. Discussion of this concept occurs in greater detail in Chapter 3.

44. This topic is woven throughout the textbook and receives in-depth discussion on historic funding methods, taxation schemes, and litigation in Chapters 3–5.

45. Consider, if you will, all the foregoing as drawing the line between individual and external benefits of education to worker productivity and economic prosperity.

46. Theodore Schultz, "Education and Economic Growth," in *Social Forces Influencing American Education,"* 16th Yearbook of the National Society of Education, ed. N. B. Henry (Chicago: University of Chicago Press, 1961), 63.

47. Edward Denison, *The Sources of Economic Growth in the United States and the Alternatives Before Us* (New York: Committee for Economic Development, 1962).

48. Edward Denison, "The Interruption of Productivity Growth in the United States," *The Economic Journal* 93 (1983): 56–77.

49. Edward Denison, *Why Growth Rates Differ* (Washington, D.C.: Brookings Institution, 1967).

50. Burton A. Weisbrod, "Education and Investment in Human Capital," *Journal of Political Economy* 70 (1962): 106–123.

51. There are certainly other methods that have been developed, but they are beyond the scope of this textbook.

52. The present discounted value method is a clear example of the error-prone nature of this concept. Accuracy of the PDV is entirely dependent on the accepted discount rate. If the rate is too high, the value of education is unrealistically deflated; if it is too low and inflation and credentialism (the process of devaluing additional education because progressively more education is required to gain entry into professions or occupations) are rampant, the value of additional education is underestimated. Decisions based on an inaccurate discount rate will clearly be inappropriate, with severe and damaging implications for policy-making.

53. This text is not intended to explore these concepts in great depth, but it should be recognized that this field is extremely complex. A more complete treatment would include explication of such concepts as social returns, opportunity costs, marginal costs and value, impacts of age, sex, and race, and so on.

54. Lee Hansen, "Total and Private Rates of Return to Investment in Schooling," *Journal of Political Economy* 71 (1963): 128–140.

55. Giora Hanoch, "An Economic Analysis of Earnings and Schooling," *Journal of Human Resources* 3 (1967): 310–329.

56. Schultz, "Human Capital Approach to Education."

57. Ibid.

58. Gary Becker, *Human Capital: A Theoretical and Empirical Analysis, with Special Reference to Education* (New York: National Bureau of Economic Research, 1964).

59. Schultz, "Human Capital Approach to Education."

60. Ibid.

61. See, for example, Richard Freeman, *Black Elite: The New Market for Highly Educated Black Americans* (New York: McGraw-Hill, 1976).

62. Becker, *Human Capital.,* 79.

63. George Psacharopoulos, "Returns to Education: An Updated International Comparison," *Comparative Education* 3 (1981): 321–341.

64. Richard Freeman, "The Decline in the Economic Rewards to College Education," *Review of Economics and Statistics* 59 (1977): 18–29; Hanoch, "Economic Analysis of Earnings and Schooling."

65. Adam Smith, *An Inquiry into the Nature and Causes of the Wealth of Nations* (New York: Modern Library, 1937), 734–735.

66. Karl Kaestle, *Pillars of the Republic: Common Schools and American Society, 1780–1860* (New York: Hill and Wang, 1983), 6–9.

67. For example, the famous Perry Preschool Project in Ypsilanti, Michigan, reported that at age 19, recipients of high-quality preschool/early childhood services made greater gains in education, employment, and social behaviors in that fewer were retarded (15% v. 35%), more completed high school (67% v. 49%), more held jobs (50% v. 32%), fewer were arrested (31% v. 51%), fewer committed crimes of property or violence (24% v. 38%), and fewer were on welfare (18% v. 32%). J.R. Berrueta-Clement, L. J. Schweinhart, W. S. Barnett, A. S. Epstein, and D. P. Weikart, *Changed Lives: The Effects of the Perry Preschool Programs through Age 19,* Monograph No. 8 (Ypsilanti, Mich.: High Scope Educational Research Foundation, 1984).

68. J. Dougherty, *A Matter of Interpretation: Changes Under Chapter 1 of the Education Consolidation and Improvement Act* (Serial No. 99-B), GPO Pub. No. 1985 50-5240 (Washington, D.C.: U.S. Congress House of Representatives Committee on Education and Labor, 1985).

69. Henry Levin, "Assessing the Equalization Potential of Education," *Comparative Education Review* 28 (1984): 11.

70. Weisbrod, "Education and Investment in Human Capital."

71. Alfred Marshall, "Education and Invention," in *Perspectives on the Economics of Education,* ed. C. S. Benson (Boston: Houghton-Mifflin, 1963), 83.

72. See another complicated argument related to the work of James Coleman, Ernst Campbell, Carol Hobson, James McPartland, Alexander Mood, Frederic Weinfeld, and Robert York, in *Equality of Educational Opportunity* (Washington, D.C.: Department of Health, Education, and Welfare, 1966). While it is not the intent of this textbook to explore either production functions or sociological phenomena to their greater complexity (for an excellent synopsis see David Monk, *Educational Finance: An Economic Approach* [New York: McGraw-Hill, 1990]), it is the purpose of this text to suggest that there are various schools of thought that have sparked heated debate. For example, the work by Coleman has been credited and alternatively blamed for providing impetus for the effective schools movement popular in the 1980s, which sought to unobjectively refute the social destiny twist many read into Coleman's works. See also Christopher Jencks, Marshall Smith, Henry Acland, Mary Bane, David Cohen, Herbert Gintis, Barbara Heynes, and Stephen Michelson, *Inequality: A Reassessment of the Effects of Family and Schooling in America,* (New York: Basic Books, 1972), who suggest that there are other limitations on the relationship between achievement, schooling, and opportunity; and a growing body of literature surrounding culture bias in the scheme of achievement testing.

73. The analogy to the earlier discussion about unexplained residuals in economic productivity attributable to education applies to this discussion as well. As will be apparent in the following paragraphs, education is the beneficiary of residuals, but at the expense of lack of

explanation. The purpose here is to look only briefly at the production-function activity inside the discipline of education finance, not to introduce doubt to the reader but to underscore the power of the assumption of the relationship of resources and achievement, rather than the confirmed causality between them.

74. Efforts to determine the rate of return on educational investment are good examples of cost-benefit analysis. Economists and other researchers have attempted to discover the benefits received for costs incurred, with the underlying assumption that wiser decisions will be made if such relationships are known. Education researchers have also engaged in cost-benefit analysis. The results of such studies have generally supported investment in education as evidenced by earlier discussion of the Perry Preschool Project (n. 67). For persons interested in the lengthy history of such exploration, research abounds. For example, Paul Mort's *Growing Edge* was an early assessment of teaching skills and knowledge, range of skills taught, discovery of aptitudes, and development of behavior patterns (Mort, Vincent, and Newelt: *The Growing Edge* [New York: Metropolitan School Study Council, 1953]); similarly, Johns and Morphet measured performance on achievement tests, characteristics of classroom practices, scope of programs, and administrative and structural settings in the hope of discovering attributes that enhance resource investment (Roe L. Johns and Edgar L. Morphet, eds., *Problems and Issues in Public School Finance* [New York: Bureau of Publications, Columbia University Teachers College, 1952]). Combined with other decades of research, their work viewed the correlation between achievement and resources in the same light as Mort's conclusion that there appeared to be no point of diminishing return on the educational investment (Paul Mort, Walter Reusser, and John Polley, *Public School Finance,* 3d ed., [New York: McGraw-Hill, 1960]).

75. Coleman et al., *Equality of Educational Opportunity.*

76. Anita Summers and Barbara Wolfe. "Do Schools Make a Difference?" *American Economic Review* 67:4 (1977): 639–652.

77. Some such research held a more cautious view of the Coleman report. See, for example, Marshall Smith, "Equality of Educational Opportunity: The Basic Findings Reconsidered," in *On Equality of Educational Opportunity,* ed. Frederick Mostellar and Daniel Moynihan (New York: Vintage Books, (1972); see also H. Averch, S. Carroll, T. Donaldson, H. Kiesling, and J. Pincus, *How Effective Is Schooling? A Critical Review and Synthesis of Research Findings* (Santa Monica: Rand Corporation, 1972).

78. For comprehensive reviews of the effective schools research, see S. Purkey and M. Smith, "Effective Schools: A Review," *Elementary School Journal* 83:4 (1983), 427–452; see also Thomas Good and Jere Brophy, "School Effects," in *Handbook of Research on Teaching,* 3d ed., ed. M. Wittrock (New York: Macmillan, 1986), 570–602.

79. Consider, for example, site-based management that relocates resource and management decisions closer to the point of impact, i.e., schools and classrooms. This concept is more fully explored elsewhere in this text. For an excellent discussion of the whole concept of microeconomic allocation issues, see David Monk and Julie Underwood, eds., *Microlevel School Finance: Issues and Implications for Policy,* 9th Annual Yearbook of the American Education Finance Association (Cambridge: Ballinger, 1988).

80. The concept of loose coupling has been popular among organizational theorists in recent years, implying that organizations have far less structure than is apparent to the casual observer and in direct contradiction to scientific management theory. For a fuller discussion of loose coupling theory, see Karl Weick, "Educational Organizations as Loosely Coupled Systems," *Administrative Science Quarterly* 21 (1976): 1–19.

81. See, for example, Amitai Etzioni, *A Comparative Analysis of Complex Organizations* (New York: Free Press, 1975).

82. Summers and Wolfe, "Do Schools Make a Difference?"

83. It has been a conscious claim of the effective schools research that much achievement

examined in this literature has been observed in schools that should have demonstrated abysmal failure given Coleman's work.

84. Peter Coleman, "The Good School: A Critical Examination of the Adequacy of Student Achievement and Per Pupil Expenditures as Measures of School District Effectiveness," *Journal of Education Finance* (Summer 1986), 71–96.

85. Stephen Childs and Charol Shakeshaft, "A Meta-Analysis of Research on the Relationship Between Educational Expenditures and Student Achievement," *Journal of Education Finance* (Fall 1986), 249–263.

86. While research design is beyond the focus of this textbook, it is nonetheless appropriate to note that control group experimentation would present interesting ethical questions. For example, assuming unlimited funds to permit an endless stream of money to some schools, a conscious decision would have to be made to deny funding to other schools to permit comparisons. Assuming such behavior were forbidden, experimental design would then resort to natural states of haves and have-nots to find its comparison groups. An ethical dilemma arises from both such behaviors: the first instance is ethically untenable because education's reach far exceeds its present grasp, while the second instance is also untenable under modern concepts of social justice. The old joke that physicians bury their mistakes while the victims of teachers must live with theirs is no joke at all, making experimental research design an improbability in education finance.

87. While some might question how such a conclusion could be reached on weak data, summative argument is presented in successive paragraphs of this text that addresses what to do when in doubt. Briefly, the argument can be captured in the ascerbic comment: "We regard the fierce resistance by rich districts to reform as adequate testimonial to the relevance of money. . . . If money is inadequate to improve education, the residents of poor districts should at least have an equal opportunity to be disappointed by its failure" (John E. Coons, William Clune, and Stephen Sugarman, *Private Wealth and Public Education* [Cambridge, Mass: Belknap Press of Harvard University Press, 1970], 26).

88. Bettye MacPhail-Wilcox and Richard King, "Production Functions Revisited in the Context of Educational Reform," *Journal of Education Finance* (Fall 1986): 191–222; see also Bettye MacPhail-Wilcox and Richard King, "Resource Allocation Studies: Implications for School Improvement and School Finance Research," *Journal of Education Finance* (Spring 1986): 416–432.

89. Such conclusions are often supported throughout the research. See, for example, Adam Gamoran, "Resource Allocation and the Effects of Schooling: A Sociological Perspective," in Monk and Underwood, *Microlevel School Finance,* 207–232. Gamoran notes that poor and minority students have on the average less access to those resources which really matter. He notes the effect of sociodemographics on achievement where (1) because socioeconomic status, race, and ethnicity are related to achievement, schools with high concentrations of disadvantaged children are likely to contain a disproportionate number of low achievers; (2) low socioeconomic status (SES) schools are less desirable locations for teachers; and (3) schools vary in physical resources according to their socioeconomic surroundings. This would tend to confirm the importance of the earlier discussion in the text on effective school structures. Numerous additional reviews are also available.

90. Monk, *Educational Finance,* 343.

91. Ibid., 345. Monk notes rather humorously and effectively that perhaps the methodology of such research has exceeded its grasp when one considers that "there is something bizarre and potentially alarming about economists and productivity analysts doing research on neurobiology."

92. Summers and Wolfe, "Do Schools Make a Difference?"

93. Monk, *Educational Finance,* 344–345.

94. It is worth reiterating, however, the moderateness of needs in these two states compared

to problems in other more populous states. The growing despair of the inner cities is chronicled throughout the literature. For an excellent review of various problems facing education related to large numbers stemming in part from demographic change, see Ward and Anthony, eds., *Who Pays for Student Diversity?*

95. Charles S. Benson, Paul Goldfinger, E. Gareth Hoachlander, and Jessica S. Pers, *Planning for Educational Reform* (New York: Dodd, Mead, 1974), 8.

96. Education for the Handicapped Act (PL 94–142).

97. These are more than academic questions, as legislatures around the nation have struggled with taxpayer issues and enacting mechanisms such as circuit breakers to provide relief to persons on low or fixed incomes. Such mechanisms provide salutation to the problem of tax equity, but they are not overly sophisticated and to date no state has systematically indexed property tax burdens to income. What may be derived from this observation is that the whole concept of taxpayer equity has received less academic emphasis than pupil equity, leaving the concept in a more infant state to await eventual development. Tax equity is discussed at greater length in Chapter 3.

98. Needless to say, this concept is most disturbing in a society that likes to claim a belief in equality and democracy but more closely resembles a meritocracy. The fundamental question is one of governmental form—equity under such a view is highly akin to communist or socialist philosophy, setting up a perplexing dilemma. But while all societies are imperfect, American society has been both blessed and plagued by its conscience in this regard. The blessing has derived from history's best example of a conscientious effort to provide as much mobility as possible under a mixed system of merit, privilege, and welfare. The plague has derived from the attempt to meld these functionally incompatible values.

99. From an action perspective, this has best been accomplished by continued research methodology refinement (discussed briefly in Chapter 4) and by pressuring legislatures through political action and litigation into a mode of scrutiny (developed at length in Chapter 5). The concept of justice is extraordinarily complex and has occupied scholars and thinkers for centuries. For an in-depth treatment of justice and education see Deborah Verstegen and James G. Ward, eds. *Spheres of Justice in Education,* 11th Annual Yearbook of the American Education Finance Association (New York: HarperCollins, 1991).

100. James W. Guthrie, Walter I. Garms, and Lawrence C. Pierce, *School Finance and Education Policy: Enhancing Educational Efficiency, Equality, and Choice,* 2d ed. (Boston: Allyn & Bacon, 1988), 2.

ADDITIONAL READINGS

American Education Finance Association. *Helping At-Risk Students: What Are the Educational and Financial Costs?* 13th Annual Yearbook, 1992. Edited by Patricia Anthony and Stephen Jacobson. Newbury Park, Calif.: Corwin Press, (1992).

———. *Who Pays for Student Diversity? Population Changes and Educational Policy.* 12th Annual Yearbook, 1991. Edited by James G. Ward and Patricia Anthony. Newbury Park, Calif.: Corwin Press, 1992.

Benson, Charles S. *The Economics of Public Education.* 3d ed. Boston: Houghton Mifflin, 1978.

Cohn, Elchanan. *The Economics of Education.* Rev. ed. Cambridge: Ballinger, 1979.

Dewey, John. *Democracy and Education.* New York: Macmillan, 1916.

Friedman, Milton. *Capitalism and Freedom.* Chicago: University of Chicago Press, 1962.

Friedman, Milton, and Rose Friedman, *Free to Choose: A Personal Statement.* New York: Harcourt Brace Jovanovich, 1980.

Galbraith, John Kenneth. *The Affluent Society.* 4th ed. Boston: Houghton Mifflin, 1978.

Marx, Karl. *Das Kapital.* Edited by Frederick Engels. Chicago: Encyclopedia Britannica, Inc., 1952.

Schultz, Theodore. *The Economic Value of Education.* New York: Columbia University Press, 1963.

——. *Investing in People: The Economics of Population Quality.* New York: Free Press, 1981.

Smith, Adam. *The Wealth of Nations.* New York: Collier, 1905.

Wildavsky, Aaron. *The Politics of the Budgetary Process.* Boston: Little, Brown, 1964.

Wirt, Frederick M., and Michael W. Kirst. *The Political Web of American Schools.* Berkeley: McCutchan, 1982.

——. *Schools in Conflict: The Politics of Education.* Berkeley: McCutchan, 1982.

CHAPTER 2

Financing Public Schools in America: Federal, State, and Local Responses

CHAPTER THEME

- For centuries, the nature and control of education has been a bone of contention among strong-willed groups, each seeking to overlay its own philosophy on the schools. Everything that exists has roots, and the development of education's financial structure is tied directly to policies that are philosophical and political in nature. It is thus important for administrators to understand how school finance structures have evolved and to understand how school funding is tied to the nation's economic, social, and political history.

CHAPTER OUTLINE

- The fundamental roots of American schooling in public (common) schools.

- The evolution of public schooling, tracing the historical roots of divided responsibility for education in the structure of basic school government and the school district as the most basic administrative unit.

- How federal, state, and local responsibility for funding education *consequently* follows from this history

CHAPTER OBJECTIVE

- A better sense of history's role in the present structure of education and a clearer understanding of the divided fiscal responsibility of each level of government for education

*Men are men before they are lawyers or physicians or merchants or manufacturers; and if
you make them capable and sensible men, they will make themselves capable and sensible
lawyers and physicians . . . Men may be competent lawyers without general education,
but it depends on general education to make them philosophic lawyers—who demand,
and are capable of apprehending, principles, instead of merely cramming their heads with
details. And so of all other useful pursuits, mechanical included. Education makes a man
a more intelligent shoemaker, if that be his occupation, but not by teaching him to make
shoes; it does so by the mental exercise it gives and the habits it impresses.*
        John Stuart Mill, "Inaugural Address at the University of St. Andrews"

The above quotation from the nineteenth century economist-philosopher John Stuart
Mill (1806–1873)[1] about the purpose of schooling lays to rest any belief that the current struggle over the importance and value of education is of recent origin. For centuries, education has been a bone of contention among strong-willed groups, each
seeking to overlay its own philosophy on the schools. For a distinct segment of society, schooling for economic survival and economic progress has been vital. For another segment, as for John Stuart Mill, schooling for civilized existence has been another. For still another segment, education for social change has been the focus.
These phenomena have been closely related to a history of struggles for economic
survival and prosperity, to establishing and forwarding the nation's revolutionary social experiment in government, and to what has seemed to some thinkers to be the
imperfections of a capitalist democracy.

  These realities have a close relationship to how education is funded on the
threshold of the twenty-first century because economic, social, political, and educational policy is never developed in a vacuum. Everything that exists has roots, and the
development of education's financial structure is tied directly to policies that are philosophical, economic, and political. It is thus important for the student of education
finance to have a basic understanding of how the nation's school finance structure has
evolved and to understand how its present condition is linked to the nation's economic, social, and political history. The purpose of this chapter is therefore to construct that linkage so that the student will have a firm basis from which to view subsequent chapter topics in a coherent whole.

  To achieve these goals, the chapter examines the emergence of public schools
in the United States, with particular emphasis on how that emergence may be seen
through the lens of education finance. The chapter begins by reviewing the origins
of public (common) schools to establish the most fundamental roots from which
American schooling has evolved. The chapter then turns to the evolution of public
schooling over the centuries by tracing the development of basic school governance, including a discussion of the school district as the most basic administrative
unit. From these roots, we then turn to how federal, state, and local units of government have become *consequently* involved in the educational enterprise up to
and including the present day. Because some critics argue that there are problems
with the organization of public schools that finally play out in the fiscal arena, we
conclude the chapter with a discussion of whether there has been sufficient development of an appropriate balance of responsibility for education among federal,
state, and local governments. From the data and discussion in this chapter, we
gather a better sense of history's linkages to the present structure of education,
and a body of knowledge on which to base a closer analysis in Chapter 3 of revenue structures for education.

COMMON SCHOOL ORIGINS: MORALITY, DEMOCRACY, ECONOMICS, AND EQUALITY

It may come as a shock to modern Americans who have grown up with the elaborate educational programs of the twentieth century to realize that formal mandated public education is a recent phenomenon. To many persons such realization would be embarrassing in a democratic society, particularly as even ancient civilizations such as the Greeks had well-developed educational systems for their day. The Greeks, for example, proclaimed education as the cornerstone of democracy, arguing that the mark of a free man was bound to his ability to read, write, think, and speak. Most Americans today would probably question the argument that widespread public education is a recent invention, believing from their own educational experiences that the Declaration of Independence proclaimed a fundamental entitlement to education when it declared that the unalienable rights to life, liberty, and the pursuit of happiness are secured in a nation governed by consent of an intelligent people. Surely, the modern American would argue, the nation's most precious document has since the very founding of the nation promised every person the education prerequisite to self-governance.

Whether that guarantee has ever existed or not is subject to question,[2] but shocking as it may seem, formal education in any form resembling how we know schools today did *not* exist before the nineteenth century. This is not to say, of course, that no schools existed or that education did not occur by other means. But it is to say that the current meaning of schooling is in sharp contrast to the historic realities of education in the United States.

Historical Roots of American Education

Only a cursory knowledge of American history is required to picture the struggles of early settlers in a vast and sometimes hostile environment. To survive the harsh climate and conquer an untamed land was challenge enough without having to cope with the problems of establishing an advanced civilization. In the earliest days of colonialization very little education occurred because settlers were too occupied with meeting basic needs. Too, there was little reason for schooling as the skills needed for survival in a new land had little to do with book learning or academic skills.

While it is true that the modern concept of education was virtually nonexistent in colonial America, it would not be true to suggest that no interest in education could be found in the young nation. But in sharp contrast to modern education, whenever schooling did occur in early colonial America it was almost always the exclusive province of the home or church. In fact, it may be argued that a concern for education was evident fairly early in the colonies, as the first law for which written history exists was the 1642 statute passed by the Massachusetts legislature requiring town fathers to determine whether children were being taught to read and to understand religion and to receive occupational guidance and training.[3] Sentiment for such education was obviously sustained because in 1647 the Ye Old Deluder Satan Act was passed in the same state to strengthen the teaching of morality to children through the reading of the Holy Scriptures. As the colonies began to flourish and grow, the concept of a required education for morality gained in popularity in the colonies as Connecticut, Maine, New Hampshire, and Vermont had all passed similar legislation by 1720.[4]

As civilizations move beyond subsistence toward more stable prosperity, they generally engage in higher order goals such as developing more formalized education. Toward the end of the eighteenth century, new interest in a more formal school setting in the various colonies began to take shape. The War of Independence in 1776 had been hard-fought, and the reasons behind the war brought about a new concern in the young nation that had long chafed under autocratic British rule. Where education for morality had been the sole purpose for early laws relating to formal schooling, a new concern was born based on a call for enlightened self-government to protect and preserve the new and fragile experiment in democracy. Thomas Jefferson, the great champion of liberty, was among the loudest voices calling for an end to ignorance through widespread education among the nation's common people. In an unprecedented departure from centuries of serfdom and political patronage of the world's peoples, Jefferson argued that citizens must be able to choose leaders wisely and defeat ambition and corruption in politics, and be politically discerning so as to protect liberty by keeping a vigilant guard on government. These skills, he argued, could not be developed except by education for the commoner—a radical social concept in a world that had had little experience with self-determination.

Yet despite the need to encourage morality and notwithstanding the demands of participatory government, widespread education, especially government-sponsored education, made only slow progress for many years after the American Revolution. Embroiled in struggling with a hostile land and the demands of aggressive expansionist activities across a rugged and vast continent, there was neither time for the luxury of education nor much sentiment for such luxury, as liberal education had left a bad taste in the mouths of many Americans whose painfully recent historical roots lay in foreign lands where education and abusive aristocracy were closely associated. For the common majority, education could be provided at home, either for morality or for economic survival, particularly since the nation's far-flung efforts were agricultural and required little book learning. Although the seeds of education for godly and democratic purposes were sown early by progressive thinkers in the young nation, in the mind of the average colonist the emergence of a morally literate and politically wise electorate was a luxury that would have to wait because liberal education was not only useless, but perhaps even undesirable given their embittered histories.

Westward expansion and desperate survival, however, could not last forever. Besides, not everyone wanted to move west, and ironically some were too poor to move into the primitive lands that lay beyond the horizon. With hordes of immigrants landing in America, great cities sprang up and began to grow rapidly beginning in the early 1800s. These populations were both the origin and result of industrialization of the nation because they provided a labor pool on which to build industry and simultaneously drew laborers who sought work in the new commerce. As cities grew, industry was attracted, fueling the need for more labor which in turn caused cities to grow again. As the cycle fed itself, industry began to recognize that not all growth was good because the skills needed for industry were not present in the vast throngs of people seeking work. The solution was to call for a third role for education by demanding schooling for vocational purposes. While the call for vocational training was by no means unanimous among industrialists who disagreed about whether education was the solution to technical needs or a potential drain by increasing labor costs, the effect was to add economics to the increasingly important role assigned to education.

The rapid growth of the nation, particularly in great cities, had the effect of accelerating demand for education. Although the nation had flung open its doors to the world's peoples in the belief that rapid population growth would aid in expansionist policies, the dizzying growth was both unexpected and problematic. Beginning around 1840, immigration skyrocketed out of control. In the 20-year period 1820–1840 the nation gained only 751,000 new residents, while in the 10-year period 1840–1850 more than 1.7 million persons entered the United States. Immigration continued to soar, as in the 60-year period 1840–1900 more than 16.6 million additional persons entered the country (see Table 2.1). While it might be anticipated that the nation was poorly equipped to deal with such population influx, problems were especially acute as many immigrants clustered in big cities and were most often poor and uneducated, with few or no skills useful to industry. The problem worsened as rural Americans began to populate cities and industrial centers, either because they had tired of the harsh frontier life or were starved or driven from the land. From 1820 to 1900, total resident population of the nation grew nearly eightfold, rising from about 9.6 million to nearly 76 million persons (see Table 2.2). As with any deprived population, severe problems beset many cities with the resultant poverty, slums, crime, vagrancy, intemperance, illiteracy, and ignorance that both breed and follow economic despair. While the latter two conditions could be claimed indigenous to rural and urban America alike, their visibility was greatly intensified in cities as people crowded together.

Under these alarming conditions, urban centers faced unprecedented social problems for which solutions had to be found. The revered purposes of educating for morality and self-governance had to be continued, argued leaders such as Horace Mann[5] and Henry Barnard,[6] but a concomitant effort to educate every person for economic productivity had to be made. Under the leadership of strong educational advocates such as Mann and Barnard, the first beginnings of what was to become a vast educational enterprise for the common good of the nation sprang into being under the Common Schools Movement. Spurred by uncontrolled immigration and population growth, the Common Schools Movement reached prominence between 1840

TABLE 2.1   Immigration, 1820–1990

Period	Number	Rate[1]	Period or Year	Number	Rate[1]	Year	Number	Rate[1]
1820–1990	56,994	3.4	1911–1920	5,736	5.7	1981	597	2.6
1820–1830[2]	152	1.2	1921–1930	4,107	3.5	1982	594	2.6
1831–1840[3]	599	3.9	1931–1940	528	0.4	1983	560	2.4
1841–1850[4]	1,713	8.4	1941–1950	1,035	0.7	1984	544	2.3
1851–1860[4]	2,598	9.3	1951–1960	2,515	1.5	1985	570	2.4
1861–1870[5]	2,315	6.4	1961–1970	3,322	1.7	1986	602	2.5
1871–1880	2,812	6.2	1971–1980	4,493	2.1	1987	602	2.5
1881–1890	5,247	9.2	1981–1990	7,338	3.1	1988	643	2.6
1891–1900	3,688	5.3	1970	373	1.8	1989[5]	1,091	4.4
1901–1910	8,795	10.4	1980	531	2.3	1990[6]	1,536	6.1

[1]Annual rate per 1,000 U.S. population. Rate computed by dividing sum of annual immigration totals by sum of annual U.S. population totals for same number of years.
[2]Oct. 1, 1819, to Sept. 30, 1830.
[3]Oct. 1, 1830, to Dec. 31, 1840.
[4]Calendar years.
[5]Jan. 1, 1861, to June 30, 1870.
[6]Includes persons who were granted permanent residence under the legalization program of the Immigration Reform and Control Act of 1986.
SOURCE: U.S. Department of Commerce, Bureau of the Census, *Statistical Abstracts of the United States 1992* (Washington, D.C.: U.S. Government Printing Office, 1992), 10.

TABLE 2.2 Population and area, 1790–1990

| Census Date | Resident Population | | Increase Over Preceding Census | | Area (Square Miles) | | |
	Number	Per Square Mile of Land Area	Number	Percent	Gross	Land	Water
Conterminous U.S.[1]							
1790 (August 2)	3,929,214	4.5	—	—	891,364	864,746	24,065
1800 (August 4)	5,308,483	6.1	1,379,269	35.1	891,364	864,746	24,065
1810 (August 6)	7,239,881	4.3	1,931,398	36.4	1,722,685	1,681,828	34,175
1820 (August 7)	9,638,453	5.5	2,398,572	33.1	1,792,552	1,749,462	38,544
1830 (June 1)	12,866,020	7.4	3,227,567	33.5	1,792,552	1,749,462	38,544
1840 (June 1)	17,069,453	9.8	4,203,433	32.7	1,792,552	1,749,462	38,544
1850 (June 1)	23,191,876	7.9	6,122,423	35.9	2,991,655	2,940,042	52,705
1860 (June 1)	31,443,321	10.6	8,251,445	35.6	3,021,295	2,969,640	52,747
1870 (June 1)	[2]39,818,449	[2]13.4	8,375,128	26.6	3,021,295	2,969,640	52,747
1880 (June 1)	50,155,783	16.9	10,337,334	26.0	3,021,295	2,969,640	52,747
1890 (June 1)	62,947,714	21.2	12,791,931	25.5	3,021,295	2,969,640	52,747
1900 (June 1)	75,994,575	25.6	13,046,861	20.7	3,021,295	2,969,834	52,553
1910 (April 15)	91,972,266	31.0	15,977,691	21.0	3,021,295	2,969,565	52,822
1920 (January 1)	105,710,620	35.6	13,738,354	14.9	3,021,295	2,969,451	52,936
1930 (April 1)	122,775,046	41.2	17,064,426	16.1	3,021,295	2,977,128	45,259
1940 (April 1)	131,669,275	44.2	8,894,229	7.2	3,021,295	2,977,128	45,259
1950 (April 1)	150,697,361	50.7	19,028,086	14.5	3,021,295	2,974,726	47,661
1960 (April 1)	178,464,236	60.1	27,766,875	18.4	3,021,295	2,968,054	54,207
United States							
1950 (April 1)	151,325,798	42.6	19,161,229	14.5	3,618,770	3,552,206	63,005
1960 (April 1)	179,323,175	50.6	27,997,377	18.5	3,618,770	3,540,911	74,212
1970 (April 1)	[3]203,302,031	[3]57.4	23,978,856	13.4	3,618,770	[3]3,540,023	[3]78,444
1980 (April 1)	226,545,805	64.0	23,243,774	11.4	3,618,770	3,539,289	79,481
1990 (April 1)	248,709,873	70.3	22,164,088	9.8	3,787,425	3,536,342	[4]251,083

—Not applicable.
[1]Excludes Alaska and Hawaii.
[2]Revised to include adjustments for underenumeration in southern States; unrevised number is 38,558,371 (13.0 per square mile).
[3]Figures corrected after 1970 final reports were issued.
[4]Comprises inland, coastal, Great Lakes, and territorial water. Data for prior years cover inland water only.
SOURCE: U.S. Department of Commerce, Bureau of the Census, *Statistical Abstracts of the United States 1992* (Washington, D.C.: U.S. Government Printing Office, 1992), 8.

and 1880 and was both rooted in education for morality and driven by the engine of education for economic productivity. In addition, the Common Schools Movement contained a fourth new thread that was to become pervasive in the national psychology underlying the meaning of American education. Because the movement had its most basic roots in peoples who had recently fled from deplorable economic and social conditions in their native lands, the movement not only embraced a commitment to moral training, self-destiny, and economic productivity, but also held the beginnings of an intense loyalty to social reform for justice and equality.

The Common Schools Movement was nothing short of miraculous and provided the basis for refinements that significantly reshaped the nature and scope of American education. One refinement in particular was to forever alter the face of education in a most fundamental way. While there could be no doubt that much of the nation's new growth and prosperity could be attributed to a climate conducive to commerce and industry, an undesirable fact of industrialization was the extensive use of child labor in the years preceding 1900. Given general laxness of educational provisions in the more primitive years of the nation, industry in the United States had followed the European model in making scandalous profits by employing children at poverty wages who had to work because of economic hardship. But with industrialization came labor unions in the last half of the nineteenth century that sought to protect and improve wages of adult members, with the corollary effect of gradually toughening child labor laws. The Common Schools Movement was thus aided in transforming education into a more organized and intensive process because child labor laws had the effect of displacing children from the work force. Because such children needed a place to be, schools were a convenient caretaker—a natural role especially given concomitant cries for common education for morality, economics, and equality.

By the dawn of the twentieth century, there was little resemblance between the American educational system and colonial education. But although the resemblance was slight, the roots were deep and the changes that had occurred could be seen to follow upon themselves. As the nation expanded from tightly knit little colonies, education for morality moved from religious instruction into a humanistic school based on the philosophies of social advocates for both the commoner and the common good. As the nation moved away from the daily insults of imperial oppression, education for intelligent self-government still held strong, but the desperation had calmed since the nation had successfully survived the first painful tests of democracy. As industry and commerce developed, education for economic productivity, scorned by suspicious colonists still smarting under the bitter tyranny of aristocratic rule, secured for itself a prominent place hastened by the crises of immigrant floods, and setting the stage for the alarms and exhortations that major organizations would issue throughout the twentieth century.[7] By the dawn of the new century, education had assumed a key role in the life of the nation that had grown increasingly far-flung and diverse—a role that was to lead to greater levels of education on the grounds of morality, democracy, economics, and equality.

THE STRUCTURE OF SCHOOL GOVERNANCE IN AMERICA

Not surprisingly, development of the educational system in the United States has had a strong influence on the governance structure of education. Within the general parameters of national educational growth noted in the previous section were other distinctively unique trends. For example, the propensity of people to cluster together on the basis of religious, political, and ethnic heritage led to very different views about education and governance structures. The wide spectrum of views was evident from the outset. For example, Webb, McCarthy, and Thomas[8] have noted that three attitudes were prevalent in colonial America, each with direct impact on the structure and governance of education. In the New England area, attitudes led to a religious state characterized by strong state regulation and taxation for education. In contrast, in the middle colonies including New Jersey, Pennsylvania, and Maryland, settlement by multiple religious denominations allowed for little sectarian regulation to keep the peace. A third model was developed as other middle colonies and the South largely held the view that public education was to be organized for paupers and orphans, with no real control or tax support from the state. These attitudes were deeply rooted, carrying over into the present day where geographic regions of the nation are noted for the prevalence or absence of private/parochial schools and where school funding schemes frequently take on characteristics empathetic to distinctly centralized or decentralized regulation and control.[9]

Development of School Organization

The extreme diversity that made up population development and westward settlement of the United States led to highly differential, if not fragmented, educational structures. In fact, it is reasonably accurate to say that, except for several highly general characteristics, educational systems have been uniquely dissimilar in organization and flavor. But given the passionate history of colonial America where religious and political freedoms were equated with a lack of strong central government, it should not be surprising that educational systems could develop without a specific or unitary organizational scheme. The extreme dislike for regulation, when coupled with westward expansion and the isolation that characterized the remote frontier, presented formidable barriers to development of educational systems patterned after any consistent model. More than any other factor, resistance was particularly pronounced, leading more than one scholar to comment in frustration on the difficulty of documenting educational history at all, much less deriving any semblance of order or unity. As Katz[10] noted:

> The conflicts between the democratic localists and the bureaucrats often assumed the atmosphere of an undeclared guerrilla war of sabotage and resistance, as local school districts refused to comply with state regulation and parents refused to comply with the state's representative, the teacher. Insofar as most of the resistance came from inarticulate people, it is the hardest and most maddening aspect of nineteenth century educational history to document. That it existed is, however, beyond doubt, as the frustrated testimony of local and state reformers testifies in almost every document they wrote.

Although educational advocates and reformers tried hard to superimpose a standardized educational system, it is apparent that many years passed before the fruits of their efforts produced the changes evident today.

Population expansion and westward migration nonetheless took their inexorable toll. As the frontier opened and the population center of the nation slowly shifted westward (see Figure 2.1), migrations and political preferences aligned themselves in

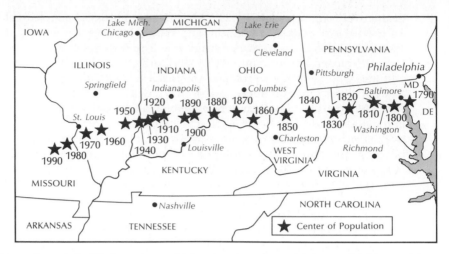

("Center of population" is that point at which an imaginary flat, weightless, and rigid map of the United States would balance if weights of identical value were placed on it so that each weight represented the location of one person on the date of the census)

Year	North Latitude			West Longitude			Approximate Location
1790 (August 2)	39	16	30	76	11	12	23 miles east of Baltimore, MD
1850 (June 1)	38	59	0	81	19	0	23 miles southeast of Parkersburg, WV
1900 (June 1)	39	9	36	85	48	54	6 miles southeast of Columbus, IN
1950 (April 1)	38	50	21	88	9	33	8 miles north–northwest of Olney, Richland County, IL
1960 (April 1)	38	35	58	89	12	35	In Clinton Co. about 6½ miles northwest of Centralia, IL
1970 (April 1)	38	27	47	89	42	22	5.3 miles east–southeast of the Mascoutah City Hall in St. Clair County, IL
1980 (April 1)	38	8	13	90	34	26	¼ mile west of De Soto in Jefferson County, MO
1990 (April 1)	37	52	20	91	12	55	9.7 miles southeast of Steelville, MO

FIGURE 2.1   Center of population, 1790–1990

SOURCE: U.S. Department of Commerce, Bureau of the Census, *Statistical Abstracts of the United States 1992* (Washington, D.C.: U.S. Government Printing Office, 1992), 9.

relative harmony as people settled into homes, formed communities, and built schools. Intolerant attitudes encouraging nonconformers to move on where local traditions did not fit with their desires, when coupled with the harsh difficulties of traveling long distances for education, were prime contributors to the establishment of countless thousands of tiny schools that increasingly dotted the continent. Although no record can recount the number of schools in early America, scholars have complained that the perceived disunity of modern educational systems is likely the result of fierce independence during the nation's developmental stages. For example, Henry C. Morrison, a school finance scholar in the mid-twentieth century, contemptuously referred to modern education as "late New England colonial . . . a little republic at every crossroads,"[11] an obvious derogatory allusion to a period in time for which he had little appreciation and whose effects he felt had never been properly overcome.

Although documented history on the number of school districts that ever existed at one time is incomplete, records do give some appreciation for the vastness and diversity of the American education system's development. Table 2.3 provides data on the number of public school districts and enrollments from 1929 to 1991, illustrating several important points. First, most citizens today can find schools still operating in their communities that seem to be unreasonably close in proximity,[12] but likely harken back to the days when travel was difficult, making neighborhood schools a true necessity. Second, it can also be safely stated that in almost every earlier time each small town had its own school, a truly startling number when one considers all the towns that have lived and died in more than 200 years of national sovereignty. Third, the number of school districts has been far greater than any other unit of government because school district boundaries in many states are not coterminous with other government entities such as counties, thereby vastly increasing the total number of school districts.[13] Fourth, while no one knows with absolute certainty how many school districts existed at the turn of the twentieth century, the number must have been truly staggering because it likely exceeded the 119,001 districts that existed in 1937 as noted in the table.[14] Fifth and finally, the relationship between state control and the number of school districts is clearly obvious, as the fragmented organization of earlier years resulted in more than 119,000 districts, contrasted to only 15,358 in 1991 following on the increased state control that has marked the latter half of the current century.

The data in Table 2.3 point up several additional historic and current realities about the structure and governance of American schools. The most obvious reality is that the school district has been *the* most basic administrative unit of schooling in America. Despite cries for more uniform education, and notwithstanding increased federal and state regulation that has followed throughout the years, practical realities of daily government and fierce protectionism of local control have kept schools a fundamentally local enterprise. The localness of schools is not to deny, however, that massive consolidation has indeed occurred, with attendant implications for conformity and uniformity. A natural result of consolidation has been to increase the size of individual schools, both as a natural product of enrollment growth and fewer school systems. In contrast to the "little republic at every crossroads" referred to by Morrison, dramatic changes have occurred. Most striking has been the decrease in the number of elementary schools, dropping from 238,306 in 1929 to only 61,340 in 1991. The number of secondary schools has remained mostly unchanged, declining from 23,930 in 1929 to 22,731 in 1991, a loss of only 1,199 schools. These changes are both reasonable and provocative: reasonable because fewer secondary schools existed initially while elementary schools were virtually on every street corner, and provocative because with current sympathy for small school size and low pupil-teacher ratios, consolidation has not met with unanimous approval. A final reality apparent in Table 2.3 is that the one-room schoolhouse, the last vestige of a quaint America, is almost extinct. No doubt surprising to many Americans, however, 617 one-room schools still existed in 1991.

Although by most accounts education has changed dramatically through a more than 700% reduction in the number of administrative units, the changes have not always focused on widescale standardization. The Constitution has allowed for wide variation in educational structure and governance by granting broad control of education to the individual states. The states have responded by creating a wide variety of educational systems, differing greatly in structure, operation, control, and fiscal support. The effect has been to preserve much local tradition and flavor in public

TABLE 2.3 Public school districts, 1929–1991

School Year	Public School Districts	Public Schools — Total, All Schools	Public Schools — Total, Regular Schools	Elementary Schools — Total	Elementary Schools — One-Teacher	Secondary Schools	Private Schools — Total	Private Schools — Elementary	Private Schools — Secondary
1929–1930	—	—	—	238,306	149,282	23,930	—	9,275	3,258
1937–1938	119,001	—	—	221,660	121,178	25,467	—	9,992	3,327
1939–1940	117,108	—	—	—	113,600	—	—	11,306	3,568
1945–1946	101,382	—	—	160,227	86,563	24,314	—	9,863	3,294
1947–1948	94,926	—	—	146,760	75,096	25,484	—	10,071	3,292
1949–1950	83,718	—	—	128,225	59,652	24,542	—	10,375	3,331
1951–1952	71,094	—	—	123,763	50,742	23,746	—	10,666	3,322
1953–1954	63,057	—	—	110,875	42,865	25,637	—	11,739	3,913
1955–1956	54,859	—	—	104,427	34,964	26,046	—	12,372	3,887
1957–1958	47,594	—	—	95,446	25,341	25,507	—	13,065	3,994
1959–1960	40,520	—	—	91,853	20,213	25,784	—	13,574	4,061
1961–1962	35,676	—	—	81,910	13,333	25,350	—	14,762	4,129
1963–1964	31,705	—	—	77,584	9,895	26,431	—	—	4,451
1965–1966	26,983	—	—	73,216	6,491	26,597	17,849	15,340	4,606
1967–1968	22,010	—	94,197	70,879	4,146	27,011	—	—	—
1970–1971	17,995	—	89,372	65,800	1,815	25,352	—	14,372	3,770
1973–1974	16,730	—	88,655	65,070	1,365	25,906	—	—	—
1975–1976	16,376	88,597	87,034	63,242	1,166	25,330	19,910	16,385	5,904
1976–1977	16,271	—	86,501	62,644	1,111	25,378	—	—	—
1978–1979	16,014	—	84,816	61,982	1,056	24,504	19,489	16,097	5,766
1980–1981	15,912	85,982	83,688	61,069	921	24,362	20,764	16,792	5,678
1982–1983	15,824	84,740	82,039	59,656	798	23,988	—	—	—
1983–1984	15,747	84,178	81,418	59,082	838	23,947	27,694	20,872	7,862
1984–1985	—	84,007	81,147	58,827	825	23,916	—	—	—
1985–1986	—	—	—	—	—	—	25,616	20,252	7,387
1986–1987	15,713	83,455	82,190	60,784	763	23,389	—	—	—
1987–1988	15,577	83,248	82,248	61,490	729	22,937	26,807	22,959	8,418
1988–1989	15,376	83,165	82,081	61,531	583	22,785	—	—	—
1989–1990	15,367	83,425	82,396	62,037	630	22,639	—	—	—
1990–1991	15,358	84,538	81,746	61,340	617	22,731	—	—	—

SOURCE: U.S. Department of Education, National Center for Education Statistics, *Digest of Education Statistics 1992* (Washington, D.C.: National Center for Education Statistics, 1992), 95.

schools. The vast differences between states, and even within states, as late as 1990, can be sensed in Table 2.4. While some might argue that land mass in the larger states accounts for higher numbers of school districts, the logic is somewhat imperfect because geographically small states occasionally contain some of the highest numbers of school districts. Of those states containing more than 500 districts, Illinois, Michigan, Missouri, Montana, Nebraska, New Jersey, New York, Oklahoma, and Pennsylvania are not geographically large compared to California and Texas with 1,012 and 1,076 school districts respectively. The logic is further faulty in that the number of school districts is not logically consistent with other governmental boundaries, as California has only 58 counties while Texas has 254. While transportation problems could account for the need to maintain some small districts, the logic is again not overwhelmingly followed, as experience in one state shows that out of 134 school districts under 500 enrollment K–12, there are 55 districts (41%) that still operate multiple small high schools within a 10-mile radius.[15] These realities are by no means uncommon and relate closely to highly localized planning and organization in schools, and resulting in the myriad of parallel organizational structures broadly summarized in Figure 2.2. While the historic evolution of schooling has deserved the many scholarly treatises devoted to it over the years, it is sufficient for this textbook to suggest that the com-

TABLE 2.4   Number of U.S. school districts, 1990

Alabama	130	Montana	528
Alaska	54	Nebraska	780
Arizona	216	Nevada	17
Arkansas	324	New Hampshire	160
California	1,012	New Jersey	592
Colorado	176	New Mexico	88
Connecticut	166	New York	718
Delaware	19	North Carolina	134
District of Columbia	1	North Dakota	268
Florida	67	Ohio	612
Georgia	185	Oklahoma	603
Hawaii	1	Oregon	296
Idaho	113	Pennsylvania	500
Illinois	955	Rhode Island	37
Indiana	294	South Carolina	93
Iowa	430	South Dakota	183
Kansas	304	Tennessee	139
Kentucky	176	Texas	1,076
Louisiana	66	Utah	40
Maine	230	Vermont	303
Maryland	24	Virginia	137
Massachusetts	360	Washington	296
Michigan	619	West Virginia	55
Minnesota	433	Wisconsin	428
Mississippi	151	Wyoming	49
Missouri	543	United States	15,181

SOURCE: National Education Association, *Rankings of the States, 1991* (Washington, D.C.: National Education Association, 1991), 12.

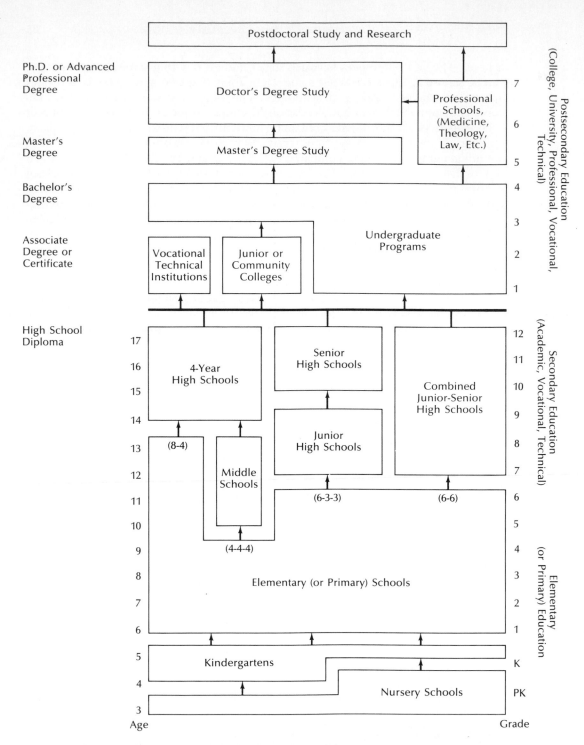

FIGURE 2.2 The structure of education in the United States

SOURCE: U.S. Department of Education, National Center for Education Statistics, *Digest of Education Statistics, 1992* (Washington, D.C.: National Center for Education Statistics, 1992), 7.

plexity of schooling and governance are both direct- and by-products of provincialism from which the countless thousands of American education systems first emerged—a history of intense local control under boards of education in school districts whose most basic characteristic has been resistance to rapid change.

FISCAL SUPPORT FOR EDUCATION

Not surprisingly, the history of education's development in the United States has also related closely to how responsibility for funding education has been established. While it is entirely true to say that education has long been of interest to federal, state, and local units of government, the types and levels of support from each of these governmental entities have varied greatly in amount and proportion to education's total costs. Given other interdependent relationships that visibly link the past to the future, it should be no surprise to learn that today's funding is for the most part a linear function of how local, federal, and state governments' responsibility for education has been defined.

Local Support for Education

If we were to conduct a survey in communities across the United States, most citizens would probably argue that because schools are guided by locally elected boards of education and operated under the direction of locally selected administrators and teachers, school budgets have also largely been a local matter. While distinguishing between budgets and finance plans is a topic that will receive refinement later in this text, citizens would mean to imply in their comments that they believe there is a high level of local fiscal support for education. Although their answers might span a continuum of emotions ranging from pride and independence in local school ownership to frustration about tax overburden, their answers would be historically correct because education in the United States has indeed had a long history of heavy local responsibility for financing schools. Some knowledgeable persons would even further argue that a heavy local fiscal burden for schools is a *current* reality, suggesting that it is an irony that much outside regulation has been placed on local schools, but that support from state and federal sources has not kept pace with education's costs.

Features of Local Support.   Dependence by school districts on local sources of revenues to carry out instructional and other related programs has indeed been very high. Table 2.5 contains several items that assist in understanding the division of responsibility assumed by all three levels of government, and is particularly illustrative of the large proportion of historic responsibility required of local districts for financing the costs of education. Although old records did not do a good job of reporting anything other than total revenue receipts from combined government sources, it may be fairly safe to assume that before 1919 fiscal support was almost entirely a local responsibility.[16] Beginning in 1919 with the first reported divisions of costs, 83.2% of all expenditures fell to local school districts. The first major shift was recorded in 1940, when the local share dropped to 68%. By 1970, it had dropped again to 43.4%, and by 1990 local responsibility accounted for 45.7% of total funding.

Although the percentage responsibility by local units of government has consistently declined over the course of the twentieth century, the picture is not as stable or

TABLE 2.5 Historical summary of school statistics, 1869–1990 (in millions of current dollars)

Item	1869–1870	1879–1880	1889–1890	1899–1900	1909–1910	1919–1920	1929–1930	1939–1940	1949–1950	1959–1960	1969–1970	1979–1980	1988–1989	1989–1990
Population, Pupils, and Instructional Staff														
Total population in thousands	39,818	50,156	62,948	75,995	90,492	104,512	121,770	130,880	148,665	179,323	201,385	224,567	245,807	248,239
Population aged 5–17 years in thousands	12,055	15,066	18,543	21,573	24,009	27,556	31,417	30,150	30,168	43,881	52,386	48,041	45,388	45,330
Percentage of total population 5–17	30.3	30.0	29.5	28.4	26.5	26.4	25.8	23.0	20.3	24.5	25.8	21.4	18.5	18.3
Total enrollment in elementary and secondary schools, in thousands	6,872	9,867	12,723	15,503	17,814	21,578	25,678	25,434	25,112	36,087	45,619	41,645	40,189	41,224
Kindergarten and grades 1–8, in thousands	6,792	9,757	12,520	14,984	16,899	19,378	21,279	18,833	19,387	27,602	32,597	27,931	28,501	29,888
Grades 9–12, in thousands	80	110	203	519	915	2,200	4,399	6,601	5,725	8,485	13,022	13,714	11,687	11,336
Enrollment as a percent of total population	17.3	19.7	20.2	20.4	19.7	20.6	21.1	19.4	16.9	20.1	22.4	18.5	16.3	16.6
Percentage of population aged 5–17 enrolled	57.0	65.5	68.6	71.9	74.2	78.3	81.7	84.4	83.2	82.2	86.9	86.7	88.5	90.9
Percentage of total enrollment in high schools (grades 9–12 and postgraduate)	1.2	1.1	1.6	3.3	5.1	10.2	17.1	26.0	22.7	23.5	28.5	32.9	29.1	27.5
High school graduates, in thousands	—	—	22	62	111	231	592	1,143	1,063	1,627	2,589	2,748	2,459	2,320
Average daily attendance, in thousands	4,077	6,144	8,154	10,633	12,827	16,150	21,265	22,042	22,284	32,477	41,934	38,289	37,268	37,779
Total number of days attended by pupils enrolled, in millions	539	801	1,098	1,535	2,011	2,615	3,673	3,858	3,964	5,782	7,501	6,835	—	—
Percentage of enrolled pupils attending daily	59.3	62.3	64.1	68.6	72.1	74.8	82.8	86.7	88.7	90.0	90.4	90.1	—	—
Average length of school term, in days	132.2	130.3	134.7	144.3	157.5	161.9	172.7	175.0	177.9	178.0	178.9	178.5	—	—
Average number of days attended per pupil	78.4	81.1	86.3	99.0	113	121.2	143	151.7	157.9	160.2	161.7	160.8	—	—
Total instructional staff, in thousands	—	—	—	—	—	678	880	912	962	1,464	2,253	2,441	—	—
Supervisors, in thousands	—	—	—	—	—	7	7	5	9	14	32	35	—	—
Principals, in thousands	—	—	—	—	—	14	31	32	39	64	91	106	—	—
Teachers, librarians, and other nonsupervisory instructional staff, in thousands	201	287	364	423	523	657	843	875	914	1,387	2,131	2,300	2,447	2,528
Men, in thousands	78	123	126	127	110	93	140	195	195	402	691	782	—	—
Women, in thousands	123	164	238	296	413	585	703	681	719	985	1,440	1,518	—	—
Percentage men	38.7	42.8	34.5	29.9	21.1	14.1	16.6	22.2	21.3	29.0	32.4	34.0	—	—
Finance														
Total revenue receipts	—	—	$143	$220	$433	$970	$2,089	$2,261	$5,437	$14,747	$40,267	$96,881	$192,016	$207,584
Federal government	—	—	—	—	—	2	7	40	156	652	3,220	9,504	11,902	12,751
State governments	—	—	—	—	—	160	354	684	2,166	5,768	16,063	45,349	91,769	98,060
Local sources, including intermediate	—	—	—	—	—	808	1,728	1,536	3,116	8,327	20,985	42,029	88,345	96,774
Percentage of revenue receipts from														
Federal government	—	—	—	—	—	0.3	0.4	1.8	2.9	4.4	8.0	9.8	6.2	6.1
State governments	—	—	—	—	—	16.5	16.9	30.3	39.8	39.1	39.9	46.8	47.8	47.2
Local sources, including intermediate	—	—	—	—	—	83.2	82.7	68.0	57.3	56.5	52.1	43.4	46.0	46.6
Total expenditures for public schools	$63	$78	$141	$215	$426	$1,036	$2,317	$2,344	$5,838	$15,613	$40,683	$95,962	$192,977	$211,731
Current expenditures	—	—	114	180	356	861	1,844	1,942	4,687	12,329	34,218	86,984	173,099	187,384
Capital outlay	—	—	26	35	70	154	371	258	1,014	2,662	4,659	6,506	14,101	17,685
Interest on school debt	—	—	—	—	—	18	93	131	101	490	1,171	1,874	3,213	3,693
Other expenditures	—	—	—	—	—	3	10	13	36	133	636	598	2,564	2,969
Percentage of total expenditures devoted to														
Current expenditures	—	—	81.3	83.5	83.6	83.1	79.6	82.8	80.3	79.0	84.1	90.6	89.7	88.5
Capital outlay	—	—	18.7	16.5	16.4	14.8	16.0	11.0	17.4	17.0	11.5	6.8	7.3	8.4
Interest on school debt	—	—	—	—	—	1.8	4.0	5.6	1.7	3.1	2.9	2.0	1.7	1.7
Other expenditures	—	—	—	—	—	0.3	0.4	0.6	0.6	0.8	1.6	0.6	1.3	1.4

SOURCE: U.S. Department of Education National Center for Education Statistics, *Digest of Education Statistics 1992* (Washington, D.C.: National Center for Education Statistics, 1992), 49.

optimistic as the data suggest, and the picture is also one of apparent contradictions. For example, it is obvious that local support in the early days was extremely high as a percentage of total costs compared to today. Local dollar amounts, however, may not have declined, either in total or in the aggregate tax burden shouldered by taxpayers. Locally contributed gross dollars have certainly continued to increase as a function of inflation and as a consequence of increased costs due to other factors, such as expanded educational programs that have come either by local choice or in response to increased federal and state regulation. Likewise, the aggregate burden of taxpayers has probably not declined much overall and may have actually increased, as the additional dollars required for complex school organizations have soared and other government units have increased their tax demands. Although the term "municipal overburden" was coined to depict the heavy demands on urban taxpayers from such diverse taxing units as schools, cities, counties, police and fire protection, central water and sewage systems, thousands of miles of paved city streets, and similar urban services, the notion of overburden across the nation in rural and urban communities alike has likely resulted in little diminution of total taxpayer burden, despite the local percentage decline in school costs resulting from increased state aid.

A second feature of the complexity of local responsibility lies in recognizing the differential realities of education finance among the various states. As indicated earlier, states have been left virtually free to develop educational services except for the occasional press of politics forcing some degree of competitive similarities between states and the occasional pressure by courts for finance reform that has occurred over the years. If one did not dig very deeply, comfort could be taken in data showing shrinking local proportions of total educational costs accompanied by increasing state and federal shares. But such a conclusion would be mostly unwarranted because although the local share may have declined in gross proportion, it may have actually increased as described earlier. Equally important is that experience in individual states has not resulted in equal shifts in proportionality of the local district's share of educational costs. Table 2.6 clearly demonstrates the uneven patterns that have been allowed to develop among the fifty states. The data indicate that while average shares assumed by local districts in the nation had dropped from 56.8% in 1959–1960 to 43.9% in 1986–1987, actual local shares in 1987 ranged from a high 90.7% in New Hampshire to a low 0.1% in Hawaii. If Hawaii's unique governance structure were excluded,[17] the range would still be great as New Mexico requires only 12.7% local contribution by the individual school districts. Under these conditions, it becomes obvious that burdens are highly differential among states and that national averages do not speak well for the differences that exist throughout the country.[18]

A third feature of the complexity of determining the extent of local responsibility rests in the fundamental nature of how local shares have in fact been determined. As will be discussed at greater length in subsequent chapters on taxation and school finance plans, school districts derive their revenues from a local tax base. Although some states tax more than one type of object to derive school revenues, almost every state relies primarily on real property ownership to define a district's local tax base. This simply means that ownership of real estate is the principal source of revenue generated at the local level. It takes little analysis to realize that no two districts contain exactly the same properties, and that the property values are likewise prone to dissimilarity. For example, urban properties are generally quite valuable with businesses, homes, vacant lots, and other types of land commanding higher prices. Rural land is generally less expensive because it is farther from commerce centers and less

TABLE 2.6 Source of school district revenues, 1959–1987 (in percentages)

	1959–1960			1969–1970			1979–1980			1986–1987		
	Federal	State	Local	Federal	State	Local	Federal	State	Local	Federal	State	Local
United States	3.7	39.5	56.8	7.2	40.9	51.8	9.2	48.9	42.0	6.4	49.8	43.9
Alabama	8.1	69.3	22.6	15.2	63.3	21.5	12.6	69.0	18.4	11.7	66.3	22.0
Alaska	17.9	50.0	32.1	27.1	53.3	19.6	13.0	70.2	16.9	11.7	63.7	24.7
Arizona	6.8	39.5	53.7	8.2	46.4	45.4	11.1	41.6	47.3	9.0	48.3	42.7
Arkansas	8.0	47.7	44.3	18.2	44.5	37.3	14.5	53.0	32.5	11.5	54.8	33.7
California	3.6	42.7	53.7	5.3	37.3	57.4	8.7	71.2	19.1	7.1	69.5	23.5
Colorado	5.7	19.9	74.4	7.6	27.8	64.5	6.1	41.0	52.9	4.9	39.0	56.1
Connecticut	3.0	26.8	70.2	2.1	25.2	72.8	6.1	31.5	62.5	4.4	40.0	55.6
Delaware	2.2	78.9	18.9	7.4	71.3	21.3	13.0	64.7	22.3	7.7	69.2	23.1
District of Columbia	0.8	—	99.2	30.2	—	69.8	15.8	—	84.2	10.3	—	89.7
Florida	2.2	57.7	40.1	9.5	55.7	34.8	11.0	55.2	33.7	7.2	54.2	38.6
Georgia	11.1	62.8	25.1	10.5	58.3	31.1	11.8	57.6	30.6	7.1	59.7	33.2
Hawaii	13.6	69.9	16.5	9.7	87.2	3.2	12.5	85.2	2.4	11.8	88.1	0.1
Idaho	5.8	33.2	61.0	8.4	37.8	53.8	9.5	55.0	35.5	8.9	62.9	28.3
Illinois	2.7	18.9	78.4	5.7	34.6	59.5	12.8	41.2	46.0	4.3	39.1	56.5
Indiana	3.1	29.8	67.1	6.8	39.4	53.8	6.9	56.1	37.0	4.9	58.1	37.0
Iowa	2.9	12.1	85.0	3.6	28.0	68.4	6.7	42.2	51.0	5.1	44.5	50.4
Kansas	5.3	21.5	73.2	5.9	31.2	62.9	6.9	43.3	49.8	4.8	42.4	52.8
Kentucky	4.7	44.9	50.4	13.6	56.2	30.2	12.5	69.7	17.8	11.6	64.5	23.8
Louisiana	2.4	67.7	29.9	11.9	56.4	31.7	14.8	54.4	30.8	11.5	55.1	33.4
Maine	4.0	30.6	65.4	6.7	32.5	60.8	9.6	48.9	41.5	6.4	50.2	43.4
Maryland	6.9	36.4	56.7	6.4	35.2	58.4	8.0	40.2	51.8	5.1	38.5	56.4
Massachusetts	2.0	20.5	77.5	6.0	20.0	74.0	6.5	36.3	57.2	4.9	45.1	50.0
Michigan	2.8	43.8	53.4	3.9	45.1	51.0	7.4	42.7	49.9	5.9	34.9	59.3
Minnesota	2.7	38.2	59.1	5.3	46.0	37.3	6.1	56.6	37.3	4.2	56.9	38.8
Mississippi	9.2	52.4	38.4	21.4	53.1	22.8	24.1	53.1	22.8	10.5	65.2	24.3
Missouri	4.8	30.5	64.7	7.9	33.7	58.4	9.7	36.7	53.6	6.3	41.2	52.5
Montana	3.7	25.4	70.9	8.5	25.4	66.2	8.4	49.3	42.2	8.5	47.8	43.7

TABLE 2.6 (*Continued*)

Nebraska	4.3	91.4	6.4	17.6	76.0	7.9	18.2	73.9	6.1	22.5	71.3
Nevada	9.4	34.2	8.8	36.5	54.7	8.6	58.5	32.9	4.4	39.5	56.0
New Hampshire	4.6	90.1	5.1	8.3	86.7	5.1	6.8	88.1	3.4	5.9	90.7
New Jersey	1.5	74.4	5.4	27.0	67.6	4.1	40.4	55.5	4.4	43.0	52.5
New Mexico	15.2	15.4	17.7	61.9	20.4	16.6	63.4	20.0	12.2	75.1	12.7
New York	1.2	59.5	4.7	46.4	48.9	5.0	40.6	54.4	4.8	42.4	52.8
North Carolina	4.7	27.0	15.6	65.7	18.7	15.2	62.4	22.3	7.9	66.0	26.0
North Dakota	1.7	67.0	9.3	25.7	65.0	7.7	46.5	45.7	9.4	50.8	39.8
Ohio	2.8	66.9	5.0	28.3	66.7	7.7	40.6	51.6	5.5	49.6	44.8
Oklahoma	7.2	50.6	11.8	43.8	44.4	11.8	43.8	44.4	5.6	63.5	30.9
Oregon	4.5	66.0	6.0	20.8	73.2	9.9	35.5	54.6	6.6	28.0	65.4
Pennsylvania	1.8	48.0	6.2	46.2	47.6	8.5	45.0	46.5	5.1	46.3	48.6
Rhode Island	4.0	77.9	5.9	38.8	55.4	5.9	38.8	55.4	4.5	42.6	52.9
South Carolina	5.8	23.3	14.0	59.5	26.4	14.9	56.8	28.3	8.9	56.0	35.1
South Dakota	5.3	86.1	11.7	13.1	75.2	13.9	20.8	65.3	11.8	27.2	61.0
Tennessee	3.7	42.3	11.9	48.0	40.1	14.0	48.3	37.7	11.1	44.5	44.4
Texas	4.6	45.5	9.3	46.4	44.3	11.0	50.1	38.9	7.1	47.1	45.8
Utah	5.3	52.8	7.6	52.8	38.2	7.8	54.0	38.2	6.1	54.4	39.6
Vermont	0.8	76.1	2.9	37.1	60.0	7.7	28.0	64.2	5.1	34.4	60.6
Virginia[1]	9.5	54.0	11.1	36.4	52.5	9.5	40.9	49.6	6.7	32.9	60.3
Washington	5.7	33.2	6.6	56.6	36.8	8.6	70.8	20.6	6.3	72.4	21.3
West Virginia	4.2	41.6	12.4	48.2	39.4	10.6	60.1	29.3	7.5	69.8	22.7
Wisconsin	2.9	75.8	2.5	31.6	65.9	5.5	37.6	56.8	4.7	34.5	60.8
Wyoming	5.7	48.6	20.2	24.8	55.0	6.6	29.6	63.8	3.7	43.0	53.3

—Not applicable.

[1]1986–1987 data for Virginia are estimated.

SOURCE: U.S. Advisory Commission on Intergovernmental Relations (ACIR), *The Structure of State Aid to Elementary and Secondary Education* (Washington, D.C.: ACIR, 1990), 12.

amenable to industrial and residential development, forcing such residents to either commute long distances or face fewer employment opportunities. Unless rural land has other features such as mineral deposits that make it attractive to nonagricultural enterprise, urban centers will have much higher property wealth. That wealth, or assessed valuation, is the basis for deriving local school revenues by applying a rate of taxation against each property. For example, an acre of land in an urban area might sell for $50,000 depending on location. In a rural area, a one-acre homesite might sell for $3,000—perhaps only $300 if that acre is remote pasture land. A tax rate of 32 mills[19] against the urban acre would yield $1,600 in school tax revenue, while the rural homesite would yield only $96, and the pasture land would yield only $9.60—a vast difference with severe implications for schools.[20]

Even the implications are complex, however, and need qualification. While the data suggest high urban wealth, the opposite might be true. For example, it is clear that urban areas naturally have a high population density. Thus high property wealth spread over large populations may in fact yield low per capita wealth. The urban condition often brings very high costs, such as disadvantaged populations and intergovernmental tax dollar competition (i.e., municipal overburden). Many times urban property owners are absentee owners, having little personal commitment to the community and interested only in bleeding off profits without reinvestment. The rural condition is equally complex. Although properties are often not expensive by comparison, ownership rests in fewer hands which increases individual tax burdens. The lack of urban problems in rural areas does not automatically result in low school costs, however, as smaller populations increase per pupil costs due to diseconomies of scale. Likewise, the reality of no two districts containing identical wealth is a vexing problem that creates vastly differential impacts on schools. A simple illustration is two contiguous rural districts with similar enrollments but very different tax bases. One rural district may contain a nuclear power plant, the other marginal pastureland. Under these conditions, the first district is likely to have perhaps $500,000 property wealth per pupil, while the second district may have only $7,500 wealth. While power plants are not common, similar situations are extremely frequent across the United States, resulting in vastly different tax burdens paid by local school patrons. Figure 2.3 illustrates the problem of varying local wealth by providing actual data on all the school districts in a state in 1991 wherein one mill of tax effort produced widely disparate amounts of local school revenue.

A fourth feature of the complexity of local responsibility for education is actually a complication of how local districts are able to determine their shares and, to some extent, their total permissible expenditure levels. This complication takes several forms. While the budget process is complicated by natural barriers including political issues surrounding the feasibility of approving budget increases, the issue is made vastly more complex by how districts' budgets are determined and the interdependency of tax bases and intergovernmental competition. The concept of municipal overburden was introduced previously, and the broader concept of tax overburden was noted to apply in some variation to almost all school districts, including rural schools. A recent by-product of tax overburden has been the increasing difficulty experienced by almost all local districts in seeking approval for increased budgets. In a significant number of states, voters are permitted to accept or reject school budgets on an annual basis. In other states, approval rests with individual boards of education, but any politically literate person can quickly comprehend that boards' willingness to approve budgets and/or budget increases is directly dependent on the amount of

School district	Amount a Mill Raises per Pupil	School district	Amount a Mill Raises per Pupil	School district	Amount a Mill Raises per Pupil
Abilene	$21.60	Cimarron-Ensign	$39.60	Goddard	$23.58
Alma	$29.51	Circle	$41.17	Goessel	$25.42
Altoona-Midway	$25.66	Claflin	$53.71	Golden Plains	$56.66
Andover	$24.66	Clay Center	$21.95	Goodland	$39.67
Anthony-Harper	$36.18	Clearwater	$27.79	Grainfield	$57.54
Argonia	$44.27	Coffeyville	$22.39	Great Bend	$26.39
Arkansas City	$18.53	Colby	$31.19	Greeley County	$76.88
Ashland	$86.51	Columbus	$25.33	Greensburg	$56.85
Atchison Public	$20.65	Comanche County	$70.73	Grinnell	$59.32
Atchison County	$27.31	Concordia	$21.23	Halstead	$24.12
Attica	$50.32	Conway Springs	$23.94	Hamilton	$64.06
Atwood	$35.50	Copeland	$100.28	Hanston	$62.87
Auburn Washburn	$38.90	Crest	$31.28	Haven	$29.55
Augusta	$17.67	Cuba	$49.37	Haviland	$67.63
Axtell	$30.15	Cunningham	$83.60	Hays	$30.37
B & B	$23.50	Deerfield	$183.78	Haysville	$16.18
Baldwin City	$20.96	Derby	$20.27	Healy	$85.19
Barber County North	$50.25	DeSoto	$26.51	Herington	$17.75
Barnes	$48.59	Dexter	$40.24	Herndon	$62.75
Basehor-Linwood	$20.94	Dighton	$50.51	Hesston	$26.30
Baxter Springs	$14.67	Dodge City	$29.99	Hiawatha	$25.57
Bazine	$73.99	Douglass	$15.00	Highland	$22.56
Belle Plaine	$15.10	Durham-Hillsboro-Lehigh	$28.75	Hill City	$41.81
Belleville	$30.35	Eastern Heights	$35.52	Hoisington	$31.59
Beloit	$30.48	Easton	$22.25	Holcomb	$168.52
Blue Valley #384	$26.49	El Dorado	$28.11	Holton	$16.90
Blue Valley #229	$60.41	Elk Valley	$26.76	Hoxie	$44.41
Bonner Springs	$23.50	Elkhart	$86.27	Hugoton	$240.82
Brewster	$70.06	Ell-Saline	$21.21	Humboldt	$24.58
Bucklin	$43.56	Ellinwood	$36.82	Hutchinson	$26.78
Buhler	$25.31	Ellis	$53.40	Independence	$24.66
Burlingame	$15.40	Ellsworth	$23.40	Ingalls	$48.08
Burlington	$554.36	Elwood	$31.42	Inman	$30.15
Burrton	$33.31	Emporia	$19.97	Iola	$14.60
Caldwell	$34.35	Erie-St. Paul	$18.70	Jayhawk	$29.05
Caney Valley	$20.67	Eudora	$13.53	Jefferson County	$19.81
Canton-Galva	$38.65	Eureka	$29.14	Jefferson West	$17.97
Cedar Vale	$38.40	Fairfield	$53.65	Jetmore	$57.43
Central	$31.44	Flinthills	$48.20	Jewell	$40.58
Central Heights	$18.50	Fowler	$71.62	Junction City	$11.72
Centre	$40.37	Fredonia	$26.28	Kansas City	$19.81
Chanute	$17.91	Frontenac	$17.95	Kaw Valley	$220.36
Chapman	$28.64	Ft. Larned	$35.14	Kingman	$47.71
Chase	$78.01	Ft. Leavenworth	N/A	Kinsley-Offerle	$41.47
Chase County	$40.39	Ft. Scott	$19.62	Kismet-Plains	$68.27
Chautauqua County	$25.90	Galena	$8.18	Labette County	$16.75
Cheney	$24.00	Garden City	$24.65	LaCrosse	$67.04
Cherokee	$20.28	Gardner-Edgerton-Antioch	$37.75	Lakin	$205.70
Cherryvale	$15.21	Garnett	$30.81	Lansing	$17.25
Chetopa	$16.28	Girard	$18.22	Lawrence	$35.90
Cheylin	$81.80				

(Continued)

FIGURE 2.3 Local ability to pay for schools: amounts raised under 1 mill tax levy

*Mill levy is the district's total levy. It includes general fund taxes, as well as taxes for building expenses, technology and other special funds.

SOURCE: Kansas Department of Education. Reprinted by Wichita Eagle, "Equal Education: A Task for the Legislature" (Wichita, Kans.: Wichita Eagle, January 26, 1992), 4.

School district	Amount a Mill Raises per Pupil	School district	Amount a Mill Raises per Pupil	School district	Amount a Mill Raises per Pupil
Leavenworth	$22.81	Olathe	$31.18	South Barber	$68.37
Lebo-Waverly	$25.23	Onaga-Havensville-Wheaton	$23.25	South Brown County	$20.29
Leon	$23.05	Osage City	$21.84	South Haven	$32.41
Leoti	$47.35	Osawatomie	$15.97	Southeast of Saline	$50.91
Leroy-Gridley	$49.87	Osborne County	$30.38	Southern Cloud	$43.67
Lewis	$74.79	Oskaloosa	$17.51	Southern Lyon County	$25.36
Liberal	$31.32	Oswego	$20.69	Spearville-Windthorst	$32.06
Lincoln	$37.15	Otis-Bison	$42.35	Spring Hill	$19.06
Lindsborg	$33.13	Ottawa	$19.50	St. Francis	$40.80
Little River	$60.88	Oxford	$25.29	St. John-Hudson	$56.86
Logan	$63.96	Palco	$98.29	Stafford	$50.55
Lorraine	$66.83	Paola	$23.43	Stanton County	$134.54
Louisburg	$22.61	Paradise	$128.05	Sterling	$27.42
Lyndon	$21.28	Parsons	$15.53	Stockton	$47.02
Lyons	$24.62	Pawnee Heights	$73.83	Sublette	$99.58
Macksville	$97.74	Peabody-Burns	$30.65	Sylvan Grove	$42.40
Madison-Virgil	$35.13	Perry	$20.98	Syracuse	$102.50
Maize	$17.84	Phillipsburg	$32.45	Tonganoxie	$18.19
Manhattan	$25.96	Pike Valley	$38.49	Topeka	$31.68
Mankato	$27.65	Piper-Kansas City	$34.85	Triplains	$87.17
Marais Des Cygnes	$20.73	Pittsburg	$20.19	Troy	$16.00
Marion	$26.24	Plainville	$59.59	Turner-Kansas City	$21.02
Marmaton Valley	$34.97	Pleasanton	$16.07	Twin Valley	$25.50
Marysville	$29.09	Prairie Heights	$55.19	Udall	$19.23
Mayetta	$13.14	Prairie View	$127.75	Ulysses	$137.40
McLouth	$19.61	Pratt	$29.74	Uniontown	$22.59
McPherson	$31.92	Pretty Prairie	$35.94	Valley Center	$18.44
Meade	$91.58	Quinter	$33.89	Valley Falls	$15.17
Midway	$39.35	Remington-Whitewater	$35.96	Valley Heights	$22.76
Minneola	$63.29	Renwick	$26.13	Vermillion	$26.95
Montezuma	$54.35	Republican Valley	$39.06	Victoria	$37.27
Morris County	$27.12	Riley County	$17.21	Wabaunsee East	$25.19
Moscow	$480.46	Riverton	$22.69	Waconda	$26.99
Moundridge	$37.36	Rolla	$316.50	WaKeeney	$39.65
Mullinville	$125.18	Rose Hill	$12.54	Wallace County	$51.70
Mulvane	$12.90	Rural Vista	$32.25	Wamego	$18.34
Nemaha	$31.84	Russell County	$50.25	Washington	$24.34
Neodesha	$19.03	Sabetha	$22.94	Wathena	$13.51
Nes Tres La Go	$127.67	Salina	$25.03	Wellington	$19.46
Ness City	$59.83	Santa Fe Trail	$15.11	Wellsville	$19.91
Newton	$19.82	Satanta	$246.49	Weskan	$70.99
Nickerson	$25.73	Scott County	$40.77	West Elk	$33.83
North Central	$45.11	Seaman	$33.32	West Franklin	$21.33
North Jackson	$17.50	Sedgwick	$15.88	West Graham-Morland	$82.85
North Lyon County	$24.57	Shawnee Heights	$23.48	West Smith County	$35.66
North Ottawa County	$29.05	Shawnee Mission	$52.20	West Solomon Valley	$72.02
Northeast	$15.61	Silver Lake	$18.43	Westmoreland	$16.77
Northern Valley	$39.69	Skyline	$57.71	White Rock	$58.50
Norton Community	$20.53	Smith Center	$33.57	Wichita	$32.98
Oakley	$48.89	Smoky Hill	$74.15	Winfield	$22.84
Oberlin	$37.01	Solomon	$31.90	Woodson	$33.88

FIGURE 2.3   *(Continued)*

vocal resistance from electors. Additionally, in many states there is local voter leeway, a concept that gives local districts the option of making additional local tax effort to improve schools. As state aid plans limiting such leeway (particularly in states with recapture provisions)[21] have come into existence and as overall tax burdens may have increased, voter approval for local leeway options has become increasingly difficult to obtain. All these considerations are finally complicated by fiscal dependence on other governmental units. In some states (see Table 2.7), local school budgets are submitted to a higher authority for consideration along with budgets of other taxing units such as cities and counties. Fiscal dependency creates severe problems because local districts in such states often have difficulty securing adequate revenues because intergovernmental competition is raised to a level of deliberate consciousness.

The list of issues surrounding local responsibility and ability to pay for educational services is endless, but discussion to this point illustrates that it is hard to tell simply from raw data whether the local share has decreased as much as it appears, because other complicated issues such as local ability to pay get in the way of otherwise apparent conclusions. What is patently obvious is that ability to pay and local

TABLE 2.7   Number of fiscally independent and dependent school districts in the United States, 1990

	Census			Census	
	Independent	*Dependent*		*Independent*	*Dependent*
Alabama	129	0	Montana	547	0
Alaska	0	55	Nebraska	952	0
Arizona	227	12	Nevada	17	0
Arkansas	333	0	New Hampshire	160	9
California	1,098	53	New Jersey	551	71
Colorado	180	0	New Mexico	88	0
Connecticut	16	149	New York	720	35
Delaware	19	0	North Carolina	0	198
Florida	95	0	North Dakota	310	0
Georgia	186	0	Ohio	621	0
Hawaii	0	1	Oklahoma	636	0
Idaho	118	0	Oregon	350	0
Illinois	1,029	0	Pennsylvania	515	0
Indiana	304	0	Rhode Island	3	37
Iowa	451	0	South Carolina	92	0
Kansas	314	0	South Dakota	193	0
Kentucky	178	0	Tennessee	14	128
Louisiana	66	0	Texas	1,113	0
Maine	88	194	Utah	40	0
Maryland	0	41	Vermont	272	0
Massachusetts	82	354	Virginia	0	140
Michigan	590	0	Washington	297	0
Minnesota	441	0	West Virginia	55	0
Mississippi	171	4	Wisconsin	433	9
Missouri	561	0	Wyoming	56	0

SOURCE: U.S. Advisory Commission on Intergovernmental Relations (ACIR), *The Structure of State Aid to Elementary and Secondary Education* (Washington, D.C.: ACIR, 1990), 14.

percentage requirements differ among districts and states. It is further strikingly clear that if local districts were still totally dependent on local tax bases, unconscionable fiscal disparities would quickly follow. What cannot be told from the data thus far, however, is the extent of federal and state involvement that may mitigate the harsh realities of fiscal differences that can be seen among local districts. To properly understand responsibility for financing schools, it is important to have a grasp of the benefits and limits of federal and state support for education.

Federal Support for Education

Our imaginary survey stated that most citizens would indicate belief in the existence of strong local fiscal support for education. If we were to next ask about the extent of federal involvement, citizens would likely tell us that they were less sure of how deeply the federal government is involved in education. Most citizens would probably also hasten to say that even if the strength of federal fiscal support is questionable, the federal government has had a pervasive influence on how education is carried out. Although the respondents would have a difficult time articulating a discrete federal role, their responses would be rather accurately reflective of the federal government's background role in education whereby it has exercised great influence, both directly and indirectly.

Although respected scholars have long argued over the proper role and relative importance of federal involvement in education (see n. 45), the federal government has had a noticeable interest in education. From one point of view, the history has been both long and meaningful. Unarguably, the Northwest Ordinance of 1787 illustrated a very early federal awareness of education's role in developing the nation for reasons pertaining to morality, economics, and equality. Although progressive reformers might argue over the interpretation of those motives, the Northwest Ordinance very clearly read: "Religion, morality, and knowledge being necessary to good government and the happiness of mankind, schools and the means of education shall forever be encouraged." The Northwest Ordinance was especially significant because it marked the beginning of a formal federal involvement by providing for the survey of lands and the reservation of the sixteenth section of every township for education. By granting such lands, the federal government made apparent its intent to encourage settlement of the frontier by people literate in the founding principles of morality, economics, and democracy. Under the Northwest Ordinance, states and territories were expected to generate income for school purposes and were given wide latitude in the use of granted lands in providing support for schools.[22]

The Northwest Ordinance of 1787 began a long history of federal support that has followed a fairly narrow path compared to the wide road traveled by local and state governments. In contrast to comprehensive local and state assumption, the role of the federal government has generally been confined to three direct thrusts, and with a fourth, indirect thrust that has nonetheless been powerful. The three direct thrusts have been national defense, higher education, and economic and social justice for disadvantaged populations. While these three have produced significant federal involvement in education, the fourth, indirect thrust has been federal court appointments that have in turn resulted in rulings on various lawsuits relating especially to economic and social justice. In many instances, these four thrusts have been overlapping in both intent and effect.

Although scholars debate the most appropriate role for the federal government in education, they generally agree with why the federal role has been rather narrowly defined. As noted earlier in this text, many of the founding fathers opposed vesting strong centralized control in a national government because they believed despotism was a natural ingredient of undiffused authority. Even Alexander Hamilton, virtually a lone sympathizer of centralization at the first Constitutional Convention in 1787, is not thought to have argued for a strong federal role in education.[23] Resistance to centralized government was so strong that only two years after the Constitution was ratified, Congress at its first meeting in 1789 immediately submitted 12 amendments to the Constitution. Virtually every one of the proposed amendments addressed deep concerns expressed by George Mason, a convention delegate who earlier opposed its ratification and refused to sign on the grounds that it failed to forbid slavery and protect individual rights. In the preamble to the resolution offering the proposed amendments in 1789, Congress noted its fear of central authority as it said: "The conventions of a number of the States having at the time of their adopting the Constitution, expressed a desire, in order to prevent misconstruction or abuse of its powers, that further declaratory and restrictive clauses should be added, and as extending the ground of public confidence in government will best insure the beneficent ends of its institution, be it resolved. . . ." Each of the amendments in the resolution was designed in some form to prevent the natural growth of government to despotic ends. The pervasiveness of such beliefs was obvious as 10 of those 12 amendments were in fact ratified.

Adoption of the amendments, known as the Bill of Rights, was of utmost importance to education because several amendments contained wording destined to profoundly impact on the development of education across the centuries. Of all the amendments, the Tenth Amendment was probably the most important because its curbs on the growth of federalism spoke most clearly to constitutional framers' intent and because it alone was to most directly mold the federal government's involvement in education. The Tenth Amendment states: "The powers not delegated to the United States by the Constitution, nor prohibited by it to the States, are reserved to the States respectively, or to the people." With these simple but powerful words, dual doctrines of sovereign limits were formed. By design, the Constitution is thus a document of limited powers, granting to the federal government only those powers specifically enumerated or reserved to it. Constitutional construction thereby *prohibits* the federal government from a direct central interest in education because the supreme document of the land is silent regarding education. At the same time, sweeping state sovereignty was granted in all matters not prohibited by the Constitution. The impact of the Tenth Amendment was enormous, as under such conditions any federal interest in education would have to be derived from other authority or limited to indirect influence.

Although the die was clearly cast making education a state function, Congress has nonetheless established a long history of involvement in education through "other authority" and "indirect persuasion." Other authority has been derived by two means. The first means has been by careful reading of the Powers of Congress found in Article 1 of the Constitution. These powers contain several sections requiring Congress to provide for a strong national defense and, as will be seen later, Congress has succeeded in providing large sums of money to education under the heading of defense. The second means has been by virtue of creative interpretations by Congress and the courts of Article 1, Section 8, of the Constitution, wherein rests a phrase usually referred to as the General Welfare Clause. In its entirety, Article 1, Section 8, reads that Congress shall have the power "to lay and collect taxes, duties, imposts and excises, to pay the debts and provide for the common defense and general welfare of the United States; but all duties, imposts and excises shall be uniform throughout the United States." Of these two means, education for national defense has been a quick and easy path by which Congress could become involved in education. More importantly, however, the General Welfare Clause has been liberally construed, allowing Congress to take an enormous interest in education, particularly in the social and economic justice reform arena. Finally, indirect influence has been powerful through other persuasive techniques such as withholding federal funds from programs unrelated to education unless contemporary federal social and economic policy reform agendas via education are accepted. As a practical observation, Congress has also been able to exercise other indirect influence through the courts because, although the federal judiciary's decisions are beyond Congress's control, appointments to the federal judgeship are congressional prerogative. Little evidence is needed to illustrate how Congress has thus exercised a powerful influence on education, particularly by appointments at the U.S. Supreme Court level.

Although obviously prohibited from direct involvement in education in its most traditional interpretation, Congress has nonetheless found means by which to exercise considerable influence. Federal involvement has closely followed the three main thrusts identified earlier, supported by cagey alignment with an often sympathetic federal judiciary. The impact has been profound, touching almost every area of education from morality to equality. As might be expected, the three main thrusts of defense, higher education, and economic and social justice have involved enormous sums of money,[24] some of which are identified in Table 2.8 (pp. 100–101).

Federalism and Defense Education.   The first thrust in stimulating education for defense purposes has a very long history. Its formal beginnings are generally marked with establishment of the U.S. Military Academy in 1802. Designed for the purpose of training military leaders, the academy gave rise to other defense colleges, with Congress establishing the Naval Academy in 1845, the Coast Guard Academy in 1876, and the Air Force Academy in 1954. Because of increasing military needs and federal interest in promoting superior leadership among officers, the Reserve Officers Training Corps (ROTC) was also established at major universities across the nation wherein future leaders could combine civilian education with military training. Other federal involvement in military aid to education followed, some of which was designed to enhance defense, while other parts were to assist veterans in moving back into civilian life.

While a complete list of all federal interests in defense-related education is impractical for a school finance text, a sampling is important to provide the flavor and breadth of federal education involvement. Congress has long anticipated future needs while attempting to assist those who have risked their lives in defense of freedom. In 1918, Public Law 178 provided disabled veterans with vocational training, and PL 16 of 1943 made similar provisions for World War II disabled veterans.[25] In 1944, Congress established the Serviceman's Readjustment Act, also known as the GI Bill (PL 78-346), which provided educational benefits to millions of servicemen. A 1941 amendment to the Lanham Act provided federal aid for construction, maintenance, and operation of schools in areas impacted by military and other federal facilities. In 1950, Congress enacted PL 81-815 and PL 81-874, which built on this aid, a program that today provides millions of dollars to school districts that have lost a portion of their tax base to tax-exempt military installations. Beginning in 1946 immediately after World War II, the military branches were authorized to establish American schools overseas for the children of soldiers stationed in foreign lands. These schools continue to operate under the Department of Defense and are commonly known as DODS (Department of Defense Schools).

The second half of the twentieth century has seen some of the largest federal outlays for defense-related education, largely sparked by cold wars and the technology race. In 1958, the National Defense Education Act (NDEA) under PL 85-865 was enacted to accelerate education in mathematics, sciences, and foreign languages in response to launching of the Soviet satellite Sputnik. The overlapping nature of federal thrusts was apparent in the NDEA because, of all defense programs affecting nonmilitary children, NDEA was by far the biggest. The NDEA provided federal aid to states and local school districts for strengthening instruction in science and math and languages, improving state statistical services, providing guidance and counseling, and establishing testing services and training institutes. The NDEA also provided higher education student loans and fellowships, foreign study, experimentation and dissemination of information on more effective utilization of media for educational purposes, and vocational training for technical occupations supporting defense. The vital interest of the federal government in defense education is typified by the national service requirements of NDEA scholarship recipients. In addition, in 1950 Congress had earlier established the National Science Foundation (to be discussed later under federal higher education interest), which served defense by training math and science teachers. More recently, the 1985 GI Bill extension in the Montgomery Act (PL 95-525) extended educational benefits to individuals entering military service after June 1985. Many other programs under other overlapping headings are typified by such laws as the Education for Economic Security Act of 1984 (PL 98-377), reflecting new thinking on the meaning of defense in the modern world. Although the overlapping nature of these programs with other federal thrusts such as higher education make it impossible to meaningfully isolate the costs of defense-related educational spending, federal education outlays in the defense arena have been very substantial.

Federalism and Higher Education.   The second thrust of aiding higher education has been a close corollary of federal defense interests. The overlap of thrusts becomes quickly apparent in this arena because higher education and defense often go hand in hand. Generally, however, there is an attempt to separate federal interest in general higher education, with the debut of the federal government in nonmilitary higher education marked by the first Morrill Act in 1862 for the establishment and maintenance of agricultural and mechanical colleges. The Morrill Act provided land grants to states in the amount of 30,000 acres, or financial remuneration in states where federal lands were not available.[26] Federal interest was sufficient to provide for a second Morrill Act in 1890 that provided money grants for the support and improvement of instruction in agricultural and mechanical colleges. In many instances, these colleges became the land grant universities of their respective states, with missions of research, teaching, and service in a practical tradition. Additionally, the formal names of many land grant universities today still identify their agricultural and mechanical origins, although most have moved far beyond their roots by becoming vast sophisticated research organizations.

Federal interest in higher education did not cease with the Morrill Act. While the list is too vast for this textbook, a sampling of highlights underscores the extensive

TABLE 2.8 Federal funds from the department of education, 1980–1991 (in thousands of dollars)

Program	1980	1982	1984	1985	1986	1988	1989	1990	1991
Total	$14,102,165	$15,089,598	$17,072,698	$18,818,201	$18,940,681	$20,897,311	$24,473,634	$25,214,653	$28,381,023
Elementary and secondary education	4,239,022	3,802,234	4,294,269	4,732,864	4,447,153	5,682,997	5,997,160	7,169,693	8,110,886
Grants for the disadvantaged	3,204,664	3,063,651	3,501,383	3,745,855	3,557,026	4,357,970	4,600,444	5,383,960	6,226,814
School improvement programs	788,918	524,730	549,117	748,000	658,676	1,067,213	1,129,444	1,524,001	1,610,678
Bilingual education	169,540	136,292	173,051	171,605	167,534	191,470	196,309	188,152	198,014
Indian education	75,900	77,561	70,718	67,404	63,917	66,344	70,963	73,580	75,380
School assistance in federally affected areas	812,873	457,227	608,791	695,746	677,055	731,241	731,768	815,573	808,286
Maintenance and operations	690,000	438,498	555,300	665,000	636,405	685,496	708,396	717,354	740,708
Construction	110,873	15,951	28,491	23,037	21,267	35,640	18,400	22,929	43,725
Disaster assistance	12,000	2,778	25,000	7,709	19,383	10,103	4,972	75,290	23,853
Education for the handicapped	1,555,253	2,023,536	2,416,799	2,666,056	2,573,399	3,075,456	3,814,846	3,480,122	5,091,091
State grant programs	815,805	933,657	1,082,180	1,245,219	1,087,249	1,115,333	1,642,647	1,258,871	2,407,086
Early childhood education[2]	38,745	40,673	53,164	27,625	15,991	210,752	319,012	280,341	612,914
Special centers, projects, and research	55,075	35,057	54,871	53,430	54,629	78,600	102,141	72,966	94,343
Captioned films and media services	17,778	11,438	14,000	35,670	36,105	13,026	13,346	15,191	16,424
Personnel training	55,375	48,911	55,540	68,025	68,339	66,153	67,023	70,838	69,289
Handicapped rehabilitation service and research	572,475	953,800	1,157,044	1,236,087	1,311,086	1,591,592	1,670,677	1,781,915	1,891,035
Vocational education and adult programs	1,153,743	751,118	954,320	856,271	1,016,302	1,000,055	1,052,470	1,138,674	1,317,000
Basic programs[3]	744,653	530,669	689,324	725,624	862,979	823,299	859,239	858,716	869,634
Consumer and homemaking	63,169	29,363	36,792	33,138	30,311	32,752	32,816	34,517	33,352
Program improvement and supportive services	162,512	91,650	117,249	5,202	—	—	—	—	—
State planning and advisory councils	13,423	8,800	11,200	7,584	6,761	7,681	7,945	7,923	9,128
Adult education, grants to States	153,724	90,636	99,755	84,723	109,791	129,183	139,771	188,280	268,903
Other	16,262	—	—	—	6,460	7,140	12,699	49,238	135,983
Postsecondary student financial assistance	5,108,534	6,584,012	7,478,401	8,534,205	8,932,803	8,807,929	11,482,608	11,112,068	12,185,673
Educational opportunity grants[4]	2,534,378	2,546,167	3,565,209	3,558,440	4,460,266	4,620,133	5,379,725	4,919,264	6,154,696
Work-study	596,065	523,910	561,322	599,467	576,145	604,445	620,644	615,269	598,574
Direct student loans	322,749	193,686	191,962	219,850	212,696	216,963	202,904	157,415	173,589
Guaranteed student loans	1,597,877	3,297,776	3,130,939	4,130,920	3,658,502	3,297,305	5,203,843	5,341,039	5,164,932
Other student assistance programs	57,465	22,473	28,969	25,528	25,194	69,083	75,492	79,081	93,882
Direct aid to postsecondary institutions	277,068	284,467	311,221	329,714	294,681	341,063	398,318	341,634	433,300
Aid to minority and developing institutions	114,680	119,829	132,081	140,374	125,895	135,222	179,062	99,812	99,542
Special programs for the disadvantaged	147,389	150,238	164,740	174,940	168,786	205,841	219,256	241,822	333,758
Cooperative education	14,999	14,400	14,400	14,400	—	—	—	—	—

TABLE 2.8 (*Continued*)

Higher education facilities	268,493	449,191	216,893	194,556	206,017	162,528	77,362	84,035	107,391
Construction loans and insurance	35,362	38,690	54,105	33,188	26,800	89,820	37,109	30,000	29,277
Interest subsidy grants	24,626	23,759	23,925	24,968	23,981	24,466	22,524	38,471	43,064
College housing loans	208,505	386,742	138,863	136,400	155,236	48,242	17,729	15,564	35,050
Other higher education programs	34,927	38,226	82,410	74,340	64,032	79,305	73,574	188,999	225,603
International education and foreign languages	19,977	23,923	30,800	32,050	—	—	—	86,337	92,224
Fund for Improvement of Postsecondary Education	12,000	11,503	11,710	12,710	62,835	65,813	67,236	99,450	120,009
Other	2,950	2,800	39,900	29,580	1,197	13,492	6,338	3,212	13,370
Public library services	101,218	80,074	107,895	116,027	117,998	135,731	141,884	132,583	155,682
Public library services	66,451	60,000	65,000	75,000	71,774	78,922	80,944	82,505	83,898
Interlibrary cooperation	—	11,520	15,000	18,000	17,226	18,395	18,826	19,551	19,908
Public library construction	—	—	21,015	16,027	17,514	23,577	27,289	14,837	32,002
Research libraries	5,992	5,760	6,000	6,000	5,742	5,744	5,675	6,593	6,831
Other	28,775	2,794	880	1,000	5,742	9,093	9,150	9,097	13,043
Payments to special institutions	273,860	251,570	249,610	253,622	255,297	271,658	284,056	292,736	311,301
American Printing House for the Blind	4,349	5,000	5,000	5,500	5,263	5,266	5,335	5,663	6,136
National Technical Institute for the Deaf	19,799	26,300	28,000	31,400	30,624	31,594	33,326	35,594	37,688
Gallaudet College	49,409	64,815	56,288	59,092	59,334	62,195	65,998	67,643	72,262
Howard University	200,303	155,455	160,322	157,630	160,076	172,603	179,397	183,836	195,215
Departmental accounts	277,174	347,943	352,089	364,800	355,944	409,348	419,588	458,536	554,810
Educational research and improvement	51,415	61,550	57,165	60,556	57,514	68,147	78,263	87,074	135,215
Departmental management account	223,857	283,906	293,351	300,885	298,397	341,171	341,286	370,844	419,579
Other	1,875	2,290	1,401	3,349	—	—	—	—	—
Trust funds	27	197	172	10	33	30	39	618	16

SOURCE: U.S. Department of Education, National Center for Education Statistics, *Digest of Education Statistics, 1991* (Washington, D.C.: National Center for Education Statistics, 1991), 358.

federal activity in this arena. Overlap can be seen not only in defense, but also in the Vocational Rehabilitation Act of 1918, which provided retraining grants for World War I veterans. The 1935 Bankhead-Jones Act (PL 74-320) authorized grants to states for agricultural experiment stations, a program which soon spilled over into K–12 education as the Agricultural Adjustment Act (PL 74-320) of 1935 authorizing agricultural commodities support that later developed into school milk and lunch programs. The 1943 Vocational Rehabilitation Act provided assistance for disabled veterans. The 1950 Housing Act (PL 81-475) authorized loans for construction of college housing facilities. Federal interest in facilities has been great, and the Higher Education Facilities Act of 1963 (PL 88-204) authorized grants and loans for classrooms, libraries, laboratories, and other facilities.

Federal interest in higher education may have also been heightened by frustration stemming from the prohibition against direct aid to public elementary and secondary education. With the dramatic social reforms attempted in the 1960s under the War on Poverty, the federal government threw itself headlong into various aids and entitlements under the Civil Rights Act of 1964 (PL 88-352), some of which were targeted for higher education. The Civil Rights Act authorized support for in-service training in higher education, particularly to address problems created by desegregation. In the K–12 arena discussed later, federal interest in this agenda was particularly pronounced as well. As Congress moved into economic and social justice concerns, a number of higher education grants became available, such as the Health Professional Educational Assistance Amendments (PL 89-290), which authorized scholarships to needy students entering health professions, and a concentrated assault was mounted by other higher education acts. The Higher Education Act of 1965 (PL 89-329) not only provided extensive grants for university community service programs, college libraries, research, teacher training, and equipment, but also heavily insured student loans and established the National Teacher Corps and many graduate fellowships. In many instances, these programs were hoped to have a significant benefit for underprivileged populations.

The federal interest in defense, higher education, and social and economic justice was sustained in other programs that followed, amounting to vast sums of federal aid. Highlights included the 1966 International Education Act (PL 89-698) for research, the Higher Education Amendments of 1968 (PL 90-575) which created new programs for disadvantaged students through summer tutorials and counseling, and the Education Amendments of 1972 (PL 92-318) which established general higher education grants and numerous committees and councils affecting higher education. Additionally, the Education Amendments of 1976 (PL 94-482) extended and revised federal assistance to higher education, vocational education, and other programs, and the 1986 Reauthorization of the Higher Education Act of 1965 (PL 99-498) increased grants and loans for postsecondary education. While again the overlapping nature of these programs with other federal thrusts makes it difficult to cleanly isolate federal outlays, Table 2.8 indicates that by 1991 federal investment in higher education was enormous as Congress was providing $12.19 billion in postsecondary student aid, $433.3 million in direct aid to postsecondary institutions, $107.4 million to higher education facilities, and $225.6 million to other higher education programs. If adult vocational programs were included, the total would increase by another $1.3 billion. Although K–12 education has been said to rest with the states, the federal government has been able to support *higher* education very handsomely.

Education and Federalist Justice.   The third thrust focusing on economic and social justice has also not been perfectly divisible from other federal interests, but it has been both the most pervasive and the most sustained concentration of all federal involvement in education. Because of the Tenth Amendment's silence on education, the overlap between thrusts has also been most apparent here as Congress has had to be highly creative to exert meaningful influence on schools. The legal basis for federal intervention into social and economic justice at the elementary and secondary school levels rests in the General Welfare Clause, which states in part: "[T]he Congress shall have power to lay and collect taxes, duties, imposts and excises, to pay the debts and provide for the common defense *and general welfare of the United States"* (emphasis added). As noted earlier, this clause has been liberally construed to grant broad powers up to the point of free congressional will unless successfully challenged in court. Needless to say, this liberal interpretation of constitutional powers has been tested. In *United States v. Butler,*[27] the U.S. Supreme Court ruled that the general welfare clause *could* be broadly construed unless Congress acted arbitrarily—a difficult judgment that would need to be made on a case-by-case basis given rules on burden of proof. A further test occurred in *Helvering v. Davis*[28] as the Court ruled that interpretation of the General Welfare Clause need not be tightly restricted to constitutional framers' intent, but could shift with the needs of the nation.[29] From a position of advantage given national defense and the General Welfare Clause, the federal government has succeeded in becoming meaningfully involved in education at virtually every level.

Despite legal wranglings to permit federal involvement in public K–12 education, the federal government's role has actually been both narrow and limited. Limitedness of federal interest relates on one hand to a convenient acceptance of state sovereignty in educational matters, and narrowness relates on the other hand to resultant congressional ability to both choose and change its interests. While Congress has been interested in both defense and higher education and their relationship to K–12 schooling, it has most often chosen to limit itself to the social and economic justice arena as these issues affect elementary and secondary education.[30] As noted, the role of the courts has at times helped Congress by supporting its aims, and at other times the courts have perhaps gone beyond legislative intent in some areas such as the massive requirements imposed through court interpretation of congressional enactments relating to special education.

The social and economic justice arena has been the center of federal educational activity for quite some time. While some might argue that Congress has inappropriately restricted its reach and has only belatedly become involved, intensive federal interest in social agendas for education can be traced back nearly 30 years.[31] Few would deny that earlier events such as the famous *Brown v. Board of Education*[32] case in 1954 had an unprecedented impact on the structure and nature of schooling, but it was not until the Civil Rights Act of 1964 that the federal government began to move into the education arena. These combined events were to have a lasting impact on education, eventually reaching far beyond the thinking of that day and sparking a massive infusion of federal aid into a wide variety of federal entitlement programs designed to improve social and economic justice.

While the list of federal involvement in K–12 education is too vast to review in this textbook,[33] several highlights deserve extended consideration. The Civil Rights Act of 1964 made a significant contribution to K–12 education, as its provisions for assistance in coping with desegregation also granted aid to public schools. Many other small programs followed over the years that collectively amounted to significant fiscal outlays. Several such programs included the 1965 Disaster Relief Act (PL 89-313) providing assistance to local education agencies suffering natural catastrophes, the 1968 Handicapped Children's Early Education Assistance Act (PL 90-538) authorizing preschool and early childhood education, and the 1970 Elementary and Secondary Education Assistance Programs extension (PL 91-230) authorizing comprehensive planning and evaluation grants, including provisions for a national commission on school finance. Many more small ventures into public K–12 education were made available as Congress chose to respond to perceived special needs relating to a particular moment in history.

Although literally hundreds of examples of federal interest in public elementary and secondary education could be cited, there were three major congressional enactments that dramatically transformed the federal relationship to education. Congress's first headlong plunge into social activism through education came with enactment of Public Law 89-910 in 1965 entitled the Elementary and Secondary Education Act (ESEA) wherein the federal government saw an opportunity for a full-scale frontal assault that would assist the War on Poverty. Not surprisingly, much of the ESEA was thus targeted toward disadvantaged children, especially since its infusion of massive aid to education was in part an outgrowth of the Civil Rights Act of 1964. Of the 11 titles in the Civil Rights Act, two were highly instrumental to federal aid for education.[34] Title IV was enacted to permit the attorney general to sue state and local governments for desegregation violations, and Title VI was an assurance that federal funds could not be used to further race discrimination. With passage of the Civil Rights Act, approval of the ESEA was also virtually assured because an activist Congress saw the opportunity to seize upon the General Welfare Clause to further its reform agenda—an agenda dually enhanced because much of the forthcoming aid would benefit children trapped by poverty and race.

Structurally, the ESEA provided grants for elementary and secondary school programs for children from low income families, provided school library resource funds, textbook funds, and money for purchase of other instructional materials for school children. Additionally, ESEA provided money for supplementary educational centers and services, made provisions for strengthening the role of state education agencies, and provided funds for educational research and training. The original ESEA legislation contained more than 40 entitlements under five titles, each addressing a specific interest of Congress. Title I provided educational services for low income children. Title II provided funds for libraries, textbooks, and visual aids. Title III provided funds for supplementary education centers. Title IV provided funds for research and training laboratories. Title V provided funds for strengthening state departments of education. In addition, other separate but impacting programs were to exist, such as Title VII bilingual education and Title IX sex discrimination laws. In fiscal outlays, however, the most important and far-reaching provisions of the ESEA were found in Title I.

Title I of the ESEA was designed to provide supplementary education services to low income and culturally disadvantaged children. The implicit assumption behind Title I was that such children are at greater risk of being low achievers, and the intent was part of a psychology suggesting that a cycle of intergenerational poverty effects could be broken through provision of supplemental educational support to such children. Children could qualify for Title I services if they met certain criteria such as the single statistic of $2,000 family income originally applied in the 1965 law. Importantly, entire schools could qualify for Title I status if the school could meet minimum numbers of qualifying children concentrated in a single school.[35] In the original law, states received federal funding that was to be flowed through to schools less an administrative cost holdback at the state level. Under the federal guidelines, schools qualified for services if they were judged needy on three criteria: the number of low income families according to census data, the number of children receiving Aid to Families with Dependent Children (AFDC), and a federally applied formula taking into account the statewide expenditure per pupil, with higher spending states receiving more federal funds.[36] Title I funding grew rapidly from $746 million at inception in 1965 to $3 billion at its peak in 1980 when Congress revised the laws with major changes affecting Title I.

In 1981 Congress repealed the ESEA in response to efforts by President Reagan to streamline the federal bureaucracy and popular sentiment to reverse erosion of state sovereignty that many persons believed had occurred from years of an activist Congress. In its place, Congress enacted the Education Consolidation and Improvement Act (ECIA), which was to take effect in 1982. The ECIA effectively continued the old ESEA, but with very different appearance and effect. The ECIA almost completely restructured federal involvement by collapsing many of the freestanding programs that had previously operated under the ESEA. The changes highlighted both the sustained and new interests of Congress, as Title I was continued as Chapter 1 and other programs were deemphasized through collapse. The new Chapter 1 was also altered, however, as many operative and reporting requirements were relaxed, granting greater local discretion and making accountability more difficult under the concept of block grants.[37] Major changes occurred elsewhere, as more than 40 programs that had previously operated under separate acts were reduced into a single unit titled Chapter 2. Chapter 2 requirements were also relaxed, creating broad subchapter categories encompassing diverse programs for basic skills development, support services, special projects, discretionary programs, and general provisions. In addition, new provisions relating to administration were made under the heading of Chapter 3 that effectively reduced the role of the federal government and returned many powers to the states under a philosophy of minimum monitoring. The ECIA did allow several old programs in addition to Title I to remain freestanding, however, including Vocational Education, Education of the Handicapped, National School Lunch, Higher Education, Impact Aid, Title VII Bilingual Education, and Title IX Women's Educational Equity. Summatively, both the ESEA and ECIA have amounted to massive federal outlays for repair of socioeconomic infrastructures (see Table 2.9). Critics have argued, however, that under the ECIA education has suffered through these changes because too little monitoring results in lowered performance, and also because although total dollars increased to $6 billion by 1991, funding increases have not kept pace with increases in other federal outlays.

The third major congressional social justice enactment dramatically transforming the federal relationship to education was passage of PL 94-142 titled Education of the Handicapped Act (EHA) in 1975. The EHA was the result of intensive litigation designed to guarantee the rights of handicapped children to free and appropriate educational programs in the public schools. While much litigation has driven continued development and expansion of the EHA, the challenge that has historically received the most press for initiating enactment of federally mandated handicapped education laws was the 1972 lawsuit brought in *Pennsylvania Association of Retarded Chil-*

TABLE 2.9 Chapters 1 and 2 appropriations under the education consolidation and improvement act, 1990–1991 and 1991–1992 (in thousands)

| State or Other Area | Chapter 1 Total, School Year 1990–1991[2] | Chapter 1, School Year 1991–1992[1] | | | State Schools | | | | | Chapter 2 | |
		Total	Concentration Grants	Local Education Agencies, Basic Grant	Handicapped Children	Neglected and Delinquent Children	Migrant Children	State Administration	Other[3]	1990 Appropriations for 1991	1991 Appropriations for 1992
Total	$ 5,318,284	$ 6,147,268	$ 555,768	$ 5,001,910	$ 148,859	$ 36,106	$ 294,592	$ 59,139	$ 50,893	$ 455,717	$ 448,908
Alabama	107,565	126,214	16,051	105,508	743	347	1,967	1,155	442	7,805	7,618
Alaska	17,920	20,475	458	8,581	2,192	176	8,581	375	112	2,262	2,228
Arizona	61,618	67,988	7,247	51,626	872	354	6,906	622	359	6,233	6,301
Arkansas	64,340	73,759	8,460	58,926	1,536	271	3,608	675	282	4,536	4,486
California	570,437	628,409	62,728	448,831	2,024	3,257	100,340	5,752	5,475	48,717	49,122
Colorado	49,032	50,078	3,279	41,041	2,565	247	2,242	458	245	5,766	5,671
Connecticut	56,847	65,595	4,433	54,075	3,004	448	2,270	600	764	5,118	5,003
Delaware	16,371	19,129	1,431	14,420	2,016	85	596	375	205	2,262	2,228
District of Columbia	24,986	29,697	3,445	22,394	2,549	615	119	375	201	2,262	2,228
Florida	235,645	268,039	27,882	208,048	4,358	1,045	23,052	2,454	1,202	18,545	18,660
Georgia	136,479	167,984	18,505	142,187	1,318	715	3,124	1,538	598	12,198	12,067
Hawaii	14,533	16,066	973	14,091	425	73	0	375	129	2,262	2,228
Idaho	17,922	20,724	973	14,991	401	97	3,765	375	122	2,262	2,228
Illinois	255,476	303,679	26,871	243,217	25,799	1,100	1,882	2,780	2,030	20,432	19,901
Indiana	79,467	93,431	3,261	81,242	4,917	793	1,434	855	931	10,226	10,016
Iowa	41,533	45,920	1,735	41,847	761	309	291	420	556	4,975	4,891
Kansas	37,222	42,528	1,873	33,794	1,448	653	4,016	389	353	4,403	4,392
Kentucky	91,515	107,189	12,060	88,610	1,424	553	2,722	981	840	6,947	6,734
Louisiana	122,622	142,760	16,580	118,024	1,728	604	3,012	1,307	1,505	8,815	8,559
Maine	27,764	32,909	2,003	25,639	663	269	3,739	375	220	2,262	2,228
Maryland	82,835	98,169	7,496	84,641	3,290	927	331	899	585	7,624	7,562
Massachusetts	128,282	148,713	11,876	116,500	12,197	752	4,351	1,361	1,676	8,901	8,681
Michigan	207,005	236,685	18,932	196,375	4,862	1,336	11,724	2,167	1,290	16,935	16,553
Minnesota	59,146	67,857	3,854	58,747	1,282	273	1,886	621	1,193	7,576	7,533
Mississippi	97,407	113,791	14,030	95,316	380	409	1,962	1,042	652	5,489	5,323
Missouri	83,951	98,586	8,866	85,106	1,511	478	710	902	1,013	8,987	8,803
Montana	14,561	15,511	855	13,482	249	133	274	375	142	2,262	2,228
Nebraska	23,866	26,445	1,603	23,137	338	192	406	375	394	2,878	2,859
Nevada	9,806	13,705	428	11,687	310	198	594	375	112	2,262	2,228
New Hampshire	13,283	14,823	340	12,596	1,026	172	117	375	197	2,262	2,228
New Jersey	167,664	194,323	17,838	164,485	4,197	1,864	1,374	1,779	2,787	12,417	12,104
New Mexico	39,376	42,644	5,347	34,838	127	267	1,337	390	337	3,002	3,010
New York	556,258	643,860	66,327	540,087	11,299	4,192	6,822	5,894	9,240	29,371	28,619

TABLE 2.9 (*Continued*)

North Carolina	118,271	141,469	13,001	121,520	982	1,019	3,238	1,295	414	11,341	11,088
North Dakota	11,208	14,704	905	12,381	346	39	473	375	186	2,262	2,228
Ohio	176,374	211,900	14,264	185,125	4,638	2,766	1,523	1,940	1,646	19,546	19,130
Oklahoma	48,665	56,394	4,986	49,073	424	202	993	516	200	6,042	5,822
Oregon	54,219	59,612	973	42,322	5,453	675	9,385	546	258	4,727	4,721
Pennsylvania	256,065	303,440	19,881	255,279	15,691	1,198	3,697	2,778	4,916	19,612	19,167
Rhode Island	19,684	22,788	2,065	19,047	619	280	170	375	231	2,262	2,228
South Carolina	76,486	89,663	9,860	76,994	472	1,011	241	821	264	6,557	6,471
South Dakota	15,465	18,134	1,694	15,348	303	91	78	375	247	2,262	2,228
Tennessee	104,102	122,095	14,983	104,211	501	737	176	1,118	370	8,758	8,596
Texas	363,056	407,948	40,135	312,438	6,782	1,322	41,617	3,734	1,920	33,335	32,654
Utah	18,906	21,588	973	18,016	1,087	192	837	375	108	4,317	4,298
Vermont	13,842	15,449	585	11,840	1,641	110	744	375	154	2,262	2,228
Virginia	100,359	118,777	10,757	103,497	1,762	863	421	1,087	390	9,911	9,781
Washington	69,258	75,249	3,297	55,333	2,372	1,138	12,034	689	386	8,034	8,079
West Virginia	45,113	48,026	4,969	41,436	750	240	25	440	166	3,469	3,320
Wisconsin	72,774	85,922	4,515	76,049	2,273	696	800	786	802	8,710	8,455
Wyoming	6,922	7,867	340	6,347	287	137	282	375	99	2,262	2,228
Other activities											
Bureau of Indian Affairs	27,345	31,276	0	31,276	0	0	0	0	0	0	0
Migrant coordination activities	8,415	8,994	0	0	0	0	8,994	0	0	0	0
Outlying areas											
American Samoa	3,014	3,430	0	3,347	19	0	0	50	15	449	446
Guam	2,988	3,399	0	3,162	172	0	0	50	15	1,270	1,261
Northern Mananas	2,210	2,499	0	2,405	29	0	0	50	15	225	224
Puerto Rico	182,317	229,294	29,545	192,039	242	188	3,309	2,099	1,872	8,390	8,280
Trust Territory of the Pacific	1,534	1,732	0	1,527	141	0	0	50	15	182	180
Virgin Islands	6,957	7,934	0	7,807	62	0	0	50	15	1,290	1,281

SOURCE: U.S. Department of Education, National Center for Education Statistics, *Digest of Education Statistics 1992* (Washington, D.C.: National Center for Education Statistics, 1992), 363.

dren v. Pennsylvania (PARC).[38] Although many states had previously provided some measure of special education services, such provision was often minimal or permissive among the states, and in some instances nonexistent. *PARC* was an excellent test for the viability of litigation, because the state of Pennsylvania provided special services for *some* children but had a provision excluding "uneducable and untrainable" children from schools.[39] Litigation under the Fourteenth Amendment's Equal Protection Clause was brought claiming violation of the uniform and equal protection of the laws and failure to provide due process based on handicapping condition. *PARC* was decided in favor of the plaintiffs, unleashing a series of lawsuits meant to force states to provide special services to all children, regardless of ability.

Partially in response to *PARC* and particularly in response to pressure from sophisticated lobbying by special interest groups, Congress enacted the EHA in 1975. Under the new law, states failing to provide special services in keeping with federal regulations were denied all federal aid to education, including federal money for special education. In the year of EHA's inception, Congress provided $300 million in federal dollars to help defray special education's costs and provided authorizing legislation allowing Congress to provide up to 40% of all special education costs if it chose to do so. Although federal support has never approached the 40% permissible limit, having peaked at 12.5% in 1979,[40] total federal education aid in all areas and pressure by courts have been sufficiently high to discourage states from refusing to provide special education services that conform to federal service mandates. Over the years since inception of the EHA, federal aid has not increased annually by equal proportions, but gross dollar amounts have. Table 2.8 illustrated significant growth, with federal aid to the handicapped totaling more than $5.09 billion in 1991.

Although federal aid to special education has increased more than 16-fold from 1975 to 1991, rising federal aid has also been accompanied by increased costs and new mandates. Federal law requires states to identify students in the categories of deaf, deaf-blind, hearing impaired, mentally retarded, orthopedically handicapped, other health impaired, seriously emotionally disturbed, specific learning disabilities, speech impaired, visually impaired, and autistic.[41] Since passage of the EHA, the number of children served by special education has increased dramatically, as seen in Table 2.10. Most of the growth has been in mild/moderate handicapping conditions such as learning disabilities, seriously emotionally disturbed, and educably mentally retarded.[42] Special education has become a vast enterprise, with powerful lobbies continuing to push relentlessly for expansion of special services. For example, it is estimated that less than half of all students qualifying for seriously emotionally disturbed or behavior disorder placements are served, and a national coalition of education and human service organizations has pressed Congress to create a new category of emotional and behavioral disorders, along with demands for a new category of attention deficit disorders distinct from learning and behavior disorders.[43] At the same time, Congress has itself increased service delivery requirements as exemplified by the 1986 amendment to the EHA titled Early Intervention Programs for Infants and Toddlers (PL 99-457), extending the right to a free and appropriate education to 3- to 5-year-olds and making new provisions for early intervention services for handicapped children aged 0-2. Congress has continued to push back the special education frontiers, enacting PL 101-476 titled Individuals with Disabilities Education Act (IDEA) in 1990, adding two new categories of autism and traumatic brain injury, and increasing existing requirements for individual education plans (IEPs). Additionally, handicapped requirements in schools have recently increased again, as in 1990 Con-

TABLE 2.10 Children aged 0 to 21 years old served in federally supported special education programs, by type of disability: 1976–1977 to 1989–1990 (number served,[1] in thousands)

Type of Disability 1	1976–1977 2	1978–1979 3	1979–1980 4	1980–1981 5	1981–1982 6	1982–1983 7	1983–1984 8	1984–1985 9	1985–1986 10	1986–1987 11	1987–1988 12	1988–1989 13	1989–1990 14
All Disabilities	3,692	3,889	4,005	4,142	4,198	4,255	4,298	4,315	4,317	4,374	4,447	4,544	4,641
Specific learning disabilities	796	1,130	1,276	1,462	1,622	1,741	1,806	1,832	1,862	1,914	1,928	1,987	2,050
Speech or language impairments	1,302	1,214	1,186	1,168	1,135	1,131	1,128	1,126	1,125	1,136	953	967	973
Mental retardation	959	901	869	829	786	757	727	694	660	643	582	564	548
Serious emotional disturbance	283	300	329	346	339	352	361	372	375	383	373	376	381
Hearing impairments	87	85	80	79	75	73	72	69	66	65	56	56	57
Orthopedic impairments	87	70	66	58	58	57	56	56	57	57	47	47	48
Other health impairments	141	105	106	98	79	50	53	68	57	52	45	43	52
Visual impairments	38	32	31	31	29	28	29	28	27	26	22	23	22
Multiple disabilities	—	50	60	68	71	63	65	69	86	97	77	85	86
Deaf-blindness	(3)	2	2	3	2	2	2	2	2	2	1	2	2
Preschool disabled[2]	(3)	(3)	(3)	(3)	(3)	(3)	(3)	(3)	(3)	(3)	363	394	422

[1]Includes students served under Chapter I and Individuals with Disabilities Education Act (IDEA), formerly the Education of the Handicapped Act.

[2]Includes preschool children 3–5 years and 0–5 years served under Chapter I and IDEA, respectively.

[3]Prior to 1987–88, these students were included in the counts by handicapping condition. Beginning in 1987–88, states are no longer required to report preschool handicapped students (0–5 years) by handicapping condition.

— Data not available.

NOTE.—Counts are based on reports from the 50 States and District of Columbia only (i.e., figures from U.S. territories are not included). Increases since 1987–88 are due in part to new legislation enacted Fall 1986, which mandates public school special education services for all handicapped children ages 3 through 5. Some data have been revised from previously published figures. Because of rounding, details may not add to totals.

source: U.S. Department of Education, National Center for Education Statistics, *Digest of Education Statistics 1992* (Washington, D.C.: National Center for Education Statistics, 1992), 64.

gress enacted the Americans with Disabilities Act (PL 101-336) requiring improved access for handicapped persons to public facilities and accommodations, employ-ment, and telecommunication aids.

The consequence of these and other programs has amounted to enormous costs for public schools. As special education is now structured, handicapped persons are entitled to a free and appropriate education under an IEP virtually from zero to 21 years of age. These span a full range of alternatives, including preschool, resource program, self-contained classroom, home or hospital care, and special residential schools.[44] Yet as seen in this chapter, federal interest in education goes beyond even these needs by also providing aid to many other areas of education. By any account, the federal government has not sat idly by, and sustained and evolving federal interest is reflected in other recent enactments, such as the 1984 Education for Economic Security Act (PL 98-377), which added new science and math programs at elementary, secondary and postsecondary levels with focus on magnet schools, excellence in edu-cation, and equal access. The Carl Perkins Vocational Education Act (PL 98-524) in 1984 continued federal assistance for education for economic thrusts, and additional concern for social welfare is evident in recent laws such as the 1986 Handicapped Children's Protection Act (PL 99-372) that allows collection of attorney's fees in cases brought under the EHA and preventing supplantation of services under other laws such as Section 504 of the Rehabilitation Act. Significant federal interest has also been evident in the Anti-Drug Abuse Act (PL 99-570) passed in 1986 providing drug educa-tion and coordination with other agencies, and followed by the 1988 Omnibus Drug Abuse Prevention Act (PL 100-690) authorizing teacher training and early childhood education. The 1988 Augustus F. Hawkins–Robert T. Stafford Elementary and Second-ary School Improvement Amendments (PL 100-297) reauthorized major programs such as Chapter 1, Chapter 2, bilingual, math-science, impact aid, Indian education, adult education, and many others. Numerous other programs have been enacted, such as the Stewart B. McKinney Homeless Assistance Act (PL 100-628) for literacy training. All these programs have focused on social and economic inequality in the belief that education is the key to resolving complex social and economic woes.

The cries of critics over narrow and limited federal interest in K–12 education are accurate from the perspective that no sweeping authority is constitutionally granted to the federal government for assumption of central educational responsibil-ity. But judging from data published by the National Center for Education Statistics on amounts and types of federal program aid, interest in K–12 education has nonetheless resulted in massive attempts to improve national security and economic and social conditions. From 1965 to 1975 growth in federal aid to K–12 education rose 189%. From 1975 to 1980, aid was stable. From 1980 to 1989 federal aid declined 17%, while funding for research increased 36%, and other programs increased nearly 38%. In 1989, about 44% of the $46.7 billion spent on education came from the Department of Education, with the remainder coming from the Department of Health and Human Services ($6.4 billion), the Department of Agriculture ($5.8 billion), the Department of Defense ($3.7 billion), and the Department of Energy ($2.4 billion). As seen in Figure 2.4, percentages had shifted slightly only a few years later. Although aid has had to be provided under the heading of defense or higher education, or creatively provided under the General Welfare Clause, federal support has been substantial—at least within the convenient narrowness of the federal government's ability to pick and choose among its contemporary agenda preferences.

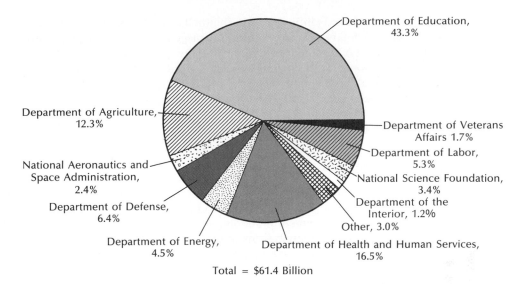

FIGURE 2.4   Federal funds for education, by agency, fiscal year 1992

SOURCE: U.S. Department of Education, National Center for Education Statistics, *Digest of Education Statistics* 1992 (Washington, D.C.: National Center for Education Statistics, 1992), 359.

It appears relatively certain that *short of a constitutional amendment to permit direct federal assumption of education,* the amount and proportion of federal aid will follow Congress's will. In recent years, there has been some question about how Congress will choose among competing goals, given fiscal exigency. The Balanced Budget and Emergency Deficit Control Act (PL 99-177), commonly called the Gramm-Rudman-Hollings Act, passed by Congress in 1985, stands as the best example of these difficult choices that may emerge. The act required the President to reduce the national debt, a difficult task that requires massive tax increases *or* program reductions. Unfortunately, the choice is not even that simple, because from these repeated attempts to reduce the deficit a struggle has developed wherein the federal government passes laws to reduce federal spending and then finds loopholes or creates exceptions to its own rules, such as guaranteed student loans and vocational rehabilitation. Likewise, other rules requiring expanded educational services continue to proliferate, such as extending aid to preschool children. At the same time, Congress continues to receive requests from interest groups, such as demands to add new special education classifications. Interestingly, efforts to reduce and expand government simultaneously are also accompanied by other proposed legislation relating to efforts such as the Regular Education Initiative (REI) seeking to return many special education children to traditional classroom settings.

The thrust for moral education may have dimmed in recent years, but it has likely only been overwhelmed by the press for economic education and social equality. Federal interest has been both limited and narrowly focused, but its impact through general welfare, defense, and indirect persuasion has been enormous. If the services supported in part by the federal government were funded only by local and/or state governments, there is little question that collapse of programs or severe reductions would quickly follow. Given the vital role played by the federal government, there is little likelihood of total federal withdrawal, but the fiscal problems facing the nation have caused some retrenchment in federal spending. Certainly there has never been enough federal funding to meet all the needs of children, and under these conditions states have been asked to take up some of the slack—a reality that has resulted in the vast majority of school costs funded by a local/state partnership, making the federal government a *very* junior partner when all dollars are considered.

State Support for Education

If our imaginary survey of school district patrons were to ask about the level of state support for education, it is likely that most citizens would hold an opinion indicating *significant* state involvement in funding for schools. Much of that public perception would be accurate, stemming from an increasingly visible and important role played by states in the overall school funding scheme. Given the understanding gained in this chapter regarding local and federal support for education, it is entirely reasonable to state that, since educational needs have outstripped available resources, it has been up to the state to create aid mechanisms that provide the level of services to which citizens have become accustomed. It should therefore be no surprise that how education is funded today is a linear product of how local, federal, and state governments' responsibility for education has been ultimately defined.[45]

Education as the State's Responsibility.   The interdependency of federal, state, and local governments in meeting the costs of education is a striking feature of Table 2.11. A second striking feature is the shifting assumption of educational costs by these levels of government over the years. In many ways, Table 2.11 is a synopsis of the interpretation of constitutional responsibility for education. This may be restated as a linear relationship containing three distinct lines of historical progression. First, as there are only three levels of government traditionally capable of assuming any share of educational costs, it naturally follows that the sum of all costs must fall in some proportion to this triad. Second, as direct federal assumption is prohibited, the federal branch is precluded from the lion's share. Third, since local fiscal capacity varies greatly along lines discussed earlier and because the Constitution grants plenary powers to states, a *major* portion of education's costs has been laid upon the states. Although states have been slow to accept responsibility, they have increasingly assumed greater proportions of education's costs out of necessity and because legal authority is vested in states through the Tenth Amendment. Where states have attempted to deny that responsibility or to delegate costs inappropriately to local districts, states have in some instances been forced by courts to accept more fully their constitutional charge.

The nature of federal, state, and local governments' changing assumption of educational costs can be seen chronologically in Table 2.11. It was pointed out in Chapter 1 that the lack of extensive recordkeeping in the early days of the nation makes exact comparison impossible, but three observations are quite clear from the table. First, although the federal share has always been the smallest and the percentage has changed over time, it has still provided a meaningful contribution to education revenues. In 1920, the federal share of education's $970 million budget was 0.3%. Federal aid peaked in 1980 at 9.8%, and tapered off to 6.2% in 1989. Although only a small

TABLE 2.11 Historical summary of public elementary and secondary school total revenues, 1869–1990 (in current dollars)

Finance	1869–1870	1879–1880	1889–1890	1899–1900	1909–1910	1919–1920	1929–1930	1939–1940	1949–1950	1959–1960	1969–1970	1979–1980	1987–1988	1988–1989	1990
Total revenue receipts from	—	—	$143	$220	$433	$970	$2,089	$2,261	$5,437	$14,747	$40,267	$96,861	$169,562	$191,210	—
Federal government	—	—	—	—	—	2	7	40	156	652	3,220	9,504	10,717	11,872	—
State governments	—	—	—	—	—	160	354	684	2,166	5,768	16,063	45,349	84,004	91,158	—
Local sources, including intermediate	—	—	—	—	—	808	1,728	1,536	3,116	8,327	20,985	42,029	74,841	88,180	—
Percentage of revenue receipts from															
Federal government	—	—	—	—	—	0.3	0.4	1.8	2.9	4.4	8.0	9.8	6.3	6.2	—
State governments	—	—	—	—	—	16.5	16.9	30.3	39.8	39.1	39.9	46.8	49.5	47.7	—
Local sources, including intermediate	—	—	—	—	—	83.2	82.7	68.0	57.3	56.5	52.1	43.4	44.1	46.1	—
Total expenditures for public schools	$63	$78	$141	$215	$426	$1,036	$2,317	$2,344	$5,838	$15,613	$40,683	$95,962	$172,400	$189,800	$198,864
Current expenditures	—	—	114	180	356	861	1,844	1,942	4,687	12,329	34,218	86,984	157,098	172,932	—
Capital outlay	—	—	26	35	70	154	371	258	1,014	2,662	4,659	6,506	—	—	—
Interest on school debt	—	—	—	—	—	18	93	131	101	490	1,171	1,874	—	—	—
Other expenditures	—	—	—	—	—	3	10	13	36	133	636	598	—	—	—
Percentage of total expenditures devoted to															
Current expenditures	—	—	81.3	83.5	83.6	83.1	79.6	82.8	80.3	79.0	84.1	90.6	—	—	—
Capital outlay	—	—	18.7	16.5	16.4	14.8	16.0	11.0	17.4	17.0	11.5	6.8	—	—	—
Interest on school debt	—	—	—	—	—	1.8	4.0	5.6	1.7	3.1	2.9	2.0	—	—	—
Other expenditures	—	—	—	—	—	0.3	0.4	0.6	0.6	0.8	1.6	0.6	—	—	—

SOURCE: U.S. Department of Education, National Center for Education Statistics, *Digest of Education Statistics 1991* (Washington, D.C.: National Center for Education Statistics, 1991), 47.

proportion of total revenues, the federal share nonetheless increased nearly 33-fold in a 69-year period. Second, the local share has dropped dramatically over the same period, decreasing from 83.2% in 1920 to 46.1% in 1989. Although gross percentages do not accurately reflect local tax burden as pointed out earlier in this chapter, the change in local shares nonetheless represents some true relief, because costs have continued to rise at the same time that the local percentage has declined. That could only be possible from the third and final observation regarding shifts in responsibility for the costs of education among the three major levels of government. Third, while the federal share has increased and the local share has declined, the difference has had to be absorbed by the state. In 1920 only 16.5% of the $1 billion in school revenue was paid by the state, but by 1989 the state's share had increased to 47.7%. If it had been left to local units to pick up the difference, catastrophe would have soon followed.

The cost of education is graphically striking. As Figure 2.5 shows, total costs have skyrocketed in recent years, increasing approximately fivefold in current dollars in the last 20 years. In constant dollars, the increase of approximately threefold is still steep. These costs could not have been met had it not been for the increasingly important role of the state. As Figure 2.6 finally shows, the shifts among government units have been historic, as in 1979 the state share exceeded the local share for the first time in history—a condition not easily achieved nor likely to be reversed any time soon.

Education is thus ultimately *the state's inescapable duty*. But states have accepted that responsibility with varying degrees of enthusiasm and impact. While state assumption by 1990 had risen to a national average of 47.7%, experience in the individual states reinforces earlier statements about how education has been left to the states and about how different states have had widely disparate school finance development. From 50 states now arise nearly 50 different methods of funding education.[46]

FIGURE 2.5 Current expenditures per student in average daily attendance in public elementary and secondary schools, 1969–1970 to 1990–1991

SOURCE: U.S. Department of Education, National Center for Education Statistics, *Digest of Education Statistics 1992* (Washington, D.C.: National Center for Education Statistics, 1992), 48.

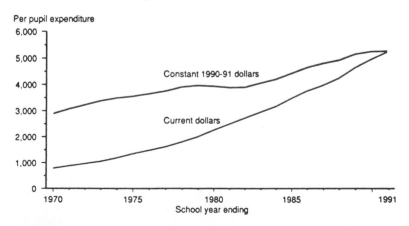

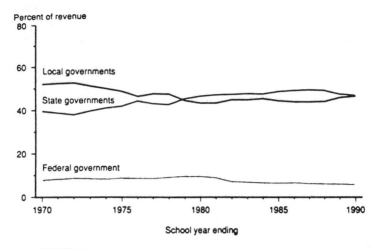

FIGURE 2.6   Revenues for public K–12 schools, 1970–1990

SOURCE: U.S. Department of Education, National Center for Education Statistics, *Digest of Education Statistics 1992* (Washington, D.C.: National Center for Education Statistics, 1992), 48.

Although a high degree of innovation has been able to emerge, the results have not been equally laudable in every instance.

Regardless of location, each of the states has chosen to financially aid education to some extent. However, the extent has been dependent on several factors. First, aid has generally depended on the wealth of each local district and, in most instances, states have tried to grant higher levels of aid to less wealthy districts. Politically, however, this has been difficult and in many states it has required legal intervention to force higher aid levels than could have probably occurred through the political process. Second, the amount of federal aid flowing to the particular state has varied. A good example is PL 874 impact aid. In some states, the amount of land exempt from local taxation because of federal installations is extremely high.[47] In such instances, although state aid has been important to local districts, the presence of impact aid may have lessened state aid requirements.[48] Third, the operation of fundamental political philosophies that have essentially driven the design of state aid formulas has also varied. For example, some states have preferred equalization formulas tying local wealth and aid together in inverse proportion. Other states have chosen minimum foundation plans that help local districts reach a minimum expenditure level before leaving the balance of costs to local choice. Only a very few states have even proposed full state funding. The bottom line is that the choice of a state aid plan is always a function of political realities. The "other bottom line" however, is that the level of state support for education has developed very unevenly in the nation, resulting in wide mixtures of federal, state, and local revenues as seen in Table 2.12.

The fragmentation brought about by virtual state sovereignty restrained only by courts, the unpredictable surges in federal aid brought on by the freedom of Congress and administrations to choose and change federal priorities, and the politicization of educational structures in the 50 states have created a vast tapestry of school finance plans. In some ways, it is highly unfortunate that such diversity has been able to de-

TABLE 2.12 Revenues for Public K–12 Schools by Source and State, 1989–1990 (in thousands of dollars)

State or Other Area	Total	Federal Amount	Federal Percent of Total	State Amount	State Percent of Total	Local and Other Amount	Local and Other Percent of Total
United States	$207,583,910	$12,750,530	6.1	$98,059,659	47.2	$96,773,720	46.6
Alabama	2,557,836	286,598	11.2	1,534,021	60.0	737,217	28.8
Alaska	909,380	116,277	12.8	567,900	62.4	225,203	24.8
Arizona	2,742,625	216,488	7.9	1,194,354	43.5	1,331,784	48.6
Arkansas	1,594,428	153,637	9.6	905,487	56.8	535,304	33.6
California	24,320,281	1,605,281	6.6	16,260,203	66.9	6,454,798	26.5
Colorado	2,767,107	132,246	4.8	1,055,366	38.1	1,579,494	57.1
Connecticut	3,554,800	161,933	4.6	1,533,343	43.1	1,859,524	52.3
Delaware	542,448	39,616	7.3	362,161	66.8	140,672	25.9
District of Columbia	557,089	54,591	9.8	—	0.0	502,498	90.2
Florida	9,589,961	595,711	6.2	4,914,474	51.2	4,079,776	42.5
Georgia	5,194,517	329,253	6.3	2,759,335	53.1	2,105,928	40.5
Hawaii	755,987	76,099	10.1	660,341	87.3	19,546	2.6
Idaho	710,841	56,891	8.0	427,757	60.2	226,193	31.8
Illinois	9,001,253	531,923	5.9	2,952,592	32.8	5,516,737	61.3
Indiana	4,349,969	211,441	4.9	2,510,251	57.7	1,628,277	37.4
Iowa	2,149,710	105,270	4.9	1,056,130	49.1	988,310	46.0
Kansas	2,085,315	103,598	5.0	920,867	44.2	1,060,850	50.9
Kentucky	2,247,379	220,813	9.8	1,540,138	68.5	486,428	21.6
Louisiana	3,058,293	309,117	10.1	1,696,645	55.5	1,052,531	34.4
Maine	1,154,667	62,805	5.4	613,447	53.1	478,416	41.4
Maryland	4,267,441	196,285	4.6	1,609,649	37.7	2,461,507	57.7
Massachusetts	5,117,504	240,192	4.7	1,765,255	34.5	3,112,058	60.8
Michigan	8,394,959	482,031	5.7	2,251,071	26.8	5,661,857	67.4
Minnesota	3,988,317	165,059	4.1	2,088,236	52.4	1,735,023	43.5
Mississippi	1,573,464	243,774	15.5	884,024	56.2	445,666	28.3
Missouri	3,699,939	205,179	5.5	1,480,193	40.0	2,014,567	54.4
Montana	707,594	63,726	9.0	324,888	45.9	318,980	45.1

TABLE 2.12 (*Continued*)

State						
Nebraska	1,359,712	79,742	5.9	314,371	23.1	965,600	71.0
Nevada	860,464	36,018	4.2	326,773	38.0	497,673	57.8
New Hampshire	900,843	24,944	2.8	75,684	8.4	800,215	88.8
New Jersey	8,763,058	336,351	3.8	3,486,521	39.8	4,940,187	56.4
New Mexico	1,225,429	150,229	12.3	893,539	72.9	181,661	14.8
New York	19,744,546	1,014,296	5.1	8,044,917	40.7	10,685,333	54.1
North Carolina	4,683,693	300,405	6.4	3,127,946	66.8	1,255,342	26.8
North Dakota	487,049	47,517	9.8	218,041	44.8	221,490	45.5
Ohio	8,617,848	462,810	5.4	3,754,896	43.6	4,400,142	51.1
Oklahoma	2,172,547	121,530	5.6	1,237,503	57.0	813,514	37.4
Oregon	2,539,734	155,250	6.1	637,971	25.1	1,746,513	68.8
Pennsylvania	10,336,060	534,118	5.2	4,511,630	43.6	5,290,312	51.2
Rhode Island	844,009	41,524	4.9	363,539	43.1	438,946	52.0
South Carolina	2,678,790	215,088	8.0	1,340,255	50.0	1,123,447	41.9
South Dakota	503,949	57,774	11.5	130,552	25.9	315,623	62.6
Tennessee	2,907,714	261,676	9.0	1,330,928	45.8	1,315,110	45.2
Texas	13,948,117	1,012,383	7.3	5,847,048	41.9	7,088,686	50.8
Utah	1,326,479	86,986	6.6	751,040	56.6	488,454	36.8
Vermont	562,543	24,464	4.3	181,330	32.2	356,749	63.4
Virginia	5,101,281	268,730	5.3	1,687,176	33.1	3,145,376	61.7
Washington	4,192,291	243,402	5.8	3,000,965	71.6	947,925	22.6
West Virginia	1,413,165	106,072	7.5	928,128	65.7	378,965	26.8
Wisconsin	4,240,432	174,249	4.1	1,703,555	40.2	2,362,628	55.7
Wyoming	581,050	29,140	5.0	297,225	51.2	254,684	43.8

SOURCE: U.S. Department of Education, National Center for Education Statistics, *Digest of Education Statistics 1992* (Washington, D.C.: National Center for Education Statistics, 1992), 151.

velop, because an inherent outcome of such latitude is that, to whatever extent money purchases educational quality, that quality may consequently become highly unequal among the various states. It is no secret that not all states have placed high priority on education, while other states have chosen in their framing documents to declare education a fundamental right. Differing beliefs about the importance of education have had a direct effect on the amount of money invested in education through state aid plans, and it is accurate to allege that states with low educational priorities have reasonably been among the lowest spending states in the nation. While it could be argued that needs and costs differ among the states, it is difficult to show that differing expenditures per pupil among the various states are the result of careful analysis of such educational needs, cost-of-living indices, and so forth. Most often, expenditure levels are the operationalization of educational values through the political process. While it is possible that such behavior was once acceptable in simpler times, the transportability of poor educational investment by states in a highly mobile society raises legitimate questions about the wisdom of 50 different educational systems on the threshold of the twenty-first century.

While it is difficult in a democracy to argue against state sovereignty and even more difficult to argue against the collective individualism that founded such sovereignty under principles of freedom from oppression, it is also difficult to uncritically accept the disparity in local education systems briefly illustrated in these first two chapters. It is further increasingly difficult to explain to school district patrons why taxes are going up, while reports like *Nation at Risk* are sounding an alarm over declining achievement. For school administrators at both the district and building levels, it is especially difficult to explain the graphic data in Figure 2.7 showing dramatic expenditure increases for schools accompanied by equally dramatic achievement declines. While the data in Chapter 1 of this text pointed to many good reasons why these changes have occurred, the public is led to be largely unsympathetic since the press has seized on the graphic impact of such data and popularized knowledge that the level of educational expenditure in the United States ($3,238) is significantly higher than its industrial competitors of Japan ($1,904) and West Germany ($1,941),[49] while foreign achievement in academics and economic marketplaces is reportedly far superior. No amount of explanation seems sufficient to satisfy the public, because the taxpayer is generally unable to appreciate the inaccuracies of international comparisons and equally unwilling to accept logical explanations. Yet such comparisons are likely to continue, and it is up to federal, state, and local units of government to meet the increasingly complex needs of children. If the past is at all predictive of the future, meeting the needs of tomorrow's citizens and leaders who are now in school will continue increasingly to fall to the state.

In Chapter 1, we explored the social and economic context of education and reached the conclusion that the countenance and mission of American schools is changing dramatically. In Chapter 2 that theme was continued and expanded to understand how responsibility for funding public schools has been assigned among federal, state, and local units of government, reaching the conclusion that, while there is a place for all three levels of government, the major responsibility has fallen to the states, but with uneven consequences. In Chapter 3 we turn to examination of sources of revenue for schools, a process that relates closely to federal, state, and local methods for funding education.

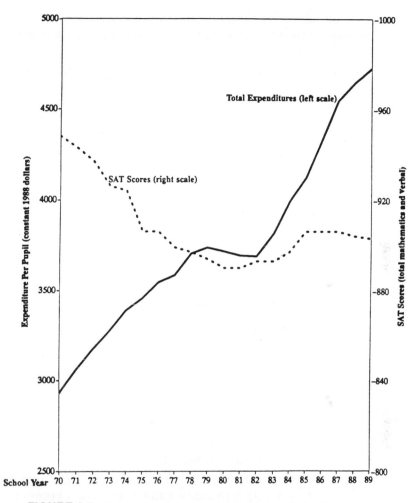

FIGURE 2.7   Total expenditure per pupil in Average Daily Attendance (ADA) in constant 1988 dollars and Scholastic Aptitude Test (SAT) scores, school years ending 1970–1989

SOURCE: U.S. Advisory Commission on Intergovernmental Relations (ACIR). *The Structure of State Aid to Elementary and Secondary Education* (Washington, D.C.: ACIR, 1990, 4.

Review Points

HISTORICAL ROOTS OF AMERICAN EDUCATION

Economic, social, political, and educational policy is never developed in a vacuum. Everything that exists has deep roots that led to its present nature.

Education's financial support structure is subject to those same forces, leaving the conclusion that the present funding scheme has deep historical and sociopolitical origins.

American education had its origins in colonial America where isolation and clustering of peoples of similar political, economic, and religious sympathies shaped schools in the same mold.

American schools were profoundly shaped by beliefs about morality, democracy, economics, and equality. Education for morality was the first purpose of colonial schools. With colonial independence, schools were also perceived to educate for enlightened government. With settlement of the nation's frontier, economic productivity became an important role of education through vocational training, particularly given the Common Schools Movement. In more modern times, the latent theme of equality has taken on special importance.

THE STRUCTURE OF SCHOOL GOVERNMENT IN AMERICA

It is both true and sensible to recognize that development of the educational system's values cannot be separated from its governmental structure.

The fierce independence of colonialism, and later the American as a special breed, was in large measure deliberately carried into educational government in its intensely local focus. When coupled with the localism that flowed inherently from geographic isolation during national expansion, American education was destined to be first a local enterprise.

Localism in public schools led to much fragmentation and very few unifying themes among the thousands of school districts that dotted the nation until very recently.

The twentieth century has brought much standardization to education, largely as a function of school district consolidation.

Consolidation has largely been forced by recognition that local districts have inadequate revenue to continue to supply equal educational opportunities.

LOCAL FISCAL SUPPORT FOR EDUCATION

From the earliest colonial times when local communities paid all educational costs, school funding has remained a heavy local responsibility, as in the 1990s nearly 50% of all school revenues are raised locally.

Throughout the twentieth century, the local share of costs has steadily declined, while spending rose.

The thousands of school districts in the nation have contributed to varying costs and varying quality and quantity of education available to children. In some instances, differences in local wealth are vast.

State funding plans have historically allowed great local leeway, adding to variations in available funding.

Because local wealth is neither equal nor adequate, other outside revenues have had to be introduced.

FEDERAL FISCAL SUPPORT FOR EDUCATION

Federal educational interest has been long-standing and selectively targeted at defense, higher education, and social justice. K–12 education has received significant funding, especially for justice concerns.

A centralized federal role in education was intentionally precluded in the Constitution. As a result, federal K–12 spending has been more indirect under the General Welfare Clause and aimed at social justice concerns. Desegregation, special education, and disadvantaged youth have been special federal targets.

The federal government has also exerted strong influence by coercion through withholding unrelated funds for noncompliance with federal views, and by appointments to the judiciary.

STATE FISCAL SUPPORT FOR EDUCATION

Given no central federal role and given inadequate and highly variable local ability to support education, states have assumed the responsibility for the ''other'' major revenue source to public schools.

Fifty different states, largely free to pursue their variable commitments to education, have created vastly different educational systems with equally variable support levels.

Given all the above, states have been forced politically and judicially to assume increasingly greater shares of education's costs, so that today average state aid exceeds 50%.

Case Study

As the new budget director for a medium-size school district in your state, you have been given the task of working with the state legislature to help them better understand the district's needs for additional revenue. It seems to be particularly bad timing for this request because the state and the district are facing some problems. Because of shortfalls in state sales tax receipts and increased statewide unemployment, state tax revenues are below estimates, and state aid distributions for the remainder of this year will be affected by a 2% across-the-board recission to each district. Additionally, you have just learned from the county treasurer's office that property tax delinquency, which historically has been very low, increased this year to approximately 8%, resulting in uncollected taxes of approximately $2.8 million. Further, you have just been informed that a U.S. Army base in your district for which you receive federal impact aid will permanently reduce enlisted personnel over the next two years by about 12,000 troops. As a result, the district will lose about 1,500 students for which you receive other federal assistance. Finally, in the last legislative session a bill was passed that increases state aid to districts whose standardized test scores are above the national average and reduces aid if scores are below the national norm. The district's curriculum director has just informed you that the district will lose 1% of next year's entitlement due to low student test scores.

As you prepare to work with the legislature, your superintendent has given you authority to spend as much time in the state capital as you need, and you have been assigned one specific objective: to obtain additional state aid. Using the following sets of information and questions to help guide your deliberations and class discussions, what do you anticipate your approach will be? Why? Defend your view through logic, data, and use of appropriate theory.

Case Study Directed Discussion

1. As you began to prepare your thoughts on the upcoming legislative session, you did some additional research into the district's demographic and financial bases. Specifically, you discovered that of the district's 7,000 students, nearly 70% are military dependents where the parent is enlisted or civilian-employed full-time at the army base. Your population projection and analysis also indicated that of these students, only 20% entering kindergarten will remain in the system until graduation. Almost 60% are racial minorities. Fully 15% of students in the district are in special education, and approximately 56% are in Chapter 1 reading programs. Academically, you discovered that scores on the ITBS *and* the ACT are nearly 15% below national averages. Financially, you found that the district has faced significant problems for several years. Specifically, you learned that the proposed state aid reductions will be added to federal aid payment deficits, wherein federal aid is sometimes as much as two years late arriving; that most of the district's wealthy business owners and many of the district's teachers commute from a nearby university town, rather than living in your school district; that there is a fairly heavy parochial school enrollment of 2,000 students, comprised mostly of the resident nonmilitary population; that spending per pupil is only $4,100, nearly $1,100 below statewide average, despite the fact that the district's nonfederal receipts are made up of nearly 79% state aid; and that property tax levies in the district have averaged almost 20% above the statewide average and are expected to increase sharply as a result of the combined effect of enrollment losses, state aid recissions, and achievement score penalties. How will such data add to your lobbying efforts for more state aid?

2. In recent years, there has been much talk among liberals of the need to better define and articulate a federal role for education. Conversely, political conservatives have resisted any federal expansion, arguing wisdom in the constitutional framers' intent and the folly of allowing the federal government to venture into yet another arena, given questionable federal success in other areas of social and economic justice. These groups extend the same general tenor to the topic of increased state aid to education. As you prepare for the upcoming state legislative session, what arguments and data do you anticipate in response to your plea from conservatives? From liberals? How will you counter adverse argument? What are your own views on federal/state/local responsibility for funding education, so that you can argue "from the heart," or alternatively in the absence of strong personal appeals, prepare yourself with effective data? In your opinion, what anticipated points by critics have merit that you must prepare to confront?

3. What sociopolitical realities, if any, in these data might be of possible harm to your efforts?

4. What short- and long-term impacts could you anticipate from the data? Use both the effects you can calculate from the data presented in the case study, and other effects you are able to discern or anticipate from your professional knowledge and experience in education.

5. If a similar scenario were to occur in your state, would the impact be greater or less than in the case study? Has there been some analogous event in your state? What is the profile of your state on issues common to this chapter: for example, the number of school districts; the number and type of federal or other tax-exempt properties, the number of students involved and amounts of "in lieu of" aid, and so forth?

6. As this case study is based in a real event, you should know the outcome. State revenues improved somewhat before the year's end, with state aid recissions only 0.75%. Similarly, delinquent tax collections improved, with nearly 80% of delinquent taxes paid before the end of the district's fiscal year (in this state, delinquent taxpayers' names and amounts are published in local newspapers—in this instance, one prominent business owned by a local board of education member paid nearly $400,000 in back taxes). Likewise, expected troop reassignments never materialized because of Desert Storm operations, with only about 200 students moving out of the district to be closer to extended family in panicked reaction to Gulf War mobilization. Finally, other issues are as yet unresolved, including a new set of anxieties that send mixed signals to the district: for example, the fall of Communism is anticipated to cause massive growth in the district due to troops in Europe returning to the United States; alternatively, the end of the Cold War expects to close hundreds of military bases, and it is rumored that this district may be targeted for closure; and, of course, low student achievement scores persist and penalties loom beginning next year. As you think about these realities, how do such school districts plan, both short- and long-term? If you were to place first-order blame for these unsettled conditions, to whom would you assign responsibility? Who should finally be responsible for seeing that education in such districts is fairly funded (there are nearly a thousand militarily impacted districts in the United States)?

NOTES

1. John Stuart Mill, "Inaugural Address at the University of St. Andrews," in *John Stuart Mill on Education,* ed. Francis Garforth (New York: Teachers College Press, 1971), 156.
2. The reader should not infer from this chapter that a full discussion of this concept has occurred nor that the framing documents of the United States make no guarantees regarding education. The discussion of education as a constitutional and legal right is reserved for Chapter 5.
3. Ellwood P. Cubberley, *The History of Education* (Boston: Houghton Mifflin, 1920), 364.
4. Cubberley, *History of Education,* 364.
5. Horace Mann was appointed the first secretary to the State Board of Education in Massachusetts in 1837.
6. Henry Barnard was the first state superintendent of public instruction in the states of Rhode Island and Connecticut.

7. See the listing of selected national reports on education in Chapter 1. These reports almost unanimously decried the state of education and called for new emphasis on education for morality, economics, and equality.

8. L. Dean Webb, Martha M. McCarthy, and Stephen B. Thomas, *Financing Elementary and Secondary Education* (Columbus, Ohio: Merrill, 1988), 3.

9. Methods of funding in the 50 states are discussed in Chapter 4. Although the focus will not deliberately construct or belabor similarities between funding schemes and religious/political ideologies, it is nonetheless true that the differences in current school finance schemes do favor political ideologies along conservative or progressive lines, and a line can be drawn between political and religious views as well. As an example, the minimum foundation program is highly popular in southern states, and it is accurate to say that the whole concept of minimum support is compatible with the slow development of southern public education systems.

10. M. Katz, "From Voluntarism to Bureaucracy in American Education," in *Power and Ideology in Education,* ed. Jeremy Karabel and A. H. Halsey (New York: Oxford University Press, 1977).

11. Quoted in Austin Swanson and Richard King, *School Finance: Its Economics and Politics* (New York: Longman, 1991), 39.

12. The authors have seen many instances of elementary school buildings only one or two city blocks apart, sometimes within eyesight of one another. In many school systems, it is not uncommon to have more than one high school serving a population of perhaps only 100–200 students in total combined enrollment. These experiences are by no means unique despite the massive changes in school organization and boundaries described in this chapter.

13. For example, there are only 3,064 counties in the United States, containing 3.6 million square miles of land area. Excerpted from *The World Almanac and Book of Facts 1992* (New York: Pharos Books, 1992), 109–127.

14. There is little risk inherent in this statement as documented in other school finance texts. For example, Odden and Picus in *School Finance: A Policy Perspective* (see n. 41), 3 concur with data in this text noting 17,108 districts in 1940; Swanson and King in *School Finance: Economics and Politics,* (42, state that there were more than 127,000 districts in 1930; Percy Burrup, Vern Brimley, and Rulon Garfield in *Financing Education in a Climate of Change,* 4th ed. (Newton, Mass.: Allyn & Bacon, 1988), 133, state that there were 127,649 districts in 1932; Johns, Morphet, and Alexander in *Economics and Financing of Education* (see n. 25), 150, state that there were approximately 130,000 districts in 1933. Except for the estimates given by Odden and Picus, and by Swanson and King (and except for the data obviously documented in this textbook), none of the estimates by other authors can be confirmed because no authority is given for their data. The lack of risk for the statement in this text thus obviously depends on the accuracy of their information.

15. Sharon Tatge, "Using Geographical Isolation Factors in State Education Funding: A Policy Option for Kansas," (Ph.D. diss., Kansas State University, 1992). The state actually contains 304 school districts, of which 134 (44%) are less than 500 enrollment. This study uses a distance factor of 10 miles as the disqualifier for state aid purposes wherein closer proximity resulted in loss of aid. If aid were removed from these districts, a $38 million savings would result. If alternate isolation factors were used, the rate of disqualification for state aid would increase sharply, with attendant increases in aid recapture. For example, using a distance factor of 12 miles would disqualify 81 districts (26%), and a factor of 15 miles would disqualify nearly 50%. The analysis also showed that many of these districts were the political remains of massive school consolidation in the 1960s, when more than 2,000 districts were reduced to slightly more than the present 304 districts.

16. Additional qualification of this statement will occur later, particularly relating to federal

interest in such matters as Section 16 lands and so forth. The statement is true, however, for purposes of overall purview because the vast majority of total education dollars has historically come from local tax bases.

17. Hawaii is noteworthy for two reasons. As Hawaii is structurally comprised of only one school district, state aid by local district is obviously not a completely valid comparison. Additionally, Hawaii operates under a full state funding plan—even if multiple districts existed, the comparison still might not be valid because the state would assume all costs regardless of local wealth.

18. In actuality, even these ranges are not totally representative because different state aid plans require greater differences in local support levels. Equalization plans, for example, often base the local share on some measure of ability to pay, offering state aid to less wealthy districts. In many states, such aid may range from 0%–90% or more. The mitigating factor is, of course, that local shares decline as ability decreases. No such implication can be drawn, however, from the suggestion that local shares differ on a state-by-state basis rather than on a methodologically sound basis as does state aid.

19. More discussion will occur later on calculating tax rates and yields. For now, 1 mill is $1 tax yield per $1,000 assessed valuation. Mathematically $(.001)($1,000) = 1.

20. In reality, even these numbers are inflated because the tax rate here is applied against market value rather than assessed value. Most states utilize fractional assessment, a concept that taxes only a portion of the total value of the property. While tax revenues in each of these examples would be less than shown here, the situation is merely worsened. Imagine, for example, the acre of pasture that would yield only $1.15 in tax revenue if the property were assessed at a fairly common rate of 12% of market value.

21. Recapture is a concept in school finance that requires wealthy districts to remit excess revenues raised due to high wealth to the state. This concept and others will be more fully discussed in Chapter 4.

22. It should be noted that not all states were recipients of identical land grants. Section 16 lands were granted to territories beginning in 1787. In 1802, Congress instituted a policy of granting Section 16 of each township on admission to statehood. Beginning with the Oregon territory in 1848, two sections were granted. In 1896, Utah was granted four sections, and the same was done for western states later admitted. Several states, however, received no grants.

23. Guthrie, Garms, and Pierce, *School Finance and Education Policy,* 160.

24. Exhaustive discussion of every federal program affecting education is beyond the scope of this textbook. This section is meant to sample the depth of federal presence in education.

25. Roe Johns, Edgar Morphet, and Kern Alexander, *The Economics and Financing of Education,* 4th ed. (Englewood Cliffs, N.J.: Prentice-Hall, 1983), 336.

26. Johns, Morphet, and Alexander, *Economics and Financing of Education,* 332.

27. United States v. Butler, 56 S.Ct. 312 (1936).

28. Helvering v. Davis, 57 S.Ct. 904 (1937).

29. This argument is a deeply divisive issue in constitutional interpretation. It has been particularly relevant in church-state relationships affecting schools, a topic not covered in this text. One faction argues that the Constitution is timeless and its meaning may not be conveniently abridged lest it fall prey to politicization. The other faction's argument is embodied in the words of Justice Brennan when he said: "We current Justices read the Constitution the only way we can, as twentieth century Americans. We look to the history of the time of the framing and to the intervening history of interpretation. But the ultimate question must be, what do the words mean in our time" (in an address to the Text and Teaching Symposium, Georgetown University, 1985). The argument is not likely to be resolved, but the federal government has succeeded in capturing current court majority, believing that a liberal construction of the General Welfare Clause is appropriate at this time.

30. It should be noted that there is a related area of aid to private schools where both Congress and the courts have been extensively involved. This issue is not discussed here due to space limitations, but the student of education finance should make a point of exploring this issue.

31. Quite literally, in a fuller discussion the interest would carry back to the Civil Rights Act of 1871 and continue through court cases including Plessey v. Ferguson (347 U.S. 483 [1896]), Brown v. Board of Education (347 U.S. 483 [1954]), and so forth in order to trace the overlapping relationships of the federal government and the courts in the educational enterprise. Some of this discussion occurs in Chapter 5; the present discussion, however, is limited to intensive aid to education.

32. Brown.

33. No discussion occurs here about the numerous and substantial federal involvement in Indian education. This topic is beyond the intent of this textbook.

34. Rosemary Salomone, *Equal Education Under Law: Legal Rights and Federal Policy in the Post-Brown Era* (New York: St. Martin's Press, 1986), 58.

35. Although there is not room here to develop this concept, qualifying individual schools arose in response to concerns about the loss of impact that occurs when spreading available funds across too large a population. The implication is that too many children were identified as needy, necessitating a change of rules to reach the "worst of the worst in need." Unfortunately, this too created a unique set of problems related to uniformity of qualification for services.

36. Successive years of Title I operation saw many rule changes. The changes related to perceived problems in Title I equity and to changes in administrations that attempted to exercise influence on the federal role in education.

37. The concept of a block grant was in direct opposition to the ESEA which had operated under categorical grants. Each concept, however, was in keeping with the political philosophy behind its origination. Under an activist Congress, categorical grants had included strict rules on how money could be spent, and stringent reporting procedures were in place in the ESEA to assure that intended recipients were indeed the beneficiaries. The old story of the administrator with two typewriters illustrates the point. Under the federal rules, equipment purchased with federal entitlements had to be clearly marked as such. The story goes that when filling out forms, the administrator had to switch between machines depending on whether or not the form was for federal reimbursement, because severe penalties would follow improper use of federal outlays. In contrast, the block grant concept under the ECIA provided a sum of money with broad guidelines and left much of its appropriate use to the local decision-making process.

38. Pennsylvania Association of Retarded Children v. Pennsylvania (PARC), 343 F.Supp. 279 (1972).

39. Thomas H. Jones, *Introduction to School Finance: Technique and Social Policy* (New York: Macmillan, 1985), 228.

40. Webb, McCarthy, and Thomas, *Financing Elementary and Secondary Education,* 242.

41. Allan Odden and Larry Picus, *School Finance: A Policy Perspective* (New York: McGraw-Hill, 1992), 218.

42. Thompson, "State Education Finance Policies," 107.

43. David C. Thompson, "Special Needs Students: A Generation at Risk," in *Who Pays for Student Diversity? Population Changes and Educational Policy.* The Twelfth Annual Yearbook of the American Education Finance Association, ed. James G. Ward and Patricia Anthony (Newbury Park, CA: Corwin Press, 1992), 107.

44. Odden and Picus, *School Finance: A Policy Perspective,* 220.

45. It should be noted with great emphasis that the order of local/federal/state funding is deliberate in that this discussion is meant to be chronological. The level and importance of

support from each unit, however, does not follow in either ascending *or* descending order. As indicated in text, a limited federal role and fewer federal dollars make it a junior, albeit powerful, force. It is important to note this since the state/local partnership is undeniably the predominant funding schema. The order here, however, is also based somewhat in another logic. Critics can easily attribute to the discussion in text a certain implication of overemphasis on federalism that leaves the impression that the state has picked up the slack left by federal and local units of government—an implication not normally accepted in school finance circles. That criticism is duly noted here, but the implication is somewhat intentional and justifiable by the chronology itself. Local funding is discussed *first* because that is the way history evolved. To the precise point, federalism is discussed *second* because that is also historical reality. The state is discussed *third* because states emerged last and because, *absent* a federal role, it was indeed left to states to "fill the void." Hence, critics are respected, but the order is intentional. Likewise, neither are federal/state/local discussions out of balance in length, in that the remainder of the book is devoted in some form to theory and practice under state/local funding schemes. The balance in this chapter between federal/state/local funding should *not* be misinterpreted or overstated.

46. Chapter 4 discusses in greater detail the various methods by which state aid can be distributed and how state aid plans have actually operated.

47. For example, Alaska, Idaho, Nevada, and Utah each has more than 50% of its land area owned by the federal government.

48. School finance scholars and practitioners can no doubt find exceptions to this generalization, as the federal government has been notorious in not making impact aid payments on time and in not fully offsetting tax base losses. The generalization is meant to indicate that federal aid has some effect on state aid plans by its presence or absence, as states with virtually no special federal assistance obviously must depend on the combination of local wealth and state aid to fully meet educational costs.

49. National Center for Education Statistics, *The Condition of Education* (Washington, D.C.: NCES, 1991). Data taken from Chart 1:26, p. 91. Comparisons are in U.S. dollars for 1986–1987. International comparisons are inexact, particularly since other nations may have different spending patterns involving both public and private education.

ADDITIONAL READINGS

Campbell, Roald F., Luvern L. Cunningham, Ralph O. Nystrand, and Michael D. Lisdan. *The Organization and Control of American Schools.* 5th ed. Columbus, Ohio: Merrill, 1985.

Counts, George S. *Education and American Civilization.* New York: Columbia University Teachers College, 1952.

Cremin, Lawrence. *American Education: The Colonial Experience 1607–1783.* New York: Harper & Row, 1970.

———. *Public Education.* New York: Basic Books, 1976.

———. *American Education: The National Experience 1783–1876.* New York: Harper & Row, 1980.

Dewey, John. *Democracy and Education.* New York: Macmillan, 1916.

Kaestle, Carl. *Pillars of the Republic: Common Schools and American Society, 1780–1860.* New York: Hill & Wang, 1983.

Polanyi, Karl. *The Great Transformation: The Political and Economic Origins of Our Time.* Boston: Beacon Press, 1957.

Ravitch, Diane. *The Troubled Crusade.* New York: Basic Books, 1983.

———. *The Schools We Deserve: Reflections on the Educational Crises of Our Times.* New York: Basic Books, 1985.

Spring, Joel. *The American School 1642–1990.* 2d ed. New York: Longman, 1990.

de Toqueville, Alexis. *Democracy in America.* 1835. Reprint. New York: Mentor, 1965.

Tyack, David. *The One Best System: A History of American Urban Education.* Cambridge: Harvard University Press, 1974.

Tyack, David, and Elizabeth Hansot. *Managers of Virtue: Public School Leadership in America, 1820–1980.* New York: Basic Books, 1982.

Wirt, Frederick M., and Michael W. Kirst. *The Political Web of American Schools.* Berkeley: McCutchan, 1982.

CHAPTER 3

Revenue Sources for Education

CHAPTER THEME

- Although Americans have firm beliefs about the value of education, the pervasive sentiment is that education has become too expensive and that school taxes are a heavy burden. These perceptions arise from growth in education and from the elaborate tax systems that distribute vast revenues to schools. The size of education makes it an easy target for disaffected taxpayers calling for reducing the size and cost of government and for a tax system that better distributes the costs of society's goals. But since neither government nor its costs is likely to be reduced given the new sociopolitical demographics straining school budgets, administrators must be informed about the issues and options in taxation.

CHAPTER OUTLINE

- A historical base for understanding taxation in the United States, continuing the view proposed in this textbook that retrospection offers insights into future solutions through broader understanding
- The general characteristics of a desirable tax system in light of current tax systems to offer a basis for critique and improvement of taxation
- The merits and limitations of the various tax bases available to government

CHAPTER OBJECTIVE

- A better appreciation of the issues surrounding school taxes, which in turn will aid administrators in working with policymakers and taxpayers

The taxes a government can impose are related to a nation's economy, its history, and the political climate at home and abroad. Citizens of Western nations will more readily support their government if its policies are seen by most people as benevolent, and if it makes moderate fiscal demands. In such circumstances governance approximates market exchange; taxes, as Justice Holmes said, are the price citizens pay for civilized government. A long history of punitive taxation, ended abruptly by revolution establishing legislative government, will have long-lasting effects on citizens' attitudes; in these places bias against central government persists for a long time. Such societies are slow to impose new taxes. When they do, remembering past injustice, reluctant taxpayers search for ways to evade.

Carolyn Webber and Aaron Wildavsky, A History of Taxation and Expenditure in the Western World

Following on the heels of the tumultuous nature of education finance described in the first two chapters in this text, the opening quotation[1] for this discussion of revenue sources for schools should come as no surprise. Although the desire of most Americans to have good schools is well documented, it is equally evident that citizens want such schools without the attendant burden of continually increasing taxes. Despite firm beliefs in the value of education, there is a pervasive sentiment that education has become too expensive and that school taxes are a very heavy burden poorly distributed through insensitive and fundamentally unfair tax policies. Revenues, that is, school taxes, have thus been the source of much dispute, and the result has been an uneasy peace punctuated by frequent reactions to changing political and economic conditions.

The vast resources devoted to education, however, speak clearly to four firm realities that flow from previous discussion in this text. The first reality states that growth of the educational enterprise has given rise to elaborate tax systems that are firmly in place whereby vast revenues are gathered and redistributed to schools. The second reality states that these systems have long been a target of disaffected taxpayers who have called for reducing the size and cost of government and for a system of taxation that better distributes the costs of society's goals. The third reality, however, states that neither government nor its costs is likely to be reduced because the needs of the nation's vast population are rapidly increasing. Finally, the fourth reality states that solutions to these difficult problems are aggressively political because they are imbedded in a context that demands both adequate and equitable revenue systems. Under such stark conditions, the enormity of these realities is almost overwhelming since resolution defies political pragmatism. But because the new demographics are straining school budgets, it should be obvious that administrators must be informed about the issues and options in taxation.

The need for adequate and equitable revenues for education is thus the focus of Chapter 3. Intimately related to the two previous chapters, this chapter takes the next step in our consideration of school finance by discussing the three most basic concepts of school revenue. The chapter first seeks to establish a historical base for understanding taxation in the United States. Because tax systems have been subject to much criticism, the chapter secondly discusses the general characteristics of a desirable tax system. Third and finally, the balance of the chapter is devoted to assessing the various tax bases available to government. Upon completion of this chapter, the administrator should have a better appreciation of the issues in school taxes, which in turn will aid in working with policymakers and taxpayers.

SYSTEMS OF TAXATION

Although it may be said that a democratic government stands only to serve the needs of the citizens who authorized its existence, a hallmark of government is the resentment it engenders in seeking to fulfill its role. Although many plausible explanations exist for the lack of gratitude felt toward government, it is reasonable to believe that such negative attitudes are a function of its most visible presence in the lives of people. Despite best intentions, the first image of government to most people is taxes. Although it is reasonable to know that taxes precede services, few persons extend their tax dollars joyfully and even fewer would do so without force. It is a basic tenet of public policy that taxation is the forcible removal of private wealth for a public purpose so important that it justifies violating the right to absolute ownership of wealth. Such reality is instantly fraught with tension, and worsened by the fact that systems of taxation have been shrouded in eons of abusive government. This has been a special legacy in the United States where tax resentment is a principle of equal proportion to liberty because the spark that triggered independence was oppressive taxation by the English crown.

Yet despite resentment toward taxation, every civilized nation in history has devised methods by which funds are transferred from the private sector to a public treasury. Although the nation was founded on bitter tax dissent, forcible wealth transfers have long been utilized to support all levels of American government, including education. These realities make clear that a broad understanding of the nature of tax systems is critical to school administrators in that taxpayers bear the final cost of schools—with varying degrees of enthusiasm, however. As a result, this section examines the development of government support in the United States as a preface to understanding tax systems and schools.

Tax Systems

Taxes are a pervasive reality. Every employed person is intimately aware that taxes are deducted from gross earnings each pay period. For example, the average educator's paycheck has deductions for Old Age Survivors and Disability Insurance (OASDI), federal income tax, and Medicare. In addition, paychecks may have other deductions for state income tax, state retirement, mandatory state health insurance, special unemployment insurance, local income taxes, and a host of other taxes. Similarly, most citizens are aware of taxes paid apart from income—for example, sales taxes are applied to millions of goods and services in the United States, and taxes on property are an omnipresent reality. Likewise, taxes at other levels exist, such as severance tax paid on minerals extracted from the earth, excise taxes on certain goods, and taxes on unearned income such as investments and retirement pensions. Overlapping taxes are often levied wherein items such as homes or automobiles may be taxed by more than one unit of government. These various levels and types of taxes have become known as tax systems.

Although no modern institution is so reviled as taxation, few people would argue for total abolition of taxes. Most citizens realize that the standard of living enjoyed by everyone regardless of social class is partly a function of taxes, and most persons realize that many privileges such as roads and parks would not exist were it not for a system of substantial taxation. For example, while people complain about taxes for such items as welfare, most citizens take some solace in knowing that the alternative is medieval wretchedness. Similarly, even wealthy citizens secretly take some comfort in the safety net of unemployment insurance, especially in uncertain times such as the last two decades when unemployment has remained high and as top management has been downsized. Likewise, virtually no one fails to recognize that national defense, police and fire protection, utilities, sewers and sanitation, consumer protection laws, and education from kindergarten to postdoctoral studies are all available at greatly reduced prices by the power of a collective public purse. Though widely viewed with distaste, taxation is tacitly approved in that people have come to expect a level of service that could not be withdrawn without negative economic, social, and political consequences.

Although no nation's tax system has ever been praised by citizens, the design of the tax system in the United States has been the product of its unique national history. As illustrated in the first two chapters, the history of the nation has been marked by continual expansion that has led to a unique form of government reflecting both growth and fierce independence. As the nation grew, new citizens with a variety of needs required tax systems that also had to expand in size and breadth as movement from an agricultural to an industrial society brought about large cities, and a far-flung geography also forced the need for new and expanded revenues. Growth in American tax systems can also be closely traced to profound economic crises that have led to increasing socialization as citizens have become more interdependent. For example, the devastating effect of the Great Depression in 1929 induced drastic changes in American collective behavior, as food lines and public works projects and social security and welfare were devised in an attempt to shelter the nation from economic disaster.

While the emergence of American taxation is multifaceted, no feature is more important than the fundamental principle on which the nation itself was founded. Directly analogous to the protectionist philosophy under which education systems were developed, tax systems have reflected the national principle of united state sovereignty. As evident in earlier discussion, a high degree of independence has always surrounded the nation, reflecting distrust of centralized authority. It was thus clearly not by accident that the states themselves figured prominently in the new nation that bound together by agreement sovereign states whose powers could not be usurped. The same defiance that led the nation's forefathers to restrict federal powers under the Constitution and to grant plenary powers to states can be seen in the multiplicity of parallel tax systems that have been developed due to lack of a strong central government. Just as federal, state, and local units of government emerged from the nation's struggle for independence, each of these levels has had to develop its own revenue sources to meet citizens' needs because each unit of government has been assigned differing roles of service. As a result, taxation has evolved into separate but interrelated *federal, state,* and *local* tax systems.

Federal Tax System.   Although many persons assume that the size and power of federal taxation are the result of long and distinguished development, the present federal tax system is actually the result of a series of awkward and ill-fated attempts at establishing a strong federal government. While the vast history of taxation is beyond the scope of this text, it is important to understand that the present revenue system for government, including education, is based in historical realities that includes the federal government. Three such realities observe that the present tax system is of relatively recent origin, highly narrow focus, and rather unflattering disputes.

From the earliest days on this continent, the nation's history has been based in taxpayer revolt against compulsory revenue systems. Indeed, the earliest recorded tax revolt can be traced to the Massachusetts Bay Colony in 1632 when the settlers of Watertown were informed that a portion of their wealth would be taken by the Massachusetts Bay Company to build fortifications for the nearby town of Cambridge. Outraged, the settlers refused to pay and demanded an audience with the governor of Massachusetts Bay, who successfully warded off their ire by eloquent explanation of the benefit of such a tax to the welfare of all citizens. Critical to his speech, however, was promise of parliamentary elections whereby colonists would be allowed to present their concerns and grievances.

The Watertown revolt was only a precursor of the unrest to come as the early colonial days were marked by constant struggle against the English Crown, which sought to tax colonists for a variety of reasons. For example, a law adopted in 1634 in the Massachusetts Bay Colony called for towns to levy a tax on every person according to his estate and abilities. Similarly, the Ye Old Deluder Satan Act of 1647 ordered towns to establish tax-supported schools. While such laws had the effect of either reflecting desires of the people or mollifying complaints, laws were often overshadowed by other events negatively viewed by colonists, especially since colonists were twice taxed at home and by the English Crown. For example, the Sugar Act of 1764,[2] the Stamp Act of 1765,[3] the Townshend duties of 1667,[4] and English efforts to force colonists to pay for the French and Indian Wars (1754–1763) were bitterly resisted by colonists. King Phillip's War (1675–1676) with Indian tribes destroyed entire towns and increased tax rates in some instances more than 18-fold. Similarly, colonial resistance to the Navigation Acts of 1763 led to English efforts to tighten control of the colonies wherein King Charles II revoked the Massachusetts Bay charter and abolished representative taxation by giving the king's emissary the power to "impose and assess and raise and levy such rates and taxes as you shall find necessary for the support of the government."[5]

These and numerous other events were signals of the anger that would lead to the Boston Tea Party in 1773 and to the American Revolution in 1776. By the conclusion of the Revolutionary War, the nation's path in tax resistance was firmly established. Virtually any tax laid on Americans ran the risk of uprising, ironically including taxation for the purpose of supporting the tax rebellion itself. The antitax mood of Americans was never more evident than when it came time to pay the price of the Revolutionary War. By 1789 the nation was facing enormous war debts, leading Congress to enact customs duties and collections laws. Obtaining such receipts was difficult, however, as typified by the Whisky Rebellion in 1794, which sought to impose an excise tax on liquor—a rebellion that ironically the new antitax government of George Washington was required to put down.

Although the nation was clearly founded on antitax sentiment, revenue was inevitably needed for expansion and internal improvement. Deriving such revenue, however, proved extremely difficult in the face of debt and antitax attitudes. The war debt required nearly 30% of all federal revenues gathered between 1789 and 1800, and the first presidents were themselves opposed to taxes. Washington warned about tax abuses, and Jefferson's frugality almost eliminated the navy and severely reduced the army and cut internal excise taxes. Despite some efforts at federal expansionism evident in federal subsidies for canals and railroads and the Morrill Act of 1787 that

TABLE 3.1 Federal government receipts, 1789–1865 (in millions of dollars)

Year or Period	Total	Customs	Internal Revenue	Other Receipts Total, Excluding Sales of Public Lands	Sales of Public Lands
1865	333,715	84,928	209,464	39,322	997
1864	264,627	102,316	109,741	52,569	588
1863	112,697	69,060	37,641	5,997	168
1862	51,987	49,056	—	2,931	152
1861	41,510	39,582	—	1,928	871
1860	56,065	53,188	—	2,877	1,779
1859	53,486	49,566	—	3,921	1,757
1858	46,655	41,790	—	4,866	3,514
1857	68,965	63,876	—	5,089	3,829
1856	74,057	64,023	—	10,034	8,918
1855	65,351	53,026	—	12,325	11,497
1854	73,800	64,224	—	9,576	8,471
1853	61,587	58,932	—	2,655	1,667
1852	49,847	47,339	—	2,507	2,043
1851	52,559	49,018	—	3,542	2,352
1850	43,603	39,669	—	3,935	1,860
1849	31,208	28,347	—	2,861	1,689
1848	35,736	31,757	—	3,978	3,329
1847	26,496	23,748	—	2,748	2,498
1846	29,700	26,713	3	2,984	2,694
1845	29,970	27,528	4	2,438	2,077
1844	29,321	26,184	2	3,136	2,060
1843	8,303	7,047	—	1,256	898
1842	19,976	18,188	—	1,788	1,336
1841	16,860	14,487	3	2,370	1,366
1840	19,480	13,500	2	5,979	3,293
1839	31,483	23,138	3	8,342	7,076
1838	26,303	16,159	2	10,141	3,082
1837	24,954	11,169	5	13,779	6,776
1836	50,827	23,410	—	27,416	24,877
1835	35,430	19,391	10	16,028	14,758
1834	21,792	16,215	4	5,573	4,858
1833	33,948	29,033	3	4,913	3,968
1832	31,866	28,465	12	3,389	2,623
1831	28,527	24,224	7	4,295	3,211
1830	24,844	21,922	12	2,910	2,329
1829	24,828	22,682	15	2,131	1,517
1828	24,764	23,206	17	1,541	1,018
1827	22,966	19,712	20	3,234	1,496
1826	25,260	23,341	22	1,898	1,394
1825	21,841	20,099	26	1,716	1,216
1824	19,381	17,878	35	1,468	984
1823	20,541	19,088	34	1,418	917
1822	20,232	17,590	68	2,575	1,804
1821	14,573	13,004	69	1,500	1,213

TABLE 3.1 (*Continued*)

Year or Period	Total	Customs	Internal Revenue	Other Receipts Total, Excluding Sales of Public Lands	Sales of Public Lands
1820	17,881	15,006	106	2,769	1,636
1819	24,603	20,284	230	4,090	3,274
1818	21,585	17,176	955	3,454	2,607
1817	33,099	26,283	2,678	4,138	1,991
1816	47,678	36,307	5,125	6,246	1,718
1815	15,729	7,283	4,678	3,768	1,288
1814	11,182	5,999	1,663	3,520	1,136
1813	14,340	13,225	5	1,111	836
1812	9,801	8,959	5	837	710
1811	14,424	13,313	2	1,108	1,040
1810	9,384	8,583	7	793	697
1809	7,773	7,296	4	473	442
1808	17,061	16,364	8	689	648
1807	16,398	15,846	13	539	466
1806	15,560	14,668	20	872	765
1805	13,561	12,936	22	602	540
1804	11,826	11,099	51	677	488
1803	11,064	10,479	215	370	166
1802	14,996	12,438	622	1,936	189
1801	12,935	10,751	1,048	1,137	168
1800	10,849	9,081	809	958	—
1799	7,547	6,610	779	157	—
1798	7,900	7,106	644	150	12
1797	8,689	7,550	575	564	84
1796	8,378	6,568	475	1,334	5
1795	6,115	5,588	338	188	
1794	5,432	4,801	274	357	
1793	4,653	4,255	338	60	
1792	3,670	3,443	209	18	
1789–1791	4,419	4,399		19	

SOURCE: U.S. Department of Commerce, Bureau of the Census, *Historical Abstracts of the United States: Colonial Times to 1970,* part 2, House Document No. 93-78 (Washington, D.C.: U.S. Government Printing Office, 1975), 1106.

granted vast quantities of public lands to states for educational purposes, federal revenues were able to rise only slowly in a general antitax climate. As seen in Table 3.1, from the first Continental Congress in 1789 to the start of the Civil War in 1860, federal revenues only increased from $4.4 million to $56 million—almost exclusively from customs taxes, punctuated by brief periods of small revenues gained by repeated efforts to tax income.

The recency and narrowness and disputatiousness of the federal tax system are especially evident in the record of attempts to enact an income tax.[6] Although the first recorded income tax was laid by the Massachusetts Bay Colony in 1643, a federal

TABLE 3.2 Federal government receipts, 1866–1915 (in millions of dollars)

Year	Total	Customs	Internal Revenue	Other Receipts — Total, Excluding Sales of Public Lands	Sales of Public Lands
1915	683,417	209,787	415,670	72,455	2,167
1914	725,117	292,320	380,041	62,312	2,572
1913	714,463	318,891	344,417	60,803	2,910
1912	692,609	311,322	321,612	59,675	5,393
1911	701,833	314,497	322,529	64,807	5,732
1910	675,512	333,683	289,934	51,895	6,356
1909	604,320	300,712	246,213	57,396	7,701
1908	601,862	286,113	251,711	64,038	9,732
1907	665,860	332,233	269,667	63,960	7,879
1906	594,984	300,252	249,150	45,582	4,880
1905	544,275	261,799	234,096	48,380	4,859
1904	541,087	261,275	232,904	46,908	7,453
1903	561,881	284,480	230,810	46,591	8,926
1902	562,478	254,445	271,880	36,153	4,144
1901	587,685	238,585	307,181	41,919	2,965
1900	567,241	233,165	295,328	38,748	2,837
1899	515,961	206,128	273,437	36,395	1,678
1898	405,321	149,575	170,901	84,846	1,243
1897	347,722	176,554	146,689	24,479	865
1896	338,142	160,022	146,763	31,358	1,006
1895	324,729	152,159	143,422	29,149	1,103
1894	306,355	131,819	147,111	27,426	1,674
1893	385,820	203,355	161,028	21,437	3,182
1892	354,938	177,453	153,971	23,514	3,262
1891	392,612	219,522	145,686	27,404	4,030
1890	403,081	229,669	142,607	30,806	6,358
1889	387,050	223,833	130,882	32,336	8,039
1888	379,266	219,091	124,297	35,878	11,202
1887	371,403	217,287	118,823	35,293	9,254
1886	336,440	192,905	116,806	26,729	5,631
1885	323,691	181,472	112,499	29,720	5,706
1884	348,520	195,067	121,586	31,866	9,811
1883	398,288	214,706	144,720	38,861	7,956
1882	403,525	220,411	146,498	36,617	4,753
1881	360,782	198,160	135,264	27,358	2,202
1880	333,527	186,522	124,009	22,995	1,017
1879	273,827	137,250	113,562	23,016	925
1878	257,764	130,171	110,582	17,012	1,080
1877	281,406	130,956	118,630	31,820	976
1876	294,096	148,072	116,701	29,323	1,129
1875	288,000	157,168	110,007	20,825	1,414
1874	304,979	163,104	102,410	39,465	1,852
1873	333,738	188,090	113,729	31,919	2,882
1872	374,107	216,370	130,642	27,094	2,576
1871	383,324	206,270	143,098	33,955	2,389

TABLE 3.2 (*Continued*)

Year	Total	Customs	Internal Revenue	Other Receipts Total, Excluding Sales of Public Lands	Sales of Public Lands
1870	411,255	194,538	184,900	31,817	3,350
1869	370,944	180,048	158,356	32,539	4,020
1868	405,638	164,465	191,088	50,086	1,349
1867	490,634	176,418	266,028	48,189	1,164
1866	558,033	179,047	309,227	69,759	665

SOURCE: U.S. Department of Commerce, Bureau of the Census, *Historical Abstracts of the United States: Colonial Times to 1970,* part 2, House Document No. 93-78 (Washington, D.C.: U.S. Government Printing Office, 1975), 1106.

income tax was not successfully enacted until the Civil War. Failure to enact the tax was not for lack of effort, however, as an income tax was first proposed in 1815 to finance the War of 1812. Although the estimated $3 million from an income tax was desperately needed, the short duration of the war stymied its adoption. It was not until 1862 that taxing income was approved by Congress, this time to defray the cost of the Civil War. The income tax passed in 1862 called for a tax of 3% on all income from various sources including property, rent, interest, dividends, salaries, and professions. Although by 1866 the tax was yielding $73 million in federal revenue, the American tax resister had reappeared. Despite support for the war, levying even a short-term income tax failed as compliance problems emerged, yielding only $38 million in 1870 or only 52% of the revenue available just four years earlier. A source of great controversy, the fledgling tax died out in 1872, leaving the nation again dependent on customs and excise taxes. Table 3.2 details early federal government receipts. Tables 3.3 (pp. 138–139) and 3.4 (p. 141) show modern data.

Demise of the first income tax, however, did not prevent efforts to restore income as a major federal tax base. As with all periods of history, the United States has faced prosperity and decline that have driven tax decisions. By 1894, the nation was struggling with a depressed economy whereby traditional excise and customs revenues were in serious decline and expansionism and war debt had taken their tolls. By 1894, tax liberals were calling for reinstatment of the income tax to be especially levied against the wealthy. Indicative of both history and an unending class struggle, social reformers and politicians scathingly attacked the existing system, while more established conservatives argued that a federal income tax ran counter to American freedom and came dangerously close to socialism. Although debate raged, economic conditions again drove Congress in 1894 to pass an income tax law that called for a 2% tax on earnings above a $4,000 personal exemption. The new law was never carried out, however, as the U.S. Supreme Court declared the law unconstitutional on the grounds that limited federal powers did not expressly authorize Congress to lay and collect such a direct tax.

With defeat of the 1894 law, a new era in federal judicial relations was opened, heralding a new strategy that would become common whenever popular laws were invalidated. Reasoning that only a constitutional amendment could correct the flaw,

TABLE 3.3 Modern federal revenue sources and growth, 1916–1970

						Excise Taxes			Manufacturers'						
Year	Total Collections	Individual Income Taxes	Corporation Income Taxes	Employment Taxes	Estate and Gift Taxes	Total	Alcohol	Tobacco	Total	Automobiles and Accessories	Tires, Tubes, and Tread Rubber	Gasoline, Lubricating Oils	Admissions	Telephone, Telegraph, Radio, and Cable Facilities	Capital Stock Tax
1970	195,722,096	103,651,585	35,036,983	37,449,188	3,680,076	15,904,264	4,746,382	2,094,212	6,683,061	2,497,382	614,795	3,517,586	−71	1,469,562	
1969	187,919,560	97,440,406	38,337,646	33,068,657	3,530,064	15,542,787	4,555,560	2,137,585	6,501,146	2,534,647	631,527	3,283,715	11	1,316,378	
1968	153,636,838	78,252,045	29,896,520	28,085,898	3,081,979	14,320,396	4,287,237	2,122,277	5,713,973	2,054,746	489,139	3,123,103	1,150	1,105,478	
1967	148,374,815	69,370,595	34,917,825	26,958,241	3,014,406	14,113,748	4,075,723	2,079,869	5,478,347	1,917,383	503,753	3,025,467	3,399	1,101,853	
1966	128,879,961	61,297,552	30,834,243	20,256,133	3,093,922	13,398,112	3,814,378	2,073,956	5,613,869	2,148,840	481,803	2,914,965	81,404	907,917	
1965	114,434,634	53,660,683	26,131,334	17,104,306	2,745,533	14,792,779	3,772,634	2,148,594	6,418,145	2,565,926	440,467	2,763,230	95,591	1,078,937	
1964	112,260,257	54,590,354	24,300,863	17,002,504	2,416,304	13,950,232	3,577,499	2,052,545	6,020,543	2,325,676	411,483	2,694,686	88,079	910,196	
1963	105,925,395	52,987,581	22,336,134	15,004,486	2,187,457	13,409,737	3,441,656	2,079,237	5,610,309	2,087,161	398,860	2,571,726	82,583	880,605	
1962	99,440,839	50,649,594	21,295,711	12,708,171	2,035,187	12,752,176	3,341,282	2,025,736	5,132,949	1,755,717	361,562	2,485,726	74,775	843,478	
1961	94,401,086	46,153,001	21,764,940	12,502,451	1,916,392	12,064,302	3,212,801	1,991,117	4,896,802	1,654,107	279,572	2,444,599	70,282	827,302	
1960	91,774,803	44,945,711	22,179,414	11,158,589	1,626,348	11,864,741	3,193,714	1,931,504	4,735,129	1,792,706	304,466	2,097,542	84,099	738,297	
1959	79,797,973	40,734,744	18,091,509	8,853,744	1,352,983	10,764,993	3,002,096	1,806,816	3,958,789	1,420,785	278,911	1,773,938	95,094	690,435	
1958	79,978,476	38,568,559	20,523,316	8,644,386	1,410,925	10,821,292	2,946,461	1,734,021	3,974,135	1,542,827	259,820	1,706,625	97,602	650,185	
1957	80,171,971	39,029,772	21,530,653	7,580,522	1,377,999	10,653,026	2,973,195	1,674,050	3,761,925	1,500,822	251,454	1,531,818	119,088	613,210	
1956	75,112,649	35,337,642	21,298,522	7,295,784	1,171,237	10,009,464	2,920,574	1,613,497	3,456,013	1,711,603	177,872	1,104,981	146,273	557,233	
1955	66,288,692	31,650,106	18,264,720	6,219,665	936,267	9,217,934	2,742,840	1,571,213	2,885,016	1,319,327	164,316	1,024,496	145,357	520,449	
1954	69,919,991	32,813,691	21,546,322	5,107,623	935,122	9,517,233	2,783,012	1,580,229	2,689,133	1,152,155	152,567	904,922	310,264	771,981	
1953	69,686,535	32,536,217	21,594,515	4,718,403	891,284	9,946,116	2,780,925	1,654,911	2,862,788	1,173,672	180,047	964,000	359,522	775,873	
1952	65,009,586	29,274,107	21,466,910	4,464,264	833,147	8,971,158	2,549,120	1,565,162	2,348,943	889,729	161,328	808,461	376,305	705,771	
1951	50,445,686	22,997,308	14,387,569	3,627,480	729,730	8,703,599	2,546,808	1,380,396	2,383,677	894,123	198,383	666,286	389,138	644,980	
1950	38,957,132	17,153,308	10,854,351	2,644,575	706,226	7,598,405	2,219,202	1,328,464	1,836,053	664,429	151,795	604,342	412,697	559,620	266
1949	40,463,125	18,051,822	11,553,669	2,476,113	796,538	7,578,846	2,210,607	1,321,875	1,771,533	589,747	150,899	585,407	434,701	535,911	6,138
1948	41,864,542	20,997,781	10,174,410	2,381,342	899,345	7,409,941	2,255,327	1,300,280	1,649,234	485,872	159,284	559,525	438,628	468,776	1,723
1947	39,108,386	19,343,297	9,676,459	2,024,365	779,291	7,283,376	2,474,762	1,237,768	1,425,395	366,711	174,927	515,691	456,223	417,690	1,597
1946	40,672,097	18,704,536	12,553,602	1,700,828	676,833	6,684,178	2,526,165	1,165,519	922,671	131,908	118,092	480,297	415,268	380,082	352,121
1945	43,800,388	19,034,313	16,027,213	1,779,177	643,055	5,944,630	2,309,866	932,145	782,511	72,845	75,257	498,428	357,466	341,587	371,999
1944	40,121,760	18,261,005	14,766,796	1,738,372	511,211	4,463,674	1,618,775	988,483	503,462	36,020	40,334	323,690	205,289	231,474	380,702
1943	22,371,386	6,629,932	9,668,956	1,498,705	447,496	3,797,503	1,423,646	923,857	504,746	26,132	18,345	332,104	154,451	158,161	328,795
1942	13,047,869	3,262,800	4,744,083	1,185,362	432,540	3,141,183	1,048,517	780,982	771,898	123,621	64,811	416,019	115,033	75,022	281,900
1941	7,370,108	1,417,655	2,053,469	925,856	407,058	2,399,417	820,056	698,077	617,373	105,234	51,054	381,242	70,963	27,331	166,653

TABLE 3.3 (Continued)

Year															
1940	5,340,452	982,017	1,147,592	833,521	360,071	1,884,512	624,253	608,518	447,152	77,847	41,555	257,420	21,888	26,368	132,739
1939	5,181,574	1,028,834	1,156,281	740,429	360,716	1,768,113	587,800	580,159	396,975	56,666	34,819	237,516	19,471	24,094	127,203
1938	5,658,765	1,286,312	1,342,718	742,660	416,874	1,730,853	567,979	568,182	417,152	58,051	31,567	235,213	20,801	23,977	139,349
1937	4,653,195	1,091,741	1,088,101	265,745	305,548	1,764,561	594,245	552,254	450,581	84,382	40,819	227,996	19,740	24,570	137,499
1936	3,520,208	674,416	753,032	48	378,840	1,547,293	505,464	501,166	382,716	62,311	32,208	204,443	17,112	21,098	94,943
1935	3,299,436	527,113	578,678		212,112	1,363,802	411,022	459,179	342,145	50,617	26,638	189,332	15,380	19,741	91,508
1934	2,672,239	419,509	400,146		113,138	1,287,854	258,911	425,169	385,291	43,271	27,630	227,830	14,614	19,251	80,168
1933	1,619,839	352,574	394,218		34,310	838,738	43,174	402,739	243,600	17,825	14,980	141,162	15,521	14,565	
1932	1,557,729	427,191	629,566		47,422	453,550	8,704	398,579	87				1,859		
1931	2,428,229	833,648	1,026,393		48,078	520,110	10,432	444,277	138				2,779		
1930	3,040,146	1,146,845	1,263,414		64,770	565,070	11,695	450,339	2,665				4,231		47
1929	2,939,054	1,095,541	1,235,733		61,897	539,927	12,777	434,445	5,712				6,083		5,956
1928	2,790,536	882,727	1,291,846		60,087		15,308	396,450	51,952				17,725		8,689
1927	2,865,683	911,940	1,308,013		100,340		21,196	376,170	66,850				17,941		8,970
1926	2,836,000	879,124	1,094,980		119,216		26,452	370,666	150,220				23,981		97,386
1925	2,584,140	845,426	916,233		108,940		25,905	345,247	140,877				30,908		90,003
1924	2,796,179	(NA)	(NA)		102,967		27,586	325,639	200,922				77,713	34,662	87,472
1923	2,621,745	(NA)	(NA)		126,705		30,358	309,015	185,117				70,175	30,381	81,568
1922	3,197,451	(NA)	(NA)		139,419		45,609	270,759	174,361				73,385	29,272	80,612
1921	4,595,357	(NA)	(NA)		154,043		82,623	255,219	229,398				89,731	28,442	81,526
1920	5,407,580	(NA)	(NA)		103,636		139,871	295,809	267,969				76,721	27,677	93,020
1919	3,850,150	(NA)	(NA)		82,030		483,051	206,003	79,400				50,920	17,902	28,776
1918	3,698,956	(NA)	(NA)		47,453		443,840	156,189	36,637				26,357	6,299	24,996
1917	809,394	180,108	207,274		6,077		284,009	103,202	775						10,472
1916	512,723	67,944	56,994				247,454	88,064	4,219						

SOURCE: U.S. Department of Commerce, Bureau of the Census. *Historical Abstracts of the United States: Colonial Times to 1970*, part 2, House Document No. 93-78 (Washington, D.C.: U.S. Government Printing Office, 1975), 1106.

on July 12, 1909, Congress proposed a Sixteenth Amendment to the Constitution, which read: "The Congress shall have power to lay and collect taxes on incomes, from whatever source derived, without apportionment among the several States, and without regard to any census or enumeration." With those words, Congress proposed to grant itself permanent power to create a federal tax system levied against the entire nation in whatever manner it might deem appropriate. After nearly four years of struggle, the amendment was finally ratified in 1913, and a new tax law was immediately enacted by Congress calling for a tax of 1% on income as variously defined, an additional "progressive" tax between 1% and 6% with the rate rising with the level of income, and a $3,000–$4,000 personal exemption based on marital status. As such, the law was designed to permanently end the era of narrow federal revenues that had plagued the nation well into the twentieth century (see Table 3.2).

Exemptions and exclusions of income in the 1913 law, however, generated little revenue for the federal government and gave rise to the practice of frequently adjusting the law to appease political factions or to generate more revenue. As congressional leaders ventured to test their new power, this tax source grew rapidly as lawmakers both reveled in new monies and scrambled to fund federal objectives that blossomed almost overnight. Corporations were quickly brought under the new federal tax code, and laws were passed to increase revenue and stabilize the flow of tax receipts. For example, stabilization was achieved through the Current Tax Payment Act of 1943 that began withholding tax liabilities from gross payrolls and requiring quarterly tax payments on nonpayroll income. Similarly, revenues were increased as lawmakers adjusted tax rates, with top rates climbing to nearly 90% in the 1940s. Revenue growth has been nothing short of phenomenal, with Tables 3.3 (pp. 138–139) and 3.4 detailing revenue growth from the first permanent success in taxing income in 1916 to the latest cumulative data for 1992. As seen by these data, federal revenue has recently grown dramatically as a result of expanded tax base.

Although federal power to levy direct tax has finally become a mighty force, these powers have still not been gained without turmoil or dissent. Attempts to appease political factions have been commonplace as Congress has been pressured into "perpetual" tax reform. For example, major revision of federal tax law occurred in the 1986 Tax Reform Act, which contained over 1,850 separate amendments. These reforms resulted in closing many loopholes and reduced tax rates to three brackets of 15%, 28%, and 33%. The 1986 reform was by no means the first or last such effort, however, as major reform had already occurred in 1954 and lesser but significant reforms had been enacted at other times, including as recently as 1990.[7] Yet revenue growth and federal tax presence have become undeniable in that Congress has recently created numerous other revenue sources that now include various forms of income tax, social insurance taxes, excise taxes, estate and gift taxes, customs duties, and Federal Reserve deposits. As seen in Table 3.4, tax collections in 1992 for individual income taxes approached $479 billion, social insurance revenues and excise taxes yielded vast monies, and there were billions more in other funds, making 1992 a record year as federal tax revenues nearly reached $1.1 trillion.

The data indicate that a powerful federal presence has been created within disputatious and narrow confines. Yet despite its vastness, the federal tax system has still not produced revenues equal to Congress's ability to spend. If the modern era in federal taxation is presumed to coincide with more aggressive congressional behavior beginning about 1945 when tax rates reached 90% in the top bracket, the record of

TABLE 3.4 Modern federal Revenue sources and growth, 1980–1992 (in millions of dollars)

Source	1980	1985	1989	1990	1991	1992, Est.	Percentage Distribution 1980	Percentage Distribution 1992, Est.
Total receipts[1]	517,112	734,057	990,691	1,031,308	1,054,264	1,075,706	100.0	100.0
Individual income taxes	244,069	334,531	445,690	466,884	467,827	478,749	47.2	44.5
Corporation income taxes	64,600	61,331	103,291	93,507	98,086	89,031	12.5	8.3
Social insurance	157,803	265,163	359,416	380,047	396,016	410,863	30.5	38.2
Employment taxes and contributions	138,748	234,646	332,859	353,891	370,526	383,663	26.8	35.7
Old-age and survivors insurance	96,581	169,822	240,595	255,031	265,503	271,784	18.7	25.3
Disability insurance	16,628	16,348	23,071	26,625	28,382	29,138	3.2	2.7
Hospital insurance	23,217	44,871	65,396	68,556	72,842	79,007	4.5	7.3
Railroad retirement/pension fund	2,323	2,213	2,391	2,292	2,371	2,329	0.4	0.2
Railroad social security equivalent account	—	1,391	1,407	1,387	1,428	1,405	—	0.1
Unemployment insurance	15,336	25,758	22,011	21,635	20,922	22,547	3.0	2.1
Other retirement contributions	3,719	4,759	4,546	4,522	4,568	4,653	0.7	0.4
Excise taxes	24,329	35,992	34,386	35,345	42,402	46,098	4.7	4.3
Federal funds[1]	15,563	19,097	13,147	15,591	18,275	21,170	3.0	2.0
Alcohol	5,601	5,562	5,661	5,695	7,364	8,219	1.1	0.8
Tobacco	2,443	4,779	4,378	4,081	4,706	4,897	0.5	0.5
Windfall profits	6,934	6,348	—	—	—	—	1.3	—
Ozone depletion	—	—	—	360	562	662	—	0.1
Other taxes	585	261	317	2,460	2,549	4,343	0.1	0.4
Trust funds[1]	8,766	16,894	21,239	19,754	24,127	24,928	1.7	2.3
Highways	6,620	13,015	15,628	13,867	16,979	17,387	1.3	1.6
Airport and airway	1,874	2,851	3,664	3,700	4,910	5,193	0.4	0.5
Black lung disability	272	581	563	665	652	627	0.1	0.1
Hazardous substance response	—	273	883	818	810	825	—	0.1
Aquatic resources	—	126	187	218	260	278	—	—
Leaking underground storage	—	—	168	122	123	145	—	—
Vaccine injury compensations	—	—	99	159	81	120	—	—
Oil spill liability	—	—	—	143	254	283	—	—
Estate and gift taxes	6,389	6,422	8,745	11,500	11,138	12,063	1.2	1.1
Customs duties	7,174	12,079	16,334	16,707	15,949	17,260	1.4	1.6
Federal Reserve deposits	11,767	17,059	19,604	24,319	19,158	18,507	2.3	1.7

For fiscal years ending in year shown. Receipts reflect collections. Covers both federal funds and trust funds. Excludes government-sponsored but privately owned corporations. Federal Reserve System. District of Columbia government, and money held in suspense as deposit funds. *See Historical Statistics, Colonial Times to 1970,* series Y 343-351, and Y 472-487, for related data.)

—Represents or rounds to zero.

[1] Totals reflect interfund and intragovernmental transactions and/or other functions, not shown separately.

SOURCE: U.S. Department of Commerce, Bureau of the Census, *Statistical Abstracts of the United States 1992* (Washington, D.C.: U.S. Government Printing Office, 1992), 316.

revenues in relation to outlays has been one of perpetual deficits. The federal budget summary in Table 3.5 shows that in 1945 federal revenues were $45 billion, but outlays for various programs including human resources and national defense were $93 billion. The $49 billion deficit obviously contributed to the $260 billion national debt, yielding a national debt 122.5% greater than the GNP in that year. While it is clear that prior deficit spending had occurred, the era beginning in 1945 marked a special frenzy of deficit spending in each successive year.[8] By 1960, federal revenue had more than doubled to $92.5 billion, but debt had grown to $290.5 billion. By 1980, revenues had more than quintupled to $517.1 billion, but outlays reached $590.9 billion, with a national debt of $908.5 billion. Only two years later, the national debt broke the trillion-dollar mark as Congress again overspent the budget by $127.9 billion. By 1990, federal revenue itself had broken all records at $1.031 trillion—but outlays again exceeded revenue by $123.8 billion, with a staggering national debt equaling 58.7% of the nation's economic output—increasing to 69.5% of GNP in 1992.

Although federal taxation and deficit spending are widely condemned, these massive amounts must be recognized in the political context that engendered them. In an odd marriage, both revenues and deficits are massive because social demands are insatiable and because resentment is innate to American tax psychology. As seen in Table 3.6, Americans expect strong national defense, international security and humanitarianism, income security, good retirement and disability insurance, cheap health care, work force training, good transportation and energy systems, and responsive government. Additionally, an educational system for world leadership is expected. Federal deficits are thus a legacy rather than a recent phenomenon, if for no other reason than citizens have steadfastly refused productive taxation. The result has been a narrow and inadequate federal tax base in that all other federal revenues are buffeted by forces beyond Congress's control. For example, excise taxes and customs duties depend on the strength of commerce, and estate and gift taxes are inconstant and easily avoidable. The combined effect is that history has established a tradition wherein the federal government has come to rely on a tax structure that is both vast and inadequate, and simultaneously seen as oppressive.

Depending on the critic's viewpoint, the federal tax system has offered much or very little to education. It was seen in Chapter 2 that federal taxation arguably offers large revenues to education under shifting and benevolent aims. Although needs outstrip aid, such a view argues that a notable portion of the federal budget goes to education because these monies add to the total deficit rather than going to reduce the federal debt. Table 3.7 (pp. 147-148) can be used to support such a view in that federal outlays in 1990 for K-12 education totaled nearly $12.8 billion, averaging 6.1% of all public school revenues. These amounts would then not reflect the huge sums paid under other federal programs that indirectly benefit the work of schools, such as income security payments, social services block grants, human development services, training and employment assistance, health services, and a host of other federal aid to states. Similarly, higher education aid is not included. In broad perspective, the sum of all related assistance is much greater than many critics allow. Opposing views, however, would argue that education ranks below other federal goals, that education's share has declined in recent years, and that the indirect support cited is wrongly placed in that many social services would not be needed if aid were applied to prevent social ills rather than to remedy social decay.

The federal tax system thus chronicles a history of false starts, frustration, and until recently, very weak effect. Despite the fear many persons hold of federal tax

TABLE 3.5 Federal budget summary, 1945–1992 (in millions of dollars)

Year	Outlays[1] Receipts	Total	Human Resources	National Defense	Percentage of GNP[2]	Surplus or Deficit (−)	Gross Federal Debt Total	Held by— Federal Government Account	The Public	Federal Reserve System	As Percentage of GNP[2]	Annual Percentage Change[3] Receipts	Outlays	Gross Federal Debt	Outlays Off-budget
1945	45,159	92,712	1,859	82,965	43.6	−48,720	260,123	24,941	235,182	21,792	122.5	3.2	1.5	27.5	0.1
1950	39,443	42,562	14,221	13,724	16.0	−4,702	256,853	37,830	219,023	18,331	96.3	0.1	9.6	1.7	0.5
1955	65,451	68,444	14,908	42,729	17.7	−4,091	274,366	47,751	226,616	23,607	71.0	−6.0	−3.4	1.3	4.0
1960	92,492	92,191	26,184	48,130	18.2	510	290,525	53,686	236,840	26,523	57.3	16.7	0.1	1.1	10.9
1965	116,817	118,228	36,576	50,620	17.6	−1,605	322,318	61,540	260,778	39,100	47.9	3.7	−0.3	2.0	16.5
1966	130,835	134,532	43,257	58,111	18.2	−3,068	328,498	64,784	263,714	42,169	44.5	12.0	13.8	1.9	19.7
1967	148,822	157,464	51,272	71,417	19.8	−12,620	340,445	73,819	266,626	46,719	42.8	13.7	17.0	3.6	20.4
1968	152,973	178,134	59,375	81,926	21.0	−27,742	368,685	79,140	289,545	52,230	43.4	2.8	13.1	8.3	22.3
1969	186,882	183,640	66,410	82,497	19.8	−507	365,769	87,661	278,108	54,095	39.4	22.2	3.1	−0.8	25.2
1970	192,807	195,649	75,349	81,692	19.8	−8,694	380,921	97,723	283,198	57,714	38.5	3.2	6.5	4.1	27.6
1971	187,139	210,172	91,901	78,872	19.9	−26,052	408,176	105,140	303,037	65,518	38.7	2.9	7.4	7.2	32.8
1972	207,309	230,681	107,211	79,174	20.0	−26,423	435,936	113,559	322,377	71,426	37.8	10.8	9.8	6.8	36.9
1973	230,799	245,707	119,522	76,681	19.2	−15,403	466,291	125,381	340,910	75,181	36.4	11.3	6.5	7.0	45.6
1974	263,224	269,359	135,783	79,347	19.0	−7,971	483,893	140,194	343,699	80,648	34.2	14.0	9.6	3.8	52.1
1975	279,090	332,332	173,245	86,509	21.8	−55,260	541,925	147,225	394,700	84,993	35.6	6.0	23.4	12.0	60.4
1976	298,060	371,779	203,594	89,619	21.9	−70,499	628,970	151,566	477,404	94,714	37.0	6.8	11.9	16.1	69.6
1976[4]	81,232	95,973	52,065	22,269	21.4	−13,336	643,561	148,052	495,509	96,702	35.9	(X)	(X)	(X)	19.4
1977	355,559	409,203	221,895	97,241	21.2	−49,745	706,398	157,295	549,103	105,004	36.5	19.3	10.1	12.3	80.7
1978	399,561	458,729	242,329	104,495	21.1	−54,902	776,602	169,477	607,125	115,480	35.8	12.4	12.1	9.9	89.7
1979	463,302	503,464	267,574	116,342	20.6	−38,178	828,923	189,162	639,761	115,594	33.9	16.0	9.8	6.7	100.0
1980	517,112	590,920	313,374	133,995	22.1	−72,689	908,503	199,212	709,291	120,846	34.0	11.6	17.4	9.6	114.3
1981	599,272	678,249	362,022	157,513	22.7	−73,916	994,298	209,507	784,791	124,466	33.3	15.9	14.8	9.4	135.2
1982	617,766	745,755	388,681	185,309	23.8	−120,003	1,136,798	217,560	919,238	134,497	36.2	3.1	10.0	14.3	151.4
1983	600,562	808,380	426,003	209,903	24.3	−207,977	1,371,164	240,114	1,131,049	155,527	41.3	−2.8	8.4	20.6	147.1
1984	666,457	851,846	432,042	227,413	23.0	−185,586	1,564,110	264,159	1,299,951	155,122	42.4	11.0	5.4	14.1	165.8
1985	734,057	946,391	471,822	252,748	23.8	−221,623	1,816,974	317,612	1,499,362	169,806	46.0	10.1	11.1	16.2	176.8
1986	769,091	990,336	481,594	273,375	23.5	−237,898	2,120,082	383,919	1,736,163	190,855	50.7	4.8	4.6	16.7	183.5
1987	854,143	1,003,911	502,196	281,999	22.5	−169,257	2,345,578	457,444	1,888,134	212,040	53.0	11.1	1.4	10.6	193.8
1988	908,954	1,064,140	533,404	290,361	22.1	−193,897	2,600,760	550,507	2,050,252	229,218	54.4	6.4	6.0	10.9	202.7
1989	990,691	1,144,169	568,668	303,559	22.1	−206,132	2,867,538	677,214	2,190,324	220,088	55.9	9.0	7.5	10.3	210.9
1990	1,031,308	1,251,778	619,327	299,331	22.9	−206,470	3,206,347	795,906	2,410,441	234,410	58.7	4.1	9.4	11.8	225.1
1991	1,054,264	1,323,011	689,691	273,292	23.5	−268,746	3,598,993	911,751	2,687,242	258,591	64.0	2.2	5.7	12.2	241.7
1992, Est.	1,075,706	1,475,439	776,900	307,304	25.2	−399,733	4,077,510	1,000,227	3,077,283	—	69.5	2.0	11.5	13.3	251.5

—Not available. X Not applicable.
[1] Includes off-budget receipts, outlays, and interfund transactions.
[2] Gross national product as of fiscal year; for calendar year GNP.
[3] Change from previous year.
[4] Represents transition quarter.

SOURCE: U.S. Department of Commerce, Bureau of the Census, *Statistical Abstracts of the United States 1992* (Washington, D.C.: U.S. Government Printing Office, 1992), 315.

TABLE 3.6 Federal outlays by detailed function, 1980–1992 (in millions of dollars)

Function	1980	1985	1989	1990	1991	1992, Est.	Percentage Distribution 1980	Percentage Distribution 1992, Est.
Total outlays	590,920	946,316	1,144,069	1,251,778	1,323,011	1,475,439	100.00	100.00
On-budget	476,591	769,509	933,258	1,026,713	1,081,324	1,223,909	80.65	82.95
Off-budget	114,329	176,807	210,911	225,065	241,687	251,530	19.35	17.05
National defense	133,995	252,748	303,559	299,331	273,292	307,304	22.68	20.83
Dept. of Defense—Military	130,912	245,154	294,880	289,755	262,389	294,039	22.15	19.93
Military personnel	40,897	67,842	80,676	75,622	83,439	79,289	6.92	5.37
Operation and maintenance	44,788	72,371	87,001	88,340	101,769	97,828	7.58	6.63
Procurement	29,021	70,381	81,620	80,972	82,028	73,952	4.91	5.01
R and D, test, and evaluation	13,127	27,103	37,002	37,458	34,589	36,145	2.22	2.45
Military construction	2,450	4,260	5,275	5,080	3,497	4,541	0.41	0.31
Family housing	1,680	2,642	3,257	3,501	3,296	3,404	0.28	0.23
Other	-1,050	553	50	-1,218	-46,229	-521	-0.18	-0.04
Atomic energy defense activities	2,878	7,098	8,119	8,988	10,004	11,685	0.49	0.79
Defense related activities	206	495	560	587	899	980	0.03	0.07
International affairs	12,714	16,176	9,573	13,764	15,851	17,811	2.15	1.21
International development and humanitarian assistance	3,626	5,409	4,836	5,498	5,141	6,154	0.61	0.42
Conduct of foreign affairs	1,366	2,043	2,886	3,050	3,282	3,560	0.23	0.24
Foreign information and exchange activities	534	805	1,106	1,103	1,253	1,343	0.09	0.09
International financial programs activities	2,425	-1,471	-722	-4,539	-3,648	-1,029	—	-0
International security assistance	4,763	9,391	1,467	8,652	9,823	7,783	0.81	0.53
Income security	86,540	128,200	136,031	147,277	170,846	198,093	14.64	13.43
General retirement and disability insurance	5,083	5,617	5,650	5,148	4,945	5,538	0.86	0.38
Federal employee retirement and disability	26,594	38,591	49,151	51,981	56,106	57,718	4.50	3.91
Housing assistance	5,632	25,263	14,715	15,891	17,200	19,438	0.95	1.32
Food and nutrition assistance	14,016	18,540	21,192	23,964	28,481	33,561	2.37	2.27
Other income security	17,163	22,715	29,706	31,404	37,030	45,145	2.90	3.06
Unemployment compensation	18,051	17,475	15,616	18,889	27,084	36,693	3.05	2.49
Health	23,169	33,542	48,390	57,716	71,183	94,593	3.92	6.41
Health care services	18,003	26,984	39,164	47,642	60,723	82,810	3.05	5.61
Health research	3,442	4,908	7,325	8,611	8,899	10,058	0.58	0.68
Consumer and occupational health and safety	1,006	1,182	1,356	1,462	1,560	1,724	0.17	0.12
Medicare	32,090	65,822	84,964	98,102	104,489	118,638	5.43	8.04
Social Security	118,547	188,623	232,542	248,623	269,015	286,732	20.06	19.43
On-budget	675	5,189	5,069	3,625	2,619	6,078	0.11	0.41
Off-budget	117,872	183,434	227,473	244,998	266,395	280,654	19.95	0.00

TABLE 3.6 (*Continued*)

Veterans benefits and services	21,185	26,292	30,066	29,112	31,349	33,819	3.59	2.29
Income security for veterans	11,688	14,714	16,544	15,241	16,961	17,193	1.98	1.17
Education, training, and rehabilitation	2,342	1,059	459	278	427	696	0.40	0.05
Hospital and medical care	6,515	9,547	11,343	12,134	12,889	13,727	1.10	0.93
Housing for veterans	(Z)	214	878	517	85	1,153	0.00	0.08
Other	665	758	843	943	987	1,050	0.11	0.07
Education, training, employment, and social services	31,843	29,342	36,674	38,497	42,809	45,025	5.39	3.05
Elementary, secondary, and vocational education	6,893	7,598	9,150	9,918	11,372	13,052	1.17	0.88
Higher education	6,723	8,156	10,584	11,107	11,961	11,140	1.14	0.76
Research and general educational aids	1,212	1,229	1,509	1,577	1,773	1,966	0.21	0.13
Training and employment	10,345	4,972	5,292	5,361	5,388	5,792	1.75	0.39
Other labor services	551	678	786	810	788	871	0.09	0.06
Social services	6,119	6,710	9,354	9,723	11,526	12,204	1.04	0.83
Commerce and housing credit	9,390	4,229	29,211	67,142	75,639	87,149	1.59	5.91
Mortgage credit	5,887	3,054	4,978	3,845	5,362	3,201	1.00	0.22
Postal service	1,246	1,351	127	2,116	1,828	1,335	0.21	0.09
Deposit insurance	−285	−2,198	21,996	58,081	66,394	80,185	−0.05	5.43
Other commerce	2,542	2,022	2,109	3,100	2,054	2,427	0.43	0.16
Transportation	21,329	25,838	27,608	29,485	31,099	34,031	3.61	2.31
Ground transportation	15,274	17,606	17,946	18,954	19,545	21,086	2.58	1.43
Air transportation	3,723	4,895	6,622	7,234	8,184	9,042	0.63	0.61
Water transportation	2,229	3,201	2,916	3,151	3,148	3,633	0.38	0.25
Other transportation	104	137	124	146	223	270	0.02	0.02
Natural resources and environment	13,858	13,357	16,182	17,067	18,552	20,231	2.35	1.37
Water resources	4,223	4,122	4,271	4,401	4,366	4,729	0.71	0.32
Conservation and land management	1,043	1,481	3,324	3,553	4,047	4,374	0.18	0.30
Recreational resources	1,677	1,621	1,817	1,876	2,137	2,474	0.28	0.17
Pollution control and abatement	5,510	4,465	4,878	5,156	5,853	6,131	0.93	0.42
Other natural resources	1,405	1,668	1,890	2,080	2,148	2,522	0.24	0.17
Energy	10,156	5,685	3,702	2,428	1,662	4,026	1.72	0.27
Supply	8,367	2,615	2,226	1,062	1,170	3,000	1.42	0.20
Conservation	569	491	333	365	386	463	0.10	0.03
Emergency preparedness	342	1,838	621	442	−235	336	0.06	0.02
Information, policy, and regulations	878	740	521	559	340	226	0.15	0.02
Community/regional develop	11,252	7,680	5,362	8,498	6,811	7,533	1.90	0.51
Community development	4,907	4,598	3,693	3,530	3,543	3,911	0.83	0.27

(*Continued*)

TABLE 3.6 (Continued)

Function	1980	1985	1989	1990	1991	1992, Est.	Percentage Distribution 1980	Percentage Distribution 1992, Est.
Area and regional development	4,303	3,117	1,894	2,868	2,743	3,144	0.73	0.21
Disaster relief and insurance	2,043	(Z)	−226	2,100	525	478	0.35	0.03
Agriculture	8,839	25,565	16,919	11,958	15,183	17,219	1.50	1.17
Farm income stabilization	7,441	23,751	14,817	9,761	12,924	14,670	1.26	0.99
Research and services	1,398	1,813	2,102	2,197	2,259	2,550	0.24	0.17
Net interest	52,538	129,504	169,266	184,221	194,541	198,820	8.89	13.48
On-budget	*54,877*	*133,622*	*180,661*	*200,212*	*214,763*	*222,673*	*9.29*	*15.09*
Off-budget	*−2,339*	*−4,118*	*−11,395*	*−15,991*	*−20,222*	*−23,853*	*0.39*	*−1.62*
Interest on the public debt	74,808	178,898	240,963	264,820	286,004	292,992	12.66	19.86
Other interest	−10,224	−23,438	−19,755	−18,191	−20,266	−16,948	−1.73	−1.15
General science, space, and technology	5,832	8,627	12,838	14,444	16,111	16,373	0.99	1.11
General science and basic research	1,381	2,019	2,642	2,835	3,154	3,612	0.23	0.24
General government	13,028	11,588	9,017	10,734	11,661	12,838	2.20	0.87
Legislative functions	1,038	1,355	1,652	1,763	1,916	2,230	0.18	0.15
Exec. direction and management	97	113	129	160	190	197	0.02	0.01
Central fiscal operations	2,612	3,492	5,517	6,004	6,097	6,790	0.44	0.46
General property and records management	327	96	−396	31	657	704	0.06	0.05
General purpose fiscal assistance	8,582	6,353	2,061	2,161	2,100	2,158	1.45	0.15
Other general government	569	521	814	800	1,280	1,505	0.10	0.10
Deductions, offsetting receipts	−351	−506	−893	−361	−718	−914	−0.06	−0.06
Administration of justice	4,584	6,270	9,474	9,995	12,276	14,061	0.78	0.95
Federal law enforcement	2,239	3,520	4,719	4,648	5,661	6,422	0.38	0.44
Federal litigative and judicial	1,347	2,064	3,255	3,579	4,352	5,029	0.23	0.34
Federal correctional activities	342	537	1,044	1,291	1,600	1,901	0.06	0.13
Criminal justice assistance	656	150	455	477	663	709	0.11	0.05
Undistributed offsetting receipts	*−19,942*	*−32,698*	*−37,212*	*−36,615*	*−39,356*	*−38,761*	*−3.37*	*−2.63*
On-budget	*−18,738*	*−30,189*	*−32,354*	*−31,048*	*−33,553*	*−32,665*	*−3.17*	*−2.21*
Off-budget	*−1,204*	*−2,509*	*−4,858*	*−5,567*	*−5,804*	*−6,095*	*−0.20*	*−0.41*
Employer share, employee retirement[1]	*−15,842*	*−27,157*	*−34,283*	*−33,611*	*−36,206*	*−36,478*	*−2.68*	*−2.47*
Rents and royalties[1]	*−4,101*	*−5,542*	*−2,929*	*−3,004*	*−3,150*	*−2,282*	*−0.69*	*−0.15*

—Represents zero.
Z Less than $500,000.
[1] On outer continental shelf.
SOURCE: U.S. Department of Commerce, Bureau of the Census, *Statistical Abstracts of the United States 1992* (Washington, D.C.: U.S. Government Printing Office, 1992), 318–319.

TABLE 3.7 Federal revenues to public school districts, 1990

State or Other Area	Total	Federal	
		Amount	Percentage of Total
United States	$207,583,910	$12,750,530	6.1
Alabama	2,557,836	286,598	11.2
Alaska	909,380	116,277	12.8
Arizona	2,742,625	216,488	7.9
Arkansas	1,594,428	153,637	9.6
California	24,320,281	1,605,281	6.6
Colorado	2,767,107	132,246	4.8
Connecticut	3,554,800	161,933	4.6
Delaware	542,448	39,616	7.3
District of Columbia	557,089	54,591	9.8
Florida	9,589,961	595,711	6.2
Georgia	5,194,517	329,253	6.3
Hawaii	755,987	76,099	10.1
Idaho	710,841	56,891	8.0
Illinois	9,001,253	531,923	5.9
Indiana	4,349,969	211,441	4.9
Iowa	2,149,710	105,270	4.9
Kansas	2,085,315	103,598	5.0
Kentucky	2,247,379	220,813	9.8
Louisiana	3,058,293	309,117	10.1
Maine	1,154,667	62,805	5.4
Maryland	4,267,441	196,285	4.6
Massachusetts	5,117,504	240,192	4.7
Michigan	8,394,959	482,031	5.7
Minnesota	3,988,317	165,059	4.1
Mississippi	1,573,464	243,774	15.5
Missouri	3,699,939	205,179	5.5
Montana	707,594	63,726	9.0
Nebraska	1,359,712	79,742	5.9
Nevada	860,464	36,018	4.2
New Hampshire	900,843	24,944	2.8
New Jersey	8,763,058	336,351	3.8
New Mexico	1,225,429	150,229	12.3
New York	19,744,546	1,014,296	5.1
North Carolina	4,683,693	300,405	6.4
North Dakota	487,049	47,517	9.8
Ohio	8,617,848	462,810	5.4
Oklahoma	2,172,547	121,530	5.6
Oregon	2,539,734	155,250	6.1
Pennsylvania	10,336,060	534,118	5.2
Rhode Island	844,009	41,524	4.9
South Carolina	2,678,790	215,088	8.0
South Dakota	503,949	57,774	11.5
Tennessee	2,907,714	261,676	9.0
Texas	13,948,117	1,012,383	7.3
Utah	1,326,479	86,986	6.6

(Continued)

TABLE 3.7 (*Continued*)

State or Other Area	Total	Federal	
		Amount	*Percentage of Total*
Vermont	562,543	24,464	4.3
Virginia	5,101,281	268,730	5.3
Washington	4,192,291	243,402	5.8
West Virginia	1,413,165	106,072	7.5
Wisconsin	4,240,432	174,249	4.1
Wyoming	581,050	29,140	5.0

SOURCE: U.S. Department of Education, National Center for Education Statistics, *Digest of Education Statistics 1992* (Washington, D.C.: National Center for Education Statistics, 1992), 151.

laws, federal tax history is rather ignominious in that it is still characterized by limited power, narrow breadth, and inadequate funds in relation to social demands. The federal tax system has been the target of so much dissent that it only recently has been permitted significant revenues—only after formidable deficits and unmet needs have accumulated for centuries. While it is likely that federal taxes will continue at a historic pace, it is unlikely that the federal tax system will increase in importance to education because constitutional limits and congressional interests will continue to drive tax revenues. As stated at the outset of this chapter, when revolution crushes punitive taxation, bias against central government persists for a very long time, forcing schools to look beyond the federal tax system for meaningful revenues.

State Tax Systems. If Americans regard federal taxation as omnipresent, there is an almost equal feeling that state tax systems have become similarly pervasive. Although every state now levies various taxes for support of government, state tax history has also been the focus of dissent and halting progress. Unlike the federal system, however, development of state taxation is more difficult to trace because the history is so vast due to a multitude of different states devising tax systems without any effort at coordination. Consequently, each state's tax system has been heavily influenced by economic and political factors within the state and further affected by the variable presence of the federal government. Although these differences make it impossible to exhaustively explore emergence of state tax systems, it is still possible to paint the broad strokes of state tax development. Central to such understanding are three basic observations, namely that the roots of state tax systems are closely intertwined with those of federal taxation, that state tax systems are once again both old and new, narrowly focused, and the object of unflattering disputes, and that despite such struggles, the present structure of revenue for education has come to rely heavily on state government.

As might be easily implied from the discussion of federal tax emergence, the history of state taxation intimately parallels federal tax evolution. It can even be argued that the origins of state tax systems were firmly in place before the birth of the new nation. For example, systems of taxation in the colonies existed long before the

Revolutionary War, and history of the individual colonies chronicles the fierce independence that frustrated both English rule and later attempts to forge and preserve a new federation. Indeed, the roots of both tax systems and tax rebellion are more related to the colonies and the original states themselves than to any federal example. As a result, understanding modern state tax systems requires briefly tracing the broad history of emergent statehood within a federal/state tax framework.

While scholars might argue gross and fine distinctions in separating federal and state issues, no argument can be made against the view that the historic development of the colonies had a powerful impact that carried over into federal-state relationships. Additionally, it is obvious that federalism suffered as a result of many years of "self-rule" in the colonies that later led to such issues as states' rights and even the Civil War. As seen earlier, colonists were generally eager to resist federal taxation, and there is evidence that taxation in the individual colonies had also been the object of dissension. As might be imagined, colonists were not appreciative of taxes in any form, their individual and collective European histories having created a strong distaste. Few modern Americans, however, realize the depth of hatred toward taxes and government that undergirds the American psyche on which the nation and various states are built.

Although much attention is accurately given to religious freedom as the basis for America, less attention is given to development of systems of government that emerged in parallel with religious freedoms. Inheriting a long struggle for liberty dating from the Magna Carta, the first settlers immediately built political systems reflecting such independence. The Virginia legislature, formed in 1619, quickly began making laws declaring its rights and resisting revocation of the Virginia Company's charter in response to legislative presumptuousness. In Massachusetts Bay, representative government was also quickly adopted, as in 1634 a legislature was seated following the tax revolt at Watertown. Similarly, in 1639 Connecticut's freemen drew up the Fundamental Orders, providing for a governor and a house of elected representatives. Likewise, in 1663 a charter granted by the Crown made Rhode Island an exemplar of self-rule, making its own laws and electing officers. By 1700, colonial government in all existing colonies had become characterized by written charters guaranteeing liberties, by conflict between appointed governors of the Crown and colonial representation, and by adamancy of colonial legislatures that purse strings were to be tightly controlled by the colonists themselves.

The existence of legislatures and closed purse strings were an admission that regardless of dislike for government, there were costs associated with civilization. Although colonial society was simple, there remained a need for citizens to band together for services including forts, prisons, roads, jails, and courts. As a result, some system of revenue for government had to be devised. Critical to such development was the reality that the colonies were not united but formed under vastly different conditions. Logically, government in each colony came to be closely related to both political views and economic bases. Although the early colonies had been church-centered, other forms of government became necessary.[9] For example, the geography of New England gave rise to small farms and villages, while the climate in the southern colonies of Virginia, South Carolina, and Georgia favored large plantations. In New England, the political center of life became the town, with councilmen popularly elected. In contrast, the South's vast expanses centered government in counties, and the nature of aristocracy and race resulted in political appointments. Between these extremes stood the middle colonies, combining various characteristics and traits of their neighbors.

Not surprisingly, systems of taxation were also related to both political and economic circumstances. As the need for revenue grew with population, the New England colonies generally developed the broadest tax systems, raising revenue by taxing personal property often defined to include possessions such as livestock and slaves. Consonant with a geography and economy that did not favor vast property holdings, these colonies also developed a tradition of taxing land and houses in an attempt to gather a tax base that would yield revenue from every person based on the various forms of wealth making up the local economy. In contrast, the economy of southern colonies dictated different taxation because the intensely agricultural base vested in only a few persons augured against taxes on individual wealth as represented by land or other property such as slaves. The southern economy consequently led to a revenue system based on exports and imports. In addition, some colonies also levied poll taxes and faculty taxes to better distribute taxation by allowing almost no one to escape taxation. The poll tax was a fee paid by each person regardless of wealth. The faculty tax refined the notion of personal worth by basing the tax on an individual's expected income by occupation. The middle colonies often used refinements of all these taxes. There were also lotteries or other revenues such as fines on immoral behavior, including failure to attend church.[10]

The roots of state rule were further encouraged by the political philosophies of the time. Encouraged by the settlers' natural proclivity toward rebellion and colonialism's physical isolation, conditions were ripe for a new generation of thinkers to propound ideas that would ultimately help shape a new nation. Among the most potent were the ideas of the philosopher John Locke (1632–1704), whose social contract theory, arguing eloquently for the rights of self-destiny and representative government, was ideally suited to tax-resenting colonists. Locke proclaimed: "Though the earth and all inferior creatures be common to all men, yet every man has a property in his own person; this nobody has any right to but himself. . . . Whatsoever then he removes out of the state that nature has provided and left it in, he has mixed his labor with, and joined to it something that is his own, and thereby makes it his property."[11] Locke continued: "The supreme power cannot take from any man part of his property without his own consent; for the preservation of property being the end of government and that for which men enter into society, it necessarily supposes and requires that the people should have property; without which they must be supposed to lose that, by entering into society, which was the end for which they entered into it—too gross an absurdity for any man to own."[12] Yet, concluded Locke, "It is fit every one who enjoys his share of the protection should pay out of his estate for the maintenance of it. But still it must be with his consent—i.e., the consent of the majority, giving it either by themselves or their representatives chosen by them."[13]

Such oratory was extraordinary in a time when taxes had long been a great burden on the masses. Such logic was also particularly suited to colonial thinking because it advanced four notions sympathetic to colonial belligerence, namely the notions of natural dignity before the law wherein consent of the governed is essential; of government solely to serve, whereby any lesser assumption was absurd; of representation; and of consent. Such thinking was radically opposed to history wherein taxes had been abusive and never the object of consent. This conceptual breakthrough gave standing and impetus to the careful thinking of economist Adam Smith (1723–1790), who argued convincingly that taxes should be proportional to the income a person receives under protection of the state and that a tax should be certain and not arbitrary. Additionally, he argued that a tax must only take an efficient minimum and that excess balances are wrong. A tax, Smith proclaimed, "may obstruct the industry of the people, and discourage them from applying to certain branches of business which might give maintenance and employment to great multitudes. While it obliges the people to pay, it may thus diminish, or perhaps destroy, some of the funds which might enable them more easily to do so."[14]

The conservative thinking of Smith and Locke was powerful in a time when the Crown was increasing its political presence in the colonies. As described earlier under federal tax development, a widening rift was further forced by British efforts to impose new colonial taxes for support of various patronages and as punishment for tax dissidence. At the same time political philosophy was urging new freedom, the Stamp Act was taxing colonists without consent, new tariffs were being levied, armies were being raised at colonial expense, and writs of assistance authorizing search and seizure of homes to detect smugglers were being carried out against colonists suspected of tax evasion. Seeing their economies destroyed, colonial legislatures began passing antitax resolutions. A boycott against England was raised by merchants in various colonies, causing trade to fall in some instances by nearly half. Intercolonial committees began staging tax protests, and the growing tension was solidified by the Boston Tea Party in 1773, when Samuel Adams led a group to destroy the cargo of British ships in protest of tax duties. Retaliation was swift, as Parliament revoked many political freedoms, closing the port of Boston until restitution was made, and forcibly quartering troops in private homes.

These growing tensions were to have permanent and drastic effects on the structure of tax policies in the colonies. While each colony had been fiercely independent, political and economic exigency drew the colonies together to form the first Continental Congress. The precursor of a new nation, the Continental Congress met in Philadelphia in 1774 with all colonies except Georgia represented. The result was a declaration of colonial rights in which it was proclaimed that the colonies had sole power to legislate their destinies, a declaration that was backed up by an agreement binding the colonies to cease all British trade and declaring that the colonies would revolt if force were used to restore trade. By these acts, the Continental Congress acting under authority of the independent colonies threw down the gauntlet that launched the Revolutionary War.

The Revolutionary War dragged on for six years, with resultant financial problems that strongly shaped both federal and state tax policy. Although the Continental Congress was a first union of states, it was an entity without money. No provision permitted taxation for any reason, and Congress was forced to request money from each colony to continue the war. Although the colonies had bound together in rebellion, raising money was nearly impossible as the colonies continued to be tax-resentful, raising only $6 million dollars by 1784 and claiming home rule as the basis for ignoring federal pleas for money. Desperate for funds, Congress borrowed nearly $18 million from domestic and foreign lenders and also began issuing paper money in the amount of nearly $240 million but which quickly depreciated to only $38 million by the end of the war in 1783. Although the war was won, it was not without a financial and political price: financial in that a Congress without power to tax sowed the first seeds of national debt, and political in that despite efforts to form a central government through the Articles of Confederation in 1781, the colonies remained sovereign. That is, Congress still had no real power, including the critical role of collecting taxes.

The first years after the war were further historic in shaping state and federal tax policy by creation of the Constitution. Desperate straits of the colonies in a postwar economy and interstate dissension led to the Constitutional Convention of 1787 in Philadelphia. With delegates chosen by the colonial legislatures, federal and state tax policy was forged that would have a profound impact for centuries, principally through the doctrine of limited and plenary powers. Under the new Constitution, the federal government was given power to lay taxes for the purpose of paying debt and for general welfare. It could borrow money and impose duties and imposts and excises, mint money, adopt weights and measures, grant patents, and build post offices, raise and maintain a military force, govern interstate commerce, manage Indian affairs, conduct international affairs, and declare war. Other federal powers were granted, but always within the limits of restricted national interest. The states, however, were granted full powers. States were given control of local government, chartering of towns, building of roads and bridges, and protection of civil liberties. But most importantly, the care of federal government was given to the states which would govern not only themselves, but also the nation by election to the Congress.

Adoption of the Constitution is critical to both federal and state tax systems because it explains many powers and limitations. Obvious is the basis for the limited and weak tax role of the federal government until very recently. Equally obvious is the plenary role of states. In a nation born of fierce resentment, it has not been accidental that states have stood firm against strong central government. Even more obvious is that in the absence of strong federalism, states have had to build upon long-standing tax systems dating from colonial times. The sovereign nature of states has been a primary force behind strong state tax systems and has been further abetted by a federal government that has frequently empathized with antitax and anticentrist emotion. For example, Thomas Jefferson argued fervently in his First Annual Message that "government shall itself consume the whole residue of what it was instituted to guard."[15] Andrew Jackson was so opposed to taxes that by the end of his term in 1836 he had reduced internal federal tax revenues to less than $500, warning that "Congress has no right . . . to take money . . . unless it is required to execute some one of the specific powers . . . and if they raise more than is necessary for such purposes, it is an abuse of taxation and unjust and oppressive."[16]

The union of antitax sentiment and federal empathy was simultaneously a depressant to strong federal tax policy and a stimulant to defining more aggressive state taxation. These realities were highly apparent as the nation moved westward. Anxious to settle a new and vast land, Congress began in the 1800s to share some of its revenues with states to hasten expansion such as railroads and canals. Although the nation had struggled financially after the Revolutionary War, the nation enjoyed some new prosperity in the early years of the nineteenth century as peace settled across the land and as new markets were found. Critical to prosperity had been the contributions of Alexander Hamilton and Thomas Jefferson, who in their terms of office had done much to financially restore the nation. Hamilton became a hero to the states as he carried out a plan to pay off a national debt of $56 million and to take over the $18 million in unpaid debts of the states. To fund these debts, he established a national mint, levied tariffs to support national industry, and enacted an excise tax on liquor. Jefferson's frugality also aided these goals, with the result that by 1806 revenues surpassed expenses, the national treasury had a $6 million surplus, and the national debt had been reduced.

In these "boom" years, expansionist policies had shared federal revenue with the states. Jefferson had created a House Committee on Roads and Canals and a Civil Engineer Corps within the Army Engineers and recommended $20 million in federal aid to canals and highways. Expansion of railroads was especially costly as the federal government both bought railroad stock and granted lands to railroads. Impatient and eager, however, many states had also borrowed against a rosy future and had begun massive projects that nearly collapsed when national fortunes fell and successive federal administrations were unsupportive in the face of new federal debt. The War of 1812 had proved an expensive event, and the Louisiana Purchase in 1803 for $15 million added greatly to the cost of government. By the Panic of 1837, many states were close to financial ruin. Although placing blame might be debatable, these events provided a breeding ground for conservative federal and state tax philosophies as many states angrily denounced public debt by passing legislation forbidding deficit spending. In 1840 no state forbade public debt; but 19 of the 32 states had adopted constitutional amendments limiting debt by 1855.[17]

A major consoling theory of both federal and state taxes had been the belief that once the nation and states were established, taxes paid by citizens could be abolished. The mounting federal and state debt, however, proved the end of such hope, particularly given the $3 billion debt incurred for the Civil War. Faced with huge debts and recognizing repeated federal failure to implement an income tax, states began seeking in earnest to systematically increase revenues. Colonial tax structures were no longer adequate given state debts and the need for services in keeping with a growing population, and the answer seemed to be raising revenue by taxing general property. True to historic form, however, widespread evasion again thwarted success in that houses and cattle were easily discovered while other property such as bonds, mortgages, and other instruments were undiscoverable. The effect was that evasion placed the entire tax burden on real property. The unfortunate aspect, however, was that farmers who had little cash income to pay taxes also held the most visible representation of wealth in the form of land, making them the recipients of the heaviest tax burden.

Whereas previous tax attempts had been strongly resisted, however, the mood of the states now generally accepted the inevitability of taxation. The trade-off was a demand for taxation that would equitably spread the cost of government. Frustrated with property tax problems, beginning in about 1880 study commissions began to examine ways to improve tax structures, especially administration of the property tax. Although highly imperfect, the introduction of systematic inquiry in an environment resigned to taxation resulted in creation of tax equalization boards, efforts to improve property assessment procedures, uncovering tax evasion, and refining tax requirements on various kinds of property. Although representing vast improvement over previous tax policies, many such efforts again met with limited success as equalization proved politically impossible and as evasion and resistance to taxation were impossible to eliminate. The numerous difficulties of property tax administration ultimately led to many recommendations that states should abandon property taxes in favor of other tax bases. Taxes on business and inherited wealth were high on the list of reforms.

Through a complex series of political tensions, the dawn of the twentieth century generally found progressiveness to be the watchword in state taxation. Faced with property tax administration problems, states began to rely less on property tax and to venture into other areas. Undaunted by federal failure to enact a broad tax base, between 1910 and 1920 several states adopted both individual and corporate income taxes. With adoption of the first state income tax by Wisconsin in 1911, the floodgates of state revenue reform seemed to open. Although no anthology meticulously traces development of state tax systems, the Wisconsin model seemed to dissolve old barriers as states adopted various taxes in rapid succession—no doubt due in part to movement of American society away from agrarian reticence toward the optimism of a new urban millennium. Although the property tax at the state level has never been uniformly abandoned, states have succeeded in securing other revenue sources. In its place, most states have enacted various types of taxes on commercial transactions such as sales and excise taxes. Similarly, Wisconsin's experiment with income encouraged many states to adopt this tax base, proving a tremendous revenue source for the support of ever-growing state government.

If the modern era in state taxation is marked with the twentieth century, the rapid development of state tax systems can be seen in Tables 3.8 and 3.9 on state tax collections, which together trace the types and amounts of state revenue from 1902 to 1990. As seen in these data, states have come far in the search for revenues. The era from 1902 to 1970 shows growth in state government not only in the amounts of revenue, but also in the types of revenue available. This era is remarkable because in 1902 states were levying only small property taxes and other nondefined taxes, while only a few years later states had adopted many new taxes including motor vehicle tax, retirement tax, unemployment tax, personal and corporate income taxes, and various sales and gross receipts taxes, such as motor fuel, alcohol, and tobacco products. Conjointly, intergovernmental revenue grew sharply, as states positioned themselves to share in local taxation and enjoy the rebirth of federal revenue sharing. Combined growth in all sources of revenue to states in this era was phenomenal, moving in less than 75 years from only $192 million in 1902 to nearly $89 billion in 1970.

The era 1970–1990 is also significant for two reasons. First, as seen in Table 3.9 this brief period showed continued rapid growth of both government and revenue. Revenues from direct state tax sources in 1970 were slightly less than $48 billion, increasing to more than $300 billion in 1990. While all categories grew significantly, the greatest increases were consonant with the search to expand the tax base beyond property. Individual income tax experienced the greatest growth in the last two decades, from about $9 billion in 1970 to nearly $96.1 billion in 1990. Equally impressive were sales and gross receipts taxes, increasing from approximately $14 billion to almost $100 billion. A third major source of state revenue lay in corporate income taxes, which increased from about $3.7 billion to almost $22 billion. Vehicle taxes also experienced large gains, rising from $2.7 billion in 1970 to nearly $10.7 billion in 1990. These data form the second reason for the importance of this era. The movement away from state property tax is apparent in that state revenues now focus primarily on user taxes, such as sales and gross receipts, and on personal income and personal property, such as automobiles.

Although state tax systems have taken on new forms and proportions, the responsibility of states has increased at least proportionally to tax bases. By Table 3.10 (pp. 159–160), Jefferson's warning that "government will consume the whole . . . of what it was instituted to guard" has been true in that states have found ways to spend all they collect. State outlays in the years 1970–1990 have been enormous and inclusive of some sympathy for activist government. Although reformers would argue that

TABLE 3.8 State government revenue by source, 1902–1970 (in millions of dollars)

	Revenue from All Sources		Intergovernmental Revenue		Revenue from State Sources	General Revenue	Taxes			Sales and Gross Receipts					
Year	Total	General Revenue (direct and intergovernmental)	From Federal Government	From Local Governments	Total	Total	Total	Individual Income	Corporation Income	Total	General	Motor Fuel	Alcoholic Beverages	Tobacco Products	Other
1970	88,939	77,755	19,252	995	68,691	57,507	47,962	9,183	3,738	27,254	14,177	6,283	1,420	2,308	3,065
1969	77,584	67,312	16,907	868	59,809	49,537	41,931	7,527	3,180	24,050	12,443	5,644	1,246	2,056	2,660
1968	68,460	59,132	15,228	707	52,525	43,197	36,400	6,231	2,518	20,979	10,441	5,178	1,138	1,886	2,335
1967	61,082	52,071	13,616	673	46,793	37,782	31,926	4,909	2,227	18,575	8,923	4,837	1,041	1,615	2,159
1966	55,246	46,757	11,743	503	43,000	34,511	29,380	4,288	2,038	17,044	7,873	4,627	985	1,541	2,019
1965	48,827	40,930	9,874	447	38,507	30,610	26,126	3,657	1,929	15,059	6,711	4,300	917	1,284	1,847
1964	45,167	37,648	9,046	417	35,703	28,184	24,243	3,415	1,695	13,957	6,084	4,059	864	1,196	1,755
1963	40,993	33,882	7,832	411	32,750	25,639	22,117	2,956	1,505	12,873	5,539	3,851	793	1,124	1,565
1962	37,595	31,157	7,108	373	30,115	23,677	20,561	2,728	1,308	12,038	5,111	3,665	740	1,076	1,448
1961	34,603	28,693	6,412	370	27,821	21,911	19,057	2,355	1,266	11,031	4,510	3,431	688	1,001	1,401
1960	32,838	27,363	6,382	363	26,094	20,618	18,036	2,209	1,180	10,510	4,302	3,335	650	923	1,300
1959	29,164	24,448	5,888	364	22,912	18,196	15,848	1,764	1,001	9,287	3,697	3,058	599	675	1,257
1958	26,191	21,772	4,461	302	21,427	17,008	14,919	1,544	1,018	8,750	3,507	2,919	566	616	1,142
1957	24,656	20,382	3,500	427	20,728	16,454	14,531	1,563	984	8,436	3,373	2,828	569	556	1,109
1956	22,199	18,389	3,027	269	18,903	15,093	13,375	1,374	890	7,801	3,036	2,687	546	515	1,017
1955	19,667	16,194	2,762	226	16,678	13,205	11,597	1,094	737	6,864	2,637	2,353	471	459	944
1954	18,834	15,299	2,668	215	15,951	12,417	11,089	1,004	772	6,573	2,540	2,218	463	464	889
1953	17,979	14,511	2,570	191	15,218	11,750	10,552	969	810	6,209	2,433	2,019	465	469	823
1952	16,815	13,429	2,329	156	14,330	10,944	9,857	913	838	5,730	2,229	1,870	442	449	740
1950	13,903	11,262	2,275	148	11,480	8,839	7,930	724	586	4,670	1,670	1,544	420	414	621
1948	11,826	9,257	1,643	97	10,086	7,517	6,743	499	585	4,042	1,478	1,259	425	337	542
1946	8,576	6,284	802	63	7,712	5,419	4,937	389	442	2,803	899	886	402	198	419
1944	7,695	5,465	926	55	6,714	4,484	4,071	316	444	2,153	720	684	267	159	323
1942	6,870	5,132	802	56	6,012	4,274	3,903	249	269	2,218	632	940	257	130	258
1940	5,737	4,382	667	58	5,012	3,657	3,313	206	155	1,852	499	839	193	97	224
1938	5,293	4,141	633	48	4,612	3,460	3,132	218	165	1,674	447	777	176	55	219
1936	4,023	3,672	719	39	3,265	2,914	2,618	153	113	1,394	364	687	126	44	173
1934	3,421	3,212	933	36	2,452	2,243	1,979	80	49	978	173	565	62	25	153
1932	2,541	2,423	222	45	2,274	2,156	1,890	74	79	726	7	527	—	19	173
1927	2,152	2,015	107	51	1,994	1,857	1,608	70	92	445		259			186
1922	1,360	1,254	99	27	1,234	1,128	947	43	58	134		13			121
1913	376	376	6	10	360	360	301			55					53
1902	192	190	3	6	183	181	156			28			2		28

(Continued)

TABLE 3.8 (Continued)

| | General revenue (continued) | | | | | Insurance Trust Revenue | | | | | |
| | Taxes (Continued) | | | | | | | Unemployment Compensation | | | |
Year	Property	Motor Vehicle and Operators' Licenses	Other	Charges and Miscellaneous	Liquor Stores Revenue	Total	Employee Retirement	Total	Contributions	Interest (credited by U.S. Government)	Other
1970	1,092	2,955	3,741	9,545	1,748	9,437	5,205	3,090	2,524	566	1,143
1969	981	2,685	3,509	7,606	1,663	8,609	4,509	3,039	2,550	488	1,061
1968	912	2,485	3,275	6,797	1,557	7,771	3,831	2,963	2,547	416	977
1967	862	2,311	3,042	5,856	1,470	7,541	3,351	3,273	2,910	363	917
1966	834	2,236	2,940	5,131	1,361	7,128	2,918	3,326	3,040	286	884
1965	766	2,021	2,691	4,483	1,270	6,627	2,638	3,234	2,994	239	755
1964	722	1,917	2,536	3,942	1,195	6,324	2,369	3,250	3,046	203	706
1963	688	1,780	2,316	3,523	1,161	5,950	2,136	3,171	2,992	179	642
1962	640	1,667	2,180	3,116	1,134	5,304	1,942	2,812	2,649	162	550
1961	631	1,641	2,133	2,854	1,119	4,791	1,745	2,511	2,317	194	535
1960	607	1,573	1,957	2,583	1,128	4,347	1,558	2,316	2,136	181	472
1959	566	1,492	1,740	2,348	1,085	3,631	1,376	1,827	1,647	179	428
1958	533	1,415	1,658	2,089	1,058	3,361	1,224	1,711	1,493	218	426
1957	479	1,368	1,701	1,923	1,065	3,209	1,063	1,719	1,510	209	427
1956	467	1,295	1,548	1,718	1,019	2,791	919	1,500	1,315	185	371
1955	412	1,184	1,306	1,608	962	2,511	837	1,325	1,138	187	350
1954	391	1,098	1,251	1,328	974	2,560	757	1,466	1,263	203	337
1953	365	949	1,250	1,198	967	2,501	634	1,551	1,370	181	316
1952	370	924	1,082	1,087	924	2,462	579	1,597	1,438	159	287
1950	307	755	888	909	810	1,831	425	1,176	1,028	148	229
1948	276	593	747	774	857	1,711	296	1,203	1,059	144	212
1946	249	439	616	482	798	1,494	193	1,162	1,034	128	140
1944	243	394	520	413	528	1,702	142	1,405	1,319	86	154
1942	264	431	472	370	373	1,366	115	1,134	1,076	58	117
1940	260	387	453	344	281	1,074	108	878	844	34	88
1938	244	359	472	328	262	890	85	726	702	24	79
1936	228	360	370	296	183	168	75	23	23	—	70
1934	273	305	294	264	90	119	64	—	—	—	55
1932	328	335	348	266	—	118	54	—	—	—	64
1927	370	301	330	249	—	137	40	—	—	—	97
1922	348	152	212	181	—	106	29	—	—	—	77
1913	140	5	101	59	—	—	—	—	—	—	—
1902	82	—	46	25	2	—	—	—	—	—	—

SOURCE: U.S. Department of Commerce, Bureau of the Census, *Historical Abstracts of the United States: Colonial Times to 1970, Part 2*. House Document No. 93-78 (Washington, D.C.: U.S. Government Printing Office, 1975), 1129.

TABLE 3.9 State government revenues by source, 1970–1990

Year, Region, Division, and State	Total[1]	State Tax Collections (in millions of dollars)							Excise Tax Rates		
		Sales and Gross Receipts				Individual Income	Corporation Net Income	Motor Vehicle and Operators' Licenses	General Sales and Gross Receipts (Percentage)[2]	Cigarettes (Cents per Package)	Gasoline (Cents per Gallon)
		Total[1]	General Sales and Gross Receipts	Motor Fuels	Alcoholic Beverages and Tobacco Products						
1970[3]	47,962	27,254	14,177	6,283	3,728	9,183	3,738	2,728	(X)	(X)	(X)
1975[3]	80,155	43,346	24,780	8,255	5,249	18,819	6,642	3,941	(X)	(X)	(X)
1980[3]	137,075	67,855	43,168	9,722	6,216	37,089	13,321	5,325	(X)	(X)	(X)
1985[3]	215,893	105,419	69,633	13,344	7,393	63,908	17,631	7,780	(X)	(X)	(X)
1990[3]	300,489	147,069	99,702	19,379	8,732	96,076	21,751	10,675	(X)	(X)	(X)
Northeast	70,961	29,696	18,960	2,659	1,937	28,282	5,935	2,151	(X)	(X)	(X)
New England	18,692	8,337	5,441	956	591	6,820	1,832	709	(X)	(X)	(X)
Maine	1,561	773	509	138	77	581	58	55	5 F&D	31	17
New Hampshire	595	271	(X)	81	50	41	127	58	(X)	25	16
Vermont	666	321	136	54	26	251	27	39	4 F&D	17	16
Massachusetts	9,369	2,852	1,956	302	223	4,910	871	319	5 F&D	26	17
Rhode Island	1,233	645	397	73	49	427	69	40	7 F&D	37	20
Connecticut	5,268	3,475	2,443	308	166	610	680	198	8 F&D	40	22
Middle Atlantic	52,269	21,359	13,519	1,703	1,346	21,462	4,103	1,442	(X)	(X)	(X)
New York	28,615	9,368	6,003	544	733	15,289	1,885	604	[4]4 F&D	39	8
New Jersey	10,434	5,444	3,291	414	256	2,952	1,123	363	7 F&D	40	10.5
Pennsylvania	13,220	6,547	4,225	745	357	3,221	1,095	475	6 F&D	18	12
Midwest	68,760	32,842	21,964	5,451	1,988	24,454	5,439	2,924	(X)	(X)	(X)
East North Central	48,330	23,004	15,389	3,721	1,376	17,055	4,176	1,927	(X)	(X)	(X)
Ohio	11,436	5,752	3,589	971	285	4,125	643	411	[4]5 F&D	18	20
Indiana	6,102	3,372	2,551	565	148	2,090	341	178	5 F&D	15.5	15
Illinois	12,891	6,468	4,077	916	385	4,288	939	651	[5]6.25	30	19
Michigan	11,343	4,414	3,188	740	377	3,927	1,816	509	4 F&D	25	15
Wisconsin	6,558	2,998	1,984	529	181	2,625	437	178	[4]5 F&D	30	21.5
West North Central	20,430	9,838	6,575	1,730	612	7,399	1,263	997	(X)	(X)	(X)
Minnesota	6,819	2,966	1,870	461	209	2,877	482	339	[4]6 F&D	38	20
Iowa	3,313	1,471	944	334	98	1,272	200	221	4 F&D	31	20
Missouri	4,939	2,509	1,899	355	102	1,791	221	213	[4]4.225 D	13	11
North Dakota	677	380	231	67	20	106	47	41	5 F&D	30	17
South Dakota	500	403	250	80	23	(X)	31	21	[4]4 D	23	18
Nebraska	1,513	827	508	209	54	496	72	59	[4]5 F&D	27	21.9
Kansas	2,669	1,282	873	224	106	857	210	103	[4]4.25 D	24	16
South[3]	87,840	51,452	33,871	7,769	3,108	19,898	4,410	3,250	(X)	(X)	(X)
South Atlantic[3]	48,576	26,069	17,741	3,713	1,549	14,557	2,879	1,516	(X)	(X)	(X)
Delaware	1,130	159	(X)	64	17	456	118	24	(X)	19	16
Maryland	6,450	2,712	1,572	450	86	2,864	293	156	5 F&D	13	18.5
District of Col.[3]	23,110	674	467	30	15	638	140	18	6 F&D	17	17.5
Virginia	6,600	2,644	1,353	622	100	3,082	306	264	[4]3.5 D	2.5	17.5
West Virginia	2,230	1,193	765	209	41	517	222	76	6 D	17	15.5
North Carolina	7,865	3,192	1,773	793	166	3,390	612	262	[4]3 D	2	21.5
South Carolina	3,934	2,137	1,448	358	144	1,380	151	89	5 D	7	16
Georgia	7,078	3,454	2,639	441	204	2,868	478	100	[4]4 D	12	[6]7.5
Florida	13,289	10,578	8,191	776	791	(X)	699	545	[4]6 F&D	33.9	4

(Continued)

TABLE 3.9 (Continued)

State Tax Collections (in millions of dollars)

Year, Region, Division, and State	Total[1]	Sales and Gross Receipts Total[1]	General Sales and Gross Receipts	Motor Fuels	Alcoholic Beverages and Tobacco Products	Individual Income	Corporation Net Income	Motor Vehicle and Operators' Licenses	Excise Tax Rates: General Sales and Gross Receipts (Percentage)[2]	Cigarettes (Cents per Package)	Gasoline (Cents per Gallon)
East South Central	14,722	8,751	5,559	1,592	467	2,864	911	530	(X)	(X)	(X)
Kentucky	4,261	1,911	1,088	360	64	1,210	279	154	[4]6 F&D	3	15
Tennessee	4,245	3,268	2,344	630	143	103	332	172	[4]5.5 D	13	20
Alabama	3,820	2,003	1,038	294	176	1,121	180	137	[4]4 D	16.5	11
Mississippi	2,396	1,569	1,089	308	84	430	120	67	6 D	18	18
West South Central	24,542	16,632	10,571	2,464	1,092	2,477	620	1,204	(X)	(X)	(X)
Arkansas	2,261	1,210	839	219	87	739	130	80	[4]4 D	21	13.5
Louisiana	4,087	2,035	1,263	399	111	737	394	80	[7]4 D	20	20
Oklahoma	3,477	1,541	844	331	127	1,001	96	275	[4]4.5 D	23	17
Texas	14,717	11,846	7,625	1,515	767	(X)	(X)	769	[4]6.25 F&D	41	15
West	72,929	33,082	24,908	3,498	1,698	23,443	5,968	2,348	(X)	(X)	(X)
Mountain	15,420	8,279	5,633	1,324	362	4,097	612	726	(X)	(X)	(X)
Montana	858	183	(X)	112	25	403	80	39	(X)	18	20
Idaho	1,139	559	383	108	27	280	73	60	5 D	18	18
Wyoming	612	217	162	37	6	(X)	(X)	43	[4]3 D	12	9
Colorado	3,069	1,337	825	325	81	1,342	123	122	[4]3 F&D	20	20
New Mexico	2,014	1,136	836	165	35	361	62	105	45	15	16.2
Arizona	4,377	2,575	1,918	333	87	1,064	180	237	[4]5 F&D	15	17
Utah	1,768	915	707	132	38	647	94	48	45 D	23	19
Nevada	1,583	1,357	802	112	63	(X)	(X)	72	[4]5.75 F&D	35	16.25
Pacific	57,509	24,803	19,275	2,174	1,336	19,346	5,356	1,622	(X)	(X)	(X)
Washington	7,423	5,564	4,471	484	252	(X)	(X)	191	6.5 F&D	34	22
Oregon	2,786	394	(X)	236	89	1,827	148	232	(X)	28	18
California	43,419	17,270	13,627	1,359	909	16,824	4,928	1,158	[4]5 F&D	35	14
Alaska	1,546	91	(X)	42	23	(X)	185	21	(X)	29	8
Hawaii	2,335	1,484	1,177	53	63	695	95	20	4 D	(8)	[9]11

X Not applicable.
[1]Includes amounts for types not shown separately.
[2]F = food exempt from sales tax; D = prescription drugs exempt from sales tax.
[3]DC excluded from total.
[4]Local sales tax rates are additional.
[5]Food and prescription drugs are subject to a 1% state tax. In addition, these items may be subject to a 1% local tax.
[6]An additional tax is levied at the rate of 3% of the retail sales price, less than the current 7.5 cents per gallon tax.
[7]Food products subject to a 2% state tax.
[8]Tax is 40% wholesale price.
[9]Combined state and county rates are: Hawaii 19.8 cents; Honolulu 27.5 cents; Kauai 21 cents, and Maui 20 cents.
SOURCE: U.S. Department of Commerce, Bureau of the Census, *Statistical Abstracts of the United States 1992* (Washington, D.C.: U.S. Government Printing Office, 1992), 290.

TABLE 3.10 State government outlays by broad function, 1970–1990 (in millions of dollars)

	General Expenditures							
Total			**Selected Functions**					
	Per Capita					**Health and Hospitals**	**Natural Resources**	**Year, Division, and State**
Amount	**Total (dollars)**	**Rank**	**Education**	**Public Welfare**	**Highways**			
77,642	383	(X)	30,865	13,206	13,483	5,355	2,223	1970
228,223	1,010	(X)	87,939	44,219	25,044	17,855	4,346	1980
345,047	1,449	(X)	128,604	67,264	33,154	27,595	6,758	1985
376,429	1,565	(X)	140,189	72,464	36,661	30,131	7,312	1986
403,942	1,664	(X)	149,901	78,454	38,273	32,131	7,816	1987
432,179	1,763	(X)	159,500	84,235	40,681	34,872	8,310	1988
469,269	1,895	(X)	173,184	92,750	42,694	38,602	9,070	1989
507,875	2,047	(X)	184,529	104,971	44,249	42,662	9,909	U.S., 1990
								Northeast
2,743	2,234	16	942	689	244	162	73	Maine
1,676	1,512	48	401	328	207	143	33	New Hampshire
1,466	2,603	9	516	274	147	66	42	Vermont
17,039	2,832	5	3,496	4,604	616	1,635	149	Massachusetts
2,658	2,741	7	782	547	189	256	23	Rhode Island
8,880	2,702	8	2,178	1,701	985	955	71	Connecticut
								Middle Atlantic
49,697	2,763	6	14,266	14,820	2,228	5,018	378	New York
18,041	2,334	15	5,390	3,456	1,324	1,237	201	New Jersey
21,234	1,787	37	6,975	5,186	2,275	1,667	331	Pennsylvania
								East North Central
20,489	1,889	32	7,720	5,058	1,700	1,585	237	Ohio
9,992	1,802	36	4,235	1,930	974	714	124	Indiana
20,055	1,754	41	6,488	4,437	2,190	1,393	279	Illinois
19,561	2,104	19	6,418	4,543	1,355	2,491	255	Michigan
10,499	2,146	17	3,685	2,221	796	692	196	Wisconsin
								West North Central
10,407	2,379	12	3,774	2,064	1,001	815	256	Minnesota
5,935	2,137	18	2,418	1,112	738	532	145	Iowa
7,703	1,505	49	3,274	1,377	779	676	188	Missouri
1,587	2,483	11	592	226	202	86	73	North Dakota
1,281	1,841	33	377	187	186	90	51	South Dakota
2,815	1,784	39	907	498	409	288	98	Nebraska
4,329	1,747	42	1,845	732	544	380	121	Kansas
								South Atlantic
1,994	2,994	4	709	228	191	147	33	Delaware
9,832	2,057	21	2,865	1,864	1,241	831	235	Maryland
11,850	1,920	30	4,723	1,484	1,680	1,265	169	Virginia
3,530	1,969	25	1,454	632	451	192	85	West Virginia
12,555	1,894	31	5,966	1,833	1,335	960	278	North Carolina
6,775	1,943	28	2,843	1,078	487	787	143	South Carolina
11,393	1,759	40	5,048	2,125	1,008	955	288	Georgia
20,558	1,589	47	7,829	3,529	1,733	1,786	616	Florida
								East South Central
7,101	1,927	29	2,945	1,419	718	441	211	Kentucky
7,879	1,616	46	2,821	1,675	1,029	646	110	Tennessee
7,400	1,831	34	3,380	1,049	716	893	143	Alabama
4,394	1,708	44	1,883	696	411	340	129	Mississippi
								West South Central
3,930	1,672	45	1,686	788	420	328	106	Arkansas
8,524	2,020	23	3,177	1,342	740	848	207	Louisiana

(Continued)

TABLE 3.10 (*Continued*)

	General Expenditures							
Total				**Selected Functions**				
	Per Capita							
Amount	**Total (dollars)**	**Rank**	**Education**	**Public Welfare**	**Highways**	**Health and Hospitals**	**Natural Resources**	**Year, Division, and State**
5,612	1,784	38	2,369	1,090	662	531	96	Oklahoma
23,630	1,391	50	10,973	4,189	2,730	1,818	364	Texas
								Mountain
1,651	2,066	20	576	276	252	97	86	Montana
1,831	1,818	35	751	228	288	80	87	Idaho
1,485	3,270	2	524	110	250	93	85	Wyoming
5,627	1,708	43	2,491	902	628	372	131	Colorado
3,891	2,568	10	1,681	436	386	319	77	New Mexico
7,535	2,056	22	2,759	1,077	1,469	316	117	Arizona
3,471	2,014	24	1,663	458	349	334	80	Utah
2,366	1,968	26	846	219	295	94	56	Nevada
								Pacific
11,389	2,340	14	5,082	2,098	864	798	350	Washington
5,563	1,957	27	1,730	934	651	502	185	Oregon
70,189	2,359	13	26,906	16,421	3,512	5,520	1,775	California
4,284	7,790	1	1,057	368	464	176	208	Alaska
3,547	3,201	3	1,113	431	202	311	134	Hawaii

SOURCE: U.S. Department of Commerce, Bureau of The Census, *Statistical Abstracts of the U.S. 1992* (Washington, D.C.: U.S. Government Printing Office, 1992), 287.

government cannot do enough, these data illustrate that the price of what government has chosen to do is high. The biggest state costs have been education, welfare, highways, health, and natural resources. In 1970 education received nearly $31 billion in state revenues, increasing to nearly $185 billion in 1990. Welfare consumed $13.2 billion in state funds in 1970, increasing to $92.8 billion in 1990. Highways were likewise a large expense, as states spending $13.48 billion in 1970 increased their contribution to $42.7 billion by 1990. Yet as all educators know, the tremendous child-based needs have not been met even by these vast resources, nor are they the sum of all education expenditures. For example, although the states' share of education budgets averages 47.2% as indicated in Table 3.11, federal and state participation still totals only 53.3%, leaving unexplained another 46.7%.

From these data, it may be concluded that state tax systems have also matured. It is important to note, however, that such growth has occurred under the three conditions stated at the outset of this discussion. First, state tax systems have been closely entangled with development of federal tax structures. Dating from the Constitution, the power of the state has been preserved and such protections were carefully built into the nation's framing documents. Second, like federal taxation, state tax systems are of both old and recent origin, predating the nation but until recently very narrowly focused and moderately effective. Third, like federal taxation, state tax systems have been the object of disputes. But unlike the federal struggle, schools have become heavily dependent on states for revenue, although such revenues may still not be said to comprise the bulk of resources nor be sufficient to meet needs. As a

TABLE 3.11 State revenues to schools, 1990 (in thousands of dollars)

| | | Revenues, by Source | | | |
| | | Federal | | State | |
State or Other Area	Total	Amount	Percentage of Total	Amount	Percentage of Total
United States	$207,583,910	$12,750,530	6.1	$98,059,659	47.2
Alabama	2,557,836	286,598	11.2	1,534,021	60.0
Alaska	909,380	116,277	12.8	567,900	62.4
Arizona	2,742,625	216,488	7.9	1,194,354	43.5
Arkansas	1,594,428	153,637	9.6	905,487	56.8
California	24,320,281	1,605,281	6.6	16,260,203	66.9
Colorado	2,767,107	132,246	4.8	1,055,366	38.1
Connecticut	3,554,800	161,933	4.6	1,533,343	43.1
Delaware	542,448	39,616	7.3	362,161	66.8
District of Columbia	557,089	54,591	9.8	—	0.0
Florida	9,589,961	595,711	6.2	4,914,474	51.2
Georgia	5,194,517	329,253	6.3	2,759,335	53.1
Hawaii	755,987	76,099	10.1	660,341	87.3
Idaho	710,841	56,891	8.0	427,757	60.2
Illinois	9,001,253	531,923	5.9	2,952,592	32.8
Indiana	4,349,969	211,441	4.9	2,510,251	57.7
Iowa	2,149,710	105,270	4.9	1,056,130	49.1
Kansas	2,085,315	103,598	5.0	920,867	44.2
Kentucky	2,247,379	220,813	9.8	1,540,138	68.5
Louisiana	3,058,293	309,117	10.1	1,696,645	55.5
Maine	1,154,667	62,805	5.4	613,447	53.1
Maryland	4,267,441	196,285	4.6	1,609,649	37.7
Massachusetts	5,117,504	240,192	4.7	1,765,255	34.5
Michigan	8,394,959	482,031	5.7	2,251,071	26.8
Minnesota	3,988,317	165,059	4.1	2,088,236	52.4
Mississippi	1,573,464	243,774	15.5	884,024	56.2
Missouri	3,699,939	205,179	5.5	1,480,193	40.0
Montana	707,594	63,726	9.0	324,888	45.9
Nebraska	1,359,712	79,742	5.9	314,371	23.1
Nevada	860,464	36,018	4.2	326,773	38.0
New Hampshire	900,843	24,944	2.8	75,684	8.4
New Jersey	8,763,058	336,351	3.8	3,486,521	39.8
New Mexico	1,225,429	150,229	12.3	893,539	72.9
New York	19,744,546	1,014,296	5.1	8,044,917	40.7
North Carolina	4,683,693	300,405	6.4	3,127,946	66.8
North Dakota	487,049	47,517	9.8	218,041	44.8
Ohio	8,617,848	462,810	5.4	3,754,896	43.6
Oklahoma	2,172,547	121,530	5.6	1,237,503	57.0
Oregon	2,539,734	155,250	6.1	637,971	25.1
Pennsylvania	10,336,060	534,118	5.2	4,511,630	43.6
Rhode Island	844,009	41,524	4.9	363,539	43.1
South Carolina	2,678,790	215,088	8.0	1,340,255	50.0
South Dakota	503,949	57,774	11.5	130,552	25.9
Tennessee	2,907,714	261,676	9.0	1,330,928	45.8
Texas	13,948,117	1,012,383	7.3	5,847,048	41.9
Utah	1,326,479	86,986	6.6	751,040	56.6

(*Continued*)

TABLE 3.11 (*Continued*)

State or Other Area	Total	Federal Amount	Federal Percentage of Total	State Amount	State Percentage of Total
Vermont	562,543	24,464	4.3	181,330	32.2
Virginia	5,101,281	268,730	5.3	1,687,176	33.1
Washington	4,192,291	243,402	5.8	3,000,965	71.6
West Virginia	1,413,165	106,072	7.5	928,128	65.7
Wisconsin	4,240,432	174,249	4.1	1,703,555	40.2
Wyoming	581,050	29,140	5.0	297,225	51.2

SOURCE: U.S. Department of Education, National Center for Education Statistics, *Digest of Education Statistics 1992* (Washington, D.C.: National Center for Education Statistics, 1992), 151.

result, the unique system of American government has placed schools in a further dependent relationship with a third level of government that has had to develop its own tax system to fund the remaining costs of government, including the bulk of education expenditures.

Local Tax Systems.   The nature of tax system development in the United States has cast unique lots to each unit of government. As described earlier, the federal revenue system has yielded an intentionally limited focus. Likewise, state revenue systems have developed from a void of central leadership and in response to preferences for state sovereignty. The third and final tier of tax systems has also developed in parallel with the other two systems, but the outcome has been even more narrow and contentious because the two higher systems have seized most available tax bases except the local property tax. These realities have the dubious benefit of severely abbreviating discussion of the development of local tax systems.

The unique nature of tax system development has led to three organizational levels known as federal, state, and local governments. Traditionally, the federal government has accepted responsibility for national defense, international affairs, interstate regulation, and general welfare of the nation. In contrast, sovereign states laid claim to all other rights and responsibilities. These plenary powers were further extraordinary in that states viewed their power to include a right to delegate almost any function to local government. The rationale was akin to "government of the people, by the people, and for the people" in which successively lesser units were thought to be better attuned to local needs, thus increasing the responsiveness of government. While federal and state governments have tended to be centrally vested, the concept of local government has been refined to consist of multiple layers including counties, cities, schools, and other even smaller incremental levels.

Although local government has been widely dispersed, its role has been less diverse and its tax structure has been extremely limited. Although careful tracing of early America would reveal self-sufficiency at the local level including such historical facts as colonial militia and minting of money, such excessive cloistering has long been defunct. Instead, federal and state governments have stepped in to care for more global concerns while local governments have taken up the mundane and immediate problems of society. At the same time, however, local government on a daily basis has assigned a huge array of affairs to lower government units. While overlapping with federal and state interest, local governments have assumed major responsibility for education, welfare, health, highways, police and fire protection, corrections, sanitation, housing and community development, utilities, and a series of other concerns about economic development and quality of life. Additionally, the high visibility of local government has laid a special burden for responsiveness whereby attitudes about all government are formed. Although diverse views can be offered about whether local government is greatest or least in importance, it is unarguable that much has been expected of local government as the most directly accessible of all formal governmental structures.

Prominent visibility and breadth of service, however, have not been joined to equally comprehensive local tax systems. Like federal and state taxation, local tax systems have had to struggle against resentment and have been handicapped by a narrow tax base. Colonial roots of such struggles have already been described, with a legacy that continued into statehood. But unlike federal and state governments, there has been an expectation that local government is needed, an expectation demanding responsiveness that has increased rapidly with the twentieth century. These expectations have been difficult due to three phenomena negatively affecting local government. First, parallel tax system development at each level has had the effect of restraining all other governments. Second, governmental hierarchy has dictated that although local expectations have grown, local units have taken a back seat to federal and state revenue systems. Third, American traditions of intense tax revolt have not missed the local level, but revolt has only recently occurred, primarily as a backlash to the first two phenomena. These realities have both shaped and strained local tax systems.

Parallel development of state tax systems should not be surprising. Just as federal and state systems developed in response to one another, local tax systems have also evolved as a result of divisions in government responsibility. The impact of tax evolution, however, has been striking at the local level because each level has acquired its revenue capacity in part by tax base domination or abandonment. This concept is clear when it is recognized that a tax is basically lost to one unit of government when it is seized by another unit. For example, it may be seen that once the federal government has reached some conceptual limit in taxing income, that portion of the income tax is lost to lower governments. States may then seek to tax income only up to some additional point. Obviously, if it is then still politically feasible to further tax income, the local unit of government may levy income tax. Each unit's share, however, is smaller by virtue of the next higher unit's actions. Conversely, if a tax is unproductive or unworkable at some level, it may be abandoned to a lower level. For example, failure of property taxes at the federal level resulted in abandonment to the states, while only limited state success has resulted in the property tax as the nearly exclusive domain of local governments.

As a result, successively higher units of government have forced lesser units into fewer tax base options. The concept of estimating how much more income taxes citizens will silently pay once federal demands are met has obviously worked to some degree because the modern mix of taxation represents considerable overlap between levels—for example, all three units of government sometimes levy income taxes, and in several states property taxes are collected by both state and local governments. The principles stand true, however, in that the income tax has become first a federal tax, with states primarily capturing sales tax and most of the remaining income tax, while local government has taken a backseat by relying mostly on property taxes supported by various other small sources.

The effect of restraining local government to a narrow tax base has yielded an interesting local revenue system. As seen in Table 3.12 local governments have come to depend on three main sources for funding. Revenue-sharing has finally become a powerful force, as in 1980 local governments received about $21 billion from federal sources and about $81 billion from the various states. By 1990 local governments had experienced decline in federal revenue to only about $18.4 billion, while state contributions to local governments increased to about $172.3 billion. States themselves, however, have carried a huge tax burden, generating about $130 billion in 1980 and increasing to over $321.6 billion in 1990. Combined total revenues to local government are staggering, as in 1980 revenues totaled more than $232.4 billion, increasing to over $512.3 billion in 1990. While no assessment can be made from Table 3.12 on how the local share was raised, the burden to taxpayers is obvious in that citizens simultaneously paid taxes to all three units of government, of which actual local tax collections were more than $201.1 billion.

Table 3.13 (pp. 167–169) shows local funding by detailing sources and amounts of revenue to all three levels of government and by showing the intended use of funds. Increasing dependence on intergovernmental revenue is evident, as in 1990 states received more than $126 billion and local governments received almost $191 billion. Tax base abandonment is evident, as the federal government received no property tax revenue, general sales tax, motor vehicle tax, or other smaller taxes. Similarly, state and local governments received no revenue from customs or other exclusively federal charges. In contrast, tax base domination is evident, as the federal government captured the vast share of income tax at almost $466.9 billion, compared to only $96.1 billion and $9.6 billion at the state and local levels, respectively. Likewise, states captured almost all sales and gross receipts taxes, receiving approximately $147.1 billion, compared to local receipts of about $30.8 billion. At the same time, however, the various local units of government received the overwhelming majority of property taxes. While the federal government collected no property tax, massive revenues of almost $149.8 billion were collected locally, compared to a mere $5.8 billion collected by states.

Despite narrow tax bases, revenues to all three levels of government still reached over $2 trillion. The expenditure patterns in Table 3.13 reveal much about current tax systems and society's expectations. Despite arguments of critics, the divisions and limits among the three governments is well defined as each level has been assigned a primary role for certain goals. The role of states has caused them to lead in higher education ($60.9 billion), welfare ($83.3 billion), highways ($36.5 billion), and corrections ($15.9 billion). Likewise, local governments led in spending for education ($212.7 billion), health ($39.1 billion), police and fire protection ($39.2 billion), sanitation ($26.9 billion), and government administration ($27.1 billion). In keeping with its limited role, the federal government spent huge sums on national debt ($187.9 billion) and defense and selected social programs (not shown). Importantly, however, it must be noted that revenue at each level was less than expenditures. For example, federal revenues fell short by more than $238 billion, while state revenues were only slightly surplus, by $59.9 billion. Although much smaller, local governments also overspent by approximately $1.01 billion.

TABLE 3.12   Local government general revenue by broad source, 1980–1990 (in millions of dollars)

Year, Division, and State	Total[1]	Intergovernmental from—		From Own Sources	
		Federal	State	Total	Taxes
1980	232,453	21,136	81,289	130,027	86,387
1985	354,119	21,724	116,380	216,014	134,473
1989	468,549	17,588	157,652	293,308	184,478
1990, U.S.	512,322	18,449	172,274	321,599	201,130
New England	23,518	931	7,589	14,999	11,767
Maine	1,802	66	600	1,137	863
New Hampshire	1,786	52	224	1,510	1,279
Vermont	825	27	239	559	465
Massachusetts	11,528	563	4,362	6,603	4,827
Rhode Island	1,405	60	406	939	810
Connecticut	6,172	163	1,758	4,251	3,523
Middle Atlantic	101,873	2,864	33,212	65,796	48,053
New York	62,417	1,604	20,275	40,538	30,150
New Jersey	17,454	389	5,436	11,629	9,038
Pennsylvania	22,002	871	7,501	13,629	8,865
East North Central	78,021	2,654	25,360	50,009	33,845
Ohio	19,231	762	6,431	12,038	8,230
Indiana	9,204	242	3,435	5,528	2,942
Illinois	21,628	938	5,483	15,208	11,132
Michigan	17,965	482	5,812	11,671	7,876
Wisconsin	9,993	230	4,199	5,564	3,665
West North Central	32,375	1,311	10,257	20,803	12,266
Minnesota	11,056	537	4,291	6,227	3,263
Iowa	5,033	186	1,689	3,158	1,912
Missouri	7,042	319	1,990	4,733	2,999
North Dakota	966	53	348	564	325
South Dakota	928	52	205	670	507
Nebraska	2,865	97	569	2,198	1,351
Kansas	4,485	67	1,165	3,253	1,909
South Atlantic	83,713	4,377	25,170	54,167	31,466
Delaware	918	41	402	476	241
Maryland	9,029	417	2,431	6,181	4,572
District of Columbia	4,405	1,599	(X)	2,806	2,310
Virginia	10,809	367	3,290	7,152	5,127
West Virginia	2,090	52	881	1,157	572
North Carolina	11,286	412	4,725	6,149	3,239
South Carolina	4,946	162	1,803	2,961	1,512
Georgia	12,570	455	3,561	8,554	4,589
Florida	27,660	872	8,077	18,711	9,304
East South Central	22,687	857	9,213	12,617	6,232
Kentucky	4,388	182	1,782	2,424	1,250
Tennessee	9,002	283	3,970	4,750	2,578
Alabama	5,361	192	1,903	3,266	1,548
Mississippi	3,936	200	1,558	2,177	856
West South Central	44,073	1,405	12,081	30,588	18,241
Arkansas	2,603	87	1,087	1,429	732
Louisiana	6,918	306	2,228	4,385	2,504
Oklahoma	4,423	154	1,497	2,772	1,478
Texas	30,129	858	7,269	22,002	13,527

(*Continued*)

TABLE 3.12 (*Continued*)

Year, Division, and State	Total[1]	Intergovernmental from—		From Own Sources	
		Federal	*State*	*Total*	*Taxes*
Mountain	26,903	1,074	9,273	16,558	9,569
Montana	1,394	78	416	901	576
Idaho	1,449	59	572	818	432
Wyoming	1,292	29	504	759	389
Colorado	7,208	231	1,821	5,157	3,273
New Mexico	2,575	157	1,292	1,126	546
Arizona	7,589	318	2,703	4,568	2,664
Utah	2,660	93	944	1,622	958
Nevada	2,736	109	1,021	1,607	731
Pacific	99,155	2,975	40,121	56,060	29,689
Washington	9,613	376	3,746	5,490	2,909
Oregon	5,739	360	1,408	3,971	2,711
California	80,298	2,058	34,048	44,193	22,837
Alaska	2,202	91	815	1,297	691
Hawaii	1,303	90	104	1,109	541

X Not applicable.
[1]Excludes duplicative intergovernmental transactions.
SOURCE: U.S. Department of Commerce, Bureau of the Census, *Statistical Abstracts of the U.S. 1992* (Washington, D.C.: U.S. Government Printing Office, 1992), 294.

Relegating local governments to a backseat has had the effect of turning the American tradition of tax revolt toward the local level. In contrast to federal and state tax resentment that prevented effective tax systems for many years, tax revolt at the local level has occurred but in reverse order by only recently swelling as a backlash to tax overburden. While many complex explanations are plausible, it is reasonable to believe that taxpayers have reacted negatively to heavy local taxes as a last resort simply because these services are most visibly perceived to benefit local taxpayers. For example, property taxes have long been seen as a "school tax" by which every citizen benefits visibly, as have taxes for roads and police and fire protection. Rapid growth of government in the twentieth century, dependence on narrow tax bases, and societal events such as court rulings contravening local ownership of school taxes, however, have recently led once again to taxpayer dissatisfaction. Its accessibility has made local government the natural target for venting frustration.

The outcry against taxes popularly known as the tax limitation movement was best evidenced in the 1978 passage of Proposition 13 in California, when a state constitutional amendment to limit government revenues was placed on the ballot through voter initiative. Although complex in impact, Proposition 13 called for the simple concept of rolling back big government by limiting property taxes to 1% of assessed value. In addition, other restrictions were placed on taxes wherein the assessed value of a property could not increase more than 2% in a year unless the property was sold. The law further reduced the tax base by requiring assessed valuations to be rolled back to 1975–1976 values and forbade any new ad valorem, sales, or transaction taxes on real property. Proposition 13 passed by a large majority, and only one

TABLE 3.13 All government revenues and expenditures, 1990 (in millions of dollars)

Source of Revenue and Type of Expenditure	All Governments	Federal	State	Local	Percentage		Per Capita[1] (Dollars)	
					Federal	State and Local	Federal	State and Local
Revenue	2,046,998	1,154,596	632,172	580,193	100.0	100.0	4,642	4,150
Intergovernment revenue	2	2,911	126,329	190,723	0.3	26.2	12	550
Revenue from own sources	2,046,998	1,151,685	505,843	389,470	99.8	73.8	4,631	3,600
General revenue from own sources	1,493,179	780,479	391,101	321,599	67.6	58.8	3,138	2,866
Percent of total revenue	73	68	62	55	(X)	(X)	(X)	(X)
Taxes[3]	1,133,886	632,267	300,489	201,130	54.8	41.4	2,542	2,017
Property	155,613	(X)	5,848	149,765	(X)	12.8	(X)	626
Individual income	572,524	466,884	96,076	9,563	40.4	8.7	1,877	425
Corporation income	117,073	93,507	21,751	1,815	8.1	1.9	376	95
Sales and gross receipts	231,855	53,970	147,069	30,815	4.7	14.7	217	715
Customs duties	16,810	16,810	(X)	(X)	1.5	(X)	68	(X)
General sales and gross receipts	121,287	(X)	99,702	21,585	(X)	10.0	(X)	488
Selective sales and gross receipts[3]	93,758	37,160	47,367	9,231	3.2	4.7	149	228
Motor fuel	33,120	13,077	19,379	664	1.1	1.7	53	81
Alcoholic beverages	9,223	5,753	3,191	279	0.5	0.3	23	14
Tobacco products	10,002	4,268	5,541	193	0.4	0.5	17	23
Public utilities	17,892	6,476	6,544	4,903	0.6	0.9	26	46
Motor vehicle and operators' licenses	11,444	(X)	10,675	769	(X)	0.9	(X)	46
Death and gift	15,355	11,500	3,832	23	1.0	0.3	46	16
Charges and misc. general revenue[3]	359,293	148,212	90,612	120,469	12.8	17.4	596	849
Current charges[3]	204,418	88,877	42,745	72,795	7.7	9.5	357	465
National defense and international relations	8,268	8,268	(X)	(X)	0.7	(X)	33	(X)
Postal service	38,202	38,202	(X)	(X)	3.3	(X)	54	(X)
Education[3]	32,840	—	23,585	9,256	—	2.7	—	132
School lunch sales	3,454	—	13	3,441	—	0.3	—	14
Higher education	26,339	—	23,224	3,115	—	2.2	—	106

(Continued)

TABLE 3.13 (*Continued*)

Source of Revenue and Type of Expenditure	All Governments	Federal	State	Local	Percentage Federal	Percentage State and Local	Per Capita[1] (Dollars) Federal	Per Capita[1] (Dollars) State and Local
Natural resources	29,205	27,385	1,347	473	2.4	0.2	110	7
Hospitals	31,191	77	9,388	21,726	(Z)	2.6	(Z)	125
Sewerage and sanitation	17,647	(X)	224	17,423	(X)	1.5	(X)	71
Parks and recreation	3,456	100	748	2,608	(Z)	0.3	(Z)	13
Housing and community development	5,843	2,997	190	2,656	0.3	0.2	12	11
Air transportation	5,193	20	556	4,617	(Z)	0.4	14	21
Water transport and terminals	2,394	906	355	1,133	0.1	0.1	4	6
Special assessments	2,427	(X)	146	2,281	(X)	0.2	(X)	10
Sale of property	5,270	3,967	246	1,057	0.4	0.1	16	5
Interest earnings	70,037	11,313	27,370	31,353	1.0	4.8	45	236
Utility revenue	55,202	(X)	3,305	51,897	(X)	4.6	(X)	222
Liquor stores	3,441	(X)	2,907	533	(X)	0.3	(X)	14
Insurance trust revenue	495,176	371,206	108,530	15,441	32.2	10.2	1,493	498
Expenditure	2,218,793	1,393,121	572,318	581,207	100.0	100.0	5,601	3,924
Intergovernment expenditure	2	146,990	175,028	5,836	10.6	15.7	591	13
Direct expenditure	2,218,793	1,246,131	397,291	575,371	89.5	84.3	5,010	3,911
General expenditure	1,686,774	855,234	333,256	498,284	61.4	72.1	3,439	3,343
Percent of total expenditure	76	61	58	86	(X)	(X)	(X)	(X)
Education[3]	305,552	17,404	75,497	212,652	1.3	25.0	70	1,159
Elementary and secondary education	202,009	—	1,798	200,211	—	17.5	—	812
Higher education	73,418	—	60,978	12,441	—	6.4	—	295
Public welfare	140,734	33,447	83,336	23,951	2.4	9.3	134	431
Health and hospitals	92,487	17,852	35,543	39,092	1.3	6.5	72	300
Highways	61,913	856	36,464	24,593	0.1	5.3	3	245
Police protection	35,921	5,344	4,487	26,090	0.4	2.7	21	123

Fire protection	13,186	(X)	(X)	13,186	(X)	1.1	(X)	53
Corrections	26,229	1,594	15,898	8,737	0.1	2.1	6	99
Natural resources[4]	96,922	70,266	11,906	14,750	5.1	2.3	283	107
Sewerage and sanitation	28,453	(X)	1,527	26,926	(X)	2.5	(X)	114
Housing and community development	32,430	16,951	1,724	13,756	1.2	1.3	68	62
Governmental administration	57,546	12,710	17,707	27,130	0.9	3.9	51	180
Interest on general debt	237,691	187,952	21,532	28,207	13.5	4.3	756	200
Other	557,710	490,858	27,635	39,214	35.2	5.8	1,974	269
Utility expenditure	74,875	(X)	7,131	67,744	(X)	6.5	(X)	301
Liquor stores expenditure	2,926	(X)	2,452	474	(X)	0.3	(X)	12
Insurance trust expenditure	454,218	390,897	54,452	8,870	28.1	5.5	1,572	255
By character and object:								
Current operation	1,190,147	490,016	258,046	442,084	35.2	60.7	1,970	2,815
Capital outlay	220,960	97,891	45,524	77,545	7.0	10.7	394	495
Construction	98,536	9,422	34,803	54,310	0.7	7.7	38	358
Equip., land and existing structures	122,424	88,469	10,721	23,235	6.4	2.9	356	137
Assistance and subsidies	106,602	79,375	16,902	10,325	5.7	2.4	319	109
Interest on debt (general and utility)	246,866	187,952	22,367	36,547	13.5	5.1	756	237
Insurance benefits and repayments	454,218	390,897	54,452	8,870	28.1	5.5	1,572	255
Expenditure for salaries and wages	*487,594*	*146,436*	*101,338*	*239,820*	*10.5*	*29.6*	*589*	*1,372*

— Represents zero or rounds to zero.
X Not applicable.
Z Less than 0.05% or $0.50.
[1] Based on enumerated resident population as of April 1.
[2] Aggregates exclude duplicative transactions between levels of government.
[3] Includes amounts not shown separately.
[4] Includes parks and recreation.
SOURCE: U.S. Department of Commerce, Bureau of the Census, *Statistical Abstracts of the U.S. 1992* (Washington, D.C.: U.S. Government Printing Office, 1992), 280.

year later Californians also passed Proposition 4 by an even greater margin, further imposing restrictions on revenue growth by tying tax increases to the cost of living and to changes in population and further authorizing fiscal accountability of government by permitting a simple majority of voters to control the spending limit of any unit of government.

The effect of Proposition 13 was dramatic and of national impact. The effect was to instantly reduce property tax by $7 billion (−60%). Proposition 4 worsened the crisis by tying state spending to the economy, permanently reducing state revenues by 16%. Under these conditions, the one-time revenue loss from Proposition 13 theoretically could have been absorbed by tax reserves, but linking revenues to the economy had a permanent effect. While all governments lost revenue, schools were hit the hardest as approximately 29% of all school revenue was lost to property tax reduction. Although the state was able to fund most of the loss by other means, tax limitation in California dramatically changed the nature of its tax system and sparked nationwide tax revolt. Almost immediately, Proposition 2 ½ was passed in Massachusetts, taking its name from an effort to limit property taxes to 2.5% of market value and calling for reduction of all taxes to that level and limiting revenue growth to 2.5% annually. In the frenzy that followed, 19 states adopted various revenue limits designed to roll back or reduce big government.

Tax revolt soured, however, as the nation learned that even tax reduction can have unwanted effects, and short-term gains of tax reduction were quickly shown to be false economy as citizens lost ground under tax limitation. For example, Californians lost big federal income tax deductions as a result of lower property tax, and enactment of user fees for many formerly tax-subsidized items such as golf courses and swimming pools turned previously deductible taxes into personal expenses. Ironically, tax revolt led to worse tax inequity because new systems were not able to stop slippage in assessments as property changed hands. The worst irony, however, was in the impact on education where revenue losses caused California's schools to slip to the bottom third of all states in expenditures—an ignominy worsened by the fact that a prime purpose of tax revolt was to restore local control of government, but had the opposite effect of requiring the state to assume almost full funding of schools. As a result, Proposition 9, which proposed cutting income taxes by 50% and indexing income tax rates to the economy, failed in 1980, as did tax initiatives in several states. By 1988, a California initiative known as Proposition 98 easily passed, reversing some of the cuts to education.

Tax systems in the United States can thus be characterized by both their uniqueness and their commonalities. First, the subjugation of all three levels of government to taxpayer dissent has made it difficult to secure a broad and comprehensive revenue base. The federal tax system has especially suffered in this regard by being limited to only a few productive taxes. Second, all three levels have reacted to the lack of broad tax base by dominating a few tax sources to the near exclusion of all other governments. To an extreme, local government has suffered in this regard as virtually only the property tax has been accessible, higher governments having preempted other tax sources. Third, while growing roles for all three governments have led to both increased revenues and demands for expenditures, resources have been insufficient. Fourth, the implications for education have been enormous when joined with other historical contexts seen in earlier chapters. Although education is vital to federal, state, and local interests, responsibility has been unequally shared and the costs are disproportionately distributed. As summarized in Table 3.14, education has been predominantly locally funded—a reality falling mostly to the local property tax.

TABLE 3.14 Revenues for public K–12 schools, federal, state, and local sources combined, 1990 (in thousands of dollars)

State or Other Area	Total	Revenues, by Source					
		Federal		State		Local and Other	
		Amount	Percentage of Total	Amount	Percentage of Total	Amount	Percentage of Total
United States	$207,583,910	$12,750,530	6.1	$98,059,659	47.2	$96,773,720	46.6
Alabama	2,557,836	286,598	11.2	1,534,021	60.0	737,217	28.8
Alaska	909,380	116,277	12.8	567,900	62.4	225,203	24.8
Arizona	2,742,625	216,488	7.9	1,194,354	43.5	1,331,784	48.6
Arkansas	1,594,428	153,637	9.6	905,487	56.8	535,304	33.6
California	24,320,281	1,605,281	6.6	16,260,203	66.9	6,454,798	26.5
Colorado	2,767,107	132,246	4.8	1,055,366	38.1	1,579,494	57.1
Connecticut	3,554,800	161,933	4.6	1,533,343	43.1	1,859,524	52.3
Delaware	542,448	39,616	7.3	362,161	66.8	140,672	25.9
District of Columbia	557,089	54,591	9.8	—	0.0	502,498	90.2
Florida	9,589,961	595,711	6.2	4,914,474	51.2	4,079,776	42.5
Georgia	5,194,517	329,253	6.3	2,759,335	53.1	2,105,928	40.5
Hawaii	755,987	76,099	10.1	660,341	87.3	19,546	2.6
Idaho	710,841	56,891	8.0	427,757	60.2	226,193	31.8
Illinois	9,001,253	531,923	5.9	2,952,592	32.8	5,516,737	61.3
Indiana	4,349,969	211,441	4.9	2,510,251	57.7	1,628,277	37.4
Iowa	2,149,710	105,270	4.9	1,056,130	49.1	988,310	46.0
Kansas	2,085,315	103,598	5.0	920,867	44.2	1,060,850	50.9
Kentucky	2,247,379	220,813	9.8	1,540,138	68.5	486,428	21.6
Louisiana	3,058,293	309,117	10.1	1,696,645	55.5	1,052,531	34.4
Maine	1,154,667	62,805	5.4	613,447	53.1	478,416	41.4
Maryland	4,267,441	196,285	4.6	1,609,649	37.7	2,461,507	57.7
Massachusetts	5,117,504	240,192	4.7	1,765,255	34.5	3,112,058	60.8
Michigan	8,394,959	482,031	5.7	2,251,071	26.8	5,661,857	67.4
Minnesota	3,988,317	165,059	4.1	2,088,236	52.4	1,735,023	43.5
Mississippi	1,573,464	243,774	15.5	884,024	56.2	445,666	28.3
Missouri	3,699,939	205,179	5.5	1,480,193	40.0	2,014,567	54.4
Montana	707,594	63,726	9.0	324,888	45.9	318,980	45.1

(Continued)

TABLE 3.14 (Continued)

Revenues, by Source

State or Other Area	Total	Federal		State		Local and Other	
		Amount	Percentage of Total	Amount	Percentage of Total	Amount	Percentage of Total
Nebraska	1,359,712	79,742	5.9	314,371	23.1	965,600	71.0
Nevada	860,464	36,018	4.2	326,773	38.0	497,673	57.8
New Hampshire	900,843	24,944	2.8	75,684	8.4	800,215	88.8
New Jersey	8,763,058	336,351	3.8	3,486,521	39.8	4,940,187	56.4
New Mexico	1,225,429	150,229	12.3	893,539	72.9	181,661	14.8
New York	19,744,546	1,014,296	5.1	8,044,917	40.7	10,685,333	54.1
North Carolina	4,683,693	300,405	6.4	3,127,946	66.8	1,255,342	26.8
North Dakota	487,049	47,517	9.8	218,041	44.8	221,490	45.5
Ohio	8,617,848	462,810	5.4	3,754,896	43.6	4,400,142	51.1
Oklahoma	2,172,547	121,530	5.6	1,237,503	57.0	813,514	37.4
Oregon	2,539,734	155,250	6.1	637,971	25.1	1,746,513	68.8
Pennsylvania	10,336,060	534,118	5.2	4,511,630	43.6	5,290,312	51.2
Rhode Island	844,009	41,524	4.9	363,539	43.1	438,946	52.0
South Carolina	2,678,790	215,088	8.0	1,340,255	50.0	1,123,447	41.9
South Dakota	503,949	57,774	11.5	130,552	25.9	315,623	62.6
Tennessee	2,907,714	261,676	9.0	1,330,928	45.8	1,315,110	45.2
Texas	13,948,117	1,012,383	7.3	5,847,048	41.9	7,088,686	50.8
Utah	1,326,479	86,986	6.6	751,040	56.6	488,454	36.8
Vermont	562,543	24,464	4.3	181,330	32.2	356,749	63.4
Virginia	5,101,281	268,730	5.3	1,687,176	33.1	3,145,376	61.7
Washington	4,192,291	243,402	5.8	3,000,965	71.6	947,925	22.6
West Virginia	1,413,165	106,072	7.5	928,128	65.7	378,965	26.8
Wisconsin	4,240,432	174,249	4.1	1,703,555	40.2	2,362,628	55.7
Wyoming	581,050	29,140	5.0	297,225	51.2	254,684	43.8

SOURCE: U.S. Department of Education, National Center for Education Statistics, *Digest of Education Statistics 1992* (Washington, D.C.: National Center for Education Statistics, 1992), 151.

EVALUATING TAX SYSTEMS

Despite the problems in developing sound taxation, it is very clear that tax systems are now well established in the United States. Problems in establishing good tax policy, however, have not been a sole function of politics because there are also innate limitations to taxes themselves that have urged legitimate resistance. While the politics of tax resistance have been highly evident throughout the first half of this chapter, little has been said about the equally fatal limitations of various types of taxes collected by government. In other words, politically acceptable taxation is almost impossible because the only fair tax is a tax someone else pays; but it is equally impossible to find a tax that has no innate weakness on some aspect of tax theory. Unfortunately, this sets an irresoluble dilemma wherein the only solution is knowing acceptance of tax mechanisms *according* to their flaws, with corresponding attempts at mitigating their deficiencies. Because tax systems, and especially school taxes, have been much criticized, the last section of this chapter examines the traits of desirable taxation, with implications for schools.

Good Tax Systems

Although no one likes to pay taxes, most citizens have finally understood that the price of civilization is related to their taxes. Under such recognition, the last century has seen sentiment shift away from abolishing taxes toward a search for fairer tax systems. Although officials might choose to argue that the shift is a fine one given recent state tax revolt and the bitterness with which patrons still complain about taxes, the distinction is nonetheless important because it argues that resignation to taxation is accompanied by at least acquiescence if taxpayers can be satisfied that taxes are fundamentally fair. Under these conditions, public officials such as policymakers and school leaders are importantly freed up to spend more effort on assuring that citizens are held accountable to tax systems that are as equitable as humanly possible. It is obvious, however, that good tax systems would already be in place if this were a simple task. Failure to produce tax fairness, however, has been due more to politics than to lack of knowledge about tax equity. In other words, knowledge about fair taxation exists, but avoiding even fair taxes has prevented the ideal tax system.

Although tax systems have never been perfectly equitable, knowing good tax system requirements has made a significant difference in the pursuit of tax equity. Tax systems with all their flaws are significantly better today than in the early eras that spawned violent outrage. While Americans grumble, they have generally come to believe more than their predecessors that the objectives of taxation in raising revenue, shifting wealth, and protecting the common good are worthy goals. While each of these three objectives has varying support, almost everyone understands and approves in principle. For example, the exclusion principle discussed in earlier chapters assures approval at the most selfish level in that benefits such as roads and fire protection are tangible rewards of taxes. At the next higher conceptual level, the externality of shifting wealth by welfare and unemployment payments to prevent desperate lawlessness likewise receives majority approval. While successively higher conceptual levels might evoke debate about whether such payments create disincentives through a permanent underclass at the expense of productive Americans or whether it is wrong to thwart personal initiative through mechanisms such as inheritance taxes, Americans have come to accept and tolerate fair taxation.

Although most citizens lack formal schooling in tax equity, the principles of fair taxation have a long history among Americans. The theories of Locke and Smith were integral in shaping the nation's basic tax beliefs from the very outset. Locke in particular argued the dignity of man's right to the fruit of his labor, setting forth the principle that government may not displace the right of wealth ownership. Locke argued that no rational person would set up a government that abused its creator and that democracy by its nature precluded an arrogant tax system. But Locke was also vocal in arguing for social responsibility, charging that a just tax should be paid in return for freedom. The power of such thought was augmented by Smith, who argued principles of representative taxation by pleading for tax systems based on four vital criteria of *equity, certainty, convenience,* and *economy.* According to Smith, equity demanded taxes in proportion to a citizen's ability to pay. Certainty demanded that taxation must fall on each citizen with clarity in amount, manner, and time of payment. Convenience demanded that tax systems must accommodate taxpayers, wherein the natural inconvenience of taxes must not be worsened by government itself. Finally, economy demanded that government not bloat itself with unneeded revenue, taking only what is needed to efficiently conduct its affairs.

Although much time has lapsed since these profound principles were laid down, modern Americans still see these goals as the essence of good tax systems. Although thinking has changed little, significant refinement has followed, yielding both a framework by which tax systems can be evaluated and resultant knowledge about the strengths and weaknesses of the various taxes levied by governments. A useful framework for evaluating tax fairness is thus to examine each tax under the headings of tax *basis,* tax *yield,* tax *equity,* tax *incidence,* and tax *administration.*

Tax Basis.   Understanding and evaluating tax systems requires that the basis of taxation must be understood. Before a tax can be levied, decisions must have been made about what to tax. Thus a basic concept of tax systems is that the object against which a tax is levied is the *basis* of the tax. Basis is both the starting and ending point because the ultimate objective is evaluation of tax basis itself. In other words, if a tax were not considered for implementation, none of the evaluation would have merit because the benefits and limitations of any tax are systemic to tax basis itself.

Although it seems that government has sought to levy many types of taxes, such perception is inaccurate because there are only four tax bases. Historically, the most important tax basis has been *wealth.* As seen earlier, all three levels of government have tried to tax wealth with varying degrees of success. Numerous examples of wealth exist, but the most historically important form is real property. Deeply rooted in tradition, it is easy to see how real property has represented wealth because land and other visible real estate suggest high financial status. Other forms of wealth also exist, however, such as personal property, estates of deceased persons, and intangible wealth such as stocks and bonds. Historically, however, wealth as a tax base has been viewed without consideration for income yielded by a possession. For example, a farm may represent a large asset, but in recent times farm income has been very low and conversion of the asset to cash may result in little gain or even loss. Likewise, a retired person's home is wealth that bears no relationship to income. Although many such problems exist, real property is the basis of wealth in most tax systems, particularly at the local level.

A second basis is *income*. Although all wealth was once income regardless of the form in which it accrued to its owner, income as a basis for taxes is distinct in looking at changes in fiscal position, usually over a single year. Examples of income are wages and salaries, corporate earnings, or income from investments—all of which result in improvement of one's ability to pay taxes. Generally, income is defined in terms of cash payments from earnings or investments, as opposed to other income such as inheritance, which is usually defined as wealth. The basis of the income tax is further separated by allowing for deductions and for expenses incurred in deriving the income, thus making the income tax contingent on the net earnings used to pay taxes. This distinction between wealth and income is an important one to later discussion of tax equity because the ability principle will consider what constitutes the most appropriate basis for taxation. Both federal and state governments have become dependent on income as the basis for revenues.

A third basis is *consumption*. Several consumption taxes have already been mentioned in this chapter. Federal excise taxes and duties, all forms of sales tax, and lotteries are all forms of consumption taxes. The basis of consumption rests in the nature of the tax wherein goods or services are taxed at the consumer level. The rule is that when tax on consumers is broadly levied against objects or services, it is called a sales tax. In contrast, a tax on specific items of a class, such as tires or alcohol, is called an excise tax. Likewise, a lottery tax is a consumption tax in that it is a tax against a particular item levied and collected by the state. A critical distinction of consumption is that revenue follows consumer demand, and within limits can be considered a voluntary tax. As seen earlier, consumption is a significant tax at federal and state levels.

The final basis of taxation is *privilege*. Privilege taxes are well named in that they are taxes levied against persons who engage in a particular pursuit. Most often privilege taxes are levied as license fees, such as professional licenses to engage in business or fees for the privilege of operating an automobile. Still other privilege taxes are levied as user fees for parks, dog tags, and so forth. In a sense, a privilege tax is an excise tax, particularly in that licensing a person to sell a skill or to conduct business is a sales tax on a specific skill or the right to pursue a career. Although analysts are correct in placing privilege last as a revenue source, money raised by privilege taxes is not small. For example, rights to public lands are often sold for large fees in return for commercial venture. The federal government has made a practice of such fees, and states also collect many "regulatory" fees.

Wealth, income, consumption, and privilege thus comprise the basis of all taxation by providing the object against which taxes are laid and collected. While the statement may seem obvious, it is important in that no tax could be collected without basis and that any deviation from these bases would require invention of some other basis. As such, evaluation of tax systems always returns to tax basis because evaluation is the process of assessing the merits and drawbacks of each basis. Consequently, evaluation of taxes is actually evaluation of tax *basis* by comparing each tax on the criteria of *yield, equity, incidence,* and *administration.*

Tax Yield.   It is reasonable to argue that the first criterion on which a tax must be judged is its performance in providing revenue. Although a despotic tax would not be justified merely because it produced enormous revenue, a tax that provides little revenue would not be worth the effort and resistance involved in levy and collection. Similarly, if a tax is not responsive or reacts adversely due to some inherent characteristic, it may be argued that there are serious problems with that tax. Revenue yielded by a tax is thus critical to good tax systems, especially by virtue of comparing the yield of various taxes in relation to costs of administration as further traded off against results of evaluating each tax's fundamental fairness.

Tax yield is generally first evaluated by considering the *elasticity* of a tax. As the name implies, elasticity is the ability of a tax to expand its yield in relation to changes in income. A tax that increases yield at a greater rate than changes in income is an *elastic* tax; inversely, tax revenues that increase more slowly than income are *inelastic.* Another condition is also possible as revenue and income change at the same rate; in this instance, the tax shows *elasticity of unity.* A useful analogy to elasticity is inflation. During the 1970s, income failed to increase as rapidly as inflation because although salaries rose with inflation, the cost of living rose more rapidly. The income tax, however, was steeply indexed, causing an effect known as bracket creep because disposable income declined at the same time that higher salaries pushed workers into higher tax brackets. Under such conditions, the income tax was elastic because government services stayed about the same while revenues rose sharply. Thus a characteristic of income tax is elasticity. Conversely, other taxes may be inelastic or show elasticity of unity due to innate characteristics. The relative elasticity of various tax bases will be seen later, but it is generally true that a good tax should not be inelastic, and elastic tendencies should be carefully monitored to prevent negative outcomes such as the inflation example given here.

Equally important in considering yield is the concept of *stability,* or the pattern of tax revenue in relation to the economy. As might be expected, a stable tax is less responsive to economic downturn by continuing to produce relatively smooth revenue patterns; conversely, a tax lacking stability tends to be highly responsive to economic changes. While in some instances economic sensitivity makes good tax policy because it empathizes with taxpayers' ability to pay, it is also true that a 1:1 ratio could cause disruption to important programs. Some taxes are more stable than others, making decisions about tax basis an important trade-off between social and economic goals.

Tax Equity. It should not be surprising that the second tenet of a good tax system is tax equity. Although each tax criterion discussed here is importantly interactive with each of the other criteria, only tax yield approaches the importance of tax equity. Further, the only rationale for placing yield and equity on the same plane is that equity without yield is a gentle but pointless exercise; it should not be presumed, however, that yield supersedes equity in an absolute hierarchy. The painful tax history of the nation is evidence of the tight balance between these goals. Indeed, tax *in*equity and tax revolt are causal. The issue, however, is more complex than choosing either yield or equity in that equity is multidimensional. For example, equity is usually discussed in the context of resource distribution to children, with some scholars claiming that tax equity is a lower priority. It is reasonable to argue, however, that children's equity both follows and requires taxes to be equitable first. For example, it can be argued that inequitable taxation is the *genesis* of children's inequity, making taxpayer equity in one sense a precondition of equal opportunity. The issue becomes even more clouded when it is admitted that tax equity is highly subjective given that the only fair tax is a tax paid by someone else. As a result, assessing tax equity is complex and requires several further criteria.

Benefit Principle.   It is inescapable that decisions about equity are finally value judgments. One of those judgments has been a decision by policymakers about whether individuals may expect to receive direct or proportional returns on taxes paid. Many aspects of taxation seem to favor this concept. For example, special assessments to property owners for utilities and paving are levied only against owners whose holdings front a paved street or are connected to a utility line. Similarly, the benefit principle seems to apply to fuel taxes, as drivers pay excise taxes on each gallon purchased for road construction. Similarly, in many states only local school district residents pay for building new schools built for the exclusive use of resident children. Under such conditions, many examples seem to provide evidence that society has judged it fair to expect people to pay for services in proportion to individual benefit.

The benefit principle, however, requires complex analysis when more fully applied to tax systems. In the previous examples, it is easy to see that the person whose home connects to utilities is the direct beneficiary of the tax. In fact, most people would agree that it is unreasonable to expect anyone else to pay for such services. Strict application of benefit, however, produces inconsistencies and inequities. For example, each person is usually assessed the same special tax on a per-lot basis. In this instance, the owner of one lot pays only one share and the owner of two lots is twice taxed. It may be impossible, however, to know if the person with two lots receives double benefit from sewer service. Similarly, there is evidence of proportionality of benefit in gasoline taxes because the person who drives more pays more tax and enjoys greater use of roads. Benefit is frustrated, however, in that the driver of a fuel-efficient car may drive more miles on less gas than the owner of a luxury car—yet greater road use at less final cost accrues to the owner of the economy car. Likewise, imperfect exclusion occurs in that anyone can use streets or receive the general benefits of sanitation provided by water and sewer systems. In effect, it seems that many taxes based on benefit do not truly adhere to its principles, raising serious equity issues about basing taxes on benefit.

Even if it were possible to restrict services to benefit, the general principle of modern taxation has become that no direct return may be expected. In keeping with earlier discussion on externalities, it is a feature of good tax systems that the benefit to society derived from good school facilities outweighs the unequal burden that may fall to some persons. An important principle thus emerges in that benefits need not be proportional and that equity is not equated to any direct return. Indeed, the use of general tax revenue to augment special road and highway taxes provides a clear example of this principle because many persons who do not drive still pay for road construction and maintenance. The justification rests in benefit to society; for example, police and fire vehicles, ambulances, and grocery delivery trucks all use roads to the benefit of nondrivers. Similarly, nearly all persons paying school taxes no longer receive direct instructional services, but everyone is benefited by their previous schooling and by the contribution of education to society. While clearly a value judgment, current tax laws and tax theory reject benefit by positing that a public good may supersede the right to private ownership of wealth.

Ability to Pay Principle.   Rejection of benefit is the conceptual lever that has opened other principles of tax equity theory. While admittedly belief in the first condition is mandatory to accept all subsequent judgments about equity, tax systems have extended the concept of nonexclusiveness to how tax revenues are raised. If it is accepted that people may not expect direct return, it can similarly be accepted that citizens may not automatically expect to pay taxes in equal amounts. A head tax, for example, could be equitable because it promotes neutral equality. Conversely, such a tax might be inherently unequal because it ignores natural and social inequalities that lead to fiscal inequality. The preference of modern tax equity has been not only to reject benefit, but also to argue that differences among people should result in differential taxes. As a result, ability to pay is a central tenet of modern tax theory.

Ability to pay, often called sacrifice theory, argues that each person should pay taxes based on financial status. Under this notion, persons with higher status are presumed more able to pay and should be made to contribute more than persons of lesser status. Although this seems to be common sense, it becomes more complex in that American society has difficulty determining if it wishes to pursue capitalist liberty or socialist equality. For example, some taxes are based on ability, while others have no relationship. The result of rejecting benefit theory and accepting ability to pay has been creation of a criterion of equity, but uniform application of either principle has not followed in that many taxes violate these conditions. For example, special assessment taxes tend toward exclusion and fall indiscriminately on those least able to pay. In contrast, income taxes are more steeply applied to larger incomes. Property taxes, however, are uniform in rate. The effect is more than mere inconsistency by causing a tax to fall into one of three classifications: *progressive, regressive,* or *proportional.* A progressive tax is one that accelerates the tax portion relative to income as income rises. A regressive tax causes the proportion of tax paid to income to fall as income rises. A proportional tax then is one in which the ratio of taxes to income is constant despite changes in income. All taxes fit one of these classes, but their effect may be inconsistent or inequitable.

Ability to pay is thus one expression of tax equity that is rooted in political philosophy and pragmatic economics. The two main reasons for a progressive tax are political and economic: political because it derives from an intent to redistribute wealth, and economic because it intends to seek the highest yield. The reason for a proportional tax is the apparent lack of favoritism among taxpayers, with less note paid to yield. The reason behind a regressive tax is always self-serving, although it may be masked by claims that low taxes on high incomes stimulate the economy by encouraging investment of wealth in economic growth. But regardless of the political or economic logic, a tax is based on decisions to accept or reject ability.

Horizontal and Vertical Equity.   Tax equity under ability to pay is further divided into *horizontal* and *vertical* equity. If equity is equality, horizontal equity requires equality of equals, while vertical equity requires action to assure equality of unequals. Achieving tax equity can thus become complex in that each level becomes more difficult in a capitalist democracy. For example, horizontal equity requires identically situated taxpayers to pay identical taxes. While conceptually appealing, it is almost impossible to find two identical persons. The imperfect solution has been to charge the same tax rate to all persons on the assumption that all other things are equal. Obviously, two people in identically priced homes probably do not have identically equal incomes or expenses, making these persons immediately unequal. Vertical equity is then required to adjust tax loads to produce equality. This is again appealing because it would only require calculating the percentage of income paid in taxes and adjusting each to the same percentage irrespective of actual dollars. Here again, however, vertical equity is spoiled because two citizens in two communities will pay from very different wealth bases. Lastly, different tax bases accept or ignore one or both conditions, making evaluation of tax equity more difficult and more important.

Although imperfect in practice, it is a principle of modern taxation that good tax systems should be both horizontally and vertically equitable. As will be seen later, however, more attention has been paid to horizontal equity, either by virtue of the forbidding task of vertical equity or by virtue of not having moved political thinking beyond horizontality. In either case, these two dimensions of equity form an important part of modern tax theory.

Tax Impact and Incidence.   Horizontal and vertical equity is further complicated by tax *impact* and tax *incidence.* The relationship to equity should be clear in a very sequential fashion. It follows that if benefit is rejected, then the ability principle must be accepted. Progressivity then follows, redistributing wealth while equalizing taxes on both horizontal and vertical dimensions. Although the logic is clear, achievement is complex because it is not always apparent who pays a tax. The difference is tax impact versus tax incidence, an issue complicated by tax shifting.

While it is easy to advocate equitable taxation, it is more difficult to evaluate whether a given system or a particular tax is equitable. Likewise, it is easy to determine the impact of a tax and extraordinarily difficult to determine incidence. Determining impact is simply knowing who makes a tax payment. For example, a landlord will make a point of paying property tax on a rental unit, both because the tax bill is sent to the owner and because these taxes reduce federal and state income tax liability. The difficulty arises in that the landlord may not be the person truly paying the tax. In other words, a wise landlord will build taxes into rents, thereby shifting incidence of the tax to renters. In this instance, the tax is being shifted forward. In other instances taxes are shifted backward, such as negotiating lower wages with workers to compensate for tax increases that otherwise would be borne by the employer. Thus tax incidence may involve shifting, with only drastic events preventing shifting, such as the rent controls and price freezes that were applied in the 1970s. For tax equity, it is important to note that some types of taxes are more amenable to shifting, making a reasonable assessment of tax equity more possible.

Neutrality.   A further major tenet of tax equity is *neutrality.* Tax neutrality is the notion that a tax should leave each citizen in the same relative financial position as was true prior to the tax. Wealthy taxpayers should thus pay more tax, but they should still have more wealth after taxes than will less wealthy citizens. Tax neutrality is thus not only a concept of equity via fair taxpayer treatment, but also an economic policy in that the theory holds that taxes should not depress the economy. For example, high taxation may drive businesses to bankruptcy or encourage other tax jurisdictions to create tax havens to attract businesses and industry, while high taxes invite inflation as businesses raise prices to shift taxes to consumers, in turn fueling higher labor costs. Modern tax policy at the federal level, however, has been to manipulate the economy through taxes to reduce the supply of money in times of inflation and to reduce taxes in recessions to stimulate the economy. Such luxury is less available at state and local levels, except through tax preferences intended to spur economic growth.

It is important to note that neutrality is often violated by various types of tax manipulation—what is less clear is whether more taxes are eventually paid through increased income and consumption taxes brought on by tax preference than is lost due to violating tax neutrality. Evaluation of tax systems will indicate that some taxes are more neutral than others; consequently, although neutrality is a condition of equity, achieving it is a complex undertaking.

Directness and Certainty.   A final condition of tax equity demands that a tax exhibit both *directness* and *certainty.* Prime tenets of Adam Smith's insightful view of taxes, directness and certainty are among the few elements of good tax policy unchallenged by government and citizens alike. Directness simply demands that taxes should not be hidden and that the purpose and use of taxes should be clear and unambiguous. Certainty also ingenuously demands that the types of taxes and amounts should be knowable in advance. The combination of directness and certainty argue against any appearance of duplicity by making government transparent. While it cannot be known whether government has always sought these conditions, it is clear that tax resistance is greatly nourished by indirect and uncertain taxation.

Ease and Cost of Administration.   Finally, a good tax system requires ease and economy of administration. As indicated earlier, a tax that requires much effort and expense may prove annoying or even counterproductive. Failed federal attempts at levying various taxes during the first 200 years of the nation are proof of problems wherein low yield, evasion, and high collection costs made mockery of the system. As will be seen, some taxes are more prone to high administrative costs compared to yield, and others are so invasive of privacy as to engender more resentment than revenue. Accordingly, a good tax system must exhibit stable yield and low costs and, of course, good public relations that make it easy and convenient to pay.

It should now be remembered that the opening headline to this chapter stated that "the taxes a government can impose are related to a nation's economy, its history, and the political climate at home and abroad." Deep wisdom is apparent in such words because the nation has never moved far from its fiercely tax-rebellious colonialism. Although a perfect tax system has never been found, the harsh lessons of nation and statehood can be combined with sound tax theory to argue that a good tax system must meet several criteria vital to productive revenue generation:

1. *Tax bases* should be considered for their performance relating to fundamental fairness. In addition, tax bases should be so broad as to avoid reliance on any one source or on groups that may be singled out to carry a disproportionate burden;

2. *Tax yield* should provide adequate revenue and be restrained by principles of tax equity that encourage willing acquiescence;

3. *Tax equity* should be balanced against yield to derive appropriate interplay. Because these goals are not compatible, a tension must be preserved to prevent domination of one aspect; and

4. *Tax administration* should be built on sound management and political

awareness so that while citizens may not appreciate taxes, they will better understand and accept the inevitability.

Tax Base Evaluation

The principles of good taxation provide a framework for evaluating the taxes levied by governments. This framework is useful in that while schools often have direct access only to the property tax, evaluation of all tax structures is informative because there is much discussion about alternative revenue sources. In one sense, tax system evaluation on the dimensions of basis, yield, equity, and administration can identify whether that discussion is useful or merely rhetorical, masking some other goal. In addition, evaluating tax bases on such criteria may aid policymakers since mechanisms such as state aid draw from more tax bases than are directly accessible to schools. For example, schools cannot levy income tax, but many states use income tax revenue to fund schools. Similarly, schools do not levy sales tax, but a state aid formula that depends heavily on sales tax may behave predictably given the nature of the sales tax. It is thus important to recognize that knowledge about each tax is useful because tax systems pervade all government funding.

Each of the four bases of taxation is reviewed in this last section using the tax evaluation framework. Wealth, income, consumption, and privilege are thereby assessed using the criteria of basis, yield, equity, and administration. The focus is both broad and specific: broad in that the generalities are widely applicable, and specific in that the interest in tax systems always rests in implications for schools.

Wealth.   The most important tax basis has been wealth, primarily because wealth is the proven source of the greatest revenue. All three governments have sought to tax wealth with varying degrees of success.

Basis.   As historically defined, the basis of wealth is ownership of any one of three kinds of property. *Real* property denotes land and/or improvements to land, such as houses or commercial buildings. *Tangible* property refers to all other physical items, such as automobiles, recreational vehicles, business equipment, or inventory, and in many states includes items not affixed to the land, such as mobile homes. *Intangible* property refers to items representing wealth but which are worthless except by the exchange value they represent. For example, stocks and bonds and cash are worthless except as valued by the ability to exchange such instruments in market transactions. As noted earlier, wealth is distinct from income in that wealth is the sum of accumulated assets at a given point in time. Because of the nature of such definition and traditional beliefs about wealth, the most historically important form of wealth is real estate. Of next importance has been tangible or personal property, only distantly followed by intangible wealth. Wealth as a basis for taxation has thus come to be characterized best by the property tax.

Before wealth can be taxed, however, it must be valued. Valuing the three kinds of wealth is at once straightforward and complex. It presents little problem to value intangibles because the exchange rate can be easily known. Intangible wealth, however, is hard to tax due to evasion. Valuing tangible property is more complex due to its use. A good example is commercial tangible property, which is often valued by depreciation—for example, business equipment can be listed on the tax rolls and depreciated over its useful life wherein each year's tax value is the original price less accumulated depreciation. That is, an item with a new cost of $10,000 could be depreciated at the rate of 14% annually to a value of zero after seven years. Conversely, private tangible property, such as automobiles, is usually taxed by its present market value. For example, a new Lincoln selling for $32,000 may only bring $17,000 one year later due to low demand among wealthy people for used luxury cars. In contrast, an economical Ford may hold most of its value. In this instance, annual market updates for each vehicle determine the tax value.

The act of valuing property is known as property *appraisal* or *assessment.* Tangible property appraisal is completed in many different fashions depending on the type of property to be valued. Tangible personal property is generally appraised by annually adjusting the value of an item to its depreciated worth. Commercial tangible property is more complex and depends on the laws of an individual state. For example, a service business may have little inventory, while industries may have large inventories that are liabilities rather than assets until products are sold.[18] The widest application to schools, however, is valuation of real property. As noted earlier, the property tax has been left almost exclusively to local governments, with schools generally receiving more than 50% of all property tax revenues.

Like other property valuation, real property appraisal begins and ends with the tax appraiser, but the process is very different. Appraisal is generally comprised of several steps. First, a tax appraiser inspects each property, using a checklist to record features of the property. In the instance of existing homes, the most critical features are square footage, type of exterior construction, number of bedrooms and baths, and special features such as fireplaces or swimming pools. At the same time, the size and features of the lot are noted, including such items as sprinkler systems. The second step usually notes any changes since the last appraisal. The third step then researches recent sales of similar nearby homes. Using an average of sales, an appraisal of market value of each home can be made with adjustments for any improvements to the property. Appraisal of new homes is much simpler in that the selling price establishes market value. In stable neighborhoods with few sales, however, difficulties can arise due to a lack of market-comparables.[19]

When the value of a property is decided, the remaining steps are mostly mechanical by applying the tax laws of the state. It should be noted that while many tax jurisdictions have authority to lay and collect taxes, the laws governing taxation are state laws. Such laws are generally constitutional provisions, with enabling statutes that regulate levy and collection. The process is to follow state law by applying the rate of assessment to a given property to derive the *assessed value.* Several states require properties to be appraised at *full market value,* while others require *fractional assessment.* The difference is mostly political. When full market value is used, taxes are laid against the full value of a property, with advocates arguing more accurate appraisal and less slippage in ratios of taxes to property values. When fractional assessment is used, taxes are laid against only a portion of market value, with fractional assessment justified as tax relief allowing part of the property to go untaxed. The point is political in that fractional assessment does not exempt any part of the property; instead, it merely requires a higher tax rate to produce the same revenue yielded by full market appraisal.[20]

Regardless of the method of appraisal, the fourth step requires applying the rate of assessment to the appraised value of the property. For example, a home valued at $100,000 under a fractional classification scheme of 12% for residential property would yield an assessed value of $12,000. This amount supplies the information needed to complete the fifth step of calculating the actual tax. When the assessed value is known, the *mill rate* is multiplied against the assessed value to generate the tax bill to be sent to the owner. The mill rate is simply the statutory tax rate of a unit of government. For example, some states require a statewide uniform tax rate for schools. Other states allow tax rates to float free, seeking only to control large differences by sending state aid to schools. In the latter instance, the mill rate is determined by dividing the budget of a government unit by the total assessed valuation of the tax district. For example, a school district with a budget of $1 million and an assessed valuation of $100 million would require a mill rate of 10 mills ($1,000,000 ÷ $100,000,000 = 0.010). Generating the $1 million would then require calculating the tax for each parcel of property and sending tax notices to each owner. Given that a mill is $1 tax yield for every $1,000 assessed value, the tax bill would be calculated as:

$$[MV * RAV * TR] = TB$$
or
$$[(\$100,000 * 12\%) = (\$12,000 * .010)] = \$120$$

where:
   Market Value (MV) = $100,000
   Residential Assessment Rate (RAV) = 12%
   Tax Rate (TR) = 10 mills
   Tax Bill (TB) = $120

The process of property valuation may vary among states, but the outcome is the same. Once tax bills are prepared, citizens owe the tax according to the legally prescribed method of payment. A school district's interest in this process is threefold. First, it is vital to assure that property appraisal is as accurate as possible, since underassessment results in inflated tax rates, thereby producing the appearance of high taxes. Second, since schools depend on property taxes, districts are concerned that properties within and between jurisdictions be uniformly assessed. Resentment arises when nearby school districts and neighboring properties in the same district are assessed at different levels. Although laws demand accuracy, error is common. For example, many states have conducted appraisal studies, often finding errors of 20% or more among tax units and variations among individual properties approaching 50%. Third, schools are interested in patterns of total assessed valuation because declining wealth means higher taxes. Because budgets are greatly shaped by tax rates, the wealth base of a district is vitally important.

Property as a basis for taxing wealth is thus highly complex. Problems of tax evasion and privacy concerns in assessing intangible wealth have virtually precluded this base, with only feeble attempts by many states to tax intangibles in conjunction with income tax reporting. Taxing tangible property has been more successful, but often limited to highly visible items such as automobiles, business equipment, and so forth. By default, real property has become the basis of taxing wealth, and its exclusive local nature has made it the mainstay of school funding.

Yield.   Table 3.13 seen earlier illustrated the enormous revenue power of property taxes, as in 1990 the property tax at all levels of government yielded more than $155 billion. Division of tax yield, however, is as important as the amount of revenue raised. As seen in Table 3.13, the federal government earned no revenue from property taxes, while state governments earned slightly more than $5.8 billion. Local governments, however, raised nearly $150 billion—more than 96% of all property tax collections. At the local level, no other tax even approached the revenue generated by taxing wealth through the property tax. Although state property tax collections lagged far behind other state tax sources, the $5.8 billion raised by states was still not trivial and local collections were truly astounding.

Productive yield of the property tax is further evident in the elasticity and stability of this tax base. Although data on the elastic performance of the property tax has been inconclusive, the traditional view is that the property tax has exhibited at least elasticity of unity and in some estimations has shown modest elasticity. More recently, some data have shown a calculated value slightly below unity—an observation that seems reasonable given recent property tax revolt in the worst cases and supported by efforts in other states to reduce overall property tax burden. Under such conditions, any tendency toward elasticity could have been undermined by tax limitations that reduced property tax revenue growth to less than the rate of growth in the economy. As a general rule, the combined evidence from both sides is encouraging in that the property tax has historically been slightly elastic and in that exclusive dependence on this tax base may have been slightly relaxed. Stability, however, has been unquestioned as the property tax exhibits many desirable qualities in that because wealth is not linked to income, it responds only slowly to economic downturn by holding property values and revenue stable, while at the same time either prosperity or inflation drives valuation and revenue upward.

The tremendous yield of the property tax is unfavorably apparent in recent events. Not surprising is that dominance of other tax bases by higher governments has resulted in heavy reliance on property at the local level. In addition, it is not surprising that tax revolts like Proposition 13 centered on the property tax if for no other reason than its size. Similarly, a local tax can be more effectively besieged, and the property tax makes an obvious target simply because no other tax base has such a high price on each taxable object. Likewise, the desirable traits of elasticity and stability can also create unwanted effects by their unresponsiveness to economic downturn. This may account for the fact that while property continues to be the mainstay of local government, property as a percentage of total taxes has declined modestly since 1978. Although the reasons are not certain, rational explanations are that other taxes have risen in response to tax limitation that has both slowed property tax growth and in some instances greatly reduced the property tax base. But despite moderation in property tax growth, the bottom line is that almost no other tax has had the yield and stability of property—and it is equally important that it has been the only powerful tax available to schools.

Equity.   It must also be recognized, however, that the unpleasantness of property tax revolt has not been exclusively due to its vast yield. While most citizens likely cannot articulate a scholarly basis of discontent, their anger is vitally important because it mostly rests in perceptions of unfairness. Unfairness, of course, is an equity discussion and Americans have long been preoccupied with ferreting out differential tax burdens. Although various local governmental units derive property tax support, the perception of unfairness in property taxes is especially important to schools because no other taxing unit is so dependent on the property tax. As a consequence, the relative performance of the property tax on the criteria of ability, progressivity, horizontal and vertical load, incidence, neutrality, directness and certainty, and administration is of critical importance to schools. In one sense, the benefit and ability to pay principles are mutually exclusive. The benefit principle expects a return on taxes paid that is roughly proportional to the amount of taxes compared to benefits and return to another taxpayer who pays a different amount. In contrast, ability presumes no such relationship. The property tax exhibits some argument favoring both principles. Property owners who have central utility lines such as water and sewer are direct beneficiaries of these taxes, while homeowners on water wells or septic systems do not seem to pay these taxes. Paved streets result in higher taxes to adjacent properties, while rural residents on dirt roads pay lower taxes. These outcomes are not mutually exclusive, however, as water treatment plants benefit everyone's health, and paved streets are public. As a result, enforcement of exclusion is impossible and unproductive. This does not mean, however, that property taxes are based on ability. This is very evident in that property tax rates are the same for every resident of a tax unit, with tax bills a sole function of property value. Only in the most contorted sense can it be claimed that lower tax bills on cheap properties reflect ability to pay since poor people live in poorer housing. It must therefore be concluded that the property tax at best provides only a modified benefit principle since higher taxes often result in better services.

This discussion can be extended to the second condition of equity wherein it is expected that tax equity will depend in part on whether a tax is progressive, proportional, or regressive. The property tax can be shown to demonstrate any one of these three conditions. Traditional justification for uniform property tax rates has been that one rate is proportional and even voluntary. Under this assumption, property owners choose homes corresponding to their incomes—an argument that finds each owner in end equality where wealthy owners buy expensive homes and pay proportionally higher taxes. A second view, however, is that proportionality is really regressive in that these same points can be turned around. In this view, a lower tax bill on a cheaper home is not proportional because taxes make up a larger percentage of disposable income for poor people—a regressive trait that is hardly voluntary. More recently, a third view favoring progressivity has emerged that basically claims that regressivity in property taxes has been in error or, worse, political philosophy. This view rejects abstract contentions about whether property taxes are tied directly to income, looking instead at the final outcome. Many arguments apply, but the concept is illustrated by the argument that the poorest people pay rent (including taxes) using public assistance—a view that returns some of the tax burden to the income-producing sector. In sum, the arguments are inconclusive, basically proving only that a regressive tax is fundamentally evil.

A third demand of good taxation is horizontal and vertical equity. Horizontal equity demands equal treatment of equals, and vertical equity requires unequal treatment of unequals—concepts closely tied to progressivity and proportionality. Property tax performance is again mixed, based on tax incidence. Horizontal equity seems a natural conclusion about the property tax since uniform tax rates fall to everyone. This is complicated, however, by four critical issues. First, absence of a link between property tax and the income used to pay taxes makes assumptions about finding equally situated taxpayers a leap of faith. Second, movement toward taxing property by classification injects questions about whether arbitrarily creating different property classes with unequal assessment rates is equitable. Third, tax incidence is a serious question in horizontal equity because it is generally possible to shift taxes.[21]

Fourth, newer views on property tax progressivity argue for some attributes of vertical equity. Similarly, vertical equity would seem precluded by a system of uniform tax rates that does not track income differences. Yet subventions such as circuit breakers and homestead exemptions have lent an element of vertical equity to a tax system unrelated to ability to pay. In sum, the mixed data report that the property tax with its basis in wealth is ill-suited to horizontal or vertical equity because it ignores the income from which taxes are paid, while subventions and political philosophy alternatively infer more or less equity to the property tax.

A fourth trait of equitable taxation is neutrality, in which a tax would leave each citizen in the same relative financial position as prior to the tax. Critics, of course, argue a perverse twist on neutrality in that the property tax indeed leaves poor people poor and rich people unharmed—an argument that cannot be easily refuted regardless of any slight progressive incidence. A more productive analysis would examine neutrality of the property tax in the economy. Probably the greatest negative impact of property tax is its highly localized nature. As stated earlier, many local governments have waged warfare to attract business or industry by granting tax abatements in return for economic development. As a result, there has been a propensity toward undervaluing some properties that would otherwise generate revenue, with the effect of increasing taxes on other taxpayer groups. A related issue is population migration that also creates a destructive tax cycle. For example, higher income persons abandon urban centers to cluster in suburbs. As suburbs grow, their lucrative base allows lower tax rates to yield high revenue. This in turn spurs higher urban tax rates to recoup lost revenue—tax rates that damage the poor who cannot move and simultaneously discourages business from locating in the city. On the whole, property tax is not neutral despite uniform rate.

The final trait of tax equity is directness and certainty. Directness requires that taxes not be hidden and that the purpose of a tax be clear and unambiguous. Certainty demands that tax amounts be knowable in advance. The combination makes government accountable. While the property tax has many flaws and an equal number of critics, most would agree that the major drawback of localism ironically also serves as a benefit via directness and certainty. In other words, while many disagree with the amount and structure and use of the property tax, almost everyone sees it as highly visible, overtly direct, and highly certain.

Administration.   Finally, a good tax system exhibits administrative ease and economy. As noted earlier, a tax that lends itself to low yield, evasion, and high costs makes a mockery of the system. While many complaints center on property taxes in regard to inequitable assessment, few complaints relate to its fiscal efficiency. Although it is costly to assess and maintain property records, the cost is extremely efficient compared to the enormous yield of the tax. Similarly, long-term evasion is virtually nonexistent as tax foreclosure sales speak clearly to the issue. Although the cost of correcting deficiencies in property appraisal might change the overall assessment of administration, especially by eliminating very small taxing units, the property tax scores well on administration in the context of productivity.

Conclusions about Wealth Basis.   Few taxes have simultaneously embodied all the traits of the property tax. Its positive attributes are weighty. The basis is broad by including real, tangible, and intangible wealth. From a pragmatic perspective, this has been mostly limited to real property, but the yield, stability, elasticity, directness and certainty, and administrative efficiency of the property tax have made it enduring. Its negative attributes, however, have caused it to be much maligned. Probably the major criticism has been the political inability to effectively tax the full scope of wealth, thereby placing a disproportionate burden on real property. In addition, severe problems in valuing property and political machinations have both depressed and skewed the true potential of the wealth tax. Likewise data on equity is mixed, with major deficiencies in the lack of relationship to ability to pay, the absence of overt progressivity, its poor horizontal and vertical equity, and general lack of neutrality. Yet as stated at the outset, yield and equity have been balanced by a real world—a balance that has made the property tax a workhorse, particularly for public schools.

Income.   If wealth has been an important tax base, an equally important basis has been income. In many respects, hierarchical primacy has depended on the particular unit of government being considered. As seen earlier in Table 3.13, property tax has been the mainstay of local units of government, while the income tax has provided the main revenue source for the federal government. In addition, income has been vitally important to states. Like other tax bases, however, income has strengths and weaknesses when evaluated by the criteria of a good tax system.

Basis.   It is obvious to point out that the basis of the income tax is income. The earlier point of distinguishing income from other wealth, however, becomes more obvious when considering the attributes of the income tax. Although all wealth was once income regardless of how it was accrued, income as a basis for taxation is distinct in looking at the change in current position of the taxpayer, usually over the course of one year. Examples of income are wages and salaries, corporate earnings, and investment income. Generally, income is thought of in terms of cash payments related to earnings or investments that come due in a tax year, in contrast to other income such as inheritances usually considered to be wealth.

The basis of income is further distinguished by the structure of income taxes. Unlike all other taxes, the income tax is based on gross and adjusted income, where gross income is the total amount of income before taxes.[22] Adjusted income turns to special tax laws permitting deduction of expenses incurred in deriving income or that promote some government interest. For example, the federal income tax code permits adjustments for such costs as medical expenses, mortgage interest, business expense, and a host of other items that serve social or economic ends. For example, deducting medical expenses is meant to lessen the financial strain of unanticipated illness. Similarly, a social goal is served by home mortgage deduction by diverting otherwise tax payments toward promoting home ownership, and business expense deductions are a recognition of costs in producing income wherein both fairness and economic stimulus are aided by reduced tax liability. Regardless of purpose, these adjustments are subtractions from gross income wherein tax rates apply only after income has been reduced. As such, the unique feature of the income basis is that it sees only current revenues—a feature that ties to other good tax criteria.

Yield.   The enormous yield of the income tax has placed it near the top of all tax structures in productivity. As seen in Table 3.13, the income tax in 1990 generated nearly $690 billion for all units of government, an amount unequaled by any other tax base. Among all three levels of government, income was a vast producer as the federal share was nearly $560.4 billion in individual and corporate income taxes, while the states received more than $118 billion. Although a distant third in tax yield, local units of government still collected almost $11.4 billion.

Yield of the income tax has primarily been a function of three factors. The first factor is analogous to property tax in that property owners cannot avoid taxes in some form. This analogy is especially true in the case of income because tight structures in federal and state income tax codes make it impossible for legitimate income to avoid taxation. This has particularly been the case following adoption of payroll withholding laws requiring periodic remittance of taxes to the government. The second factor relates to the rate and manner in which income is taxed. Income tax rates are sufficiently high to generate great revenue, and the structure of these rates assures that since everyone who works pays income taxes, revenues increase each time income increases. Although there are serious exceptions to this view, stated later under equity evaluation, it has been true that over the course of the twentieth century, incomes have steadily increased, with income taxes at least keeping pace.

The third factor of great yield is that the income tax shows considerable elasticity. Unlike almost all other tax bases, the income tax has historically been structured to accelerate tax receipts faster than growth in income. Success rests in a progressive tax rate scheme wherein higher incomes pay not only more dollars, but also higher percentages on each dollar—a factor that also pushes taxpayers into higher tax brackets as income increases.[23] The federal income tax has been variously progressive with rates reaching nearly 90% around World War II and with states generally following in moderation. In keeping with both tax protest and social agendas, income tax rates have fluctuated over time to where presently three federal tax rates of 15%, 28%, and 31% apply to taxpayers based on marital status. State income tax rates are lower in percentage and more moderate in graduation, but the combination of federal and state income taxes demands significant income tax payments. Although income tax revenues have never been enough to fund all government spending, substantial rates and graduation inherently guarantee elastic and significant revenue. Relatedly, revenue has been stable even under economic stress, mostly due to the smoothing effect of constant payment by a vast work force.

Equity.   If property has been targeted for inequity, the tax revolt history of the United States also stands as evidence of concern about equity in taxing income. People simply do not like taxes, and each type of tax engenders special resistance. For example, property tax is paid in lump sum and thus requires taxpayers to part with large amounts of money at one time. Sales taxes are less obvious by trickling into government coffers, except on big-ticket items like automobiles and appliances. Income tax departs more frequently, but it is highly visible by its regularity, and the annual accounting to the Internal Revenue Service is a hated event. Unlike other taxes, however, there have been many attempts to reform income taxation based on principles of tax fairness. Although success might be debatable, evaluation of the income tax on equity results in a different outcome than for many other taxes.

There can be little doubt that while traces of the benefit principle are evident in income tax structures, the overwhelming order of the system is ability to pay. While some benefit can be construed in that individuals with large incomes still have large amounts of money left after taxes compared to lower income persons who are left with smaller amounts, the progressive structure of the income tax is proof of the ability principle. The current progressive tax rates of 15%, 28%, and 31% argue a theory of declining utility wherein it is presumed that someone with an income taxed at

31% is less needful of each additional dollar that resulted in the higher tax bracket. Inversely, a tax bracket of 15% presumes additional utility to each dollar by which income declines. Further, differentiation by marital status is proof of ability wherein social policy has deemed that more dependents reduces ability to pay. Similarly, the rationale of deductions from gross income is testimony to ability. For example, single taxpayers are allowed a personal deduction of only $3,450, while a joint return can deduct $5,700—however, if itemized deductions are greater than these amounts, taxpayers can choose to list expenses. Similarly, other deductions such as old age or blindness are permitted. The ability principle is clearly evident in Table 3.15. As income tax is the only one that considers ability, on this dimension the income tax is the most equitable tax in the United States.

Performance of income tax on horizontal and vertical equity is also superior. In large part, improved performance stems from interaction between its progressive structure and its inherent strengths on the additional aspect of tax incidence. The

TABLE 3.15   Federal income tax structure, 1991

Single	
Tax Rates	**Bracket**
15%	$0–$20,350
28%	$20,351–49,300
31%	Over $49,300
Married Filing Jointly or Qualifying Widow(er)	
15%	$0–$34,000
28%	$34,001–$82,150
31%	Over $82,150
Married Filing Separately	
15%	$0–$17,000
28%	$17,001–41,075
31%	Over $41,075
Head of Household	
15%	$0–$27,300
28%	$27,301–$70,470
31%	Over $70,470
1991 Basic Standard Deduction	
Single	$3,450
Married filing jointly or widow(er)	$5,700
Married filing separately	$2,850
Head of household	$5,000
1991 Additional Standard Deduction	
Single or head of household, age 65 or over	$850
Single or head of household, age 65 or over and blind	$1,700
Married filing jointly or widow(er), age 65 or over and blind	$650
Married filing jointly or widow(er), age 65 or over and blind per person	$1,300
Married filing separately, age 65 or over or blind	$650

very nature of a tax on income injects horizontal equity simply because tax liability is a mathematical product of a tax rate applied uniformly to income. This simply means that all persons with income will pay taxes, and that the first taxable dollar will be taxed at the same rate for everyone. This is especially appealing in America because it represents equality and is supported by the fact that all tax is paid from income — an inherent weakness to the property tax, for example. But while income tax is innately equitable on a horizontal plane, it can become less equitable as attempts at verticality are applied. This is ironic since the purpose of verticality is to produce equity among unequals. Whether income tax is horizontally equitable thus depends in large part on how vertical equity is managed.

Vertical equity intends to make exception for conditions that cause taxpayers to be unequal. One such condition maintains that a family of four requires more income than a husband and wife to secure equal maintenance. Another scenario expects that medical bills will reduce the level of equality given otherwise identical incomes. Similarly, there is social engineering in policies that permit home interest deductions because it is believed that otherwise excluded people given this indirect tax subsidy will buy houses. Clearly the progressive tax rate plan is an attempt to inject economic justice into capitalist society; indeed, the whole of itemized deductions is a vertical equity scheme that seeks to mitigate income inequality. The balance is delicate, however, and horizontal or vertical equity is easily upset as social or economic engineering is courted. For example, economic stimulation through tax-exempt municipal bonds may reduce both types of equity because the effect is to lower taxable income for wealthy investors by offsetting the progressive rate structure. In the extreme, this "loophole" could allow zero taxes on an income of millions if the income were all from tax-exempt instruments. At the other end, the mortgage interest deduction may not aid either form of equity because very low income persons who cannot afford any mortgage are still excluded.

Attempts at vertical equity may thus enhance or hinder horizontal equity. Although instances of either condition can be posed, the income tax is generally believed to be the most equitable tax on both vertical and horizontal dimensions due to its progressivity and performance on the final criterion of tax incidence. Unlike many taxes, impact and incidence are identical because income cannot be shifted.[24] Similarly, the income tax is viewed by most experts to be reasonably neutral in that wealthy taxpayers remain wealthy even after progressive tax rates are applied, and less wealthy persons pay lower tax rates and lower tax amounts. While the ethical and social merits of progressivity (i.e., liberty versus equality) are contentious among proponents of opposing camps, the dimensions of equity seem fairly well served by the income tax (see data on tax burdens in Table 3.16). The data consistently illustrate a progressive effect where despite loopholes threatening the balance of equity, the wealthiest pay the most while the poorest pay the least.[25] These data argue that top end slippage is not endemic, and that the degree of equity is greater than reformers like to admit.

If the income tax falls short of equity, it is likely in directness and certainty. Directness requires that taxes and purposes not be hidden, while certainty demands that tax amounts should be known in advance. Performance of the income tax is mixed on these dimensions. The tax is clearly not hidden — if anything, it suffers from unfavorable exposure in that people fear and resent its administration. The purpose of income tax, however, is neither always clear nor always clearly favored. At the federal level, the income tax seems removed from daily life and the press agitates resentment

TABLE 3.16   Tax burden by income class, 1985

Income Decile	Effective Individual Income Tax Rate (1985, percentage)
Progressive Assumptions	
Lowest	3.8
Second	3.5
Third	5.2
Fourth	7.4
Fifth	9.2
Sixth	9.9
Seventh	10.9
Eighth	11.9
Ninth	13.3
Highest	13.5
Regressive Assumptions	
Lowest	4.0%
Second	3.4
Third	5.1
Fourth	7.1
Fifth	8.7
Sixth	9.5
Seventh	10.4
Eighth	11.5
Ninth	13.0
Highest	14.5

SOURCE: Joseph Pechman, *Who Paid the Taxes in 1966–86,* rev. ed. (Washington, D.C.: Brookings Institution, 1986).

with exposés of waste and abuse. Additionally, known uses are not always popular among citizens who often perceive others as the beneficiary of federal gratuitousness. At the state level, some similar sentiment is evidenced by tax revolt claims of out-of-touch and grossly bloated government. Likewise, some disfavor accrues to income taxes on the criterion of certainty in that filing federal and state tax returns is a dreaded event that may involve underpayment of taxes. Although equitable on many fronts, the income tax is a pale performer in the arena of directness and certainty.

Administration.   The tremendous yield and entrenched nature of the income tax gives clear indication that success on the criterion of administration is assured. Although bad press about tax evasion abounds, compliance is quite high in that most salaried workers are subject to involuntary withholding tax. Compliance is also high due to rapid growth in sophistication of electronic reporting—for example, banks must report not only interest earnings to the government but also deposits above $2,500. The cost of administration is at once high and minimal. On one hand, costs are high because the complexity of both federal and state income tax codes supports an entire industry of accounting and tax services. On the other hand, costs are low from an efficiency view because yield is so vast that the cost of compliance and administration is negligible. From a simple profit perspective, administration is quite efficient unless one also considers the underground economy of unreported income widely believed to exist. Although costs have recently increased in keeping abreast of the tax reform that has become almost an annual recurrence, the income tax represents an administratively efficient and effective tax base.

Conclusions about Income Basis.   Like property, few taxes have yielded the enormous revenue of the income tax. At the same time, income has many positive attributes lacking in other taxes. The basis of income is ultimately logical in that income is the source of all tax payments. As government has grown, income tax yield has been phenomenal and its progressive structure has produced a high degree of elasticity. Likewise, its progressivity has produced evidence of fairness by tax theory standards, including sensitivity to horizontal and vertical equity due to its focus on ability to pay. Similarly, it has been made administratively efficient by payroll withholding and severe laws on evasion. Its negative attributes, however, have caused it to be maligned. Probably the major criticism has been the political unpopularity of a progressive tax exacerbated by common perception of loopholes. Likewise, disconnectedness of citizens from government and questions about the validity of aggressive income redistribution have yielded negative consequences. Importantly, domination of the income tax by federal and state governments has resulted in only secondary benefit to schools in that school participation in the income basis has only been through state aid derived from the income tax. As a result, income as a revenue base for education has been greatly underutilized.

Consumption.   If property and income have been primary, an almost equally important tax basis has been *consumption.* Like the other two taxes, the role of consumption in hierarchical order of importance has depended largely on the unit of government being considered. As seen in Table 3.13, property taxes have been the mainstay of local government, while income tax has provided a major revenue source for both federal and state governments. At the state level, however, consumption taxes have served as *the* single most important tax base. Like other tax bases, however, consumption has strengths and weaknesses when evaluated by the criteria of a good tax system.

Basis.   The basis of a consumption tax is sales. Several types of consumption taxes were mentioned earlier in this chapter. These taxes run a full range in scope and nature and are levied in some form by all three levels of government. For example, federal efforts to raise revenue by excise taxes and duties are actually consumption taxes. Similarly, all forms of general sales tax are consumption-based and are levied by almost all states and by many local governments throughout the nation. Although the form of a consumption tax depends on what goods or services are taxed, all consumption taxes fall into the category of either general sales tax or excise tax. The difference rests in selectiveness of the tax. The general rule is that when tax is broadly levied against objects or services it is a sales tax, while a tax only on specific items such as tires or alcohol is an excise tax. Under these conditions, it is important to note that a lottery is an excise tax levied and collected by the state. Similarly, severance taxes are a form of excise tax.[26]

The specific basis of a tax within the general concept of consumption is a function of choices made by policymakers at a given level of government. The federal government presently levies no general sales tax, but its historic reliance on excise taxes and customs duties has continued into the present. Likewise, state and local governments charge no customs duties, but states have chosen to seize control of general sales and some excise taxes. Local units of government have obviously had less choice in that higher governments have dominated some tax bases, leaving local units mostly dependent on the property tax. Whether a unit of government can levy a particular tax, however, is a function of political decisions within constitutional or statutory provisions. At the federal level, Congress has refused to adopt a general sales tax. This has proved crucial because it has left states as next heir to seize this tax base. As seen in Table 3.17, states have so aggressively pursued consumption taxes that 45 states and the District of Columbia now levy a sales tax. Many states, however, also allow local governments access to sales tax as an add-on. As a result, significant consumption taxes are paid at all three levels via excise or general sales taxes.

Yield.   As seen earlier, consumption taxes make up a large revenue source at all three levels of government. Table 3.13 showed heavy federal reliance on income taxes, but it also showed federal revenues of more than $53.9 billion in sales and gross receipts. These revenues were obviously excise taxes because no general federal sales

TABLE 3.17   General sales tax rate, 1990

State	Percentage	State	Percentage
Alabama	4	Nebraska	5
Alaska	None	Nevada	5.75–6
Arizona	5	New Hampshire	None
Arkansas	4	New Jersey	7
California	6–7	New Mexico	5–6.75
Colorado	3	New York	4–8.25
Connecticut	8	North Carolina	5
Delaware	None	North Dakota	5–6
Florida	6	Ohio	5
Georgia	4	Oklahoma	4
Hawaii	4	Oregon	None
Idaho	5	Pennsylvania	6
Illinois	6.25	Rhode Island	7
Indiana	5	South Carolina	5
Iowa	4	South Dakota	4
Kansas	6.25 maximum	Tennessee	5.5
Kentucky	6	Texas	6
Louisiana	6	Utah	6.25
Maine	4	Vermont	5
Maryland	5	Virginia	4.5
Massachusetts	5	Washington	6.5
Michigan	4	West Virginia	6
Minnesota	7.25	Wisconsin	5
Mississippi	6	Wyoming	3
Missouri	4.225	District of Columbia	6
Montana	None		

SOURCE: *The World Almanac and Book of Facts, 1992.* (New York: Pharos Books, 1992), 626–651.

tax exists. At the state level, consumption taxes were enormous, as states collected more than $147 billion in sales and gross receipts and another $47.4 billion in selective sales taxes. These sums made consumption the biggest state revenue producer, proving state domination of the consumption basis. Still other consumption taxes were collected, however, as sales taxes are often significant add-ons at the local level. Local governments collected more than $30.8 billion in consumption taxes in 1990, with approximately $21.6 billion in general sales tax and about $9.2 billion in excise taxes. The sum of consumption at all levels was more than $231.8 billion, a sum clearly assigning a major role to consumption.

The large yield of consumption basis is a function of four factors. First, general sales tax is levied by most states against most items sold. This in itself guarantees that as long as sales occur, revenue will flow. Second, general sales tax is levied aggressively. As seen in Table 3.17, state sales tax rates range from a low 3% to a high 8.25% for an average of 4.8%. This does *not* include local add-ons or excise taxes. Third, the general sales tax base is broad by including most sales. The only exceptions in most states are prescription drugs, real estate, and rent—a small majority also do not tax food or utilities. Other exemptions are less uniform. For example, several states tax retail sales but exempt professional services, while excise taxes steeply target some items, such as, alcohol, tobacco, and motor fuel. Fourth, general sales tax has proved somewhat elastic because sales tax revenue has grown faster than income. The reasons are debatable. One view argues that growth has been caused by tax rate increases, another, that taxing staples (given inflation) causes revenue growth regardless of income; and a third, that elasticity of unity exists because consumer behavior mirrors income—a factor also arguing tax base instability as inherent to consumption. On the whole, however, revenue is large mostly due to aggressive consumption taxation.

Equity.   Performance of consumption taxes on equity standards is more mixed than is true for either wealth or income. This is mostly true because the inherent nature of consumption taxes has been the target of more intervention policies that impact its eventual performance.

Modern equity principles prefer a tax based on ability. Examination reveals that consumption, however, more closely adheres to the benefit principle and tends to reject ability to pay. For example, there is no link between the income of a consumer and the amount of tax on the sale of a commodity because both general sales and excise taxes apply equally to any purchase. As a result, it is easy to see that consumption taxes likely violate several equity requirements related to ability. First, horizontal equity seems unlikely in that two consumers of equal income can be affected differently. For example, it was seen earlier that finding two persons of identical income is difficult enough—adding the element of consumer preference, however, could make radical differences, as when two people earning $50,000 may choose to buy a Ford and a Porsche, respectively. In the first instance, sales tax at 4% might be $800, while in the second instance it might exceed $2,800. Each person's tax liability and contribution to tax yield thus reflect a 7:1 differential. Consequently, horizontal equity is not met in that the tax burden of each person is unequal, self-determined, and variable in yield.

Second, vertical equity also seems endangered by a consumption tax in that low-income persons automatically spend more of their incomes in sales taxes. Although it can be argued that consumption is a voluntary tax, for low incomes this is less true.

For example, there might be some merit in seeing voluntarism in choices about Fords and Porsches. There is no merit, however, to voluntarism in beans versus steak or unreliable transportation versus luxury cars. Everyone must eat, and almost everyone must have transportation to earn an income. In these instances, sales tax on food or an old Ford will both be larger proportions of a lower income. These arguments are well supported by data on whether consumption taxes are progressive, regressive, or proportional. As seen in Table 3.18, the burden of consumption taxes on the lowest income class ranges from about 7% of income to only 1.9% for the highest income group. It is also notable that the degree of regressivity to all classes is perfectly linear. As a result, neither horizontal nor vertical equity is well satisfied by the consumption basis.

These realities also apply to the third equity consideration of tax incidence. Determining tax impact is easy because collection falls to retail merchants. It is entirely unreasonable, however, to believe that incidence also falls to the merchant. Under retail conditions it is said that the tax is shifted forward to the consumer—in which case one must immediately return to the difficult issues of horizontal and vertical equity. The nature of a consumption tax is such that tax incidence always falls to the

TABLE 3.18 Consumption of tax burden by income class, 1985

Income Decile	Tax as Income Proportion (1985, percentage)
Progressive Assumptions	
Lowest	7.0
Second	5.9
Third	5.0
Fourth	4.6
Fifth	4.3
Sixth	4.1
Seventh	3.9
Eighth	3.7
Ninth	3.3
Highest	1.9
Regressive Assumptions	
Lowest	7.2
Second	5.7
Third	4.9
Fourth	4.6
Fifth	4.2
Sixth	4.0
Seventh	3.8
Eighth	3.7
Ninth	3.2
Highest	1.9

SOURCE: Joseph Pechman, *Who Paid the Taxes in 1966–86,* rev. ed. (Washington, D.C.: Brookings Institution, 1986).

consumer because it is useless to shift the tax backward. If this were even possible, it would only have the effect of increasing wholesale prices wherein the supplier would simply shift the tax forward to the merchant, who in turn would shift it forward again to the consumer. Tax incidence thus undergirds regressivity of consumption by laying the tax on persons who are unequal in ability to pay.

The equity condition of neutrality argues that consumption taxes should have no effect on consumer behavior. The reality of consumption, however, is that neutrality is at once observed and violated. Neutrality is supportable in that it can be shown that many items will be purchased regardless of changes in tax rate or incidence on in-come class—for example, tobacco and liquor are unaffected. On the other hand, con-sumption tax rates and changes in income can severely affect consumer behavior. For example, income changes affect borrowing for big items like cars or appliances. If income drops, a buyer might not qualify for a loan, thus negatively impacting dealer sales and tax revenues. Equally valid is the view that income drives consumer deci-sions wherein sagging income causes consumers to wait. Even without income varia-bles, sales tax rates can affect consumer behavior because add-on local sales taxes can greatly impact the price of expensive items. For example, consumers can be expected to shop wisely when buying a $20,000 car in a state with a 4% sales tax rate if one dealer must also collect an added 3% local sales tax, compared to a more distant dealer with no local tax. In sum, such examples make the consumption tax a poor performer on the criterion of neutrality.

The final equity conditions of directness and certainty are better satisfied by con-sumption taxes. The sales tax is highly visible, and there are no signals that any aspect of the sales tax is hidden. Directness is only harmed in that consumer choices may follow the reality that taxes vary by location; alternatively, resentment may be engen-dered if citizens learn about tax rate differences only after a purchase is already made. Excise taxes may be a bit less direct in that they are often built into the price—for example, large taxes are included in gasoline prices. Certainty is more mediocre in that like many taxes, the use of the tax is unclear—on the other hand, the tax is expected.

Administration. Administration of consumption taxes is probably the greatest strength of this tax base. Unlike other taxes, no taxpayer effort is needed since these taxes are collected and remitted by the merchant. In administrative terms, this is par-ticularly beneficial to cost, compliance, and efficiency. Costs are reduced because collection is assured at the point of sale and no individual taxpayer accounting as with income tax is required—the effect is to reduce the number of actual taxpayers to only the number of merchants collecting the tax. No great cost is involved in calculating the tax, since cash registers compute the tax and can also provide a monthly total to the merchant who then remits that amount. The efficiency of the tax is aided by all the foregoing, and has an added benefit in that consumption taxes represent a con-stant stream of revenue that impacts taxpayers almost imperceptibly. As a result, con-sumption scores well on this criterion and generally meets greater tolerance by tax-payers who fail to recognize the accumulation of total sales taxes.

Conclusions about Consumption Basis. The tremendous yield of the consump-tion tax is generally exceeded only by wealth and income taxes. Yet despite its enor-mous yield, the consumption tax has long been frowned upon by critics who see it as highly regressive. Regressivity is undeniably innate to consumption, but declaring consumption taxes to be totally regressive and inequitable is not entirely accurate in that artificial subventions such as exemptions for food, medical services, and so forth restore some vertical equity to an otherwise poor performer. Performance of consumption on all other elements of equity, however, is poor. Yet like the property tax, equity and yield have been set against each other in an imperfect real world. Under these conditions, yield has triumphed over equity as consumption taxes presently represent a formidable basis for tax revenues—a basis that has indirectly supplied much revenue to schools, as state aid is paid from state budgets that are often heavily funded by sales taxes.

Privilege.   Property, income, and consumption have thus been primary tax bases, but they are not the sum of all taxes levied by governments. Although much smaller in proportion, various units of government have also collected revenues on the basis of *privilege*. A few of these taxes were included earlier in Table 3.13 where the sources of revenue for federal, state, and local governments were identified. Data on privilege taxes are quite sparse, but the existence of the privilege tax requires some comment because it represents the final basis of taxation. Like other taxes, the privilege tax has both strengths and weaknesses that deserve brief comment.

Basis and Yield.   Privilege taxes are well named in that they are taxes levied against persons who engage in a select group of pursuits. As such, privilege taxes are essentially a form of excise tax wherein government has decided that regulation of an activity is in the public interest. As a general rule, privilege taxes are most often levied as license fees. For example, licenses to engage in business or licenses for operating a motor vehicle all fit the definition of a privilege tax. Still other privilege taxes are levied in the form of user fees for parks, dog tags, and vehicle license plates. Most often these taxes are defended as the cost of regulating a public interest. For example, it is difficult to argue that no regulation is needed in determining whether lawyers and doctors and educators are qualified to engage in practice. Similarly, dog tags prevent spread of rabies through vaccination as a prerequisite to licensure, and the rules of business licenses can discourage dishonorable firms from engaging in bad business practices. It is also noteworthy that these taxes are paid voluntarily in that there is no requirement to engage in any activity demanding such tax.

The fact that privilege taxes do not yield revenue at the same rate as other tax bases should not be taken as an indication that privilege is unimportant to any of the three levels of government. The federal government's role in excise taxes can be seen as a very productive privilege tax. Likewise, there is significant federal activity in this arena when federal lands are involved. For example, commercial rights to public lands are sometimes sold for large fees in return for permitting a commercial venture. Recent rulings on mining in national parks and the timber industry's activities on federal lands are examples of commercial ventures. Similarly, selling grazing rights to national grasslands is common federal practice, as is the sale of franchises. State governments also levy productive privilege taxes, but local governments collect only modest revenues. Although the privilege basis is much smaller than other bases, it represents the final means by which governments can levy direct taxes.

Although tax analysts are correct in ranking privilege last as a tax source, the amount of money raised is not insignificant and generally far exceeds the cost of administration. Although lack of sophistication and lack of agreement on the full scope and definition of privilege taxes prevent accurate totals, governments collect a fair amount of revenue by taxing privileges, as shown in Table 3.13. For example, using only the category of motor vehicle and operators' licenses, state revenues in 1990 exceeded $10.6 billion, and local revenues were $769 million. If fuller data were available, it is likely that these sums would be greatly increased.

Other Criteria and Conclusions about Privilege Basis   It is difficult to evaluate the privilege tax beyond describing its basis and noting its yield. For example, little extensive development can be made about yield in the context of elasticity and stability. This is true because the voluntary nature and low impact of the privilege tax on the vast majority of citizens prevent these criteria from having much importance. No real effort to assess the elasticity of the privilege tax is apparent, and stability can be reasonably presumed because businesses in fiscal exigency are pressed by concerns such as low sales or high property taxes and generally do not cease operation because of privilege taxes. Similarly, other conditions of equity are basically nonapplicable or functionally absurd—for example, any effort to make privilege taxes adhere to vertical equity would not only be administratively impossible, but would also result in a nuisance tax wherein yield would be counterproductive. As a result, it is more helpful to note that privilege taxes serve a useful regulatory role that fortunately yields revenue in excess of the costs of regulation. To expect more of this tax base is as counterproductive as assessing its nature at great length, particularly as it provides no known revenue for schools.

TAX SYSTEM APPLICATION TO SCHOOLS

It should not be assumed that because schools have been restricted to only a few revenue sources that examination of the various tax systems is unimportant. On the contrary, the narrow tax base of schools heightens the need to be informed about the history of taxation in the United States because it can be seen that school revenue systems have not been engendered vacuously. There is wisdom to be gained from historical perspective, and the recent cries for a broader tax base for education can be better addressed when it is recognized that Americans themselves have created the present system and must be willing to break free of their own deeds if improvement is to occur. In other words, it is as important to understand why some tax is not accessible to schools as it is to understand the limitations of the property tax for the support of schools. In sum, history has made the nation what it is—a reality that expects several final observations.

First, there should be no doubt that taxes have held an unquestioned tyranny of the mind in the United States. The history of tax rebellion is legendary and unequaled in sophistication. Similarly, the adamancy of Americans on the topic of taxation clearly indicates that the nation keeps a watchful eye on its policymakers because it is naturally suspicious and preoccupied with fairness. this has been particularly evident in that although the nation is more than 200 years old, its tax systems have become productive only within the present century. Although Americans have finally shown resignation to taxes as an unwelcome responsibility, they are ever vigilant and jealous in guarding against abuses and unfairness.

Second, it should be recognized that the revenue collected by the many units of government has been enormous. The combined total of revenues now exceeds $2 trillion, and it can be seen from the data in this chapter that revenues have been substantial for every level of government. Equally staggering, however, is the number of governmental units that collect these revenues. Table 3.19 shows that in 1987

TABLE 3.19 Number of local governments, 1982 and 1987

State	1982			1987					Special District Governments			
	All Local Governmental Units[1]	School District Governments	Special District Governments	All Local Governmental Units	County Governments[2]	Municipal Governments[2]	Township Governments[2]	School District Governments	Total[1]	Natural Resources	Fire Protection	Housing and Community Development
United States	81,780	14,851	28,078	83,186	3,042	19,200	16,691	14,721	29,532	6,360	5,070	3,464
Alabama	1,018	127	390	1,053	67	436	—	129	421	69	4	156
Alaska	156	—	6	172	9	149	—	—	14	—	—	13
Arizona	452	232	130	576	15	81	—	227	253	82	116	13
Arkansas	1,424	372	505	1,396	75	483	—	333	505	245	33	130
California	4,102	1,111	2,506	4,331	57	442	—	1,098	2,734	521	389	93
Colorado	1,544	185	1,030	1,593	62	266	—	180	1,085	188	213	56
Connecticut	479	16	281	477	—	31	149	16	281	1	55	91
Delaware	217	19	139	281	3	57	—	19	202	197	—	3
District of Columbia	2	—	1	2	—	1	—	—	1	—	—	—
Florida	969	95	417	965	66	390	—	95	414	133	48	98
Georgia	1,268	187	390	1,286	158	532	—	186	410	28	6	208
Hawaii	18	—	14	18	3	1	—	—	14	14	—	—
Idaho	1,018	117	659	1,065	44	198	—	118	705	169	119	13
Illinois	6,467	1,049	2,602	6,627	102	1,279	1,434	1,029	2,783	913	801	114
Indiana	2,865	305	897	2,806	91	567	1,008	304	836	129	—	45
Iowa	1,871	456	361	1,877	99	955	—	451	372	234	69	15
Kansas	3,795	326	1,370	3,803	105	627	1,360	324	1,387	271	—	101
Kentucky	1,241	180	517	1,303	119	437	—	178	569	127	85	24
Louisiana	468	66	39	452	61	301	—	66	24	2	—	—
Maine	806	98	195	800	16	22	471	88	203	13	—	28
Maryland	439	—	264	401	23	155	—	—	223	165	—	20
Massachusetts	798	81	354	836	12	39	312	82	391	16	20	249
Michigan	2,643	599	184	2,699	83	534	1,242	590	250	85	1	—
Minnesota	3,529	436	356	3,555	87	855	1,798	441	374	119	—	169
Mississippi	858	169	315	853	82	293	—	171	307	227	—	59
Missouri	3,117	557	1,195	3,147	114	930	325	561	1,217	155	145	172
Montana	1,029	399	450	1,243	54	128	—	547	514	117	128	18
Nebraska	3,324	1,069	1,157	3,152	93	534	454	952	1,119	110	427	134

(Continued)

TABLE 3.19 (*Continued*)

State	1982 All Local Governmental Units[1]	1982 School District Governments	1982 Special District Governments	1987 All Local Governmental Units	1987 County Governments[2]	1987 Municipal Governments[2]	1987 Township Governments[2]	1987 School District Governments	1987 Special District Governments Total[1]	Natural Resources	Fire Protection	Housing and Community Development
Nevada	184	17	134	197	16	18	—	17	146	29	15	14
New Hampshire	517	160	113	524	10	13	221	160	120	9	15	22
New Jersey	1,591	548	454	1,625	21	320	247	551	486	16	172	84
New Mexico	319	89	101	331	33	98	—	88	112	73	—	7
New York	3,249	726	923	3,302	57	618	929	720	978	2	898	—
North Carolina	905	—	321	916	100	495	—	—	321	142	1	108
North Dakota	2,795	325	692	2,787	53	366	1,355	310	703	83	279	34
Ohio	3,393	669	377	3,377	88	940	1,318	621	410	100	30	55
Oklahoma	1,702	638	406	1,802	77	591	—	636	498	110	17	119
Oregon	1,454	352	825	1,502	36	240	—	350	876	213	270	23
Pennsylvania	5,198	514	2,050	4,956	66	1,022	1,548	515	1,805	5	1	88
Rhode Island	122	3	80	125	—	8	31	3	83	3	39	26
South Carolina	645	92	242	707	46	269	—	92	300	46	86	43
South Dakota	1,767	196	199	1,762	64	309	984	193	212	102	31	38
Tennessee	913	15	469	904	94	334	—	14	462	124	—	94
Texas	4,180	1,124	1,681	4,415	254	1,156	—	1,113	1,892	399	70	396
Utah	504	40	211	530	29	225	—	40	236	71	13	11
Vermont	664	273	83	673	14	55	237	272	95	20	19	9
Virginia	407	—	83	430	95	229	—	—	106	43	—	—
Washington	1,734	300	1,130	1,779	39	266	—	297	1,177	161	411	48
West Virginia	633	55	292	630	55	230	—	55	290	15	—	32
Wisconsin	2,592	408	263	2,719	72	580	1,268	433	366	150	—	204
Wyoming	395	56	225	424	23	95	—	56	250	114	44	—

— Represents zero.

[1] Includes other types of governments not shown separately.

[2] Includes "town" governments in the six New England states and in Minnesota, New York, and Wisconsin.

SOURCE: U.S. Department of Commerce, Bureau of the Census, *Statistical Abstracts of the U.S. 1992* (Washington, D.C.: U.S. Government Printing Office, 1992), 296.

there were 83,186 *local* units of government, a total that includes school districts but does not include the various states or the federal government or other special district governments. The combined total makes government truly vast, but it is vitally important to recognize that these thousands of governmental units must turn to only four tax bases for financial survival. The criticalness of these points is astounding when it is remembered that these governments do not enjoy equal support from each tax base. The federal government depends almost exclusively on income and selective excises, while states depend on general sales and income; local units, however, depend almost entirely on the property tax.

Finally, these realities have compounded the many problems of schools. Government has many roles, and education is only one responsibility. Although educators rightly cannot be convinced that education is not the most important role, it is important to understand that government could not correct every problem even if revenues were unlimited. Because choices must be made, governments have chosen to delegate responsibilities—a reality that has caused education to be funded at the local level first. Local taxpayers, however, have been strained beyond their willingness in many instances, and it has been the property tax that has absorbed both the load and resentment. The system has not worked well, with the result being that schools have had to look outside the local community for assistance. The development of education in the United States, however, has denied turning to the federal government, leaving only the state as a final recourse. Therefore, we turn to the state in Chapter 4 to examine how state aid formulas have been developed to fill a void in revenue systems for public schools.

Review Points

SYSTEMS OF TAXATION

Although democracy is based on willing consent of the governed, taxes are not welcomed, making it necessary to implement mandatory taxation to conduct the affairs of society.

Tax systems have become pervasive in modern society, with multiple overlapping levels among various units of government that provide a host of visible and background services.

The American tax system's multiple layers are a function of parallel development of local, state, and federal governments.

Taxation can be traced to the earliest colonial days, with dislike for taxes predating the birth of the nation.

The nation's preoccupation with tax resistance is evident at every turn, as tax rebellions formed a national identity that has powerfully impeded government growth until very recently.

The federal tax system has developed only recently, after a series of lame attempts spanning more than a century.

State tax systems are, in part, a response to resistance to federal taxation, in that states have encountered less resistance to inventing and levying new taxes.

American tax systems in the various states often reflect state and local economies.

While vigorously protested, local taxes have been more palatable to citizens because their use is more visible and believed to be of more local benefit.

Parallel federal/state/local tax system development has resulted in abandonment of tax bases to each unit of government, with each level significantly dependent on only a few tax bases.

EVALUATING TAX SYSTEMS

Good tax systems demonstrate many qualities, among which the most important are broad basis, adequate yield, sensitivity to equity, appropriate incidence, and efficient administration.

The four principal bases of taxation are wealth, income, consumption, and privilege.

As government has grown, demand for revenue has severely pressed the capacity of tax bases. The result has been increased concern for assuring that tax systems are based in the benefit principle when appropriate, and that other taxes are sensitive to ability to pay. This has created much concern about the progressivity of taxes and about other equity characteristics.

Heavy dependence by local governments on the property tax has resulted in massive revenues, complex administration, and complaints about imbalance in who pays for government. While the property tax cannot be abandoned because of its tremendous yield, it presents serious equity concerns as presently structured.

Heavy dependence by state and (to some extent) local governments on consumption taxes also results in massive revenues, but with fewer administrative problems. Equity, however, is complex and disputatious, depending on the advocate's or the critic's point of view.

Similar federal and state dependence on income taxes effectively denies this tax to local government. Income, however, is thought to be the most equitable because of its innate ability-to-pay characteristics and by its present progressive structure.

Privilege taxes produce considerable revenue, but the nature of this tax prevents wide-scale application as a primary tax base for government services.

TAX SYSTEM APPLICATION TO SCHOOLS

As schools have historically received the bulk of revenues from local tax sources, they have been primarily dependent on the property tax.

As tax systems at all levels almost never produce sufficient revenue to meet demands, schools have increasingly had funding problems.

Because local property tax bases have been both inadequate and widely variable in tax capacity, schools have had to increasingly rely on state aid.

Case Study

You have recently been appointed as a new principal in your school district after having taught in the system for several years. Shortly after you were hired, the superintendent explained to you that part of your responsibility is to attend board of education meetings and to work with various committees that are seeking to draw patrons into a more active understanding of the issues and problems facing schools. At last month's board meeting, it was decided that the district should become actively involved with the legislature's plans to revise state aid to schools during the upcoming session. To initiate this activity, the board appointed a committee of three board members, one administrator, eight lay citizens, and one area legislator who agreed to sit in on the committee's deliberations. On the following day, your superintendent assigned you to serve as the committee's chair.

After organizing a schedule, you called the first meeting of the committee, which decided that its first task was to educate itself about school finance generally and about how schools in the state are funded. While the group was not particularly knowledgeable about school finance, a major interest was expressed in knowing more about how schools could be financed differently. As chair, the group asked you to devote the next scheduled meeting to exploring three specific topics: the sources and amounts of revenue available to schools in your state, the revenue sources used to fund schools in other states, and an evaluation of the strengths and weaknesses of the various revenue sources that could be available. The group also requested that you take the initiative in drafting a proposal of an alternative funding plan.

Using the following sets of questions to help guide your deliberations and class discussions, what information do you think you will present to the committee?

Directed Discussion Questions

1. As you prepare your thoughts on organizing for the tasks at hand, what do you perceive your task to be? What types of information will you need to respond to each of the three major areas of study? Where do you think you should turn for information? Assuming that this case study applies to you in the state where you now live, what organizations are likely candidates to assist you? What data systems do these organizations maintain? What types of technical assistance from these organizations are available for your research? What other questions should you ask to intelligently respond to your committee's needs? How will you distill all this information into a format usable and nonthreatening to your lay audience?

2. This committee has expressed a fairly avid interest in school finance in other states. In your opinion, is it a worthwhile activity? What can be gained from such research and information? Conversely, what potential drawbacks or logical extensions do you see from this behavior? Based on the information in this chapter, what data do you expect to find on revenue sources and amounts in other states? Assuming your professor asks you to prepare some comparative analysis of tax bases and revenues between your own and other states, what generalizations from your research could you usefully present to this committee?

3. Based on what you learned in this chapter and your own research in preparing to meet with this committee, how will you respond to the task of evaluating the strengths and weaknesses of potential tax bases? What assessment of your own state will you present? As you judge your state in comparison to other states' tax structures, what is the outcome?

4. Inasmuch as your task is to present a tentative school tax scheme to this committee, what tax sources would you recommend, assuming you could design the perfect system? What logic and empirical knowledge will you use to justify your choices? How similar (or different) is your proposed scheme from the present tax mix in your state? Are there states which you think represent a better tax system design? If your proposed plan is similar to reality in your state, what fine-tuning would you do to make it even better? If your plan is significantly different from your state's present system, what political or economic problems would you reasonably anticipate if this commitee lobbies for adoption? What tax system modifications have been previously proposed in your state, and what was the outcome? If your plan is meaningfully different, why do you think a similar plan has not been accepted by the legislature? What weaknesses do you see in your own plan?

5. Finally, as you contemplate the broad and diverse makeup of your committee, how will you coalesce these interests into a consensus? What common ground do you think the group shares? What do you anticipate will be the potentially large hurdles? How do you read the sociopolitical makeup of the group? What special interests exist, and what will their reactions be to your proposed tax plan? Generally, what is your role, and what must you do or not do to carry out your assigned task successfully?

NOTES

1. Carolyn Webber and Aaron Wildavsky, *A History of Taxation and Expenditure in the Western World* (New York: Simon & Shuster, 1986), 333.

2. In an effort to reduce smuggling to avoid taxes, the English government cut the duty owed on molasses to less than the bribe needed to carry on this illicit activity. The logic was to cut the duty in half and still increase tax revenues by bringing smuggled goods into the legal tax channel. The result, however, was to simply adjust the market and at the same time invoke great ire.

3. An act requiring all commercial and legal documents and newspapers to display a stamp purchased through payment of a tax.

4. A tax imposed on American imports of glass, lead, paper, paint, and tea. The proceeds were to be used to pay for English expenses incurred in reducing British land taxes by 25%.

5. In Nathan Matthews, *The Proposed Amendment to the State Constitution; Shall the word "proportional" be eliminated from the Clause which restricts the Power of the Legislature in the Matter of Taxation to the Imposition of "proportional and reasonable Assessments, Rates, and Taxes"? Argument for the Remonstrants* (Boston: Little, Brown, November 1909), 25.

6. This discussion is not to imply that the federal government has had no revenues or has levied no taxes. For example, the first tariff act was adopted shortly after the War of Independence when in 1789 a duty tax of 5%–15% was levied on more than 80 manufactured

articles imported into the United States. Generally, it may be stated that federal revenues were limited almost exclusively to excise and customs taxes. It is to imply, however, that such taxes have been extremely narrow compared to the modern conception of a broad tax base—a comparison that is also meant to define the income tax as a singular and narrow conception of tax base.

7. Lesser reforms have been the hallmark of continual flux in federal taxation. For example, such reforms were evident in repeated amendments to the tax code in 1921, 1924, 1926, 1928, and 1929. Similarly, renewed efforts to reduce the federal tax brackets occurred in 1964, 1971, 1975, and 1981. The 1981 amendment marked the path leading to the 1986 Tax Reform Act by significantly reducing long-term decrease of 23%. Even the 1986 Tax Reform Act has again been amended, reducing the top rate to 31%, confirming the continual state of change that marks American tax systems. For further development on these topics, see generally Webber and Wildavsky, *A History of Taxation.*

8. The only exceptions were in 1960 and 1969 when revenues exceeded outlays by 0.03% and 3.2%, respectively.

9. For example, the relationship of the Church of England to colonists in Virginia quickly led to taxation for the church, as in 1632 when the legislature passed an act compelling each settler to annually give the church a tithe from crops and herds. Church control was even stronger in some colonies, as in Massachusetts and Connecticut where the Puritan Church operated an ecclesiastical monopoly.

10. Webber and Wildavsky, *A History of Taxation,* 361–363.

11. John Locke, *The Second Treatise on Government* (Indianapolis: Bobbs-Merrill, 1952), 17.

12. Ibid., 79.

13. Ibid., 80.

14. Adam Smith, *An Inquiry into the Nature and Causes of the Wealth of Nations* (New York: Modern Library, 1937), 816.

15. Thomas Jefferson, "First Annual Message," December 8, 1801, in *A Compilation of the Messages and Papers of the Presidents 1789–1897,* vol. 1, ed. James D. Richardson (Washington, D.C.: Government Printing Office, 1896), 328–329.

16. Joseph Blau, *Social Theories of Jacksonian Democracy,* American Heritage series (New York: Liberal Arts Press, 1954), 9.

17. B. U. Ratchford, *American State Debts* (New York: AMS Press, 1966), 121–122.

18. The problem is to arrive at an accurate estimate of the value of an item—a complex task beyond the scope of this book. It is important to note, however, that administrators should be vitally interested in tangible property valuation, as businesses are often major school tax contributors.

19. Valuing other types of real property can be problematic. For example, vacant lots have no utility until sold and are often appraised too high in relation to their present value. Similarly, appraising businesses is complex in that property valuation generally does not lend itself to the unique nature of the business enterprise or take into account that such properties may not sell often enough to provide good market-comparables. Because valuation is so complex and because the vast majority of schools' tax interaction is with properties under private ownership such as homes, the example here focuses for greater simplicity on home ownership.

20. Property assessment in some states is further complicated by classification of property that taxes different types of property at different rates. For example, residential property might be assessed at 12% of market value, agricultural land at 30% of use value, and commercial properties at 30%.

21. In the case of renters or businesses, this is obviously true as discussed earlier. In the case of homeowners, there is often an assumption that no shifting can occur. This is likely not true, however, as property taxes can be deducted from federal and state tax liabilities. Since

federal and state tax rates are progressively indexed, the value of property tax deduction is not equal in that each dollar deducted at a higher tax bracket represents a greater savings.

22. This discussion is in broad generalities to understand overall concepts. This text is not concerned with distinctions such as adjustments to business properties that allow for deducting upkeep and repairs that can be equated to gross and adjusted basis.

23. Although historically true, President Reagan was successful in persuading Congress to index tax brackets to inflation to prevent bracket creep. Indexation was put into effect in 1985 and had the effect of canceling out the rate of inflation so that a higher income would not actually result in less after-tax income because of a higher tax rate coupled with less purchasing power. The effect depends on one's point of view, with critics of indexation pointing to lost opportunity to expand spending for social and economic programs, and with proponents arguing that indexation will work to restore the economy and reduce tax inflation.

24. Some critics could take broad exception because there are provisions in the tax code for gifts. The point here is not to argue the finer nuances. In this instance, it is still maintained that such income is not shifted in the traditional meaning of shifting tax payments to others while retaining the object, for the gift is truly no longer of financial benefit to the giver (short of fraudulent gifts—that, however, is a criminal matter).

25. It is notable that this conclusion holds true under both progressive and regressive assumptions, with only one deviation from perfect ascending order by income. At the same time, it is important to note that the deviation occurs at the poorest level where the lowest decile pays slightly more income tax than the second. This glitch in an otherwise perfect ordering deserves further consideration to determine whether it is primarily a flaw in the tax structure that needs correction to prevent inequity to the most poor, or if other explanations are possible (e.g., whether intergovernmental transfer payments to the nation's poorest could ironically cause a regressive pattern that negatively affects the second decile).

26. It should be noted that an additional type of consumption tax, not discussed, is the *sumptuary* tax whose purpose is to discourage some activity generally believed to be undesirable—for example, illicit or immoral behavior such as drinking, smoking, and gambling. In most instances, however, these have more recently been considered consumption taxes, a difference based partially on semantics, partially on reality. Sumptuary taxes were designed to discourage a behavior; generally, such discouragement has been ineffective. In addition, it is ironic that if such a tax is successful, its yield becomes merely annoying. Conversely, if it fails to suppress behavior, its purpose has been frustrated. Consequently, considering these taxes merely consumption taxes is as meaningful as giving them separate treatment in the modern context.

ADDITIONAL READINGS

Aaron, Henry J. *Who Pays the Property Tax? A New View*. Washington, D.C.: Brookings Institution, 1975.

Break, George. *Financing Government in a Federal System*. Washington, D.C.: Brookings Institution, 1980.

Due, John F. *Sales Taxation*. Urbana: University of Illinois Press, 1957.

Gold, Steven. *Property Tax Relief*. Lexington, Mass.: D.C. Heath & Co., 1979.

Gold, Steven, ed. *Reforming State Tax Systems*. Denver: National Conference of State Legislatures, 1986.

Grubb, W. Norton, and Stephen Michelson. *States and Schools: The Political Economy of Public School Finance*. Lexington, Mass.: Lexington Books, 1974.

Musgrave, Richard, and Peggy Musgrave. *Public Finance in Theory and Practice*. New York: McGraw-Hill, 1989.

Netzer, Dick. *Economics of the Property Tax.* Washington, D.C.: Brookings Institution, 1966.

Oates, Wallace. *Fiscal Federalism.* New York: Harcourt Brace Jovanovich, 1972.

Pechman, Joseph. *Who Paid the Taxes, 1966–85.* Washington, D.C.: Brookings Institution, 1985.

Pechman, Joseph, and Benjamin Okner. *Who Bears the Tax Burden?* Washington, D.C.: Brookings Institution, 1974.

Seligman, Edwin. *The Income Tax: History, Theory, and Practice of Income Taxation.* 2d ed. New York: Augustus M. Kelley, (1970).

Webber, Carolyn, and Aaron Wildavsky. *A History of Taxation in the Western World.* New York: Simon & Schuster, 1986.

Wildavsky, Aaron. *The New Politics of the Budget Process.* Glenview, Il: Scott, Foresman, 1988.

CHAPTER 4

Funding Education in the 50 States

CHAPTER THEME

- It is fundamentally true that inequity in school funding is a function of failure to redress the inadequacies of local tax base. Since taxable wealth varies among communities in a state, equity demands fiscal equalization. Because education is a state responsibility and because states are free within reason to design their own education funding schemes, it is critical that administrators understand the nature of funding schemes and to be able to analyze the relative effectiveness of various state aid plans in redressing fiscal and educational inequality.

CHAPTER OUTLINE

- The nature and evolution of basic state aid formulas, from the premise that tax base equality can never be achieved without active intervention and that states have been given the role of assuring more equal educational opportunities

- Examination of formula adjustments that seek to move beyond simple equality of school revenues, in light of state aid formulas that have had to move beyond basic equity concerns, becoming extremely complex by their increasing focus on ever-expanding definitions of equity

- Exploration of state aid formulas in the context of how to measure whether fiscal equity is improved by a given state aid formula, given that the history of state aid formula development has been long and imperfect

CHAPTER OBJECTIVE

- A basic understanding of the dominant characteristics of common state aid schemes, thereby laying a foundation for discussing school finance equity litigation in the next chapter.

School finance inequities derive from the way states finance public elementary and secondary schools.

> *Allan Odden,* School Finance in the 1990s

The simplicity of the opening quotation[1] in this chapter is powerful for both its logic and its tersely accurate assessment of reality. While many longer paths to the same truth could be found, nothing is more fundamentally true than the fact that inequity in school funding is a function of failure to redress the inadequacies of local tax base. Since wealth distribution varies naturally, inequity must follow unless active intervention occurs. In school finance, intervention in unequal wealth distribution is especially mandatory because equal educational opportunity is in part a function of purchased resources. The method of intervention is distribution of state aid to local schools to offset the effects of tax base differences. Yet school finance formulas have not been perfectly successful in this attempt because variations in available resources persist even after formula intervention. From the quotation it then follows that formulas may either fail to redress inequality or, worse, create inequality themselves. As Monk perceptively notes, "Something that does not vary cannot be a function of anything else."[2] But since fiscal resources do vary greatly, inequity is either inadequately redressed or even provoked by how some states fund education.

The logic of the preceding paragraph is the basis for this chapter on state methods of funding education. The focus in the preceding chapter on tax fairness provided a foundation for the concept of equity, and proposed that the defense of any school tax or revenue distribution plan should be tied to its effect on educational opportunities for children. The present chapter sequentially extends that concept. First, if taxation is meant to provide school revenue, then money should flow to schools. Second, if equal opportunity is required, then equity in revenue distribution should follow. Third, since tax equity is not natural, the local nature of schools prevents natural equity in revenue distribution. Fourth, the logical tool to redress revenue inequity becomes financial aid to schools. Fifth and finally, then, the merit of an aid plan rests in its contribution to equal opportunity through its ability to equalize the financial resources that purchase education.

These postulates form the basis of the three main sections in this chapter. Because natural tax base inequality has been acknowledged, there have been attempts to devise aid formulas to offset the fiscal inequality among local districts that follows. As seen in earlier chapters, this role has especially fallen to states. As a result, this chapter first discusses the evolution and nature of basic state aid formulas. Basic formulas, however, have become extremely complex by their increasing focus on vertical equity. Consequently, the second section examines formula adjustments that seek to move beyond simple horizontal equality of revenues. But because formula development has been long and imperfect, the third section finally explores state aid formulas in the context of how fiscal equity can be measured. The purpose of the chapter is thus twofold in identifying the dominant characteristics of state aid schemes, and in laying a foundation for the next chapter on school finance equity litigation.

EVOLUTION AND NATURE OF STATE AID FORMULAS

The point has been made repeatedly throughout this text that almost nothing occurs vacuously. Everything has genesis, so much so that Newton's law of physics seems axiomatic even to many theoretical constructs. School finance is no exception in that the present methods and status of education revenue structures can be traced to prior events that led to decisions about how schools should be funded. Just as tax systems are a product of their history, state aid schemes are likewise deeply rooted in the development of theory and practice. As such, it becomes critically important to understand the evolution and basic nature of state aid formulas so that criticism will at least be founded on knowledge, rather than on emotional responses.

Evolution of State Aid Concepts

The roots of state aid to schools have been implicit in the three preceding chapters. Chapter 1 provided a basis for the role of education in society in which its contributions were seen to be invaluable to the economic and social order. At the same time, that discussion noted that failure to fund education adequately has enormous consequences that threaten to destroy the fabric of a free nation if not sufficiently nurtured. These observations led to Chapter 2 where the development of schools in the United States was traced, drawing conclusions that wisdom and shortsightedness had both contributed to how schools have been organized. Of major impact was the decision to deny strong federal control of education, instead making education a state responsibility that in turn was almost unanimously delegated to the local level. Chapter 3 emerged from these realities, noting that tax systems and revenue sources for education closely paralleled other historical events wherein education was first funded locally, with only minimal support from state and federal governments. At the same time, however, it was noted that local tax base inadequacy has caused the state's role to become increasingly important.

Many of the reasons for increasing state importance have been outlined in previous discussion, but all such reasons fall into a two-dimensional schema that ultimately finds every rationale relating to either adequacy or equity of revenues. Enough revenue must be not only available but also distributed by rules of fairness. However, equity has largely superseded adequacy in most circles, primarily because the principle of unlimited needs and limited resources creates despair that finally focuses available energies on assuring better distribution. Because local tax bases have been inadequate to fund the growing educational needs described in this book, the result has been creation of numerous state assistance schemes that seek to offset fiscal inequalities among districts. State aid plans have thus been attempts to improve adequacy of revenues, accompanied by efforts to distribute such revenue fairly. But even states have experienced limits to available revenue. Thus while it would be incorrect to say that state aid formulas have not sought adequacy, it is accurate to say that the primary focus has been on distributing finite resources by some equitable scheme.

Simply intending to distribute revenues equitably, however, has not been enough to turn aside arguments about fairness because even the purest motivation can be said to be lacking. In some instances, inequity may be no more than the politics of envy; on the other hand, growing sophistication about the true meaning of equality has contributed much to national integrity. As seen in Chapter 3, the United States has proved fertile ground for such growth as the nation has long been preoccupied with ever-expanding views of fairness. In contrast to a nation content in its early years with natural rights to life, liberty, and the pursuit of happiness, the nation has marched untiringly toward a definition of equity that extends well beyond mere equality. Evolution has been painful, however, in that accord has not been simple as liberty and social equity have competed for attention. This struggle can be summed up by the work of philosopher John Rawls, who developed a theory of social justice much acclaimed by equity advocates who often reject liberty as a basis for social justice. Rawls conceptualized *justice as fairness,* arguing that the major institutions of society distribute all fundamental rights. "Justice," Rawls wrote, "is the first virtue of social institutions."[3] According to this view, educational equity is paramount among all rights because schools are a central social institution.

Rawls's thinking led to the formulation of two principles of social justice. The first principle dealt with the rights of individuals wherein he stated the limits of individual liberty. Each person was believed to have equal rights to basic liberties compatible with the liberties granted to all. The second principle, however, addressed social and economic disparities and moved equity beyond mere frontal equality by arguing that social and economic inequality are permissible only when two conditions are met. First, any inequality must be attached to positions open to everyone; and second, any inequality must be of the greatest benefit to the least advantaged members of society. It thus follows that equity is most complex to achieve because it permits inequality only when it elevates disadvantaged persons above those who are advantaged. Obviously, to effect this requires immediate conflict since people *innately* prefer a larger to a lesser share. Equity, then, is an induced state because it requires selflessness—a trait seldom seen among mortals.

Intending equity is thus far from achieving it, and it may be argued that if equity is fully understood, some impurity of intent always follows. Yet there has been sufficient acceptance of the equity ideal to cause pursuit of the closest proxy that can be gained given the imperfect human nature. Conceptual acceptance has been able to concede that schools indeed offer social and economic opportunities—a concept that then demands that these rewards must be equally available. Likewise, there has been some approval of Rawls's solution in which he envisioned a society where the distribution of social and economic benefits follows distributive justice—a radical concept that demands redistributing social and economic rewards to the least privileged. The radical nature of distributive justice, however, has only been partially accepted because it violates the innate human propensity to acquire and preserve wealth. In fact, it can be argued that perfect equity would require income equality—a requirement hardly suited to the American psyche.

Representative government confronted with perfect equity has thus wavered in that income equality is not acceptable to capitalist democracy. Yet the need to closely emulate equity has led to several realities and interventions. First, equality is conceptually ingrained in Americans, although they cannot come to accept its actualization. Second, embarrassment has thus led to government structures that operate from at least charity-based equity, if not honest pursuit of true equity. For example, social services such as welfare and unemployment speak to beliefs about fairness and justice. The best example, however, is public schools as the benefits of society are offered in a quasi-meritocracy that both offers reward for competition and encourages the disadvantaged to reverse their fortunes. Third and most importantly, however, the pursuit of equity is never more evident than in fiscal aid schemes for schools whereby the least able are afforded an opportunity to change their lives—a benefit that would be totally inaccessible were it not for public fiscal support. While critics vehemently argue the imperfection of such schemes, it is incontrovertible that representative government has sought distributive justice through financial aid to schools.

However, state aid schemes have not always been unanimously championed or warmly welcomed, and the difficult development of tax laws seen earlier stands as clear proof of the struggle between liberty and equity. Yet efforts to provide aid to schools have been persistent, and some data belie the notion that all aid has been penurious or laboriously extracted. Although previous chapters pressed the point that government has often been only reluctantly sanctioned, it must be noted that fiscal aid to schools is a long-standing concept even by modern standards. By 1890 the states were providing nearly $34 million in aid to schools, amounting to nearly 24% of revenues.[4] Although poor records prevent analysis of the purpose of such aid, these data are nonetheless indicative of an emergent state responsibility for education—a responsibility engendered in part by the economic ramifications of industrialization and no doubt due in part to growing awareness that local districts could not meet their educational needs by historically total local funding. Emergence and growth in state aid can thus be seen to be a response to both economic and fairness concerns.

Although progress toward fiscal equity has been difficult, the momentum has been fairly steady due in large part to the systematic analyses of school funding that began in the early twentieth century. Although struggles over school funding predate the present century,[5] formal adoption of state aid plans was given special impetus by early leaders in the field, when inquiry began to reveal embarrassing differences in educational revenues and expenditures among school districts. The historical antecedents of modern school finance began with the dissertation of Ellwood P. Cubberley, who published in 1906 a monograph based on his doctoral work. Cubberley argued revolutionary concepts, stating that it was the state's responsibility to provide minimum education programs and encourage innovative educational behavior in schools. Cubberley's principal theses were embodied in only two sentences that were to form the basis of modern school finance theory:

> Theoretically all the children of the state are equally important and are entitled to have the same advantages; practically this can never be quite true. The duty of the state is to secure for all as high a minimum of good instruction as is possible, but not to reduce all to the minimum; to equalize the advantages to all as nearly as can be done with the resources at hand; to place a premium on those local efforts which will enable communities to rise above the legal minimum as far as possible; and to encourage communities to extend their educational energies to new and desirable undertakings.[6]

Cubberley's hypotheses formed the basis of his subsequent studies about the effect of school finance plans on educational opportunity, which in turn led to his greatest contributions in the new field of education finance. In studying various states, he concluded that few, if any, had met these demands because educational quality varied greatly and in seeming response to local wealth. By observation and postulation, Cubberley's work thus made four great advances. First, his hypotheses were a giant step by stating the impact of money on education. Second, in advocating the notion that all children in a state are entitled to the same advantages, he moved the focus of school funding into the fairness and justice arena. Third, his subsequent studies confirmed his hypotheses by showing that some children were indeed disadvantaged by the extremely local nature of school funding. Fourth and perhaps most importantly, his advocacy for a state tax to more equally distribute the costs and benefits of education was an enormous stride in that it marked the beginning of a shift from benevolence to active state responsibility for education.

It was natural for other theorists to build on the work of contemporary scholars and thus move thinking forward. Harlan Updegraff's work[7] in 1922 was the next major force as he studied rural schools in New York State, reaching many of the same conclusions as Cubberley and extending the frontier of state responsibility along three important lines. First, like Cubberley he argued that the state had a responsibility to aid communities in support of schools. Second, he added a dimension arguing that state aid should vary by local district wealth and according to tax effort. This concept was unique because it heralded equalization and reward for tax effort, wherein districts could qualify for state aid based on their willingness to tax themselves. Updegraff was thus the first to argue for an equalized foundation level of state support conditioned by local effort. Third, Updegraff made a major contribution as he advocated funding a standardized teacher unit, rather than granting funds based on the number of teachers employed by a district.[8] As a consequence, Updegraff actually made a fourth contribution by advocating aid to districts with higher efficiency levels.

A third major breakthrough in school finance theory occurred at about the same time with publication in 1923 of *The Financing of Education in the State of New York* by George D. Strayer and Robert M. Haig.[9] Probably more than anyone else's, the contribution of these researchers to the field of school finance was monumental because the time was right for them to be able to successfully advance the concept of a minimum education for all children in a state, and the contribution was increased by the mechanics of their proposal. Based on the notion of equalized educational opportunity, their minimum foundation contained three revolutionary elements: that schools be required to make uniformly available to every child in the state some prescribed minimum level of education, that the same requirement of minimum uniformity reflect ability to pay in a state or local education tax, and that a state department of education assume responsibility for direct fiscal administration.

The minimum foundation program was to eventually have a powerful impact on school funding.[10] Although probably not envisioned by its authors, the program was revolutionary because it called for equality of students and taxpayers in educational program and tax effort in the belief that equality of educational opportunity would arise from these requirements. The foundation concept was appropriately named in that the state would provide a foundation upon which the local district could build—a total reversal of the thinking of the day when state aid was an add-on to primary local support. The growing support for primary state responsibility was especially evident in their work as they argued the state's obligation to intervene on behalf of both students and taxpayers. As such, their clear presumption that equality of educational opportunity could not occur without equalized school funding was a striking feature highly predictive of the future. The power of their thinking was best illustrated in these words:

> There exists today and has existed for many years a movement which has come to be known as the "equalization of educational opportunity" or the "equalization of school support." These phrases are interpreted in various ways. In its most extreme form the interpretation is somewhat as follows: The state should insure equal educational facilities to every child within its borders at a uniform effort throughout the state in terms of the burden of taxation; the tax burden of education should throughout the state be uniform in relation to tax-paying ability, and the provision for schools should be uniform in relation to the educable population desiring education. Most supporters . . . would insist that there be an adequate minimum offered every-

where, *the expense of which should be considered a prior claim on the state's economic resources* (emphasis added).[11]

In the tradition of building on other theorists, a fourth major advancement was made by Paul Mort in 1924 in his doctoral dissertation. In *The Measurement of Educational Need,*[12] Mort sought to overcome a void in the work of Strayer and Haig wherein they had advocated a minimum program but failed to define criteria by which such a program could be judged and linked to school funding. Mort argued that a minimum program should meet three criteria. First, he argued that the cost of an educational program was equivalent to the measure of educational need. This was an important concept because it argued that "it costs what it costs" and that cost ought not to drive decisions about a program's necessity. Second, he argued that the educational need of a community is quantifiable as the composite of all those elements that affect the cost of those programs that the state requires, meaning that districts be differentiated based on actual costs. Third, he argued that a satisfactory minimum opportunity was synonymous with a satisfactory equalization program, meaning that when the minimum program was universally available, equalization was satisfied. When these criteria were met in every district, a minimum program would be in place.

The translation of Mort's postulates of a satisfactory minimum educational program were profound in their implications. First, educational activities common to communities throughout a state must be available in all communities—an equal-access criterion. Second, a vertical equity criterion was included by demanding redress for any unusual expenditures that might be required to provide a minimum educational program due to factors over which local communities had no control. And third, where communities offered more schooling or more costly educational programs than were otherwise common, and if it could be established that unusual conditions required such expenditures to meet the minimum, these expenditures would be included in the equalization program. Under these conditions, Mort required the same program everywhere and devised the weighted pupil concept as the measure of educational need. Using linear regression, he estimated the relationship between the number of teachers and the average daily attendance in schools of various sizes. This served to quantify the number of teachers needed in schools by size—a number that then allowed prediction of costs and need, yielding the weighted pupil to be funded. Mort's own words graphically portray his intent:

> A satisfactory equalization program would demand that each community have as many elementary and high school classroom or teacher units, or their equivalent, as is typical for communities having the same number of children to educate. . . . It would demand that each of these classrooms be provided with a teacher, course of study, equipment, supervision, and auxiliary activities meeting certain minimum requirements. It would demand that some communities furnish special facilities, such as transportation.[13]

Under these conditions, Mort linked educational opportunity with standards of visible equality and summed up his hypothesis that state money should provide such uniform equality to all children.

A final early contribution to the field of school finance was made by Henry Morrison in 1930 in his book *School Revenue.*[14] Morrison's ideas were even more extreme than his contemporaries as he saw only failure in seeking equal educational opportunity without radical reforms. Morrison's pessimism led him to advocate abolition of all school districts and to turn funding over to the state. In Morrison's view, this was not radical as he reasoned that states were constitutionally required to control education, and he observed that differences in educational opportunity were a direct function of taxing subdivisions of the state. Morrison reasoned a fundamental flaw in such organization—that is, it is inherently wrong to vest education in a unit of government that does not bear the equivalent burden of fiscal support. Morrison then argued that this inconsistency could be resolved, along with fiscal inequality, only if the state's tax base were used to fund the state's responsibility for education. Although his ideas hardly seem radical today, Morrison outpaced the thinking of his time by effectively advocating full state funding. Although his ideas never received contemporary acclaim, Morrison made a fundamental contribution to school finance equity theory that would later gain some popularity.

The research of these early theorists is remarkably consonant with Rawls's principles of social justice. In one sense this should not be surprising as these theorists and the philosopher were both concerned with justice, viewing fairness as the only means of achieving equity. Rawls's second principle of justice requiring that legitimate inequality must be to the greatest benefit of the least advantaged was especially reflective of school finance theory in that revenues and educational opportunity have not naturally adhered to this principle. Grounded in fairness, equalization of educational opportunity came to be operationalized in school finance by resources inversely related to educational need wherein all children are initially equal, with some then having greater needs requiring more resources. In Rawlsian fashion, school finance theory found it to be the duty of government to fund those costs—a duty that has fallen to states through school funding formulas.

The Nature of State Aid Formulas

The work of early theorists was so powerful that legislatures began intensive study and development of state aid formulas. Although it was seen earlier that before the turn of the century states had begun to provide aid to local districts, interest in state aid formulas only intensified as states took on more responsibility for education. From one perspective, much has been gained by the many years of developmental school finance in that many different state aid plans have been created and states are now highly sensitive to claims of unfairness in school finance schemes. From another perspective, however, it is possible to argue that little has been recently gained as it can be shown that innovative thinking in school finance formulas mostly occurred in the early years of the twentieth century. Both views are partially correct because it can be argued that while little major formula innovation has recently occurred, research has contributed much to refinement and assessment of formula equity. Thus, a long history of formula development stands as testimony to growing sophistication in providing equal educational opportunity.

The nature of state aid formulas has indeed remained fairly constant across the years in that formulas have only three intended purposes. The first purpose is to increase the level of revenue in school districts. This purpose is obvious in that no need for aid would exist except by virtue of recognizing that districts are often inadequate to fund their own needs. The second purpose is to provide some uniformity or smoothing to the differing quality of education among districts that flows from inadequate and highly uneven wealth bases. This purpose is also obvious in that states intuit unequal program quality by their decisions to introduce state aid, because simply adding money without presuming an educational impact is nonsensical. The third purpose of state aid formulas is to satisfy government's moral and legal obligations to education. While all three purposes are critical, it is particularly the latter that has both spurred and retarded school finance equity because state responsibility is simultaneously affected by political philosophy and available formula technology. Although our discussion will indicate that technical sophistication has increased during the developmental stages of school finance formulas, it will be evident that political readiness has not always kept pace.

Development of state aid plans has occurred in three sequential stages since the turn of the twentieth century. Although it must be stated that these stages have at times been blurred, it is true that the stages both reflect growing knowledge about equity and correspond to the political thinking of the times. For example, the technology of full state funding as proposed by Morrison was available in the 1930s, but political readiness has never generally occurred. Similarly, states have often continued to use an "inferior" plan long after newer technology has become available. As such, no crisp lines of historical demarcation exist. As a general rule, however, the three stages follow the thinking of early theorists, to be later succeeded by refinement of basic concepts and slowed only by political readiness. Viewed in terms of both their chronology and their degree of technological sophistication, development of aid formulas has followed a path of *flat grants,* multiple forms of *equalization grants,* and *full state funding.*

Flat Grant Programs.   Among the earliest forms of state aid to schools, the flat grant reflected both the political thinking of the time and the level of sophistication in understanding the meaning of equity. Politically, it was seen as highly efficient because it contained something for everyone. Technologically, the flat grant can be defined as a warrant paid to local school districts without concern for a local share or the ability of local patrons to pay for the services it funds. This simply means that the state gave no consideration to whether districts qualified for the grant on some basis of need—rather, the basis of qualification was simply that the district existed. This was politically convenient since all that was required of the state was to determine the object and amount of the grant. For example, a flat grant might be given on the basis of the number of pupils in the district. This merely required multiplying the number of pupils by the grant amount to derive aid entitlement. Under these conditions, wealthy districts received the same "dollar per scholar" as poor districts—an aid mechanism that served contemporary beliefs about equity, as almost everyone saw flat grants as neutrally distributed.

The operation of a flat grant is graphically striking as seen in Figure 4.1 which shows two school districts with different abilities to pay for education. District A has an assessed valuation of $100,000 per pupil; District B, $500,000 per pupil. Assuming that the state's share of the costs in each district is a flat grant of $2,000 per pupil and assuming that the actual costs are $3,000 per pupil, it is clear that each district must generate $1,000 from local tax sources. Under these conditions, several favorable attempts at equality can be seen. First, the districts are equal in the amount of money that must be raised locally. Second, every child has equal merit in that the state uniformly awards $2,000 per pupil to pay for educational services. Third, the level of the flat grant is quite high in that local districts must only raise one-third of the total costs

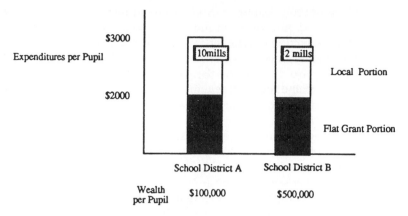

FIGURE 4.1   Graphic representation of the flat grant

per pupil. Fourth, districts' tax rates are lower than would be true if the total program costs were locally funded. These conditions provide immediate benefits that relate to both adequacy and equity. Most obvious is that the grant increases available revenues or, alternatively, allows for local tax relief. Equally obvious is that the grant is seen to be highly neutral.

Neutrality, however, is only evident *until* tax load is analyzed. Although front-end equality is present, true equality is actually poorly served by the flat grant because it can be shown that the districts are not really initially equal. In fact, the equal tax amounts to be raised and equal revenues from the state provide an appearance of neutrality that masks a deeper inequality because the districts do not start on an even playing field. Despite apparent neutrality, the problem relates to the discussion in Chapter 3 of property wealth wherein District A is much poorer than District B. This basic reality observes that although taxpayers in both districts need to raise exactly equal amounts, District A must tax itself at a rate of ten mills ($1,000 ÷ $100,000 = .010), while taxpayers in District B need to pay only two mills ($1,000 ÷ $500,000 = .002), a direct function of a tax base inequality of 5:1. Thus, the apparent neutrality of a flat grant is misleading in that taxpayers in poor districts pay higher tax rates to fund the same expenditure. If one accepts the view that equity is the aim of state aid, this result is unacceptable. Consequently, a flat grant can actually be *dis*equalizing unless it covers the entire cost of a program, which it can never do for political and technical reasons.[15]

At the turn of the century, however, 38 states were using flat grants to aid schools.[16] These grants did not usually cover the entire cost of programs and additional local funds were needed. Rich districts could raise additional revenue from the local property tax base with minimal tax effort, while poor districts were forced to levy higher tax rates or forgo equal programs at the expense of students. In historical perspective these districts were often rural, which in turn related to widespread attempts at consolidation. Additionally, the level of the flat grant was generally much lower than the ratio in Figure 4.1. Yet despite obvious weaknesses in flat grants, the monumental stride represented by this aid mechanism must be noted. First, simply achieving state aid was remarkable at that time. Second, flat grants can actually be said to offer some equalization in that it can be shown that equity increases with the size of a flat grant—a phenomenon most easily seen in the hypothetical "full-cost" grant. Third, introduction of state aid was a first indication of state awareness of a need for minimum educational program definition, and the flat grant was an attempt to invoke such a standard. Fourth, the flat grant greatly augmented expenditures or provided tax relief. Finally, later refinements based on weighted units of need, such as rural or urban location, size, or exceptionalities, were evidence of increasing awareness of equity.

The combination of these realities caused flat grants to continue in popularity for a number of years, tapering off only as progressive states experimented with newer finance plans and as more traditional legislatures eventually sought to "stay in line" with their sister states. As late as 1971, flat grants were still the primary funding mechanism in 10 states,[17] and Connecticut continued to fund a flat grant of $235 per pupil until 1975 when it moved to an equalization formula. Popularity diminished rapidly, however, as school finance litigation began to escalate in the 1970s so that by the present time no state now relies solely on flat grants as the principal finance scheme. This does not mean that flat grants are no longer used, however, as flat grants are still used in most states to provide categorical or supplemental aid, particularly for special operations and programs such as transportation, special education excess costs, food services, textbooks and libraries, vocational education, and driver education. As such, the flat grant has never disappeared despite its inability to equalize educational opportunity, and its continued use may be seen as a function of its original popularity—the politics of granting aid to nearly everyone in seeming neutrality, tempered only by occasional efforts to qualify districts on some needs basis.[18]

Formula Equalization Plans.   The era of flat grants slowly gave way to numerous forms of equalization plans that represented both new political sophistication and new equity technology. Like most other aspects of change, these plans moved forward in concert with the pace of political thinking and as technology became available. As such, their emergence is chronological, but their adoption has been popularized or avoided based on emerging conceptions of justice and fairness. Each equalization plan, however, is a representation of progress toward a greater awareness of the value of education and the importance of equalizing educational opportunity.

While the conceptual breakthrough of state aid by flat grants was historically monumental, a second enormous stride was taken in the movement beyond blind equality into the era of attempting to equalize the differing wealth capacities of school districts. Formula equalization thus represented a major conceptual shift in that its most fundamental premise was an overt admission of four critical tenets of taxation and equal opportunity: first, that differential resources can lead to uneven quality, and that equalizing differences is mandatory if equal opportunity is to be achieved; second, that the state must redress inequality to overcome local tax base inadequacy; third, that "neutral" aid is inadequate in that blind equality at best has no effect, or at worst aggravates the problem by giving funds to unneedy groups; and fourth, that inequality is first a tax base problem and that intervention must be proactive rather than benevolent. As a result, conceptual acceptance of state responsibility required new aid schemes that embraced state and local sharing of school costs.

The response to these new concepts was the creation of various aid plans that were available in the context of political viability and emerging technology. Again the work of theorists in combination with political readiness produced several different plans, all of which sought to provide a better relationship between educational opportunity and local ability to pay. More precisely, these plans sought to reduce dependence of educational opportunity on local ability to pay, and the vehicle was state aid plans designed to meet the objectives of more revenue at the local level and revenue in greater proportion to those districts with the least local fiscal capacity. Although various equalization schemes over many years all sought to achieve these goals, each scheme was technologically different based on political preferences and economic realities. Political realities were formidable by requiring resolution to three central policy concerns: first, whether the state should set expenditure levels and local tax rates; second, whether the state should allow each district to set its own costs with corresponding aid; and third, whether the state should simply set minimum expenditures that could be exceeded by local option. The answers were also economic in that fiscal constraints could drive responses.

Answers to these questions were most often determined by political readiness and availability of technology. Generally, political readiness has moved from right to left, preceded by technological understanding of equity performance of an aid scheme. As such, response to the three questions has been in reverse order, with the earliest equalization plans based on belief that states should provide only minimum aid to some predetermined level while leaving local decision making intact. In next order of appearance were plans seeking strong local control while linking state coffers to local decision making. Finally and most recently, the response has tended toward centralization, perhaps born of the same pessimism that earlier led Morrison to observe the oxymoron of strong local control and state constitutional responsibility. The result, however, was several equalization schemes that fall into the typology in Figure 4.2. Each scheme is discussed in order of chronological appearance, with brief detail of both its conceptual and mechanical underpinnings.

Minimum Foundation Plans.   Foundation plans were the next level of sophistication to emerge after flat grants began to fall into disfavor among theorists and policymakers. Observing the disequalizing nature of flat grants, pioneering work by Strayer and Haig in 1923 caught the attention of legislatures as they argued for a new aid scheme that would address the fiscal inadequacy problems of poor districts which they believed to have detrimental effects on educational program quality. Their solution was a *minimum foundation* concept that granted aid to districts based on ability to pay for a minimum educational program. The conceptual shift was profound. Whereas flat grants had sought to provide school revenues through political neutrality, the minimum foundation formula granted aid inversely by ability to pay—thereby placing under each district a minimum fiscal foundation on which to build educational programs. According to Strayer and Haig, a foundation formula should reach several goals. First, educational programs should be based on the wealthiest district. Second, a minimum foundation should encourage local initiative. Third, the plan should reward efficiency. Fourth, the plan should make districts fiscally competitive so that differences would reflect local choices rather than the effects of local ability or inability to pay.

These key elements of a minimum foundation formula proved attractive in the policy arena, because a *minimum* foundation met several important political goals. First, legislatures are often attracted to concepts that assure some competitive mini-

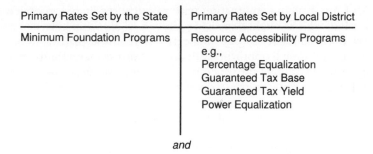

Primary Rates Set by the State	Primary Rates Set by Local District

Minimum Foundation Programs	Resource Accessibility Programs
	  e.g.,
	  Percentage Equalization
	  Guaranteed Tax Base
	  Guaranteed Tax Yield
	  Power Equalization

and

Combination Foundation and Resource Accessibility Programs
  e.g.,
  Foundation and Guaranteed Tax Base
  Foundation and Guaranteed Tax Yield
  Foundation and Flat Grant
  Guaranteed Tax Yield and Flat Grant
  Percentage Equalization and Flat Grant

FIGURE 4.2 Typology of equalization plans categorized by degree of local and state control

mum for economy reasons, and they are also attracted to concepts that speak reassuringly of local control. Second, the minimum foundation concept spoke to contemporary concerns about districts that failed to finance some reasonable educational program because it required a base expenditure that could be said to satisfy some quantity of minimum education. Third, Strayer and Haig were politically astute in building competitive aspects into the foundation formula. The emphasis on setting a high minimum was meant to prevent low effort or token aid, and demand for efficiency was meant to discourage reward for low enrollments and underassessment of property. Fourth, focusing on a minimum educational program was politically wise because it allowed districts to exceed minimums and encouraged establishment of lighthouse districts. The motivation was both educational and political—educational because lighthouse innovation would increase quality, and political because legislators would seek to increase state aid to make the lighthouse the new norm.

Finally, the foundation concept was especially radical and ingenious by its demand for a minimum local tax effort. Equity was immediately better served by front-end equality where each district paid the same tax rate to fund the minimum expenditure. It was equally clever, however, that each district would be required to levy the minimum tax rate to qualify for state aid, with aid distribution inversely related to ability to pay. The basic premise underlying the foundation plan was thus radically different. Under flat grants, tax rates had varied greatly even after state aid because the tax base remained unchanged. In contrast, the foundation plan actually caused the state to set a minimum local property tax rate as a condition of state aid, and the state likewise determined a minimum required expenditure level in all districts. The concept reversed prior thinking in at least three ways. First, districts were placed on an even footing by requiring them all to initially levy the same tax rate if they wished to receive state aid. Second, all districts were expected to spend a minimum amount that was implicitly equated with a minimally adequate educational experience. Third, equity was met by variable aid according to ability to pay. Hence the formula was meant to equalize a definable educational program.

Operationalization of the minimum foundation formula was only slightly more complex than a flat grant scheme. The basic formula for a foundation plan was simple in concept, although it could appear forbidding when expressed as an equation. The formula is stated as

State Share = Total Costs − Local Share

This is straightforward when it is recognized that the cost of a minimum program less some legislatively determined local share leaves the state to fund the difference. Importantly, the initial tax rate and the initial expenditure per pupil are the equality factors, with the state share varying in direct proportion so that the effect is to initially flatten expenditures per pupil and tax rates across all districts. But because costs vary by district and the local share will vary by local wealth multiplied by a uniform tax rate, the equation is solved for different dollar amounts of aid to each district. Mathematically expressed, the foundation formula would thus read:

$$S_i = \left(\sum P_i \times F_{state} \right) - \left(\text{Val}_i \times r_{state} \right)$$

where:

S_i is the state aid to the i-th district;

P_i is the sum of the number of students as calculated in the state (e.g., by ADA, ADM, weighted by FTE, etc.) for the i-th district;[19]

F_{state} is the foundation dollar-per-pupil expenditure set by the state;

Val_i is the assessed valuation for the i-th district; and

r_{state} is the tax rate set by the local district.

The effect of the foundation formula can be shown mathematically. In the example below, there are three districts with different wealth and enrollment. The minimum foundation concept is first evident in that the state has decided that a minimum educational program is satisfied when districts spend $2,500 per pupil. The second requirement is seen in the state's order that all districts levy at least five mills. Differences among districts are then quickly evident in their wealth and enrollment data. Districts A and C each have wealth of $100,000 per pupil, while District B's wealth is $500,000 per pupil, or a ratio of 5:1. Multiplying the five-mill minimum tax rate against district wealth produces the tax yield in each district, with Districts A and C each generating $500 per pupil ($100,000 × .005 = $500), while District C generates $2,500 per pupil ($500,000 × .005 = $2,500). This local share is then simply subtracted from the state minimum expenditure to solve for state aid. Districts A and C will receive $2,000 per pupil ($2,500 − $500 = $2,000) in state aid, while District C will receive no state aid ($2,500 − $2,500 = $0) due to local wealth. These data are then multiplied by the enrollment to derive total aid. If District A had 1,000 pupils, District B had 1,500 pupils, and District C had 2,000 pupils, the formula in each district would be calculated as follows:

District A S_a = (1,000 pupils × $2,500) − (5 mills × 1,000 pupils × $100,000)
            = $2,500,000 − $500,000
            = $2,000,000 or $2,000 per pupil

District B S_b = (1,500 pupils × \$2,500) − (5 mills × 1,500 pupils × \$500,000)
                      = \$3,750,000 − \$3,750,000
                      = \$0 or \$0 per pupil

District C S_c = (2,000 pupils × \$2,500) − (5 mills × 2,000 pupils × \$100,000)
                      = \$5,000,000 − \$1,000,000
                      = \$4,000,000 or \$2,000 per pupil

The requirements of a minimum foundation formula are well served in this example because a state can be assured that its constituencies are substantially aided in reaching the legislature's policy goals. As discussed earlier, these goals are often both political and substantive. First, the example is politically and substantively effective in that front-end equality is met by both expenditure and tax rate. Second, the formula works because the state can no longer be embarrassed by districts that fail to fund a minimum educational program because a base program of \$2,500 is required. Third, constituents are usually pleased because a minimum foundation encourages additional local spending discretion. Fourth, the high level of aid in the example is substantive by ensuring that aid goes beyond tokenism. Fifth, efficiency is served by such a high level of aid because it almost guarantees that the state will look critically at districts' efficiency before making policy decisions about tax rates and minimum expenditures. Sixth, the "local leeway" option to tax and spend more is an inducement to lighthouse districts and to increased aid in future years. Last, the costs are obviously better equalized as aid is inversely granted on ability to pay.

Minimum foundation plans thus represented significant improvement over earlier finance schemes. The nature of a minimum foundation, however, was not without deficiencies. Ironically, its flaws were inherent to its most fundamental attributes. The first concern was that districts could choose not to exceed the base expenditure and minimum tax rate, thereby thwarting a central goal of a *minimum* foundation. Ironically, however, when districts take the challenge to exceed the minimum, many equity gains are lost because a minimum foundation does not automatically redress wealth inequality above the minimum expenditure and tax rate. In this example, if the state permitted local discretionary millage, District B could generate additional funds with lower tax effort because each additional mill generates \$500 per pupil (\$500,000 × .001), compared to only \$100 per pupil in either District A or District C. Three problems thus emerge. First, a basic foundation formula does not equalize above the minimum tax rate. Second, if voters in poorer districts refuse to approve additional millage, then that district must spend less. Third, even if poor districts approve additional tax effort, spending is still less because the yield per mill above the minimum is not equalized.

These flaws are inherent to foundation formulas, and the impact on equity is graphically seen in Figure 4.3. The graph shows that the foundation works well up to a point when it becomes dysfunctional to its original equalization aim. The formula works well in the bottom two-thirds of the graph as the foundation amount (\$2,500) is set at the highest district wherein five mills yields zero aid, with the other districts receiving aid to equalize local tax base inadequacy. In the upper third, however, discretionary millage allows District B to spend at a ratio of 5:1 for each additional mill. The problem is perplexing. If the state equalizes local leeway, the scheme is no longer a minimum foundation. If it fails to equalize discretionary millage, it restores the inequality it first sought to eliminate. If the state does not permit discretionary millage,

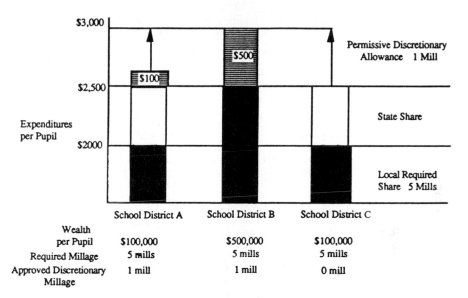

FIGURE 4.3   Graphic representation of foundation program showing the effect of discretionary millage on per-pupil expenditures

the minimum concept is again thwarted. Political and substantive realities further apply in that it is easier to generate support for additional millage in wealthy districts. Thus, the formula is irresolubly imperfect because any unaided discretionary millage is disequalizing, while minimum intent is violated if local leeway is denied. The only other option is to limit the amount of discretionary millage, but it is clear that this is compromising and a depressant to the lighthouse concept.

Despite its inherent limitations, the foundation plan has been the single most popular equalization formula. As seen in Table 4.1, foundation schemes continue to dominate school finance, as several states presently use some form of the foundation plan as the primary scheme for distributing state aid. Still other states depend heavily on a foundation plan in combination with other aid programs. Although more sophisticated and technically superior formulas exist, the popularity of the minimum foundation program is not surprising due to its political and substantive benefits. First, it is still politically expedient to embrace the minimum philosophy. Second, it is clear that front-end equality of expenditures and tax rates serves both politics and equity. Third, local tax and spending leeway are political necessities in most states. Fourth, both politics and economics are well served by the minimum philosophy because states can control costs while offering local control to districts. Lastly, there is no question that the foundation formula meets the test of aid in inverse relationship to ability to pay—at least within the base expenditure covered by the formula. As a consequence, the minimum foundation has been popular as states have chosen either to overlook its deficiencies or to alter its pure form.[20]

Resource Accessibility Programs.   As seen earlier in the typology in Figure 4.2, all equalization schemes can be grouped into one of two philosophies. The first philosophy of minimum foundation held as its aim to impose certain minimum stan-

TABLE 4.1 Classification of states according to formula used to determine state aid, 1991

State	Formula
Alabama	Modified foundation
Alaska	Foundation
Arizona	Foundation
Arkansas	Foundation: two-tiered
California	Foundation with flat grant
Colorado	Modified foundation
Connecticut	Percentage equalization
Delaware	Flat grant with equalization
Florida	Foundation
Georgia	Foundation with GTB
Hawaii	Full state funding
Idaho	Modified foundation
Illinois	Modified foundation/GTB with flat grant
Indiana	Foundation with flat grant
Iowa	Foundation with flat grant
Kansas	Percentage equalization
Kentucky	Foundation with GTB
Louisiana	Foundation
Maine	Modified foundation
Maryland	Foundation with flat grant
Massachusetts	Percentage equalization
Michigan	GTB with flat grant
Minnesota	Foundation
Mississippi	Foundation
Missouri	Foundation with GTB and flat grant
Montana	Foundation with GTB
Nebraska	Foundation
Nevada	Foundation
New Hampshire	Foundation
New Jersey	Foundation
New Mexico	Foundation, near full funding
New York	Percentage equalization with flat grant
North Carolina	Flat grant
North Dakota	Foundation
Ohio	Foundation
Oklahoma	Foundation with equalization
Oregon	Foundation
Pennsylvania	Percentage equalization
Rhode Island	Percentage equalization
South Carolina	Foundation
South Dakota	Foundation
Tennessee	Foundation
Texas	Foundation with guaranteed yield
Utah	Foundation
Vermont	Foundation with flat grant
Virginia	Foundation
Washington	Full state funding
West Virginia	Foundation
Wisconsin	GTB, two-tiered
Wyoming	Foundation

SOURCE: Steven Gold (ed.), *School Finance in the Fifty States* (Albany: The American Education Finance Association and the National Center for Education Statistics, State University of New York at Albany 1992).

dards on local districts and to grant state aid to help them reach those standards, giving rise to greater sophistication in state thinking about equal educational opportunity. Beginning with foundation plans, preferences for blind neutrality were dropped in favor of greater uniformity in educational programs, and the variability of wealth capacity began to be the object of state intervention. The problems of minimum provision, however, caused this line of thinking to be extended to the next tier of equalization formulas that fall into the classification of *resource accessibility* programs. Following a tradition of increasing sophistication, these plans moved equalization to the next higher plane by going more directly to the unequal tax base itself.

In many ways, all equalization programs are alike. Resource accessibility and foundation programs both seek to equalize educational opportunity by offering aid in inverse relation to ability to pay, and both schemes argue that resources have a meaningful impact on educational opportunity. Their solutions, however, are fundamentally different despite the fact that they both see differences in tax base as the root of inequality. In most instances, their different approaches rest in how aggressively each seeks to confront inequality, the level at which inequality is redressed, and the political and technical preference for adjusting wealth bases. The foundation program follows a less aggressive minimum provision philosophy, while resource accessibility programs focus on a more aggressive equal access philosophy or even an equal total provision philosophy.[21] In addition, resource accessibility programs are much more heavily vested in local decision making, despite the foundation's interest in local leeway. Thus, there is one premise that especially distinguishes resource accessibility plans from foundation plans. This premise is profound in that it demands that the state share in educational costs at a level determined *by the local district,* and also focuses more intensively on end opportunity instead of uniform effort or program.

Resource accessibility programs are thus appropriately named because they require equal access to resources, rather than initially uniform levels of funding. The difference is more than semantic because the foundation formula is satisfied when some definition of equality is reached because it theoretically releases the state's obligation to further consider differences above the foundation. In contrast, resource accessibility formulas are interested in whether students have equal access to resources and are less philosophically concerned about whether resources are initially uniform or even finally equal as long as the opportunity to access the same amount was available at no disadvantage. Thus, while foundation plans seek minimum equality, resource accessibility schemes attempt to balance wealth, or ability to pay, in each district through formulas that technically adjust for tax base differences, theoretically on an infinite continuum of local choice. The vehicles have been various percentage equalization (PE) plans, and these formulas have been further refined to include newer variations discussed later.

Chronologically, resource accessibility programs are both old and relatively recent. PE programs were actually first promoted by Updegraff in the 1920s in response to his observation that low financial support for foundation plans was forcing many school districts to levy unequalized additional taxes to support education. The irony, of course, was that state support was not enough to provide the minimum education purported by the foundation plan so that the need for local unequalized add-ons prevented attainment of the foundation plan's goals. This was not surprising for two reasons. First, legislatures never have sufficient revenue to meet all their goals, and the natural response is to set a low foundation amount that the state can afford to fund. Second, the only other alternative of deriving a higher foundation amount is to set the minimum tax rate high enough to recapture excess revenues in wealthy districts for redistribution to poorer districts. As might be expected, the political improbability of recapture assured that foundation amounts would be less than adequate. The PE program as conceived by Updegraff was meant to vest control in local decision making about spending levels and to require states to follow in partnership.

The technology of PE was straightforward. Local districts would determine a cost of education that reflected both local prices and local preferences and would inform the state of their decisions. For its part, the state would decide on a support level to be applied equally to all districts, generally expressed as a percentage of costs to be paid in the average district after local ability to pay was subtracted. For example, a district might decide the price of an education was $2,000, and the state would have agreed that districts could expect the state to fund 50% adjusted to local district wealth.[22] Under this scenario, a district of average wealth with an expenditure of that same $2,000 would receive approximately half from the state, while a poor district with identical expenditures would receive more. Similarly, a wealthy district might receive no aid. These factors would remain constant regardless of the expenditure level chosen by the district. Unlike the foundation, state aid was thus variable on two factors. The first factor still varied aid on the basis of wealth, but the second factor caused aid to vary based on local decisions with state partnership guaranteed.

Updegraff's view was both theoretically and politically alluring. First, his view argued local decision making and reward for effort in the same breath. In his view, districts were guaranteed that costs could reflect local desires and unique needs. At the same time, districts were assured that increased tax effort would be matched in ratio based on wealth. The state could also gain because the formidable cost of a high foundation often precluded such a program, but a PE scheme would require high aid only to poorer districts. At the same time, the state would effectively shift the politically explosive burden of minimum program definition to the local districts. The assumption from the school finance theory side was that offering districts a partnership with the state would encourage extra tax effort, driving up educational quality. The assumption from the state side was that local control would placate districts and that the strain on the treasury would be less than in the case of a sufficiently high foundation. A tempering state reality, however, was that vesting control locally can be discomfiting because states may fear an open checkbook.[23] At the same time, shoving decision making back to local districts would reopen quality questions that had earlier been hard-fought.

Although PE was a more sophisticated response to the problems of foundation formulas, this scheme did not receive popular acclaim until the 1970s following a spate of lawsuits seeking greater equalization. Although the new plans were actually modifications of older percentage equalization, there was an important difference in that the new schemes focused intensely on redistributing tax base. As such, these new resource accessibility formulas were designed to distribute aid *as if* the tax base per pupil in every district were identical. The vehicles became known as guaranteed tax base (GTB) and guaranteed tax yield (GTY) formulas, with a special variation also known as district power equalization (DPE). The differences between GTB and GTY were semantic, differing somewhat in design while achieving the same mathematical result.

The GTB makes a theoretical assumption that all school districts have the same tax base wealth per pupil. Obviously this is not true, but by some process such as finding the average assessed valuation per pupil for the state as a whole, the state would determine a tax base amount to be equally guaranteed to every district. Under this condition, all students are instantly equal. The features of the PE formula would remain, however, in that local districts would still make the decisions about local expenditures and would also set the tax rate. When that decision is made, the district would simply multiply the local tax rate against the GTB, while the state would be required to make up any difference. For example, if two districts established the same tax rate, they would be guaranteed the same expenditure per pupil. The GTB thus guarantees taxpayer equity such that each taxpayer in the state has equivalent capacity to generate revenue. Mathematically, the GTB is expressed as follows:

$$\text{State Share} = \text{Local Tax Rate} \times (\text{GTB} - \text{Local Tax Base})$$

The GTY formula is very similar in operation except that the state sets a tax yield level for all property in the state. Very often the tax yield generated by a given tax rate for the wealthiest districts in the state represents the starting point for policy deliberations, obviously because the state has only three options: setting the GTY so that the formula provides zero aid to the wealthiest district to avoid recapture, setting the GTY above the wealthiest district to provide aid to everyone, or setting the GTY below the wealthiest district to recapture excess revenue. Politically, only the second option is usually available. Regardless of the option, however, the formula is solved so that poor districts receive the same revenue per pupil as the wealthiest district using the same tax rate. The GTY formula is mathematically expressed as follows:

$$\text{State Share} = (\text{Wealth}_w \times \text{Tax Rate}_w) - (\text{Wealth}_i \times \text{Tax Rate}_i)$$

In solving the formula, the revenue per pupil generated in the i-th district (wealth per pupil of the i-th district times its tax rate) is subtracted from the revenue per pupil generated in the wealthiest district (wealth per pupil of the wealthiest district W times its tax rate), with the difference yielding the state aid per pupil.

In practice, resource accessibility formulas are not this simple. The detailed formula for the PE, GTB, and GTY is identical and is expressed as follows:

$$\text{State Share} = \text{Total Costs} - \text{Local Share Ratio}$$
$$S_i = (\textstyle\sum P_i)(\text{Exp}_i) - [1 - (C \times \text{Adj. Val}_i)]$$

where:

S_i	is the state aid to the i-th district;
P_i	is the sum of the number of students as calculated in the state (e.g., by ADA, ADM, weighted by FTE, etc.) for the i-th district;
Exp_i	is the dollar-per-pupil expenditure set by the i-th district;
C	is the state share percentage factor; and
Adj.Val$_i$	is the ratio of assessed valuation per pupil for the i-th district compared to that of the average assessed valuation for all districts.

Solving the equation requires several steps. First, the total number of pupils (P_i) is multiplied by the dollar-per-pupil expenditure level (Exp$_i$) set by the district. To solve for the state share, (S_i), the far right set of parentheses must be known wherein the adjusted valuation[24] of the school district is multiplied by the state constant (C) factor and subtracted from 1. S_i is then the sum of pupils multiplied by the district expenditure per pupil minus the product of 1 minus the constant multiplied against the assessed valuation of the district. Although complex, the outcome is sensible in that districts receive the same revenue per mill of tax effort regardless of wealth and all districts are equal in their ability to choose their expenditure levels by varying their equalized tax rates. From the state perspective, the value of C in a given year can be leveled up or leveled down to control costs. The same three district example used above would each calculate as follows:

Average wealth of the state: $266,666,667
State share factor (C):　　0.5

District A　S_a = (1,000 pupils × $2,500) − [1 − (0.5 × 1,000,000 ÷ 2,666,667)]
　　　　　　= $2,500,000 × 1 − 0.187
　　　　　　= $2,031,853 or $2,032 per pupil

District B　S_b = (1,500 pupils × $2,500) − [1 − (0.5 × 5,000,000 ÷ 2,666,667)]
　　　　　　= $3,750,000 × 1 − 93.7
　　　　　　= $234,815 or $235 per pupil

District C　S_c = (2,000 pupils × $3,000) − [1 − (0.5 × 1,000,000 ÷ 2,666,667)]
　　　　　　= $6,000,000 × 1 − 0.1874
　　　　　　= $4,875,600 or $2,438 per pupil

　　　　Aid to these districts under a resource accessibility formula is different than when a foundation formula is applied. Districts A and B have chosen to spend the same $2,500 in both examples, but aid is now different. Under a foundation aid formula, District A received aid of $2,000 per pupil while wealthier District B received nothing. Factoring in a more sensitive wealth variable and setting the state share at 50% adjusted to wealth, however, changes District A aid to $2,032 per pupil, and supplies District B with aid of $235 per pupil. In contrast, District C has chosen to set its expenditure even higher at $3,000. Remembering that Districts A and C have equal wealth, it can now be seen that a higher budget per pupil will demand higher aid, but it must also be remembered that a higher tax rate has been chosen. But since all ratios are proportional, this is acceptable because the amount of state aid is adjusted according to the relative wealth of each district, with wealthy districts receiving less state aid than poor districts for equal tax effort.

　　　　The operation of the resource equalization formula is graphically visible in Figure 4.4. Stated simply, Districts A and C have the same wealth but District C has approved a higher expenditure level of $3,000. The state thus pays a higher share in support of District C than it does for District A, but taxpayers in District C pay approximately 20% more local taxes as a result ($562 compared to $468). Under these conditions, however, both strengths and weaknesses become evident. Updegraff's goals of local decision making and reward for effort are met, and the formula supplies aid inversely. At the same time, the state has shifted minimum program definition to local districts. School finance theory has also prevailed in that state partnership has encouraged extra tax effort and extra aid, and perhaps increasing program quality. However, the state's hypothetical fears about an open checkbook are made manifest if local districts set expenditure levels that the state cannot match. A major flaw then appears in that if the state must exercise its only option of increasing the constant (C), districts at higher expenditure levels would be hurt more than those at lower levels. This would be ironic for poor districts by making them the recipients of the severest loss. Finally, there is merit in noting that local decision making can reopen quality questions.

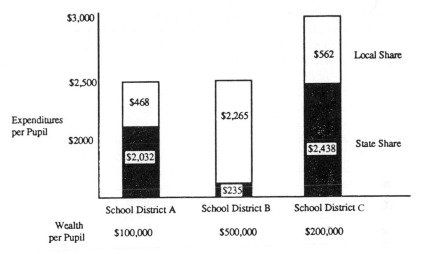

FIGURE 4.4 Graphic representation of percentage equalization program for three school districts showing per-pupil expenditures and resulting local share amounts

Finally, the DPE formula is a plan that carries the resource accessibility concept to its ultimate potential of recapture. Although each of the previous schemes had the technical capability to achieve this same end, in practice all have generally sought to set the level of state support near zero for the wealthiest district, due to the political unpopularity of recapturing excess revenues that could be generated in the wealthiest districts. As a product of the late 1960s and early 1970s, however, DPE plans were a deliberate departure from the traditional political model by simply extending percentage equalization to intentionally embrace recapture. Operationally simple, DPE plans require that every district with an assessed valuation greater than the state's guaranteed valuation per pupil must pay back the difference to the state to be redistributed for support of poor districts. Unlike the other resource accessibility plans, setting the constant would intend that districts exert significant tax effort because recaptured amounts would be needed to fully fund the formula. As with all other resource accessibility plans, the intent of DPE is to equalize the spending power of the mill without concern for the level of actual spending or the tax ability of each district.

Despite mostly unenthusiastic legislatures, a few states have adopted resource accessibility plans. No adoption has been pure in form, however, as most states have sought ways to limit the politically unattractive features of these plans. As seen in Table 4.1, equalization schemes were in place in only a few states in 1991, and with some indication that support is weakening.[25] More popular has been the practice of multitier formulas that include an equalization aspect as discussed next. Yet equalization schemes have served a very useful purpose. First, school finance reform in the 1970s gave much impetus to state self-scrutiny of their school aid formulas, with resulting improvements in equalization regardless of the aid scheme in place. Second, as almost all states have moved incrementally toward greater equalization, this genre of state aid formulas advanced equity well beyond the basic foundation schemes that preceded this era. Third, although reform did not fully eradicate the minimum philosophy, considerable movement away from this concept was evident as states began to seek more comprehensive equalization. Fourth, there is no question that equalization formulas better meet the test of ability to pay. As a result, theory may often have an impact that exceeds its direct adoption.

Combination Programs.   As seen earlier in the typology in Figure 4.2, all equalization schemes can be grouped by either minimum foundation or resource accessibility characteristics. In the purist tradition this statement is entirely true. In the policy arena, however, the inherent deficiencies of pure formulas have led modern policymakers to create less pure alternatives that nonetheless still fall within the equalization philosophy. As seen at the bottom of Figure 4.2, the vehicle has been to straddle the principles of foundation aid and equalization aid by combining one or more types of formulas in an effort to secure the benefits of each. The intent, of course, is that the strengths of one plan may help offset the weaknesses of another.

Describing mathematical operations of combination programs is less useful at this point since it can be observed that each part of a combination will function exactly as described earlier. In addition, the numerous combinations seen in Table 4.1 that have actually been adopted indicate that illustration would require extended space because the mix is quite broad. The operation of a combination plan can be easily seen, however, in Figure 4.5 where a foundation program is combined with a fully equalized one-mill local leeway option. The horizontal line of $2,500 marks the foundation amount, and in keeping with earlier discussion it can be seen that the state variably supports each district to that foundation level. For example, Districts A and C can only raise $2,000 per pupil under the required five mills, while District B can raise the full amount. As a result, foundation aid to Districts A and C offsets the lack of tax base required for a minimum program offering. The add-on local option resource

FIGURE 4.5   Graphic representation of a multitier foundation and equalization aid scheme showing the effect of discretionary equalized millage

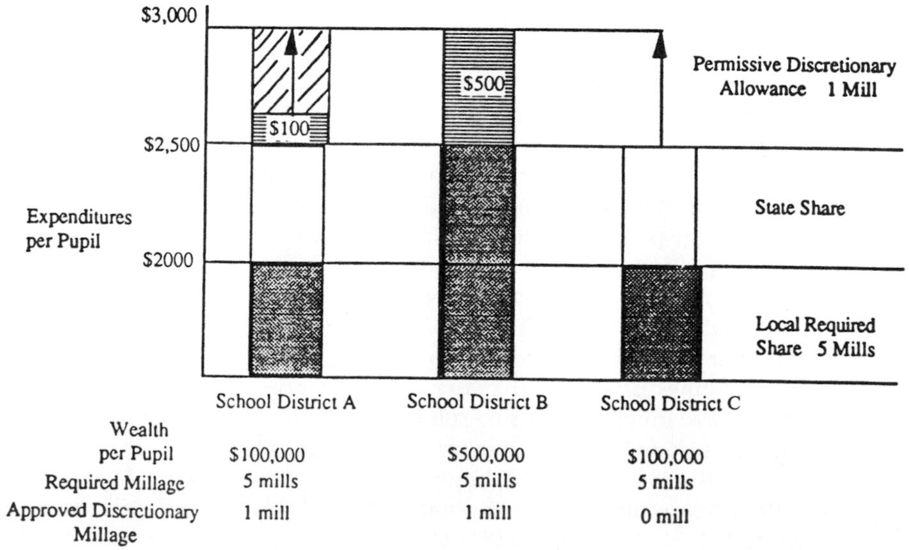

	School District A	School District B	School District C
Wealth per Pupil	$100,000	$500,000	$100,000
Required Millage	5 mills	5 mills	5 mills
Approved Discretionary Millage	1 mill	1 mill	0 mill

equalization scheme, however, kicks in above $2,500. In this example, a one-mill discretionary tax in Districts A and C yields only $100 per pupil while yielding $500 per pupil in District B, requiring the state to equalize the one mill to the highest level for poorer districts choosing to exercise the local option. As seen in Figure 4.5, the remaining $400 in District A will be funded by the state, while District C will receive no additional aid since it chose not to participate.[26]

As seen in Table 4.1, there are presently several states that employ a combination of formula programs to set the state's share of the costs of public education. These states have usually mixed flat grants or foundations with some form of percentage equalization. As a general rule one scheme provides "base" aid, while the other formula is added on to meet some policy goal. For example, Georgia and Missouri combine foundation schemes with a GTB component that balances district wealth under a local leeway option. In Georgia, education is thus funded first by a five-mill foundation, supported by equalization of a three-mill local option. Similarly, Montana combines foundation and GTY to assure a set amount of revenue after uniform effort, with an additional local option millage equalized to all districts. Still other states may use predominantly one scheme but may also build in features of another plan in less obvious ways.

Multitier formulas thus represent the newest trend among the states as the deficiencies of "pure" formulas have been revealed. Yet even these plans have their strengths and weaknesses, underscoring the importance of vigilance in an era heavily characterized by balancing political viability against equity. The greatest strength of these schemes is obviously that they are proof of the imperfect performance of other plans: if any one plan had fully achieved some set of criteria, no combination would be needed. For example, a common combination calls for equalization above a foundation for several apparent reasons. First, the fondness for minimum provision has not faded even with the advent of technically superior formulas, particularly in the context of assuring initially flat expenditures and tax rates, more uniform program quality, and local discretionary leeway. The major flaw of a foundation is corrected by overlaying equalization wherein local option preserves its strength by guaranteeing equal revenues for equal effort if the choice is exercised. Indeed, the strength of combination is so great that its major weakness seems to relate to the care that must be taken not to combine two inferior plans to create a slightly less inferior union.[27] While it can be argued that Table 4.1 is real proof of this concern, the combination scheme has seemed to some states to be the best alternative in a world where politics and equity must be balanced.

Full State Funding Plans

Although the policy arena has steadily moved through the eras of flat grants and foundation formulas and equalization aid schemes, school finance theory has considered other alternatives that have been even less enthusiastically welcomed. As such, chronological adoption and technological sophistication have not always coincided. This has particularly been true when considering more radical schemes such as full state funding. Chronologically, full state funding was first proposed in the early 1930s by Morrison, a harsh critic of state aid plans that did not fully meet the criterion of equity. He was especially critical of contemporary aid plans because he had no patience with delaying available technological superiority to await political readiness. As stated earlier, Morrison's views were particularly advanced as he noted that it is fundamentally illogical to fund education by any plan that does not reflect state responsibility for education as constitutionally mandated. Considering education a state responsibility, Morrison argued that nothing less than full state funding could guarantee equity for all children—a view in which he called for the state to assume all fiscal administration of schools.

In contrast to the oftentimes complex state aid formulas considered in this chapter, full state funding is both conceptually and operationally simple. As the name implies, the concept of education as a state responsibility is embraced so that funding likewise becomes the state's obligation. Operationally, full state funding places all the resources of a state in reach of every child, generally by requiring a statewide tax initially apportioned equally to every child without regard to location or wealth.[28] Three critical features follow, however, that further distinguish full state funding from all other aid plans. First, there can be no local spending leeway because localities no longer factor into a statewide scheme. Second, all revenue belongs to the state as the "local" tax has become a tax on local wealth remitted to the state for redistribution without regard for location. Third, this last reality effectively legitimizes and operationalizes recapture as a distinguishing feature of full state funding. These features are radically different from the benevolent nature of foundation plans, and particularly run counter to the intensely local preferences of resource accessibility schemes.

Although Morrison's arguments are no longer viewed as radical, it is easy to see how the technologically superior equity performance of full state funding has outstripped political viability, preventing all but a very few states from adopting full state funding and almost universally being adopted in the wake of extenuating circumstances. This is immediately evident in that only Hawaii follows the classic de jure full state funding model, a reality coinciding with its unique lack of local property taxes and its lack of "traditional" local school districts. Within seven taxing jurisdictions, school "districts" in Hawaii simply send budget requests to the state for legislative consideration. Extenuating circumstances also describe the only other full "state" funded school system, as the District of Columbia receives its operating funds directly from Congress. A few other states qualify as "almost full state funded," also under unusual circumstances, as in California and Florida where local property tax limitations have created de facto full state funding.[29] For example, the Florida legislature sets a range of approved local property tax rates and also determines allowable costs per pupil, with the state funding the difference. Since almost every district exercises the maximum millage, Florida effectively has full state funding without ever having formally adopted it.

Despite recognition that full state funding represents a technically correct way of achieving a high level of fiscal equity, the political unpopularity of shifting decision making to the state has effectively prevented its adoption in all but the most unusual instances. Yet it is easy to see that full state funding is the easiest and best expression of the nature of defining educational responsibility, and Morrison's observation of fundamental incorrectness of vesting conceptual responsibility at the state and operational responsibility at lesser levels was entirely accurate. It is also important to note that full state funding is the only plan that assures horizontal equity among all children of the state. But with few exceptions, the technology of full state funding has always exceeded its political popularity, thus predicting the foreseeable future with relative confidence.

The Best Aid Scheme

Examination of the various aid schemes raises the question of whether one plan is preferable to the others. The answer, however, is less obvious than all the foregoing discussion implies because deep-seated values play a strong part in the response. It is relatively easy to rank state aid plans according to equity achievement, and it is reasonable to read into the discussion that the various aid plans have been presented in ascending order of equity achievement. Technology must still be weighed against political realities, however, and the response must be twofold. First, it is at once possible to be on the cutting edge *and* to be tilting at windmills because nothing will occur before its time. Yet as evidenced by the chronology of this chapter, frontiers are continually opened by pioneering thought. Each plan has been an improvement on history, and there is reason to believe that the future will also represent improvement as political readiness and available technology continue to combine almost imperceptibly, backward momentum seldom being an enduring reality. Second, it must be remembered that progress will be slow because the argument is *fundamentally* difficult since liberty and equality are at odds. If liberty through minimum provision or local leeway wins, equity loses; likewise if equity wins, liberty and individuality must lose.

Johns, Morphet, and Alexander proposed a series of options in selecting the best finance plan that are provocative when restated as "if . . . then" postulates. They argue that the choice among competing plans is made on the basis of values, and that differing value structures dictate different outcomes. As such, it would seem that no finance plan will ever meet all the criteria applied by everyone because people are innately different and hold diverse views of the world. Under these conditions, it would seem that each person must individually decide to take sides on the issue of a best finance plan and allow the imperfections to be resolved by the democratic process of majority rule. Since majority rule can be wrong, it is imperative that knowledge should guide and temper the decisions of both individuals and society. As democracy is presently structured in the United States, policymakers are held accountable to both the will of voters and the courts, which provide a needed tension of checks and balances. The queries proposed by Johns, Morphet, and Alexander place these choices in perspective when restated as follows:

1. *If* it is believed that a basic educational opportunity should be available to all and that wisdom and merit rests in liberty, *then* an equalization model should be chosen; or
2. *If* it is believed that educational opportunities must be equal without variation, *then* full state support is the only answer.

Thus, the answer to the "best" finance plan must be that tension of informed choice is necessary, since the alternative is suppression of at least one premise of democracy.

FORMULA ADJUSTMENTS

Discussion of the various school finance formulas in this chapter thus far has been predicated on the assumption that all children are equal. But as stated at the outset, that assumption is only partially true. Obviously, all children are of equal worth, and that premise has been the basis of presenting state aid formulas without discussion of any other adjustments that would be required if children were not equal. It is thus the first premise of state aid distribution that horizontal equity must be present if an aid scheme merits adoption. As seen in this chapter, however, many state aid plans have only imperfectly provided horizontal equity, and it will be seen in the next chapter that states have suffered much anxiety over this issue through the course of lengthy equity litigation. But it should not be assumed that horizontal equity is the sufficient end of formula design because it is obvious that children are not equal on economic, social, or physical planes. As a result, it has been necessary to adjust aid formulas to consider the differences among children in the belief that elements of verticality will better lead to ultimate horizontal equity—that is, initial equality should be carried to end equality insofar as possible.

Formula adjustment to reflect vertical equity is an exceedingly complex topic that has long preoccupied school finance scholars. In fact, it is accurate to say that the vast majority of the professional literature in school finance is concerned in some way with improving vertical equity and testing the means by which equity can be measured. This text briefly introduces the most common formula adjustments applied in the modern school finance arena. These adjustments fall within the broad headings of *need equalization* and *cost equalization*. The traditional view has been that need equalization aligns most closely with vertical equity adjustments or formula add-ons for programs such as compensatory, bilingual, and special education, while cost equalization focuses on vertical adjustments for differences such as economies of scale and market baskets. The assumption, of course, is that horizontal equity will be aided by vertical adjustment because children will be more nearly equal through the unequal treatment of unequals.

Need Equalization

If all children in a school district were exactly equal in economic, social, physical, and intellectual status, state aid formulas would not need to be concerned with vertical adjustment. But as seen in earlier chapters, children suffer increasingly from myriad complex problems that negatively affect their future life chances. In addition to inequality on such dimensions, these children are seldom evenly distributed across all school districts. For example, urban schools have large minority populations, and the frequency and nature of problems relating to poverty is likewise unevenly concentrated among districts. Of particular merit in need equalization is the extreme disadvantage many children face as a result of special handicapping conditions that affect their ability to learn. As awareness and identification of these complex issues has grown, states have recognized the need to provide additional resources in an attempt to offer these children a more equal footing in a competitive society. As a consequence, there have been special efforts to concentrate additional resources on three need areas of *compensatory, bilingual,* and *special* education.

Compensatory Education. As seen in Chapter 2 of this text, compensatory education has long been a major federal thrust. Appropriately named for its interest in compensating social and economic disadvantage among deprived groups, compensatory education has also attracted the attention of some states. Although various states have long provided some such support, the greatest interest has occurred since the War on Poverty, which began the federal practice of granting Title I money under the

Elementary and Secondary Education Act of 1965 to give additional instruction to children from poverty families. Title I caused several states to initiate their own compensatory education programs, not only because of the political popularity of social programs at that time, but also because of growing concern for other vertical equity issues, such as new awareness about the need for special education. Through a series of complex social and political events, compensatory education programs were in place in more than half the states by 1990.

The level of fiscal support for compensatory education, however, has varied greatly among the individual states. Likewise, the means by which states have chosen to aid these children has also varied widely. Although there has been common consensus that poverty is the best indicator of need for compensatory services, the aid mechanisms have varied widely. In some states, flat grants have been used to supplement regular education expenditures, while other states have sought a greater degree of equalization based on local ability to pay. In addition, in some states the various aid mechanisms have been attached to the general state aid formula, while in other instances they have stood as separate formulas with separate fund accounting schemes. Although uniformity has not been widely apparent, all these formulas have sought to provide extra aid on the assumption that these children can benefit from more intensive services due to their backgrounds.

As a general rule, states with aid for compensatory education have followed three general patterns. First, the costs of compensatory education have been viewed as an add-on to the costs of regular education that disadvantaged children also receive. Second, states have generally required that local districts share in the extra costs. Third, states have generally provided such aid in philosophic parallel to their general aid schemes so that compensatory aid formulas either reflect a minimum approach or a fairly equalized intent. As a result, in some states aid is at such a low level that it serves only as an incentive to establish and operate programs. In a few other instances, cost schemes have been heavily state supported. Generally, the first philosophy has been supported by the use of flat grants. In contrast, the second philosophy has been more prone to base aid on some equalized formula. In the latter instance, the common methods have been either to include these programs into the regular aid formula by a system of pupil weightings, or to create categorical aid in the form of a system of equalized entitlements.

The concept of pupil weighting has been popular in all of the various vertical adjustments discussed here. Weighting is simply the process of determining how much more it costs to provide a special service and adding that amount to the cost of a regular education child for inclusion in the general aid formula. Weighting schemes are always based on a regular education child at a weight of 1.0 wherein the cost of a child with no special needs is defined as the uniform expenditure level for all such children. The cost of a special needs child can then be calculated as some amount greater than 1.0 where the weight will be the program's cost divided by the number of children served. For example, a regular education child funded at $3,600 provides a base weight of 1.0. If the cost of remedial reading programs across a state are found and averaged at an additional 25%, then the state may choose to fund that child at a total weight of 1.25. This does not mean that the state will fully pay for either the 1.0 or the additional .25 weight, but it does mean that this child will be run through the regular state aid formula at a higher weight than if these services were not received. This same concept is commonly applied to all vertical programs in a state so that this discussion describes other weights that will appear later under bilingual, special education, or costs programs, which take each child at 1.0 and sum all other weights to produce the weighted pupil.

The weighting scheme is important both for its functional operation in providing aid for compensatory and other vertical adjustments and for its inherent philosophy. States using this scheme are more likely to view education rather holistically, focusing on recognition of special pupil needs while seeking the highest practical inclusion of these students in the total educational program of the district. There is likewise an inclusion theme to running weights through the regular education formula in that the same philosophy that drives regular education funding also drives vertical adjustments. The issues in such states have less to do with whether these services should be provided than with the weights that should be attached to each identified condition. Weights have been fairly common in compensatory education programs.

The common alternative to pupil weighting has been a system of categorical aids, or money sent to a district to be used for a special purpose such as compensatory education. Categorical aids have several traits that distinguish them from weights. First, a categorical aid is generally restricted to the specific program and requires separate fund accounting to assure that these monies are in fact spent as intended. Second, categorical aid generally bears some relation to actual program costs in that aid per pupil should approximate average program costs, but there is less explicit expectation that aid is an intense function of cost studies. For these reasons, there is no implicit assumption that the method of distribution of categoricals will reflect the philosophy of the general aid formula because there is no dependent relationship. However, a system of categorical aid may reflect either a minimum philosophy or a high level of concern in that the categorical formula may be more equalized or may be funded at a higher level than the general aid formula. The result is that categorical programs have often provided flat grants, or alternatively have followed an excess cost reimbursement scheme that refunds most or all of the costs of programs above the price of regular education in the local district. The latter has been more common in special education, with compensatory education more often aided by weights or flat grants.

Table 4.2 broadly details the compensatory education plans in place in those states that have chosen to accept special responsibility for this vertical equity question. These data illustrate a wide variation in the approaches of states, but there are themes on three major aspects. First, the two most common methods are weighting schemes and flat grants. Second, the more prevalent is the weighting scheme, with numerous states utilizing weights compared to few states using flat grants. Weighting schemes vary widely, however, in impact. For example, weights range from a low .18 in one state to a high 1.1 in another, with an average in all states of about .25. Third, it is noteworthy that many of these states use schemes consistent with their general aid formulas. For example, Hawaii is the only full state funded general aid formula and likewise has a fully funded compensatory education program. Likewise, states that tend toward equalization in general aid are more prone to adopt compensatory education formulas reflecting weighting or variable grant structures. There is less linear relationship in those states using flat grants, although one of two assumptions is valid. One assumption is that aid is sufficiently high to represent significant state concern, while the other assumption is that the flat grant represents an add-on minimum approach.

On the whole, compensatory education has been of some vertical equity interest to slightly more than half the states. Among those states there has been a presumption

TABLE 4.2   State methods of aiding compensatory education, 1991

State	Method
Arkansas	Flat grant
California	Complex needs formula
Connecticut	Flat grant per needy pupil
Delaware	Flat grant with equalization component
Florida	Weighted
Georgia	Weighted
Hawaii	Full funding
Illinois	Multilevel grants
Indiana	Weights and competitive grants
Kentucky	Flat grant
Louisiana	Flat grant
Maryland	Equalized
Massachusetts	Weighted
Michigan	Needs-based formula scale
Minnesota	Weighted
Mississippi	Flat grant
Missouri	Flat grant
New Jersey	Weighted
New York	Weighted
North Carolina	Flat grant
Ohio	Equalized
Oklahoma	Weighted
Oregon	Special grant only to Portland
South Carolina	Matching grant
Texas	Weighted
Virginia	Equalized
Washington	Weighted
Wisconsin	Competitive grant
Wyoming	Flat grant

SOURCE: Excerpted and modified from American Education Finance Association, *Public School Finance Programs of the United States and Canada 1990–91,* ed. Steven Gold. (Albany: American Education Finance Association, State University of New York at Albany, 1992).

that federal interest in Title I and other disadvantaged legislation is appropriately placed, no doubt augmented by each state's experiences in student achievement relating to unique population characteristics. Whether compensatory education will take on new dimensions in the future is not known, but it can be hypothesized that interest may grow as demographic change increasingly focuses attention on at-risk children.

Bilingual Education.   A second area of vertical concern to states has been in relation to students who are linguistically handicapped in an English-dominant instructional setting. Obviously this has been a greater concern in some states due to larger populations from non–English-language backgrounds, but it has been a legitimate policy question in every state to some extent. It has particularly been of recent merit, as states have had to respond to pressure from the courts brought on by the

California lawsuit in *Lau v. Nichols*[30] in 1974, which ruled that Title VII of the Civil Rights Act of 1964 also embraced language deficiency. In its decision, the U.S. Supreme Court ruled that equal educational opportunity is not adequately provided merely by supplying all students with the same teachers and textbooks. While lower courts in the wake of *Lau* have not been consistent in determining the extent of special equal educational opportunity requirements for language-deficient children,[31] the rulings have caused many states to make provisions for bilingual education as they feared lawsuits or loss of federal funding if they failed to comply. Although some critics argue recent losses in bilingual status,[32] pressure has continued as Congress has amended the Bilingual Education Act on several occasions, with reauthorization debate scheduled for 1993.

Although designed to compensate for educational disadvantages brought on by inability to compete from the dominant language base, states have taken very different approaches to providing bilingual education services. Whereas the common theme of regular compensatory education programs was extra tutoring in basic skill areas, bilingual education has been the subject of some debate regarding the best and most economical method of service delivery. Among the states providing bilingual services, variable enthusiasm is reflected in both the method of delivery and in aid formula design. The level of commitment is generally reflected in both these aspects, as different delivery systems have different costs. Generally the states with the highest bilingual populations also have the highest expenditures, a reality accompanied by a propensity to teach children in true bilingual programs. States with lower bilingual numbers likewise spend less, and are more likely to provide services through English as a Second Language (ESL). Aid formulas have fallen in line with these realities, as states exhibiting reluctance to provide services use rather minimum aid plans, while other states have more fully incorporated bilingual education into the mainstream of school funding.

Table 4.3 illustrates the variable interest in bilingual education among the 50 states, as it can be seen that only 26 states have formal state aid structures for bilingual services. These mechanisms are generally reflective of the approach to compensatory education seen earlier, although some greater degree of variability in funding schemes can be seen. Slightly less than half of the states use weighting schemes that attach to their general aid formulas, with a small increase in the number of states using flat grant mechanisms. This variability seems reflective of the different approaches among states to service provisions, as some states seek to provide more extensive bilingual programs while others provide ESL support or various transitional programs to move children quickly back into the mainstream of regular English instruction. Although bilingual education remains controversial and subject to the flow of political thought, it can be seen that vertical equity as expressed by improving a child's ability to function in an English-dominant setting is a meaningful consideration in a significant number of states' vertical need equalization schemes.

Special Education.   Although compensatory and bilingual education have been assigned some priority among various states, vertical formula adjustments for the purpose of equalizing needs are most strikingly apparent in special education provisions. Special education has been a reality in many states for decades, as states voluntarily provided some services to children with special physical or intellectual needs that could not be effectively served in the regular classroom. In many instances, these programs were funded at special schools designed for these children, and in a few

TABLE 4.3 State methods of aiding bilingual
programs, 1991

State	Method
Arizona	Weighted
California	Complex need formula
Colorado	Flat grant
Connecticut	Flat grant
Delaware	Flat grant
Florida	Weighted
Georgia	Weighted
Hawaii	Full funding
Idaho	Flat grant
Illinois	Limited reimbursement
Iowa	Weighted
Kansas	Flat grant
Maine	Variable grant
Massachusetts	Weighted
Michigan	Flat grant
Minnesota	Classroom unit grant
New Jersey	Weighted
New Mexico	Weighted
New York	Percentage equalized and competitive
North Carolina	Flat grant
Oklahoma	Weighted
Texas	Weighted
Vermont	Equalized and other grants
Virginia	Equalized
Washington	Flat grant
Wisconsin	Percentage grant

SOURCE: Excerpted and modified from American Education Finance
Association, *Public School Finance Programs of the United States and
Canada 1990–91,* ed. Steven Gold (Albany: American Education
Finance Association, State University of New York at Albany, AEFA,
1992); and Education Commission of the States, *School Finance at a
Glance,* ed. Deborah Verstegen (Denver: Education Commission of
the States, 1988). Where sources are in disagreement, the latest
source is used.

instances programs were carried out in regular school settings. It is important to recognize, however, that special education schemes have only reached their present level within the last 20 years as these programs have moved from strictly voluntary offerings to mandated programs aimed at vertically equalizing children's educational opportunities. As a result of several lawsuits involving the right to an appropriate education, a wide variety of special services has become an integral part of state aid schemes in all 50 states.

The impetus for special education was produced by two nearly simultaneous forces. The first force was a series of lawsuits beginning in the early 1970s that sought to require states and school districts to provide appropriate education to all children regardless of their physical or mental abilities. One of the earliest cases was *PARC v. Pennsylvania*[33] in 1972 which tested the constitutionality of a law that excluded mentally retarded children from school if they had been certified as uneducable or untrainable or could not test to the mental age of a normal five-year-old child. Through an unusual series of circumstances involving consent decree wherein settlement was reached between the plaintiffs and the state, a historic legal requirement was laid down, stating that all children must be provided access to a free public education "appropriate to his learning capacities."[34] Although agreement to provide appropriate services was reached in this instance, special education litigation was to grow to immense proportions over the next two decades. The second force was the passage of the Education of the Handicapped Act (EHA)[35] by Congress in 1975 mandating special education services in any state that wished to continue receiving federal education aid.

The rulings by various courts and federal threats were sufficient to quickly bring states into compliance with special education service requirements. An enormous maze of statutes and regulations quickly followed, all of which were intended to provide equal educational opportunity for handicapped children. As seen earlier in this text, this included ever-expanding definitions and redefinitions of handicapping conditions so that new handicapped classifications continue to be proposed to Congress. The general result, however, was to force states to provide funding for the 12 special education categories mandated by federal law that include deaf, deaf-blind, hearing impaired, mentally retarded, multiply handicapped, orthopedically handicapped, other health impaired, seriously emotionally disturbed, specific learning disabilities, speech impaired, visually handicapped, and autistic. Although efforts to reduce the impact of special education have occurred in such forms as the Regular Education Initiative (REI), special services to handicapped children have remained a powerful force wherein states and school districts alike closely monitor compliance to avoid costly lawsuits.

As a result of the attention to special education, states have developed rather elaborate funding mechanisms. In all fairness, however, it should be said that these mechanisms are thought to be more elaborate primarily because of the level of mandated intensity and the level of funding, rather than for their technological complexity. In other words, states generally fund special education in much the same way as other vertical needs are funded, but the mandated nature of these programs and the vast dollars caused stricter oversight and monitoring than may be true for more permissive programs. As such, states are inclined to fund special education by weighting handicapping conditions or to use categorical grants that often operate as excess cost reimbursement schemes. Weighting schemes operate exactly as described earlier, wherein each handicapping condition is usually examined to track historic cost data in order to calculate a weight above the regular education child. Excess cost reimbursement is often designed in other states to develop similar cost data, from which states either pay such costs or reimburse some percentage of costs. A third alternative is to calculate the costs of each instructional organization and reimburse part or all of such costs to districts.

Table 4.4 broadly defines various state plans for funding special education. These data show that many states either weight pupils by handicapping condition or make other weighted provisions of instructional units. Likewise, another set of states fund special education by classroom units to produce nearly the same effect, while others use a cost reimbursement scheme wherein the state either pays the excess costs or reimburses school districts some percentage of those costs. Finally, a small number of states use other arrangements, as a few states fund special education with flat grants or combinations of various aid plans. As expected, Hawaii continues its consistent behavior by funding special education in its full state funding plan.

TABLE 4.4 State methods of aiding special education, 1991

State	Method	State	Method
Alabama	Instructional unit	Montana	Percentage reimbursement
Alaska	Instructional unit	Nebraska	Excess cost
Arizona	Weighted	Nevada	Flat grant
Arkansas	Weighted	New Hampshire	Excess cost
California	Instructional unit	New Jersey	Weighted
Colorado	Excess cost	New Mexico	Weighted
Connecticut	Equalized grant	New York	Combination
Delaware	Weighted	North Carolina	Flat grant
Florida	Weighted	North Dakota	Excess cost
Georgia	Weighted	Ohio	Combination
Hawaii	Full funding	Oklahoma	Weighted
Idaho	Combination	Oregon	Excess cost
Illinois	Combination	Pennsylvania	Excess cost
Indiana	Weighted	Rhode Island	Excess cost
Iowa	Weighted	South Carolina	Weighted
Kansas	Instructional unit	South Dakota	Percentage reimbursement
Kentucky	Per-pupil unit	Tennessee	Weighted
Louisiana	Instructional unit	Texas	Weighted
Maine	Percentage reimbursement	Utah	Weighted
Maryland	Excess cost	Vermont	Combination
Massachusetts	Weighted	Virginia	Equalized
Michigan	Percentage reimbursement	Washington	Combination
Minnesota	Percentage reimbursement	West Virginia	Weighted
Mississippi	Instructional unit	Wisconsin	Percentage reimbursement
Missouri	Instructional unit	Wyoming	Percentage reimbursement

SOURCE: Excerpted and modified from American Education Finance Association, *Public School Finance Programs of the United States and Canada 1990–91,* ed. Steven Gold (Albany: American Education Finance Association, State University of New York at Albany, 1992); and Deborah Verstegen and Cynthia Cox, "State Models for Financing Special Education," in *Helping At-Risk Students: What are the Educational and Financial Costs?* 13th Annual Yearbook of the American Education Finance Association, ed. Patricia Anthony and Stephen Jacobson (Beverly Hills: Sage, 1992), 146–147.

Special education has become a mighty force that few states want to offend for both educational and political reasons. When compensatory, bilingual, and special education are considered in tandem, vertical equity takes on important dimensions in state funding schemes as formulas now attempt to adjust educational opportunities on the basis of needs equalization. From this perspective, much progress has been made in that basic formulas can seek to equalize education for regular students, while vertical adjustments care for students with unequal needs.

Cost Equalization

Although needs equalization has been a primary method of aiding vertical equity, a number of states have also attempted to redress other differences that may result in inequality among students. As stated earlier, these efforts have generally focused on differences in costs that occur among school districts as a consequence of economies of scale and market baskets. In this sense, formula adjustment for economies of scale is simply a recognition that different costs may arise as a result of size of a school district, since education may be considerably more expensive per child when districts are either very small or quite large—an observation more correctly stated as adjust-ments for either economy or *dis*economy of scale. The other common cost equaliza-tion factor considers market baskets, wherein districts are analogous to consumers in a marketplace of goods and services that may be more or less expensive according to geographic location. In these instances, urban districts may pay higher prices due to the need for competitive salaries or for higher costs of other goods and services. Alter-natively, rural districts may face problems of distance, as attracting good teachers may be difficult. As a general rule, it is helpful to conceptualize such adjustments as modifi-cations to basic state aid formulas on behalf of regular education children who may be disadvantaged for some reason unrelated to socioeconomics or special handicapping condition.

The economy of scale adjustment is best conceptualized when it is understood that economies of scale occur when larger organizations can produce the same out-comes as smaller organizations for less cost. As such, economies of scale are generally traced to two sources. The first source involves the problems faced by small organiza-tions when they seek to buy smaller amounts of relatively indivisible inputs. The re-sult may be a tendency for small organizations to purchase more inputs than is opti-mal in terms of efficiency. For example, rural schools may be forced to fund smaller class sizes than the state prefers. To the extent that student learning is unaided by small classes, the teacher resource is being underutilized because of indivisibility. This underutilization erodes the efficiency of the school, leading to the further obser-vation that small organizations cost more to achieve the same result. A second source of scale economies involves the gain in specialization that can accompany increases in scale. For example, a common scenario involves 30 students and one teacher in one district and 240 students and eight teachers in a second district. The pupil-teacher ratio is 30:1 in both cases, but in the latter case each teacher can specialize to a degree that is nearly impossible in the first instance. To the degree that specialization is linked to learning, the second district will produce more than the first at the same cost, suggesting that a smaller district can produce equal outcomes only if it spends more to hire more teachers.

While most states have not become politically sophisticated in maximizing a pro-duction function of economy of scale, numerous policy deliberations paralleling that logic have occurred. For example, legislatures often seek answers to why costs are higher in some districts, and the answers are generally found in the variable costs of inputs such as personnel, buildings, teaching materials, transportation, and other fixed costs wherein the cost of producing educational outcomes is found to be di-rectly related to the size of district membership. Research has thus generally shown that economies of scale can be graphically proved by a U-shaped cost curve as seen in Figure 4.6. That is, the cost per pupil for a given level of educational outcome de-creases as the size of student membership increases to the point of maximum effi-ciency where the costs are lowest. Beyond that point, costs per pupil increase again.[36] The explanation for this phenomenon is that teachers or other inputs are not fully utilized at very low enrollments, that is, the fixed costs of salaries and building mainte-nance and operations are essentially the same whether 10 or 20 students are taught. The cost per pupil, however, changes dramatically if the costs are spread over 20 students instead of 10. It can thus be easily seen that this phenomenon encouraged school consolidation during the first half of this century.

At the opposite end of the scale, costs can increase as district size passes the point of maximum efficiency. Large urban districts rely on efficiency curves to ex-plain their higher costs in that they are often asked to provide higher levels of ser-

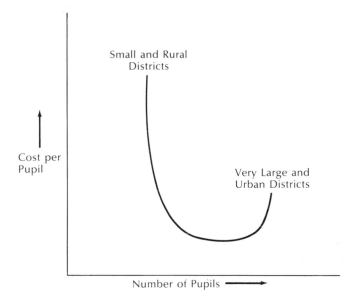

FIGURE 4.6   Graphic representation of economy of scale

vices, particularly in relation to disadvantaged populations that cluster in urban areas. This argument takes two forms, the first encompassing the enhanced service function, the second relating to the market basket concept. The first form argues that vast organizations require more costly structures, with attendant costs not experienced in smaller districts. For example, data developed in a recent urban lawsuit noted that as many as 50% of all students in some schools in the district were served by at-risk programs, that approximately 10% of all students were served in federally aided disadvantaged programs, that 12% of all students were in special education programs where additional spending ranged from a low $3,558 to a high $16,374 per pupil, and that another 10% of the district's budget was spent on other social services not included in these costs.[37] The second form then follows, wherein a market basket is applied. Usually, urban costs are linked to higher teacher salaries, more expensive local economies, extra security needs, vandalism, and a host of other urban issues to justify the upward trend of the U-curve. Finally, the second argument is also applied to rural districts in that these schools often must pay more for teachers, transportation, and so forth to attract staff and serve children in large or isolated areas.

As a result of these and other concerns, many states have enacted vertical formula adjustments that can be attached to the regular aid scheme for the purpose of aiding conditions believed to hinder initial horizontal equality. These structures are without exception cost equalization strategies, although overlap does occur. For example, compensatory, bilingual, and special education can be quickly observed to blur into the matrix of various cost equalization schemes. Cost equalization, however, has been legislatively courted—a phenomenon that likely follows the desire of legislators to visibly serve their own constituencies. The formulas have again been typical of the foregoing discussion, as cost equalization has been addressed through categorical aid schemes or through weightings that may attach to the regular aid plan. A summary of major cost equalization plans is seen in Table 4.5 where the data show that 30 states

TABLE 4.5   General fund cost equalization schemes[1]

State	Density/Sparsity	Enrollment Decline/Increase	Grade Level
Alabama		✓	✓
Alaska	✓		✓
Arizona	✓	✓	✓
Arkansas			
California	✓	✓	✓
Colorado	✓	✓	✓
Connecticut	✓		
Delaware			✓
Florida	✓	✓	✓
Georgia	✓	✓	✓
Hawaii			
Idaho	✓	✓	✓
Illinois			✓
Indiana		✓	✓
Iowa	✓	✓	
Kansas	✓	✓	
Kentucky	✓	✓	✓
Louisiana	✓		
Maine	✓	✓	✓
Maryland			✓
Massachusetts	✓		✓
Michigan			
Minnesota	✓		✓
Mississippi			
Missouri			✓
Montana	✓		✓
Nebraska	✓	✓	✓
Nevada	✓	✓	✓
New Hampshire			✓
New Jersey			✓
New Mexico	✓	✓	✓
New York		✓	✓
North Carolina	✓		✓
North Dakota	✓		✓
Ohio	✓	✓	
Oklahoma	✓	✓	✓
Oregon	✓	✓	✓
Pennsylvania	✓		✓
Rhode Island			
South Carolina			✓
South Dakota	✓		
Tennessee			✓
Texas	✓		
Utah	✓		
Vermont		✓	✓
Virginia			
Washington	✓	✓	✓
West Virginia			
Wisconsin			
Wyoming	✓	✓	✓

[1]Broadly interpreted for effect of explicit categories and implicit provisions built into regular funding schemes. Does not include any provisions for vocational, special education, or other.

SOURCE: Excerpted and modified from American Education Finance Association, *Public School Finance Programs of the United States and Canada 1990–91,* ed. Steven Gold (Albany: American Education Finance Association, State University of New York at Albany, 1992).

provide aid for enrollment density or sparsity, 22 states grant aid to declining enrollment or growth, and 34 states provide aid to grade level differences. In a few instances, there have been attempts to use price differential indices, although this practice has never gained strong support due to its technical complexity. A more common practice has been special legislative appropriation to districts presenting strong cases or by implicit inclusion of price indices in other adjustments, such as school size, or various state-specific techniques, such as using the more advantageous of the current or prior year's enrollment for calculating state aid.

Summary of State Aid Formulas

Our discussion of state aid formulas permits several final conclusions. First, it has long been recognized that state responsibility for education creates a special obligation on the part of states to assure equal educational opportunity. Second, that responsibility has resulted in increasingly sophisticated aid mechanisms that have grown to encompass not only horizontal equity, but also vertical equity. Third, these recognitions have played well to formula design because state aid plans are first constructed under assumptions of equality and then adjusted to reflect differences among pupils that are inherent to a real world. Fourth, progress toward more equitable aid schemes has been slowed at times by the operation of politics seeking to resist the costs of improvement, but in other instances progress has been accelerated because of the political benefit to be gained from advocating contemporary social issues. Fifth, although no state has adopted a "perfect" aid scheme, there has been overall genuine improvement since the beginning of this century, and there have likewise been major gains in the humane treatment of all persons. As a consequence, the new frontiers of school finance formulas lie either in refinements to the ever-expanding definition of equity, or in an unprecedented breakthrough that would shift education responsibility to a more national arena.

MEASURING FORMULA EQUITY

The intensely local nature of education has been raised throughout this text with the blunt implication that variation in program quality is partly a function of differing resources. While it is equally conceded that absolute fiscal equality would not automatically result in equally absolute quality, it can be shown that variations in funding at least accompany and perhaps impact the level of educational services and productivity represented by the nearly 16,000 school districts in the nation. There has been a further intentional implication that the highly state-specific nature of school finance results in differential funding, induced in large part by different aid mechanisms that perform variably under equity examination. In fact, this chapter's epigraph makes a statement so direct and blunt that it is impossible to be more clear about the causes of inequality. Under these conditions, three options remain: to argue that little more can be accomplished because great gains have been made, to seek national assumption of education in the belief that a more global view will at worst level a vast playing field, or to closely scrutinize funding formulas for the purpose of making continual equity adjustments. While the latter views are preferable, the most realistic immediate truth is vested in close scrutiny.

Two paths are available by which scrutiny and improvement may occur. One path of scrutiny examines production functions at increasingly smaller units through microlevel analysis as discussed in Chapter 1. This path is particularly promising, both as a function of newer and more sophisticated knowledge about educational productivity and as a function of realizing that radical formula redesign is less likely to occur than at any point in the past. A second path has a longer tradition by scrutinizing the equity of state aid formulas in distributing fiscal resources. Although this path is more traditional, its utility will likely continue for two principal reasons. First, school finance is not immediately destined to leave the control of states; a reality that notes that states, in turn, control local districts. Second, this observation is supported by the reality that states are becoming more, rather than less, responsible for education. Both paths thus need to be pursued simultaneously, but vigilance over state aid formulas will continue to be a primary thrust of school finance analysts, the courts, and state policymakers. As a result, some knowledge about measuring formula equity is incumbent upon everyone who occupies a position of responsibility for education.

Measurement of formula equity is generally focused along three dimensions that relate to horizontal and vertical equity. Most policymakers concentrate on horizontal equity, if for no other reason than it is more easily understood and measured. In addition, vertical equity is extraordinarily complex so that agreement about measurement or achievement is not assured, and its costs are often thought to be prohibitive. Further, vertical equity may presume a focus on educational outcomes among unequal populations—a topic that makes policymakers distinctly uneasy and for which the technology for accurate measurement has not been fully developed.[38] As a result, the bulk of equity measurement has occurred in horizontal generalities about state aid schemes along the three dimensions of *resource accessibility, wealth neutrality,* and *tax yield.* Resource accessibility refers to the now familiar concept of measuring whether all students in a state have equal access to resources. Wealth neutrality carries that notion to the next level by asking whether the available resources are related to the accident of location, that is, district wealth. Tax yield naturally goes to the issue of unequal wealth by asking whether a state aid formula offsets these inherent inequalities. At once singular and interdependent, the equity performance of any state aid formula may be tested on these dimensions using a set of common statistical tools.[39]

Resource Accessibility

Resource accessibility is primarily concerned with determining whether all students have equal access to the resource pool represented in a given state. This is obviously problematic in a policy sense because most states do not have a statewide education tax, offering prima facie violation of this standard. However, if it were to be discovered that no substantive differences in wealth existed, then the standard could be technically violated while substantively vacuous. Reality, however, suggests the unlikelihood of a smooth wealth distribution. As a result, the task of determining resource accessibility is one of measuring degrees of noncompliance. In most states, this means comparing the level of resources among districts with a common set of statistical tools and making a judgment of the relative achievement of equity among all districts in the state.

While there are numerous ways of reaching that goal, several measures of equity used to evaluate resource accessibility include the *mean, range, restricted range, federal range ratio, standard deviation, coefficient of variation,* and *variance.* These statistical tests are usually applied, by group, to a number of variables that represent items such as budgets, expenditures, wealth (the dollar value generated by one mill), budget surplus, and tax millage for each district in a distribution. The groups in these analyses can be selected to represent any number of comparisons. For example, an analysis might examine all districts or only large or small districts, or it might select groups of large and small districts for specific comparison purposes. Analyses can be built in almost infinite ways, making a thorough discussion the subject of another text. The purpose and outcome can be easily understood, however, given two important observations. First, the analysis will be specific to the given structure of a state and the hypotheses that initially sparked the investigation. Second, an understanding of these basic tools is needed to know whether their application is appropriate to a given situation. As such, each analysis will be different and may not include every tool discussed here, or alternatively, may use other tools not identified in this text.

Mean.   Although not a highly sophisticated tool, the mean is often the first tool to be applied in considering resource accessibility. The mean is a measure of the central tendency of the distribution of observations, that is, the mean represents the average value in the distribution of a variable. The mean takes into account all the observations in the distribution. The mean is calculated by a simple formula

$$\sum X_i \div N$$

where:

$\sum$ is the sum of all districts;
X_i is the value of a given variable in district i, and
N is the number of districts.

Solving this formula yields a single number for comparison purposes. For example, finding the sum of wealth of all districts in a state and dividing by the number of districts yields the mean wealth. Using dummy data, this can be illustrated as \$2,000,-000,000 ÷ 100 = \$2,000,000 where the sum of district wealth is \$2 billion, the number of districts is 100, and the mean district wealth is \$2 million. Each district, however, will not have exactly \$2 million in local wealth. Individual districts can then be compared to the mean for a crude estimation of variation. While the mean alone does not prove anything about resource accessibility, it is an excellent first step in assessing wealth variation because wide differences from the mean *unredressed by the state aid formula* could suggest inequity.[40]

Range.   A second measure that can be used to demonstrate simple differences in a distribution is the range, defined simply as the difference between the highest and lowest observations in a distribution. The smaller the value of the range, the smaller the variation in the distribution of a variable; likewise, the smaller the variation, the better the equity of the distribution. The range is easily found by the formula

$$\text{Highest } X_i - \text{Lowest } X_i$$

where:

X_i is the variable considered in district i.

Solving the formula yields a single number for the entire distribution. Using the same example but expressed as per-pupil wealth, the highest wealth district might have wealth of $500,000 compared to the lowest district with wealth of only $6,000 per pupil. In this case, the range is $500,000 – $6,000, or $494,000. Obviously, as a measure of equity the usefulness of the range is limited because it is based on only two values, does not show patterns of variation, and is not sensitive to changes in the distribution. Yet it is a useful tool for raw wealth measurement in that a wide range *unredressed by the aid formula* could suggest inequity.

Restricted Range.   The restricted range is a third measure that overcomes some of the problems of the range. The restricted range is defined as the difference between the observations at the 95th and 5th percentiles of the distribution. This is useful in viewing the total distribution because it eliminates the effect of misrepresentative values above and below these extremes. The restricted range is easily calculated by the formula

$$X_i \text{ at 95th percentile} - X_i \text{ at 5th percentile}$$

where
X_i is the variable considered in district i.

Solving this formula yields a single number for the distribution. Using the same example of per-pupil wealth, the highest wealth district at the 95th percentile might have wealth of $100,000 compared to the 5th percentile district wealth of $35,000 per pupil. As such, the restricted range is $100,000 – $35,000, or only $65,000. A very different picture is thus obtained in which extremely wealthy and poor districts at the top 5% and bottom 5% of the state distorted the total picture. As the restricted range decreases, equity increases. Although crude, the restricted range is helpful by reducing the distortion of a few extreme districts.

Federal Range Ratio.   Originally designed as a federal test to measure whether states met federal wealth neutrality guidelines in distributing federal funds, the federal range ratio is simply the restricted range divided by the revenue per pupil per district at the 5th percentile. The federal range ratio is calculated as

$$\text{Restricted Range} \div X_i \text{ at 5th percentile}$$

where
X_i is the revenue per pupil in district i.

Solving the formula yields a value expressed as a ratio wherein the smaller the value, the less variation or inequity in distribution. Using the same example of per-pupil wealth, the federal range ratio would be found as $65,000 ÷ $35,000, or 1.857. This number has utility primarily as an alternative expression of relative equity achievement and is subject to the same uses as the restricted range because it is based on that measure.

Standard Deviation.   The standard deviation is defined simply as the square root of the variance as calculated by the formula

$$\sqrt{\Sigma P_i \, (X_p - X_i)^2 \div \Sigma P_i}$$

Like the other measures described here, the smaller the calculated value, the smaller the variation in the distribution of revenues per pupil, and thus, the greater the equity. The standard deviation is based on assumptions about normal distributions in a bell curve and may thus be instructive about how a school finance formula affects various groups. For example, examination of a state aid formula might reveal that medium-size school districts received less revenue than all other districts and that their revenues were more than two standard deviations below the mean. Under these conditions, additional questions could arise about whether these districts are underfunded. The advantage of the standard deviation is that all observations are included in the calculation and the units of measurement are in the original scale. However, it is sensitive to outliers that could skew the distribution.

Variance.   The variance is defined simply as the average of the squared deviations from the mean as calculated by the formula

$$\Sigma P_i \, (X_p - X_i)^2 \div \Sigma P_i$$

where
  Σ is the sum of pupils in all districts;
  P_i is the number of students in district i;
  X_p is the mean of some tested variable for all pupils; and
  X_i is the same variable in district i.

When the results of the formula are obtained, the smaller the variance, the smaller the variation in the distribution of a given variable, and thus, the greater the equity. Although the variance is useless in descriptive statistics, it is highly important in inferential analysis because it permits testing for significant differences between groups. For example, a school finance lawsuit might seek to test if mean revenues of plaintiff and nonplaintiff districts are statistically different based on some illegitimate criterion such as district wealth variables. Under these conditions, analysis of variance could be used to infer various properties to the state aid scheme.

Coefficient of Variation.   The coefficient of variation is simply the standard deviation divided by the mean, or the square root of the variance divided by the mean. The coefficient of variation is expressed as the ratio of the standard deviation of the distribution to the mean of the distribution, calculated by the formula

$$\sqrt{[\Sigma P_i \, (X_p - X_i)^2 \div \Sigma P_i]} \div X_p$$

where
  X_p is the mean of some variable for all districts.

Solving the formula yields a single value between zero and one wherein smaller values demonstrate smaller variations in the distribution, thereby indicating greater equity.

While many uses of the coefficient of variation can be found, one example could compare differences in expenditure levels among districts in a state aid scheme that uses economies of scale as a basis for different levels of expenditure per pupil authority. For statistical purposes, the coefficient of variation can be important when sensitivity to outliers, but not to changes in scale, is required.

These measures of resource accessibility should be recognized as overlapping and almost redundant in some instances. As such, not all of these measures need to be used in analyzing resource accessibility, but each measure has assumptions and weaknesses implicit that should govern the selection among alternative choices. In addition, resource accessibility is merely a first step in measuring school finance equity. It is an important step, however, because equal access to resources is an obvious precondition of equal educational opportunity. It is equally important, however, to go beyond resource accessibility to determine whether differences are related to variations in wealth or whether other explanations are possible.

Wealth Neutrality and Tax Yield

Analysts often want to determine whether wealth neutrality and equal tax yield are demonstrated by a school finance formula. Like resource accessibility assessment, the range of choices in tools for evaluating wealth neutrality and tax yield is large. The conditions surrounding each project are different, and the suspicions of the analyst and the vagaries of each state can help establish the most appropriate tools. Three of the more common statistical measures used to assess wealth neutrality and equivalency of tax yield, however, are the *McLoone Index*, the *Gini coefficient*, and *correlational analysis and regression*.

McLoone Index.   The McLoone Index is a measure unique to school finance that was designed to demonstrate the degree of equity in the bottom half of a distribution. The McLoone Index is the ratio of the sum of observations below the median to the sum of all observations that would be required if all observations below the median were brought up to the median level. This can be better grasped in the example of expenditures per district. In this instance, the McLoone Index is the ratio of the sum of expenditures per district for all districts below the median to the sum of all expenditures that would be required if all districts below the median were brought up to the median level expenditure. The McLoone Index is calculated, using the expenditure example, by the formula

$$\Sigma(1 \ldots j) \, P_i X_i \div M_p \, \Sigma \, (1 \ldots j) \, P_i$$

where:

    districts 1 through j are below the median;

        Σ is the sum of pupils in all districts 1 to j,

        P_i is the number pupils in district i;

        X_i is the expenditure per pupil in district i; and

        M_p is the median expenditure per pupil for all districts.

Solving the formula gives a value where the larger the value of the McLoone Index, the closer the lower half of the distribution to the median of the distribution. This index is usually between zero and one; however, if the group of districts being compared has a mean value close to the median, this value can be greater than one.

Gini Coefficient.   The Gini coefficient is actually an economist's measure of income equality that indicates how far the distribution is from providing each percentage of a population with the same percentage of a variable, such as how far the distribution of expenditures is from providing each percentage of students with the same expenditure, or expenditure inequality. The Gini is calculated, using the expenditure example, by the rather complex formula

$$\Sigma_i \ \Sigma_j P_i P_j \ (X_i - X_j) \div 2(\Sigma_i \ P_i)^2 \ X_p$$

where:
  Σ is the sum for all pupils in districts i and j;
  P_i is the number of pupils in district i;
  P_j is the number of pupils in district j;
  X_i is the expenditure per pupil in district i;
  X_j is the expenditure per pupil in district j; and
  X_p is the mean expenditure per pupil for all districts.

Solving the formula yields a value from zero to one where the smaller the value of the Gini coefficient, the more equitable the distribution of expenditures in providing a specified percentage of students with the same percentage of expenditures. The coefficient compares expenditures at each level with expenditures at every other level so that perfect equity grants exactly equal proportions of expenditures to exactly equal proportions of the population. For example, 50% of a population should receive 50% of all resources. The Gini is sensitive to changes throughout the distribution, though not to extreme outliers.

Simple Correlation and Regression.   In assessing school finance equity, it is important to be able to estimate relationships that may vary in association. While all the measures described up to this point are highly useful by providing different kinds of data about variables such as wealth and revenues and expenditures, they are insufficient to do more than simply describe some variable. As such, all the foregoing measures are univariate in that they deal with the dispersion or variation of a single variable. To complement these tools, there are many other measures that describe relationships between two variables.[41] Regression-based measures are especially helpful in that they describe how variables perform in relation to each other and further allow, in some instances, inference about causation. Correlations and slopes are two regression-based measures that are included in this discussion of wealth neutrality and tax yield because they can indicate the degree to which district wealth and revenue are associated. Similarly, these measures are useful in assessing taxpayer equity by examining tax yield as measured by wealth neutrality.

   Simple correlation is a statistical tool that describes the degree to which two variables are associated with each other. For example, the two variables of wealth of school districts and expenditures per pupil could be examined for possible association. When these two variables are thus examined, the result is viewed as a description of the fiscal neutrality of a state aid formula. These variables are tested through correlation and regression analysis to confirm or deny a state's contentions that the formula is fiscally neutral. If the formula is indeed neutral, the analysis will indicate that there is no relationship between wealth and revenue per pupil.

   Several correlation procedures are possible based on the types of variables in question. For most purposes, the Pearson correlation coefficient is the appropriate tool and is calculated, using the expenditure example, as

$$P_i(X_i - X)(W_i - W) \div [\sqrt{} \sum P_i(X_i - X)^2][\sqrt{} \sum P_i(W_i - W)^2]$$

If the above example of correlating wealth and expenditures were the object of inquiry, the formula would be run

where:

- $\sum$ is the sum of pupils in all districts;
- P_i is the number of pupils in district i;
- X_i is the expenditure per pupil in district i;
- X is the mean expenditure per pupil for all districts;
- W_i is the wealth per pupil in district i; and
- W is the mean wealth per pupil for all districts.

The correlation coefficient would then yield a value ranging from −1.0 to +1.0. When two variables are positively associated, larger values of one tend to be accompanied by larger values of the other; conversely, if two variables are negatively related, larger values in one tend to be accompanied by smaller values of the other. A value of +1.0 indicates a perfect positive linear relationship and a value of −1.0 a perfect negative linear relationship, while a value of zero indicates no relationship. As a measure of fiscal neutrality, a correlation coefficient of zero would indicate no wealth to expenditure relationship. Generally, inference about causation is available as well through accompanying regression analysis wherein the square of the correlation coefficient explains the amount of change in one variable caused by the other.

The results of all these tests yield a set of observations about the equity of a school finance formula. As stated earlier, other tests can be run as well, but the objective is always to gain the best picture of a state's aid scheme on the three dimensions of resource accessibility, wealth neutrality, and tax yield. Under these conditions, a formula should yield proof that resources are equally available to all children, that variation in resources is not related to local wealth patterns, and that equal tax yield follows from equal tax effort. If the analysis fails to yield favorable results, the formula should be adjusted or abandoned.

A Sample Formula Analysis

As will be seen in Chapter 5, school finance formulas have been the focus of much bitter dissent over equity achievement. Plaintiffs have alleged formula inequity, and states have most often defended their formulas vigorously. Analysis of equity performance has been an important factor in judicial rulings, and almost every state has taken precautions to assess the equity performance of its state aid scheme. Because the statistical tools described here are in fact much more than abstract musings about equity, it is important to illustrate concretely how formula analysis can help guide researchers and policymakers in the pursuit of equal educational opportunity.

The following analysis is excerpted from a lawsuit in which most of the tests for equity discussed in this chapter were included.[42] The lawsuit was brought by plaintiff school districts, alleging that the state aid formula was unconstitutionally denying them equal access to fiscal resources based on differences in local district wealth that permitted more urban districts to raise more revenue at lower tax rates. Additionally, the plaintiffs contended that the state aid formula was biased against rural districts and restrained them from access to equal tax base. The state naturally chose to argue that differences were more a function of local inability to pass permissive tax levies and that the state could not be responsible for the operation of local politics. As such, both sides presented classic arguments. In anticipation that the data would prove or disprove either set of contentions, analyses were drawn by both sides.

Resource Accessibility.   Selected data developed on resource accessibility by one set of litigants are shown in Table 4.6 and Figure 4.7. Table 4.6 shows that for the state as a whole, the range in expenditures was $14,737 per pupil. When the restricted range removed the outliers, the difference was $6,570.50. Similar observations were made on yield per mill of tax effort, wherein it can be seen that the range measure of wealth varied by $911.20 per mill per pupil, with restricted range varying by $129.50. By these data, it seemed that wide disparities existed in the state. Yet these data were not sufficient to conclude the investigation because no causality was shown and because other data appeared to mitigate these results. For example, the restricted range greatly reduced disparities by removing a few extreme districts. More importantly, examination of mean expenditures showed that plaintiffs spent a mean $5,407.50 per pupil, compared to a mean $4,388.40 for nonplaintiffs. Obviously, these data did not appear to favor plaintiffs' claims of low expenditures compared to nonplaintiffs, despite wealth differences.

Figure 4.7 shows the results of analysis of variance that was conducted to see if

TABLE 4.6   Descriptive measures including range calculations for expenditures per pupil and mill value per pupil by group (in dollars)

Group	Mean	Standard Deviation	Minimum	Maximum	Range	Res. Range[1]
All Districts						
Exp/pupil	4,537.31	2,178.50	1,832.78	16,570.70	14,737.00	6,570.50
Mill value/pupil	44.84	67.80	0.26	911.45	911.20	129.50
Plaintiffs						
Exp/pupil	5,407.50	2,426.50	2,562.31	14,014.90	11,452.70	6,820.00
Mill value/pupil	52.36	44.58	6.912	230.62	223.70	150.00
Nonplaintiffs						
Exp/pupil	4,388.40	2,100.20	1,832.78	16,750.69	14,737.91	6,625.00
Mill value/pupil	43.56	70.94	0.264	911.45	911.20	129.45
Matched Nonplaintiffs						
Exp/pupil	5,440.02	2,691.00	2,020.35	14,344.35	12,324.00	8,960.00
Mill value/pupil	45.77	36.93	0.26	183.58	183.32	109.50

[1]Restricted range
SOURCE: R. Craig Wood, David C. Thompson, David S. Honeyman, and M. David Miller, *Funding Public Education in Montana Based on the Concept of Cost of Living Indices in Montana Rural Education Association v. State* (Gainesville, Fla.: Wood, Thompson and Associates, 1992); see also David S. Honeyman, M. David Miller, R. Craig Wood, and David C. Thompson, *The Study of Resource Accessibility, Wealth Neutrality, and State Yield in Montana Rural Education Association v. State* (Gainesville, Fla.: Wood, Thompson and Associates, 1992), 16.

ANOVA Table for EXP/P

	DF	Sum of Squares	Mean Square	F-Value	P-Val
P-NP	1	68276650.196	68276650.196	14.764	.00
Residual	525	2427938739.460	4624645.218		

Model II estimate of between component variance: 484049.158

Means Table for EXP/P
Effect: P-NP

	Count	Mean	Std. Dev.	Std. Err.
1	77	5407.453	2426.466	276.521
2	450	4388.416	2100.202	99.004

Scheffe for EXP/P
Effect: P-NP
Significance Level: 5 %

	Mean Diff.	Crit. Diff	P-Value	
1, 2	1019.037	521.007	.0001	S

ANOVA Table for MILVALUE

	DF	Sum of Squares	Mean Square	F-Value	P-Value
P-NP	1	5093.055	5093.055	1.109	.2928
Residual	525	2411073.771	4592.521		

Model II estimate of between component variance: 3.806

Means Table for MILVALUE
Effect: P-NP

	Count	Mean	Std. Dev.	Std. Err.
1	77	52.356	44.588	5.081
2	450	43.555	70.946	3.344

Scheffe for MILVALUE
Effect: P-NP
Significance Level: 5 %

	Mean Diff.	Crit. Diff	P-Value
1, 2	8.801	16.418	.2928

FIGURE 4.7 Analysis of variance for expenditures and mill value comparing plaintiffs with nonplaintiffs

SOURCE: Data drawn from *Montana Rural Education Association v. State*. Developed by Wood, Thompson and Associates (1992).

there were significant differences among plaintiffs and nonplaintiffs on the expenditure and tax rate variables. If statistically significant differences were shown by this procedure, additional questions would have to be asked about whether differences in expenditures and tax rates derived from some illegitimate basis. The data showed, however, that no statistically significant differences were found in either expenditures or tax rates, weakening the argument that plaintiffs as a class were discriminated against on these variables. The implications for resource accessibility were thus that wealth indeed varied greatly, but that no meaningful differences could be shown between plaintiffs and nonplaintiffs, which, barring other evidence, would suggest successful operation of the state aid scheme.

Wealth Neutrality and Tax Yield.   To test the assumptions stemming from the resource accessibility data, the analysis finally turned to examination of wealth neutrality and, by inference, tax yield. Again selected data developed by one set of litigants on these standards are shown in Figure 4.8 and Table 4.7. Figure 4.8 shows the

FIGURE 4.8   Correlation and regression analysis for the plaintiff districts merged with matched nonplaintiff districts

SOURCE: Data drawn from *Montana Rural Education Association v. State.* Developed by Wood, Thompson and Associates (1992).

Regression Summary
EXP/P vs. MILVAL

Count	154
Num. Missing	0
R	.015
R Squared	2.227E-4
Adjusted R Squared	•
RMS Residual	2562.087

Regression Coefficients
EXP/P vs. MILVAL

	Coefficient	Std. Error	Std. Coeff.	t-Value	P-Value
Intercept	5388.788	280.530	5388.788	19.209	<.0001
MILVAL	.009	.051	.015	.184	.8542

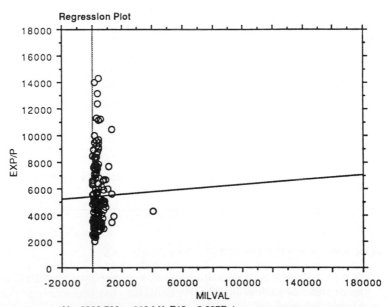

Regression Plot

$$Y = 5388.788 + .009 * X; R^2 = 2.227E\text{-}4$$

TABLE 4.7 McLoone's Index and Gini coefficient for all groups

Group	McLoone Index	Gini Coefficient
All districts	0.657	0.036
Plaintiffs	1.37	0.029
Nonplaintiffs	0.589	0.03
Matched nonplaintiffs	1.47	0.028

SOURCE: Data drawn from *Montana Rural Education Association v. State*. Developed by Wood, Thompson and Associates (1992).

results of correlation and regression analysis on matched sets of plaintiff and nonplaintiff districts. While full explanation of these data is quite complex, three points are especially germane for purposes of this illustration. First, the effect of outliers on perceptions of widespread inequity is upheld in that districts are much more closely clustered on expenditures and tax rates than plaintiffs contend. Second, there is only a very slight positive relationship between wealth and expenditure per pupil. Third, these observations permitted initial conclusion that the state was in fact highly (although not perfectly) wealth- and tax-neutral.

Table 4.7 contains examples of the final data prepared to confirm these observations, showing the results of the McLoone Index and the Gini coefficient, wherein plaintiffs actually can be argued to receive more favorable treatment under the state aid scheme than is true for nonplaintiffs. For example, the higher McLoone value for plaintiffs reflects their higher expenditures per pupil, while the low Gini illustrates that plaintiffs again cannot show mistreatment by over-representation in the bottom half of the wealth and expenditure distribution. Additional data not shown here were also developed on the tax yield standard with similar results.

Although much more extensive data were developed to fully explain the findings, these brief descriptions illustrate the nature of formula equity analysis. Yet equity is elusive, and the same data can be used to show other perspectives on the same issues. The complexity of school finance formulas is readily apparent, and it can be seen that equity is both temporal and difficult to achieve and/or prove. That these realities are omnipresent is clearly illustrated as we explore in Chapter 5 school finance litigation where state aid formulas have been taken to task for their imperfect equity performance.

Review Points

EVOLUTION AND NATURE OF STATE AID FORMULAS

As with other facts of education as seen in previous chapters, state aid formulas are the product of sociopolitical and economic environments operating in the context of the individual states.

Transcending total isolation of states has been pressure for better equalizing educational opportunity through introduction of state aid into local school districts.

States have a long history of aiding schools, but the percentage of aid has only recently surpassed an average 50%, as legislatures have been pressured by the public, scholarly studies, and the courts to better equalize educational opportunity.

Modern aid formulas have generally fallen into categories of minimum foundations, equalization grants, and full state funding, with each plan underlaid by political philosophy.

Highly popular minimum foundation plans have intended to make available a basic educational program, leaving local districts free to supplement expenditures.

Equalization plans have also been relatively popular, seeking to assure aid in inverse relation to local wealth and leaving districts free to supplement expenditures.

Full state funding plans have received much scholarly acclaim for equity achievement, but have proved politically unpopular for a variety of reasons.

Combining one or more aid schemes has become an increasingly popular method of addressing the technical and political weaknesses of the various basic aid schemes.

FORMULA ADJUSTMENTS

Because basic aid schemes generally address only horizontal equity, vertical equity adjustments have been devised.

Formula adjustments may be generally classified as either *need* equalization or *cost* equalization.

Need equalization has most often occurred in compensatory, bilingual, and special education.

Cost equalization has generally sought to adjust for market differences and economies of scale affecting the price of education among various school districts.

The most common method of formula adjustment has been weightings.

MEASURING FORMULA EQUITY

To know if a formula is equitable requires data-based measurement that considers how widely and why variations occur.

Formula equity may be considered on horizontal or vertical planes.

Equity measurement usually considers whether resources are accessible to all students, whether local wealth conditions available revenue, and whether equal tax effort produces equal yield.

Common statistical measurement of resource accessibility includes the mean, range, federal range ratio, standard deviation, coefficient of variation, and the variance.

Common statistical measurement of wealth neutrality and equal tax yield includes the McLoone Index, Gini coefficient, and correlational analysis and regression-based techniques; many other statistical tools are also available.

Data analysis is a common yardstick of "proof" when school finance formulas are challenged in court.

Case Study

As a principal in your district for the last five years, you have recently been involved in the state building level administrators' organization. You have attracted considerable attention because your experience in another state was similar to the set of issues now facing education in the state where you work. Specifically, education reform is now sweeping your state wherein all facets of the educational process are under great scrutiny. The legislature seems favorably inclined to shift education to a more centralized state-level focus through outcome-based measures and to revise other support mechanisms, including how schools are funded.

At the last meeting of the state principals' organization, a task force was formed and instructed to study a school finance bill that will be introduced in the legislature during the upcoming session. The bill has already passed out of a joint legislative interim committee and has received tentative support from the chairs of the education committees in both houses, but it is expected that full legislative approval may be difficult because of radical changes sought in tax base and distribution formula. Unless amended, the bill will abolish the current equalization aid formula because its critics charge that districts have become too disparate in both tax rate and expenditure per pupil. Current mill levies now span from a low 8 mills to a high 119 mills, and per-pupil expenditures last year ranged from a low $2,800 to over $10,000 in a small wealthy district. The new bill seeks three fundamental changes. First, the formula will be changed to a high-level foundation program that sets a base expenditure per pupil at $4,000. Second, the base expenditure will be adjusted by a series of program weights for bilingual and vocational education, and another series of weights based on at-risk classification, transportation, and school size. An additional 20% unequalized local leeway will be permitted, subject to a voter protest petition. Third, a uniform statewide tax rate will be levied with recapture provisions.

Your committee has been instructed to report back to the principals' group with an analysis of this proposal. Since your advanced degree course work centered on school finance, you have been asked to lead the discussion. Specifically, the group has asked for comparative data and recommendations based on three issues: how other states generally fund education, the general advantages and disadvantages of weighting schemes and the scope and type of weights used in other states, and justification and criticism on principles of sound school finance theory of the proposed formula. Using the following questions to help guide your deliberations and class discussions, what information will you present? Defend your views through logic, data, and appropriate use of school finance theory.

Directed Discussion Questions

1. As you prepare your responses to the committee's requests, what particular issues do you believe merit your greatest attention? What types of information will you need to respond to each of the three major areas of study? Where will you turn for information? Specifically, relating to the first task of how other states fund education, what resources can you find that will help you distill this information into a usable format? Assuming your professor asks you to actually research this question, what were the results of your analysis?

2. The topic of school finance formulas is a fairly complex arena that often bewilders even reasonably knowledgeable people, including legislators who are responsible for enactment of these laws. One of your tasks will certainly be to present your information in a useful and understandable format. As you contemplate the second task of exploring weighting schemes, what process and information will you use to instruct the group about the operation of basic aid formulas and vertical equity adjustments? Assuming that your professor asks you to actually prepare such an analysis, what were the findings of your research?

3. Having explored school finance funding schemes in this chapter, what are your present philosophical inclinations in responding to the third task of critiquing the proposed state aid formula revision? In your opinion, is the proposed plan theoretically sound? What strengths do you find that are supportable by modern finance theory? What weaknesses, if any, do you see? Based on your knowledge and research of funding methods generally and in other states, how favorably does the proposed plan compare with other current practices?

4. Based on your learning to this point, how favorably does your own state's school aid formula compare to other states' funding schemes? What is your assessment of your state's aid scheme based on the criteria in this chapter? Have significant studies of school funding been recently performed in your state? If so, what were the findings? Have any changes in the funding scheme been adopted, or are any changes under consideration? If so, what is your evaluation of their appropriateness to the goals of sound school finance theory? If no such studies have occurred, why not, and what questions do you think should be asked about school funding in your state? What data can you present from your experience or your research that indicate a need for systematic review of your state's aid plan?

5. This case study, like several others in this textbook, invokes formal scrutiny of school finance by various levels of administrative hierarchy. In this case study, the state principals' organization is taking school time to study finance. In your opinion, is this a worthwhile activity for principals, or should school finance be reserved to higher ranks? What arguments can you present favoring principal involvement? What arguments can you construct against involvement in legislative and policy issues in school finance? In your own state, what is the current status of such affairs?

NOTES

1. Allan Odden, *School Finance in the 1990s,* Policy Brief no. 1 (Los Angeles: USC Center for Research in Education Finance, June 1991), 1.
2. David Monk, *Educational Finance: An Economic Approach* (New York: McGraw-Hill, 1990), 211.
3. John Rawls, *A Theory of Justice* (Cambridge: Belknap Press of the Harvard University Press, 1972), 4.
4. Paul R. Mort, *The National Survey of School Finance: State Support for Public Education* (Washington D.C.: The American Council on Education, 1933), 24–26.

5. See, for example, Chapter 5's discussion of school finance lawsuits. The famous case of Stuart v. School District No. 1 of the Village of Kalamazoo (38 Mich. 69 [1874]) stands as early proof of efforts to formally analyze responsibility for education. Many other cases indirectly impacting school finance exist, such as the pre-1900 civil rights cases discussed elsewhere in this text and other writings of the authors.

6. Ellwood P. Cubberley, *School Funds and Their Apportionment* (New York: Columbia University, 1906), 17.

7. Harlan Updegraff, *Rural School Survey of New York State: Financial Support* (Ithaca, N.Y.: Author, 1922).

8. The distinction is an important one as historically a focus of state aid formulas has been on funding the teacher unit, but meaning aid in proportion to the number of teachers a district chooses to employ. Updegraff argues that such a scheme can harm equity, for example, wealthy districts can afford to employ more staff and thus receive additional (unneeded) aid. Updegraff's scheme would have set standardized conditions such as low enrollment, grade level, and so forth to justify each teacher, thus making each position the object of approval prior to funding.

9. George D. Strayer and Robert M. Haig, *The Financing of Education in the State of New York,* vol. 1 (New York: Macmillan, 1923).

10. It will be seen later in this chapter that the minimum foundation program first advanced by Strayer and Haig has formed the most popular basis for funding education in the 50 states. Additionally, most other finance plans typically discussed apart from foundation schemes are in fact highly analogous to the foundation.

11. Strayer and Haig, *Financing of Education,* 173.

12. Paul R. Mort, *The Measurement of Educational Need* (New York: Columbia University Teachers College, 1924).

13. Mort, *Measurement of Educational Need,* 8.

14. Henry C. Morrison, *School Revenue* (Chicago: University of Chicago Press, 1930).

15. Politically, flat grants were never designed for such sophistication in equity. Technically, if a flat grant were to cover the total program costs, it would become a full state funding scheme as discussed later.

16. James W. Guthrie, Walter I. Garms, and Lawrence C. Pierce. *School Finance and Education Policy: Enhancing Educational Efficiency, Equality, and Choice,* 2d ed. (Boston: Allyn & Bacon, 1988), 133.

17. Flat grants were still the principal funding mechanism in 1971 in Arizona, California, Connecticut, Oregon, Arkansas, Delaware, Nebraska, New Mexico, and North Carolina and South Carolina.

18. Ironically, a common current application of the "disequalizing" flat grant is in those arenas where equity is intended to be the central focus. For example, many states grant general aid on a highly equalized basis using one of the formulas discussed later, but continue to use flat grants to aid programs initially intended to induce greater vertical equity, such as the excess costs of special education, which are often funded at a very high flat grant level (e.g., ≥90% reimbursement). This excess cost is routinely reimbursed to rich and poor districts alike. The irony, of course, is overlaying a nonequalizing grant mechanism on a program born of recognition of inequality. The same is true of transportation (e.g., 80%–100% reimbursement) where many states never attempt to tie the level of transportation aid to district wealth. Worse, the noncovered excess costs usually fall outside any formula and must be absorbed by the local tax base. No firm estimates of wasted revenues or slippage outside the formula in such programs exist, although the sums may be hypothesized to be enormous and ripe for reform.

19. Methods of calculating the number of students has historically varied among the states. Average Daily Attendance (ADA) counts an average of students in attendance. Average

Daily Membership (ADM) ignores attendance and counts students officially enrolled at some legal point in time. Full-Time Equivalency (FTE) counts students for the demand on instructional time—for example, half-day kindergarten counts each student as 0.5 rather than 1. Each method has a different appeal. For example, poor city districts with high truancy rates prefer ADM because it does not look at attendance. States have historically based student count methods on political goals rather than a firm theoretical foundation.

20. Altering the minimum foundation has been fairly frequent. The most common methods have been to equalize local leeway up to some predetermined point or to restrict discretionary millage so that wealthy districts cannot financially embarrass the state. The latter has been most common because it carries no state cost. The former is generally placed on a sliding scale that decreases the level of equalization of each additional discretionary mill—a cost-saving technique that, while inferior to fully equalizing each mill, at least has the effect of tempting poorer districts with a higher equalization rate for local discretionary tax effort. However, if a state were to fully equalize each discretionary mill, the state could be said to actually have adopted a resource equalization scheme as discussed next.

21. Although common throughout the research literature, the exact terms *minimum provision* philosophy and *equal access* philosophy, and particularly *total equal provision* philosophy (as used later in this discussion), are derived here from Guthrie, Garms, and Pierce, *School Finance and Education Policy,* 132–133.

22. Actual formulas for PE are not shown here for three reasons. First, it is easier to understand new versions of the same outcome discussed next under GTB and GTY. Second, the point of this discussion need not be clouded by digression into an old complex formula. And third, all these equalization plans are algebraically identical in their results, making display of multiple repetitive formulas redundant.

23. This perception is largely ungrounded except politically because the state maintains control of the state ratio. For example, if district spending outstrips the legislative purse, the legislature can simply adjust the state ratio downward and control costs. Politically, however, this places the difficult decisions on the legislature.

24. Districts are never required to provide this figure. This is simply the value of property in the district adjusted at a common assessment level throughout the state compared to the average adjusted value of all similar property for each district in the state—that is, the ratio of the tax value of local property compared to the average taxable value of all property for all districts in the state.

25. For example, Kansas dropped its equalization formula in 1992 in response to a lawsuit that effectively challenged the constitutionality of an equalization scheme that failed to fully equalize educational opportunity. Several other states in Table 4.1 that have equalization formulas are also facing lawsuits. For example, Pennsylvania and South Dakota are presently in litigation, and suits have been threatened in Colorado, Rhode Island, and other states.

26. The effects of various nuances such as fully equalized local option should not be regarded as unimportant. For example, it could be argued that the combined programs in Figure 4.5 are really a higher level foundation since foundations are themselves equalized. This would be true except for the local option exercised by District A but not by District C. Many such nuances are critical to defining aid plans. For example, if a foundation aid plan is set sufficiently high, there is little to distinguish it from a full state funding plan as described next. Thus, the attention in Figure 4.5 to one-mill discretionary millage is not unimportant.

27. The exceptions and proofs of this statement are important. First, although it may be troublesome to some that any scheme of local choice violates horizontal equity, there are a few issues in the real world that are philosophically troubling but totally irresoluble, such as the incompatibility of perfect liberty and perfect equity noted in earlier chapters. In this instance, liberty seeks freedom to choose and claims that equity is served by equalized oppor-

tunity that can be seized or rejected, while equity must claim that deviation from absolute horizontality is impermissible. Thus, the search for perfect equity will never yield a solution in a democracy where differing views are permitted. The argument is more than academic, however, in that absolute equity would require tyranny, while tyranny itself rejects absolute equality because it is based in hierarchical authority. Second, care must be taken to choose wisely among combinations, as the use of primitive formulas or improper balance between schemes can detract from the total scheme. For example, Table 4.1 clearly illustrates the combination of flat grants with other more equalized aid schemes. The primitive nature of the flat grant automatically injects negative performance into the combination unless the level of the flat grant is extremely high—in which case it is effectively no longer a flat grant. Further, only token presence of equalization in a combination plan might actually offer little substantive equalization. Hence, care should be taken in assuring apolitical combinations and in assuring that the choices will indeed offset the inherent deficiencies of each plan.

28. Although no extensive development of this point is made here, the key word in text is *initially* equal apportionment. There is nothing in a full state funding scheme that denies vertical differentiation in resources based on need; in fact, it would be a great irony if full state funding prevented unequal resources based on conceptions of vertical equity such as special education services. The point is that all children in the state are equal and will continue to be equal by vertical treatment on a statewide basis—the end result may still be very different resources to each child, but the differences will relate only to educational needs.

29. See the earlier discussion in Chapter 3 on property tax limitation movements. The California example actually goes beyond the extenuating circumstance concept because full state funding was clearly an ironic and unintended effect brought on by seeking greater local government accountability.

30. Lau v. Nichols, 414 U.S. 653 (1974).

31. See, for example, Castaneda v. Pickard, 648 F.2d 989 (5th Cir. 1981); see also Keyes v. School Dist. No. 1, 521 F.2d 465 (10th Cir. 1974), *cert. den.,* 423 U.S. 1066 (1976). Relatedly on the same topic of alien children and educational deprivation, see Plyler v. Doe, 457 U.S. 202 (1982).

32. Jennifer Sevilla, ''Bilingual Education: The Last 25 Years,'' in *Helping At-Risk Students: What Are the Educational and Financial Costs?* 1992 Yearbook of the American Education Finance Association, ed. Patricia Anthony and Stephen Jacobson (Newbury Park, Calif.: Sage, 1992), 43–46.

33. Pennsylvania Association of Retarded Citizens (PARC) v. Pennsylvania, 343 F.Supp. 279 (E.D.Pa. 1972) (consent decree); see also Mills v. Board of Education, 348 F.Supp. 866 (D.D.C. 1972), which extended the right to education beyond mentally retarded children to include a broad range of handicapped children and began the practice of forbidding exclusion of handicapped children from regular school assignment unless provided with due process. An entire history of litigation began with these two cases that led to much change in handicapped rights to education.

34. PARC.

35. Education of the Handicapped Act (EHA), PL 94–142. This act is discussed in some greater detail in Chapter 2 of this text.

36. There are, however, mitigating factors that may cause hesitation over blind adherence to this concept. This is particularly true when the U-curve is used to justify chronically low levels of aid over time. For example, building subsequent years of permissible expenditures per pupil on the U-curve may serve to suppress expenditure growth into a self-fulfilling prophecy, rather than reflecting any true efficiency. In effect, this difficult notion argues the alternative view that state aid limitations may *cause the curve* through expenditure constraints, when an unrestrained *curve should cause* state aid determinations. If so, a

great inequity can occur because districts are expected to have certain efficiencies falsely "proved" in reverse. For further development of this concept, see David C. Thompson, R. Craig Wood, and David S. Honeyman, *Educational Fiscal Equality in Kansas under the School District Equalization Act: Consultants' Analysis on Behalf of Newton USD 373 et al. v. State of Kansas* (Manhattan, Kans.: Wood, Thompson & Associates, 1991); see also David C. Thompson, R. Craig Wood, and David S. Honeyman, *Fiscal Equity in Kansas under the School District Equalization Act: Consultants' Analysis on Behalf of Turner USD 202 in Mock v. State of Kansas* (Manhattan, Kans.: Wood, Thompson & Associates, 1990).

37. David C. Thompson, *Report to USD 259 on the Impacts of Hold-Harmless Aid on Select School Districts in Kansas* (Manhattan, Kans.: UCEA Center for Education Finance, 1991).

38. This implies neither that vertical equity is impossible to measure nor that it should not be measured, only that its measurement is beyond the scope of this text. Other more extended resources are available; see, for example, Robert Berne and Leanna Stiefel, *The Measurement of Equity in School Finance: Conceptual, Methodological, and Empirical Dimensions* (Baltimore: Johns Hopkins University Press, 1984).

39. The statistical tools presented here are not a complete list, since this text is only an introduction to the concept of measurement. Further, the complexity of several advanced statistical treatments would only cloud the issue. The tools presented here provide the most straightforward introductory analysis, beyond which successively higher studies should be pursued.

40. These numbers can be expressed at various levels. For example, it might be more useful to express the mean as differences in per-pupil dollar amounts.

41. Other tools are available beyond this level. For example, contributions of multiple variables can be assessed at successively more complex statistical levels, such as various kinds of multiple regression analysis.

42. See R. Craig Wood et al., *Funding Public Education in Montana Based on the Concept of Cost of Living Indices in Montana Rural Education Association v. State* (Gainesville, Fla.: Wood, Thompson & Associates, 1992); see also David S. Honeyman et al., *The Study of Resource Accessibility, Wealth Neutrality, and State Yield in Montana Rural Education Association v. State* (Gainesville, Fla.: Wood, Thompson & Associates, 1992); in the broader context, see earlier expert reports from Kansas; see also David C. Thompson, R. Craig Wood, and David S. Honeyman, *Adequacy of Educational Revenues in Oklahoma School Districts: Expert Analysis on Behalf of Plaintiff in Fair School Finance Council, Inc., v. State of Oklahoma* (Manhattan, Kans.: Wood, Thompson and Associates, 1992); see also other expert reports in litigation produced by the author(s) in various states.

ADDITIONAL READINGS

Berke, Joel. *Answers to Inequity.* Berkeley: McCutchan, 1974.

Berne, Robert, and Leanna Stiefel. *The Measurement of Equity in School Finance: Conceptual, Methodological, and Empirical Dimensions.* Baltimore: Johns Hopkins Press, 1984.

Burke, A. J. *Financing Public Schools in the United States.* Rev. ed. New York: Harper & Row, 1957.

Cohn, Elchanan, and Stephen Millman. *Economics of State Aid to Education.* Lexington, Mass.: Lexington Books, 1974.

Coons, John, William Clune, and Stephen Sugarman. *Private Wealth and Public Education.* Cambridge: Belknap Press of Harvard University, 1970.

Cubberley, Ellwood P. *School Funds and Their Apportionment.* New York: Columbia University Teachers College, 1906.

Gold, Steven. *Public School Finance Programs in the United States and Canada 1990-1991.*

Vols. 1–2. Albany: American Education Finance Association and the National Center for Education Statistics, State University of New York at Albany, 1992.

Kozol, Jonathan. *Savage Inequalities.* New York: Crown, 1991.

Morrison, Henry. *School Revenue.* Chicago: University of Chicago Press, 1930.

Mort, Paul R. *State Support for Public Schools.* New York: Columbia University Teachers College, 1926.

Strayer, George, and Robert Haig. *The Financing of Education in the State of New York: Report of the Educational Finance Inquiry Commission.* Vol. 1, New York: Macmillan, 1923.

Verstegen, Deborah. *School Finance at a Glance.* Denver: Education Commission of the States, 1988.

Wise, Arthur. *Rich Schools, Poor Schools.* Chicago: University of Chicago Press, 1967.

Updegraff, Harlan, and Leroy King. *Survey of the Fiscal Policies of the State of Pennsylvania in the Field of Education.* Philadelphia: University of Pennsylvania, 1922.

CHAPTER 5

Court Reform
in Education Finance

CHAPTER THEME

- The truths and beliefs about the importance of education in a democratic society have fueled a great struggle over fiscal resources because the absence of money with which to buy school inputs, such as teachers, negatively impacts children. Because money is envied by people who believe they do not receive equal educational opportunities, litigation seeking to force states to restructure school funding formulas has become common, making public school funding schemes a direct product of litigation because state legislatures have not been unanimously willing to voluntarily increase state funding to local schools. In an increasingly litigious environment, it is important for school administrators to understand how litigation impacts on the construction and operation of school funding plans.

CHAPTER OUTLINE

- A broad overview of federal school finance litigation issues that have played a central role in defining who is responsible for school finance
- Because the history of federal litigation has been largely unsuccessful for plaintiffs' claims, the outcome of the most important lawsuits that have been brought at the state level and a summary of cases currently before state courts
- The broad principles laid down by federal and state courts and the future role of litigation in an increasingly litigious educational environment

CHAPTER OBJECTIVE

- Recognition of the integrated nature of broad school finance policy concerns, serving as an overarching umbrella under which the remainder of this textbook can turn to the more operative aspects of daily administration of school fiscal affairs

Whatever it is that money may be thought to contribute to the education of children, that commodity is something highly prized by those who enjoy the greatest measure of it. If money is inadequate to improve education, the residents of poor districts should at least have an equal opportunity to be disappointed by its failure.

John Coons, William Clune, and Stephen Sugarman,
Private Wealth and Public Education

In many ways, the provocative opening quotation[1] for this chapter is the essence of this text. As noted at the close of Chapter 4, there has been a great struggle over fiscal resources in education. While it is clearly true that tightly perfect linkages between money and educational productivity cannot yet be drawn, there are at least six other truths that render powerless any hesitancy about the importance of school finance. First, schools indeed distribute economic and social opportunities in a nation fueled by competitiveness. Second, these opportunities depend in large measure on the quality of schools children attend. Third, despite lack of strong productivity equations, school quality is heavily conditioned by resources such as teachers that are purchased with money. Fourth, absent ability to purchase these inputs, schools must fail because altruism is not a sufficiently offsetting condition. Fifth, people who argue for the irrelevance of money still prefer a larger share. Sixth, until money is *irrefutably* shown to make no difference, its effect must be presumed from the behavior, rather than the rhetoric, of wealthy people—a presumption powerfully stated by Coons and coworkers.

It should therefore not be surprising that our examination of state aid plans in Chapter 4 ended by discussing equity in resource distribution and by remarking that school funding has been taken to task through litigation challenging the imperfect equity performance of state aid distribution schemes. Money has been the object of envy, and a long history of litigation stands as proof of the intensity of beliefs and emotions about the power of education. Bitter litigation wars have been waged at both federal and state court levels, and it is accurate to say that the outcome has led to massive restructuring of funding formulas and continues to drive reform in many states. The nature of current public school revenue schemes is fundamentally a product of litigation because we have seen that political readiness seldom moves at the same quick pace as knowledge about school finance equity. In a system of necessary tensions among various competing forces, litigation has played a critical role in shaping school finance policy in the name of equal educational opportunity.

The central role of litigation in school finance is the focus of this chapter, providing a necessary next step from the preceding chapters and closure and prediction to a complex federal and state policy arena wherein successive chapters will focus on more intensely local concerns. This chapter therefore has three major goals: first, a broad overview of school finance litigation issues in light of the historical roots undergirding school finance challenges, especially at the federal level; second, consideration of the outcome of the most important suits that have been brought at the state level, and a summary of cases currently before the courts; and third, a summary of the broad principles laid down by courts and a brief discussion of the future role of litigation in an increasingly litigious educational environment. These three goals thus weave a continuous thread and provide a capstone to all the preceding chapters. Upon completion of this chapter, the reader will be sufficiently well grounded in the broad issues of school finance policy to focus next on the operative aspects of daily administration of school fiscal affairs.

THE ROOTS OF SCHOOL FINANCE CHALLENGES

For more than 100 years, school finance has been of vital concern to both courts and policymakers. Although it was indicated in Chapter 4 that school finance as a discipline has emerged only during the present century, it was also seen that issues of taxation have been at the forefront of thought since the early days of the nation, and it is only a small step to move school finance into that stream of activity. This is especially true when the wider implications of school finance are considered, such as equality of educational opportunity as it relates to matters of discrimination. As such, the study of school finance litigation can actually begin long before the birth of the discipline of school finance. Although the full range of equality lawsuits is too broad to examine here,[2] these threads should be remembered as we limit discussion to those questions of law that have emerged in direct school finance challenges.

The history of school finance litigation has centered on questions of law brought in both federal and state courts. Since courts do not create controversies and are limited in redress only to interpreting whether an extant law has been violated, school finance litigation has been at once constitutional and statutory. At the federal level, litigation has focused on interpreting the constitutional limits of federal responsibility to embrace education and on any guarantees construed in the Constitution. At the state level, litigation has been dually focused on constitutional and statutory provisions of the individual states. At both levels, these questions have been complex, as constitutional interpretation is nebulous, particularly when overlaid by the presence or absence of statutory provisions. Regardless of whether a lawsuit has been brought in federal or state court, litigants have had to be first concerned with questions of law in order to create an actual controversy. In both instances, litigants have sought to determine the meaning and extent of equal opportunity and to test the strength and limits of constitutional and statutory language. Depending on the level at which a lawsuit is brought, the attacks have centered on three strategies: education as a *fundamental right,* the *equal protection* of the laws, and the *education articles* of the individual state constitutions.

Federal Roots[3]

Often believed to be of recent origin, school finance litigation has a lengthy history, raising questions based on particular strategies aimed at various features of federal and state laws. Plaintiffs have first sought to bring equality in fiscal resources at the federal level in a logical attempt to capture a U.S. Supreme Court ruling as the highest law of the land. The logic of a first assault in the federal courts has been that if a favorable ruling could be obtained, such a ruling would in turn be binding on the states. Both at the same time and as a consequence of the results of federal litigation, litigants have also earnestly sought grounds on which states can be held liable for equalizing fiscal resources in schools. The issues on which both federal and state litigation has been pursued have theories in common, as well as differences, that have contributed to their respective outcomes.

In a historical context, bringing a school finance lawsuit first at the federal level was an ultimately sensible act. As seen in earlier discussion, concern for equality has been a hallmark of American society dating from the colonial charters that sought liberation from oppression. Indeed, the Declaration of Independence was itself a ring-ing call for equality, as the nation's framers boldly proclaimed "We hold these truths to be self-evident, that all men are created equal, that they are endowed by their Creator with certain inalienable Rights; that among these are Life, Liberty and the pursuit of Happiness."[4] These concerns were the basis of the Bill of Rights,[5] and the incessant watchfulness against tyranny carried to the rights and privileges that were quickly written into individual state constitutions. Preoccupation with equality was the basis for the Emancipation Proclamation in 1863 and equality was carried forward into the Thirteenth Amendment in 1865, which abolished slavery.[6] But it was especially the Fourteenth Amendment to the U.S. Constitution that gave genesis to equality under the law. The Fourteenth Amendment not only assured citizenship to all persons born or naturalized in the United States, but also applied to the individual states the rights and prohibitions of the amendment. The amendment provided in salient part:

> No State shall make or enforce any law which shall abridge the privileges or immunities of citizens of the United States; nor shall any State deprive any person of life, liberty, or property, without due process of law; nor deny to any person within its jurisdiction the equal protection of the laws.[7]

These words were to prove particularly powerful in both federal and state litigation in a wide-ranging variety of equality lawsuits. While no federal school finance lawsuits existed before the mid-twentieth century, the foundations were laid by American preoccupation with equality and supported by a series of broader cases with school finance overtones that would only later become apparent. The Fourteenth Amendment's equality provisions led to three litigation strands[8] that were to have a powerful impact on school finance. The first strand was a series of lawsuits under the heading of segregation, in which enforcement of equality before the law for all persons was sought.[9] The second strand was a series of cases known as the reapportionment decisions, establishing the principle of "one man, one vote."[10] The third strand sprang from lawsuits that became known as the indigent defendants and administration of criminal justice cases, which established that defendants may not be denied the right of appeal simply because of inability to pay for a transcript of trial proceedings because such denial is tantamount to wealth discrimination.[11] Although seemingly unrelated to school finance, these strands were to lay a framework for equal protection in resource distribution.

These and other lawsuits were instrumental in placing before the courts a series of questions that formed the basis of equality under the law. Although each word and clause of the Fourteenth Amendment is poignant and far-reaching, the third clause was particularly powerful as it declared that no citizen may be treated unequally under the Constitution. Under these conditions, segregation cases were obvious for their eventual impact on schools, as active desegregation became a hotly contested issue for many years, with great overtones for the costs and structure of education. The reapportionment decisions fueled the equality struggle, as all people were brought under federal protection and given equal status under the law. The third strand, however, was to prove critically important because it raised the question of whether differential wealth could be a barrier to equality under the law. If this were true, an entirely new meaning to equality would be formed that could shake the nation to its very foundations.

These three strands were actually the expression and extension of judicial sympathy to a fairly liberal construction of the meaning of equality that had already resulted in establishment of certain fundamental rights under the law. In addition to the rights and liberties specifically guaranteed by the Constitution, the U.S. Supreme Court had enumerated several other rights it found to be so fundamental as not to be abridged or denied except by the most exacting due process of law. Several of these rights were established in the cases that formed the three strands; for example, the Court had found a fundamental right to interstate travel,[12] procreation,[13] voting,[14] and the right to criminal appeal.[15] The essence of fundamental rights, however many or few, was to assure the equality of each citizen so that arbitrary abridgment of certain freedoms could never be countenanced in a democratic nation. With the Fourteenth Amendment in place, there could be no doubt that all persons great and small would be assured full protection against arbitrary discrimination.

The effect of the Fourteenth Amendment's nondiscrimination clause was to devolve two distinct lines of litigation. The first line resulted from unequal treatment of a suspect class. As defined by the courts, various conditions might lead to establishment of a suspect class wherein "prejudice against discrete and insular minorities may be a special condition, which tends seriously to curtail the operation of those political processes ordinarily to be relied upon to protect minorities, and which may call for a correspondingly more searching judicial inquiry."[16] Subsequent litigation was to create suspect classes for race,[17] national origin,[18] and alienage,[19] with special empathy for other sensitive constitutional concerns. The first line thus drew its basis from illegitimate differential treatment on the basis of immutability whereby people were discriminated against for characteristics they could not change. The second line of litigation resulted from abridgment of some fundamental right. The second line thus drew justification from Constitutional provisions or, alternatively, whether the Court would newly construe a fundamental right for reasons of its own.

The concepts of suspect class and fundamental right were vitally important to equal protection litigation because if a court could be persuaded that a fundamental right or suspect class were discriminated against, courts would evaluate an act or a law with searching scrutiny. For example, race was clearly immutable, and alleged violation of the rights of a member of this suspect class would trigger an exacting analysis under antidiscrimination equal protection laws; similarly, abridgment of a fundamental right would trigger the same sharp scrutiny. Under these conditions, establishing the characteristics of suspect classes and increasing the number of suspect classes became paramount to successful equal protection challenges. The second line of fundamentality was equally critical in that any right declared to be fundamental would demand strict scrutiny under the law. These key concepts were thus the first strategy of equal protection analysis because if violation of a fundamental right were shown or if a suspect class was established, then the burden of proof would shift to the defendant to show a compelling interest in the law. This test of strict scrutiny became the sought-after judicial standard, as the only other standard of rational basis would require only some sensible reason to allow a law to stand.

As Kurland notes, the concepts derived from these three broader strands were quickly applied to education,[20] wherein litigants launched concerted efforts to establish suspectness and fundamentality in education. Although the origins of equality in American law are more complex than briefly stated here, these strands make plain why it was ultimately sensible in a historical context to bring lawsuits over education at the federal level first. Regardless of whether the topic were race discrimination or fiscal resources, the goal of any such lawsuit would be to seek federal protection wherein inequality would be alleged and from which it would be claimed that equal educational opportunity was denied. Thus, from a simple hierarchical perspective, if education were found in some way to merit the protections of the Fourteenth Amendment, especially in areas where abridgment would be severely proscribed, new federal law would be written that would also be controlling on the states. By analogy, then, the only two paths to this goal were simple and profound. The first path required a ruling that education is a fundamental right. Failing this, the only alternative was to establish a protected class against whom illegitimate discrimination in education could be shown.

Winning a federal lawsuit was thus critical. If the broader cases could be analogized to education, their successful application meant the establishment of constitutional protections in a totally new arena. If neither fundamentality nor suspect class could be established, failure was assured because the doctrine of limited federal powers given the Tenth Amendment's silence on education would release the coveted claims of federal protection; worse, failure of a federal case meant that equality of educational opportunity would either be lost or turned to the states without the power of the federal Constitution. The stakes were thus high because a challenge would have to prove that unequal treatment violated the Fourteenth Amendment's equal protection clause to invoke the strict scrutiny test. With a basis in the three equality strands, the search for educational equality was first tested in the school desegregation arena, followed by federal school finance litigation.

The Federal Response.   Although federal litigation on racial equality spanned many decades,[21] it was in the 1954 *Brown v. Board of Education*[22] case where equality of educational opportunity under the law received its greatest impetus. In a landmark ruling, the U.S. Supreme Court struck down the "separate but equal" provisions in most states whereby segregated school systems were maintained for black and white children. In a decision that shook the social and economic foundations of society, the Court held that separate but equal is inherently unequal, and that education is vital to the health and well-being of the nation and its citizens. The famous words of the Court rang throughout the nation as it proclaimed:

> Education is perhaps the most important function of state and local governments. Compulsory school attendance laws and the great expenditures for education demonstrate our recognition of the importance of education to our democratic society. It is required in the performance of our most basic public responsibilities, even service in the armed forces. It is the very foundation of good citizenship. Today it is a principal instrument in awakening the child to cultural values, in preparing him for later professional training, and in helping him to adjust normally to his environment. In these days, it is doubtful that any child may reasonably be expected to succeed in life if he is denied the opportunity of an education. Such an opportunity where the state has undertaken to provide it, is a right which must be made available to all on equal terms.[23]

With the words of the Supreme Court in *Brown,* the struggle for equality and equal educational opportunity seemed destined to succeed as reformers were overjoyed at the apparent strength of the Court's language. Invoking the equal protection clause of the Fourteenth Amendment, *Brown* spoke strongly to the value of education, calling it one of the most important functions of government and noting its central role to preservation of a literate and free people. At the crux of the matter, the Court in *Brown* struck a powerful blow as it declared that education is a right that must be made available on equal terms. Couched in such strong language, *Brown* contained all the hopes of reformers as it seemed to speak condemningly to violation of the Fourteenth Amendment in terms of race as a suspect class and a fundamental right to education. As such, *Brown* opened a new era of justice from which a whole field of civil and educational rights litigation would occupy the nation's court system for many decades.

Racial equality, however, was not the full extent of dreams held by social and educational reformers. Flushed with the victory in *Brown,* litigants soon turned their attention to inequality in financing as they reasoned that these same standards could be applied to inequality in school funding. Reformers felt justified in arguing that if the Court's apparent mandate in *Brown* were to be fully satisfied, equal educational opportunity would have strong application to fiscal resources since uneven revenues are at the root of most other inequality. Reformers recognized, however, that it would not be as easy to obtain a favorable ruling simply because there was no precedent for such litigation. Although it had not been a simple matter to force condemnation of racial inequality, at least there had been a long record of discrimination lawsuits against which concepts and theories could be empirically tested. In school finance inequality, however, there was no rich history on which to rely. The question first became one of moral, rather than legal, imperative from which litigants would be forced to argue. The only other alternative was to make analogy to the three strands cited earlier, supported by the strong language of *Brown.* By the 1960s, plaintiffs had formulated arguments and were ready to launch an assault for resource equality.

The first strand of unequal treatment under the law seemed well established in *Brown* because children must be provided equal opportunity. The second strand also seemed viable because it was reasonable to draw an equal protection analogy to geographic discrimination since it was widely known that educational opportunity varied greatly based on residence. The third strand also seemed applicable, as there was sufficient case law to argue that wealth may not serve to bar equality under the law. Of particular support to the latter theory was the belief that school district wealth could be the basis of wealth discrimination, that is, leading to establishment of a new suspect class. In plaintiffs' minds, wealth suspectness was grounded in case law and it was simply a matter of transferring the *Brown* logic condemning racial inequality to fiscal inequality. Plaintiffs were encouraged in their thinking, as the Court had long ago said in *United States v. Carolene* that "prejudice against discrete and insular minorities may be a special condition, which tends seriously to curtail the operation of those political processes ordinarily . . . relied upon to protect minorities, and which may call for a correspondingly more searching judicial inquiry.[24] In addition, there were the voting rights and criminal appeals cases cited earlier in which the Court had held that classifications based on wealth were to be strictly scrutinized.[25]

These conditions seemed ripe for a federal decision extending equality of educational opportunity to include fiscal equality. The first suit to be filed was *Burruss v. Wilkerson,*[26] brought in Virginia in 1968. The plaintiffs in *Burruss* based their claims on the Fourteenth Amendment, arguing that inequality in Bath County's physical and instructional facilities resulted in a lack of equal protection of the law because the quality varied among districts. A three-judge U.S. District Court that heard oral arguments rendered a decision in May 1969, stating that while "the existence of such deficiencies and differences is forcefully put by plaintiffs' counsel . . . we do not believe they are creatures of discrimination by the State. . . . our reexamination of the Act confirms that the cities and counties receive State funds under a uniform and consistent plan . . . we can only see to it that the outlays on one group are not invidiously greater or less than that of another . . . no such arbitrariness is manifest here."[27] The court added that although "plaintiffs seek to obtain allocations of State funds among the cities and counties so that the pupil in each of them will enjoy the same educational opportunities . . . the courts have neither the knowledge, nor means, nor the power to tailor the public monies to fit the varying needs of these students throughout the state."[28]

A second federal case of *McInnis v. Shapiro*[29] was decided in Illinois in the same year. Again heard in U.S. District Court and affirmed by the U.S. Supreme Court,[30] *McInnis* was also a Fourteenth Amendment equal protection suit seeking to overturn the state funding scheme on the grounds that unequal educational expenditures based on variable property values at tax rates of local districts were arbitrary and unreasonable denial of equal protection of the law. The court ruled for the defendant state, however, noting several features that were to become summative of the federal position in school finance litigation. While acknowledging wide variations in expenditures per pupil based on wealth, the court stated its helplessness before the law in three respects. First, variations in revenue are not on their face invidious and arbitrary. Second, the legislature's decision to allow local choice and experimentation was reasonable, particularly since the common school fund placed a $400 minimum base under each student. Third, the court ruled that there is no constitutional requirement establishing rigid guidelines for equal dollar expenditures under the Fourteenth Amendment's equal protection provisions. And fourth, the court was clear in stating that allocation of revenue is a policy decision better suited to legislatures.

Although plaintiffs in the *Brown* legacy had reasoned well, the decisions in *Burruss* and *McInnis* were not supportive of their logic. In fact, in both instances federal courts had uniformly refused to intervene on three importantly consistent grounds. The first rationale was a plain reading of the Fourteenth Amendment, noting no equal protection mandate for unequal revenues. The second rationale was equally important, as the court deferred to the legislative branch by calling on the separation of powers in the absence of blatant invidious discrimination. The third rationale applied to the court's bewilderment as it noted its lack of judicially manageable standards, even if it were to rule for plaintiffs. Equality, then, to the federal court was a negative standard in that no affirmative duty was owed by the state to each child for resource equality—rather, the absence of something was not the same as invidious denial of that object. From a federal perspective, the first two cases were thus totally abject failures in that solutions were found to be both legislatively and judicially unmanageable.

The optimism of plaintiffs in the post-*Brown* tradition, however, did not flag in the face of early adversity. Confident of the logic and cognizant that the ultimate opportunity and test finally lay with the U.S. Supreme Court, plaintiffs launched an all-out assault in *San Antonio Independent School District v. Rodriguez.*[31] The case had actually been filed in 1968, and a three-judge panel had rendered a decision in 1971 holding the Texas system of school finance unconstitutional under the Fourteenth Amendment.[32] The case was then taken on appeal by the U.S. Supreme Court. Wiser and more sophisticated than in earlier federal cases, the plaintiffs argued key points taken from earlier successful but broader litigation and contended that the Texas funding system violated the federal equal protection clause by discriminating against a class of poor and that students were denied their right to an education. As such, plaintiffs were actually arguing for wealth as a suspect class and for fundamentality at the highest level in an all-out effort to force strict judicial scrutiny.

The Court, however, refused to accept plaintiffs' arguments since it found no identifiably suspect class. The injured class was argued by plaintiffs to be comprised of all students living in poor school districts, rather than poor students themselves. Justice Powell, writing for the majority, noted that wealth discrimination in prior cases had historically been confined by the Court to personal wealth, and that the class in *Rodriguez* was not one for which special protection is usually provided; that is, it was neither politically powerless, discrete, or an insular minority.[33] The Court further noted that individual income did not necessarily correlate with district wealth, and that even if the correlation had been strong, the Court's historic application of wealth discrimination under strict scrutiny had been limited to absolute deprivation rather than relative differences.[34] Under these conditions, the Court found no distinct suspect class and held that since no student was absolutely deprived of an education, fiscal inequalities were of only relative difference and not entitled to wealth suspectness.

The Court then turned to plaintiffs' claims for fundamentality, again refusing to accept their arguments. Plaintiffs had recognized the difficulty of this argument and had based their claims on the relationship of education to other extant fundamental rights in an effort to establish nexus.[35] According to this theory, education was inextricably tied to other existing fundamental rights wherein the intelligent exercise of the right to vote and the right to free speech were said to depend on education. The Court refused these arguments, however, stating that it saw no more connection between education and these rights than it could find between housing, food, or other subsistence and the right to vote.[36] The Court especially noted a difference between hindering a child from an education and the state aid scheme that, in its view, instead sought to improve available offerings.[37] Although the Court noted wide disparities among Texas school districts, it rejected strict scrutiny, stating that a rational relationship is all that is required to defend an aid plan where no invidious discrimination can be found. In the case of Texas, a rational basis could be found in the state's goal of promoting local control of schools—a view supported by the Court's own words:

> Education, perhaps even more than welfare, presents a myriad of intractable economic, social, and even philosophical problems. The very complexity of the problems of financing and managing a statewide public school system suggests that there will be more than one constitutionally permissible method of solving them, and that, within the limits of rationality, the legislature's efforts to tackle the problems should be entitled to respect.[38]

The federal case was thus turned aside at the highest level by *Rodriguez,* striking a death blow in the minds of reformers who had cherished high hopes for this next step in securing equal educational opportunity. But contrary to *Brown,* there was apparently no fundamentality, no suspect class, and no equal protection for education except in cases of total education deprivation or in the established instances of invidious discrimination such as race. The strong words of the Court rang hollow to reformers, who recalled the earlier high promise of *Brown.* In the harsh light of day, it appeared from *Rodriguez* that little equality of educational opportunity could be had apart from race, as the Court had sanctioned legislative prerogative and declared judicially unmanageable standards, while unwilling to go beyond the historically narrow application of race relations.

The Court ruling in *Rodriguez* had two particular effects on school finance litigation. One was to refocus efforts in federal lawsuits, while the other was to turn litigants' attention to state courts in hopes of finding greater sympathy for reform. Both tactics experienced some success, although the balance clearly favored the state reform strategy. Yet the successive federal lawsuits following after *Rodriguez* had a persistent thread that needs to be cited before discussing state litigation.

The Post-Rodriguez Aftermath.   Although *Rodriguez* did indeed turn reform toward the states, there were three other federal cases coming after *Rodriguez* that have contributed to speculation about the future of a federal claim for equal educational opportunity as defined by fiscal resources.[39] The first case followed 13 years later in *Papasan v. Allain*[40] as plaintiff districts in Mississippi argued violation of federal equal protection in revenue differences based on Section 16 land income lost during the Civil War. Although the state had provided aid to help offset those losses, by 1981 state funds were only $.63 per pupil compared to $75.34 per pupil in districts whose lands had not been lost. Originally dismissed in federal district court, the Fifth Circuit Court of Appeals held that equal protection would not be barred by the Eleventh Amendment,[41] but also held that *Rodriguez* was the controlling standard on disparate funding. The U.S. Supreme Court upheld the immunity decision,[42] but reversed on the equal protection issue and remanded the case for development because the countenance of discrimination absent a legitimate state interest was sufficient to state a cause of action. *Papasan* is thus important both for what it stated and for what it failed to state. The complaint did not raise the issue of fundamentality, so that the federal court dealt only with a narrow legal question. In addition, a glimmer of federal interest in education finance was seen on remand as the Court noted that unreasonable government action would be scrutinized.[43]

The second important federal case after *Rodriguez* was also found in Texas as the Supreme Court ruled in *Plyler v. Doe*[44] that refusal by a state to educate illegal aliens involved an area of special sensitivity that would merit constitutional pleas of equal protection. While the Court in *Plyler* stopped short of declaring education a fundamental right, it stated a higher level of scrutiny and interest in cases of educational deprivation, using language that seemed less closed to fundamentality under such conditions. The *Plyler* majority stated that while its ruling in *Rodriguez* remained intact, it was deeply concerned that education is more than a mere service and convenience to citizens. In the Court's own words:

> Education provides the basic tools by which individuals might lead economically productive lives to the benefit of us all. In sum, education has a fundamental role in maintaining the fabric of our society. We cannot ignore the significant social costs borne by our Nation when select groups are denied the means to absorb the values and skills on which our social order rests.[45]

The third and final important federal case occurred in 1988 in *Kadrmas v. Dickinson Public Schools,*[46] in which plaintiffs argued that charging for bus service was denial of equal protection since the plaintiff child was wealth-disadvantaged. Although the Court found for the defendant state, its 5–4 vote was sharply divided and indicative of the constantly unsettled nature of a federal claim to education and further noted in strong language that there are variances and exceptions that preclude absolutism in interpreting *Rodriguez*. *Kadrmas* stands as the most recent proof of this indeterminateness, as dissenting opinion sharply stated:

> The Court therefore does not address the question whether a state constitutionally could deny a child access to a minimally adequate education. In prior cases this court explicitly has left open the question whether such a deprivation of access would violate a fundamental constitutional right. That question remains open today.[47]

Contrary to post-*Rodriguez* depression, the federal test of fiscal equality has thus been incomplete and awaits further development. From the early suits, however, several observations may be stated. First, it can be gathered that the Supreme Court is sympathetic to the problems of judicially manageable standards. Second, the Court is quick to uphold legislative prerogative. Third, the Court is reluctant to declare education a fundamental right, and any reversal is not likely to occur lightly. Fourth, the Court is not yet willing to create new suspect classifications. Fifth, in the case of education the Court has narrowly interpreted equal protection to mean racial equality or, alternatively, absolute deprivation with fiscal overtones. Sixth, *Rodriguez* has been the controlling precedent in subsequent litigation, and the Court itself has used *Rodriguez* to reject further assaults on a federal educational right. But seventh, all assaults following after *Rodriguez* have been narrowly drawn, and it is clear the Court holds an undefined interest in education that will eventually emerge. As such, reformers can continue to hold out hope, as a future federal case will depend on changes in the Court makeup and as cases like *Plyler* and *Kadrmas* repeatedly chink the armor by exceptions, causing the Court to revisit and qualify its rulings. But it is finally clear that no firm federal case yet exists—a reality that has in fact effectively turned most traditionally pure school finance litigation to the state courts for adjudication.

STATE COURT TESTS

Although school finance litigation is often believed to be of recent origin, legal struggles over the financing of schools actually predate the present century. The perception of recency is particularly misguided for two reasons. First, federal claims beginning in 1968 lend the appearance that school finance litigation is only a modern phenomenon. Second, the intensive state-level reform following the failed federal test in *Rodriguez* has confirmed the impression of recency. But while a lengthy history of school finance litigation could be drawn,[48] it is more instructive in the modern context to examine the state court test in the post-*Rodriguez* light because the nearby events have had the greatest impact in shaping current school finance practices.

The State Response[49]

As seen in the previous discussion, there has been considerable overlap in the chronology of federal and state lawsuits, and in the issues framing the various challenges to unequal fiscal resources. Chronological overlap occurred as lawsuits were brought in both federal and state courts in the early days of reform. For example, *Burruss, McIn-*

nis, and *Rodriguez* were brought in federal court under Fourteenth Amendment claims in the 1960s, but *Serrano v. Priest* had already been decided at the state supreme court level before the U.S. Supreme Court finally reached its ruling in *Rodriguez* in 1973. Overlap of issues occurred in like form, as the federal cases obviously grieved federal equal protection and as state cases such as *Serrano* also commonly brought both federal and state constitutional claims. As such, there are no crisp lines of demarcation as might be implied from the earlier federal discussion—but it is true that state litigation has become the standard fare in the post-*Rodriguez* era. It is equally true that state litigation has far outnumbered federal lawsuits, making it possible to review only the highlights and principles that have emerged from the complex task of litigating equal educational opportunity without firm federal precedent.

The state test is usually marked with the historic ruling of the California Supreme Court in *Serrano v. Priest.*[50] Destined to become the classic model for state school finance litigation, this lawsuit charged that the state scheme for aiding public schools violated the federal and state constitution's guarantees of equal protection. Inherent to these allegations were concepts of fundamentality, wealth suspectness, and equal protection under the state constitution to which reformers had earlier pinned their hopes in the failed federal test. The complaint thus set out three causes of action. First, the plaintiffs alleged that as a direct result of the state financing scheme for schools, substantial disparities existed in the quality and extent of educational opportunities. Second, plaintiffs alleged that as a result of such a scheme, they were likewise required to pay higher tax rates to obtain the same or lesser educational opportunity. And third, plaintiffs alleged that these realities worked jointly to deny children the equal protection of the laws, to deny them their fundamental right to education, and to make the quality of education a function of residence wherein quality varied in response to local district wealth. Given these causes, the plaintiffs sought to invalidate the state aid scheme under the federal and state constitutions.

The landmark ruling in *Serrano* completely reversed every evident trend in school finance litigation, as the California Supreme Court found for plaintiffs on every cause. The court provided numerous condemning statements about unequal educational opportunity as it justified its ruling. In establishing the facts, the court first noted that the root of disparity was unmistakable in that aid was insufficient to offset the widely disparate assessed valuation per pupil in Baldwin Park of $3,706, compared to Beverly Hills's valuation of $50,885 per pupil, a ratio of 1:13. Second, the court noted that state aid actually widened the gap between rich and poor districts, as aid was distributed irrespective of wealth wherein rich and poor districts alike were aided by the state. Third, the court noted that such aid was effectively meaningless to poor districts. The court then turned to the legal questions at bar. In ruling on wealth suspectness, the state supreme court rejected the state's traditional claim that suspectness lay only with individual wealth, stating that "to allot more educational dollars to the children of one district than to those of another merely because of the fortuitous presence of . . . property is to make the quality of a child's education dependent upon the location of private commercial and industrial establishments—surely this is to rely on the most irrelevant of factors as the basis for educational financing."[51] The court went on to say that "we reject defendants' underlying thesis that classification by wealth is constitutional so long as the wealth is that of the district, not the individual. We think that discrimination on the basis of district wealth is equally valid."[52]

Similarly, in ruling for fundamentality the court turned to both law and logic to justify its position, stating that education in a modern industrial state was indispensable and noting that education had two major distinguishing attributes that qualified it as a fundamental right. First, the court stated that education is a major determinant of an individual's chances for economic and social success in a competitive society. Second, the court noted that education is a unique influence on the development of citizens and their place in political and community life. The court then turned to its own thinking and the state constitution in declaring fundamentality. In comparing education to other fundamental rights, the justices stated: "We think that from a larger perspective, education may have far greater social significance than a free transcript or a court-appointed lawyer."[53] The court then considered the education article of the California state constitution,[54] declaring fundamentality on five bases. First, education is essential to free enterprise democracy. Second, education is universally relevant. Third, unlike other government services, public education continues for a lengthy period of time. Fourth, education is unmatched in molding youth and society. And fifth, education is so important that the state has made it compulsory.[55] The court then ruled that plaintiffs were entitled to strict scrutiny equal protection, and that the federal and state equal protection clauses were both impermissibly violated.

Although *Rodriguez* would later invalidate the federal claims in *Serrano,* the case was powerful and decisive for school finance reform. First, *Serrano* proved that the meaning of equal educational opportunity could be so broadly sweeping as to include school finance. Second, *Serrano* proved that states could be vulnerable to constitutional attack, even though the federal courts had been unassailable. Third, under state provisions *Serrano* successfully established all three claims of fundamentality, wealth suspectness, and equal protection. Fourth, *Serrano* had an immediate and profound effect, sparking dramatic reform of state aid formulas in many states as discussed in earlier chapters. Although these reforms were later thought to have been a premature overreaction given later developments, *Serrano* was the impetus for reform as many states believed their own courts would adopt identical standards that would cause their formulas to fall before court scrutiny. Fifth and finally, *Serrano* compelled the flurry of reform both through legal standards and by the court's view on how inequity might be redressed. While the *Serrano* court had stopped short of mandating a solution, it proposed several alternatives, including full state funding and statewide taxation. Although multiply misconstrued, many states took *Serrano* to be an absolute mandate for sweeping reform.

The impact of *Serrano* was accelerated by the nearby New Jersey Superior Court decision in 1972 in *Robinson v. Cahill.*[56] Plaintiffs had alleged that the state school finance scheme violated federal and state equal protection laws and their fundamental right to education, in that tax revenues varied greatly by district wealth and were inadequately equalized by the state. This, according to plaintiffs, denied equal educational opportunity and equal protection by making the quality of education dependent on the wealth of each local district. According to plaintiffs, the state had abrogated its responsibility to education because the laws were not equal in effect on all citizens where equal tax effort did not produce equal tax yield, despite the fact that state aid provided approximately 28% of all district revenues. The trial court agreed in principle, and the case was taken on appeal by the state supreme court.

The 1973 New Jersey Supreme Court ruling that came after *Rodriguez,* however, was notable for many important reasons. First, the court refused to rule for fundamentality, perceptively noting a profound hesitancy in *Rodriguez* that had been overlooked by plaintiffs. The U.S. Supreme Court had said that "every claim arising under the Equal Protection Clause has implications for the relationship between national and state power under our federal system. . . . It would be difficult to imagine a case having a greater potential impact on our federal system than the one now before us, in which we are urged to abrogate systems of financing public education presently in existence in virtually every State."[57] Second, the court noted that the U.S. Supreme Court had never cited *Brown* as a case involving the "fundamental right" concept, stating that *Brown* would point the opposite direction since it declared education to be a most important function of state and local governments.[58] Third, the New Jersey court refused to find wealth a suspect class, noting that "if this is held to constitute classification according to 'wealth' and therefore 'suspect,' our political structure will be fundamentally changed."[59] Under these conditions, the court could find no basis for fundamentality or federal equal protection. But critical to reform, the court nonetheless ruled the system unconstitutional by invoking the education article of the state constitution, which demanded a "thorough and efficient" system of education—a requirement not met by the lack of equalization in revenues and thereby violating the state's equal protection clause.

Although some critics believed *Robinson* had reversed some *Serrano*-like gains and had thus failed the important test of generalizing litigation across states, the decision of the state court in *Robinson* was equal to or greater in significance than either *Serrano* or *Rodriguez*. First, as the first test to follow the federal debacle in *Rodriguez, Robinson* was proof that plaintiffs could prevail at the state level. Second, while a ruling for fundamentality and suspectness would have strengthened reform, critics overlooked an enormous lever in that *Robinson* showed that school finance litigation did not necessarily have to turn on fundamentality. Third, *Robinson* found no need to rely on tenuous *Brown* analogies. Fourth, the genuine effect of *Robinson* was not in its failure to establish coveted claims, but rather in prevailing solely on the education article of the state constitution. Fifth, *Robinson* thereby opened wide the door to technical examination of state aid formulas wherein analysis could be centered on whether the aid scheme worked sufficiently well so as to not deny equal protection of state laws. In sum, *Robinson* greatly aided reform by helping shake free from high-risk litigation strategies that depended too heavily on ephemeral constitutional analysis.

The ruling of the *Robinson* court laid bare the third prong of an emerging school finance litigation strategy. Although the federal case had failed, *Serrano* and *Robinson* taken together indicated that plaintiffs could still bring claims for equal protection and fundamentality wherein an adverse federal ruling on the latter would not negatively affect equal protection claims under interpretation of the education clause of the individual state constitutions. Since the Tenth Amendment had cast educational responsibility to the states, this strategy would apply universally since all states had included some statement in their respective constitutions about education. The fundamentality claim, while not equally universal, should also be uniformly made since it might succeed in some states. The strategy thus shifted to multiple prongs with subparts—the first prong directing the assault toward state courts, the second seeking relief under both federal and state provisions for equal protection, the third seeking a ruling for fundamentality in hopes of securing strict scrutiny, and the fourth challenging the formula under analysis of the education article, wherein chances for success could depend on court analysis of the constitutional framers' intent, the inclinations of each court, litigation from sister states, and the strength of language of the education article itself. In this manner, a rational basis test might also be sufficient to win.

The decisions and strategy derived from *Rodriguez, Serrano,* and *Robinson* have provided a legacy of intense litigation in most of the 50 states. Since 1971, state aid plans have been held unconstitutional at the supreme court level in the states of Arkansas,[60] California,[61] Connecticut,[62] Kentucky,[63] Montana,[64] New Jersey,[65] Texas,[66] Washington,[67] West Virginia,[68] and Wyoming,[69] spurring the hopes of reformers as each instance has provided another opportunity for determining the elements of successful constitutional analysis. The universality of winning strategy has not been perfect, however, as state courts have reached different conclusions when confronted with the unique provisions of each state's laws. While litigation has succeeded in many states, school finance schemes have also been upheld in other states where courts have refused to follow reform logic, finding no language in state constitutions to compel an adverse decision. As such, school aid plans have been upheld by supreme courts in the states of Arizona,[70] Colorado,[71] Georgia,[72] Idaho,[73] Maine,[74] Maryland,[75] Michigan,[76] Montana,[77] New York,[78] North Carolina,[79] Ohio,[80] Oklahoma,[81] Oregon,[82] Pennsylvania,[83] South Carolina,[84] and Wisconsin.[85] Still other states' aid plans have been ruled on by lower courts not reported here.

From these rulings, significant features have emerged. First, the supreme courts in 8 states have declared that education is a fundamental right. Second, there are 10 states in which the highest court has declared that education is *not* a fundamental right. Third, there has been no perfect pattern whereby establishing fundamentality has *automatically* invalidated a school finance plan by virtue of invoking coveted strict scrutiny. For example, the Arizona Supreme Court found that education was a fundamental right, but nonetheless ruled for the state in *Shoftstall v. Hollins* in 1973. Similarly, the Wisconsin court declared in *Buse v. Smith*[86] that education is a fundamental right, but later noted in *Kukor v. Grover* that a rational basis is all that is required to uphold the state aid scheme when absolute denial of education is not at question. Fourth, the harshness of this reality has been somewhat softened by the logic of *Robinson,* as several state supreme courts including Arkansas, New Jersey, and Texas have ruled for plaintiffs by finding equality a requirement, even absent the one feature of fundamentality that would invoke strict scrutiny analysis. Fifth and finally, only one state other than California has declared wealth a suspect class, as the Wyoming court in *Washakie County School District No. 1 v. Herschler*[87] invalidated its aid scheme, establishing that no equality could exist until funding is also equal. The results of these decisions are seen in Table 5.1

The checklist indicates an uncertain patchwork of decisions wherein some argue that winning at the supreme court level is analogous to rolling dice. Yet despite the uneven record, there are indicators of which claims have consistently received the most court sympathy or rejection. First, it is extraordinarily rare to reach wealth as a suspect class. As stated very early in *Robinson,* the unintended implications for society are too broad in that all other government services could be immediately subject to the same claim. Second, fundamentality is only slightly less rare, as courts are slow to construe new rights from state constitutions and for which federal precedent is adverse. Third, federal equal protection is de rigueur in claim, but state equal protection is a key to overturning state aid plans—a strategy that does not usually work well unless the education article can also be invoked in a plain reading that requires the state to accomplish what it set out to do. For example, the Texas Supreme Court in *Edgewood v. Kirby* in 1989 stated: "Whether the legislature acts directly or enlists local government to help meet its obligation, the end product must still be what the constitution demands."[88] Taken collectively, this suggests that favorable rulings de-

TABLE 5.1 Litigation Checklist[1]

Filed on State	Name of Case	Filed Federal Court	State Supreme Court	Case Won	Case Lost	Case Suspect	Ruled Fundamentality	Ruled Education Article	Filed on Equal Protection
Alabama									
Arizona	*Shofstall*		x		x		x		x
Arkansas	*Dupree*		x	x				x	
California	*Serrano*		x	x		x	x		x
Colorado	*Lujan*		x		x			x	x
Connecticut	*Horton*	x	x			x	x	x	
Delaware									
Florida	*Askew*		x	(vacated)					
Georgia	*McDaniel*		x		x			x	x
Hawaii									
Idaho	*Thompson*		x		x			x	x
Illinois	*McInnis*	x			x				x
Indiana									
Iowa									
Kansas									
Kentucky	*Rose*		x	x			x	x	x
Louisiana	*Scarnato*	x			(dismissed)				x
Maine									
Maryland	*Hornbeck*		x		x			x	x
Massachusetts									
Michigan	*Milliken*		x		x				x
Minnesota	*VanDusartz*	x		x					x
Mississippi	*Papasan*	x			x				x
Missouri									
Montana	*Helena*		x	x			x	x	x
	Woodahl		x		x			x	x
Nebraska									
Nevada									
New Hampshire									

TABLE 5.1 (Continued)

State	Case						
New Jersey	*Robinson*			X		X	X
	Abbott			X		X	X
New Mexico							
New York	*Levittown*			X		X	X
	Spano			X		X	X
North Carolina							
North Dakota	*Kadrmas*	X		X			X
Ohio	*Walter*			X		X	X
Oklahoma	*Fair*			X		X	X
Oregon	*Olsen*			X		X	X
Pennsylvania	*Danson*			X		X	X
Rhode Island							
South Carolina							
South Dakota							
Tennessee							
Texas	*Rodriguez*	X				X	
	Edgewood		X	X		X	X
Utah							
Vermont							
Virginia	*Burruss*	X				X	X
Washington	*N.Shore*					X	X
	Seattle		X	X			X
West Virginia	*Pauley*		X	X	X	X	X
Wisconsin	*Buse*		X	X	X	X	X
	Kukor		X	X	X		X
Wyoming	*Washakie*		X	X	X	X	X

¹Includes only decisions rendered at the state supreme court level and federal court decisions. Does not include active or threatened litigation.

pend at least in part on specific language in state constitutions. While the relationship may not be perfectly incremental as language increases, in most instances the opportunity for success does diminish rapidly as language becomes more vague. For example, the probability of success in Mississippi would be much lower than in Wyoming or Washington; similarly, litigants in states with only moderate language can be less certain about the outcome. States indeed have great language differences, as well as significant commonalities:

State Education Articles

Alabama
The legislature shall establish, organize and maintain a liberal system of public schools throughout the state for the benefit of the children thereof between the ages of seven and 21 years. *Ala. Const. art. 14, sec. 256.*

Alaska
The legislature shall by general law establish and maintain a system of public schools open to all children of the State, and may provide for other public educational institutions. *Alaska Const. art. VII, sec. 1.*

Arkansas
The State shall ever maintain a general, suitable and efficient system of free schools whereby all persons in the State between the ages of six and twenty-one years may receive gratuitous instruction. *Ark. Const. art. 19, sec. 19.*

Arizona
The University and all other State educational institutions shall be open to students of both sexes, and the instruction furnished shall be as nearly free as possible. The Legislature shall provide for a system of common schools by which a free school shall be established and maintained in every school district for at least six months each year, which school shall be open to all pupils between the ages of six and twenty-one years. *Ariz. Const. art. II, sec. 6.*

California
A general diffusion of knowledge and intelligence being essential to the preservation of the rights and liberties of the people, the Legislature shall encourage by all suitable means the promotion of intellectual, scientific, moral, and agricultural improvement. *Cal. Const. art. 9, sec. 1.*

Colorado
The general assembly shall, as soon as practicable, provide for the establishment and maintenance of a thorough and uniform system of free public schools throughout the state, wherein all residents of the state, between the ages of six and twenty-one years, may be educated gratuitously. *Colo. Const. art. IX, sec. 2.*

Connecticut
There shall always be free public elementary and secondary schools in the state. *Conn. Const. art. 8, sec. 1.*

Delaware
The General Assembly shall provide for the establishment and maintenance of a general and efficient system of free public schools and may require by law that every child, not physically or mentally disabled, shall attend the public school, unless educated by other means. *Del. Const. art. X, sec. 1.*

Florida
Adequate provision shall be made by law for a uniform system of free public schools and for the establishment, maintenance and operation of institutions of higher learning and other public education programs that the needs of the people may require. *Fla. Const. art. IX, sec. 1.*

Georgia	The provision of an adequate education for the citizens shall be a primary obligation of the State of Georgia, the expense of which shall be provided for by taxation. *Ga. Const. art. VIII, sec. 1.*
Hawaii	The State shall provide for the establishment, support and control of a statewide system of public schools. . . . *Hawaii Const. art. IX, sec. 2.*
Idaho	The stability of a republic form of government depending mainly upon the intelligence of the people, it shall be the duty of the legislature of Idaho to establish and maintain a general, uniform and thorough system of public, free common schools. *Idaho Const. art. IX, sec. 1.*
Illinois	A fundamental goal of the People of the State is the educational development of all persons to the limits of their capacities. The State shall provide for an efficient system of high quality public educational institutions and services. . . . *Ill. Const. art. X, sec. 1.*
Indiana	Knowledge and learning, generally diffused throughout a community, being essential to the preservation of a free government; it shall be the duty of the General Assembly to encourage, by all suitable means, moral, intellectual, scientific, and agricultural improvement; and to provide, by law, for a general uniform system of Common schools. . . . *Ind. Const. art. 9, sec. 1.*
Iowa	The Board of Education shall provide for the education of all the youths of the State, through a system of Common Schools. . . . *Iowa Const. art. IX, sec. 3.*
Kansas	The legislature shall provide for intellectual, educational, vocational and scientific improvement by establishing and maintaining public schools, educational institutions and related activities which may be organized and changed in such manner as may be provided by law. *Kan. Const. art. 6, sec. 1.*
Kentucky	The General Assembly shall, by appropriate legislation, provide for an efficient system of common schools throughout the State. *Ky. Const. sec. 183.*
Louisiana	The legislature shall provide for the education of the people of the state and shall establish and maintain a public education system. *La. Const. art. 8, sec. 1.*
Maine	A general diffusion of the advancement of education being essential to the preservation of the rights and liberties of the people; to promote this important object, the Legislature [is] authorized . . . to require, the several towns to make suitable provision, at their own expense, for the support and maintenance of public schools. *Me. Const. art. VIII, sec. 8.*
Maryland	The General Assembly, at its first session after the adoption of this Constitution, shall, by law, establish throughout the state a thorough and efficient system of free public schools. *Md. Const. art. VIII, sec. 1.*
Massachusetts	Wisdom, and knowledge, as well as virtue, diffused generally among the body of the people, being necessary for the preservation of their rights and liberties; . . . it shall be the duty of legislatures . . . to cherish the interests of literature and the sciences. . . . *Mass. Const. ch. 5, sec. 2.*

Michigan	Religion, morality and knowledge being necessary to good government and the happiness of mankind, schools and the means of education shall forever be encouraged. *Mich. Const. art. VIII, sec. 1.*
Minnesota	The stability of a republican form of government depending mainly upon the intelligence of the people, it is the duty of the legislature to establish a general and uniform system of public schools. The legislature shall make such provisions by taxation or otherwise as will secure a thorough and efficient system of public schools throughout the state. *Minn. Const. art. XIII, sec. 1.*
Mississippi	The legislature may in its discretion provide for the maintenance and establishment of free public schools for all children between the ages of six and twenty-one years. *Miss. Const. art. 8, sec. 201.*
Missouri	A general diffusion of knowledge and intelligence being essential to the preservation of the rights and liberties of the people, the general assembly shall establish and maintain free public schools. . . . *Mo. Const. art. X, sec. 1(3).*
Montana	It is the goal of the people to establish a system of education which will develop the full educational potential of each person. Equality of educational opportunity is guaranteed to each person of the state. *Mont. Const. art. X, sec. 1.*
Nebraska	The Legislature shall provide for the free instruction in the common schools of this state of all persons between the ages of five and twenty-one years. *Neb. Const. art. VII, sec. 1.*
Nevada	The legislature shall provide for a uniform system of common schools. . . . *Nev. Const. art. 11, sec. 2.*
New Hampshire	It shall be the duty of legislators and magistrates, in all future periods of this government, to cherish the interest of literature and the sciences. *N.H. Const. art. 83.*
New Jersey	The legislature shall provide for the maintenance and support of a thorough and efficient system of free public schools for the instruction of all the children in the state between the ages of five and eighteen years. *N.J. Const. art. 8, sec. 4.*
New Mexico	A uniform system of free public schools sufficient for the education of, and open to, all the children of school age in the state shall be established and maintained. *N.M. Const. art. XII, sec. 1.*
New York	The legislature shall provide for the maintenance and support of a system of free common schools, wherein all the children of the state may be educated. *N.Y. Const. art. 11, sec. 1.*
North Carolina	The General Assembly shall provide by taxation and otherwise for a general and uniform system of free public schools . . . wherein equal opportunities shall be provided for all students. *N.C. Const. art. IX, sec. 2(1).*
North Dakota	A high degree of intelligence, patriotism, integrity and morality on the part of every voter in a government by the people being necessary in order to insure the continuance of that government and the prosperity and happiness of the people, the legislative assembly shall make provision for the establishment and maintenance of a system of public

	schools. . . . This legislative requirement shall be irrevocable without the consent of the United States and the people of North Dakota. *N.D. Const. art. VIII, sec. 1.*
Ohio	The general assembly shall make such provisions, by taxation, or otherwise, as, with the income arising from the school trust fund, will secure a thorough and efficient system of common schools throughout the state. *Ohio Const. art. VI, sec. 2.*
Oklahoma	The Legislature shall establish and maintain a system of free public schools wherein all children of the state may be educated. *Okla. Const. art. 13, sec. 1.*
Oregon	The Legislative Assembly shall provide by law for the establishment of a uniform and general system of common schools. *Or. Const. art. VIII, sec. 3.*
Pennsylvania	The General Assembly shall provide for the maintenance of a thorough and efficient system of public education to serve the needs of the Commonwealth. *Pa. Const. art. 3, sec. 14.*
Rhode Island	It shall be the duty of the general assembly to promote public schools and to adopt all means which they may deem necessary and proper to secure to the people the advantages and opportunities of education. *R.I. Const. art. 13, sec. 1.*
South Carolina	The General Assembly shall provide for the maintenance and support of a system of free public schools open to all children of the state. . . . *S.C. Const. art. XI, sec. 3.*
South Dakota	The stability of a republican form of government depending on the morality and intelligence of the people, it shall be the duty of the legislature to establish and maintain a general and uniform system of public schools wherein tuition shall be without charge, and equally open to all. . . . *S.D. Const. art. VIII, sec. 1.*
Tennessee	The General Assembly shall provide for the maintenance, support and eligibility standards of a system of free public schools. *Tenn. Const. art. 11, sec. 12.*
Texas	A general diffusion of knowledge being essential to the preservation of the liberties and rights of the people, it shall be the duty of the legislature of the state to establish and make suitable provision for the support and maintenance of an efficient system of public free schools. *Tex. Const. art. VIII, sec. 1.*
Utah	The Legislature shall provide for the establishment and maintenance of a uniform system of public schools. . . . *Utah Const. art. X, sec. 1.*
Vermont	Laws for the encouragement of virtue and prevention of vice and immorality ought to be constantly kept in force, and duly executed; and a competent number of schools ought to be maintained in each town unless the general assembly permits other provisions for the convenient instruction of youth. *Vt. Const. ch. II, sec. 64.*
Virginia	The General Assembly shall provide for a system of free public elementary and secondary schools for all children throughout the Commonwealth and shall seek to ensure that an educational program of high

quality is established and continually maintained. *Va. Const. art. VIII, sec. 1.*

Washington   The legislature shall provide for a general and uniform system of public schools. *Wash. Const. art. IX, sec. 2;* and

It is the paramount duty of the state to make ample provision for the education of all children residing within its borders. . . . *Wash. Const. art. IX, sec. 1.*

West Virginia   The legislature shall provide, by general law, for a thorough and efficient system of free schools. *W. Va. Const. art. XII, sec. 1.*

Wisconsin   The legislature shall provide by law for the establishment of district schools, which shall be as nearly uniform as practicable. . . . *Wis. Const. art. 10, sec. 3.*

Wyoming   The legislature shall provide for the establishment and maintenance of a complete and uniform system of public instruction. . . . *Wyo. Const. art. 7, sec. 1.*

Active Lawsuits

The high-risk stakes of constitutional litigation, however, have not deterred unhappy plaintiffs around the nation from persistently bringing new school finance lawsuits. Some current litigation is a function of compliance monitoring, but the 1990s has brought an intense wave of new filings seeking judicial review of state aid plans. The present record stands as proof. As of 1992, plaintiffs had won at the state supreme court level in four states (Arkansas, Connecticut, Kentucky, and Texas) with no further filings. Plaintiffs in another six states (California, Montana, New Jersey, Washington, West Virginia, and Wyoming) had also won at the state supreme court level, but further compliance litigation had occurred wherein the courts had either retained jurisdiction or plaintiffs had refiled, resulting in review of progress. Compliance litigation had either followed or was actively in place in 1992. In nine states (Colorado, Georgia, Maine, Maryland, Michigan, North Carolina, Oregon, South Carolina, and Wisconsin), plaintiffs had lost at the supreme court level with no further filings, or alternatively had lost further complaints as well. In addition, plaintiffs in another six states (Arizona, Idaho, New York, Ohio, Oklahoma, and Pennsylvania) had lost at the supreme court but had filed further complaints that have not been heard.

The nature of modern school finance litigation is so fluid that an accurate account of actions before the court can never be compiled. Plaintiffs initiate lawsuits on a daily basis, and in many instances withdraw almost as quickly. In addition, some suits are never reported as they may involve small issues that are quickly resolved at the lowest court level. Further, lawsuits may be dismissed by the court, as it is expected that states will immediately file motions to dismiss. Additionally, the status of lawsuits is altered as decisions are finally handed down. Yet much can be observed by a freeze-frame of current litigation because it monitors the nation's pulse. At this writing, the pace of litigation is escalating rapidly as a new wave of school finance equity challenges swells to unequaled and historic proportions. As 1992 drew to a close, litigation was present in at least 27 states in which no supreme court decision had been rendered, with active suits before the courts in many states including Alabama,[89] Alaska,[90] Arizona,[91] California,[92] Florida,[93] Idaho,[94] Illinois,[95] Indiana,[96] Kansas,[97] Louisiana,[98] Massachusetts,[99] Michigan,[100] Minnesota,[101] Missouri,[102] Montana,[103] New

Hampshire,[104] North Dakota,[105] Nebraska,[106] Pennsylvania,[107] Rhode Island,[108] South Dakota,[109] Tennessee,[110] Vermont,[111] Virginia,[112] Washington,[113] Wyoming,[114] and West Virginia.[115] In addition, rumors were rampant that additional filings would soon occur, as one national advocacy group had threatened new filings in half the states. When these instances are added to compliance monitoring, the school finance climate of recent years has indeed been intense.

PRINCIPLES AND DIRECTIONS
OF COURT CHALLENGES

The critical nature of education finance has been graphically illustrated in all the foregoing chapters. No matter how much citizens complain about taxes and despite the reality that people would purchase differing amounts of education if left to their own discretion, Americans believe in the power of education. As stated in the opening quotation for this chapter, the proof of that belief is that the measure of how deeply people believe in education and money is apparent in how hard wealthy districts seek to gather their resources to themselves. Alternatively, a negative proof would state that money matters to people in poor districts as well, and proof is in the record of bitter litigation that has come to characterize the late twentieth century. This chapter is therefore a fitting capstone to all the foregoing chapters because it makes real the contentions of this book on which later chapters will examine current professional practice—that is, money matters so much that society can afford to entrust education only to highly skilled leaders.

The realities of a litigious society that simultaneously covets resources and equality virtually assure that school leaders of the future will experience school finance litigation at some point in their professional careers. While opposing views might take heart or discouragement at such a statement, reality suggests that administrators should both be knowledgeable about the broad principles that have governed school finance litigation thus far and have some sense of future direction. Obviously new directions in litigation are tenuous and highly fluid, and court decisions should never be predicted with confidence. There are, however, broad principles to be gleaned from the turbulent and perplexing history of school finance lawsuits, and future directions can at least be surmised.

Principles and New Directions in Litigation

First, it may be safely stated that litigation will not achieve great success in federal courts. The only exceptions to this principle rest in events that might cause the Supreme Court to abandon its traditional position on fundamentality, wealth suspectness, or broadened interpretation of Fourteenth Amendment equal protection. Given the Court's historic reluctance to create new fundamental rights, that path will disappoint reformers unless nexus to other fundamental rights can be better established. Despite waverings such as *Plyler*, the Court has stood firm in calling education a most important responsibility of state and local governments. Similarly, wealth as a suspect class is an unfruitful attack unless the Court unexpectedly reverses itself or plaintiffs can show overwhelming and consistent wealth-education discrimination against individuals. Likewise, federal equal protection will remain largely unavailable except when established suspect classes can be linked to school finance. For example, a vastly overlooked genre of school finance–related litigation exists in desegregation suits, and it may be said that analogy to such strategy will be required to gain federal attention. The only other alternative is by changes in the Court itself, as incumbents leave and are replaced, under which conditions a federal plea will receive sympathy only by dramatic breakthroughs or new political appointments.[116]

Second, it may be confidently stated that litigation will continue in state courts at historic levels into the foreseeable future. Although the record in state courts has been mixed, plaintiffs have achieved their only successes at this level. Within state courts, it is equally evident that the plea for fundamentality will experience very limited success, as these courts will frequently apply the federal test in the absence of strong state constitutional provisions. It must, of course, be noted that few states have the language needed to unquestioningly require strict scrutiny. Even when such language is present, it should still be recognized that many courts will hesitate at fundamentality because of the powerful analysis found long ago in *Robinson,* in which the court perceptively recognized that society itself could be unintentionally transformed by hasty declarations of fundamentality because even a noble goal could be twisted under law by turning other mere social conveniences into fundamental rights. As such, litigation in state courts will continue to turn on issues other than fundamentality or wealth suspectness.

Third, it is likely that *Serrano* logic will have only limited utility in that courts have generally moved beyond striking down unequal systems without evidence that inequality results in an inadequate education. While this may appear regressive, an attractive logic underlies it. The court in *Serrano* presumably did not care that the system could be adequate without being equal—in contrast, the predominance of subsequent decisions has attempted to determine if inequality is in fact followed by inadequacy. While the standard appears to be lowered, it may be ultimately beneficial in that the linkages between resources and equal opportunity will be resultantly strengthened because plaintiffs will be required to demonstrate these effects if they are to prevail. While it is a harsh requirement, there may be a silver lining that moves equity forward through new technology that will have to focus on educational productivity.

Fourth, the potential demise of *Serrano* logic also speaks to the dubious survival of strategies based only in noble theories and moral outrage. While all persons should carry high conscience for children's causes, it is nonetheless true that few lawsuits have been won based on exhortation or shame. The failure of this strategy is evident in the shambles of federal hopes after *Brown,* leading to the conclusion that there is high regard for conscience in the context of the law, but lawsuits are generally won by constitutional requirements. Instances of "soft" litigation are rare, and the outrage in *Pauley v. Kelly* is generally nonreplicable at the state level as well, as is its level of judicial prescription.[117] Likewise, Wyoming's requirement of equal expenditures is not generally likely to recur elsewhere. This view is especially reinforced in compliance litigation, as even in *Serrano II*[118] the court was satisfied when most fiscal variation was erased. This logic was also echoed in *Horton II,*[119] as the court under fundamentality required only that disparities not be so great as to be unconstitutional. As a consequence, litigants may generally expect to overprepare in the expectation that minimal scrutiny will be the standard.

Fifth, it is likely that the *Robinson* strategy of scrutinizing the education clause of individual state constitutions will continue to be the most immediately promising strategy. This is consistent with all the foregoing in that the greatest scrutiny will likely rest in how closely the state achieves its aims when held up to its constitutional requirements. *Robinson* demonstrated that fundamentality and suspectness are not absolute prerequisites to success, and most subsequent winning litigation stands as further proof to this truth. The ephemeral and intangible nature of fundamental rights and wealth suspectness is frustrating to courts, which in contrast can usually make plain reading of state education articles and apply the more tangible concept of equal protection. This reality is aided by the fact that while litigants may feel helpless before the law, courts likewise feel helpless on the slippery grounds of constitutional analysis. Given that courts have no dispositive proof to presuming the linkage between wealth and opportunity, tying specific language to factual analysis in the context of equal protection likely explains the success of the *Robinson* strategy.

Sixth, it is likely that different decisions will continue to be handed down by state courts using the *Robinson* strategy for several reasons. One reason is obviously that different constitutions say different things. A second reason is that courts themselves cannot look at language so dispassionately as to read nothing into the language except the words, making words subject to perceptual filter. A third reason is that the language in many state education articles is nearly empty. In these cases, courts are exhibiting an interest in constitutional debate analysis wherein the court looks back to the framing of the constitution to determine legislative intent in the education article. Although it has been suggested that many legislatures had no motive deeper than copying other states' education articles, the recent decisions in Kentucky and Texas seriously looked to framing intent to determine the meaning of ''thorough and/or efficient'' phrases. An increasingly common strategy combines framers' intent, litigation from sister states, and jurisdictional precedent to cast a ''plain'' reading of the education article. Thus, decisions will be different among the states, with some influence by other reform aided or deterred by the inclinations of the court itself.

Seventh, it is likely that courts will always be reluctant to engage in specific judicial prescription as a remedy to school finance problems because courts are bound to respect the separation of powers. For decades, courts have hesitated to intervene in legislative affairs, remarking that they have neither the power nor the expertise to prescribe solutions to political questions. Instead, courts have held themselves aloof, ruling only on questions of law brought before them by plaintiffs and sending the problem back to the legislatures for resolution. As such, in one sense courts are poor tools to force reform as they will almost always stop short of providing solutions.[120] In addition, the courts can actually frustrate reform since a favorable decision for plaintiffs by no means guarantees immediate or receptive legislative response; for example, response to *Edgewood* was a call for a constitutional amendment that would nullify the court's decision.[121] Alternatively, however, much progress has been wrought by litigation. As a consequence, a natural tension will continue to slow reform as courts will not readily pursue direct intervention strategies.

Eighth, it is likely that reform will be slow and will remain incomplete for many years. In one sense, it is discouraging that the root of the problem was identified so many years ago in *Sawyer* in 1912 when the court stated ''[t]he method of distributing the proceeds of a tax rests in the wise discretion and sound judgment of the Legislature. If this discretion is unwisely exercised, the remedy is with the people, and not with the constitution,''[122] a view consistently upheld and confirmed by *Rodriguez*. Under these conditions, it would seem that reform has gained little ground in this regard. Yet on the other hand, it is encouraging to note that standards do change with the times, as contemporary views of inequality have led to significant judicial intervention by state courts. Indeed, *Sawyer v. Gilmore* may have been right for the wrong reasons—that is, justice makes few errors of haste, and rapid change is often available only at the voting polls. Thus, litigants expecting dramatic events may be disappointed, although breakthroughs such as Kentucky and Texas offer some solace. But it still should be stated that deliberateness may be beneficial, as dizzying change may not be well planned.

The net sum of nearly a quarter century of intense reform litigation finally proves that the outcome of future lawsuits cannot be known. Too many variables impact on an ever-changing social milieu, and the courts themselves are never certain of whether to lead or reflect society's thinking. Courts seem at times to be ahead of the political readiness, while in other obvious ways they are behind. The political climate of legislatures adds greatly to the litigation equation, as states themselves shape the frequency and intensity of litigation by their relative vigilance to equity concerns. While no amount of money can ever satisfy litigants, they are better satisfied when distribution is fair—legislatures, however, are generally faced with competing demands from all corners of society for which sufficient funding is beyond their grasp. Yet there has been great change flowing from litigation: states have assumed greater shares, taxes have been better equalized, and expenditures are higher. In addition, reform has become a political agenda seized upon by presidents and governors and legislators. Thus, while equity has far to go, the power of a court should never be underestimated—if it were not for litigation, it is absolutely certain that less progress toward fundamental fairness in school finance would exist today.

Although these conditions indicate that only uncertainty itself is certain, the long-range view still demands optimism. The pendulum swings, and equity will continue to rise and fade in cycles. It cannot be otherwise because people will protect their resources, giving rise to disputes. But in the context of this book, education remains a great and noble cause since life's opportunities are in large measure a product of the education received by children. As stated at the outset of this chapter, if money is inadequate to these ends, then children in all social and economic circumstances should experience its inadequacy on equal terms.

Under these conditions, we turn next to more operational aspects of school districts where the outcome of all the foregoing chapters is set in motion by school district budgets.

Review Points

THE ROOTS OF SCHOOL FINANCE CHALLENGES

School finance has been of interest to federal and state courts for more than a century. This dual thrust sought federal protection first, since a ruling would likely bind states to compliance.

Plaintiff claims have their deepest roots in federal constitutional litigation, dating from the provisions of the Declaration of Independence and the U.S. Constitution.

American preoccupation with equality is widely evident, as the developing nation adopted the Bill of Rights and other legislation and constitutional amendments aimed at equality under the law.

Equality litigation received its first great impetus, however, with passage of the Fourteenth Amendment, giving rise to a series of broad civil rights lawsuits beginning in the nineteenth century that would later influence school finance litigation strategy.

Of paramount importance to school finance challenges were the concepts of establishing education as a fundamental right and seeking to apply the Fourteenth Amendment Equal Protection Clause to education.

Drawn from broader civil rights litigation, school finance strategists sought to have courts declare education as a fundamental right since it would require strict judicial scrutiny. Similarly, strategists sought similarities between education and previously defined suspect classes to invoke Fourteenth Amendment equal protection. These strategies were necessary, given the Tenth Amendment's silence on a federal role in education.

The modern civil rights movement beginning with *Brown v. Board of Education* (1954) provided the vehicle to initiate direct school finance litigation, as the Supreme Court spoke to the value of education to a child in modern society. Given this decision, reformers believed that fiscal equality was also required.

The result of these events was an assault on state school finance schemes in federal courts beginning in the 1960s, with a similar strategy directed toward states shortly afterwards that also included a sharp scrutiny of state constitutional provisions under the respective education articles, wherein tight analysis of state constitutional language was sought.

PRINCIPLES AND DIRECTIONS OF COURT CHALLENGES

The promising federal reform future suggested in *Brown* never materialized, as federal courts refused to make the same applications of fundamentality, suspect class, and equal protection to education. Rather, federal courts have used the logic of *San Antonio Independent School District v. Rodriguez* (1973) to defer to states in the absence of educational deprivation, claiming unmanageable judicial standards, the imperfect analogy of money and suspect class, and generally avoiding the question of fundamentality of education.

State reform litigation has been much more successful, as state constitutional provisions may be more restrictive than the federal provisions.

The decision in *Serrano v. Priest* (1971) in California provided a template for subsequent state litigation, as that state supreme court found for fundamentality and equal protection under both the federal and state constitutions.

An equally important template was provided in *Robinson v. Cahill* (1972) when the New Jersey Supreme Court overturned the state aid plan without the prerequisite ruling for fundamentality, instead reaching its decision under the "thorough and efficient" clause of the state constitution.

Although *Rodriguez* nullified federal claims, state litigation has followed these strategies with some success—however, no consistently perfect strategy has emerged, as state courts are reasonably free to interpret state constitutional requirements differently.

The present inclination of federal courts offers no immediate reversal, and the attitude of state courts augurs against fundamentality and suspect class. The better strategy is to scrutinize the language of state education articles under equal protection analysis in the vein of *Robinson.*

Finally, the imperfect record of plaintiff victories has not discouraged further litigation, as a new wave of lawsuits is sweeping the nation, with no signs of abatement.

Case Study

As the new superintendent of schools in your district, you are facing a difficult decision that must be reached before the next board meeting. At last month's meeting, several of your board members were quite upset that this year's state aid entitlement has declined by more than 50% over the previous year. As you are new to the state, you spent several days discovering why the district has lost so much aid. From your work, you learned that the legislature had reacted to a lawsuit filed by poor districts, alleging discrimination in various aspects of the state equalization aid formula. To render the lawsuit moot, a new finance plan was enacted calling for a foundation program with local option leeway. More specifically, the plan placed a uniform base expenditure of $4,000 per pupil under each district, adjusted by weightings of enrollment size where the median enrollment for the state will calculate at a weight of 1.0. In addition, the new plan required a uniform tax rate of 25 mills and allowed an unequalized 10-mill local option leeway. Finally, the plan contained a recapture provision.

After calculating aid entitlements, the effect on your district was severe. As your district enrollment is at the median for the state, it will receive only the base amount per pupil for regular education children. Last year your district spent $4,700 per pupil at a tax rate of only 22 mills. As a result of the new law, your expenditure per pupil will decline approximately 15% while your tax rate will increase more than 13%. Because a neighboring district's power plant has been a source of local envy, you began by first looking at available tax revenue. Article XI, Section 1, of your state constitution reads: "The legislature shall provide for a uniform and equal basis of valuation and rate of taxation on all property." In checking with the county appraiser, however, you discovered that the state sales-to-assessment-ratio study performed annually by the state property valuation department shows substantial noncompliance with the constitutionally required appraisal rates. Second, state statutes provide that property exempt from property taxes shall not be included in the computation of assessed valuation of a school district. In checking with the state department of education, you found that property in excess of $850 million in District ABC was exempted, and property in excess of $700 million was exempt in District XYZ. Third, you also learned that both Districts ABC and XYZ will receive more state aid this year. In contrast, your loss will be several million dollars in operating funds your district has historically received.

Having contemplated your research, you visited with the board's attorney to explore the feasibility of litigation. The attorney seemed to think that a lawsuit challenging the new aid formula might be possible on three grounds. First, the attorney suggested that the uniform taxation provision might be violated by applying a statewide tax rate to unequally appraised property as shown by the sales-ratio study. Second, the unequal amounts of tax-exempt property in school districts might violate both equal protection and equal taxation laws in that taxpayers throughout the state would be required to pay higher taxes due to local decisions in some districts to exempt large amounts of property. Third, the reduction in permissible expenditure per pupil under the new foundation plan might be arbitrary and capricious since it does not have any basis in fact or law by failing to take into account those factors establishing an adequate educational expenditure since it was derived by dividing available resources by the number of pupils in the state, adjusted for weighting on district size. Based on your research and legal consultation and estimate of large legal fees, you must make a decision before the next board meeting on whether to recommend court action to enjoin the distribution of state aid.

Using the following set of questions to help launch your class discussion, what do you anticipate your decision will be? Why? Defend your views through logic, data, and what you have learned from this chapter.

Directed Discussion Questions

1. As you prepare to make your recommendation to the board of education, what are the salient legal points in the data on this hypothetical lawsuit that seem particularly logical, given your learning in this chapter? How would you explain the attorney's thinking to the board so that lay people could easily grasp the logic and mandates of law?

2. Given your studies from previous chapters of this textbook, what are the salient technical points of the state aid formula with which you agree philosophically? Why? Conversely, what technical points do you disagree with philosophically? Why? In your opinion, what is your overall evaluation of the formula in terms of sound school finance theory? In what areas, if any, do you express reservations? In generalities, do you think the state aid formula as presently written will pass constitutional muster? Why or why not?

3. Given your studies in the previous chapter on school finance formulas, how favorably does the state aid formula in this case study compare to the general patterns of practice in the United States? How does the formula in this case study compare to your own state's aid plan? Where is it superior to your state's plan? Where is it deficient? In your opinion, what are the potential legal vulnerabilities of your state's aid formula? If your state's school funding plan has been challenged in court, what was the outcome? What were the legal arguments? What data were provided to support plaintiffs' claims? What were the defendants' responses? In reading your state's constitution, what are the provisions on which plaintiff attorneys might argue for a favorable decision for their clients?

4. If you were asked to design a state aid plan that would be as invulnerable as possible to legal challenge, how would you structure its tax and distribution provisions?

5. Given the historical record of federal and state school finance litigation and recognizing that constitutional litigation is generally referred to as "high risk" litigation and knowing that the lawsuits may take years in trial and appeals and cost several hundred thousand dollars, what will you recommend?

NOTES

1. John Coons, William Clune, and Stephen Sugarman, *Private Wealth and Public Education* (Cambridge: Belknap Press of Harvard University Press, 1970), 36.
2. For an in-depth treatment of the whole concept of equality in the law with broad-ranging implications including school finance, see Rosemary Salomone, *Equal Education Under Law* (New York: St. Martin's Press, 1986).
3. These arguments generally, and sections in part, of this discussion have been developed elsewhere by the authors. Specifically see David C. Thompson, "School Finance and the Courts: A Reanalysis of Progress,"; West's *Education Law Reporter,* 59:4 (1990), 945–961; see also David C. Thompson, Julie K. Underwood, and William E. Camp, "Equal Protection under the Law: Reanalysis and New Directions in School Finance Litigation," in *Spheres of Justice in Education,* ed. Deborah Verstegen and James Ward, 11th Annual Yearbook of the American Education Finance Association (New York: HarperBusiness, 1990).
4. In Congress, July 4, 1776. A Declaration By the Representatives of the United States of America, In General Congress assembled.
5. Ten Original Amendments: The Bill of Rights. In force December 15, 1791.
6. The Thirteenth Amendment to the Constitution states: "Neither slavery nor involuntary servitude, except as a punishment for crime whereof the party shall have been duly convicted, shall exist within the United States or any place subject to their jurisdiction."
7. Proposed by the 39th Congress, June 13, 1866, and ratified in a proclamation by the Secretary of State, July 28, 1868.
8. Philip Kurland, "Equal Educational Opportunity: The Limits of Constitutional Jurisprudence Undefined," *University of Chicago Law Review,* 35 (1968), 583–600.
9. The history of racial equality is too complex to fully describe here. In an educational context, it is obvious that Brown v. Board of Education, 374 U.S. 483 (1954), is the most critical as discussed later. However, this analysis is aided by recognition that a long history of such equality preceded Brown, which in an educational context included, for example, Gong Lum v. Rice (275 U.S. 78 (1927); Missouri ex. rel. Gaines v. Canada, 305 U.S. 337 (1938); Freeman v. County School Board, 82 F.Supp. 167 (E.D. Va. 1948); Butler v. Wilemon, 86 F.Supp. 397 (N.D. Tex. 1949); Pitts v. Board of Trustees, 84 F.Supp. 975 (E.D. Ark. 1949); McLaurin v. Oklahoma State Regents, 339 U.S. 637 (1950); Sweatt v. Painter, 339 U.S. 629 (1950); Carter v. School Board, 182 F.2d 531 (4th Cir. 1950); and Davis v. County School Board, 103 F.Supp. 337 (E.D. Va. 1952).
10. These cases are also multiple and meaningful. For example, see Baker v. Carr, 369 U.S. 186 (1962) where accident of geography and arbitrary boundaries of governments may not be a basis for discrimination among otherwise equal citizens, in this instance forbidding the requirement that one must pay property taxes to vote; see also Gray v. Sanders, 372 U.S. 368 (1963); Wesberry v. Sanders, 276 U.S. 1 (1964); Reynolds v. Sims, 377 U.S. 533 (1964); Davis v. Mann, 377 U.S. 678 91964); and others.
11. These cases are also multiple and far-ranging. But see, for example, Shapiro v. Thompson, 394 U.S. 618 (1969), where a law against bringing indigents into a state violates the right to interstate travel; see also Lubin v. Panish, 415 U.S. 706 (1974), where a filing fee as prerequisite to the right to vote is wealth discrimination; see also Harper v. Virginia Board of Elections, 383 U.S. 663 (1966), where a state poll tax is wealth discrimination; and Griffin v. Illinois, 351 U.S. 12 (1956), where denying an indigent defendant a transcript of trial for appeal is wealth discrimination.
12. See, for example, Shapiro, 394 U.S. 618 (1969).
13. See, for example, Skinner v. Oklahoma, 316 U.S. 535 (1942).
14. See, for example, Reynolds, 377 U.S. 533 (1964).
15. See, for example, Griffin, 351 U.S. 12 (1956).

16. United States v. Carolene Products Co., 304 U.S. 144 at 153 (1938).

17. See, for example, Loving v. Virginia, 388 U.S. 1 (1967).

18. See, for example, Oyama v. California, 332 U.S. 633 (1948).

19. See, for example, Graham v. Richardson, 403 U.S. 365 371 (1971).

20. Kurland, "Equal Educational Opportunity."

21. Litigation on this issue is indeed long-standing. For example, a Massachusetts court in 1850 addressed school segregation under Massachusetts's 1780 equality statute in 59 Mass. (5 Cush.) 198 (1850).

22. Brown.

23. Brown, at 493.

24. Carolene, n.4 (dictum).

25. Griffin; Douglas v. California, 372 U.S. 353 (1963); and Harper. This logic was especially supported as the Court had stated in Harper, in ruling against a poll tax: "Lines drawn on the basis of wealth or property, like those of race, are disfavored" (at 668).

26. Burruss v. Wilkerson, 310 F.Supp. 572 (1969) *affirmed mem.,* 397 U.S. 44 (1970).

27. Ibid., 310 F.Supp. 572 at 574 (1969).

28. Ibid.

29. McInnis v. Shapiro, 293 F.Supp. 327 (N.D. Ill. 1968).

30. Aff'd sub nom. McInnis v. Ogilvie, 394 U.S. 322 (1969).

31. San Antonio Independent School District v. Rodriguez, 411 U.S. 1 (1973).

32. San Antonio Independent School District, 337 F.Supp. 280 (W.D. Tex. 1971).

33. Rodriguez, at 27–28.

34. Rodriguez, at 20–22, noting Griffin on transcripts, Douglas on hiring counsel, and others.

35. It will be seen under state review later that this claim was not entirely novel, as it had been successfully used in Serrano v. Priest, 487 P.2d 1241 (1971), in California. It had not, however, been tried at the federal level even though the state court in Serrano invoked the Fourteenth Amendment in its decision. The lack of cleanliness between overlapping federal/state chronology should be noted, as state litigation had already begun following the debacle of McInnis and Burruss, but before Rodriguez.

36. Rodriguez, at 37.

37. Ibid., at 39.

38. Ibid., at 42.

39. This section is based on Thompson, "School Finance and the Courts."

40. Papasan v. Allain, 478 U.S. 265 (1986); Papasan v. United States, 756 F.2d 1087 (5th Cir. 1985).

41. The Eleventh Amendment to the Constitution reads: "The judicial power of the United States shall not be construed to extend to any suit in law or equity, commenced or prosecuted against one of the United States by citizens of another State, or by citizens or subjects of any foreign state."

42. Papasan, 106 S.Ct. 2932 (1987).

43. Although only four federal cases are discussed here, there were actually five such cases, as in 1987 plaintiffs in Livingston v. Louisiana State Board of Elementary and Secondary Education, 830 F.2d 563 (5th Cir. 1987), claimed equal protection, arguing that the state aid plan was arbitrary and discriminated against districts with large homestead exemptions. This case is in footnote here since, like Papasan, it was narrowly drawn and did not claim inadequate education or a fundamental right. Livingston stood, however, as another case of federal escape from facing the basic issues. This analysis also considers only Supreme Court cases—thus, perfect correlation with Table 5.1 will not occur; for example, Scarnato v. Parker, 415, F.Supp. 272 (1976), granting summary judgment and dismissing, does not factor into this analysis.

44. Plyler v. Doe, 457 U.S. 202 (1982).

45. Ibid., at 221.
46. Kadrmas v. Dickinson Public Schools, 487 U.S. 450, 108 S.Ct. 2481 (1988).
47. Ibid., 108 S.Ct. at 2491 (1988).
48. School finance litigation could be readily traced into the nineteenth century where complex roots of other issues impacting school finance can be understood. For example, school finance-related litigation can be seen in Stuart v. School District No. 1 of the Village of Kalamazoo, 30 Mich. 69 (1874), where a court determined the power to levy and collect taxes for the support of secondary schools; similarly, see Sawyer v Gilmore, 109 Me. 169 (1912), in which a court enunciated the Rodriguez-like principle of legislative discretion in the manner and amount of tax distributions to schools; similarly, Morton Salt Co. v. City of South Hutchinson, 177 F.2d 889 (10th Cir. 1949), in which the court noted that no direct benefit need accrue to taxpayers if the taxes are uniform and for public purposes benefiting the entire public; and Lewis v. Mosley, 204 So.2d 197 (Fla. 1967), in which the court ruled that laws providing for taxation must be construed in favor of the taxpayer when questions of court discretion arise. These cases are not discussed in text here since the focus is on modern school finance policy.
49. These arguments have been developed elsewhere by the authors. Specifically, see Thompson, "School Finance and the Courts"; see also Thompson, Underwood, and Camp, "Equal Protection under the Law." There is a wealth of professional literature in the field.
50. Serrano.
51. Ibid., at 1253.
52. Ibid., at 1252.
53. Ibid., at 1258.
54. Article IX of the California Constitution states: "A general diffusion of knowledge and intelligence being essential to the preservation of the rights and liberties of the people, the Legislature shall encourage by all suitable means the promotion of intellectual, scientific, moral, and agricultural improvement."
55. Serrano 1258–59.
56. Robinson v. Cahill, 287 A.2d 187 (N.J. Super. 1972), *aff'd as mod.,* 303 A.2d 273 (N.J. 1973).
57. Rodriguez, 93 S.Ct. at 1302 (1973).
58. Robinson, 303 A.2d 273 at 284 (N.J. 1973).
59. Ibid., at 283.
60. Dupree v. Alma School District, 651 S.W.2d 90 (1983).
61. Serrano, 487 P.2d 1241 (1971) ("Serrano I"); 557 P.2d 929 (1976) ("Serrano II").
62. Horton v. Meskill, 376 A.2d 359 (1977) ("Horton I"); 486 A.2d 1099 (1985) ("Horton II").
63. Rose v. The Council for Better Education, 790 S.W. 186 (Ky. 1989).
64. Helena School District v. Montana, 769 P.2d 684 (Mont. 1989).
65. Robinson; Abbott v. Burke, 119 N.J. 287 (1990).
66. Edgewood v. Kirby, 777 S.W.2d 391 (Tex. 1989).
67. Seattle v. Washington, 585 P.2d 71 (Wash. 1978).
68. Pauley v. Kelly, 255 S.E.2d 859 (W. Va. 1979).
69. Washakie County School District No. One v. Herschler, 606 P.2d 310 (Wyo. 1980).
70. Shofstall v. Hollins, 515 P.2d 590 (1973).
71. Lujan v. State Board of Education, 649 P.2d 1005 (Col. 1982).
72. Thomas v. McDaniels, 285 S.E.2d 156 (Ga. 1981).
73. Thompson v. Engleking, 537 P.2d 635 (Idaho 1975).
74. Sawyer v. Gilmore, 83 A. 673 (Me. 1912).
75. Hornbeck v. Somerset County, 458 A.2d 758 (Md. 1983).
76. Milliken v. Green, 212 N.W.2d 711 (Mich. 1973); East Jackson Public Schools v. State, 348 N.W.2d 303 (1984), ev. den., 419 Mich. 943 (1984).

77. State ex rel. Woodahl v. Straub, 520 P.2d 776 (Mont. 1974).

78. Board of Education v. Nyquist, 57 N.Y.2d 27 (1982), app. dismissed, 459 U.S. 1138; also Spano v. Board of Education, 328 N.Y.S.2d 229 (N.Y. 1972); also R.E.F.I.T. v. Cuomo (citation omitted [1992], dismissed by the state supreme court under Nyquist, awaiting appeal.

79. Britt v. State Board of Education, 357 S.E.2d 432, app. dismissed, 361 S.E.2d 71 (1987).

80. Board of Education v. Walter, 390 N.E.2d 813 (1979), *cert. den.,* 444 U.S. 1015 (1980).

81. Fair School Finance Council v. State, 746 P.2d 1135 (Okla. 1987).

82. Olsen v. Oregon, 554 P.2d 139 (Ore. 1979); Coalition for Educational Equity v. Oregon, 811 P.2d 116 (Ore. 1991).

83. Dansen v. Casey, 399 A.2d 360 (1979).

84. Richland County v. Campbell, 364 S.E.2d 470 (S.C. 1988).

85. Kukor v. Grover, 436 N.W.2d 568 (Wisc. 1989).

86. Buse v. Smith, 247 N.W.2d 141 (Wis. 1976).

87. Washakie, at 334.

88. Edgewood, at 398.

89. Two suits were present in 1992: Alabama Coalition for Equity v. Hunt, CV-90-883-1 (1990) and Harper v. Hunt, CV-91-000117 (1991).

90. Matanuska-Susitna Borough v. Alaska (1989).

91. Roosevelt Elementary School District No. 66 v. Bishop No. CV 91-13087 (1991).

92. ABC United School District v. State (Orange Co. Sup. Ct.) (pending).

93. Ford-Coates v. Glasser, 91-02-336 (Ct. App. 2nd Dist.) (1991).

94. Frazier et al. v. Idaho, Case No. 938821 (Dist. Ct., 4th Jud. Dist., County of Ada) (1990).

95. The Committee v. Edgar, No. 90CH11097 (Cir. Ct. of Cook County) (1990).

96. Lake Central v. Indiana (1987). This suit was dropped in late 1992 but was being considered for refiling.

97. Four cases were consolidated in 1992: Mock v. State, Case No. 90-CV-918 (1990), Newton USD et al. v. State, Case No. 90-CV-2406 (1990), USD 259 v. State, Case No. 91-CV-1009 (1991), and Hancock v. State, Case No. 90-CV-1795 (1990). After intervening legislative action, these suits were dismissed by letter decision. The Newton plaintiffs, however, were permitted under amendment of the decision to join under a new suit filed in USD 229 v. State, Case No. 92-CV-1099 (1992). In addition, several other districts have filed new actions challenging the new 1992 state aid formula.

98. Charlet v. Legislature of State of Louisiana (19th Jud. Dist. Ct.) (1992).

99. McDuffy v. Robertson, SJC 90-128 (1990).

100. Schmidt v. State, Ct. App. No. 132677 (1990); also Durant v. Dept. of Ed., 463 N.W.2d 461 (1990); Hamtramack School District v. Board of Education, Ct. App. No. 130580 (pending).

101. Skeen v. Minnesota, No. C7-88-1954 (Wright Co. Dist. Ct., Dec. 17, 1991) (1991).

102. The Committee v. Missouri, Consolidated Case No. CV190-510CC (1990); also Lee's Summit P.S.U. v. Missouri, Consolidated Case No. CV190-1371CC (1990).

103. Montana Rural Education Association v. State, No. BDV-91-2065 (1991); also Helena Elementary School District v. State, No. BDV-91-1334 (1991).

104. Claremont, New Hampshire v. Gregg, Sup. Ct., Merrimack County (1991).

105. Bismarck Public Schools v. North Dakota, Civ. No. 41554 (1989).

106. Gould v. Orr 91-0097 Cir. Ct. (1990); also Meyer v. Nebraska Dept. of Ed., 105-188 Dist. Ct. Line. City (1990).

107. Pennsylvania Association of Rural and Small Schools v. Casey, No. 11 M.D. 1991 Commonwealth Ct. of Pa. (1991).

108. Central Falls v. Lippit (1992); also City of Pawtucket v. Sundlun (1992); also Exeter-West v. Rhode Island (1992).

109. Bezdichek v. South Dakota, CIV. 91-1073 Sixth Jud. Cir. (1991).

110. Tennessee Small School Systems v. McWherter, No. 01-A-01-9111-CH-00433 Tenn Ct. App. (1992).

111. Board of School Commissioners v. Wilson (1992); Coalition for Equity in Educational Funding v State (1992).

112. Scott v. Commissioner (1992).

113. Yakima School District v. Washington, No. 91-2-02133-1 (1991); also Tronson v. Washington, 91-2-00555-6 (1991).

114. Campbell County School District v. Sullivan (1992).

115. West Virginians for Community Schools v. Marockie, Civil Action No. 92-C-553 (1992).

116. This discussion is confined to changes brought about by the legal system itself. It does not consider other strategies such as congressional action or amendment to the U.S. Constitution to achieve the same ends. It should be noted that this text does not take upon itself to suggest that these changes are wise or foolish; hence, it is not a political primer in that it seeks only to consider foreseeable realities. As a result, the reader should not presume any political overtones to any of this chapter's discussion.

117. Pauley. Pauley stands almost alone in the court's willingness to engage in judicial remedy for fiscal inequities. The court ordered creation of a master plan addressing in minute detail each deficiency of educational program and its support mechanism, which today has resulted in millions of new dollars to education and massive restructuring of education on a statewide basis linked to student outcomes. To some extent, the same "revolution" can be seen in Kentucky where Rose required total reconstruction of the educational system.

118. Serrano II.

119. Horton II.

120. Even where courts have become enthusiastic in judicial prescription, they have usually later modified their zeal. See, for example, Pauley.

121. William E. Camp and David C. Thompson, "School Finance Litigation: Legal Issues and Politics of Reform," *Journal of Education Finance* (Fall 1988), 221–238.

122. *Sawyer,* at 677.

ADDITIONAL READINGS

American Education Finance Association. *The Impacts of Litigation and Legislation on Public School Finance: Adequacy, Equity, and Excellence.* 10th Annual Yearbook. Edited by Julie K. Underwood and Deborah A. Verstegen. New York: Harper & Row, 1990.

———. *Spheres of Justice in Education.* 11th Annual Yearbook. Edited by Deborah A. Verstegen and James G. Wards. New York: HarperCollins, 1991.

Benson, Charles S. *The Cheerful Prospect: A Statement on the Future of Public Education.* Boston: Houghton Mifflin, 1965.

Berger, R. *Government by Judiciary.* Cambridge: Harvard University Press, 1977.

Bork, Robert. *The Tempting of America.* New York: Free Press, 1990.

Coleman, James S., Ernest Campbell, Carol Hobson, James McPartland, Alexander Mood, Frederick Weinfeld, and Robert York. *Equality of Educational Opportunity.* Washington, D.C.: U.S. Government Printing Office, 1966.

Coons, John, William Clune, and Stephen Sugarman. *Private Wealth and Public Education.* Cambridge: Belknap Press of Harvard University, 1970.

Gardner, John W. *Excellence: Can We Be Equal and Excellent Too?* New York: Harper & Row, 1961.

Hayek, F. A. *The Constitution of Liberty.* South Bend, Ind.: Gateway Editions, 1960.

Lieberman, J. K. *Milestones! 200 Years of American Law: Milestones in Our Legal History.* New York: Oxford University Press, 1976.

Mosteller, Frederick, and Daniel P. Moynihan. *On Equality of Educational Opportunity.* New York: Random House, 1972.

Murphy, W. F. *Elements of Judicial Strategy.* Chicago: University of Chicago Press, 1964.

Perry, M. J. *Morality Politics and Law.* New York: Oxford University Press, 1988.

Rae, D. *Equalities.* Cambridge: Harvard University Press, 1981.

Rawls, John. *A Theory of Justice.* Cambridge: Harvard University Press, 1971.

Salomone, Rosemary C. *Equal Education Under Law: Legal Rights and Federal Policy.* New York: St. Martin's Press, 1986.

Wise, Arthur. *Rich Schools, Poor Schools.* Chicago: University of Chicago Press, 1960.

Wood, R. Craig, and David C. Thompson. *Education Finance Law: Constitutional Challenges to State Aid Plans.* Topeka: National Organization on Legal Problems of Education, 1993.

PART II

Primary Functions of School Fiscal Leadership

CHAPTER 6

Effective Budget Planning: Concepts and Practices

CHAPTER THEME

- The enormous pressures on education brought about by demographic change, intense local control, varying ability to pay, involvement of multiple levels of government, intense court struggles, and emerging emphasis on educational quality have a powerful influence on how districts provide leadership and management in fiscal resource distribution. It is therefore vital that administrators understand the fundamental concepts and processes of budget planning in modern school districts.

CHAPTER OUTLINE

- An overview of major concepts and assumptions governing school district budgets to provide administrators with the proper perspective for controlling the budget planning process
- Principles of organizing a framework for the budget process, including a review of different philosophical approaches to budgeting
- The process of budget construction, wherein universal events involved in fiscal planning are reviewed, including identification of major cost determinants and general steps in the budget process, and methods of balancing revenues and expenditures as required by law in most states

CHAPTER OBJECTIVE

- A better appreciation for the mix of policy and practice, and the readiness to relate the budget to the more technical aspects of fiscal planning in school districts that follow in later chapters

The basis for proper control is established with good planning. Planning establishes the aims and objectives, how they are to be achieved, and the appropriate time lines. The functions for each area of responsibility within the business function should be clearly defined. These include providing machines, money, land, buildings, equipment, materials, services and other resources to schools; assisting all personnel in attaining the goals and objectives of the district; hiring sufficient professional personnel to conduct the district's business successfully; controlling the operations of the district in the areas of administration, plants and budgets, and monitoring progress to assure good performance; engaging in long and short range planning to assure availability of adequate resources; and following good management so that the business division can realize the most from its people.

Association of School Business Officials,
Control Points in School Business Management

The goals of school finance and school business administration stated by the Association of School Business Officials, International, in the opening quotation[1] for this chapter illustrate the complexity of fiscal leadership and fiscal management in a complex modern school district. The importance of this area of administration is underscored by our studies in previous chapters, and it is axiomatic that the role of finance in schools is increasing dramatically with competition for scarce revenues. Given the enormous pressures on education through demographic change, a history of decentralized financing, widely varying ability to pay for education, an increasingly complex interrelationship of the three main branches of government, intense court struggles over responsibility for the costs of education, and emerging emphasis on educational quality, it is appropriate to turn now to how school districts build and administer budgets at the local level. While many other aspects of finance such as accounting, personnel planning, purchasing, risk management, and other fiscal functions of school districts will add to the complexity of school finance in future chapters, it is appropriate now to broadly examine the budget process in preparation for more minute detail in later chapters.

The purpose of this chapter is to introduce the student of education finance to the fundamental concepts and basic processes of budgets in modern school districts. Although development of 50 state systems for financing education makes accurate generalization an impossible task, it is appropriate to examine school budgets from a viewpoint that seeks underlying concepts governing all budget development and outlines the steps and issues that surround budgets in all states. As a consequence, this chapter first presents an overview of major concepts and assumptions governing school budgets. The chapter then turns to principles of organizing for budgeting, including different philosophical approaches to budgets because each district must adopt a framework on which all budget activities are based. The chapter finally considers the process of budget construction wherein universal events involved in fiscal planning are considered. This includes such issues as identifying major cost determinants and general steps in the budget process. Because district revenues are seldom adequate to cover every expenditure districts need to make, this section also considers methods of balancing revenues and expenditures as required by law in most states. On completion of this chapter, the student of school finance should be prepared to engage the more technical aspects of fiscal planning in school districts that follow in later chapters.

CONCEPTUALIZING SCHOOL DISTRICT BUDGETS

The importance of school budgets is increasing dramatically with competition for scarce resources. Our exploration in earlier chapters revealed that education is currently undergoing enormous changes related to populations served, increased understanding of the different needs of children, and greatly increased public expectations that schools should become the major caretaker of children in an advanced society. Schools have historically been ill-equipped to meet such demands because although education has been held by the nation's highest court to be an exclusive state function, local school districts until very recently have had to fund the vast majority of education's costs. Although increasing state assumption of educational costs has marked the latter half of the twentieth century, demands on government at all levels have resulted in scarcity of school funds. At the same time, increasing disenchantment with the outcomes of education has combined with taxpayer revolt over the costs of all government to create an atmosphere of general hostility toward government and taxation for any purpose.

The result of recent history has been an increased interest in the fiscal operations of school districts. As citizen participation in school finance has grown, administrators have increasingly had to become more conversant in the language of budgets. Whether the administrator functions at the central office or building level is irrelevant to the need to understand the budget process and to have a good grasp of the basic concepts that control effective school budgeting.

Basic Budget Concepts

The new realities of life on the threshold of the twenty-first century deny and invalidate many old assumptions about school budgets, and condescending "green eyeshade" attitudes of educators toward the finance function no longer serve any purpose in the intense context of educational productivity.[2] Although every discipline within education sees itself as the most important factor in the educational enterprise, modern realities demand recognition of the key role of money in schools. While all wise educators understand that the purpose of schools is to prepare young people for survival and prosperity in a capitalist democracy, it is nonetheless true to say that such preparation would not occur except by appropriate funding because no person is so altruistic as to serve schools without compensation. Even if such persons could be found, no buildings would be available in which to teach children and no supplies or equipment or textbooks would assist in their learning. Thus, the first and most fundamental concept of school budgets is that educational programs cost money: without funds, there are no schools.

The second fundamental concept is that the primary purpose of a budget is to translate educational priorities into programmatic and fiscal terms. The phrase "money talks" is entirely true of the educational enterprise. While education is indeed the most noble of all professions and while education's professionals need to focus on achieving the highest level of outcomes possible with the school's clients, it is important for administrators and others to internalize the view that the school's budget is a statement of priorities. Because programs cost money, a budget is the operationalization of the individual and collective programs that exist in a school district. And because money is finite in relation to infinite needs, prioritization of programs occurs through the budget process wherein top priorities are funded first while other programs' survival may become a function of economic fortunes. Thus, a budget is not only the translation of a district's educational goals and priorities into programs that are included in the school's budget, but also the fiscal expression of the educational philosophy of the school district.

A third fundamental concept of budgets is that they are not natural phenomena that occur spontaneously in educational environments but are created by people charged with carrying out a school district's legal educational obligations, which are influenced by philosophical and fiscal realities. While it is clearly true that all districts must provide educational programs in conformance with state mandates relating to years, days, hours, and minutes of instruction and various required and elective course offerings, the budgets that surround these required events are also influenced by the attitudes and persuasiveness of the persons charged with their performance. Those persons obviously include the community at large, which approves (or sometimes vocally disapproves) of total school operations, the locally elected school board legally charged with school operation, and school personnel who design and carry out the district's educational programs. Although they all play important budget roles, none are more critical than the professionals hired by the board to build the district's financial plan because these persons provide the philosophical leadership and technical expertise used by lay boards of education when budgets are constructed. For example, administrators are usually the key influencers in decisions to engage in curriculum innovation and in wise fiscal planning. As a result, a key concept is for administrators never to underestimate the power flowing from their expertise and influence.

A fourth fundamental concept is that budgets must be seen as a powerful political tool in school districts. The process by which money talks within budgets is highly political. Anyone experienced in school district fiscal affairs recognizes that the budget is the means by which public approval or disapproval of the school is expressed, that school board attitudes about proposed budgets are determined by the political arena, and that individual programs within schools may flourish or languish due to such environments. Although politicization is often regarded as unfortunate and unacceptable, in many instances such earthy realities are desirable. For example, failure to engage the public in the budget process would be a serious mistake because ownership and approval of the school is vital to effective school operation at all levels. The concept of budgets as political creatures must be known to all administrators and regarded as a useful tool because it must be remembered that budgets are the fiscal expression of a district's educational philosophy. Administrators must therefore learn to accept and ethically utilize the political benefits of the budget process.

While many other principles also underlie school budgets, these four basic concepts suggest several important belief structures for good school administrators in the future. First, it is unfortunate that so many people see budgets as dry financial documents generally attended to by accountants and clerks, because budgets must be viewed as the central enabling feature around which schools are structured and that permit operationalization of the entire educational enterprise. Second, it is unfortunate that so few persons in a community ever consciously realize that the budget is the fiscal expression of the educational philosophy of the school district. Public school administrators thus have great responsibility to inform citizens and school personnel of the processes involved in budgeting and to engage them at every possible opportunity. Third, it is unfortunate that many administrators fail to appreciate their own importance in the budget process, or alternatively refuse to capitalize on their persuasive power by mistakenly keeping the budget at a technical level that discourages wide understanding and involvement by all constituents. Fourth and finally, it is unfortunate that so many educators have viewed the political nature of budgets with distaste instead of learning to take ethical advantage of the benefits of political systems.

These concepts provide the basis for an operational definition of a budget. First, a budget should be defined as the *description of a desirable educational program.* Second, a budget should be defined as an *estimate of expenditures* required to carry out the desired programs. Third, a budget should be defined as an *estimate of revenues* available to meet the defined expenses. Such a definition is therefore three-dimensional. Although this definition is different from the accountant's view of budgets, which considers only revenues and expenditures, the three-dimensional view more accurately expresses the budgeting philosophy stated earlier wherein programs should drive both revenue and expenditure dimensions. In fact, viewing educational budgets as two-dimensional is a historical mistake that has prevented much educational innovation and progress.

It is thus not accidental that in Figure 6.1 the educational program forms the base of an equilateral budget triangle. Although fiscal problems often cause the revenue and program sides to be reversed as programs are constrained by available resources, community members, parents, board members, administrators, teachers, and other vested persons must not lose sight of the fact that budgets should first be established on the basis of sound educational programs. As the budget triangle illustrates, the definition of a budget is first based on quality educational programs, and supported by revenue and expenditure plans that make the envisioned outcomes possible.

From these basic budget concepts, it may easily be seen that common attitudes toward school budgets are badly misinformed. Budgeting is not a preoccupation with ledgers and accounting, application of profit business principles to education, or an exercise in fiscal conservation. In contrast, budgeting is multidimensional, governed by principles of sound educational and fiscal management, and characterized by a purposeful integrated educational plan. As a consequence, budgeting is the principal planning system, a vehicle for public review and approval of the educational program, the legal basis from which to execute educational plans, a control device, and a tool

FIGURE 6.1   The ideal budget triangle

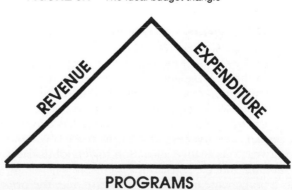

PROGRAMS

for evaluation of various types of district performance.[3] To achieve these ends, however, a budget must be comprised of a series of orderly and thoughtful processes and steps organized in such a way as to conform to law and result in quality educational opportunities for children.

ORGANIZING FOR SCHOOL DISTRICT BUDGETING

The critical nature of budgeting to the educational enterprise demands that a high degree of organization surround the activities that lead to establishment of a school district budget. Historically, however, budgeting has been an intensely local affair with only minimal state regulation relating to a few reporting procedures involved in qualification for the amounts of state aid received by districts. Although state reporting requirements have increased enormously with the growth of state aid, which in many states now exceeds 50% of all revenues, the budget process has continued to be fairly loosely structured in most school districts. Various efforts to devise thoughtful budgeting systems have occurred, however, whereby school districts can adopt a budget framework consistent with the overall vision and operational philosophies of the district. Knowledge of the most commonly proposed models is useful to administrators who must organize themselves and their districts to engage in the critical educational function known as budgeting.

Approaches to Budgeting

Efforts to systematize budgeting have led to establishment of six principal organizational approaches to the budget process. These include *incremental* budgeting, *line item* budgeting, *program* budgeting, *program, planning, and budgeting* systems, *zero-based* budgeting, and *school site* budgeting wherein the models have followed the increasing sophistication of school operations. As such, the order in which they are identified relates to both their chronological invention and the political processes that have increasingly surrounded the educational enterprise. Although the main purpose of any approach to budgeting is to detail where resources are directed, there is a corollary level of politicization that also surrounds each model. As a result, each approach to budgeting has both benefits and drawbacks inherent to the model itself and to its political utility. It is therefore important for administrators to understand that adoption of a budget model must include consideration of both technical advantages and suitability to district belief systems.

Incremental Budgeting.   Historically the most common technique by which districts build budgets, incremental budgeting is a highly simplistic model that assumes that the previous level of expenditure is a reasonable base for estimating needs and revenues for the next budget cycle. As such, incremental budgeting acquires its name from the assumption that each budget entity will receive the same "increment" as a percentage increase or decrease for the next budget cycle.

The process of incremental budgeting has certain bases in logic that provide it with a certain attractiveness. Obviously, there is common sense in assuming that the following year's legislative allocation to school districts will be related to the prior year's funding. Indeed, legislatures themselves generally state new school appropriations as a percentage increase or decrease over the prior year. Additionally, there is apparent reason to think of budgets in terms of comparing multiple years to gauge changes in revenues and costs. In fact, many states' budget documents require that budget administrators show several prior years' revenues and expenditures by line item to help the state determine fiscal health of districts and to alert taxpayers to the ever-changing amounts of money invested in schools. As a consequence, incremental budgeting's straightforward simplicity is appealing in a highly complex budget world.

Despite its longevity, there are several drawbacks associated with adopting a budget philosophy that goes no further than comparing each year to the previous one. Obviously, this technique focuses on aggregate trends and does not consider the effects of revenue and expenditure changes within a budget unless deliberate efforts are made to track such changes. Additionally, incremental budgeting has historically failed to pay much attention to the uses of money within budgets because it was developed in a time when little concern was evidenced over school productivity. Finally, it should be fairly obvious that rigid application of incremental budgeting results in uncritical incremental increases to each budget line item in equal proportions when such neutrality may result in overfunding or underfunding of individual areas. As a result, this technique does little more than reveal gross trends and does not speak intelligently to either methods of internal allocation or returns on investment in the educational enterprise. Interestingly, however, many districts still conceptually believe that incremental budgeting is neutral and fair in that no area of the budget can be said to receive less than another area.

Line Item Budgeting.   Because incremental budgeting does not speak well to allocation within budgets, a by-product has been development of line item budgeting. This technique has been widely used for many years in assigning amounts to each expenditure category of the budget. In line item budgeting, the emphasis is placed on the specific objects for which funds are expended wherein each line item shown in the budget document is assumed to be the proper base for an expenditure. As a result, budgets are planned around each line separately, and the new budget is based on increases applied to each line's base—usually the expenditure level of the previous budget cycle. For example, the line items in a typical budget might include instructional salaries, administrative and clerical salaries, repair and upkeep of grounds, supplies, and capital construction. Operationally different from incremental budgeting, each line receives separate consideration wherein lines may be increased by different amounts.

Line item budgeting holds several advantages over blind incremental methods. The major benefit is obviously that the budget is now considered a sum of its parts, with each part considered separately in terms of some measure of need. Further, line item budgeting permits some tracking of expenditures over time. Finally, line item budgeting suggests some consideration of programmatic needs, although the concept is not as sophisticated as other techniques discussed later. Because line item budgeting has been in place for many years and because it is easily understood, it has survived despite the advent of other more sophisticated budgeting techniques.

Despite historic popularity, there are several drawbacks to line item budgeting that deserve consideration. A major drawback is that this technique depends on the budget document almost exclusively for allocation decisions. Most state budget documents are not very informative because they are quite general by often providing broadly inclusive lines such as "teacher salaries," "instructional supplies," or "miscellaneous expenses." Too little information is provided about how allocations are made, the process is too dependent on experience, and little or no record of decision processes is evident. Additionally, use of this method is not considered totally appropriate to determine levels of expenditure for particular grade levels, programs, or projects. Obviously, the use of such a method fosters the cloistered appearance of budgets, vests decisions in only a few persons, and does not facilitate the greater degree of accountability required of today's educational planners.[4] This traditional budgeting method was by far the most popular until the 1960s, and although its use has faded, a number of school districts continue to operate under line item budgeting. Because many high-ranking persons in schools were trained under this procedure, it is likely that this technique will remain evident for a number of years.

Program Budgeting.   Development of program budgeting represents movement of the budget process into a more modern phase. Also known as functional budgeting[5] or function-object budgeting,[6] program budgeting differs from line item budgeting in that the various funds in a budget are internally organized by the district according to their specific objective or purpose. This is most obvious in that the budget document as required by the state no longer serves as the decision document of the district because a more sophisticated method of fund structures is used for internal decision and control processes. Enabling this process is an elaborate system, developed with the advent of electronic accounting systems using various national reporting standards,[7] wherein various fund subaccounts break expenditures in a budget into incrementally smaller parts related to how the money is used. For example, subcodes make it possible to identify the amount of money spent on teacher salaries at the elementary school level. Using standards recommended by either the U.S. Office of Education or the National Center for Education Statistics, a budget code might read 110-1100 where 110 indicates regular elementary education and 1100 indicates instructional salaries. Additional code numbers may further identify exact grade levels, the building where a specific grade is located, and the teacher of the particular class. For example, 01-0200-0240-1111 might indicate an expenditure in the general fund (01) for the budget function of instruction (0200) for the salary object (0240) at the kindergarten level (111) in Washington Elementary School (1).

Program budgeting thus has several advantages over earlier forms of fiscal decision making. Obviously, the emphasis is placed on the program being supported by a set of funds. This conceptually moves the budget process into a conscious recognition of the relationship between money and programs, and the opportunity now becomes available to think of the budgeting process as an educational enterprise. Additionally, the advent of electronic cataloging of expenditures and programs introduces possible productivity questions that were previously uninteresting or unavailable. The major benefit, of course, is that greater data are available for districts that choose to view budgets and instruction as interdependent functions.

The increased benefits of program budgeting over earlier forms of decision making minimize the drawbacks, which derive from the chronological development of the program budgeting wherein the infant system was not used widely or pressed to its potential. Development of the concept was a historic breakthrough, however, laying the groundwork for subsequent sophistication in program, planning, and budgeting systems discussed next.

Program, Planning, and Budgeting Systems **(PPBS).**   Given the progress represented by program budgeting, the next logical step was greater refinement through a system that linked programs, planning, and budgeting into a more integrated whole. Also further refined to become Program, Planning, Budgeting, and Evaluation Systems (PPBES),[8] this approach extended program budgeting to require each individual budget unit within a district or school to establish its own goals and direction through a systematic planning process. The process required development of an educational plan wherein each unit developed individual plans for programs to meet instructional objectives, supported by a plan for spending justified by educational needs. Funds were then to be allocated according to the plan. With refinement in PPBES to include evaluative activities, the system was expanded to include expectations that identifiable outcomes resulting from fiscal investment decisions would be evident. Instead of designing budgets around the organizational structure of the district, budgets were to be conceptualized around instructional objectives.

The benefits of PPBS should be highly apparent. Obviously, this structure marked a major conceptual shift in the operation of schools by linking for the first time educational programs and school expenditures into a model that presumed some cause-and-effect interaction. Further, PPBS contributed powerfully to the concept of accountability, both as a consequence of its focus on outcomes and by its ability to continue and extend the object-function code account system to include analysis of success. This ability sparked interest by school systems in tracking student progress, developing data bases, and measuring their performance against the resources invested in the school enterprise. For example, Figure 6.2 illustrates the ability to electronically assemble expenditures by major source code broken out by building and classroom, wherein the individual teacher was required to state the outcomes of an expenditure that would then be tracked by account code and linked to some assessment criteria such as standardized test scores. As such, PPBS marked the beginning of modern productivity analysis, described in greater detail in Chapter 13 of this text. Consequently, PPBS was a major contributor to the modern instructional environment of today's schools.

Despite the conceptual breakthrough represented by PPBS, there were drawbacks, among the most significant of which was that both thinking and technology can outpace organizational readiness for change, particularly in schools unprepared for the dramatic philosophical shift underlying PPBS. As a result of the different value structures inherent to the model, significant discord often developed in school systems as programs and staff members became competitors for resources. In many instances this led to confusion due to inconsistency between budgetary objectives, existing organizational patterns, and new organizational structures required by PPBS.[9] Additionally, because PPBS is heavily data-driven, significant investments of time, processes, and machinery were necessary to gather and interpret information required by the system's logical demands. As a result, most school systems that attempted to institute PPBS were larger schools with the resources and expertise to engage in lengthy and complex planning. Although this method was popular in the 1960s and 1970s, its use is less prevalent today because of its complexity and basic incompatibility with the historically nonaccountable culture of schools.

***Zero-based Budgeting* (ZBB).**   As stated earlier, political overtones often overshadow school finance and budget structures. For example, despite the merits of program budgeting its utility was limited because of tremendous logistical problems and political environments. The logic of politicization also applies to zero-based budgeting (ZBB), although in a rather reverse fashion. Whereas program budgeting was often initially courted from *within* schools, ZBB is an example of *external* political realities pressing change on educational organizations during an era of fiscal austerity and retrenchment in the nation.

Although the concept of ZBB preceded its initiation in education by many years,

(1) Program Name _____ KINDERGARTEN _____ (2) Account Number _____ 00-0200-0240-1111 _____
(3) Building Name _____ (4) Program Administrator _____

(5) Program Function or Purpose:

The kindergarten provides a transition from the important learning experiences of the home to the more formalized learning program of the school. The kindergarten curriculum provides a carefully planned sequence of learning experiences in all subject areas. Each activity has a serious purpose relating to some phase of the child's growth and development.

Kindergarten is:

1. *An environment for learning* which is designed to provide an atmosphere in which each child may develop to full potential.
2. *A level of development* which considers the child's basic needs.
3. A program of day-to-day experiences which is appropriate for this specific level of development.
4. *Democratic living within a group.*
5. *The foundation for future learning.*
6. *The beginning of academic learnings.*

(6) Performance Standard(s) to be Reached by Program.

The students will:

Social & Emotional Development
1. Show self control
2. Work & play well with others
3. Show a feeling of success
4. Happy & secure in the school environment

Visual Perception
1. Distinguish between left/right
2. Demonstrate left to right sequence
3. Recognize colors, shapes
4. Identify likeness & differences
5. Follow pattern sequences
6. Recognize capital/lower case letters

Auditory Perception
1. Listen to & follow simple directions
2. Hear rhyming sounds
3. Hear differences in sounds
4. Hear likenesses in sounds

Language Development
1. Speak clearly & distinctly
2. Relate experiences in a simple sentence
3. Tell a story in sequence
4. Dramatize a story

Math Development
1. Identify a number of objects in a set of ten
2. Recognize numerals 0–10
3. Write numerals 0–10
4. Rote count to 20
5. Rational count to 10
6. Know address & telephone number

Physical Development
1. Can run, skip, gallop, jump, march
2. Use kindergarten tools effectively—pencil, crayons, scissors
3. Walk balance beam forward, backward

FIGURE 6.2 Sample program description form

its appearance in schools resulted primarily from fiscal problems that began to surface during the high inflation years of the 1970s. Often thought to be a military concept, ZBB was first instituted in the federal government under President Carter as an effort to trim federal spending through implementation of sunset laws designed to zero out unproductive or unjustified government programs. Popular with antitax constituencies, ZBB was subsequently implemented by many local governments in response to taxpayer unrest, and it was naturally only a matter of time until schools were asked to experiment with the concept. Broadly appealing psychologically, the basic premise supporting ZBB is that all budget categories must be completely rejustified each fiscal year to cut waste and thus improve organizational and fiscal efficiency. From an operational perspective, all budget categories must be set at zero and those responsible for preparing budgets must carefully justify the amount of money to be placed in each fund. To complete each budget cycle requires rebuilding the need for every staff position, every piece of new equipment, and every supply purchase.

Many school districts also adopted modified ZBB approaches.[10] One generally accepted procedure was to build the new budget based on a percentage reduction over the previous year wherein restoration of the prior year's funding level required extensive justification. The rationale was that efficiency could be injected into any operational fund and that percentage reductions as a matter of course would achieve that end. New resources to programs were particularly viewed askance, and proposed improvements in school operations that cost money were microscopically examined. Another form of modified ZBB required administrative personnel to prepare multiple scenarios and justify expenditure levels for each. Most often three alternative scenarios were demanded, the first requiring extensive description of the organizational plan with the new budget set at a specified percentage below the current year's funding, the second requiring maintenance of both the educational plan and the budget at the same level as the current year, and the third permitting improvements to the plan and budget increases by a specified percentage over the current year. Each scenario had to detail any differences between the current year's operation and the operation as it would exist during the next budget cycle with full expenditure justification.

The conceptual benefits of ZBB are obvious. The product of an era of high inflation and discontent with government waste, ZBB represented a better chance of assuaging taxpayer anger by giving the impression of strong government action to reduce both waste and government growth. Additionally, the concept had other legitimate bases, particularly that budget growth should not continue unchecked without serious questions about positive contribution to the educational enterprise. Additionally, the concept of multiple scenarios was sound in principle in that organizational planning would improve when rampant growth in expectations was systematically restrained. Finally, common sense dictated that the district would be better prepared to deal with potential reductions if systematic groundwork was laid well in advance of actual need.

Despite ZBB's conceptual strength, many problems were experienced in its operationalization. Like PPBS, the process of zeroing budgets was extremely complicated for a variety of important reasons. ZBB was also often criticized as a cost reduction method that required more resources for effective preparation than could be saved by the process. The same problems of internal strife seen in PPBS were also inherent to zero-based budgeting, as elective and enrichment courses were indiscriminately asked to exhibit the same justification for existence as core areas of instruction. Additionally, the notion of zeroing core courses was inherently impossible, creating both incredulity and requiring substitution of the modified ZBB techniques described earlier. Although most persons would likely describe ZBB as a fundamentally good idea, its problems were so significant that many districts have abandoned the concept in recent years. Vestiges of ZBB still linger, however, as many districts have continued the concept of preparing best case–no growth–worst case scenarios given the present uncertain revenue prospects commonly faced by schools in many states.

School Site Budgeting.   The modern successor to all the foregoing budget structures is school site budgeting, a site-based management technique following closely on the popularity of decentralized school administration wherein budget-related decisions are made at the individual school building level. As such, it can be said that school site budgeting is an extension of program budgeting applied to each individual building site within a single district. Under this plan, each school site is allocated resources each year based on some district-level allocation formula that takes into account the number of students served at each site in each specific grade level and in each specific program. The principal and a school site council comprising patrons, parents, and staff from the building are generally responsible for developing and managing the school budget within the confines of the total allocation. These persons usually have authority to make decisions in such areas as salaries, supplies, sports and student activities, and capital outlay, while carefully avoiding violation of various items such as collective bargaining agreements, federal regulations concerning federally funded programs, statutory requirements such as class size, and district policies such as school calendar or length of the school day.

The advantages of school site budgeting are numerous, and they are particularly appealing because they relate soundly to the philosophical underpinnings of site-based management. Conceptually, school site budgeting represents the most recent sophistication in learning theory because it finally recognizes the importance of resources at the point of actual utilization—that is resources are only truly meaningful when they arrive at the individual classroom under the care of the individual teacher as applied to the individual student. School site budgeting is also conceptually sound in that it involves all stakeholders, especially parents and teachers, in the total education of the child. Such a concept is particularly attractive in a time when parental involvement in schools is at historic low point, and it acknowledges the critical role of the home and community in each child's educational development. While the advantages of school site budgeting are unquestionably enormous, the special value of this technique is in providing a more holistic and inclusive view of education, making school site budgeting a reality long into the foreseeable future.[11]

School site budgeting is not without disadvantages, however. Among the primary disadvantages is the complexity of the process wherein the historic environment of schools is once again asked to take on new roles and accept new power brokers. Throughout history schools have been fairly closed social systems, and the addition of community members and parents to central decision structures is a complex and time-intensive undertaking. The process of site-based budgeting requires much learning and training for all stakeholders as administrators, teachers, and parents must learn about organizational and technical structures of funding and learn to work together in a cooperative and collegial, nonthreatening environment. Additionally, there are real dangers inherent to the concept. Unless strict attention is paid, equity among schools within a district may be endangered by site-based budgeting in that some schools will have greater participation levels and greater advocacy in these processes. Similarly, some schools will eventually do a better job with available resources, inherently making a child's education dependent on the happenstance of residence. Likewise, there is great danger in allowing site decisions about salaries and related matters, raising infinite legal, ethical, and moral questions. As a consequence of current persistent trends, however, school site budgeting is a likely companion for the foreseeable future, but its success depends on wise and ethical administrators who are courageous and skilled in the complex budget process.

Adopting a Budget Framework

The various choices in budget philosophies demand that good school administrators individually develop a consistent framework for budgeting to be implemented in their districts. This applies regardless of whether the administrator is at the building or district level because all administrators and their staffs are increasingly being asked to take on new and expanded decision roles. Many questions about each type of budgeting philosophy need to be asked, and administrators need to be certain that both the district's temperament and their own value structures are satisfied by the adopted choice. As a consequence, there are several considerations in adopting a budget framework that must be understood so that administrators do not naïvely seize upon a "good idea" that later proves unworkable for reasons that could have been anticipated in advance.

A full set of issues must be considered by administrators when adopting a budgeting philosophy. Although one might question why a personal philosophy is important to school district or building operation, it should be readily apparent that the administrator's attitudes about fiscal control must substantially align with that of the district, or chaos and discontent will follow. Additionally, the administrator's philosophy will be the operational style of that individual, and considerable disharmony can follow when fundamental value structures are at cross purposes. Very importantly, a strong administrator should reasonably be expected to exercise considerable influence on the district's fiscal decision-making structures. As argued at the outset of this chapter, one might legitimately wonder about the effectiveness of the administrator if no such influence were ever apparent. Because administrators, boards, staffs, and communities must all work together to assure success in schooling, it is vitally important to adopt a budget framework that meets the expectations of all the various stakeholders in the educational enterprise.

Hartman has proposed a set of issues and questions that must be taken into account when adopting a financial structure for districts and educational leaders.[12] These relate primarily to style, preference, and congruency of stakeholders in the budget process. Hartman proposes that administrators must take strong account of the history of the district to avoid resistance and failure resulting from rapid or abrupt changes in budget policies and operations. For example, if the district has a long history of constituent apathy in budget affairs, the opportunity for dramatically increased patron involvement is unlikely except over a very long period of time wherein fundamental attitudes are reversed. Similarly, decision structures about budgets must be carefully designed in light of the historic role of the board of education in that districts with a history of strong centralized board control will likely experience much strife if administrators try to move too quickly to more decentralized structures such as site-based budgeting. Likewise, the fiscal condition of the district must be analyzed, as districts in poor economic health should probably not consider decentralization until fiscal strength is restored due to the high costs and inefficiency inherent to diffused decision making. As Hartman warns, these and other issues should be carefully considered before "jumping on the bandwagon" in the naïve faddist fashion that has long characterized education.

The inherent problems in each of the six common budget philosophies give rise to yet another option if carefully structured. As an alternative to rigid devotion to any one budgeting philosophy, the administrator may prefer to consider learning from past errors while taking the best aspects of each type of budget framework and meld-ing them into a workable compromise. Although there is danger in assembling incompatible elements, there is also benefit from appreciating the value each philosophy has given to the field of budgeting because none of the six philosophies is inherently useless. The value of incremental budgeting is obvious in working with state legislatures, although the administrator should encourage legislators to understand the value of looking at the various tasks that schools perform. Line item budgeting also has utility in that every final budget eventually ends up with amounts of money assigned to each line of the budget. Program budgeting is inherent to the basic work of schools, and the systematization and justification inherent to PPBS has served to bring budgeting into the modern era. ZBB also helps by questioning protectionism, and school site budgeting is highly consistent with the new organization of schools. Although inconsistency is potentially omnipresent, the best features of each model could be highly beneficial in the hands of experienced administrators. For example, regardless of whether a district is highly centralized or decentralized, the obvious benefits of function-object tracking for productivity analysis should not be lost. In addition, administrators should continually stay alert for innovations in budget frameworks.

Organizing for school budgets and developing a consistent philosophy to budgeting are thus essential parts of a budget framework on which informed practice can be based. Organization and philosophy are inherently consonant with the purpose of budgets, which is to identify the needs of districts, to prioritize those needs, to match available resources and needs, and to make the goals of education operational. Although there is no way to ever become so fully skilled in budget affairs that there is no room for further improvement, administrators who have deliberately developed an informed framework for budgeting are better prepared to understand the various techniques and problems associated with the actual construction of school budgets.

CONSTRUCTING SCHOOL DISTRICT BUDGETS

Development of the basic principles of budgeting and consideration of budget frameworks lead naturally into discussion of how school budgets are actually built. In approaching this section, it must be clearly noted that constructing school budgets demands three kinds of knowledge. The first type of knowledge is the general appreciation for the critical relationship of budgets to the total educational enterprise as developed at the outset of this chapter. Such knowledge is crucial if administrators are to work effectively with legislatures and local boards and communities in assuring the best possible educational environment. The second type of knowledge is understanding of the technical processes that surround budgets on a general level. While such knowledge is complex, a good grasp of procedures can be gained in a textbook of this nature in that there are elements common to budget construction that generally apply irrespective of location. The third type of knowledge is understanding of state-specific practices that have developed as a result of the diffused nature of education in the United States. Although crucial to survival in the world of practice, a textbook cannot hope to competently cover the complexities of state-specific budgets. By firmly establishing knowledge in the first two areas, however, administrators can expect to be well prepared to add the details unique to individual states at an appropriate time. As a consequence, a study of school budgets should primarily focus on the process of budget construction in a general context.

The Process of Budget Construction

The process of budget construction follows a similar pattern in most states. Although each state establishes specific statutory time lines and forms to which final budgets must conform, the process generally follows the format of the budget model graphically depicted in Figure 6.3 The model is inclusive of much of the information presented in earlier chapters of this text wherein the interdependent nature of schools and external agencies such as federal, state, and local government units is highly apparent. Because the figure is inclusive of the total political and technical dynamics of the budget process, this model provides an accurate and convenient basis from which to consider the various fiscal aspects of school district budgeting contained in the remainder of this chapter.

The Budget Model. If we were to ask the average citizen how school budgets are built, we would no doubt be told that the local school board and administration work together to determine needs and set the budget. While such description is certainly not false, it does illustrate a basic belief that budget construction is a local activity. The budget model in Figure 6.3, however, argues that the budget process is far more complex than most people generally understand because it may be seen that the budget process actually begins long before the amount of revenue available to a district becomes known. The model reaffirms our learning from prior chapters wherein it was seen that money flows to school districts from a variety of sources. Although most districts receive the largest share from state and local government units, amounts vary by individual state to a great extent, making the budget process unique to each state and each district. For example, districts in states with high concentrations of federal land ownership may receive a much larger proportion of total revenue from federal sources than states with very little federal presence. Similarly, the balance between state and local revenues is highly variable as indicated in Table 2.6. The mixture of revenue sources to school districts thus has a powerful impact on budget processes, and mixtures are determined long before amounts of funds are ever known in any district.

The budget model also illustrates that revenue balance between the various

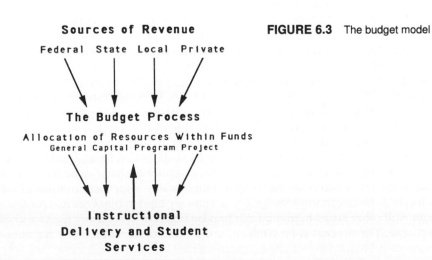

FIGURE 6.3   The budget model

sources is achieved almost entirely by the political process. For example, we noted in Chapter 2 that federal aid to school districts has generally been indirect and limited to contemporary interests. Additionally, federal aid has varied with the changing attitude of the majority in Congress and the administration. Under President Johnson, for example, federal aid increased as a result of liberal social programs, while under President Reagan significant conservatism was reflected in the federal role. Similarly, the budget process in each state is dependent on political and philosophical inclinations of state legislatures. For example, states utilizing a nearly full state funding formula will differ significantly in amount and type of aid to local school districts from states preferring minimum foundation aid formulas. Likewise, state economic health often helps determine intergovernmental revenue balance, since stagnant or depressed states may be more likely to shift the costs of education to local districts, whereas states experiencing thriving economies are often more willing to assume a greater state role in school budgets. In all instances, however, balance is determined at political levels far above the local district, making participation in the political process a necessity for modern survival.

The budget model in Figure 6.3 thus notes that federal and state shares are established beyond local district control and that this process is necessary to bring about three subsequent events: First, the amount of federal and state revenue is the engine that drives local revenue generation because the balance of revenue needed to fund proposed educational programs must be raised by local taxation. Second, the local revenue requirement is the engine that drives many education program decisions because there are both legal and practical limits to the amount of local taxes that can be raised. Third, once federal, state, and local revenues are determined, budget processes at the local level can finally be undertaken in earnest wherein allocation of resources to the educational plan through construction of the actual budget document is carried out. As the figure shows, the total process finally results in direct impacts on instruction through downward linearity of fiscal cause and effect. The model thus notes that although the level of federal and state revenues is generally beyond the control of local school districts, in many states the local share can vary with local taxpayer willingness to fund the balance of a proposed budget through application of such mechanisms as local leeway, excess levies, or similar conventions.

The budget model finally illustrates that depending on the amount of local discretion in funding education budgets, determination of the local share can be a complex process. The process is obviously simplest in the few states that attempt to approach full state funding because distinction between federal, state, and local revenues becomes virtually unnoticeable when all funding is effectively provided by the state through reallocation of these various revenues to local districts. In states where a uniform local tax rate limit is required, the process is also simple in that federal, state, and local revenues are easily calculated, leaving discretion only in allocation of funds to individual lines within a budget document. In states where some form of local option exists, however, determining the local share can be a sensitive political process. For example, some states require local school budgets to be voted on annually by the qualified voters in the district. Other states with local options grant school districts authority to raise budgets to a statutory limit subject only to protest referendum. Still other states permit boards to raise budgets to statutory limits without voter recourse. The process is probably most difficult in states that allow tax rates to vary, because taxpayers pay more attention to changes in tax rates than to total dollars in a school budget.

Examination of the budget model in Figure 6.3 thus describes the general budget process rather graphically. First, budgets are intensely complex creatures with multiple players who have different interests and operate at different levels of government power structures. Second, budgets at the local level experience a high degree of predestination in that the bulk of revenues is determined prior to local budget processes and further limited by statutory restrictions placed on districts by the various states. Third, budgets are dependent on the willingness of local constituents to support the proposed expenditure level because residents will make their satisfaction or dissatisfaction known in unmistakable ways. Fourth, except for the opportunity to politically influence appropriations at each of the three primary revenue source levels, school district budget processes generally center around allocational issues in providing the best educational program possible under revenue constraints, thus generating the average citizen's impression that school budgets are a local affair. Fifth and finally, the effect of budgets on educational programs is undeniable because, as noted earlier in this chapter, educational priorities must be set within the context of finite resources. As a result, administrators should understand the budget model and develop a high level of knowledge about the general budget process in their respective states.

The General Budget Process.   The general budget process is usually regarded as consisting of four sequential and interrelated activities: estimating the revenues a district will receive for the upcoming budget cycle, envisioning the educational program, estimating the expenditures required to support the proposed program, and balancing program needs against revenue and expenditure realities. Consequently, the general budget process is the operationalization of the budget triangle discussed earlier in this chapter. Ideally, the budget triangle demands that educational programs be determined before revenue and expenditure estimates are made, but in many instances the budget triangle is rotated so that revenues drive both expenditures and programs. Although such realities are unfortunate and should be intelligently resisted to keep proper focus on a district's fiscal belief structures, administrators must understand that the budget process normally calls first for revenue estimation. Each of these four activities is developed below.

Estimating Revenues.   Although the various states use different methods to calculate federal, state, and local revenues,[13] these amounts usually become known to local school districts in a typical pattern. Federal revenues are determined at the national level and usually flow through a state agency with notice sent to each district of the amount of local entitlement. State revenues are determined for the entire state through the legislative process, and each district's share is calculated through the state aid formula so that notification can be sent to the local district of the amount of entitlement. The local district can then calculate its tax requirement in accordance with state limits on spending. For example, states with aid formulas based on a classroom unit of funding may permit a total instructional cost of $30,500 per unit where the state aid formula allocates $20,000 aid per classroom. If federal aid is the equivalent of $500 per classroom, an additional $10,000 must be raised through local taxation. A variation achieving the same result might be through an aid plan requiring a local tax rate of 20 mills to be paid to the state, with state aid reimbursed to the district through a statewide staffing formula and salary schedule that pays for 55 professional staff positions for every 1,000 students. If local option leeway is permitted, the remainder of costs would have to be funded under a local option levy. Likewise, in states funded on a per-pupil basis, the formula might determine the local tax share by providing aid in an equalized ratio between 0% and 100% where the unfunded portion must be met by whatever local tax rate is required to raise the necessary funds. Many other highly state-specific configurations exist in that each state's funding mechanism determines how resources are raised. An example of revenue estimation for an actual school district in one state is shown in Figure 6.4.

In most instances, revenues are estimated by individual funds using state-prepared worksheets and information obtained from the appropriate agencies. In this arrangement, separate funds are established for specific organizational aspects of the school district and are usually named according to the purpose of the fund. For example, a state may specify that all revenue and expenditures for normal educational purposes be made from one of the following funds: general, vocational education, special education, capital outlay, bond and interest, food service, transportation, adult education, bilingual, or in-service. The purpose of such funds is twofold. First, fund-based budgets permit accounting distinctions to determine how monies are spent. Second, a fund-based system permits the state to categorically aid various operations of school districts based on the state's educational philosophy. For example, rural states often place high priority on transportation to improve educational opportunities for children in remote areas. Fund-based budgets permit the state to choose to aid transportation at a high level, while aiding some other aspect such as the general fund at a lower level. Similarly, urban states may choose to provide greater aid to an adult education fund to reduce adult illiteracy. Under these conditions, districts must repeat the revenue estimation process for each fund that exists in the district. An example of one state's revenue estimation method for the General Fund is shown in Figure 6.5.

In many states, revenue estimation by fund may also include ability (or necessity)

FIGURE 6.4   Annual revenue percentages by source: General Fund Budget

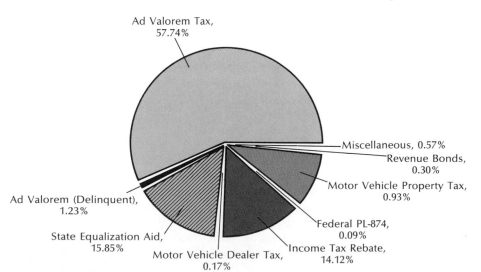

	Code 06 Line	12 mo. 1990–91 Actual (1)	12 mo. 1991–92 Actual (2)	12 mo. 1992–93 Budget (3)
GENERAL				
UNENCUMBERED CASH BALANCE JULY 1	01	618,983	683,106	703,202
UNENCUMBERED CASH BALANCE FROM TRANSPORTATION, BILINGUAL ED AND VOCATIONAL ED FUNDS	02			23,365
REVENUE:				
1000 LOCAL SOURCES				
1110 Ad Valorem Tax Levied				
89 $	05	354,615		
90 $	10	655,282	323,748	
91 $	15		857,787	386,784
92 $	20			435,968
1140 Delinquent Tax	25	15,285	13,897	32,752
1300 Tuition				
1312 Individuals (Out-Dist)	30			
1316 Indiv (Summer Out-Dist)	35			
1320 Oth Sch Dist in State	40			
1330 Oth Sch Dist Out State	45			
1700 Student Activities (Reimb)	50			
1900 Oth Rev From Local Source				
1910 User Charges	55			
1980 Reimbursements	60	43,312	38,792	
2000 COUNTY SOURCES				
2400 Motor Vehicle Tax	70	264,038	267,966	289,713
2800 In Lieu of Taxes IRBs	85			
3000 STATE SOURCES				
3110 General State Aid	95	2,029,617	2,135,672	2,964,776
3120 Income Tax	105	260,411	270,103	
3130 Mineral Production Tax	115			
3212 Aids & Human Sexuality	125			
4000 FEDERAL SOURCES				
4590 Other Res Grants in Aid				
4591 Chapter I	130			
4592 Chapter II	135			
4599 Other	140	14,365	13,654	
4820 PL 874 (Exclude Extra Aid for Children on Indian Land and Low Rent Housing)	145	32,483	42,484	40,000
5000 OTHER				
5208 Transfer From Supp Gen	165			
RESOURCES AVAILABLE	170	4,288,391	4,647,209	4,876,560
TOTAL EXPENDITURES & TRANSFERS	175	3,605,285	3,944,007	4,876,560
UNENCUMBERED CASH BAL JUNE 30	190	683,106	703,202	
EXCESS REVENUE TO STATE	200			0

FIGURE 6.5 General Fund revenue estimation

to levy different amounts of local taxes for each individual fund. For example, the uniform tax rate common to many states usually refers only to the general fund from which the bulk of educational expenditures is made. Many states without an aid scheme for capital outlay or bonded indebtedness therefore permit or require local districts to levy a special tax for these funds. As a result, the series of funds operated by districts in most states can result in many different revenue estimations and numerous separate tax levies. For wise administrators, revenue estimation by fund is also a political issue in that it must be remembered that other governmental agencies also tax citizens for various services and likewise operate under a fund-based budget system that may require numerous different tax levies. As seen in Figure 6.6, the list of additive tax rates assessed by all units of government may be quite lengthy, emphasizing the importance of remembering that in most states the school tax is only one of many types of taxes citizens pay. In many instances, revenue estimation by fund can result in a total aggregate tax rate for services including city, county, townships, and special assessments two or three times higher than the school tax.[14]

Revenue estimation is thus usually the first step in preparing a school district budget. The process is usually the simplest of the four budget steps because federal and state revenues cannot be altered significantly except by the political process, and legislative decisions are generally complete before districts actually begin to estimate their revenues or calculate the local tax requirement. In addition, revenue estimation is often simpler because of restrictive limits on discretion in raising local school taxes. Although the process varies by individual state, revenue estimation therefore generally involves estimating federal, state, and local revenues by individual operating fund and entering those amounts into the prescribed state budget document form for comparison to program description and adjustments based on program expenditures.

Envisioning the Educational Program.   The second activity in the budget process is review and establishment of the educational program envisioned by the school district. Although school districts engage in different versions of planning activities for determining education programs, the general process usually calls for maintaining the present program and considering potential improvements. As will be seen later, in some instances fiscal issues may also force consideration of educational program reductions, but generally districts strive hard to maintain or improve the educational services provided to children.

Envisioning the educational program may therefore take numerous forms. One method is to assume that the present educational structure is adequate for the following year and to build the budget around the cost of maintaining the current structure. A second method is to propose program improvements based on consultation with various constituencies in the school district. This method has gained much popularity in recent years with the advent of school reform movements. Many districts have begun school improvement plans modeled on various research designs including the Effective Schools Movement, Site-Based Management, Outcomes-Based Education, and other innovative programs intended to increase academic excellence or to address the multiple needs of at-risk children. Such school improvement designs may include standing school curriculum committees, special curriculum councils, special board task forces, school site councils, community-school consultation models, educational partnerships with business and industry, and a host of other creative arrangements. Generally all such efforts are intended to take a hard look at the school's educational program with improvement and

All Levies are Dollars per $1,000 or fraction thereof.

Educational Building Fund	1.000	
State Institutions Building Fund	.250	
State Correctional Institutions Building Fund	.250	1.500

County General Fund	.460	
Road and Bridge	4.381	
Special Bridge	1.455	
Agriculture Extension	1.148	
Noxious Weed	.730	
Health	.864	
Memorial Hospital Maintenance	1.993	
Fair Building and Premium	.420	
Mental Health Clinic	.617	
Historical Records	.430	
Wharton Manor - Maintenance	.622	
Election Expense	.266	
Soil Conservation District	.053	
Park System	.422	
Jr. College Tuition	.381	
Employees Benefits	.414	
Mentally Retarded	.629	
County Building	.652	
Ambulance	.998	
Law Enforcement	2.331	
Appraiser's Cost Fund	1.213	
Council on Aging	.830	
Economic Development	.973	
Bond and Interest	1.997	
Workers Compensation	-0-	24.279

TOTAL STATE AND COUNTY   25.779

CITY LEVIES

CITY

General Operating	17.139
Library	5.222
Library Employee Benefits	.729
Industrial Promotion	.853
Fire Equipment Reserve	.517
Bond and Interest	15.432
City Total	**39.892**
State	1.500
County	24.279
U. S. D.	73.452
Total City	**139.123**

CITY

General Operating	-0-
Law Enforcement	25.601
Bond and Interest	3.325
Employee Benefit	5.239
City Total	**34.165**
State	1.500
County	24.279
Fire District	2.282
U. S. D.	73.452
Township	-0-
Cemetery	.225
N. C. Library	.994
Total City	**136.897**

CITY

General Operating	17.316
Library	2.025
Bond and Interest	8.100
City Total	**27.441**
State	1.500
County	24.279
Fire District	2.282
U. S. D.	82.158
Township	-0-
Total City	**137.660**

CITY

General Operating	17.256
Bond and Interest	5.344
City Total	**22.600**
State	1.500
County	24.279
Fire District	2.282
U. S. D.	82.158
Township	-0-
Cemetery No. 3	.873
N. C. Library	.994
Total City	**134,686**

CITY

General Operating	14.197
City Total	**14.197**
State	1.500
County	24.279
Fire District	2.282
U. S. D.	69.346
Township	-0-
Cemetery No. 6	1.889
N. C. Library	.994
Total City	**114,487**

---

*North Central Library	General	.826
	Retirement	.168	.994

Fire District	2.282
Mill Creek Watershed	2.600
University Park Sewer and Water District	8.845
University Park Improvement District	4.969
Tatarrax Hills Sewer and Water	8.817
Terra Heights Sewer District	8.125
Cemetery District May Day No. 1	.974
Cemetery District Bellegard Jt. 1	1.796
Cemetery District Bala Jt. 2	2.429
Cemetery District No. 3	.873
Cemetery District E. F. & G. No. 4	.648
Cemetery District Walsburg No. 5	1.062
Cemetery District Fancy Creek No. 6	1.889
Cemetery District Crooked Creek	2.489
Cemetery District Lasita	.737
Cemetery District Rose Hill	2.304
Cemetery District Swede Creek	1.044
Cemetery District Czech Moravian	1.122

*North Central Libraries System; Chase, Clay, Dickinson, Marion, Marshall, Morris, Washington Counties and Riley County except Manhattan and Leonardville Cities.

TOWNSHIP LEVIES

TOWNSHIP	GENERAL	ROAD	NOXIOUS WEED	MISC.		TOTAL
Ashland	.000	6.601				6.601
Bala	.000	6.865	.891	Special Road	3.017	10.773
Center	.000	9.866	.443			10.309
Fancy Creek	.000	5.625		Special Road	1.664	7.289
Grant	.000	1.668				1.668
Jackson	.000	7.183	-0-			7.183
Madison	.000	3.259				3.259
Manhattan	.000	4.066				4.066
May Day	.000	5.473	-0-			5.473
Ogden	.000	4.294		Cemetery	.225	4.519
Sherman	.462	6.132				6.594
Swede Creek	.000	5.115	1.130	Special Road	3.123	9.368
Wildcat	.000	7.355	.298			7.653
Zeandale	.000	5.213		Hall Maint.	-0-	5.213

SCHOOL DISTRICTS

U-COUNTY		
General	63.235	
Capital Outlay	3.677	
Bond and Interest	15.246	
Total	**82.158**	

U-		
General	63.623	
Adult Education	.395	
Capital Outlay	3.164	
Bond and Interest	6.270	
Total	**73.452**	

U-		
General	61.509	
Capital Outlay	2.000	
Bond and Interest	5.837	
Total	**69.346**	

U-		
General	31.832	
Capital Outlay	3.324	
Bond and Interest	12.139	
Total	**47.295**	

U-		
General	60.160	
Capital Outlay	3.900	
Total	**64.060**	

U-		
General	51.093	
Capital Outlay	2.000	
Total	**53.093**	

U-		
General	45.114	
Capital Outlay	3.165	
Total	**48.279**	

U-		
General	55.429	
Capital Outlay	3.003	
Bond and Interest	7.732	
Total	**66.164**	

Special assessment taxes and intangible taxes are in addition to the above levies.

State of _____ County of _____

I, _____, County Clerk, do hereby certify the foregoing to be a true and correct statement of the levies of the taxing units of _____ County, _____ for the year 1990.

FIGURE 6.6   Sample tax levies in one county in 1990

redesign as the major goal. As a general rule, envisioning the educational program is undertaken to create an integrated and balanced curriculum with stated outcomes in return for resources invested.

Regardless of the method schools use to examine their educational programs, there is an implicit assumption that programs cost money. The purpose of program description in a budget cycle is therefore to identify the *physical* requirements of the proposed program so that these requirements can be translated into *fiscal* statements for inclusion in the next budget cycle. If program maintenance is the goal, the district can generally use the prior year's data as the basis for a new budget cycle, giving consideration to any funding problems that occurred during the current year and making allowance for increased costs of doing business. If program improvements are being considered, the district generally turns to its proposed educational program description, which should be designed to include statements about resources required to achieve the envisioned goals. A budget development calendar such as the one in Figure 9.8 in Chapter 9 may assist the process wherein the district's hierarchy may have already established the procedures for identifying needed resources for the following year. Obviously, it is assumed that the district's budgeting philosophy such as school-site budgeting will have a powerful impact on the process utilized in designing and monitoring the educational program. For example, the process used in Figure 6.2 earlier in this chapter is a good illustration of how school curriculum goals are translated into statements that can be quantified for budgetary purposes in the expenditure estimation process.

Envisioning the educational program is thus usually the second step in preparing a school district budget. The process can be quite complex and may be thought of as the heart of school district operations. Unless program vision is thoughtfully accomplished, nothing more than program maintenance can ever occur, and the program being maintained may therefore not be of the best quality because the proper time has not been invested in this critical school function. Although the process varies by individual district with many controls often established by the state, program envisioning is the vital link between estimating revenues and estimating expenditures.

Estimating Expenditures.   Estimating the expenditures required to support the educational program is usually the third activity in preparing a school budget. Like revenue estimation, expenditure plans must follow state budgeting requirements. While many unique features of expenditure estimation apply to different states, the process usually calls for tentative allocation of amounts of anticipated revenue to the various lines of each fund contained in the budget document. While it is difficult to say that any one procedure in the budget process is the most important step, expenditure estimation is one of the most critical because underestimation of program costs could result in disaster. For example, failure to accurately calculate the costs of a new salary schedule could result in lawsuits for breach of contract and force school closures because estimated revenues must be sufficient to cover all contracted expenditures. Consequently, the major aspects of expenditure estimation deserve greater development in this text.

Expenditure estimation normally requires identification of major cost determinants and estimation of changes in these amounts for the following year. Estimating general fund expenditures, for example, requires determining negotiated salaries and benefits for various employee groups, determining the number of positions required in each employee category, determining the next year's location of each staff member on the various salary schedules approved by the board,[15] determining quantities and costs of supplies in the various operations of the district,[16] determining needs and costs for additional or replacement equipment, estimating operational costs allocable to the General Fund by law, and calculating costs of various support services such as in-service, legal services, auditing, insurance, printing, data processing, security, and so forth.[17] The exhaustive nature of these activities is illustrated in Figure 6.7, which details one state's General Fund expenditure estimation process. It is likewise critical for the administrator to understand that these steps are repeated for each of the various separate funds the district operates. Estimating expenditures is critical not only to determining revenue requirements, but also to balancing revenues and expenditures as described later.

Although Figure 6.7 illustrates that many separate facets are involved in expenditure estimation, it must be remembered above all that in most states every item of the budget is driven by student enrollment. Staffing requirements, quantities of supplies and equipment, sizes and numbers of buildings, and every other feature of all the different funds operated by a school district are at some time an absolute function of the number of children in school. Similarly, revenue projections are a function of enrollment wherein a budget will increase in response to higher enrollment. Likewise, although there is recognition in many states for diseconomy of scale based on lower numbers of pupils, it is still a fundamental law of budgets that enrollment is the key factor driving revenues and expenditures, with attendant implications for program breadth and maintenance. The interdependency of the various steps in the budget process is most evident in enrollment estimation, wherein enrollments are the prime factor in revenues, expenditures, and programs. Accurately estimating enrollment is thus critical in that enrollments determine revenues and drive expenditures, and inversely, enrollment estimation drives expenditure estimation that in turn may help drive revenue requirements. While accuracy in all aspects of budgets is absolutely essential, enrollment projection is the single most important task because it typically drives all other budget aspects.

While there are a variety of methods that can be used to estimate enrollment, it is critical to understand that no single system is always 100% accurate. Even with powerful computer mapping and population analysis software where the number of children by age and grade in each house on every street in the school district are counted and plotted for enrollment and bus routing, sudden inmigrations and outmigrations of families due to human factors and economic shifts prevent perfect accuracy. Predictive assumptions under several enrollment projection techniques are remarkably accurate, however, because all such techniques are based on two important features: first, the expectation that conditions experienced in the past will continue "predictably" into the future and second, the mitigation of the inherent foibles of such assumption through constant monitoring, reevaluation, and updating of the various models. Trend analysis and cohort survival technique are the most common methods used to estimate enrollment, each having strengths and weaknesses that must be clearly understood by administrators.

Trend analysis is simply the application of least-squares regression to predicting district enrollment based on the enrollment figures from a series of previous years. In its simplest form, trend analysis predicts future enrollment based on the manner in

GENERAL EXPENDITURES	Code 06 Line	12 mo. 1990–91 Actual (1)	12 mo. 1991–92 Actual (2)	12 mo. 1992–93 Budget (3)
1000 Instruction				
100 Salaries				
110 Certified	210	1,632,956	1,688,504	1,800,000
120 Non-Certified	215	27,833	25,682	28,000
200 Employee Benefits				
210 Insurance (Employee)	220	24,282	28,949	34,600
220 Social Security	225	122,075	131,083	139,000
290 Other	230	2,914	3,039	3,600
300 Purchased Professional and Technical Services	235			
500 Other Purchased Services				
560 Tuition				
561 Tuition/oth St LEA's	240			
562 Tuition/other LEA's outside the State	245			
563 Tuition/Priv Sources	250			
590 Other	255	8,948	9,241	11,000
600 Supplies				
610 General Supp (Teaching)	260	110,500	85,984	103,000
644 Textbooks	265	63,468	52,486	62,800
680 Miscellaneous Supplies	270			
700 Property (Equip & Furn)	275	3,163	4,685	5,600
800 Other	280	62,039	51,863	62,070
2000 Support Services				
2100 Student Support Serv				
100 Salaries				
110 Certified	285	58,533	60,504	65,000
120 Non-Certified	290			
200 Employee Benefits				
210 Insurance (Employee)	295	434	562	700
220 Social Security	300	4,296	4,630	5,000
290 Other	305	52	59	100
300 Purchased Professional and Technical Services	310	7,453	7,982	10,000
500 Other Purchased Services	315			
600 Supplies	320			
700 Property (Equip & Furn)	325	3,163	4,291	5,100
800 Other	330			
2200 Instr Support Staff				
100 Salaries				
110 Certified	335	89,106	91,860	97,400
120 Non-Certified	340			
200 Employee Benefits				
210 Insurance (Employee)	345	687	1,072	1,300
220 Social Security	350	6,553	7,070	7,500
290 Other	355	82	112	150
300 Purchased Professional and Technical Services	360			
500 Other Purchased Services	365			
600 Supplies				
640 Books (not textbooks) and Periodicals	370	15,193	14,389	17,200
650 Audiovisual and Instructional Software	375	12,435	12,684	15,180
680 Miscellaneous Supplies	380			

FIGURE 6.7 General fund expenditure estimation

GENERAL EXPENDITURES	Code 06 Line	12 mo. 1990–91 Actual (1)	12 mo. 1991–92 Actual (2)	12 mo. 1992–93 Budget (3)
700 Property (Equip & Furn)	385	3,163	4,066	4,900
800 Other	390			
2300 General Administration				
100 Salaries				
110 Certified	395	36,561	38,184	40,500
120 Non-Certified	400	48,523	49,860	53,700
200 Employee Benefits				
210 Insurance (Employee)	405	651	984	1,200
220 Social Security	410	6,205	7,115	8,500
290 Other	415	78	103	200
300 Purchased Professional and Technical Services	420	16,313	17,054	20,400
400 Purchased Property Serv	425			
500 Other Purchased Services				
520 Insurance	430			
530 Communications (Telephone, postage, etc.)	435	4,267	4,643	5,600
590 Other	440			
600 Supplies	445	7,781	8,106	9,700
700 Property (Equip & Furn)	450	11,614	7,964	9,600
800 Other	455	12,500	13,165	17,000
2400 School Administration				
100 Salaries				
110 Certified	460	201,228	211,864	225,000
120 Non-Certified	465	83,935	84,286	89,300
200 Employee Benefits				
210 Insurance (Employee)	470	2,171	4,995	6,000
220 Social Security	475	20,993	25,005	27,000
290 Other	480	261	324	400
300 Purchased Professional and Technical Services	485			
400 Purchased Property Serv	490			
500 Other Purchased Services				
530 Communications (Telephone, postage, etc.)	495	1,684	1,792	2,200
590 Other	500			
600 Supplies	505			
700 Property (Equip & Furn)	510	3,163	4,001	4,800
800 Other	515			
2600 Operations & Maintenance				
100 Salaries				
120 Non-Certified	520	187,529	192,386	204,000
200 Employee Benefits				
210 Insurance (Employee)	525	1,429	1,995	2,400
220 Social Security	530	13,860	15,750	17,000
290 Other	535	171	209	X50
300 Purchased Professional and Technical Services	540		1,248	1,500
400 Purchased Property Serv				
411 Water/Sewer	545	7,115	8,150	9,750
420 Cleaning	550			
430 Repairs & Maintenance	555	74,775	161,745	193,600
440 Rentals	560			

FIGURE 6.7 (*Continued*)

		12 mo.	12 mo.	12 mo.
GENERAL EXPENDITURES	Code 06 Line	1990–91 Actual (1)	1991–92 Actual (2)	1992–93 Budget (3)
460 Repair of Buildings	565	53,249	237,312	417,071
490 Other	570	36,967	37,984	45,460
500 Other Purchased Services				
520 Insurance	575	29,615	32,345	38,710
590 Other	580	11,000		
600 Supplies				
610 General Supplies	585	41,488	42,387	50,730
620 Energy				
621 Heating	590	43,078	45,190	54,100
622 Electricity	595	63,540	67,810	81,200
626 Motor Fuel-not sch bus	600			
629 Other	605	19,824	22,196	26,560
680 Miscellaneous Supplies	610			
700 Property (Equip & Furn)	615	3,163	4,284	5,100
800 Other	620	1,392	2,361	2,800
2500, 2800, 2900 Oth Supp Serv				
100 Salaries				
110 Certified	625			
120 Non-Certified	630			
200 Employee Benefits				
210 Insurance	635			
220 Social Security	640			
290 Other	645			
300 Purchased Professional and Technical Services	650			
400 Purchased Property Serv	655			
500 Other Purchased Services	660			
600 Supplies	665			
700 Property (Equip & Furn)	670			
800 Other	675			
3300 Community Serv Operations	680	2,951	3,064	3,700
3400 Student Activities	685	27,124	28,564	34,200
4300 Architectural & Eng Serv	690			
5200 TRANSFER TO:				
932 Adult Education	695			3,000
934 Adult Suppl Education	700			
936 Bilingual Education	705			
938 Capital Outlay	710	68,759	75,246	94,406
940 Driver Training	715		5,000	5,000
942 Educ Excellence Grant Prog	720			10,000
944 Food Service	725	15,000		
946 Inservice Education	730		2,000	9,798
948 Parent Education Program	735		14,539	26,855
950 Special Education	740	130,000	100,000	200,000
952 Transportation	745	54,000	66,000	323,070
954 Vocational Education	750	2,000	6,000	16,000
955 Area Vocational School	752			
956 Disabil Income Benfs Resrv	755			
958 Health Care Services Resrv	760			
960 Risk Management Reserve	765			

FIGURE 6.7 (*Continued*)

GENERAL EXPENDITURES	Code 06 Line	12 mo. 1990–91 Actual (1)	12 mo. 1991–92 Actual (2)	12 mo. 1992–93 Budget (3)
962 School Workers' Comp Resrv	770			
966 COOP Data Processing 1/	775			
968 COOP Elementary Guidance 1/	780			
970 Contingency Reserve	785			
TOTAL EXPENDITURES & TRANSFERS	xxxx	3,605,285	3,944,007	4,876,560

FIGURE 6.7   (*Continued*)

which previous enrollments deviate from a straight line. The formula for this regression line (a straight line) is given as

$$Y = Mx + b$$

where

Y is the enrollment being forecast;
M is a coefficient calculated during the regression operation;
x is some future year for the prediction; and
b is a constant showing the relationship between enrollment and year at some starting date.

If accurate data are available, a future year is entered into the equation and the result is a predicted enrollment. Figure 6.8 shows sample enrollment data and the result after being entered into the computer which then calculates the regression equation. According to the regression formula which casts a line of best fit to the data, the projected enrollment for next year (Year 6) is calculated as

$$Y = Mx + b$$

or:

$$\text{Future Enrollment} = 57.6(6) + 2339 = 2684$$

Results of trend analysis for these given data therefore indicate a steadily increasing enrollment trend for this district, with Year 1 enrollments at 2,350 students and increasing to 2,622 students by Year 5. By substituting other years for the x variable, projections for additional future years can be obtained.

Trend analysis is an enrollment projection technique primarily useful to larger school districts because the averages inherent in a line of best fit do not harm the district to the extent that would be true for smaller districts where the loss of each student represents an incrementally larger proportion of the total enrollment. The "misses" inherent to a line of best fit are better absorbed when population numbers are high than when enrollments are low simply because each student in a small district is proportionally a greater part of the total budget. Because of this and other limitations relating to the complexity of calculation of trend analysis, many school districts prefer to use the cohort survival technique, which is more arithmetically

DATA FOR TREND ANALYSIS

Year	Enrollment
1	2350
2	2500
3	2555
4	2532
5	2622

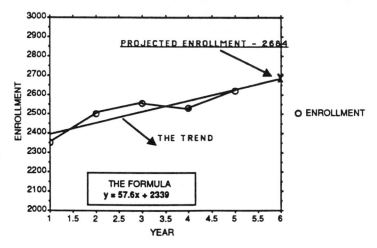

FIGURE 6.8   Trend line analysis for enrollment projection

straightforward, more intuitive, and more sensitive to changes in each individual headcount.

Cohort survival analysis is an enrollment projection technique that groups students according to grade level at entry to school and tracks them through each year they remain in the school district. In concept, cohort survival looks at entering kindergarten students in Year 1 and calculates how many enter the first grade in Year 2, the second grade in Year 3, and so on until high school graduation. Cohort survival is thus a method that evaluates the relationship over time of the number of students who pass from one grade to the next in the following year. Such a system therefore more minutely accounts for grade failures, dropouts, and migratory trends that impact the school district's student population.

The cohort survival model requires enrollment data from the previous and present years for each grade level in the district, calculating percentage change by grade level and survival as a percentage of the previous year's grade. For example, the middle part of Figure 6.9 shows that historically enrollments from first grade to second grade averaged only 76% of the prior year's population, indicating that although children cannot be identified by name, outmigrations or other reasons such as grade failure have resulted in −24% average loss between first and second grade. This allows entry of the six-year average into the bottom part of the analysis wherein the actual current 1992–1993 first grade enrollment can be multiplied by 0.76 to project only 99 students in second grade next year compared to 25 students in first grade in the pre-

Part I.
Historic Enrollments

Grade	86–87	87–88	88–89	89–90	90–91	91–92	92–93	Avg
K	28.0	30.0	34.0	26.0	27.0	15.0	22.0	26.0
One	17.0	25.0	32.0	32.0	34.0	23.0	25.0	26.9
Two	25.0	17.0	15.0	22.0	21.0	26.0	20.0	20.9
Three	17.0	25.0	16.0	11.0	16.0	20.0	21.0	18.0
Four	12.0	20.0	24.0	22.0	9.0	16.0	22.0	17.9
Five	16.0	14.0	21.0	21.0	16.0	12.0	16.0	16.6
Six	13.0	14.0	16.0	19.0	17.0	18.0	12.0	15.6
Seven	17.0	15.0	19.0	15.0	13.0	23.0	16.0	16.9
Eight	17.0	20.0	16.0	13.0	15.0	16.0	17.0	16.3
Nine	18.0	19.0	19.0	16.0	15.0	20.0	15.0	17.4
Ten	11.0	18.0	17.0	20.0	10.0	19.0	15.0	15.7
Eleven	13.0	15.0	18.0	16.0	23.0	13.0	17.0	16.4
Twelve	19.0	13.0	11.0	17.0	14.0	18.0	11.0	14.7
TOTAL	223.0	245.0	258.0	250.0	230.0	239.0	229.0	

Part II.
Survival Ratio

Grade	86–87	87–88	88–89	89–90	90–91	91–92	92–93	6 Yr Avg
One		0.89	1.07	0.94	1.31	0.85	1.67	1.12
Two		1.00	0.60	0.69	0.66	0.76	0.87	0.76
Three		1.00	0.94	0.73	0.73	0.95	0.81	0.86
Four		1.18	0.96	1.38	0.82	1.00	1.10	1.07
Five		1.17	1.05	0.88	0.73	1.33	1.00	1.03
Six		0.88	1.14	0.90	0.81	1.13	1.00	0.98
Seven		1.15	1.36	0.94	0.68	1.35	0.89	1.06
Eight		1.18	1.07	0.68	1.00	1.23	0.74	0.98
Nine		1.12	0.95	1.00	1.15	1.33	0.94	1.08
Ten		1.00	0.89	1.05	0.63	1.27	0.75	0.93
Eleven		1.36	1.00	0.94	1.15	1.30	0.89	1.11
Twelve		1.00	0.73	0.94	0.88	0.78	0.85	0.86

Part III.
Enrollment Projection 1998

Grade	6 Yr Avg	1992–93 Actual	1993–94	1994–95	1995–96	1996–97	1997–98
0→K	0.187	22.0	24.0	21.0	18.0	19.0	19.0
One	1.12	25.0	24.7	26.9	23.5	20.2	21.3
Two	0.76	20.0	19.1	18.8	20.5	18.0	15.4
Three	0.86	21.0	17.2	16.4	16.2	17.7	15.5
Four	1.07	22.0	22.5	18.4	17.6	17.4	18.9
Five	1.03	16.0	22.6	23.1	18.9	18.0	17.8
Six	0.98	12.0	15.6	22.0	22.5	18.5	17.6
Seven	1.06	16.0	12.7	16.6	23.4	23.9	19.6
Eight	0.98	17.0	15.7	12.5	16.3	23.0	23.5
Nine	1.08	15.0	18.4	17.0	13.6	17.6	24.9
Ten	0.93	15.0	14.0	17.1	15.9	12.6	16.4
Eleven	1.11	17.0	16.6	15.5	19.0	17.6	14.0
Twelve	0.86	11.0	14.7	14.4	13.4	16.4	15.2
TOTAL		229.0	237.8	239.8	238.8	239.8	239.1

FIGURE 6.9 Enrollment projection analysis, sample school district cohort survival

sent year. This process is repeated for each grade for up to five years into the future, and enrollments are totaled by individual grade and all grade levels.[18] Obviously, these numbers are used in determining staffing needs, staff assignments, purchasing of supplies and equipment, facility utilization, and many other aspects of revenue and expenditure estimation. Thus, significant predictive value resides in enrollment projections, particularly in states where school budgets are fundamentally enrollment-driven. Because of its sensitivity to changes in population, cohort survival is the best choice of the various techniques for estimating enrollments for most districts.

Expenditure estimation is therefore crucial to the budget process because it is based on three critical issues: first, expenditures are tightly tied to enrollments; second, accurately estimating expenditures becomes the key to the revenue required to fund the envisioned educational plan; and third and most importantly, accurate revenue and expenditure estimations combine in the final budget preparation activity wherein revenues and expenditures must usually be balanced. As stated earlier, the budget process is sequential and interrelated wherein errors hopefully become apparent during the planning process, rather than at the point of final execution.

Balancing the Budget.   The fourth activity in the budget process consists of comparing estimated program costs for each fund against the revenues estimated for each fund. Again the process is easier in states that tightly control school revenues through mechanisms such as allocating classroom units to each district. For example, it takes little time for a district to calculate salary costs if the state allocates 55 professional positions for each 1,000 students. In such states, districts will spend more time deciding how to meet all the instructional needs of children given a set staff size because no options regarding staff size are available. Where less state control is present, districts may spend considerable time experimenting with reallocation of amounts to various lines in the budget to achieve the best balance given available resources. In states where tax rates are allowed to float more freely through local leeway options, districts may also consider raising taxes to more fully achieve the desired program. The process in all states, however, calls for comparing the revenue and expenditure sides of the budget because most states forbid deficit school spending,[19] regardless of the importance of educational program needs in the budget triangle.

Balancing revenues and expenditures thus has a cause-and-effect impact wherein adjustment usually affects the dimension of instruction. Again the interactive nature of budgets is evident wherein the first activity called for revenue estimation, followed by envisioning the educational program and estimating expenditures required to support these programs. The fourth activity of balancing revenues and expenditures may have a reactive effect, however, as recalculation or adjustment to those estimates and plans may be required. For example, revenues may need to be reassessed if program needs exceed available funds, or the program may have to be scaled back if it is clear that revenues are decreasing. While state-specific conditions control such interactions, these budget-balancing activities are generally called budget adjustments and usually involve one of three common funding scenarios: either legislation results in increased revenue available to the school district, or revenues are static, or decreased revenue is made available for educational purposes. Each possibility has been faced at some time by every school district, and the procedures for dealing with each can be quite complex.

The first scenario involving additional revenue is the "problem" many administrators would like to face. Although it is thought to be the least common scenario, the history of revenue to school districts seen in Chapter 2 suggests that ever-increasing revenues are more prevalent than is typically believed. For example, Odden and Picus contend that despite the enormous demands that have pressed upon schools in recent years, educational agencies have been the beneficiaries of meaningful revenue increases wherein *real* revenues increased by 100% from 1920 to 1930, an additional 67% in the 1960s, and by another 36% in the 1970s. The subtle nature of revenue increases is striking, as Odden and Picus comment that small increases of only 1%–3% per year amount to as much as one-third more real revenue in only a 10-year period.[20] Inasmuch as districts have commonly incurred such increases and notwithstanding the vast demands illustrated earlier in this text, districts need to have a plan for dealing with revenue increases.

As a general rule, increased revenues are the result of only a few unusual occurrences. Throughout the 1980s, revenue increases were often associated with legislative efforts to engage in school reform. Consequently, many such revenues were targeted at special areas intended to strengthen the quality of education in schools. Under such conditions, dealing with new revenues often simply meant expending funds in the categories that the state wished to improve. For example, much money in recent years has been poured into special needs such as at-risk programs and expanded curricula. As seen in Table 1.13, in a 20-year period one state instituted new and increased expenditures in the areas of special education, teacher retirement, motorcycle safety, in-service education, human sexuality, parent education, and innovative programs. At the same time, general state aid increased more than fourfold and total state aid, more than sixfold. Expenditure increases throughout the nation have been illustrated throughout this text, noting that despite inflation, dollars flowing to education have greatly expanded due in great part to school reform.

A second occurrence leading to increased revenues has occurred in many states due to inflation of tax bases. For example, school tax rates have not declined in recent years, despite rapid increases in property values in many states. Such parallel phenomena naturally result in increased revenue as the same tax rate applied to property whose value has increased will resultantly produce windfall revenue. This phenomenon has had negative results, however, as taxpayer protests have occurred throughout the nation and in the worst instances have resulted in tax limitation referenda. For example, Proposition 13 in California in 1978 reduced property tax revenues by $7 billion (−60%) and was followed the next year by Proposition 4, which constitutionally tied state spending limits to the state economy, permanently reducing spending by nearly 16%.[21] In states where no such taxpayer initiatives have been passed, school districts have most generally benefited by increased revenues brought about by inflation. If such windfall does occur, administrators often have the option of committing the additional dollars to various funds within the budget or establishing or enlarging capital outlay and contingency funds.

More common, however, is the need to increase revenues in a district. Highly specific to state revenue and budget structures, increasing revenues can be difficult if not impossible. As discussed earlier, intentionally increasing revenues is easiest in states that permit local leeway options because such leeway is usually subject only to legislatively established limitations. Commonly such limits are fairly restrictive because of state attempts at equalization and because such equalization is less expensive to the state if it simply caps local leeway rather than providing extra aid to poor districts under a cost-share arrangement. Under such conditions, districts are often limited in their choices for increasing revenues, usually taking advantage of a variety of techniques such as improved cash management, charges for services when permitted, seeking donations and partnerships with businesses and other organizations, and utilizing volunteers in lieu of various purchased services. Unless wide tax latitude is available, the most profitable activity is improved cash management, wherein the goal is to increase investment income and to underspend the budget if permitted by law in order to build cash reserves and offset tax increases in the following year. On the whole, districts have experienced revenue increases primarily through inflation and state aid and wise management, but they have generally managed to find ways to spend the money rather than to create an ample treasury.

The scenario of static revenue is not unlike the problems that occur when revenues actually decline. In fact, the difference may only be one of degree, as static revenues in a constantly changing economy are tantamount to active decline. Because the problems and outcomes are so similar, the second and third scenarios of balancing expenditures against static and declining revenues can be discussed simultaneously.

The scenario of static or declining revenue is the event most dreaded by administrators and boards of education. Although the history of revenue trends outlined above suggest that the problem is not common, the reverse is actually quite true. Despite their dramatic growth, it must be remembered that trends are a summation of all the gains and losses experienced in all the districts in a state or the nation. When dissected for impacts on individual districts, they present a very different picture. In many states, districts have experienced static or declining revenues in response to faltering state economies, declining enrollment, depressed land prices reducing tax bases, decreased sales and income taxes, and a host of other elements that comprise the state aid equation. For example, energy-dependent states have had a particularly hard time in recent years due to mineral price declines, and agricultural states have seen losses in assessed valuations greater than 50% in some instances. Similarly, populous states have seen massive influx of student enrollments outstripping revenue growth while rural states have experienced sharp enrollment declines. Despite overall growth, for individual districts such growth is much like the old saying that "a hand in the fire and a hand in the freezer on average is quite comfortable."

Regardless of reasons for fiscal exigency, static or declining revenues force the need to devise some method of balancing the difference between revenues and expenditures. Unfortunately, there are few ideal solutions to this difficult problem. From a practical perspective, often only two solutions are available wherein districts must either find replacement revenue from alternative sources or reduce expenditures. Although combination of these two approaches is the preferred compromise, restrictions on revenue enhancement in many states force reliance on expenditure reductions. As all administrators know, the unfortunate reality is that personnel reduction in force (RIF) is the most significant method simply because salary-related costs make up 80%–85% of the typical district's budget. Such decisions are more than fiscal considerations, as administrators at all levels should be mindful that budget reductions cannot violate federal regulations, state statutes, district policies, collective bargaining agreements, or other legal and moral obligations. Such realities make it difficult to fix on any reduction strategy. As a result, educational decision makers should endeavor to involve as many staff and community members as possible because decisions made from a single point of view (e.g., the superintendent or the board) can have severe legal and political repercussions.

Although RIF is the major method of balancing a district's revenues and expenditures, other efforts should be made that can amount to some significant cost savings. The best approach is to cut costs through various strategies aimed at improving the efficiency of the school organization. Examples of successful strategies actually used by districts have included:

1. *Improved energy conservation.* Such efforts may include reducing monthly costs by lowering temperatures, reducing cooled spaces, or turning off lights, or may involve new expenditures designed to reduce costs in the long run. The latter is problematic in that the need to reduce a budget hardly places a district in position to spend its way out of a budget deficit, but consultation with experts can make such efforts worthwhile.
2. *More efficient purchasing techniques.* These efforts are often attempts to streamline the purchasing activities of the district by not purchasing "elective" items, and bulk discounts or alternatively "just-in-time" purchasing strategies. The benefits and problems involved in purchasing are discussed in greater detail in Chapter 9, where it will be seen that some districts claim significant cost savings through such strategies.
3. *Improved cash management.* Cited earlier under revenue enhancement, cash management also serves as a vehicle for offsetting revenue losses. Although each state has strict rules about how districts can invest idle funds, wise management dictates that all monies not yet spent work every moment while in the district's possession. Depending on state law, cash management may also include underspending the budget to rebuild reserves, reducing annual cash carryover amounts, and so forth. While several of these are principles of wise fiscal management, administrators should be reluctant to engage in some techniques such as reducing reserves because long-term negative effects will invariably follow.
4. *Improved risk management techniques.* These efforts, many of which are discussed in Chapter 10, are designed to curb costs of insurance for staff, buildings, and equipment. These include raising deductible amounts, assessing the benefits of self-insurance, bidding insurance coverages, and so forth. As will be stressed later, however, caution must be exercised in risk management to avoid penny-wise and pound-foolish behavior.
5. *Deferral or elimination of certain expenditures.* Although the same admonition of false economy applies to this strategy, many districts have put off new purchases such as equipment, supplies, and maintenance until better times. Such strategy obviously creates as many problems as it solves; for example, delaying bus purchases results in old and possibly unsafe equipment, raising liability questions. Similarly, the vast facility needs seen later in Chapter 12 are ample proof of what deferral or elimination of expenditures can mean. A variation on this strategy could include make-or-buy decisions wherein the district performs more tasks in-house.
6. *Use of more efficient equipment and technology.* Although many problems associated with spending to obtain benefits from the newest technology and equipment again surface, many districts have benefited by such strategies. For example, necessary bus replacement can involve smaller, more economical buses, and environmentally smart thermostats can reduce energy costs at a very low investment price. Care should be taken in all instances to deliberately calculate the cost-benefit ratio of contemplated strategies.
7. *Refinancing of long-term debt.* In recent years school districts have become heavily involved in refunding bond issues to take advantage of interest rates that follow economic decline. Many thousands of dollars can be saved annually by refinancing a district's bonded indebtedness. However, care must be taken not to increase costs in the long run by extending bond payments over a longer period of time.

8. *Implementing early retirement programs.* Many school districts have become involved in contract buy-outs of higher-cost teachers nearing retirement to replace these persons with newer teachers at lower salaries — or alternatively to leave these positions vacant. Although some evidence in Chapter 8 indicates lower-than-expected benefits due to costs of buy-outs, this strategy has become popular in many districts.

9. *Changes to collective bargaining agreements.* Although most experienced educators would doubt the likelihood of success in negotiating salaries and benefits downward, the theory is that a job at a lower salary is better than RIF. So few districts have succeeded in this strategy that it is hard to evaluate its merit, but it is reasonable to believe that the stress it would create is second only to extensive employee RIFing. Administrators must be extremely careful to avoid violating any contractual or due process rights.

10. *Reduction in force* (RIF). As gathered from this discussion, reducing the number of employees should be the last option considered. As stated earlier, however, the vast majority of district costs are for personnel, leaving few options if deep and permanent cuts must be made.

These methods are structured in a loose continuum from preferable to undesirable. It is possible, however, that even these measures may prove insufficient to fully balance the budget. In such a scenario, the only remaining alternative is to engage in program cuts. These include reducing course offerings, shortening the school day, increasing class size, and reducing "nonessential" services not legally mandated in a given state, such as extended day programs or extracurricular activities. Much care must be exercised, however, not to violate contracts or state laws. For example, in many states length of school day, hours of work, and class schedules are part of negotiated agreements, and many states have also begun to mandate preschool and extended day programs to help bridge latchkey and at-risk conditions. Although cuts are never helpful, reductions in staff and program are the most deleterious because they negatively affect educational services and students. As a result, such measures should be used only as a last resort.[22] Fortunately, most districts have been able to avoid deep cuts, but hard times have pressed many school districts in recent years. As a consequence, administrators must understand the value of such options to effectively deal with the more unpleasant scenarios.

Completing the Budget Process. Budget construction is nearly complete when programs have been envisioned, revenues and expenditures have been estimated, and a balanced budget has been recorded on paper. One further critical activity is required, however, in that the budget must still be approved. Budget approval follows different procedures in different states, but the process is always designed to achieve legal adoption of the budget according to statutory provisions. For example, in states where school districts are fiscally dependent on some other unit of government, approval usually means that the proposed budget is forwarded to a higher authority, often a city or county board. In states where school districts are fiscally independent, approval processes are more complex in that several events usually must occur sequentially. While highly state-specific, a general procedure often calls for publication of a budget summary in an official organ, most usually a newspaper of general local circulation (see Figure 6.10), followed by consecutive publication, a waiting period, public hearing,

NOTICE OF HEARING 1992–93 BUDGET

The governing body of __School District__ will meet on the __5th__ day of __August__ , 1992 at __7:00__ P.M., at _____ for the purpose of hearing and answering objections of taxpayers relating to the proposed use of all loans and the amount of tax to be levied. Detailed budget information is available at _____ and will be available at this hearing.

BUDGET SUMMARY

The Amount of 92 Tax to be Levied and Expenditures (published below) establish the maximum limits of the 1992–93 Budget. The "Est. Tax Rate" in the far right column, shown for comparative purposes, is subject to slight change depending on final assessed valuation.

Fund	Code 99 Line	1990–91 Actual		1991–92 Actual		PROPOSED BUDGET 1992–93		
		Actual Expenditures (1)	Actual Tax Rate* (2)	Actual Expenditures (3)	Actual Tax Rate* (4)	Expenditures (5)	Amount of 92 Tax to be levied (6)	Est. Tax Rate* (7)
OPERATING								
General	06	19,448,264	63.62	21,415,832	74.17	24,851,412	5,258,330	32.00
Supplemental General	08					81,033	73,053	.44
SPECIAL REVENUE								
Adult Education	10	138,287	.40	145,681	.40	189,038	65,239	.40
Adult Supplemental Education	12	61,079		49,866		35,420		
Bilingual Education	14	5,334		4,927				
Capital Outlay	16	1,235,010	3.16	655,488	2.73	1,150,000	657,291	4.00
Driver Training	18	106,284		114,795		127,786		
Educational Excellence Grant Prog	20	31,619		195,901		78,410		
Food Service	24	1,209,159		1,275,270		1,672,774		
Inservice Education	26	84,283		82,631		106,610		
Parent Education Program	28	71,606		98,815		174,364		
Special Education	30	2,077,814		2,448,444		3,227,975		
Technology Education	31							
Transportation	32	776,803		830,666		1,016,002		
Vocational Education	34					80,000		
Area Vocational School	36	2,217,829		2,303,240		2,734,502		
Judgments	40							
Special Liability Expense	42							
School Retirement	44							
Disability Income Benefits Reserve	46							
Health Care Services Reserve	48							
Risk Management Reserve	50							
School Workers' Comp Reserve	52							
Student Material Revolving	54							
Textbook Rental	56							
DEBT SERVICE								
Bond and Interest #1	62	1,197,021	6.27	1,154,418	5.29	1,109,955	942,570	5.74
Bond and Interest #2	63							
No-Fund Warrant	66							
Special Assessment	67				.24	37,824	8,523	.05
Temporary Note	68							

*Tax rates are expressed in mills
#Sponsoring district only

FIGURE 6.10 Sample notice of budget hearing

| Fund | Code 99 Line | 1990–91 Actual | | 1991–92 Actual | | PROPOSED BUDGET 1992–93 | | |
		Actual Expenditures (1)	Actual Tax Rate* (2)	Actual Expenditures (3)	Actual Tax Rate* (4)	Expenditures (5)	Amount of 92 Tax to be levied (6)	Est. Tax Rate* (7)
COOPERATIVES#								
Bilingual Education	72							
Data Processing	74							
Elementary Guidance	76							
Special Education	78							
TOTAL USD EXPEND	100	28,660,392	73.45	30,975,974	82.83	36,673,105		42.63
Less: Transfers	105	1,242,246	xxxxxx	1,279,950	xxxxxx	1,894,082	xxxxxxxxxxxx	xxxxxx
NET USD EXPEND	110	27,418,146	xxxxxx	29,696,024	xxxxxx	34,779,023	xxxxxxxxxxxx	xxxxxx
TOTAL USD TAXES LEVIED	115		xxxxxx		xxxxxx		7,003,006	xxxxxx
OTHER								
Historical Museum	80							
Public Library Board	82							
Recreation Commission	84							
Rec Comm Emp Benf & Spec Liab	86							
TOTAL OTHER	120							
TOTAL TAX LEVIED	125							
ASSESSED VALUATION	130	159,061,864		162,217,116		164,322,821		

Outstanding Indebtedness July 1		1990		1991		1992		
General Obligation Bonds	135	6,285,000		5,645,000		4,995,000		
Capital Outlay Bonds	140							
Temporary Note	145							
No-Fund Warrant	150							
TOTAL USD DEBT	155	6,285,000		5,645,000		4,995,000		

*Tax rates are expressed in mills
#Sponsoring district only

FIGURE 6.10   (*Continued*)

formal adoption of the budget, and certification of the proposed or amended budget to some governmental unit, such as a county clerk. The purpose of publication is to inform the public of the proposed budget. A waiting period is often required to permit citizens an opportunity to be present at the hearing if they wish to speak to the proposed budget. Statutes also generally call for voting by the board in open meeting. The proposed or amended budget must then be adopted at the hearing and certified according to statute. Because these laws are meant to guard against improper behavior, they must be rigidly observed or angry taxpayers could conceivably force school closures until a budget is properly adopted under statutory requirements.[23]

The purpose of budgets is to identify the needs of school districts, to prioritize those needs, to match available resources with needs, and to make educational goals operational. Budgets should thus be used to structure the educational plan, to read progress toward the plan, to evaluate its relative achievement, and to make adjustments when discrepancies arise. Operationalizing the educational plan, however, requires resources, forces value decisions, and requires linking inputs and outcomes in a structured and integrated budget plan. Unfortunately, the equilateral budget triangle is often turned on its side by economics in a less-than-ideal world. Administrators must therefore guard vigilantly against losing sight of the purpose of budgets and must be true leaders rather than accountants and clerks with green eyeshades. As Ward suggests so poignantly, the field of education finance is not a "technical and sterile area of study employing complex mathematics, arcane algebraic formulas [nor] a refuge for the methodologically minded . . . to be avoided by those humanists in education who see their emphasis as being on children, instruction, and qualitative aspects of schooling."[24] Instead, a budget is the fiscal expression of the educational philosophy of a school district. Under these conditions, we turn next to the language of accounting to better understand how budgets reveal this philosophy.

Review Points

CONCEPTUALIZING SCHOOL DISTRICT BUDGETS

The importance of school budgets is increasing dramatically, as competition for scarce fiscal resources grows; given the changes and disputes seen in earlier chapters, allocating resources through budgets is critical to equal educational opportunity.

These realities require abandoning "green eyeshade" attitudes about budgets, calling instead for strong and visionary leadership by those charged with the fiscal affairs of the district, and further calling for all school people to become informed and skilled in budgetary matters.

The importance of school finance and budgets is irrefutable when it is realized that *budgets buy education.*

This is underscored by recognition that the budget is a fiscal expression of educational philosophy in the district.

Budgets do not evolve spontaneously; they must be created by knowledgeable, trained people.

Budgets are a powerful political tool wherein success or failure of school goals is tied to administrative leadership.

For accounting purposes, budgets are two-sided revenue and expenditure documents. For educational purposes, however, budgets have a third dynamic planning side: the educational program, which should be at the core of all budget planning.

ORGANIZING FOR SCHOOL DISTRICT BUDGETING

Historically, finance and budgeting have been local affairs; given new external aid plans and accountability demands, budgets have become better organized.

Districts and administrators at all levels need to organize budgeting around consistent planning behaviors.

Incremental budgeting no longer fits modern-day demands for planning and for accountability.

Similarly, line-item budgeting is outmoded, but it is still in use in districts that have not moved conceptually beyond this simple technique.

Program budgeting is at least conceptually practiced in school districts by virtue of state accounting codes for reporting revenue and expenditure data, but some districts have not taken full advantage of its application to tracking expenditure data to educational programs.

PPBS budgeting has enormous potential, but its demands on district human resources are severe, particularly given the nonaccountable social and political structures of most school districts.

Zero-based budgeting offers only minimal benefits to school districts when practiced vigorously.

School site budgeting promises to restore some of the lost potential of PPBS *if* it can be politically and culturally permitted to link resources and achievement in a productivity equation.

Although schools and districts should adopt a budget framework to consistently guide resource decisions, the process of selecting a model should be conducted carefully so as to not violate knowledge about appropriate management or the norms of deeply imbedded school culture.

CONSTRUCTING SCHOOL DISTRICT BUDGETS

Administrators need to fully conceptualize the vast reach of the budget model seen in Figure 6.3, which takes in the total social, economic, and political milieu of the nation, state, and local communities.

Administrators must accept the role of leader and facilitator of school budgets if they are to show strong leadership.

The general budget process is composed of estimating revenues, envisioning the educational program, estimating expenditures, balancing the budget, and assuring that the budget is legally adopted and administered.

Revenue estimation is guided by state-specific procedures tightly linked to each state's funding formula.

Envisioning the educational program must be made consciously prominent by administrators to prevent revenues from unduly restraining and driving educational decisions.

Expenditure estimation is also guided by state-specific procedures on how money can be spent. Administrators play a critical role, both by their discretionary judgments and by skills such as enrollment forecasting.

Balancing the budget particularly requires strong leadership, as trade-offs inevitably occur given finite revenues.

Reducing expenditures to balance budgets requires sensitive treatment to do the least educational damage.

Finally, assuring legal adoption of the budget is critical to avoid serious disruption to the learning process.

Case Study

At last month's board of education meeting, several members of the board expressed interest in generating proposals for restructuring the educational government process in your school district. Of particular interest to the board was the spontaneous suggestion by one member that ways be devised to involve the community in the total operation of the school district with particular emphasis on curriculum design, monitoring of student outcomes, and citizen participation in the budget process. The board was particularly impressed by the superintendent's suggestion that part of their deliberations should include formation of a community-wide study group to consider various structural options available to increase community cooperation. The board instructed the superintendent to develop a proposal for moving the district into the twenty-first century that would involve as many as 100 community members in redesigning district operations, and the superintendent was also instructed to build the proposal around adoption of a decentralized approach to school district and school building management.

As the most experienced building principal in the district, you were asked to work with the associate superintendent for finance in developing plans for involving community members in the forthcoming discussion. The associate superintendent has given you the task of envisioning the overall process, with instructions to suggest possible structures by which patrons can become involved in the school district's fiscal affairs and to prepare a list of problems that may arise. Because you hope to move into a central office role shortly, you want to be exhaustive in your approach. Given the following sets of questions to launch your class discussion, what avenues and problems will you propose?

Directed Discussion Questions

1. Using your own experience and formal learning about educational administration, where should you conceptually begin in this planning process? What are the factors that need to be taken into account? What do you believe are the critical elements leading to success of the proposed organizational changes? What do you believe will be the single most important causal reason if this plan succeeds? Conversely, what should you guard against to prevent failure?

2. In general, do you believe the process this district is embarking upon is wise? Why or why not? What advantages do you see? What disadvantages might reasonably be anticipated to follow from this process? How can this process be implemented so that involvement by nonadministrators can be meaningful? Conversely, how can this process be implemented so that involvement by nonadministrators is neither token nor inappropriate to legal district prerogative?

3. A scenario such as this present case study could easily occur in many school districts today, particularly given the restless desire for change in many districts. Using your own community as the source of data, what would happen as a result? Recognizing that any group brings distinct interests to bear on the task at hand, what interests do you anticipate would likely emerge? How do

you read the sociopolitical environment of your community? What commonalities would you expect of the group? What "negative" issues would likely emerge? What special interest groups would want to be involved, and why? What groups would you deliberately seek to involve? Conversely, what groups would you hope to avoid, if any? What organizational and inclusionary features would you incorporate as you seek to do the board's bidding? How would you avoid the mistakes made by other districts? Assuming you were successful in generating the desired discussion with an operative plan upon eventual committee adjournment, how would you sustain momentum and meaningful involvement?

4. If you had been the superintendent of schools, would you have chosen the same course? Why or why not? If not, what would you have done differently?

NOTES

1. Excerpted and condensed from Association of School Business Officials, *Control Points in School Business Management* (Park Ridge, Ill.: Association of School Business Officials, 1979), 4.
2. The relationship of educational productivity to school finance is undertaken in greater detail in Chapter 13 by discussing how information technology can be integrated with school budgets to assess fiscal impacts on student learning.
3. William T. Hartman, *School District Budgeting* (Englewood Cliffs, N.J.: Prentice-Hall, 1988), 7-8.
4. Hartman, *School District Budgeting*, 25-27.
5. Walter I. Garms, James W. Guthrie, and Lawrence C. Pierce, *School Finance: The Economics and Politics of Public Education* (Englewood Cliffs, N.J.: Prentice-Hall, 1978), 46.
6. Ellen Kehoe, "Educational Budget Preparation: Fiscal and Political Considerations," in *Principles of School Business Management*, ed. R. C. Wood (Reston, Va.: Association of School Business Officials, 1986), 156-157.
7. U.S. Department of Education, *Handbook II, Financial Accounting and Classification and Standard Terminology for Local and State School Systems* (Washington, D.C.: U. S. Government Printing Office, 1973); see also U.S. Department of Education, *Financial Accounting for Local and State School Systems 1990* (Washington, D.C.: U.S. Department of Education, Office of Educational Research and Improvement, 1990).
8. Kehoe, "Educational Budge Preparation," 165.
9. Hartman, *School District Budgeting*, 28-29.
10. Sam W. Bliss, *Zero-Based Budgeting: A Management Tool for School Districts* (Reston, Va.: Association of School Business Officials, 1978).
11. John C. Greenhalgh, *School-Site Budgeting: Decentralization of School Management* (Lanham, Md.: University Press of America, 1984).
12. This section borrows heavily from Hartman, *School District Budgeting*, 38-42.
13. This discussion seeks to flow as an inverted pyramid from broad to somewhat more specific concepts of operation. Some danger is inherent therein because of the interrelationship of numerous events that are discussed here as if they were discrete. As the most important example, school enrollment is the driving force behind revenue estimation, program envisioning, and expenditure estimation. Yet because of the technicality of enrollment projection techniques, such description is reserved for later development under expenditure estimation. Consequently, the steps in budget development are highly interrelated.

14. A full list of separate tax levies by all governing bodies can be formidable. For example, in 1990 one county's total list of tax levies included millages for county general operation, county ambulance, county appraiser, county bond and interest, county community college tuition, county conservation, county economic development, county elections, county employee benefits, county extension council, county fair, county health, county historical society, county home for the aged, county hospital, county library, county mental health and retardation, county noxious weeds, county reappraisal, county road and bridge, county services for the elderly, and county tort liability. School levies included school general fund, school capital outlay, school bond and interest, and other special school taxes. City levies included city special assessment, city general obligation bonds, city utility, city temporary notes, city no-fund warrants, city general fund, and city levy. The total mill rate in the county for all three units of government was over 200 mills assessed against a tax base of $2.57 billion, yielding over $514 million in tax revenues for a single county with a population of less than 100,000 permanent residents.

15. See Chapter 8 for discussion and illustration of costing out salary schedules and other employee expenditures.

16. See Chapter 9 for discussion of the purchasing and procurement function of school districts.

17. See generally Chapter 10 on risk management, Chapter 11 on food service and transportation, Chapter 12 on school facilities, and Chapter 13 on data processing.

18. Data on kindergarten are obviously not obtainable from school attendance records. To project kindergarten enrollments, several methods are used including looking at past enrollment trends, reviewing birth records for the previous five years, obtaining data from preschool programs, estimating migratory patterns, conducting kindergarten roundup, and so forth. Estimating kindergarten enrollments is likely to become easier as preschool moves into many formerly K–12 systems. The problem will simply move downward, however, as estimating progressively lower entry years will replace the kindergarten data hole.

19. This statement is neither fully accurate nor inaccurate. For example, there are a few states that permit school districts to borrow money for operating expenses. In addition, a broad exception to the statement is seen in almost all states where districts are permitted by law to engage in bonding against future revenues for capital facilities acquisition. The statement is generically true in most instances, however, as deficit spending in school budgets for ongoing operations is not normally permitted, and many states have cash basis laws that strictly prohibit encumbering any funds by purchase order or any other means until the actual cash is deposited to the appropriate account. In such states, all transactions are closely audited to verify purchase order dates and bank balances on all such dates, and specific queries are run to determine whether purchase order and other instruments were postdated.

20. Allan Odden and Lawrence Picus, *School Finance: A Policy Perspective* (New York: McGraw-Hill, 1992), 5–6.

21. John Kirlin, "Fiscal Policy Choices," in *California Policy Choices,* vol. 5, eds. John Kirlin and Donald Winkler (Sacramento: University of Southern California Center of Public Administration, 1989), 9–18; see also California Taxpayers Association, *Growth Within Limits: Reshaping Article XIIIB* (Sacramento: Author, 1988).

22. Hartman, *School District Budgeting,* 189–196.

23. The political nature of budgets is that failure to lay the groundwork for a successful budget hearing may result in defeat of a budget. In such case, the budget process must be redone. Given statutory requirements for hearings, this can be most stressful. For example, reworking a budget in time for republication and rehearing in time for certification deadline can be very difficult or even impossible. Although it is small comfort, much political activity should occur prior to the budget hearing. The best advice is probably to "have the budget

hearing on the street long before the official hearing" to gauge the pulse of the community, since board members' attitudes at the hearing are directly related to the public pressure they receive.
24. James G. Ward, "An Inquiry into the Normative Foundations of American Public School Finance," *Journal of Education Finance* (Spring 1987), 463.

ADDITIONAL READINGS

American Education Finance Association. *Managing Limited Resources: New Demands on Public School Management.* 5th Annual Yearbook. Edited by L. Dean Webb and Van D. Mueller, eds. Cambridge: Ballinger, 1984.

Association of School Business Officials, International. *Educational Resources Management System.* Reston, Va.: Association of School Business Officials, 1971.

Candoli, Carl. *School District Administration: Strategic Planning for Site-Based Management.* Lancaster, Penn.: Technomics Publishing, 1990.

Candoli, Carl, Walter Hack, and John Ray. *School Business Administration.* 4th ed. Boston: Allyn & Bacon, 1992.

Gramlich, Edward. *Benefit-Cost Analysis of Government Programs.* Englewood Cliffs, N.J.: Prentice-Hall, 1981.

Greenhalgh, John. *School Site Budgeting: Decentralized School Management.* Lanham, Md.: University Press of America, 1984.

Hartley, Harry. *Educational Planning-Programming-Budgeting: A Systems Approach.* Englewood Cliffs, N.J.: Prentice-Hall, 1968.

Hartman, William T. *School District Budgeting.* Englewood Cliffs, N.J.: Prentice-Hall, 1988.

Hentschke, Guilbert. *Management Operations in Education.* Berkeley: McCutchan, 1975.

———. *School Business Administration: A Comparative Perspective.* Berkeley: McCutchan, 1986.

Kirst, Michael W. *Who Controls the Schools?* New York: W.H. Freeman and Co., 1984.

Wildavsky, Aaron. *Budgeting: A Comparative Theory of Budgetary Processes.* Boston: Little, Brown, 1975.

———. *The Politics of the Budgetary Process.* Boston: Little, Brown, 1984.

Wholey, Joseph S. *Zero Base Budgeting: Budgeting and Program Evaluation.* Lexington, Mass.: Lexington Books, 1979.

Wood, R. Craig, ed. *Principles of School Business Management.* Reston, Va.: Association of School Business Officials, 1986.

CHAPTER 7

Planning for Accounting, Reporting, and Auditing

CHAPTER THEME

- Effective education cannot occur without leaders highly skilled in the many fiscal operations of school districts. Since the budget is the vehicle that enables schools to operationalize their educational visions, it follows that the budget is a principal means by which to control the educational enterprise. As such, it is mandatory that administrators understand the tools by which budgets are controlled—that is, the tasks of accounting, reporting, and auditing.

CHAPTER OUTLINE

- The role of accounting and the principles of fiscal control, taking a broad view of the accounting base, wherein governmental accounting is distinguished from private enterprise accounting, development of the concept of fund accounting through the role of function-object tracking for accountability purposes

- The reporting function in the accounting cycle, including the various financial reports that school districts should use to properly conduct fiscal affairs

- The auditing function, including the purposes of audits, the various types of audits that apply to schools, and procedures that assist in preparing for smooth audit operations

CHAPTER OBJECTIVE

- A greater appreciation for the grave responsibility of administering a public school budget

School accounting is manifest in several ways and places throughout the school system. It is an important means of providing vital information for districtwide as well as site- or building-level financial decisions. It is crucial in providing a structure for holding the institution as well as specific policy makers and administrators accountable for their decisions and performance. Lastly, school accounting is an important vehicle for providing information to the public that they can use in formulating basic policy or responses to specific ballot issues pertaining to the operation of the schools.

Carl Candoli, Walter Hack, and John Ray,
School Business Administration: A Planning Approach

This chapter's opening quotation[1] is especially appropriate following our study of budgets in Chapter 6. Although it has been a firm principle of this textbook that good school administrators are first educators and then financial experts, it is an equally important principle that effective education cannot occur without leaders who are highly skilled in the fiscal management of school districts. As stated in the previous chapter, the budget is the vehicle that enables schools to operationalize their educational visions. Without proper accounting for the budget, however, there is no means by which to control the educational enterprise.

The tasks of accounting, reporting, and auditing are the tools by which school district budgets are controlled. Although few educators have a deep interest in the more technical aspects of the accounting cycle, it is critical that administrators understand the overall process of tracking revenues and expenditures and the set of activities that lead to smooth fiscal operation of school districts. In this chapter we explore the most important characteristics of accounting, reporting, and auditing to help school administrators understand that these functions are neither unimportant nor something to be avoided. The first part of the chapter considers the role of accounting in schools and sets out several important principles of fiscal control. Additionally, a broad view of the accounting base of school districts is provided wherein governmental accounting is distinguished from private enterprise operations. This section develops the concept of fund accounting introduced in Chapter 6 through the role of function-object tracking. The second part of the chapter examines the reporting function by considering various financial reports school districts can use to properly conduct fiscal affairs. Finally, the third part explores the auditing function by considering the purposes of auditing, the various types of audits that apply to schools, and procedures that assist in preparing for smooth audit operations. This chapter should give the school administrator a greater appreciation for the grave responsibility of administering a public school budget.

THE ROLE OF ACCOUNTING

The importance of the accounting function has increased in recent years, in response to both closer public scrutiny of school operations and heightened demands of the various governmental agencies that provide funds to local school districts. As the importance of accounting has grown, it has become important for adminstrators to be skilled in the more technical aspects of the fiscal operations of school districts, whether they serve at the building or central office levels. Although individual schools have always handled money for such events as lunch payments, textbook rental charges, yearbook purchases, various project fees, and activity funds, these functions have at times been problematic, and the growing popularity of decentralized administration has resulted in even greater need for administrators at all levels to be informed about the role of the accounting function. This section explores the purposes and tasks performed by the accounting operation.

Purposes of the Accounting Function

Most educators are completely unaware of the scope and nature of the accounting function in schools. Although the budget is the operationalization of the school district's educational plan, educators are largely naïve about how the budget operates and are even less informed of the purposes and operational assumptions that underlie the accounting function. While it is beyond the scope of this textbook to engage in detailed inquiry into each accounting function, a broad description of the purposes and principles of accounting is needed to provide the operational overview from which administrators should base a study of the total accounting, reporting, and auditing functions in school districts.

While the purpose of a budget is to state the educational goals of a district in fiscal terms, the accounting function serves several other very important purposes. The first purpose of an accounting system is to provide a process by which the various fiscal transactions of a school district can be accumulated, categorized, reported, and controlled, each step serving a specific purpose. Accumulating transactions collects into a central location a record of the district's financial activities. Categorizing transactions distinguishes the various fiscal activities by similarities or dissimilarities in a way that is useful to district operation. Reporting transactions makes available information about the accumulated and categorized transactions. Controlling transactions requires that the purchase of goods and services not exceed available resources.

The second purpose of accounting is to provide a means by which districts can read progress toward their goals. Although school districts use many tools to gauge goal attainment, such as standardized testing and other indicators of achievement, the accounting function also provides an invaluable tool in assessing progress. As indicated in Chapter 6, no amount of good intention can overcome a lack of resources. One way in which the accounting function is therefore able to assist in gauging goal attainment is through tracking the fiscal activities of a district wherein a constant barometer is held to the financial condition of the school district. For example, regardless of the size of a school district, it is the responsibility of the accounting function to monitor all financial activities that may result in changes in various fund balances. If only 50% of the amount budgeted for utilities is remaining by the end of third month of the school year, the accounting function will indicate a potentially serious problem for the remaining two-thirds of the year. As will be discussed in Chapter 13, the accounting function can also help read progress in academic goals through combining fiscal information with student achievement data. Thus, a major purpose of the accounting function is statements at various levels about whether expenditures and educational programs are in proper alignment.

The third purpose of accounting is to provide proper evidence to the state as to whether school districts as extensions of the state are satisfying the state's primary responsibility for the educational enterprise. Although states have only reluctantly assumed their constitutional responsibilities for education, the development of state aid has required that states receive vast amounts of information not only to track educational revenue and expenditure patterns, but also to provide differing amounts of state aid to the various school districts. States invariably require local school districts to conform to standardized budget documents so that the state can accumulate comparable data on all districts and provide state aid according to principles of equity. Additionally, states use such fiscal data in meeting their obligations for federal reporting wherein states become eligible for numerous federal grants. The accounting function thus assures availability of more standardized data for use at state and federal levels.

The fourth purpose of accounting is to assist in budget preparation. As seen in Chapter 6, school districts are expected to assign amounts of money to line items in the budget for the purpose of carrying out the district's educational plan. The accounting function is satisfied in part by such assignment, and the budget preparation activity is made possible by this accounting device. For example, no method of assuring delivery of services would be available if districts were not required to budget to accountable funds and individual lines within those funds, because there would be no way of determining where monies were located and how such monies were spent. Indeed, there would be no apparent educational plan if budgeting and accounting conventions were not available. In fact, the roles of budgeting and accounting cannot be separated because each is the source and product of the other. Just as budgeting requires an accounting process to facilitate the educational plan, accounting requires a budget from which to report the fiscal information that describes the educational plan.

The fifth purpose of accounting is to assure proper handling and use of the public trust given to schools. Although few persons inside education are dishonest, it is a purpose of the accounting function to assure taxpayers that all fiscal affairs of schools meet proper standards for the position of public trust schools hold. There is no higher trust than that which is placed in the hands of public school personnel, because the public treasury and the future lives of children are at stake. While very few dishonest acts are ever found in education, many instances of naïve or careless accounting practices can be observed. Most experienced educators can easily recall instances of loose or shoddy handling of activity funds, lunch monies, expense accounts, and petty diversion of goods and materials from their intended uses. The accounting function helps assure proper handling and trust in this critical arena of educational leadership, and the importance of preserving public confidence cannot be overstated.

The role of accounting is thus one of planning and stewardship. As accounting is the tool that provides structure and organization for the budget, the budget is the entity around which the accounting function itself is structured. Accounting is the tool that makes it possible to monitor the district's fiscal health, wherein fiscal health can be viewed as a statement about educational goal attainment. Whereas budgeting is necessary to prioritize allocation of resources to operationalize the school's educational mission, accounting allows administrators to systematically monitor the flow and use of resources on a continuous basis. As a consequence, the role of accounting can be summarized as:

1. Providing a complete record of all financial transactions of the school system;
2. Summarizing with reasonable promptness the financial transactions of the school system in financial reports required for proper, effective, and efficient administration;
3. Providing financial information that would be helpful for budget preparation, adoption, and execution;

4. Providing financial controls or safeguards for the school system's money and property;
5. Providing a basis whereby the governing board can place administrative responsibility and minimize the possibility of waste, carelessness, inefficiency, and possible fraud;
6. Providing clear and concise financial reports to the public as a basis for judging past, present, and future financial operation; and
7. Providing a historical record that, over a period of years, can be studied and analyzed critically and constructively to aid citizens, the governing board, and the school system's administrative officers in keeping pace with the changing concepts of education.[2]

The Accounting Basis for Schools

The purposes of accounting suggest that the budgetary affairs of school districts would be in total disarray were it not for a system of organizing all of the thousands of fiscal transactions engaged in each year by the average school district. Because even the smallest district in the late twentieth century likely spends in excess of a million dollars per year for the various operations of a modern school system, the importance of proper fiscal handling and accounting is apparent. From our study of budgets, it is also clear that many rules and forms are involved in preparing and accounting for school district revenues and expenditures. Because the amount of money is so large and also involves the public trust, each state has generally required school districts to operate from a common accounting basis.

The basis of accounting refers to "the method to be used in recognizing revenues and expenditures in the accounts."[3] Districts receive revenues from various sources and are statutorily authorized to make expenditures for the purpose of carrying out the educational mission, accounting for revenues and expenditures through various state-prescribed budget documents throughout the school year to build a continuous history of financial activity. Several methods of building a financial record are available, and statutes in each state usually prescribe the method that school districts must use. Generally, the basis of accounting is either the *accrual* or *cash basis* method, although it will be seen shortly that schools have modified these methods to meet unique problems in reporting their revenues and expenditures. The fundamental differences between accrual and cash basis accounting systems must be understood, however, to understand the basis of accounting in schools.

Accrual accounting is a system of financial records that recognizes income in the period in which it is earned or becomes measurable and expenses in the period in which they are incurred. Since schools do not really earn income, the term *revenues* is substituted, and *expenditures* is likewise substituted for expenses. In nontechnical language, accrual accounting thus requires notation of a revenue or expenditure when any amount of school district money is committed, whether such commitment results in receipt of money to the district or indicates the intent to expend money. For example, property tax distributions from the county treasurer or state aid payments are forms of revenue commitment. Similarly, an expenditure commitment is formed when teacher salary contracts are issued, and a commitment is likewise created on issuance of a purchase order even though actual payment will not occur until delivery of the goods or services. Accrual accounting requires that revenues and expenditures be recognized in the school district's financial records in the proper period regardless of whether the funds have actually been received or a purchase claim has been paid out. Although such a system seems complicated, its purpose is to accurately reflect the financial position of the organization at any given point in time. As will be seen shortly, the benefits of accrual accounting offset its greater complexity.

In contrast, *cash basis* accounting records only those transactions involving an exchange of cash when it actually occurs. A cash basis transaction therefore requires completion of a fiscal agreement before any recordkeeping occurs. For example, knowledge of future state aid payments is not sufficient to trigger the cash basis method because actual transfer of the funds must occur to initiate entry into the district's books. Similarly, issuance of a purchase order indicating intent to pay upon delivery of the goods or services is irrelevant in a cash basis accounting system. To illustrate more simply, the checkbook of a private individual is an example of cash basis accounting. When a paycheck or gift of money is received, the income is entered into the owner's ledger only on deposit to an account at a local bank. Similarly, expense notation is made to the ledger only when a check is written for groceries or other items. The critical difference rests in the ability to calculate a true balance to the account. Using the example of a checkbook, there is no provision for the house payment due in three weeks but as yet unpaid. As seen in the following example, cash basis accounting is much simpler, but it carries inherent risks because the balance might not reflect unpaid commitments.

The accrual method is generally considered a superior basis for accounting since it gives a more accurate picture of the health and condition of an organization than cash basis accounting procedures.[4] While true for either private persons or organizations, the value of an accrual system increases with the size of an organization and the number of its commitments and by the fiduciary nature of public schools. Figure 7.1 illustrates the fundamental difference between a cash basis accounting system and an accrual basis accounting system using a simple income statement for a school activity fund.[5] The critical point illustrated by the figure is that the true bank balance is different depending on the accounting method used. The cash basis method indicates that the "financial health" of the school is an excess of income over expenses in the amount of $1,220. The accrual method, however, indicates that the financial health of the district is an excess of income over expenses in the amount of only $940. There is an obviously important difference between the two accounting methods not attributable to mathematical error.

The difference is that the cash basis method shows only those transactions that have actually occurred while the accrual basis shows all income and expenditures for the accounting period. For example, cash basis records only sales revenue collected to date ($1,035), while the accrual system shows all expected sales ($1,500). Interest ($150) has not yet been collected, and several promised donations ($750) have not been received and do not appear on the cash basis side. Bookkeeping expenses for the last month of the year ($20), outstanding bills for supplies ($900) used to generate the sales income, travel ($700) arranged for later in the year, and other miscellaneous expenses ($25) also have not been paid and therefore do not appear in the cash basis report.[6] In contrast, the accrual method shows anticipated income and encumbrances against the fund. As a result, the fundamental difference in these two accounting bases is illustrated. The cash basis report does not consider all available income or expenses and implies that there is more money than is actually the case. In reality, only $940 is truly available, making the opportunity to overcommit organizational resources a distinct possibility.

Interestingly, most small nonprofit organizations use a cash basis accounting sys-

The School District Activity Foundation
Income Statement for the End of the Current Year

Basis	Cash Basis	Accrual
Income		
Revenue from sales	$1,035	$1,500
Interest income		150
Donations	1,250	2,000
Total	2,285	3,650
Expenses		
Bookkeeping	340	360
Supplies	100	1,000
Travel	500	1,200
Miscellaneous	125	150
Total	1,065	2,710
Excess of Income over Expenses		
	$1,220	$940

FIGURE 7.1   Income statement comparing cash basis entries with accrual entries

tem.[7] Cash basis is obviously simple and can be adequate as long as it meets the financial reporting and analysis needs of the organization. The importance of handling money in the public sector, however, demands special care, and school systems are not small organizations. As a result, accrual accounting systems are better suited for use in school systems. In practice, however, neither the cash nor accrual basis for accounting in schools is uniformly adopted due to the uniqueness of government organizations in a nonprofit environment. Instead, a hybrid accounting basis utilizing aspects of both cash and accrual accounting procedures is often used and is known as *modified accrual.*

The *modified accrual* accounting system (also called *modified cash basis*) permits certain revenues and expenditures to be recorded on an accrual basis while permitting others to be recorded on a cash basis. "According to this basis revenues are recorded when they are susceptible to accrual, *i.e.,* both measurable and available, and recognized in the accounting period in which the liability is incurred."[8] While there are many variations to this procedure, unpaid bills are accrued by a system of encumbrances indicating pending payment, while revenue is entered on a cash basis when it is actually received.[9] The system can be illustrated using the modern convenience of automatic payment deductions to a private checkbook. Many persons arrange with a local bank to have mortgage payments automatically deducted from checking or savings accounts on a specified day each month. The individual, however, must remember to record the payment to keep an accurate balance on the account. If the individual keeps a regular checkbook ledger that records income and expenses as they occur but writes an entry subtracting the mortgage payment prior to the date that payment is due, a modified accrual accounting system is being used.

Although several reasons underlie a modified accrual basis for school district accounting, the most important reason rests in the nature of governmental taxing units.

On the revenue side, school districts have the power to levy taxes, thereby assuring themselves of future revenues. On the expenditure side, school districts are empowered to spend tax monies and to commit to expenditures such as salary contracts on an annualized basis. Thus, schools need an accounting system that documents anticipated revenue, but the nature of tax collection may cause revenues to accrue in the present year even though unavailable until future years. At the same time, school districts in many states are subject to statutes that require them to operate on a cash basis wherein money must actually be in the bank before it can be spent. Yet as seen earlier, cash basis may unfairly inflate cash balances where no encumbrances are made. Under these conditions, strict adherence to either cash or accrual bases is inappropriate. As a result, standardized accounting procedures have identified the modified accrual basis as the appropriate method to be used by governmental organizations.[10] In the language of one state:

> The modified accrual accounting system has been established by accounting authorities (GASB) as the standard for governmental fund accounting and reporting. In recognizing revenue, this basis requires that revenues be recorded on the accrual basis only if the amount is measurable and available for financial operations during the year. For example, property taxes for the year are to be accrued when levied (not when collected). Expense is to be recorded at the time services are provided or goods are received regardless of when actual payment for these goods and services was made.[11]

School districts must therefore account for money they receive and expend according to fairly uniform accounting procedures.[12] These standards also call for fund accounting for schools wherein revenues and expenditures are segregated by type and purpose.

Fund Accounting Operation

As will become apparent in this chapter, numerous accounting devices simultaneously apply to school districts. From the previous section, several possible options for basis were identified, and it was noted that schools generally use the modified accrual method to better assure good control over district monies. Control is simultaneously enhanced by another accounting convention used in the public sector, as schools and other tax-supported units of government generally also account for revenues and expenditures by a system known as *fund accounting,* wherein different funds are maintained by the district to which basis also applies.[13] As discussed in Chapter 6, fund accounting is a system that provides for financial organization and reporting according to types of revenues and expenditures by their intended purposes.

The fund accounting system allows for separate reporting of the financial condition of the many funds over which school districts and other nonprofit organizations have control. As public entities, school districts are legally responsible for guaranteeing that each fund is used only for specific purposes and that funds are not commingled. According to the Governmental Accounting Standards Board (GASB):

> Governmental accounting systems should be organized and operated on a fund basis. A fund is defined as a fiscal and accounting entity with a self-

balancing set of accounts recording cash and other financial resources, together with all related liabilities and residual equities, or balances, and changes therein, which are segregated for the purpose of carrying on specific activities or attaining certain objectives in accordance with special regulations, restrictions, or limitations.[14]

A fund is thus a collection of revenue and expenditure information specific to a given operation within the school system. The modern nature of intergovernmental grants requires a fund accounting structure in order to meet the demands involved in monitoring and reporting back to the granting agency (e.g., federal, state, local, or private) that provides income to schools and typically expects some service in return. Functionally, a fund accounting system provides an organizational vehicle and a permanent record of money allocated for specific or general purposes in the operation of a school district. For example, schools must usually deposit state transportation aid only to the transportation fund for exclusive use in transportation-related expenditures, and special education aid may not be used for any activity other than educational services to exceptional children. The purpose of fund accounting is therefore to recognize the discrete fiscal operations of school districts, to track revenues and expenditures by discrete function, and to provide information on these functions that can be used in assessing financial health and organizational productivity.

Within the broad concept of fund accounting, the various funds of modern school districts can be further subdivided. By convention, the fund system is divided into four general categories of *governmental* funds, *proprietary* funds, *fiduciary* funds, and *account* groups.[15] Each of these categories also includes specific subcategories wherein many of the terminologies will be familiar from our earlier study of budgets.

Governmental Funds.   *Governmental* funds constitute the majority of the various funds of educational organizations, and they further constitute the bulk of actual money received and expended by a school district. The reason is self-evident in that generally four types of governmental funds are identified and because school districts receive the vast majority of their monies from public tax sources. It should also be clear that governmental funds need to be maintained as separate entities in order to assure the public trust, to monitor operations in which the state has a constitutional or categorical interest, and to evaluate the financial health of each of the various operations of the school district. The four types of governmental funds are generally identified as:

1. *General Fund.* As seen in Chapter 6, the general fund is the major operating fund in every school district because the vast majority of money needed to operate a school is housed here. All money not specifically reserved to other separate funds is placed into the general fund. The general fund may be thought of as the heart of the school budget in that most instructional expenditures are made from the general fund. It is the intent of the general fund to provide a mechanism for monitoring the money required to provide a basic education and to guarantee equal educational opportunity to all children in the district.[16]
2. *Special Revenue Funds.* Special revenue funds are designed for depositing and expending monies restricted to specific educational purposes. Prime

examples are various types of federal aid, such as compensatory education or handicapped programs. Special revenue funds serve two primary purposes. The first purpose is to earmark monies to ensure they are spent by specified purpose. For example, federal and state categorical aid to special education is funded separately and strictly audited to assure compliance with mandates and prohibitions against commingling or supplantation of other revenues. The second purpose is to allow for accounting structures for temporary special projects. For example, if money from an outside source is provided for an innovative science project not otherwise funded by general fund support to the basic educational program, a special fund can be established. When these monies are expended and not renewed, the special fund can be abolished by board action. Other special funds like transportation, however, are permanent funds.

3. *Capital Projects Fund.* The capital projects fund is designed to permit deposit and expenditure of monies from a variety of sources (usually bond revenues) generally used to finance long-lived fixed assets including instructional buildings, equipment, land, or other facilities. A capital fund may be restricted to a given building or project, or it may be unrestricted in that monies can be used for unspecified future capital project plans. A capital project fund is temporary if the assets of the fund have been expended for a project and all encumbrances have been paid. Under these conditions, any remaining funds may be transferred to another fund or returned to the original source depending on the terms of the granting agency and the actions of the school board. A capital projects fund is distinct from other operating funds such as capital outlay and debt service funds.

4. *Debt Service Fund.* A debt service fund is established to provide a mechanism for receiving and expending money used to pay off specific long-term debt obligations, including bond issues used to finance school facilities. In fact, bond issues usually require establishment and use of debt service funds, with a separate fund established for separate bond issues. As debt is repaid from such a fund, a variance between obligations and revenues often occurs at the end of each year. If the fund generates more money than needed to pay the annual obligation, the excess funds are recorded to a retained earnings account and "saved" for future needs. If the reverse is true and there is insufficient revenue, the retained earnings account is debited and school officials should take action to avoid continued losses and the threat of default on the district's obligations.

Proprietary Funds.   Although the vast majority of school revenues and expenditures is made from governmental sources, not all revenues received by school districts are distributions from governmental taxing units. As a result, a mechanism for separating and accounting for nongovernmental monies is needed. The accounting convention for depositing and expending certain nongovernmental monies under the fund system is through the use of separate fund structures called *proprietary* funds. Similar to accounts used in private businesses, proprietary funds are distinguishable because they are partially financed through service charges actually paid by the entity receiving services or through a charge-back billing system operating internally within the district. The structure of proprietary funds is highly specific to the needs of an organization based on the nature and complexity of such services. Generally, however, propriety funds can be identified as one of two types:

1. *Enterprise Funds.* Various enterprise funds can be established in a district and are designed to handle monies derived from certain revenue-generating activities carried on in the organization, such as athletic events, school newspapers, bookstore operations, and so forth. The concept is that these activities generally operate much like private enterprises wherein services are provided to consumers in return for certain charges. As a consequence, enterprise fund revenues and expenditures are treated differently than revenues and expenditures in governmental funds, including separate maintenance in the accounting process.

2. *Internal Service Funds.* Many school districts have become so elaborately structured that they have a need for accounting procedures that recognize costs of doing business within the organization itself. For example, larger districts often have the capability to produce goods or services within the school organization that are consumed by another part of the school organization in the same district. For example, districts may operate "self-supporting" divisions of central purchasing, central printing, central maintenance, or central computing services. Under such an arrangement, districts may charge back the cost of services to the various units of the district. In addition, it becomes possible to engage in cost-accounting to determine the cost of operating these various services. Internal service funds are used to account for such transactions involving goods and services used exclusively within the district, and the nature of these operations results in the need for separate accounting procedures.

Fiduciary Funds.   Not all revenues received by school districts fall neatly into the categories of governmental or proprietary funds. One type of revenue gaining popularity in some areas is money received from nongovernmental organizations external to the school. For example, business partnerships, gifts and donations, and other types of charitable trust arrangements have been secured by many school districts. While the number of school districts with such agreements is relatively small compared to those districts seeking such arrangements, there is an increasing trend toward such revenues in many parts of the nation. As a result, *fiduciary* funds are structured to account for revenue and expenditure of such monies.

Fiduciary funds are thus actually trust funds set up to account for monies for which the district acts as legal trustee. Revenue is deposited to a fiduciary fund, and expenditure is usually covered by a trust agreement detailing the purpose of the fund, how the fund is to be managed, and providing for the disposition of the fund's balance at such time as it may be legally dissolved. The school board must authorize establishment of all such funds and, in addition, the board is empowered to establish fiduciary funds for specific purposes from its own resources. While the arrangements are complex, in general fiduciary funds include three basic types:

1. *Nonexpendable trust funds.* The organization has trusteeship over these funds, but the principal (the original amount of the gift or contribution) must be kept intact. The school organization generally has control over the various accounts within the fund and responsibility for wise investment of

the fund's principal amount. Examples of nonexpendable trust funds include scholarship awards or outstanding teacher awards. Since the fund's principal cannot be touched, the amount of an award from the fund can only be derived from interest earned on investment of the principal. Although all trust funds are subject to the restrictions of the grantor, it is often a rule of such funds that awards will be less than total earnings of the fund to continually increase the fund's assets.

2. *Expendable trust funds.* As the name implies, expendable trust funds are similar to nonexpendable trusts, with the only major distinction being that the organization may spend all or part of the fund's principal amount. In general, the rules of nonexpendable trusts pertain to expendable trusts as well, including control by the grantor.

3. *Agency funds.* Agency funds are very similar to trust funds except that the school organization simply acts as the agent and has no administrative or managerial responsibility. Such funds may also be internal to the school district and are usually established to consolidate certain activities of the school district such as payroll through a central payroll fund, or cash management activities through the use of a central treasury fund. For example, a central payroll fund reduces the number of separate accounts needed to account for payroll transactions to all the various operating entities within the district, (i.e., teachers, administrators, support staff, or food service workers). Under one central fund all information concerning such items as wages, fringe benefits, withholding tax payments, and worker's compensation can be efficiently monitored.

Account Groups.   In addition to the foregoing funds, additional *account groups* are established in many school districts. Specially designed for fixed asset and long-term debt accounting, these accounts monitor monies provided for the construction of buildings, the acquisition of land, and other major projects. The value of account groups rests in separating fixed assets and debts from general operating revenues and expenditures. These include:

1. *General Fixed Assets.* This account group includes financial information concerning assets available to the district at large and differs from fixed assets used in operations covered by enterprise funds, internal funds, or trust funds. These long-lived assets can be acquired through the general fund, the capital projects fund, or other such funds. Revenues accounted for in these funds include proceeds from the disposition of land, buildings, equipment, and the sale of other types of fixed assets.

2. *Long-Term Debt.* This account group includes financial information concerning the disposition of long-term debt instruments, such as bond issues, legal settlements, unfunded pension payments, penalties, or special assessments owed to city or county governments.

The types of funds generally established by school districts are important for administrators in conceptualizing the structure of a school district's accounting system as an inverted pyramid beginning with the broadest perspective. From the broadest view, the administrator should understand that the total accounting system is framed by establishment of these various types of funds. The simplest view is to state that all districts in all states utilize a general fund and special revenue funds, and most school districts also need to utilize capital project and debt service funds. Similarly, almost all school districts utilize proprietary funds to some degree, particularly regarding common operations such as activity funds, and many districts have developed highly sophisticated internal service funds. Fewer school districts make extensive use of fiduciary funds, but in some areas of the nation their importance is growing. Finally, many school districts have established fixed asset and long-term debt accounts to keep these functions separate from annualized operating revenues and expenditures. While establishing such fund structures is dependent on good professional advice from trained accountants, administrators need to grasp the broad operation of fund accounting to understand how the accounting transaction occurs within the individual funds.

The Accounting Transaction

The various funds thus provide a structure for grouping the major financial activities of a school district. Simply establishing appropriate fund structures, however, is not sufficient to transact business or to adequately allocate monies to the educational program or to track such expenditures in the growing context of educational accountability. Accounting convention has therefore called for establishing individual accounts within each fund wherein the actual process of financial transactions occurs. These accounts make up the record of assets, revenues, and expenditures that occur in the broader context.

Generally, five classifications of accounts are established within a given fund such as the General Fund. The five accounts include *expense, income, asset, liability,* and *net worth* or *fund balance* accounts. These may be known by different names in different states, and identifying these accounts may be difficult for administrators whose training is outside the field of accounting. These accounts are important, however, because all specific transactions involving revenue or expenditures, or increases or decreases in the value of assets, are entered or ''posted'' to these accounts.[17] Educational organizations use the *double entry* posting method, which involves entering both a *debit* (an entry on the left hand side of the account ledger) to one account and a *credit* (entry on the right hand side) to another account for each transaction. Asset and expenditure accounts (on the left) are increased by debiting and decreased by crediting. Conversely, an income account (on the right) is decreased by a debit and increased by a credit.

To illustrate double entry posting, take for example a school district that has received a general fund tax distribution of $100,000. Using a double entry system, this payment involves two general fund account groups: the income account and the asset account (the cash account). The income account will increase as the transaction is entered as a credit. The cash account will also increase as the transaction is entered as a debit to its side of the ledger. If the school district then hires a new teacher at a salary of $25,000, a new transaction in the general fund has occurred. The categories affected by this new transaction are the cash account and the appropriate expenditure account containing salaries. As a result, the cash balance in the asset account is credited (decreased), and the expenditure account for salaries is debited (increased). The purpose of such a complicated process is important for reasons similar to earlier discussion of accrual accounting. Double entry is simply a process that creates a self-balancing set of books in the district wherein the actual assets of the district are not improperly inflated. The double entry method is superior to single entry because it provides a series of checks and balances on the status of accounts and enables the organization to prepare a balance sheet and income statement reporting accurate financial data at any time.[18]

The individual accounts within each fund are listed in the official book of accounts called a *general ledger*. Each financial transaction is recorded into the general ledger by a complicated process. Before being written in the general ledger, revenue and expenditure transactions are recorded in a *general journal*, which is simply a chronological listing of transactions as they were initiated. Transactions are transferred from the general journal and posted to the appropriate accounts on the general ledger using double entry.[19] This process brings together or summarizes all similar accounts. Figure 7.2 shows a typical journal entry of the unpaid bills and the charges to the appropriate expense and asset accounts for a given day. The figure illustrates how the double entry system creates a self-balancing set of books wherein expenses are debited in the amount of $2,151, thus increasing the expense account, while assets are credited $2,151, thus decreasing the district's assets. From this transaction, the district can know exactly how much it owes in relation to its assets. As illustrated earlier, this process requires that debits and credits are applied to the proper fund and the proper account.

The listing of all accounts and subaccounts by fund is referred to as the *chart of accounts*. Several guidelines have been used in establishing the chart of accounts for public schools. These criteria are designed to allow the school district to develop accurate recordkeeping and reporting systems:

1. The Chart of Accounts encourages full disclosure of the financial position of the Local Education Agency (LEA). Emphasis is placed on the accurate classification of financial transactions. Expenditures are recorded in the accounting categories applicable, regardless of the implications of some of those decisions;

2. Comprehensiveness of financial reporting is encouraged. The LEA should incorporate all the financial activities of a district into a single accounting and reporting system for full disclosure. Accounts for such activities as food service, student activities, community services and commercial enterprises should be included in the financial reports of the LEA;

3. Simplified reporting is encouraged. Only a minimum number of funds consistent with legal and operating requirements should be established;

FIGURE 7.2   A typical journal entry

For the Journal Period Ending June 1, 1993

Expense Accounts

Debit No.	10	Supplies	$ 525.50
	25	Fees to delivery	250.00
	22	Miscellaneous	175.00
	17	Furniture	1,200.50
			$ 2,151.00

Asset Account

Credit No.	30	Accounts Payable	$ 2,151.00

4. Financial reporting emphasizes the results of LEA operations less than the resources applied. The account code structure emphasizes program accounting and the application of support service costs to the products of the "educational" enterprise;

5. The account classification system is flexible and meets the needs of both small and large LEAs while retaining comparability of reported data; and

6. The classification of accounts and recommended reporting structure remain in accordance with generally accepted accounting principles.[20]

The general process as described above is repeated for as many funds and transactions as apply in a given accounting period. These events are part of the larger accounting cycle. Each accounting transaction is part of 10 steps described by Tidwell as: (1) journalizing transactions; (2) posting transactions; (3) preparing a trial balance; (4) preparing a work sheet; (5) preparing financial statements; (6) journalizing closing entries; (7) posting closing entries; (8) balancing, ruling, and bringing forward balances of balance sheet accounts; (9) ruling temporary accounts; and (10) preparing postclosing trial balances.[21] Although there is not sufficient room to detail each of these accounting steps in an introductory school finance text, the description of the complex fund and transaction structures adequately illustrates the need to properly account for all revenue and expenditure activity in a public tax-based organization. The complexity of the system illustrates the need for professional assistance and equal need to secure trained employees charged with daily entry and maintenance of the district's financial transactions into the various books of record. At the administrative level, however, most of the administrator's time on accounting tasks will be spent working at the next lower level of revenue and expenditure structure within the budget where the primary task is to make educational decisions within fund and account structures.

Revenue and Expenditure Structure

The broader fund and account structure described above is finally broken down into more descriptive classification within the district's accounting system. It is at this level that daily administrative decisions involving the budget are made, with the support of the accounting function that provides the overall structure needed to carry out revenue and expenditure activities. While administrators are generally unacquainted with the more intricate details of professional accounting, they are familiar with revenue and expenditure structures because these structures are parallel to the budget document about which administrators are understandably more knowledgeable. Few school administrators, however, pause to consider the close relationship between accounting and the budget document. It is therefore critical that school decision makers understand the system of classifying revenues and expenditures, because this system is the superstructure supporting the budget discussion in Chapter 6 and because there is significant information about the educational process that can be derived from revenue and expenditure data.

Revenue Structure. The structure of revenue classification is generally less complex than that for expenditures for at least two reasons. First, as discussed in the budget chapter, the bulk of decisions about sources and amounts of revenue is normally beyond the control of administrators. As a result, there is little purpose in elaborate revenue structures beyond the amount of detail required by the granting agency to sustain its interests and direct revenues to their appropriate locations. Second, administrators are consequently more involved in decision making about expenditure of monies. As a result, greater structure is needed in the expenditure area to prevent inaccurate or improper use of monies and to be able to track the expenditures districts make. Therefore, classification of revenues primarily serves organizational purposes, whereas complex expenditure classification is needed for proper educational planning.

Revenue structures in educational organizations generally involve a three-tiered classification: the *fund,* the *source,* and the *type* of revenue. Each of these concepts relates to earlier discussion and requires additional development to understand their interrelationship.

The *fund* classification is now a familiar concept, as revenue received by the district must be placed into one of the various separate funds maintained by the district. Under this concept, it is easy to see that revenues earmarked for a categorical use such as transportation aid will need to be placed into the special transportation fund, and aid for any other categorical purpose will likewise be placed into the appropriate special fund. Similarly, it is easy to see that revenues not reserved to special funds will initially be placed into the General Fund, although in many states it is possible to shift monies later through a transfer process. The fund classification is used for both expenditures and revenues. Money placed into a fund will be expended from that same fund according to accounting procedures such as encumbrances, purchase orders, and so forth, using such techniques as double entry and modified accrual accounting and numbering each for automation. The fund is the overall revenue and expenditure structure in a school district wherein administrators will exercise their greatest influence.

The *source* classification refers to the granting entity that provided the revenue to the school district. Referring back to Figure 6.5 in the budget chapter, we can easily see that the source of revenue is important in that the budget document identifies revenue sources as part of the statutory expenditure authorization process. Five sources of revenue are recognized and accepted by convention:

1. *Revenue from local sources* refers to money generated within the boundaries of the local district itself. Such amounts are in the vast majority derived from local taxation, generally the local property tax. The amount and type of local sources will vary greatly between states due to state aid provisions, and the amount of local sources will vary among districts within a state based on wealth factors.
2. *Revenue from intermediate sources* includes money derived from a government entity that serves as an administrative unit between the local district and the state. Often this source is used by fiscally dependent school districts that rely on the taxing authority of a separate local government body for its revenue.
3. *Revenue from state sources* refers to money generated within the boundaries of the state in which the educational organization resides. The amount and type of state sources will also vary greatly between states due to different state aid provisions, and the amount of state sources will vary among districts within a state based on wealth factors.
4. *Revenue from federal sources* is money collected by the federal

government and distributed to the local district, either directly or through the state or another intermediate level of government. Federal monies are usually categorical aids.

5. *Revenue from other sources* does not involve money received from a certain level of government. This source is strictly used for accounting distinctions and generally involves funds related to the sale of bonds and interfund transfers.

The *type* of revenue refers to both the source and purpose of the revenue. Types under locally derived revenues, for example, include proceeds from ad valorem property taxes, tuition amounts paid, student transportation fees, earnings on investments under the management of the school district, student organization fees, revenue from textbook sales, and so forth. Types of intermediate and state revenues to local school districts would include such items as unrestricted grants-in-aid and revenue in lieu of taxes under tax exemptions or abatements granted by various other taxing units. Types of revenue from federal sources would include either unrestricted grants-in-aid received directly from the federal government or restricted federal grants-in-aid distributed through the state.[22] As can be seen in Figure 7.3, there is a rather extensive classification system for revenue receipts in a school district.

The system of revenue classification is important to administrators because it is used by states to allocate monies to the separate funds that the states themselves have created within a school district's budget. As seen in Chapter 6, these funds are reflected in the various states' school district budget documents, and the revenue classification system is used to distribute revenues to the individual funds. As can be seen in Figure 7.3, the classification of revenue is integral to the earlier fund concept. Revenues are thus first classified by fund and source, and then broken out into governmental, proprietary, fiduciary, and account group types for further distinction according to fund, source, and type. For example, food service sales revenue to full-price adults would be assigned to the food service fund (code 1600) in the local sources series (code 1000) as a daily nonreimbursable program (code 1620). This system of numbering on the revenue side of the budget is related to an equivalent numbering system located on the expenditure side of the budget, thereby providing the means to receive, segregate, and expend revenues for their intended purposes.

Expenditure Structure. The structure of expenditure classification is generally much more complex than that for revenues for several reasons. First, whereas revenue sources are quite limited for school districts and generally fit into five categories, expenditures can be broken out into hundreds of classifications if desired. Second, when revenues are received it may be assumed that the granting agency has satisfied its eligibility requirements as a condition to disbursement. In contrast, expenditure of monies deposited to each fund is beyond the daily control of the grantor, making a tight expenditure structure mandatory to control the use of various revenues. Third, interest in equity and special projects such as at-risk students make close scrutiny of general and special fund expenditures a necessity in the complex modern school world. Fourth, growing interest in accountability for educational outcomes has sparked even greater interest in tracking expenditures to the point of utilization. Consequently, the complex budget document coupled with the even more complex accounting activities can make expenditure classification an extensively detailed affair.

Regardless of the budget framework used by an individual district, expenditures

Code	Description	
1000		**Revenue from Local sources**
	1100	Taxes levied/assessed by the Local Education Agency (LEA)
	1110	Ad valorem taxes
	1120	Sales and use taxes
	1130	Income taxes
	1140	Penalties and interest on taxes
	1190	Other taxes
	1200	Revenue from local governmental units other than LEA's
	1210	Ad valorem taxes
	1220	Sales and use taxes
	1230	Income taxes
	1240	Penalties and interest on taxes
	1280	Revenue in lieu of taxes
	1290	Other taxes
	1300	Tuition
	1310	Tuition from individuals
	1320	Tuition from other LEA's within the State
	1330	Tuition from other LEA's outside the State
	1340	Tuition from other sources
	1400	Transportation fees
	1410	Transportation fees from individuals
	1420	Transportation fees from other LEA's within the State
	1430	Transportation fees from other LEA's outside the State
	1440	Transportation fees from other sources
	1500	Earnings on investments
	1510	Interest on investments
	1520	Dividends on investments
	1530	Gains or losses on sale of investments
	1540	Earnings on investment in real property
	1600	Food services
	1610	Daily sales—reimbursable programs
	1611	Daily sales—school lunch program
	1612	Daily sales—school breakfast program
	1613	Daily sales—special milk program
	1620	Daily sales—non-reimbursable programs
	1630	Special functions
	1700	Student activities
	1710	Admissions
	1720	Bookstore sales
	1730	Student organization membership dues and fees
	1740	Fees
	1790	Other student activity income
	1800	Community services activities
	1900	Other revenue from local sources
	1910	Rentals
	1920	Contributions and donations from private sources
	1930	Gains or losses on sale of fixed assets (proprietary funds only)
	1940	Textbook sales and rentals
	1941	Textbook sales

FIGURE 7.3   Classification of revenues and other sources, descriptions and codes

SOURCE: *Financial Accounting for State and Local School Systems, 1990* (Washington, D.C.: U.S. Department of Education, Office of Educational Research and Improvement, 1990), 19–23.

1942	Textbook rentals
1950	Services provided other LEA's
1951	Services provided other LEA's within the State
1952	Services provided other LEA's outside the State
1960	Services provided other local governmental units
1970	Services provided other funds
1990	Miscellaneous

2000 **Revenue from Intermediate sources**

2100	Unrestricted grants-in-aid
2200	Restricted grants-in-aid
2800	Revenue in lieu of taxes
2900	Revenue for/on behalf of the LEA

3000 **Revenue from State sources**

3100	Unrestricted grants-in-aid
3200	Restricted grants-in-aid
3800	Revenue in lieu of taxes
3900	Revenue for/on behalf of the LEA

4000 **Revenue from Federal sources**

4100	Unrestricted grants-in-aid direct from the Federal Government
4200	Unrestricted grants-in-aid from the Federal Government through the State
4300	Restricted grants-in-aid direct from the Federal Government
4500	Restricted grants-in-aid from the Federal Government through the State
4700	Grants-in aid from the Federal Government through other agencies
4800	Revenue in lieu of taxes
4900	Revenue for/on behalf of the LEA

5000 **Other sources** (governmental funds only)

5100	Sale of bonds
5110	Bond principal
5120	Premium
5130	Accrued interest
5200	Inter-fund transfers
5300	Sale or compensation for loss of fixed assets

FIGURE 7.3 (*Continued*)

in almost every state are classified in a program budgeting format. As seen in Chapter 6, this means that expenditures are classified hierarchically by *Fund, Program, Function,* and *Object*,[23] each level having a discrete code number for calculation and reporting purposes. These levels are hierarchical, progressively reducing the expenditure from broad to narrow definition. For example, the General Fund is a very broad entity, while the object breaks a function into various subcodes. As discussed in the previous chapter, districts may go beyond reporting purposes by further classifying expenditures for such purposes as productivity analysis.

Fund.   In examining expenditure structure classification, it is again evident that the *fund* is the basic level in a school accounting scheme. All expenditures are thus classified at the first level according to fund in conformance with the chart of accounts. Thus, any expenditure is classified as an expenditure from a governmental, proprietary, or fiduciary fund or from an account group. The purpose of starting with the fund should now be clear. *Revenue* is assigned to a fund on the basis of its intended use. Its intended use is for *expenditure* in support of some phase of the educational process. It is therefore implicit that each expenditure be assigned to the corresponding fund wherein revenue has been recorded. By the process of purchase orders, encumbrances, dual entry, and so forth, the expenditure reduces the proper fund. For example, transportation aid received is placed in the transportation fund, and expenditures for transportation must then be made from the transportation fund. This process is quite intuitive and is supported by the detail inherent to further breakdown through program codes.

Program.   The second level of expenditure classification by *program* refers to the educational plan of the district that has been designed to accomplish certain objectives. Although still quite broad, this classification takes the next step by assigning codes on the basis of program description to assure that all expenditures will be related to the program for which money is intended. Examples of school program classification include regular programs (elementary and secondary), special programs (e.g., learning disabled, gifted, bilingual), vocational programs, adult and continuing education programs, and enterprise programs.[24] It must be remembered that each classification level does not remove any previous classification in a broader category. For example, regular education is a program classification within the general fund. As discussed earlier, the purpose of breaking programs out is to assist policymakers in identifying and aiding discrete district operations and in evaluating those programs. Figure 7.4 contains a listing of useful program codes.

Function.   The third level, *function,* refers to the general activity for which the good or service is being acquired. While different states may require different numbering systems for these codes, in general "function" categories for school districts describe the areas of *instruction, student support* services, *business support* services, *operation and maintenance of plant* services, and *plant* services. These functions and their respective subfunctions, providing even greater detail, are grouped together in both the accounting system and the budget document. The coding system reflects areas and types of expenditures with similar purposes, as illustrated in Figure 7.5 (pp. 366–368). For example, Student Support Services (code 2100) has many subfunctions describing various activities of that operation. While each subfunction is discrete, all are similar and are grouped together accordingly. Under the broader code of Student Support Services (2100), the attendance and social work category (2110) is subcoded, while supervision of attendance activities is further subcoded (2111). Likewise, Supervision of Health Services (2131) is subcoded under the broader category of Operation of Health Services (2130). In both instances, the accounting codes make it possible to group and track similar expenditure needs in two different operational areas of student services and health.

Object.   The fourth level, *object,* refers to the specific good or service acquired by an expenditure. While different states again can use different object codes, in general "object" includes such items as salaries, employee benefits, purchased professional services, purchased property services, supplies, and so forth.[25] These objects and their codes are even further divided into subcodes to provide increased detail for

Code	Program
100	Regular Programs—Elementary/Secondary
200	Special Programs
	210 Mentally Retarded
	211 Educable Mentally Retarded
	212 Trainable Mentally Retarded
	220 Physically Handicapped
	221 Hard of Hearing
	223 Deaf-Blind
	224 Visually Handicapped
	225 Speech Impaired
	226 Crippled
	227 Other Health Impaired
	230 Emotionally Disturbed
	240 Learning Disabled
	250 Culturally Deprived
	260 Bilingual
	270 Gifted and Talented
300	Vocational Programs
	310 Agriculture
	330 Health Occupations
	340 Home Economics
	341 Occupational
	342 Consumer and Homemaking
	350 Industrial Arts
	360 Office Occupations
	370 Technical Education
	380 Trades and Industrial Occupational
	390 Other Vocational Programs
400	Other Instructional Programs: Elementary/Secondary
	410 School-Sponsored Co-curricular Activities
	420 School-Sponsored Athletics
	490 Other
500	Nonpublic School Programs
600	Adult/Continuing Education Programs
700	Community/Junior College Education Programs
800	Community Services Programs
	810 Community Recreation
	820 Civic Services
	830 Public Library Services
	840 Custody and Child Care Services
	850 Welfare Activities
	890 Other Community Services
900	Enterprise Programs
	910 Food Services
	990 Other Enterprise Programs
000	Undistributed Expenditures

FIGURE 7.4   Classification of expenditures by program code

SOURCE: *Financial Accounting for State and Local School Systems, 1990* (Washington, D.C.: U.S. Department of Education, Office of Educational Research and Improvement, 1990), 24–26.

Code	Function
1000	Instruction
2000	Support Services

  2100 Support Services Students
     2110 Attendance and Social Work Services
         2111 Supervision of Attendance and Social Work Services
         2112 Attendance
         2113 Social Work
         2114 Student Accounting
         2119 Other Attendance and Social Work Services
         2120 Guidance Services
         2121 Supervision of Guidance Services
         2122 Counseling
         2123 Appraisal
         2124 Information
         2125 Record Maintenance
         2126 Placement
         2129 Other Guidance Services
     2130 Health Services
         2131 Supervision of Health Services
         2132 Medical
         2133 Dental
         2134 Nursing
         2139 Other Health Services
     2140 Psychological Services
         2141 Supervision of Psychological Services
         2142 Psychological Testing
         2143 Psychological Counseling
         2144 Psychotherapy
         2149 Other Psychological Services
     2150 Speech Pathology and Audiology Services
         2151 Supervision of Speech Pathology and Audiology
         2152 Speech Pathology
         2153 Audiology
         2159 Other Speech Pathology and Audiology Services
     2190 Other Support Services-Students
  2200 Support Services Instructional Staff
     2210 Improvement of Instruction Services
         2211 Supervision of Improvement of Instruction Services
         2212 Instruction and Curriculum Development
         2213 Instructional Staff Training
         2219 Other
     2220 Educational Media Services
         2221 Supervision of Educational Media Services
         2222 School Library
         2223 Audiovisual
         2224 Educational Television
         2225 Computer Assisted Instruction
         2229 Other Educational Media Services
     2290 Other Support Services Instructional Staff
  2300 Support Services—General Administration

FIGURE 7.5 Classification of expenditures by function code

SOURCE: *Financial Accounting for State and Local School Systems, 1990*
(Washington, D.C.: U.S. Department of Education, Office of Educational
Research and Improvement, 1990), 26–29.

2310 Board of Education Services
2311 Supervision of Board of Education Services
2312 Board Secretary/Clerk
2313 Board Treasurer
2314 Election
2315 Tax Assessment and Collection
2316 Staff Relations and Negotiation
2319 Other Board of Education Services
2320 Executive Administration Services
2321 Office of the Superintendent
2322 Community Relations
2323 State and Federal Relations
2329 Other Executive Administration Services
2330 Special Area Administration Services
2400 Support Services—School Administration
2410 Office of the Principal Services
2490 Other Support Services—School Administration

2500 Support Services-Business
2510 Fiscal Services
2511 Supervision of Fiscal Services
2512 Budgeting
2513 Receiving and Disbursing Funds
2514 Payroll
2515 Financial Accounting
2516 Internal Auditing
2517 Property Accounting
2519 Other Fiscal Services
2520 Purchasing Services
2530 Warehousing and Distributing Services
2540 Printing, Publishing, and Duplicating Services
2590 Other Support Services—Business

2600 Operation and Maintenance of Plant Services
2610 Operation of Buildings Services
2620 Care and Upkeep of Grounds Services
2630 Care and Upkeep of Equipment Services
2640 Vehicle Operation and Maintenance Services (Other than Student Transportation Vehicles)
2650 Security Services
2690 Other Operation and Maintenance of Plant Services

2700 Student Transportation Services
2710 Vehicle Operation
2720 Monitoring
2730 Vehicle Servicing and Maintenance
2790 Other Student Transportation Services

2800 Support Services—Central
2810 Planning, Research, Development, and Evaluation Services
2820 Information Services
2821 Supervision of Information Services
2822 Internal Information
2823 Public Information
2824 Management Information
2829 Other Information Services
2830 Staff Services
2831 Supervision of Staff Services

FIGURE 7.5 (*Continued*)

		2832	Recruitment and Placement
		2833	Staff Accounting
		2834	Inservice Training (for non-instructional staff)
		2835	Health
		2839	Other Staff Services
	2840	Data Processing Services
		2841	Supervision of Data Processing Services
		2842	Systems Analysis
		2843	Programming
		2844	Operations
		2849	Other Data Processing Services
	2900	Other Support Services
3000		Operation of Non-Instructional Services
	3100	Food Services Operations
	3200	Other Enterprise Operations
	3300	Community Services Operations
4000		Facilities Acquisition and Construction Services
	4100	Site Acquisition Services
	4200	Site Improvement Services
	4300	Architecture and Engineering Services
	4400	Educational Specifications Development Services
	4500	Building Acquisition and Construction Services
	4600	Building Improvements Services
	4900	Other Facilities Acquisition and Construction Services
5000		Other Uses (governmental funds only)
	5100	Debt Service
	5200	Fund Transfers

FIGURE 7.5 (*Continued*)

reporting purposes. As seen in Figure 7.6, there is less similarity at the object code level between similar account codes and the purposes they represent. For example, overtime for personal services (code 130) in the 100 series is completely distinct from repair and maintenance services (code 430) under the 400 series detailing the classification of purchased property services.

Future Expenditure Classifications.   Revenue and expenditure classification in the various states generally conforms to a minimum of reporting detail designed to satisfy state interests in the educational process as related to state aid and to satisfy reporting requirements to the federal government for various federal aid entitlements. Beyond that minimum, however, it is the prerogative of school districts to further classify revenues and expenditures in greater detail only if they choose to do so for reasons of their own. Expenditure classification realistically receives the greatest attention, both because revenue is limited in the number of sources and because the utility of expenditure classification is much greater. Districts are required to perform up to a minimum standard, and the quality of revenue and expenditure information is thus highly dependent on the motivation of the district to study its own activities. Because of these wide variations, some thought has been given to expanding the classification system to provide better comparable data.

Although many districts have developed considerable detail through budget frameworks discussed in Chapter 6, such as Program, Planning, Budgeting, and Evalu-

Code		Function

100 Personal Services-Salaries
    110 Of Regular Employees
    120 Of Temporary Employees
    130 For Overtime
    140 For Sabbatical Leave

200 Personal Services—Employee Benefits
    210 Group Insurance
    220 Social Security Contributions
    230 Retirement Contributions
    240 Tuition Reimbursement
    250 Unemployment Compensation
    260 Workmen's Compensation
    290 Other Employee Benefits

300 Purchased Professional and Technical Services
    310 Official/Administrative
    320 Professional-Educational
    330 Other Professional
    340 Technical

400 Purchased Property Services
    410 Utility Services
    411 Water/Sewer
    420 Cleaning Services
        421 Disposal
        422 Snow Plowing
        423 Custodial
        424 Lawn Care
    430 Repair and Maintenance Services
    440 Rentals
        441 Rental of Land and Buildings
        442 Rental of Equipment and Vehicles
    450 Construction Services
    490 Other Purchased Property Services

500 Other Purchased Services
    510 Student Transportation Services
        511 Student Transportation Purchased from Another Local Education Agency (LEA) Within the State.
        512 Student Transportation Purchased from Another LEA Outside the State.
        519 Student Transportation Purchased from Other Sources
    520 Insurance. Other than Employee Benefits
    530 Communications
    540 Advertising
    550 Printing and Binding
    560 Tuition
        561 To Other LEA's Within the State
        562 To Other LEA's Outside the State
        563 To Private Schools
        569 Other
    570 Food Service Management
    580 Travel
    590 Miscellaneous Purchased Services
        591 Services Purchased Locally

(Continued)

FIGURE 7.6   Classification of expenditures by object code

SOURCE: *Financial Accounting for State and Local School Systems, 1990* (Washington, D.C.: U.S. Department of Education, Office of Educational Research and Improvement, 1990), 26–29.

592   Services Purchased from Another LEA Within the State
593   Services Purchased from Another LEA Outside the State

600   Supplies
    610   General Supplies
    620   Energy
        621   Natural Gas
        622   Electricity
        623   Bottled Gas
        624   Oil
        625   Coal
        626   Gasoline
        629   Other
    630   Food
    640   Books and Periodicals

700   Property
    710   Land and Improvements (governmental funds only)
    720   Buildings (governmental funds only)
    730   Equipment (governmental funds only)
        731   Machinery
        732   Vehicles
        733   Furniture and Fixtures
        739   Other Equipment
    740   Depreciation (proprietary funds only)

800   Other Objects
    810   Dues and Fees
    820   Judgments Against the LEA
    830   Interest
    840   Contingency (for budgeting purposes only)
    890   Miscellaneous Expenditures

900   Other Uses of Funds (governmental funds only)
    910   Redemption of Principal
    920   Housing Authority Obligations
    930   Fund Transfers

FIGURE 7.6 (*Continued*)

ation Systems (PPBES), recent recommended extensions of expenditure classification promise much greater knowledge than is now generally available. Recommendations for changes in school accounting and reporting practices have focused on expanding the detail of expenditure classification to include numerous additional dimensions, such as individual building and discrete program levels within individual buildings.[26] Although the number of classifications is infinite, it has been recommended that the next step include dimensions that could help local school districts improve the level of knowledge about instructional operations and include classifications for *level of instruction, operational unit, subject matter,* and *job.* These recommended changes would be expected to provide data as follows:

Level of Instruction.   This classification code is designed to include code numbers for all organizational grade level units within the school district, to identify and report expenditure data for each level of instruction operated by the school district. For example, financial data would be standardized to include such areas as elementary education subcoded into prekindergarten, kindergarten, and other elementary grades, middle school as a separate accounting code, and subdivisions of secondary and postsecondary education. Data gathered by level of instruction would allow pursuit of many productivity questions, as well as significant benefits to cost-accounting among programs and organizational levels. Examples of levels of instruction codes are shown in Figure 7.7.

Operational Unit.   This classification is designed to gather data by individual school building site and other operations that occur within specific educational facilities. These account code entries would allow the district to monitor and report activities based on expenditures that occur at each building and operational site within the district. These classification codes are usually arranged by budgetary unit or by the actual building where the activities could be monitored separately by function. Examples of budget units include classifications for the purchasing department, health department, and each individual school within the district. Examples of physical facilities include administrative divisions such as central office or transportation services. A fuller list of possible operational units and appropriate codes can be seen in Figure 7.8.

Subject Matter.   This classification code is designed to allow the district to monitor the costs of programs operated at multiple locations or levels within the school district. These account codes would permit gathering of financial and other data according to the curricular function of the school district and would greatly assist in accountability activities alluded to in Chapter 6 and more fully developed under the heading of productivity analysis in Chapter 13. Figure 7.9 suggests a potential list of subject classifications wherein cost-accounting could be performed or linkages to

FIGURE 7.7   Examples of level of instruction, description, and codes

SOURCE: *Financial Accounting for State and Local School Systems, 1990* (Washington, D.C.: U.S. Department of Education, Office of Educational Research and Improvement, 1990), 33.

Code	Level
10	Elementary
11	Pre-Kindergarten
12	Kindergarten
19	Other Elementary Grades
20	Middle
30	Secondary
31	Junior High
32	Senior High
39	Other Secondary
40	Postsecondary
41	Adult/Continuing
42	Junior College
00	General Districtwide

Example A: Budgetary Units

     01 Purchasing Department
     02 Principal's Office
     03 Health Department
     04 Custodial Office
     05 Peter Elementary
     06 Smith School
     07 Madison High School

Example B: Physical Facilities

     01 Central Administrative Office
     02 District Warehouse
     03 District Bus Garage
     11 Adams Elementary School
     21 Churchville Middle School
     31 York High School
     32 Lincoln Vocational-Technical School
     42 Davis Junior College

FIGURE 7.8   Examples of operational units and appropriate codes

SOURCE: *Financial Accounting for State and Local School Systems, 1990* (Washington, D.C.: U.S. Department of Education, Office of Educational Research and Improvement, 1990), 34.

FIGURE 7.9   Subject matter codes and descriptions

SOURCE: *Financial Accounting for State and Local School Systems, 1990* (Washington, D.C.: U.S. Department of Education, Office of Educational Research and Improvement, 1990), 35.

Code	Description
01	Agriculture
02	Art
03	Business
04	Distributive Education
05	English Language Arts
06	Foreign Languages
07	Health Occupations Education
08	Health and Safety in Daily Living, Physical Education, and Recreation
09	Home Economics
10	Industrial Arts
11	Mathematics
12	Music
13	Natural Sciences
14	Office Occupations
15	Social Sciences
16	Technical Education
17	Trades and Industrial Occupations
18	General Elementary/Secondary Education
19	Differentiated Curriculum for Handicapped Students
20	Cocurricular Activities
21	Safety and Driver Education
22	Junior ROTC

productivity constructed. Other codes could be added as needed by the state or local education agency.

Job. Finally, addition of a job classification allows the school district to monitor patterns of expenditure related to salaries and employee benefits. Since this category of expenditure is usually the largest single area of expense in the school district's general fund, it is important to know exactly how these funds are being spent. Because the function is both vast and customizable, different school districts will want to review different aspects of their salary expenditure patterns. Some may wish to do a comparative analysis of certified and noncertified staff salaries. Others may want to examine salary expenditures by bargaining unit. The possibilities are limited only by ability of the district to conceptualize its needs. Figure 7.10 provides several examples of options for various job classifications and their possible codes. As the figure shows, grouping by job is flexible according to the purpose to be served. For example, the first option may be of interest to administrators and boards in recruiting activities wherein comparison to other school districts is better facilitated. The second option may be of interest in assuring that salary differentials are wide enough to assure proper remuneration of employees. The third option may be of interest to administrators and boards in labor negotiations wherein various salary proposals can be analyzed and compared.

FIGURE 7.10   Three options for job classification account codes and description

SOURCE: *Financial Accounting for State and Local School Systems, 1990* (Washington, D.C.: U.S. Department of Education, Office of Educational Research and Improvement, 1990), 35.

Option 1: Personnel Purposes

1   Official/Administrative
2   Professional-Educational
3   Other Professional
4   Technical
5   Office/Clerical
6   Crafts and Trades
7   Operative
8   Laborer
9   Service Work

Option 2: Certificated/Noncertificated

1   Certificated
2   Noncertificated

Option 3: Bargaining Unit

1   American Federation of Teachers
2   National Education Association
3   Custodial Organization
4   Food Service Organization
5   Craftsman Organization
6   Transportation Drivers' Organization

The process and options involved in classification of expenditures are best illustrated schematically as seen in Figure 7.11. In this visual illustration of an actual school district's expenditure classification, the foregoing discussion can be readily seen wherein the computerized accounting database can gather information by all of the classifications shown. In the first group of numbers, each expenditure is coded by fund. For example, coding for the general fund is 06. In the second group of numbers, the expenditure is custom coded to this particular district's interests by function, subfunction, service area, and area of responsibility. For example, coding for the general area of support services yields code 2000.[27] The support services subfunction of General Administration further defines the code to 2300. The further definition of Service Area confines the expenditure to code 2310. The final digit defines the level of responsibility to the board treasurer in code 2313. In the third group of numbers, the district further defines the expenditure by object, subobject, and category. For example, object code 600 indicates supplies or materials. The subject code 610 notes the expenditure is for general supplies. Finally, category code 614 yields paper as the purchase.

As seen by the computer accounting system, the expenditure classification code reads 06-2313-614. To the administrator evaluating the code, it represents a general fund expenditure for the service function to be used for support services of general administration to the board of education under the responsibility of the board treasurer. Obviously a system focusing on cost-accounting and accountability, this classification scheme can provide a vast amount of useful information to the district's administrators. In an instructional context, the code could be structured to read:

Fund→Level of Instruction→Function→Object→Location→Course→Responsibility

or

General Fund→Elementary→Instruction→Tests→Morrison Elementary→6th grade English→J. Doe

Using such an expenditure structure, the district could choose to engage in either cost-accounting or productivity analysis at any of the various code-defined levels. Of course, the district could choose to further extend the analysis to almost any level, limited only by the cost-benefit of such analysis. For example, test scores could be linked to expenditures in a process similar to the productivity analysis described in Chapter 13. Most districts, however, have not moved expenditure classification to the level of individual teacher accountability, although the potential is attractive and imminent. A series of several expenditure classification schemes actually used by one district is shown in Figure 7.12.

The accounting structure of a school district is thus complex and indispensable. Districts utilize accounting to structure revenues and expenditures into a legal and informational framework honoring the public trust. To achieve these ends, school districts account for revenues and expenditures by individual fund wherein each fund has a specific purpose. Each fund is meant to receive revenue and make expenditures for educational purposes, and each fund generally operates on a modified accrual basis that states that revenues should be recognized in the period when they become available and expenditures should be recognized when a district becomes liable.[28] This is facilitated by double entry bookkeeping systems in an accounting cycle made up of checks and balances. Revenues are received to each fund and spent only for

```
 0   0  –  0   0   0   0  –  0   0   0
FUND       FUNCTION              OBJECT
           SUBFUNCTION           SUBOBJECT
           SERVICE AREA          CATEGORY
           AREA OF
           RESPONSIBILITY
```

FUND   (Appropriate Fund?)

```
 0   6  –  0   0   0   0  –  □   □   □
GENERAL
```

FUNCTION   (What Function is the 2000 series?)

```
 0   6  –  2   0   0   0  –  □   □   □
SUPPORT SERVICES
```

SUBFUNCTION   (2300 is what Subfunction?)

```
 0   6  –  2   3   0   0  –  □   □   □      (NOTE: MAXIMUM STATE
GENERAL ADMINISTRATION                              REQUIREMENT)
```

SERVICE AREA   (2310 is what Service Area?)

```
 0   6  –  2   3   1   0  –  □   □   □
BOARD OF EDUCATION SERVICES
```

AREA OF RESPONSIBILITY (2313 is what Area of Responsibility?)

```
 0   6  –  2   3   1   3  –  □   □   □
BOARD TREASURER
```

OBJECT   (What Object is the 600 Series?)

```
 0   6  –  2   3   1   3  –  6   0   0
SUPPLIES & MATERIALS
```

SUBOBJECT   (610 is what Subobject?)

```
 0   6  –  2   3   1   3  –  6   1   0
GENERAL SUPPLIES
```

CATEGORY   (614 is what Category?)

```
 0   6  –  2   3   1   3  –  6   1   4
PAPER
```

```
 0   6  –  2   3   1   3  –  6   1   4
GENERAL FUND

        SUPPORT SERVICE
           GENERAL ADMINISTRATION
              BOARD OF EDUCATION
                 BOARD TREASURER

                    SUPPLIES AND MATERIALS
                       GENERAL SUPPLIES
                          PAPER
```

FIGURE 7.11   Example of expenditure classification in an actual district

SOURCE: Courtesy Great Bend (Kansas) Public Schools.

Professional Development (In-Service Meetings)—Senior High (General Fund)

☐☐ - ☐☐☐☐ - ☐☐☐ ┆ ☐☐☐ - ☐☐☐

FUND   FUNCTION   OBJECT   LOCATION   DEPARTMENT/
                                                                  COURSE

Learning Center Salaries—Principals (General Fund)

☐☐ - ☐☐☐☐ - ☐☐☐ ┆ ☐☐☐ - ☐☐☐

FUND   FUNCTION   OBJECT   LOCATION   DEPARTMENT/
                                                                  COURSE

News/Periodicals—Eisenhower Elementary Library (General Fund)

☐☐ - ☐☐☐☐ - ☐☐☐ ┆ ☐☐☐ - ☐☐☐

FUND   FUNCTION   OBJECT   LOCATION   DEPARTMENT/
                                                                  COURSE

Postage—Washington Elementary (General Fund)

☐☐ - ☐☐☐☐ - ☐☐☐ ┆ ☐☐☐ - ☐☐☐

FUND   FUNCTION   OBJECT   LOCATION   DEPARTMENT/
                                                                  COURSE

Water Usage—Senior High (General Fund)

☐☐ - ☐☐☐☐ - ☐☐☐ ┆ ☐☐☐ - ☐☐☐

FUND   FUNCTION   OBJECT   LOCATION   DEPARTMENT/
                                                                  COURSE

Textbooks—Special Services (Textbook Rental Fund)

☐☐ - ☐☐☐☐ - ☐☐☐ ┆ ☐☐☐ - ☐☐☐

FUND   FUNCTION   OBJECT   LOCATION   DEPARTMENT/
                                                                  COURSE

Voc. Ag. Teaching Supplies—Senior High (Vocational Education Fund)

☐☐ - ☐☐☐☐ - ☐☐☐ ┆ ☐☐☐ - ☐☐☐

FUND   FUNCTION   OBJECT   LOCATION   DEPARTMENT/
                                                                  COURSE

Truck Repairs—Food Service (Food Service Fund)

☐☐ - ☐☐☐☐ - ☐☐☐ ┆ ☐☐☐ - ☐☐☐

FUND   FUNCTION   OBJECT   LOCATION   DEPARTMENT/
                                                                  COURSE

Human Sexuality Grant (Chapter Fund)

☐☐ - ☐☐☐☐ - ☐☐☐ ┆ ☐☐☐ - ☐☐☐

FUND   FUNCTION   OBJECT   LOCATION   DEPARTMENT/
                                                                  COURSE

(If you have two separate grants, you can use the year in the course line.)

FIGURE 7.12   Possible expenditure classification schemes

SOURCE: Courtesy Great Bend (Kansas) Public Schools.

intended purposes. Expenditures are coded according to fund, program, function, and object to allow for accurate accounting and educational accountability. Districts should be looking toward additional subcodes leading to greater understanding of the educational process and also provide greater control over the district's resources. As such, the role of accounting is a vital contribution to the educational process.

THE ROLE OF FISCAL REPORTING

Accounting processes themselves are widely misunderstood by lay persons. For most people, accounting is mysterious and highly technical, and the natural human response is either to ignore financial information or to be aggressively critical. Because neither response is helpful in a school setting, deliberate effort on the part of administrators is required to communicate clear information to constituents. Likewise, the accounting process itself demands that fiscal reports be prepared, both to assist in the audit function discussed later in the chapter and in response to the audit's findings. As a result of need to preserve and communicate fiscal information and to satisfy reporting requirements to various organizations, this section devotes some space to discussion of the role of financial reports issued by districts during a fiscal year. Although such reports are often specific to individual states' accounting and reporting structures, there are general elements to fiscal reporting employed in almost every school setting.

Financial Reports

Regardless of the state where a school district is located, all districts issue financial reports at various times. Although the number of reports may differ according to district needs, and while exact terminology may differ just as budget terms differ among the individual states, all school districts issue a minimum set of financial reports summarizing the fiscal activities of the district. At a minimum these reports are designed to be sufficient to meet the audit requirements discussed in the last section of this chapter.

Although districts engage in different amounts of reporting, it can be said that all districts at least prepare a report that is the equivalent of a Comprehensive Annual Financial Report (CAFR) at the end of the school fiscal year.[29] The CAFR was initially given its impetus by the Revenue Sharing Act of 1972, which required all recipients of federal revenue sharing activities to use a uniform accounting system.[30] This set of standardized reports describes the school district's financial condition and indicates the many changes in fiscal position that occurred during the year. As a general rule, the CAFR usually includes a letter of transmittal prepared by the district, a list of officials, an organizational chart, financial statements on combined and individual funds, notes to the financial statements, a single audit section on federal fiscal assistance, and a statistical section that contains school system data.[31] While some districts choose to make an elaborate affair of the CAFR, in many instances the annual audit report prepared in most school districts may serve the same purpose. It should be noted that the comprehensive annual audit outlined later in Figure 7.17 (p. 390) is generally organized around the concept of CAFR.

Most agencies controlling the fiscal operation of public schools recommend that at a minimum the following financial reports should be developed on an annual basis:

1. A combined balance sheet listing all funds which can be compared to the previous year's entries;
2. Combined statements of revenue and expenditure and changes in fund balances for all governmental funds;
3. Combined statements of revenue, expenditure, and changes in fund balances (budgeted and actual) for general and special funds;
4. Combined statements of revenue, expenditure, and changes in retained earnings (equity) for all proprietary funds; and
5. Combined statement of changes in financial position for all proprietary fund types.[32]

The combined balance sheet and combined statements of revenue and expenditure and changes in fund balances are the basic tools in this set of reports. As can be seen, these reports are issued for each of the various funds so that the same reports are repeatedly generated in parallel with the separate fund structure of the district. Consequently, these two reports are extremely important management tools.

Combined Balance Sheet.   A tool designed to summarize the overall financial condition of a school district at a given date is called the *combined balance sheet.* In most instances, combined balance sheets are prepared at the end of the school district's fiscal year wherein this report provides information on the assets, liabilities, and fund balances of the district. The combined balance sheet logically has three main parts: a statement of the *assets,* a statement of the *liabilities,* and a statement of the *fund balances* of the district. The asset side lists all the assets of the school district, such as cash, investments, and assets owed to the organization (receivables). The liabilities side summarizes everything the district owes, including long-term debt, payroll amounts yet to be paid, and other payables. The subtracted difference between assets and liabilities equals the unencumbered balance for each fund and for total fund equity. As noted earlier, changes in the level of fund balances indicate the overall financial condition of the school district.

An example of a combined balance sheet (Figure 7.13, pp. 380–381)[33] shows all assets and liabilities and resulting fund balances for each of the separate funds. As each fund is a set of self-balancing accounts, this report is also self-balancing in that assets must equal the sum of liabilities plus fund balances. For example, Figure 7.13 contains a column labeled "General" (general fund), wherein total assets equal $502,900. Similarly, the column labeled "Liabilities" for the general fund equals $300,850. The remaining balance of $202,050, identified as "Total Fund Equity" ($502,900 − $300,850 = $202,050), is distributed among several reserve funds, including $104,350 left as unreserved. Thus it can be easily seen that total assets of $502,900 equal the sum of liabilities and fund balances in the amount of $502,900 ($300,850 + $202,050 = $502,900). From one year to the next, it is thus possible to properly balance the district's financial records *and* to monitor changes in any of the fund balances to assure solid economic health in the various funds. Although Figure 7.13 is calculated as a year-end financial statement, a combined balance sheet can be prepared at any time. By understanding how to read a combined balance sheet, administrators can instantly know the overall financial condition of the district and make management decisions accordingly.

Statements of Revenue and Expenditure and Fund Balance.   Although the combined balance sheet shows the financial condition of the district summatively, it is largely uninformative about revenue and expenditure detail. A tool designed to report summation in greater detail is a *statement of revenue and expenditure and changes in fund balances.* This report tracks revenues and expenditures and fund balances within each of the various types of funds maintained by the district. In a combined statement, separate reports on governmental funds, proprietary funds, and so forth are reported in one combined statement. Although the detail is not extensive, the type and amount of revenues and expenditures are easily seen, and fund balances are also readily apparent. Greater detail of each individual fund is usually available in separate reports for each fund, from which the combined statement is often constructed.

Figure 7.14 (p. 382) is a sample statement of revenues, expenditures, and fund balances for all governmental fund types and expendable trusts (i.e., funds the district could spend during the year). It offers a summary of transactions that occurred in each fund during the year. For example, the column labeled "General Fund" had revenues totaling $1,597,450 and total expenditures for all operations during the year of $1,546,470. This obviously resulted in a net excess of revenues over expenditures of $50,980. During the year $50,000 was transferred from the General Fund to some other separate fund, resulting in a true net increase of $980 in the General Fund balance over the previous year ($201,050), for a total fund balance of $202,050. Remembering that a statement of revenues and expenditures and changes in fund balances is one item in a set of financial reports in a school district, it can be seen that this $202,-050 is the same Total Fund Equity amount appearing on the combined balance sheet shown in Figure 7.13. By properly reading the combined statement of revenues, expenditures, and fund balances, administrators can make many leadership decisions. For example, the excess of revenues over expenditures could be used to reduce taxes in the next year or to eliminate textbook rental fees. The possibilities are limited only by availability of excess revenue, legal and statutory limitations, and the political climate of the school district.

Financial data from summary reports can thus be used in infinite ways to review fiscal health and make operational decisions. One use of financial data is to generate supplemental reports. Figure 7.15 (p. 384) is a useful alternative form of revenue and expenditure statement that compares data on budgeted and actual amounts in each budget category of the general and special funds maintained by the school district. The format of this statement is similar to Figure 7.14; however, additional columns comparing amounts by budget, actual, and over-under budget are included. Presenting revenue and expenditure data in this manner gives school district planners a more comprehensive view of the effects of certain transactions on the financial health of the school district. For example, Figure 7.15 shows that the general fund balance was projected ("Budget" column) to be $319,070, but the actual year-end amount was in fact only $202,050. The district thus has a −$125,550 shortfall in revenue projections. However, district leadership succeeded in spending −$8,530 less than it planned to spend, reducing net loss to −$117,020, therein yielding the ending fund balance of $202,050. Such additional analysis might cause administrators to hesitate before reducing taxes or eliminating textbook fees as suggested previously. Obviously, such estimation variances need to be identified and explained to the board of education to avoid serious financial problems and a crisis of confidence. By utilizing data in this fashion, the reporting function can help modify and improve the total budgeting process.

In addition to these summative reports, school districts produce many other financial reports during a school year. Many are internal documents used in administrative budget planning, while others are intended to be nontechnical information for

Assets and Other Debits	Governmental Fund Types				Proprietary Fund Types		Fiduciary Fund Types	Account Groups		Totals (memorandum only)
	General	Special Revenue	Debt Service	Capital Projects	Enterprise	Internal Service	Trust and Agency	General Fixed Assets	General Long-Term Debt	
Current assets:										
Cash	$56,050	$23,310	$34,210	$12,700	$78,090	$10,500	$5,620			$219,480
Cash with fiscal agents			92,000							92,000
Investments	215,000	65,000	132,000	419,000			270,000			1,101,000
Taxes receivable (net of allowances for estimated uncollectibles, see notes to financial statements)	62,000	2,660	4,250							68,910
Interfund receivables	67,000			15,000	2,000	11,200	11,000			106,200
Intergovernmental receivables	30,000	75,260								105,260
Other receivables (net of allowances for estimated uncollectibles, see notes to financial statements)	950				3,900					4,850
Bond proceeds receivable				10,000						10,000
Inventories	27,200	9,400			45,900	18,200				101,500
Prepaid expenses	32,500	31,300			1,480	1,480				66,760
Other current assets	12,200	900								13,100
Total current assets	502,900	206,830	262,460	457,500	131,370	41,380	286,620			1,889,060
Fixed assets:										
Sites								$192,000		192,000
Site improvements (net of accumulated depreciation, $4,240)								39,260		39,260
Buildings (net of accumulated depreciation, $429,480)								3,994,320		3,994,320
Machinery and equipment (net of accumulated depreciation, see notes to financial statements)					52,050	54,950		709,080		816,080
Construction in progress								892,000		892,000
Total fixed assets					52,050	54,950		5,826,660		5,933,660
Other debits:										
Amount available in debt service funds									$169,710	169,710
Amount to be provided for retirement of general long-term debt									2,630,290	2,630,290
Total other debits									2,800,000	2,800,000
Current liabilities:										
Interfund payables	$35,200	$2,000		$4,000	$65,000					$106,200
Intergovernmental payables	9,250						$42,000			51,250
Other payables	87,950	36,150		48,600	15,000		16,400			204,100

Contracts payable	57,600	18,000		69,000	26,100					170,700
Matured bonds payable			$50,000							50,000
Loans payable	60,000									60,000
Interest payable	3,000		42,250							45,750
Accrued expenses	34,300	19,900			2,280	4,260				60,740
Payroll deductions and withholdings	3,900	1,780			210	380				6,270
Deferred revenues	18,000									18,000
Other current liabilities	900	800								1,700
Total current liabilities	300,850	87,880	92,750	121,600	44,990	82,640	42,000			774,710
Long-term liabilities:										
Bonds payable									$2,700,000	2,700,000
Notes payable									90,000	90,000
Lease obligations									10,000	10,000
Total long-term liabilities									2,800,000	2,800,000
Fund equity:										
Investment in general fixed assets								$5,826,660		5,826,660
Contributed capital					50,000	8,000				58,000
Retained earnings:										
Reserved for property purchases					8,000					8,000
Unreserved					80,430	3,690				84,120
Fund balances										
Reserved for inventories	27,200	9,400								36,600
Reserved for prepaid expenses	32,500	31,300								63,800
Reserved for encumbrances	38,000	46,500								84,500
Reserved for construction				300,800						300,800
Unreserved	104,350	31,750	169,710	35,100			244,620			585,530
Total fund equity	202,050	118,950	169,710	335,900	138,430	11,690	244,620	5,826,660		7,048,010
Total liabilities and fund equity	502,900	206,830	262,460	457,500	183,420	94,330	286,620	5,826,660	2,800,000	10,622,720

FIGURE 7.13 Sample combined balance sheet (in millions of dollars)

SOURCE: *Financial Accounting for State and Local School Systems, 1990* (Washington, D.C.: U.S. Department of Education, Office of Educational Research and Improvement, 1990), Appendix A, 123–132.

	Governmental Fund Types				Fiduciary Fund Type	Totals (memorandum only)
	General	Special Revenue	Debt Service	Capital Projects	Expendable Trust	
Revenues:						
Local sources:						
Taxes	$1,016,660	$238,000	$110,000			$1,364,660
Tuition	17,440					17,440
Earnings on investments	2,200	1,000	17,840	$42,050	$200	63,290
Textbook rentals	9,250					9,250
	1,045,550	239,000	127,840	42,050	200	1,454,640
State sources:						
Unrestricted grants-in-aid	413,000					413,000
Restricted grants-in-aid	30,000	2,400	14,000			46,400
	443,000	2,400	14,000			459,400
Federal sources:						
Unrestricted grants-in-aid	8,900					8,900
Restricted grants-in-aid	100,000	19,000				119,000
	108,900	19,000				127,900
Total revenues	1,597,450	260,400	141,840	42,050	200	2,041,940
Expenditures:						
Instruction services						
Regular education programs	680,590	19,010				699,600
Special programs	134,200	161,230				295,430
Vocational education programs	86,270					86,270
Other instructional programs	42,090					42,090
Nonpublic school programs	1,290	4,760				6,050
Adult/continuing education programs	10,430					10,430
Community services programs	3,710					3,710
	958,580	185,000				1,143,580
Supporting services:						
Student	78,500	14,800				93,300
Instructional staff	51,350	9,200				60,550

	General Fund	Special Revenue	Non-instructional Services	Debt Service	Capital Projects	Total
General administration	52,100	18,000				70,100
School administration	141,980					141,980
Business	19,970					19,970
Operation and maintenance of plant	169,080					169,080
Student transportation	17,250					17,250
Central	10,840					10,840
Other	46,820					46,820
	587,890	42,000				629,890
Operation of non-instructional services			2,420			2,420
Facilities acquisition and construction services					813,800	813,800
Debt service				114,420		114,420
Total expenditures	1,546,470	227,000	2,420	114,420	813,800	2,704,110
Excess of revenues over (under) expenditures	50,980	33,400	(2,220)	27,420	(771,750)	(662,170)
Other financing sources (uses):						
Proceeds from the sale of bonds					950,000	950,000
Operating transfers in			2,530		18,000	20,530
Operating transfers out	(50,000)					(50,000)
Total other financing sources (uses)	(50,000)		2,530		968,000	920,530
Excess of revenues and other sources over (under) expenditures and other uses	980	33,400	310	27,420	196,250	258,360
Fund balances—July 1	201,070	85,550	26,560	142,290	139,650	595,120
Fund balances—June 30	202,050	118,950	26,870	169,710	335,900	853,480

The notes to the financial statement are an integral part of this statement.

FIGURE 7.14 Sample statement of revenues, expenditures, and fund balances

SOURCE: *Financial Accounting for State and Local School Systems, 1990* (Washington, D.C.: U.S. Department of Education, Office of Educational Research and Improvement, 1990), 123–132.

	General Fund			Special Revenue Funds		
	Budget	*Actual*	*Over (under) budget*	*Budget*	*Actual*	*Over (under) budget*
Revenues:						
Local sources:						
Taxes	$1,202,700	$1,146,660	(556,040)	$89,000	$109,000	$20,000
Tuition	14,000	17,440	3,440			
Earnings on investments	3,500	2,200	(1,300)			
Textbook sales and rentals	8,600	9,250	650			
	1,228,800	1,175,550	(53,250)	89,000	109,000	20,000
State sources:						
Unrestricted grants-in-aid	485,000	413,000	(72,000)			
Restricted grant-in-aid				34,000	32,400	(1,600)
	485,000	413,000	(72,000)	34,000	32,400	(1,600)
Federal sources:						
Unrestricted grants-in-aid	9,200	8,900	(300)			
Restricted grants-in-aid				112,000	119,000	7,000
	9,200	8,900	(300)	112,000	119,000	7,000
Total revenues	1,723,000	1,597,450	(125,550)	235,000	260,400	25,400
Expenditures:						
Instruction services						
Regular education programs	685,000	680,590	(4,410)	20,000	19,010	(990)
Special programs	137,000	134,200	(2,800)	165,000	161,230	(3,770)
Vocational education programs	83,000	86,270	3,270			
Other instructional programs	45,000	42,090	(2,910)			
Nonpublic school programs	1,000	1,290	290	5,000	4,760	(240)
Adult-continuing education programs	10,000	10,430	430			
Community services programs	4,000	3,710	(290)			
	965,000	958,580	(6,420)	190,000	185,000	(5,000)
Supporting services						
Student	79,500	78,500	(1,000)	13,000	14,800	1,800
Instructional staff	50,900	51,350	450	11,500	9,200	(2,300)
General administration	54,800	52,100	(2,700)	20,500	18,000	(2,500)
School administration	152,000	141,980	(10,020)			
Business	18,000	19,970	1,970			
Operation and maintenance of plant	142,000	169,080	27,080			
Student transportation	30,800	17,250	(13,550)			
Central	12,000	10,840	(1,160)			
Other	50,000	46,820	(3,180)			
	590,000	587,890	(2,110)	45,000	42,000	(3,000)
Total expenditures	1,555,000	1,546,470	(8,530)	235,000	227,000	(8,000)
Excess of revenues over (under) expenditures	168,000	50,980	(117,020)		33,400	33,400
Other financing sources (uses) operating transfers out	(50,000)	(50,000)				
Excess of revenues and other sources over (under) expenditures and other uses	118,000	980	(117,020)		33,400	33,400
Fund balances—July 1	201,070	201,070		85,550	85,550	
Fund balances—June 30	319,070	202,050	(117,020)	85,550	118,950	33,400

The notes to the financial statements are an integral part of this statement.

FIGURE 7.15   Alternative statement of revenues, expenditures, and fund balances

SOURCE: *Financial Accounting for State and Local School Systems, 1990* (Washington, D.C.: U.S. Department of Education, Office of Educational Research and Improvement, 1990), Appendix A, 123–132.

public relations purposes. Still others are periodic reports prior to board meetings by which board members are apprised of the district's financial activities. School districts thus use numerous financial reports produced by the accounting function for internal uses involved in managing resources and external activities designed to work with constituencies in assuring an atmosphere of trust and financial integrity. In addition, the reporting function includes a full set of reports that informs external agencies, such as state and federal aid grantors, as discussed earlier. All such reports must obviously conform to good accounting principles wherein the purpose of accounting is to verify accuracy and to provide the basis for sound management decisions at all levels. While much reporting is elective, at a minimum school districts must maintain sufficient fiscal records to satisfy the requirements of higher units of government, to provide information useful to management decisions, and to assist in various types of financial audit activities.

THE ROLE OF AUDITING

While the accounting and reporting functions are vital to successful operation of a school district, accounting and reporting would have little authority without the critical element of auditing. Auditing is the study of accounting systems generally and specific accounts in particular in order to assure the accuracy and completeness of the accounting records of a district.[34] The role of auditing in a district is complex, but its purpose is to always to provide "a series of procedures followed by an experienced professional accountant to test, on a selective basis, transactions and internal controls in effect, all with a view to forming an opinion on the fairness of the presentation of financial statements for the period."[35] As such, school administrators need not only to understand the purpose of auditing, but also to become familiar with the various types of audits, the various reports produced by auditing, and the general preparations that should precede an audit to avoid problems. Accordingly, this section on the role of auditing is structured on these bases.

Purposes of Audits

Administrators should not mistake the purpose of audits. Many fine school people seem to believe that audits are to be both feared and dreaded. The basis for such attitudes is entirely reasonable given the nonaccounting background of most educators, but these attitudes are inherently wrong and even harmful. While audits do sometimes reveal problems in accounting and even on occasion detect intentional misrepresentation, they are in fact the best protection for administrators because without auditing, a variety of innuendoes and accusations are possible. Without proper accounting and auditing in a district, such allegations may be totally false but factually difficult to disprove.

The general statements in the previous two paragraphs about the role of auditing in a school district are sufficient to reveal the purposes of audits. First, audits are clearly designed to detect error of any sort in the accounting process. With the enormity of fiscal data handled by a modern school district, it is easy to see how errors can occur. Obviously errors can be accidental, and in a few instances, intentional. In addition, auditing serves a second valuable purpose of recommending changes in accounting procedures and improving the overall fiscal operation of a school district. Finally, a third purpose of auditing is to provide a means of demonstrating to fiscal grantors, such as state and federal governments and local taxpayers, that the educational mission of the school district is being fiscally supported according to statutory requirements. Given these purposes of auditing, administrators should be familiar with the general aspects of auditing from both professional interest in the educational enterprise and from the perspective of the ability of audits to protect their professional reputations.

Types of Audits

Auditing is therefore a key protection for school districts, boards, and administrators in the discharge of the educational enterprise. To achieve such protection, several different types of audits have been devised, with each type of audit serving a unique and important purpose. The different types of audits fall within two broad categories: *internal* and *external.* Audits may further be distinguished by their timing wherein examination of a district's fiscal records may be called a *preaudit,* a *postaudit,* or a *continuous audit.* Finally, within these categories the actual various types of audits are carried out. As a general rule, all school district external audits may be identified as *general comprehensive* audits, *state* audits, or *special* audits. Each type of audit has its own purpose and design.

Internal Audits.   As the name implies, internal auditing is a set of procedures that occurs within an organization designed to provide a system of self-checks on a regular basis. Internal auditing can range from a fairly informal system of monthly reports to the board of education to a complex system of continuous internal monitoring wherein highly skilled accountants are specifically employed by an organization to study and improve the accounting system. All systems in fact engage in some amount of internal auditing, and school districts are no exception. For example, the series of reports on the financial status of the school district sent to board of education members prior to each meeting is a form of internal auditing because employees had to engage in auditing activities to produce such reports. A monthly statement to the board requires maintaining journals and ledgers that permit issuance of income and expense statements. Similarly, the financial records maintained for state reporting requirements demand internal auditing because districts are often severely penalized for sloppy accounting practices. As a result, internal auditing exists in every school district, although the degree of formal design varies by individual district.

Most generally, internal audits are either *preaudits* or *continuous* audits. The difference between these two forms of internal auditing is implicit in their names. A preaudit is designed to assure proper accounting procedures in advance of a transaction. A continuous audit implies constant observation of the accounting system. In an informal sense, continuous internal auditing occurs through the system of checks and balances in place in most districts where multiple layers of approval must be secured to expend funds. The hierarchy from one actual school district (Figure 7.16, pp. 388–389) is proof of checks and balances wherein every fiscal operation is carefully identified and multiple protections are in place to guard against error or wrongdoing. Similarly, the encumbrance system whereby an employee checks to see that the proper accounts and cash balances are in order before making a financial commitment on behalf of the district is a form of internal preaudit.[36] Although internal auditing is never sufficient to guard against all the errors and design flaws that can occur in an accounting structure, internal auditing is an important aspect of good fiscal management that should be consciously developed in modern school districts.

External Audits.   A more familiar form of auditing to lay persons is the *external* audit. As the name implies, an external audit is a formal examination of the financial records of a school district by a qualified outside person to verify accuracy of those records and compliance with all statutory provisions. Such audits are always conducted by an independent auditing organization, such as a certified public accounting firm, or in some instances may be performed by state auditors checking for compliance with various aid entitlements. External audits are thus designed to ensure professional competence and objectivity.

Because an external audit is generally a purchased service, a thorough and exhaustive examination is usually expected, requiring that a report with recommendations be issued on the audit findings. This is generally true whether the external audit is aimed at testing only part of the total accounting structure or is a general comprehensive audit as described later. External audits are thus usually accompanied by a letter of transmittal stating the purpose of the audit, the procedures followed, a statement of findings, and a list of recommendations. In addition, the audit report is generally accompanied by a set of tables, figures, and summaries comparing multiple years' financial data on the district. In almost all instances, the auditing function is timed to coincide with issuance of the district's final annual report. As a general rule, most external audits are general comprehensive audits occurring at the close of an accounting period, usually an entire year.

General Comprehensive Audits.   When school districts prepare for an audit, they are usually anticipating a *general comprehensive audit* of the district's financial records. General comprehensive audits are designed to review all the financial records of a district to test for proper accounting procedures and good fiscal management. During a comprehensive audit, the district may expect that representatives of the auditing firm will be in the school district for several days and will request copies of all financial records and supporting materials. These items are used to perform the various analyses carried out by certified professional accountants in the discharge of an objective and unbiased examination of the fiscal integrity and accounting accuracy of a school district.

As stated earlier, a general comprehensive audit will normally result in a formal written report issued by the independent auditing firm. The report provides a permanent record of the audit findings, identifies problems that need to be corrected, and makes recommendations for improvements in the total accounting system. The report generally contains summaries of revenues and expenditures, and compares cash balances against encumbrances to ascertain whether statutory requirements on cash basis laws are observed. Additionally, the report provides results of examination of the financial records of all budgetary accounts, wherein each individual fund operated by the district is reviewed. The table of contents taken from a typical audit report (Figure 7.17, p. 390) illustrates much of our foregoing discussion. Governmental funds are examined separately under statements of budgetary accounts, and other funds maintained by the district, such as fiduciary expendable trust funds, and proprietary funds, such as enterprise funds, are likewise examined.

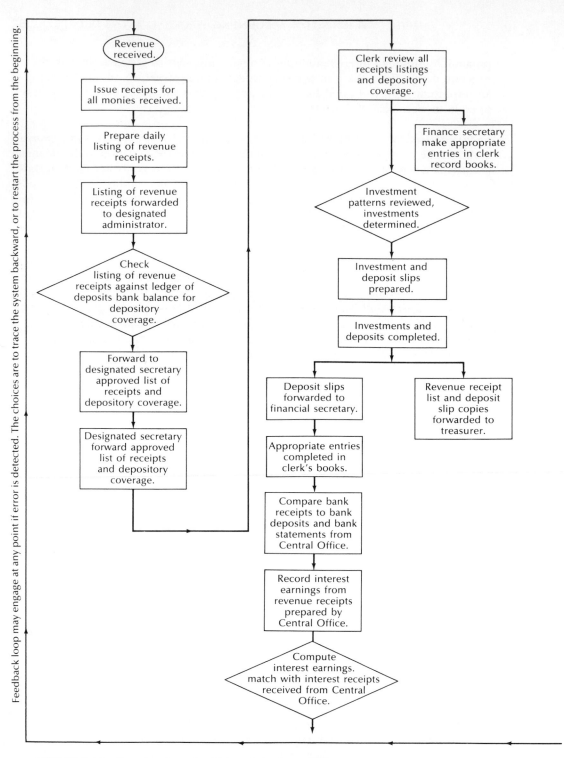

FIGURE 7.16 Sample schematic of internal checks and balances

SOURCE: Courtesy Great Bend (Kansas) Public Schools.

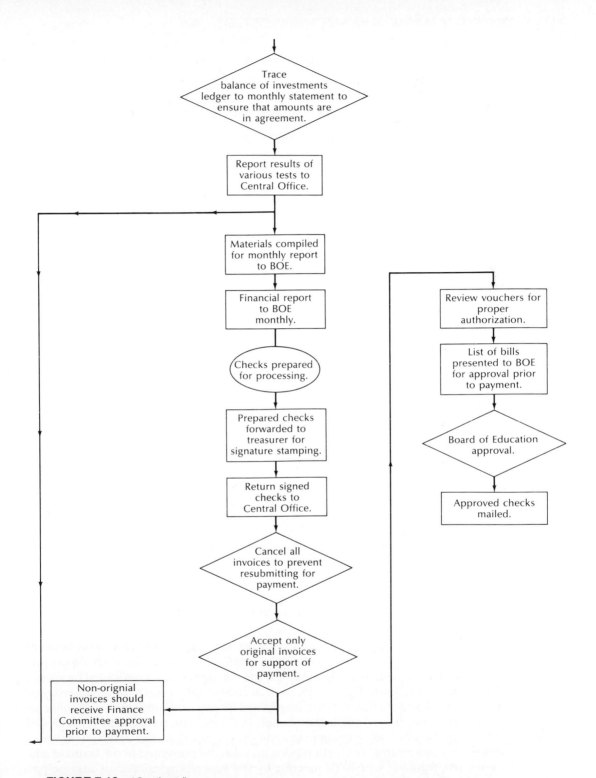

FIGURE 7.16 (*Continued*)

Table of Contents

FIGURE 7.17   Sample audit report Table of Contents

The completed audit provides statements and reports on the various financial records examined. If no items of particular concern are noted, the audit report provides the financial statements listed in the table of contents, accompanied by a letter similar to the example in Figure 7.18. Such an audit report is said to be an *unqualified opinion* because its statements are unqualified by any *audit exceptions.* If concerns surface, the letter may resemble the example in Figure 7.19, wherein the report is said to be a *qualified opinion* containing audit exceptions that state reservations about accounting procedures. The audit reports may then be presented to the board of education at a regularly scheduled meeting by the supervising auditor or may be presented by the district administration. Generally, boards of education are expected to

REPORT OF CERTIFIED PUBLIC ACCOUNTANTS

_____
_____
_____

We have examined the financial statements of Unified School District No. _____ at June 30, _____ and for the year then ended, as listed in the table of contents. Our examination was made in accordance with generally accepted auditing standards and the _____ Minimum Standard Audit Program and, accordingly, included such tests of the accounting records and such other auditing procedures as we considered necessary in the circumstances. The financial statements of Unified School District No. _____ for the year ended June 30, _____ were examined by other auditors whose report dated September 6, _____ expressed an unqualified opinion on those statements on the basis of accounting described in Note 2 (see Note 8).

As described in Note 2, the District's policy is to prepare its financial statements on a basis of accounting which demonstrates compliance with the cash basis and budget laws of the State of _____ . These practices differ in some respects from generally accepted accounting principles. Accordingly, the accompanying financial statements are not intended to present financial position and results of operations in conformity with generally accepted accounting principles.

In our opinion, the financial statements listed in the table of contents present fairly the cash and unencumbered cash balances of the various funds of Unified School District No. _____ at June 30, _____ and the revenue and expenditures of such funds for the year then ended, on the basis of accounting described in Note 2, which, except for the change with which we concur, in classifying the cash balances of the agency funds as a liability instead of unencumbered cash in the summary statement of revenue, expenditures and comparison of cash balances with encumbrances, and reclassification of certain agency funds as expendable trust funds as described in Note 9, has been applied in a manner consistent with that of the preceding year.

The accompanying additional information as listed in the foregoing table of contents is not necessary for a fair presentation of the financial statements, but is presented as additional analytical data. The additional information has been subjected to the tests and other auditing procedures applied in the examination of the financial statements listed in the foregoing table of contents and, in our opinion, is fairly stated in all material respects in relation to the financial statements taken as a whole.

_____
_____

FIGURE 7.18   Report of Certified Public Accountants—no exception

reflect receipt of the audit report in board minutes and to show proper action to correct accounting deficiencies in accordance with state law.

The comprehensive audit is designed to assure full compliance with the law and to improve the financial and accounting operations of a district. As such, the money spent for professional independent auditing services is well invested. Board members, administrators, and members of the public have a right to expect absolute conformance with the law, and administrators in particular need to be certain that auditing occurs. Because it is much easier to closely monitor the financial affairs of a district than to explain shoddy errors that cast ineradicable shadows on professional reputations, the general comprehensive audit is the best protection for every stakeholder in the educational enterprise.

Dear Board Members:

We recognize that to properly serve you the involvement of _____ & Company must extend beyond the normal services involved in an annual audit. In keeping with this philosophy, one of our objectives in the performance of our audit engagement is to assist you in controlling operations and improving efficiency. To accomplish this objective, we are issuing this management letter which sets forth significant areas we believe are worthy of your attention. The comments included herein were given consideration in the issuance of our report dated October 14, ____ and do not represent any modifications thereof.

STATUTORY NONCOMPLIANCE

__.S.A. 10-1113 prohibits creating indebtedness in excess of the amount of funds available. At June 30, ____ the Textbook Rental Fund was in violation of the above statute in the amount of $5,624. We would recommend that expenditures be monitored more closely to avoid such statutory violation.

__.S.A. 9-1401 requires that the governing body shall designate by official action recorded upon its minutes the state and national banks which shall serve as depositories of its funds. This action was not noted in the minutes of the Board of Education. We recommend that at its annual organizational meeting in July, the Board take such official action in order to comply with the above statute.

GRADE SCHOOL ACTIVITY FUND

During our examination we noted that at certain times during the year, monies received were not always deposited timely. In one instance, a deposit was not made for over 30 days after the receipt of the funds. We urge that deposits of receipts be made daily to insure the proper safeguarding of assets.

The comments in this letter are intended to be constructive suggestions and reflect a desire on our part to assist you in administering of the day-to-day business of the District. If we can be of assistance in implementing any of the above recommendations, please contact us.

Also, we would like to thank the District personnel for their cooperation and assistance extended to us during our examination.

Sincerely,

_____

_____

FIGURE 7.19 Report of Certified Public Accountants—audit exception

State Audits. In addition to internal auditing and external general comprehensive audits, a variety of external *state* audits may occur in a school district. State audits usually serve an entirely different purpose from general audits and are designed to monitor compliance with statutes and regulations involving distribution of state or federal monies.

The diversity of individual state auditing requirements makes it difficult to generalize about the specifics of state audits. The differences rest primarily in varying state philosophies about the control of education. In states that closely observe local control of education, state audits may be restricted to periodic compliance checks on a minimum set of statutory regulations. In states where education is more centrally vested in state government, state audits may more closely resemble comprehensive audits, at least in terms of thoroughness.

The similarities of state audits rest in one main goal of determining whether the state's financial interests in education are protected. Generally, state audits are therefore designed around auditing the various funds to which the state either supplies aid directly or acts as a channel for federal aid to local school districts. In the case of federal funds, states are usually interested in proper maintenance of applications, expenditure reports, and transmittal documents. In the case of state funds, states are usually interested primarily in all documentation related to state aid claims. Obviously, since school districts are required by law in all states to operate under a fund system, state audits will likely examine each fund according to level of state participation in each of those funds. For example, a state that places high emphasis on transportation services is likely to audit transportation claims very tightly, including verification of mileages by actually driving the routes to determine efficiency of student transportation services. Similarly, audits of federal funds by state agencies responsible for administering pass-through grants will closely check to assure that equipment purchased with federal monies has not been diverted to nonapproved uses. As a result, state audits are highly state-specific, although their purpose is always a singular interest in verifying that the state's educational obligations and priorities are properly served.

Special Audits.   Finally, school districts are sometimes subject to one other form of external audit. The *special* audit is seldom utilized in schools, but its purpose generally relates to suspicion of serious error or fraud in the financial operation of a school district that has been brought to the attention of officials in any of a variety of ways.

Probably one of the more common ways special audits are initiated is through normal state audit reviews. For example, a transportation audit might reveal that a district has claimed more children for reimbursement purposes than actually qualify. Similarly, a general fund state aid formula operating on an official head count basis might determine that too much state aid had been paid in a given year. While normal procedures might simply deduct the difference from the next year's aid entitlement, uncircumspect conditions might trigger a special audit if misrepresentation of transportation or attendance counts was suspected. In addition, internal auditing might cause a district to voluntarily undertake a special audit. For example, inability to reconcile expense account claims with receipts could result in a special audit, as might other events such as inventory loss. For example, investigation of the transportation function due to the loss of tires or gasoline purchased by the district could be brought about by employee reports regarding the actions of other employees. The possibilities for special audits are unlimited, but the honest nature of most educators fortunately prevents frequent application of this audit tool.

Preparing for an Audit

The auditing process should not be feared or dreaded by responsible school administrators. One of the reasons audits are not viewed with enthusiasm, however, is that the basic work of schools is not focused on the financial detail required to produce a smooth and uneventful audit. Schools are intensely human organizations, and the predominance of "green eyeshade" attitudes has already been pointed out. But despite this attitude, the level of anxiety involved with auditing will always be in direct proportion to the level of preparation engaged in by the district before the audit occurs.

The most obvious path to a successful audit is a properly designed fiscal accounting system that functions smoothly at every moment in a given accounting cycle.

While the importance of such procedures cannot be overemphasized, there are additional preparations districts should undertake to prepare for an audit. Advance preparation for internal auditing is implicit in actually carrying out internal audit procedures. External audit preparation, however, demands special care at two distinct levels. The first level considers that only proper accounting procedures can prevent special audits and protect the district if a special audit in fact occurs. The second level considers all other external audits wherein knowledge of the audit process will help carry out an uneventful audit. As a result, general preparation guidelines apply equally to both state and comprehensive general audits.

Advance Preparation for Audits.   As a general rule, the external audit operation in school districts will be greatly aided by the following preparations:

1. The district should strengthen internal accounting procedures, including segregation of duties. Multiple levels of accounting responsibility should be evident, and proper procedures for security of data and revenues and expenditures should be in place. As stated earlier, the best preparation is continuous preparation wherein the accounting function is designed to produce an uneventful audit.

2. The district should allow the internal staff enough time to do all the necessary work of accounting and audit preparation in advance without overtime, and allow enough time before the books are closed to anticipate and resolve problems. The old adage of "haste makes waste" is doubly true in financial affairs, and the risk is greatly increased because financial errors are among the worst kind.

3. The district should assemble all documents in advance that the external auditor will require. The best advice is to contact either the independent comprehensive auditor or the state auditor in advance to determine which documents will be needed. Generally, these documents include:

   a. copies of each tax levy, budget, and adopted amendment, if any. Copies of the budget must include all funds managed by the district, whether governmental or otherwise. This will allow the auditor to check proper certification of tax levies, calculate estimated tax proceeds, and check tax levies and budgets for statutory compliance;

   b. copies of the minutes of each board meeting and copies of any financial statements. Auditors use board minutes to verify proper expenditure procedures, and financial statements form the basis of the audit;

   c. a copy of the current organizational flow chart, including the names of each person responsible at each accounting level in the district. As seen earlier in Figure 7.16, a flow chart should be informative by showing all accounting steps, such as multiple security levels for signatures on checks issued;

   d. a copy of the district's document flow chart. The auditor must be able to trace each transaction from initiation to completion. The flow chart should be accompanied by a copy of the district's written accounting policies and procedures;

   e. copies of all monthly bank reconciliations for each bank account, including all canceled checks and statements for the period being examined;

   f. a list of official district depositories and their addresses. This list should also contain all bank account numbers, facsimiles of all authorized signatures, and evidence of compliance regarding signatures;

g. a schedule of investment transactions for the accounting period;

h. a schedule of insurance policies, including names of insurance companies, types of coverages, and so forth;

i. a reconciliation of salary amounts and related items, including payroll deductions;

j. a copy of details of any new bond issues, teacher contracts, leave schedules, or other agreements that commit future revenues of the district;

k. a copy of the previous year's audit report;

l. all canceled bonds and interest coupons;

m. a list of fixed assets owned by the district;

n. a summary of all past, present, and pending litigation affecting the district;

o. a schedule of all interfund loans or advance listing;

p. access to canceled and current invoices and purchase orders; and

q. all documents submitted for state aid or other intergovernmental transfer payments at any level.

The importance of proper auditing is underscored in that external audits are generally required by the various levels of government that provide funding to the organization. Under such conditions, results of audits may have a direct bearing on future funding for the school organization. When the accounting process functions properly, auditing will result in praise and can only suggest improvements. Thus, administrators should welcome the role played by auditing and take willing refuge in its ability to protect the public trust.

For most people, the complex processes of accounting, reporting, and auditing are probably the least understood aspect of fiscal leadership in schools. These functions are vital, however, as data concerning the fiscal health of a school district must be available to decision makers in a timely and accurate manner. Without such operations, school personnel would be unable to effectively plan for the other ongoing operations of a modern school district described in the following chapters, and the delivery of education to students would be fundamentally disrupted. While accounting procedures appear complex to educators who typically have no background in professional accounting, with a little effort even the most complicated financial statements can be deciphered and understood. It is on this note that we now turn our attention in Chapter 8 to other fiscal planning operations of school districts through a study of the fiscal side of the personnel function.

Review Points

THE ROLE OF THE ACCOUNTING FUNCTION

Increasing scrutiny of government expenditures, including school funds, has heightened the demands for efficiency and thorough accounting.

The purpose of the accounting function is to report and control fiscal resources; to read progress toward goals on which money is spent; to account to higher authority for resources expended; to provide feedback to the budget process; and to assure proper fiduciary execution.

Most school organizations use the modified accrual accounting method, mixing cash basis and accrual reporting to more accurately reflect resource flows and encumbrances in the nonprofit government sector.

Schools are subject to fund accounting procedures wherein receipts and disbursements are separated by purpose.

Schools usually operate three types of funds: governmental, proprietary, and fiduciary. The bulk of school monies are governmental funds. Schools further establish accounts within each given fund.

Schools usually follow accounting procedures based on double entry methods wherein assets and liabilities zero out.

The chart of accounts in a school district is a picture of all the accounts and subaccounts by all funds.

Revenues are three-tiered structures made up of the *fund,* the *source,* and the *type* of revenue.

Expenditures are multi-tiered, usually made up of at least the *fund,* the *program,* the *function,* and the *object.*

Numbering each tier allows for revenue and expenditure aggregation and disaggregation for reporting and performance accountability.

Carrying out the accounting cycle can be envisioned as the reflection of the executed budget prepared by the district.

The accounting cycle is made up of 10 steps, including: journalizing transactions; posting transactions; preparing a trial balance; preparing a work sheet; preparing financial statements; balancing, ruling, and bringing forward balances; ruling temporary accounts; and preparing postclosing trial balances.

THE ROLE OF FISCAL REPORTING

At a minimum, the role of reporting is to assure sunshine, or public access, into the financial affairs of the district, and to comply with state laws and uniform accounting procedures relating to independent audit requirements.

Districts differ greatly in the amount of financial reporting they choose to provide, but all districts must conform to state-specific laws and should seriously consider the political benefits of comprehensive reporting.

Fiscal reporting in the accounting cycle requires statements that report on the assets, liabilities, and fund balances of the district.

Agencies that monitor public funds recommend that all schools should prepare at least a combined balance sheet for all funds; a combined statement of revenue and expenditure and changes in fund balances for all governmental and general and special funds; a combined statement of revenue, expenditure, and changes in retained earnings for all proprietary funds; and a combined statement of changes in financial position for all proprietary funds.

By accounting procedures that accurately reflect true fund balances after encumbrances and liabilities, important judgments follow about the financial health of the district that permit long-range systematic educational planning to occur.

THE ROLE OF AUDITING

The role of auditing is to verify the accuracy of the accounting and reporting functions, and to recommend changes and improvements to the accounting process.

Auditing offers the only protection available to public officials who have a fiduciary responsibility.

Audits are either *internal* or *external.*

Audits may be further classified by timing, wherein they are either *preaudits, postaudits,* or *continuous* audits.

Internal auditing is generally an internal control device, and usually occur as preaudits or continuous audits.

External audits are independent verifications, generally occurring as postaudits.

The external audit is never an expense—it is an investment that handsomely repays taxpayers, boards, and administrators.

External audits are further categorized as *general comprehensive* audits, *state* audits, or *special* audits, each with its own purpose and value.

Auditing should go smoothly if preparations are made, beginning with strengthening internal accounting and auditing procedures.

Case Study

At last night's first board of education meeting of the new fiscal year, you became aware of several board concerns about the accounting structure in the school district. As the new associate superintendent for finance in this district of approximately 4,500 students, you were invited into executive session with the board, where numerous concerns were expressed.

As board members spoke, you became alarmed regarding some of the allegations raised about the accounting structure of the financial services division under your control. First, according to last year's comprehensive audit, problems exist in the cash receipts and disbursement operations in the activity fund wherein auditors noted 73 instances of cash entries to the student yearbook account for which no prenumbered receipts were found. Second, support for expenditures at the district level was incomplete, in that bank statements for the months of July and August were missing. Third, the auditors found three instances where no invoice or purchase order could be identified to support disbursements totaling more than $3,000 from the general fund. Fourth, the auditors noted that monies received were not always deposited in a timely manner, wherein on several occasions deposits were not made until 10 days after receipt. Fifth, several accounts showed a negative balance, wherein expenditures were greater than revenues. Sixth and finally, the auditors were quite concerned that there were insufficient controls over the activity fund in the district, wherein loose cash handling was apparent and only one signature line appeared on activity fund checks.

As a result of last night's meeting, you were asked to present a proposal at the next board meeting that would improve the integrity of accounting in the district. Using the following sets of questions to help launch your class discussion, what improvements and structures will you propose to the board?

Directed Discussion Questions

1. Using your own experience and formal learning to this point about school finance and school business management, what elements of this case study are really serious issues of concern? Why do you think these audit exceptions were mentioned by the auditors? What might be the outcome of ignoring or minimizing the problems cited by the board? Alternatively, are there some issues that are being overblown by lay board members? Which ones, if any?

2. As you plan your recommendations to the board, where will you begin? What issues and roles need examination? Why? Since these issues seem to have developed over time and since they are only now coming into harsh light, what actions should you take to protect yourself and the district? Since internal accounting procedures seem relatively lax, what steps will you take, if any? What other steps are needed, if any, to further examine the district's financial records? Where will you turn for help?

3. Using your own experience as a professional educator, what examples, if any, of poor accounting and financial practices have you encountered? What examples, if any, of financial wrongdoing do you recall? If you have had any type of responsibility for handling school monies or district funds at any time, what training did you receive? When you accept a new position as an administrator in a school district, what questions, if any, should you ask about the district's financial affairs and about your role? When taking a new position, what steps, if any, do you think you should take to protect your reputation? Practically, what are the protections that administrators can reasonably demand? How can administrators who remain in a district over a long period of time assure that subordinates will secure and protect the financial integrity of the district?

NOTES

1. Carl Candoli, Walter Hack, and John Ray, *School Business Administration: A Planning Approach,* 4th ed. (Needham Heights, Mass.: Allyn and Bacon, 1992), 141.

2. Sam B. Tidwell, *Financial and Managerial Accounting for Elementary and Secondary School Systems* (Reston, Va.: Association of School Business Officials, 1984), 8.

3. Florida Department of Education, *Financial and Program Cost Accounting and Reporting for Florida Schools* (Tallahassee: Florida Department of Education, 1988), 1–3.

4. Roger Hermanson, James Edwards, and Gayle Rayburn, *Financial Accounting,* 4th ed. (Homewood, Ill.: Richard D. Irwin, Inc., 1989), 858.

5. Given the distinctions regarding income and expenses, some note is needed to lessen confusion over terminology used in this example. It should be noted that Figure 7.1 is an income report on an activity fund, rather than a fund that receives traditionally defined

revenue. The difference will be more obvious later in discussion of various types of funds maintained by districts, but for now it is sufficient to note that income and expenses are proper terminology in an activity account where sales of items in fact occur.

6. The confusing nature of cash basis accounting is apparent in this illustration. The student of education finance may be wondering how it is known, for example, that bookkeeping expenses are $20 when this expenditure item is not identified anywhere in Figure 7.1. The answer is simple insofar as the $20 amount can be found by simple math — $360 – $340 = $20 — but becomes complex when the misleading aspect of cash accounting is therein illustrated as well. While cash basis seems simpler, it is actually more complex because the authors knew that an unpaid expense claim for $20 had been entered into the accrual system. The same process is true for all the other difference shown in the example.

7. Malvern J. Gross and William Warshauer, *Financial Accounting Guide for Nonprofit Organizations* (New York: Wiley & Sons, 1979), 13.

8. Sam B. Tidwell, "Educational Accounting Procedures," in *Principles of School Business Management,* ed. R. Craig Wood (Reston, Va.: Association of School Business Officials, 1986), 121.

9. Gross, *Financial Accounting,* 13.

10. For detailed discussions on the use of Handbook II, see U.S. Government Printing Office, *State Educational Records and Reports Series: Handbook II, Revised* (Washington, D.C.: U.S. Government Printing Office, 1973); for the new standards recommended by the National Center for Educational Statistics, see U.S. Department of Education, *Financial Accounting for State and Local School Systems 1990* (Washington, D.C.: U.S. Department of Education, Office of Educational Research and Improvement, 1990).

11. Florida Department of Education, *Financial and Program Cost Accounting,* 1–4.

12. The inexactness of this statement is apparent in several ways. First, efforts to standardize reporting procedures over many years indicate a lack of conformity. For example, one of the major difficulties in interstate comparisons of educational data is the lack of uniformity in reporting. Second, there are variations in accounting procedures that are permitted by statute. For example, statutes themselves often create standards and then provide exemption. As an illustration, many states have statutes requiring municipalities to use Generally Accepted Accounting Principles (GAAP) in preparing financial reports and statements. At the same time, there are numerous states that have provided additional statutory authorization for some units such as school districts to waive GAAP requirements. The purpose of the statement in text is accurate for its purpose, however, which is to indicate that present standards represent vast improvement of accounting practices compared to history by virtue of events such as *Handbook II,* modified accrual basis, and fund accounting, which follows.

13. As used in this section, funds are not synonymous with monies, but are entities containing monies. Although this is confusing, it is a language discipline that needs to be developed by school administrators so that they at least use the term *fund* advisedly, if not discriminatingly.

14. Governmental Accounting Standards Board (GASB), *Codification of Governmental Accounting and Financial Reporting Standards* (Stamford, Conn.: Governmental Accounting Standards Board, 1987), sec. 1100.102.

15. GASB recommendations relevant to educational organizations and information on the efforts of the National Center for Educational Statistics efforts to standardize financial reporting systems for public schools may be found in *Financial Accounting for Local and State School Systems 1990.* The majority of this section is referenced to that document, Chapter 3, "Account Classifications," 17–40, and Chapter 7, "Account Classification Descriptions," 77–85.

16. For further detail see Tidwell, "Educational Accounting Procedures," 107–131.

17. William G. Droms, *Finance and Accounting for Nonfinancial Managers* (Reading, Mass.: Addison-Wesley, 1979), 34.
18. U.S. Department of Education, *Financial Accounting 1990,* 3–4.
19. Droms, *Finance and Accounting,* 36–37.
20. U.S. Department of Education, *Financial Accounting 1990,* 9.
21. Tidwell, *Financial and Managerial Accounting,* 17.
22. Ibid., 18–23.
23. Ibid., 10–11.
24. Ibid., 24–25.
25. Ibid., 24–33.
26. U.S. Department of Education, *Financial Accounting 1990,* 78.
27. The student of education finance should not be confused by the overlapping nature of these codes wherein zero is equal to undefined. For example, code 2000 support services further defined as support services to general administration becomes 2300. These are not separate numbers: the successive zeroes become defined wherein 2 represents support services, 3 represents general administration, and the remaining zeroes are as yet undefined.
28. GASB, *Codification of Standards,* sec. 1100.108.
29. Details for this section are taken from U.S. Department of Education, *Financial Accounting 1990,* 123–132.
30. Candoli, Hack, and Ray, *School Business Administration,* 159.
31. Ibid., 162.
32. William T. Hartman, *School District Budgeting* (Englewood Cliffs, N.J.: Prentice-Hall, 1988), 247.
33. Figures 7.5, 7.6, 7.7 are taken from U.S. Department of Education, *Financial Accounting 1990,* 123–132.
34. Candoli, Hack, and Ray, *School Business Administration,* 160.
35. Gross, *Financial Accounting,* 370.
36. Candoli, Hack, and Ray, *School Business Administration,* 160.

ADDITIONAL READINGS

American Institute of Certified Public Accountants. *Accounting and Financial Reporting by Governmental Units, Statements of Position 80-2.* New York: AICPA, 1980.

Droms, William G. *Finance and Accounting for Nonfinancial Managers.* Reading, Mass.: Addison-Wesley, 1979.

Gross, Malvern J., and William Warschauer. *Financial Accounting Guide for Nonprofit Organizations.* New York: Wiley & Sons, 1979.

Hay, L.E. *Accounting for Governmental and Municipal Entities.* 6th ed. Homewood, Ill.: Richard D. Irwin, Inc., 1980.

Hermanson, Roger, James Edwards, and Gayle Rayburn. *Financial Accounting.* 4th ed. Homewood, Ill.: Richard D. Irwin, Inc., 1989.

Lynn, E.S., and R.F. Freeman. *Fund Accounting: Theory and Practice.* 2d ed. Englewood Cliffs, N.J.: Prentice-Hall, 1983.

Tidwell, Sam B. *Financial and Managerial Accounting for Elementary and Secondary School Systems.* Reston, Va.: Association of School Business Officials, 1974.

U.S. Department of Education. *Financial Accounting for State and Local School Systems.* Washington, D.C.: Office of Educational Research and Improvement, 1990.

U.S. Government Printing Office. *State Educational Records and Reports Series: Handbook II, Revised.* Washington, D.C.: U.S. Government Printing Office, 1973.

CHAPTER 8

Planning for Personnel Administration

CHAPTER THEME

- Because labor costs are greater than just teacher salaries and because education's fiscal resources are overwhelmingly consumed by the labor function, the interaction between school finance and the personnel function is strong. As a result, administrators must understand this relationship and develop appropriate skills.

CHAPTER OUTLINE

- The role of the personnel function, including decisions about staffing, recruitment, and selection
- An in-depth review of issues and problems in personnel compensation policies
- Other important personnel-finance related issues, including merit pay, staff reduction, and due process concerns

CHAPTER OBJECTIVE

- A greater appreciation for the magnitude of personnel issues and a better understanding of the interrelationship of school finance to all other areas of school operation

In 1869, the average salary of instructional staff in public schools was $189 per year. By 1900, salaries had risen only to $325 annually over the 30-year period. But by 1930, salaries more than quadrupled, to $1,420 annually and the number of teachers was growing rapidly. By 1950, salaries had again more than doubled, to $3,010, and by 1970 had nearly tripled again, to $8,840. By 1990, salaries again quadrupled, to $33,041. These salaries were distributed to 2.7 million public K–12 teachers in the United States in 1990. At the same time, estimates place annual growth in the number of teachers at more than 200,000 new positions beginning in 1990 and continuing to the year A.D. 2000, while estimates also indicate dwindling numbers of students planning on teaching careers.

Under the conditions cited from various sources[1] with which we open this chapter, public school budgets appear to be in a state of crisis. Instructional salaries in the United States in 1990 reached the staggering sum of $91 billion. At the projected rate of increase in teaching staff and holding all salaries at 1990 levels, another $66 billion would be needed by the year A.D. 2000 to fund only those new positions. The sum of current and new salaries would reach $157 billion and, despite having more than doubled in only 10 years, would actually represent great losses in teacher salaries because no pay adjustments would have occurred over an entire decade. Given the other enormous amounts of money needed in education, the administrator may reasonably wonder whether the American public can continue to fund its educational system.

The enormous costs of public elementary and secondary education drive home the point that wise leadership in the arena of school finance is a vital prerequisite for a new generation of school administrators. Because labor costs go beyond teacher salaries and education's resources are overwhelmingly consumed by the labor function, no textbook on school finance should ignore the role of personnel. This chapter is therefore designed to help broaden the administrator's understanding of the personnel function in school finance by providing a better working knowledge of the major fiscal aspects of school personnel administration. The chapter begins by briefly considering the role of the personnel function, including decisions about staffing, recruitment, and selection. Because this textbook focuses on school finance, the subsequent section provides an in-depth review of issues and problems in personnel compensation policies. The last part of the chapter deals with several other important personnel-finance related issues, including merit pay, staff reduction, and due process concerns. The administrator should thus gain a greater appreciation for the magnitude of personnel issues and a better understanding of the interrelationship of school finance to all other areas of school operation.

THE PERSONNEL FUNCTION

No thinking person can deny that public elementary and secondary education in America is a labor-intensive industry. Well over 75% of nearly every school district budget in the United States is directly linked to personnel salaries and benefits. At the same time, however, these vast expenditures also have a positive effect on the economy, as teachers and other school personnel are consumers in the public marketplace. In the vast majority of school districts, salaries are returned to the local economy for housing, clothing, food, and luxuries. Additionally, school personnel also pay local taxes to support the education of all children. In a complex cycle, while the personnel function in public schools results in a salary cost to the public because money is removed from its owner to be used for "nonvoluntary" public good, the money is also invested because fully three-fourths of such dollars is used for salaries of personnel who in turn generally buy within the same school district and thus actually create far more employment than they consume.

The Scope of the Personnel Function

When most people think of school personnel, they think first about the professional teaching staff. While citizens are absolutely correct in placing teachers at the center of the school and in presuming that teachers outnumber all other personnel, their view is incomplete because the personnel function embraces a much larger group of persons by taking in both certified staff (i.e., teachers and other professional employees) and classified personnel (i.e., custodians, school bus drivers, teacher aides, cafeteria workers, and other noncertified workers). All of these persons occupy indispensable roles throughout the various operational aspects of the school district. As school districts have grown more complex and inclusive of the multiple concepts of equal educational opportunity, employment of both certified and noncertified employees has increased dramatically. The school personnel function is therefore a vast and comprehensive enterprise supporting one of the largest industries in the nation.

The size of the personnel function is exceeded only by its importance in successful district operations. Regardless of the efficacy of excellent management in the fiscal operations of a school district, the success of any school organization depends ultimately on the personnel who perform the multifaceted work of education. Selection, employment, and retention of quality people are thus *the key* to the most cost-effective operation of a school district. The critical nature of the personnel function has led most districts throughout the United States to centralize this key operation under a single office, with one person generally appointed to line authority over these operations. Although the titles vary among districts according to custom and even district size, an assistant superintendent for personnel, a director of human resource development, or even the superintendent of schools may have first responsibility for the personnel function of the school district. In many large school districts the responsibility is further subdivided. For example, the chief fiscal officer may also serve as the personnel director for support staff, while the director of human relations may serve as personnel officer for certified staff. Very importantly, in such districts certain aspects are likely centralized between the two offices, while others are clearly separated. The purpose of a centralized office is to ensure coordination of all vital aspects of the school district.

Regardless of how local personnel operations are structured, good personnel administration demands certain characteristics that assist in achieving the work of the district and link all areas of the school district under one umbrella. The umbrella and linkages should be provided in a board of education policy manual that contains written school board policies governing all aspects of personnel administration. Written policies assure uniform communication and, if properly prepared, assure a thoughtful relationship between the overall goals of the school district and expectations of personnel in achieving those goals. Policies must be clearly stated so as not to create confusion or ambiguity for either the employer or employee and to further form the basis for legal interpretation in the event of personnel disputes. An added benefit of such policies is to provide a blueprint for administrative action, which in turn has a greater opportunity for consistent actions enhancing employee morale and productivity. Because the quality of educational programs is obviously a product of the quality and harmony of all certified and noncertified staff, coordinated personnel operations are vital to an effective and efficient school district.

When the personnel function is properly assigned to an individual or a formal office, governed by written policies and procedures, and carried out in such a way as to enhance school productivity, a district can view the personnel function as one of simultaneous leadership and management. Implications for leadership are obvious, as a district that merely maintains the status quo cannot be constantly improving its performance in instructional programs. On the other hand, reliance on charismatic leadership to the neglect of proper management of the personnel function endangers the school district in many ways, including liability for the numerous problems that can arise. The district's overall goals and objectives cannot be fully met except through proper control and management of both instructional and noninstructional staff. Although it is sometimes hard to distinguish between the nuances of leadership versus management, the organizational and directive functions of personnel must be addressed if the district is to function properly because the entire school revolves around its personnel.

Personnel leadership and management are thus vital to successful educational operations. Accordingly, the personnel function can be viewed as having the following desirable and necessary goals:

1. *Determining staffing needs;*
2. *Recruiting and retaining* the most competent people;
3. *Assisting in the individual development* of competencies;
4. *Assuring that employees are assigned* and utilized efficiently;
5. *Increasing and improving employee satisfaction;* and
6. *Establishing clearly defined work expectations* along with competent evaluations.[2]

The personnel function thus involves leadership for improvement and management for performance assurance. Proper attention to these areas requires direct and active administrative involvement in determining staffing needs and in the recruitment, selection, orientation, compensation, evaluation, and retainment of each employee, as well as many other areas including potential termination. While a full exploration is beyond the scope of this textbook, four of these roles are so intimately related to both the personnel and finance functions of a school district that some discussion is warranted. These areas are determination of staffing needs, recruitment and selection of quality staff, employment compensation policies, and other general considerations relating to liabilities of districts under dismissal of employees.

Determining Staffing Needs.   Ability to properly determine staffing needs is generally a function of organizing and utilizing information about the district and potential employees. Because of their state aid reporting requirements and information needed to calculate federal and state payroll taxes, most school districts possess a relatively sophisticated database of employee information. Very often the database will include basic and descriptive data, such as each individual's salary, insurance costs, cost of sick leave days, and even projected retirement information for predicting voluntary and induced staff turnover. Information about the district is likely to be less well organized, especially since many districts believe they are too small to devote the necessary time and resources to forecasting district needs. Although districts are required to keep much information on their current employees, they should further develop and maintain an extensive database on staffing needs not only because the lack of comprehensive information can be devastating, but also because usage of data nearly always rises to meet its availability. Although data maintenance on such items as transportation and insurance is important, it is surprising that many districts fail to recognize the usefulness of extensive staffing files.

Information about the district and staffing are interrelated and should not be constructed separately. In every instance, the district's profile will drive staffing needs. The database should include current populations of the community and schools, percentage of households with children in school, the ages of all children preschool through twelfth grade, immigration and outmigration trends, commercial and industrial characteristics of the district, major sources and types of employment, income and age information on residents, and of course financial data on the needs of the school district. This information should then be used to project annual population estimates on three levels: high, moderate, and conservative.[3] In most states, population of the schools drives school funding, so it follows that the population of the community drives the school's population. In addition, the demographic information on the district is extremely helpful to finance and personnel functions in understanding and predicting the community's reactions to school expenditures. Under these conditions, it is also readily apparent that school population drives staffing needs.

Staffing needs are thus in large part a function of predicting the future of a community. Unfortunately, while many districts keep much employee information on file, it is not really organized or intended to assist in formally projecting future staffing needs. In the thousands of small districts today, information on employee certification is often kept in manual paper files and referred to only as needed. In larger districts, electronic databases are more common and almost always contain information on the qualifications of individuals, including areas such as professional certification or other qualifications and experience important when considering noncertified personnel. In larger districts, these files are also more likely to contain information on prospective employees and to have built-in projections of employee attrition rates by area and level.

Regardless of district size, however, a deliberate effort to build a community profile and employee database of comprehensively descriptive information should be made because such a database can be utilized to project whether the staffing needs of the district can be met internally and whether it will be necessary to engage in a traditional search for new employees or, under the worst conditions, make staff reductions at some future time. The employee database should go beyond retrieval of areas of certification and include the ability to make other useful projections, such as calculating the costs of early retirement programs and other personnel issues. Such information also overlaps with the finance function in that the cost of comparing early retirement to other alternatives, such as hiring less expensive staff, must be available for wise personnel decisions; similarly, projections indicating a need for new staff also require budget planning. Efficient use of a current database makes it possible for the district to engage in both descriptive assessment of present realities and future scenarios—an obviously critical function for the budget side of district planning and organization. In most instances, the basic database is established and maintained by the personnel office and should be electronically coordinated with the finance side.

Although each district develops it own database according to special needs, the end purpose is the same. The personnel and finance functions share similar information needs on many occasions, most frequently when staffing needs are being considered. For current employees in the system, the personnel function annually considers contract renewal, coordinating its decision with the finance function, which must secure the necessary revenue to pay for their continued presence. There are many times when the scenario is reversed, as the finance function determines that staffing is too costly and the personnel function must find a way to deal with economic realities. But although these functions are interdependent, the realities of the modern comprehensive school causes the personnel function to drive the fiscal side most often by informing the business office of next year's staffing needs.

Although a comprehensive community and staff database is essential to good personnel and finance practices, the technical process involved in determining staffing needs differs between states and among districts. For example, some states calculate the number of pupils at each grade level and allocate funds to each district on a per-classroom basis. Under such a scenario, the district has little control over the most basic personnel function of determining how many teachers the district will hire because it can obviously only afford to hire those teachers that the state aid formula permits and reimburses. In other states, local districts independently determine how many teachers to hire by choosing among competing expenditure categories within overall budgetary constraints, wherein for example the choice to reduce class sizes may be made at the expense of enlarging athletic programs. Among the individual districts in such states, these decisions are further driven by a variety of factors, including negotiated agreements and board policies. These differences make thorough discussion impossible in this introductory textbook, but the administrator needs to understand that personnel and finance are simultaneously driven by one another and sometimes additionally driven by external forces beyond district control and that all such forces help determine staffing needs.

Generally, staffing needs are thus a function of two distinct but interdependent events. First the state funding formula in all instances directly or indirectly determines the amount of freedom each individual district has in staffing decisions. That determination is a product of either statutorily allocating approved classroom units or by actively imposing fiscal constraints that do not mandate the number of positions but nonetheless effectively prevent unlimited staff hiring. Second, the discretionary design of local staffing policies determines the remainder of decisions about how staffing needs are met. It is especially important for administrators to appreciate the multiplicity of complex pressures on staffing decisions.

Both state and local governments thus exert powerful influences on determining staff needs. As a general rule, either or both governmental units tend to adopt some type of staffing ratio. At the state level, an example of a strongly centralized state formula allocating teacher positions to individual school districts is West Virginia's efficiency-driven staffing formula allocating each district 55 teacher positions for every 1,000 students (55:1000) and providing a 34:1000 service personnel ratio. Under this formula, severe reductions in staff have recently been required in rural areas that cannot meet the efficiency mandate given low enrollments and comprehensive programs.[4] Another state-driven example from the opposite perspective of concern about overly large classes is Oklahoma's reform mandates under House Bill 1017 passed by the 1990 Legislature, which mandated class size reductions to a 20:1 pupil-teacher ratio by 1995.[5] An example of localized decisions driving staffing needs is easily seen in districts with board policies or negotiated agreements on class sizes.

Most boards of education have become concerned about high pupil-teacher ratios, and in many instances have adopted policies calling for the hiring of new staff whenever class sizes in a grade level exceed stated maximums. A more complicated but common situation is similarly found when boards either have been required under state law to negotiate class size or have voluntarily negotiated such agreements. In any of the above instances, it should be clear that personnel and finance are tightly tied together.

Once the policies or law governing staffing in a district are known, it is a simple matter to apply a staffing formula when enrollment information becomes available. Whatever formula is used, the number of prospective students at each grade level is ultimately divided by the approved ratio, yielding the number of permissible staff positions. For example, the process can be mathematically expressed as:

$$\text{Enrollment/Approved Ratio} = \text{Staffing Needs}$$
$$\text{or}$$
$$1,327 \text{ fourth graders/20:1 ratio} = 66 \text{ fourth grade positions}$$

Funding these positions is thus clearly more difficult than calculating the staff requirements, and at times adjustments are required if funding is not available. Fortunately, the comprehensive database should be designed to assist in this process when combined with other personnel and finance activities, such as long-term enrollment projections. If the database reveals, for example, that other elementary grades in the district will lose the equivalent of more than 66 teaching positions, then the district can use the personnel database to reassign fourth grade teachers to other grades if their certification matches upcoming vacancies. Under such a scenario, the district might even have surplus teachers in the given year. Obviously this situation is more likely to occur as the size of districts increases because small districts may have only one person teaching at a single grade level. More likely, however, is that other grade enrollments will not offset these changes, necessitating still other personnel decisions about reassignment or reductions in force.

Determining staffing needs is thus both simple and complex—simple mathematically, but complex in that these decisions involve humans and multiple layers of governmental restraints that may apply and impact the district negatively. Regardless of the circumstance, good decisions cannot be made without a reliable and comprehensive database that takes into account both community and employee profiles. For example, administrators in the scenario just described might be able to relieve the anguish of involuntary staff reductions if the database provided information useful in statistically projecting future retirements or early contract buy-outs for employees approaching retirement. In a more positive vein, comprehensive data systems can be used for selective information sharing, such as in-house mailings to qualified employees when vacancies occur. For numerous reasons, a rational and deliberate plan for determining staffing is the first primary function of the personnel and finance offices.

Recruiting and Selecting Personnel.   When staffing needs have been determined, the next consideration must be recruitment of personnel. Regardless of the type of position, every employee classification should have an orderly recruitment plan. The school district needs to make decisions regarding the number and types of positions, as well as the minimal and desirable standards for each classification of

employee. For the school finance and personnel functions, the most obvious relationship occurs in issues of applicable pay and employee placement on the pay scale.

While in many states the pay scale is largely a function of collective bargaining
laws and the negotiations process in individual school districts, the goal of the finance
and personnel functions must be to attract and retain the most highly qualified individuals who may otherwise accept employment in the private sector. This goal is
obviously difficult to obtain because the purposes are at odds with a competing goal
of protecting the public treasury and the taxpayers of the school district. While no
good solutions are available, there are certain procedures in the recruiting process
that may lessen the harshness of these realities.

At the outset of the recruiting process, the finance and personnel functions
should collaborate to produce a written guidebook to the district. This book is so
important that it should be given to all current and prospective employees to familiar-
ize them with the rules and benefits the school district has provided to employees.
This document should set out a thorough description of the hiring process, beginning
with the application procedure and continuing through descriptions of how screen-
ing committees, interviews, contract offers, and pay periods and amounts will occur.
In addition, every current and prospective employee should be informed about training requirements and opportunities, and this information should convey a high degree of standardization consistent with the classification of each class of employees.
These procedures should be closely tied to any advertising by the district and standardized as to both internal and external search procedures consistent with race-neu-
tral hiring and selection of the best candidate for each vacancy.

When the policies and procedures for recruitment have been determined, the
district must engage in active recruiting. For larger districts this sometimes means
hiring on the basis of anticipated vacancies. Large school systems often visit teacher
recruitment fairs across the nation every year, hiring candidates for vacancies that
have not yet occurred but which from experience the district knows will become
available. In many instances, these districts are not engaging in risky behavior because
they know from unfortunate history that they will not be able to hire as many staff as
they have available positions. In other areas of the country, the process is less strenu-
ous, as districts advertise vacancies through placement bureaus and simply wait for
applications to arrive. Even here, however, the personnel and finance functions continue to overlap, as success is in part related to how well the teacher salary schedule is
designed and funded. Because many states do not have statewide teacher salary
schedules and in other instances allow local districts to pay more than the statewide
salary schedule, recruitment is a combined responsibility of wise personnel and finance planning.

When the district has successfully determined its staffing needs and recruited as
effectively as it can given any local limitations, the selection process follows. Because
the success of all district goals depends on the quality of personnel present in the
district, the selection process is a highly critical dimension. Even though the candidate field and price must interact in candidate selection, the first obligation of the
district is to select employees on the quality of skills the candidate brings to the position. Skills must be judged on the basis of specific training, experience, and prior
performance in like or similar positions. Additionally many positions, whether certified or not, require specific licensure from a state agency. Every position should be
filled only after the appropriate person, generally the superintendent, has made the
final recommendation to the board of education. A legal offer of employment cannot

be made unless the school board has made such an offer in a duly constituted public school board meeting in a lawful manner pursuant to applicable state statutes.

The overlapping and conflicting goals of the personnel and finance functions are most apparent at the time of selection. The goal of the personnel function is to select the most qualified person to perform the tasks associated with a given position. This goal is perfectly applicable whether the person is being interviewed for a classroom teaching position or a custodial position in the school district, and persons who are not qualified should be eliminated from consideration. The goal of the finance function is also to hire that same person, but under conditions that are impossible to optimally satisfy. The old adage "20 years old with 20 years' experience and willing to work for $20,000" poignantly describes the dilemma of parallel and cross purposes of the finance and personnel functions in the selection process. Because this is impossible and because resources in education are always too limited to achieve ideal conditions, some satisfactory middle ground must be found that assures selection of quality staff within current budgetary constraints.

The selection process involves several steps throughout the school district. Again, the selection process has the goal of employing the best candidate with the least possible employee turnover. From the beginning of the process to the end, the relationship between the personnel and finance functions should be apparent in that whatever employee is chosen, that person will be financially compensated by the district. Thus, the first step of personnel planning relates to the last step of placement in the most appropriate position and at the appropriate salary schedule amount. These interactive finance and personnel steps are best summarized as follows:

1. *Describing the role expectations* for the position;
2. *Assessing personal characteristics* needed to fit the role;
3. *Compiling appropriate information* on candidates;
4. *Evaluating candidates* on role and personal expectations;
5. *Rating the eligible candidates* on the criteria;
6. *Making the employment decision* from among choices;
7. *Making the employment offer* to the best candidate; and
8. *Placing the employee* in the most appropriate position.[6]

PERSONNEL COMPENSATION POLICIES AND PROCEDURES

Although many other personnel functions such as induction, orientation, and the like overlap with finance operations because they require money and make better trained and happier employees, we next turn to personnel compensation policies and procedures because this arena is where school finance and school business management are most conspicuous in personnel considerations. Additionally, personnel compensation is the next immediate focus after recruitment and selection, continuing throughout the employment relationship between a district and its employees. With rare exception, compensation of personnel is a centralized school district function housed in the school business office. This is not to say that the finance function assumes the total role, however, because in the vast majority of situations the personnel office continues to work closely with the finance office, especially regarding applicable statutes dealing with collective bargaining for teachers and support staffs.

Compensating Personnel

It is sufficient here, however, to recognize continued overlap and to focus on the financial compensation of employees, which takes many forms. Compensation must be seen as more than salaries because the amount of money a district provides to employees is much greater than their earned income. For example, compensation in all districts includes legal requirements for workers compensation insurance, unemployment insurance, and Social Security to name just a few. Additionally, employee compensation includes other voluntarily negotiated payments, such as various forms of health insurance and leave benefits. For example, time away from the job is often not deducted from pay, such as sick leave, bereavement leave, and personal leave days. There are also many other forms of direct and indirect compensation, such as supplemental salaries and merit pay awards.[7] Additionally, state retirement systems and district perks add to a long list of compensation items that most educators forget to include as nonsalary income for public school employees.

General Issues.   Because of the large number of teachers and school employees in the United States, the vast amount of compensation to these persons should not be surprising. The data in this chapter's epigraph noted that teacher salaries have increased from $189 per year in 1869 to an average $33,041 in 1990 and that in 1990 more than 2.7 million public school teachers were employed at a total average cost of more than $90 billion per year. The epigraph also noted that growth in the number of teachers is likely to continue, requiring more than 200,000 new positions by the end of the century. Needless to say, these amounts do not include the vast expenditures for nonteaching personnel, bringing the total to a truly phenomenal sum. Yet while the aggregated dollars are vast, individually there is no great capturing of wealth by public school teachers, as seen by the average teacher salaries for 1990–1991 in Table 8.1. The sum total of dollars, however, indisputably makes compensation an important topic for all school administrators.

Typically, however, most people first think of public school compensation structures in terms of direct salary payments. All school districts pay salaries to all employees, and by far the majority reward employees, particularly teachers, on a single salary schedule. Historically, the single salary schedule was the method of correcting great inequities that intentionally discriminated in compensation between black and white, male and female, and elementary and secondary teachers. Additionally, in many rural and urban school districts, teachers were paid based on political party affiliations and other nonmeritorious bases. The practice was so prevalent that in 1918 the National Education Association stated that no single salary schedule existed in a city school district in the nation.[8] Although the single salary schedule has many modern opponents arguing that a lockstep schedule promotes a flat organizational model and depresses individual merit, proponents have long held that the plan is vastly superior to other choices because it is said to promote positive noncompetitive working relations, is relatively inexpensive to administer, and avoids a host of problematic areas, such as favoritism and punishment for select teachers.[9] The concept has even affected states themselves, as many states have a minimum salary schedule specified in state statute.

The administration of all forms of compensation begins with determination and formulation of a job description for each person working in a school district. Complete and detailed written job descriptions should be developed for every classifica-

TABLE 8.1 Estimated average salaries of public school teachers, 1990–1991

1.	Connecticut	$43,808	27.	Florida	$30,555
2.	Alaska	43,435	28.	Kansas	29,767
3.	New York	42,080	29.	Georgia	29,172
4.	California	39,598	30.	North Carolina	29,165
5.	District of Columbia	39,568	31.	Kentucky	29,089
6.	New Jersey	38,411	32.	Wyoming	28,988
7.	Maryland	38,382	33.	Maine	28,531
8.	Michigan	38,326	34.	Missouri	28,492
9.	Rhode Island	37,674	35.	Texas	28,321
10.	Massachusetts	36,090	36.	South Carolina	28,300
11.	Pennsylvania	36,057	37.	Tennessee	29,248
12.	Delaware	35,200	38.	Iowa	27,977
13.	Illinois	34,605	39.	Alabama	27,300
14.	Minnesota	33,130	40.	Montana	26,695
15.	Wisconsin	33,100	41.	Nebraska	26,592
16.	Washington	33,075	42.	Louisiana	26,240
17.	Ohio	32,615	43.	New Mexico	26,194
18.	Hawaii	32,541	44.	West Virginia	25,967
19.	Virginia	32,382	45.	Idaho	25,485
20.	Oregon	32,300	46.	Utah	25,045
21.	Nevada	32,209	47.	Mississippi	24,366
22.	Indiana	32,044	48.	Oklahoma	24,284
23.	Colorado	31,819	49.	North Dakota	23,578
24.	New Hampshire	31,273	50.	Arkansas	23,040
25.	Vermont	30,986	51.	South Dakota	22,363
26.	Arizona	30,733			
	Mean $33,041				
	Median $30,773				
	Range $21,445				

SOURCE: National Education Association, *Rankings of the States, 1991* (Washington, D.C.: NEA), 21. Reprinted by permission.

tion of employee. If done properly, these are based on surveys, interviews, and assessments of what every job classification will be expected to perform if efficient utilization of staff is to occur. The job description should be designed so that it is not ambiguous, and job descriptions should be very clear so that all parties can reach agreement regarding the nature, duties, and expectations of each position. Every position should thus have a specific and performance-oriented job description that includes statements about the method and amount of compensation. Evaluation of performance based on the goals of job descriptions can then systematically follow, and performance should form the basis for an employee's position in the salary structure. Obviously, job descriptions vary from position to position. For example, the job description of an elementary building principal would be significantly different and more complex than the job description for a secretary in that building. Examples of job descriptions and their differences are given in Figures 8.1 and 8.2.

While the job description should result in neutral salary decisions based on systematic employee placement according to district salary schedule policies, administrators should recognize that the actual salary structure itself is typically a function of two discrete realities affecting certified and classified employee groups. In some

Position Title Elementary School Principal
Reports to Assistant Superintendent
Supervises Certificated Staff Assigned. Classified Staff Assigned

Basic Function:

Administers the program of the elementary school according to the policies of the Board of Education and under the supervision of the Assistant Superintendent. Provides educational leadership to both faculty and students; manages and directs all activities concerned with the supervision and administration of an elementary school.

Performance Responsibilities:

*   Demonstrates leadership through values, beliefs, skills, and personal characteristics that inspire people to accomplish the District/school mission.
*   Ensures that teachers plan and provide effective instruction to accomplish the school's goals based on the tenet that teachers believe all students can learn and expect them to succeed.
*   Monitors, assesses, and supervises the implementation of the approved District curriculum.
*   Develops an effective staff development program for all members of the staff based on needs assessments, including recommendations from participants.
*   Promotes positive school climate by encouraging capabilities and emphasizing the worth of all individuals, while maintaining enthusiasm and learning among students, teachers, and parents.
*   Uses a variety of data to improve the school's instructional program, such as surveys and interviews regarding climate for learning, attendance, parent participation, as well as other measures of student assessment and evaluation based on defined outcomes of the curriculum.
*   Coordinates the cooperative development of a written statement of the school's beliefs and goals, and uses them in planning and updating the school's educational objectives, annually.
*   Determines whether the individual educational needs of pupils are being met: develops plans to improve the quality and adequacy of instruction, annually.
*   Evaluates the performance of the certified and classified staff members regularly assigned, and offers guidance, support, and assistance, as needed.
*   Interprets, implements, and maintains the integrity of Board policies, State school laws, and administrative practices and procedures.
*   Develops a program of public relations to further community understanding and support of the school's and School District's educational program.
*   Administers the school's budgeted allocations and recommends annual budget requirements.
*   Directs activities involving pupil/parent contacts concerning registrations, credits and transfers, suspensions, expulsions, pupil progress and adjustment, pupil placement, guidance and counseling matters, and other matters of a personal nature.
*   Possesses a thorough understanding of practical applications of child growth and development.
*   Identifies/applies effective strategies for dealing with political issues and forces that impinge upon the school's operation.
*   Engages in a program of continuing professional development; participates as a member of local, state, and national professional groups.
*   Orients newly assigned staff members and ensures their familiarization with school policies/procedures, teaching materials and school facilities, and assists in their development, as appropriate.
*   Creates a strong sense of togetherness through effective human relations techniques.
*   Possesses skills in the use of conflict resolution methods, various decision-making techniques, and the process of consensus building.
*   Performs other related duties as requested.
*   Requirements: Minimum of Master's degree in elementary education or school administration: possession of a valid certificate or the ability to obtain it prior to employment. Five years elementary teaching experience. Salary commensurate with experience by placement on the administrative salary schedule. Broad in-depth knowledge of elementary programs: ability to plan, organize, supervise, and evaluate; ability to resolve conflicts; ability to communicate effectively in both speaking and writing; ability to work with professional and lay publics; knowledge and appreciation for the ethnic and cultural diversity of the District's population.

FIGURE 8.1 Sample position description

SOURCE: Adapted and modified from the Denver Public Schools, Division of Personnel Services.

Qualifications: Ability to type, file, keep records, and take shorthand at 80 words per minute.

Reports to: Principal

Job Goal: To provide the necessary secretarial services to properly operate the public school system.

Job Functions:

1. Assigns duties to and supervises the work of all clerical personnel within the school.
2. Provides input to the administrator on the evaluations of clerical personnel.
3. Responsible for typing and processing all confidential correspondence.
4. Provides the technical skills of typing, filing, record keeping, and taking and transcribing shorthand and all other means of communication.
5. Maintains and updates reports, prescribed administrative lists, inventories, attendance records, and other similar records which are modified frequently.
6. Serves as one of the school office receptionists and as the first-line public relations staff member when answering phone calls, responding personally to staff, students, parents, and community members, when greeting people in person.
7. Understands and is able to operate office equipment including typewriters, dictating equipment, duplicating machines, photo-copiers, adding machines, and other similar equipment.
8. Prepares certain administrative reports, communications, memoranda, legal notices, employment and vendor contracts, purchase orders, and work orders.
9. Coordinates the activities and schedule of the supervising administrator permitting him/her to perform as efficiently and effectively as possible.
10. Responds appropriately to all concerns and complaints from the public and staff and assists in providing an answer or remedy.
11. Conducts special activities in accordance with the specific job assignment, such as the annual school election and high school graduation.
12. Has a working knowledge of the business and budgeting procedures as well as the legal obligations of the department in which he/she works.
13. Receives and distributes mail and other messages.
14. Provides other necessary secretarial services as requested by the supervising administrator.
15. Salary shall be paid according to years of experience and educational training in strict accordance with the district's board-approved secretarial salary schedule.

FIGURE 8.2 Job description: Middle school secretary

SOURCE: Adapted and modified from Galloway Township Public Schools (New Jersey).

states, collective bargaining procedures apply to both groups. In other states, teacher organizations bargain under collective negotiations while classified employees and administrators are outside the collective negotiations law. In such instances, nonteaching staff salaries are often a function of prevailing wages obtained through informal comparisons between competing school districts. Once salaries are in place, however, the annual adjustments to salaries across employee classifications are more likely to be a function of relatedness between percentage increases. For example, it is normally unlikely for administrators to receive a much higher percentage salary increase than teachers simply because of the negative aspect of public relations and employee harmony. In states where nonteaching staff do not have legal bargaining status, it is far more likely that such salaries will be determined immediately after collective negotiations for teachers are completed, and percentage increments will follow fairly closely.

Negotiations.   The financial aspect of collective bargaining can be quite intensive and complex. Because so much is at stake, both financially and in terms of harmonious productivity, it is important that all parties develop significant trust and respect for each side's information and position. Many school districts hold informal discussions on a frequent basis throughout the year regarding mutual areas of concern, including compensation practices. These discussions should always be with the appropriate association leaders so as not to commit an unfair labor practice. School districts in the state of New York, for example, heavily utilize labor management committees for this purpose.[10] Throughout each school year and even in multiple year contracts, it is important to establish clear and concise communications with all bargaining groups so as to better facilitate the negotiations process.

The negotiations process is different in every state because of different collective bargaining laws. In principle, however, the steps are fairly similar depending on the extent to which arbitration is required. At whatever time of year discussions actually begin, the financial office is generally called upon by the personnel division to produce finance data, determine the validity of fiscal projections, and engage in cost analyses of all salary proposals. The reason is that the actual true short- and long-range costs must be determined for all proposals before the board of education can agree to a given plan. The finance office must be skilled in providing cost analyses for every proposal and must include not only the direct costs of salary and fringe benefits, but also the issues of cash flow, costs of employee time, and other items requested to be negotiated. Each of these issues must be analyzed in terms of both present and future costs and in terms of the long-range impact on the financial health of the district.

After these data are collected and verified by both sides, the true negotiation process begins. The school administrator should understand that agreement on the facts makes collective bargaining easier because management's position at the bargaining table, the potential of favorable settlement at impasse and arbitration, and the union's level of openness will all be enhanced. The data on which agreement should be reached include cash flow projections, the impact of such data on the school district, historical data related to the issue, and data showing how the school district compares to other school districts of similar financial status within the state and region.[11] Such careful and meticulous preparation and presentation will always enhance the potential for prevailing at the bargaining table as well as favorable treatment in potential fact-finding reports and arbitration awards.

The goal of both sides during the bargaining process is to have a reasonable discussion and agreement on the facts necessary to determine a fair and just salary. When that agreement is reached, the amounts will be applied to the various salary schedules. For example, for certified teaching staff, the most direct impact is on adjustment to the single salary schedule, both in dollars applied and in changes to the structure of the schedule itself. For noncertified staff, the impact will occur either in similar application to a salary schedule or in specific adjustment to each individual's contracted salary amount. These goals of fairness must also be extended to the fringe benefit package for employees of the school district. Thus, data that reflect the need to attract and retain quality personnel, as well as to encourage the professional growth of employees, must be balanced with the ability of the local school district to sustain the costs of the contract.

During the negotiation process, both sides generally come to the table with pre-planned items they wish to negotiate. Preparation on the part of the administrative unit generally focuses on collection and examination of several types of fiscal data relating to general knowledge required to negotiate and any other concerns held by the district. The employee organization also has an interest in these items, although for a somewhat different purpose. Generally, the items both sides bring to the table are fairly common and include:

1. *The strengths and weaknesses* of the current schedule and the entire contract;
2. *The current salary schedule,* including the number and actual costs of each cell of the matrix over the life of the contract and a reasonable projection into the near future;
3. *Basic data* regarding the minimum, maximum, and actual average cost per employee over the life of the contract;
4. *Comparative salaries* in competing school districts and industries;
5. *The living standards* of the local community;
6. *Personnel turnover* as well as pending retirements;
7. *Movement on the salary schedule* due to advanced training as well as scale movements;
8. *New programmatic needs* and curtailments; and
9. *Future revenues* and expenditures, including school district levies and state aid projections.

In addition, the school district and employee group will need to gather and bring other data of a nonfinancial qualitative nature. Most generally this consists of such issues as:

1. Which portions of the contract have worked well and have not worked well in the past;
2. Which sections of the contract have presented particularly difficult situations for management or employees;
3. Which sections of the contract should be modified or dropped entirely;
4. What comments or complaints have been raised by employees during the life of the contract;
5. Whether there has been a pattern of grievances over portions of the contract; and
6. What new issues have been raised by employees that may prove to be problematic.[12]

These data are vital to the negotiations process and to compensation policies, since without these data the costs are unobtainable and ability to fund a future contract is largely unknown. Thus, the fiscal integrity of the school district may be jeopardized through a lack of such fiscal data. It is also important to note that these data must be constantly updated based on the latest and best information available to the school district for up-to-date decision making.

While terms and conditions of employment make up a significant part of collective negotiations, the most elemental aspect comes when salary is discussed, for it is then that the personnel and finance functions are most intimately related—if a satisfactory contract agreement cannot be made, the personnel function suffers badly through staff attrition. Children are likely to be harmed as well, because low employee morale cannot but be revealed in various ways, no matter how diligently professional people guard against it. It is therefore helpful for administrators to know and understand the most common areas of potential problems in salary negotiations and to recognize and be wary of predictable pitfalls.

For certified staff, discussions over salary are likely to center on changing the structure of the salary schedule and on increasing the dollar amount at the base. Figure 8.3 illustrates a salary schedule for a small school district as a good example of how contract negotiations will likely occur in the majority of districts. The student of school finance is most likely very familiar with such schedules, but three observations should be stated before looking at probable scenarios surrounding salary discussions. First, the actual salary schedule itself appears at the top of the figure. Second, the location of every teaching staff member can be found by cell location in the middle portion of the figure. Third, the costs to the district of changing the schedule can be found at the bottom. Figure 8.3 thus provides a basis for some extended discussion of the negotiations process.

Although no two districts negotiate in exactly the same way, it is highly likely that teachers will propose three changes to the salary schedule seen in Figure 8.3. The first proposed change will be to increase the base salary amount. Both the teachers and the district know this has the effect of changing every other step in the schedule because salary schedules are almost always step-dependent. In other words, increasing the base salary will increase every other salary that appears on the schedule. The second proposed change will likely be increasing the number of columns beyond the master's degree, perhaps to embrace a specialist or doctorate degree. Salary schedules now commonly go well beyond the master's degree and in some instances take in a doctorate. The third proposed change will likely be to add steps at the bottom of some or all columns to increase rewards for longevity of service. Board proposals, on the other hand, will attempt to negotiate more restrictive language on nonsalary items such as leaves, and try to minimize the amount of changes to the salary schedule itself. Almost everyone recognizes the futility of board attempts to negotiate any other items—for example, negotiating a salary decrease is highly unlikely.

As a probability of occurrence, the three changes proposed by the teacher group have a sizable chance for success. Further, these changes seem reasonable to almost everyone. But all three changes must be considered very carefully by both the personnel and finance functions of the district. The first change of increasing the base is illustrated in Figure 8.3, in which the proposed salary schedule has built in an increase of 2.9% in the base, up from $17,100 in the current year. By increasing the base 2.9%, a ripple effect will occur throughout the schedule, as every other step will take at least the same increase and perhaps more. This is because each step is a function of the prior step. For example, a teacher on Step 1 will get not only the 2.9% base increase, but also another 2.4% reward for staying in the district and moving to Step 2. Thus for just one teacher, the cost to the board for raising the base by 2.9% is actually 5.3%. Often increments between steps are progressively greater with more years' experience. Given the relative maturity of teaching staffs in the United States, care must be taken because as salary schedules load to the right side, they become surprisingly costly. The first change proposed by teachers is thus usually far more expensive than the apparent increase in base salary.

The financial cost of the second teacher proposal to increase the number of columns beyond the master's degree cannot be calculated precisely from the data in the figure because many decisions would have to be made about how a new column should be constructed. The general impact of such a proposal can be seen, however.

APPROVED SALARY SCHEDULE FOR

BA + 0	BA + 15	BA + 30	Master's
17,600	17,865	17,946	18,302
18,024	18,296	18,380	18,747
18,589	18,728	18,815	19,192
19,155	19,301	19,393	19,785
19,578	19,880	19,972	20,378
20,144	20,456	20,552	20,972
20,710	21,031	21,131	21,566
21,416	21,608	21,710	22,159
	22,184	22,289	22,753
	22,760	22,868	23,345
		23,302	23,790
		23,737	24,384
			24,978
			25,720
			26,460
			27,202
			27,944
			28,686

Name	Current Cell	New Cell	Frozen?	Current Salary	Proposed Salary	Cost Inc. Increment	Fringe Package	Proposed Package	% Package Increase
	C14	C14(F)	YES	22,114	22,760	646	1,549	24,309	102.73 %
	A5	A6	No	17,100	18,024	924	1,549	19,573	104.96 %
	G18	G19	No	24,989	26,460	1,471	1,549	28,009	105.54 %
	E16	E16(F)	YES	23,063	23,737	674	1,549	25,286	102.74 %
	G17	G18	No	24,268	25,720	1,452	1,549	27,269	105.62 %
	A9	A10	No	19,022	20,144	1,122	1,549	21,263	105.45 %
	E16	E16(F)	YES	23,063	23,737	674	1,549	25,286	102.74 %
	A8	A9	No	18,611	19,578	967	1,549	21,127	104.90 %
	A11#.70+250	A12#.57	YES	14,815	12,457	2,358	883	13,340	84.98 %
	G22#.40+250	G22#.40	YES	11,398	11,724	326	619	12,343	102.72 %
	G21.5	G22	No	27,511	28,686	1,175	1,549	30,235	104.01 %
	A7.5	A8.5	No	18,336	19,366	1,030	1,549	20,915	105.18 %
	E16	E16(F)	YES	23,063	23,737	674	1,549	25,286	102.74 %
	E16	E16(F)	YES	23,063	23,737	674	1,549	25,286	102.74 %
	E15	E16	No	22,640	23,737	1,097	1,549	25,286	104.54 %
				9,138					
	C14	C14(F)	YES	22,114	22,760	646	1,549	24,309	102.73 %
	C14	C14(F)	YES	22,114	22,760	646	1,549	24,309	102.73 %
	C14	E16	No	22,114	23,737	1,623	1,549	25,286	106.86 %
	C14	C14(F)	YES	22,114	22,760	646	1,549	24,309	102.73 %
	C10#.5+250	C11#.50	No	10,187	10,766	579	774	11,540	105.28 %
	E16	E16(F)	YES	23,063	23,737	674	1,549	25,286	192.74 %
	A6	A7	No	17,512	18,589	1,077	1,549	20,138	105.65 %
	E16	E16(F)	YES	23,063	23,737	674	1,549	25,286	102.74 %
TOTALS				$509,464	$518,915	$9,451	$34,805	$553,720	103.27 %

CURRENT PACKAGE IN DOLLARS: 544,992
PROPOSED PACKAGE COST IN DOLLARS: 553,720

DOLLARS TO FUND NEW: $ 8,727.71

APPROXIMATE EFFECT ON MILL RATE (ALL OTHER FACTORS CONSTANT)
APPROXIMATE COST TO FUND PROPOSED SCHEDULE IN LOCAL MILLS

FIGURE 8.3 Sample salary schedule matrix

For next year, only those teachers with college credits beyond the master's degree would qualify for horizontal movement to a new column. Assuming all teachers now in the masters column could move, a very expensive impact could result from this proposal. Presently three teachers would qualify. As might be expected, these teachers are experienced and well educated, with the least experienced person having been in the district for 18 years. By adding another column, these persons again would be nearly at the bottom right side. The effect is cumulative: each of these teachers will have yet another year's experience by next school term, entitling them to an additional 2.6% vertically in the master's column. If the other columns are predictive of the salary increase gained by adding additional columns, these teachers could receive another sizable increase. For example, teachers with 12 years' experience and a master's degree now receive 2.7% more than a 12-year teacher with a bachelor's plus 30 hours. On this assumption, adding another column could give 2.6% vertically and 2.7% horizontally for a total cost of 5.3% in addition to the proposed base increase of 2.9%. The total percentage involved in adding another column could thus run as high as 8.2%. Salaries at the top end of the salary schedule can therefore become expensive. Although boards often want to increase the base salary amount, there are drawbacks of a costly nature.

The third teacher proposal to add steps to existing columns can be expensive as well. The purpose of such a proposal, of course, is to "unfreeze" teachers who have bottomed out on experience in a given salary schedule column. In Figure 8.3 there are 10 frozen teachers. Adding steps will immediately multiply against their salaries. The cost is potentially much higher than it first appears, however, as we should note from data in the middle of the figure that none of these persons is frozen in the last column. In other words, unknown to the district, each teacher could have returned to a college campus during the year and be planning to move horizontally on the salary schedule. Adding vertical steps to existing columns is always expensive, and in this instance could be a very big expense.

The data contained in this simple salary schedule has many benefits to the administrator. One of the most important benefits is the ability to automate the salary schedule for instant "what if" scenarios. Figure 8.3 was prepared in a microcomputer spreadsheet with each cell referenced to another cell, so that if the base amount is changed, all other cells containing calculated values instantly update. Another important benefit accrues to both sides. When the data are agreed upon, both sides can see the effect and reasonableness of proposals. It should be recognized that both sides also profit from the entire negotiations process in that although the board will have to increase salaries next year, it does so in exchange for the least amount possible at which it can still purchase happy employees. It is thus important that school board members and administrators, as well as the public as a whole, understand that collective bargaining is a series of compromises and that it is rare when one side has complete success on every point.[13] By anticipating staffing needs, recruiting and selecting the best staff, and preparing and using data appropriately for personnel compensation, both sides have a better chance of reaching an acceptable level of compromise.

Whatever the set of proposals that come to the table, several features must be recognized and accepted. Negotiations have the potential to be highly confrontive, but such opportunity should be minimized through openness and trust whenever possible. Neither the personnel nor finance functions should take negotiations lightly because these costs reverberate throughout the district's budget—that is, a decision to meaningfully improve the salary schedule will likely negatively impact other operations, while not improving salaries is destructive to long-term district health. An average increase of 3% in teacher salaries, for example, will also likely result in 3% increases for all nonteaching staff, including administrators. The multiplicative nature of these events can be costly when a simple 3% increase is costed out across vertical and horizontal dimensions of the teachers' single salary schedule, across noncertified salary structures, and across all district administrators. In most instances, state aid increases are not sufficient to cover these costs, making it necessary to either raise taxes or rob some other district operation.

It can therefore be clearly seen that instead of sitting on the sideline, the personnel and finance functions are often directly involved in the negotiations process through production of data, costing out proposals, and working with both sides in search of agreement. In many instances, the board's negotiator may actually be a district administrator. In some districts, the superintendent of schools serves as the chief negotiator, even though consensus of the field and literature suggest that this role may be counterproductive. In other instances, the assistant superintendent for personnel and/or finance may serve in the lead board role. In still other instances, the chief negotiator is an attorney, selected either for adroitness or "impartiality." Regardless of who serves as the board's chief negotiator, the personnel and finance officers of the district should be intimately aware of the progress of negotiations and consulted frequently to determine the viability of actions under consideration.

No matter who serves in the lead role for the board, there are requisite skills and knowledge that must be present. The chief negotiator must be knowledgeable about the collective bargaining statute in effect and the conditions of unfair labor practice and experienced in such matters in the public sector. Additional attributes include personal skills such as maturity, articulation, and flexibility in thinking and the ability to reject proposals without invoking the fury of the opposing side.[14] In addition to factual knowledge and specific training and skills, the negotiator must have certain additional qualities that remain consistently evident throughout the process:

1. the spokesperson should be articulate and mature;
2. the spokesperson should have the ability to continually assess the impact of events;
3. the spokesperson should have the ability to keep accurate negotiating records;
4. the spokesperson should have the ability to organize and engage in orderly communication; and[15]
5. the spokesperson should have the ability to work constructively with every member of the negotiations committee.[16]

Beyond the spokesperson, the bargaining team normally consists of the chief financial officer, a recorder, a subcommittee of the school board, and others as deemed appropriate. This team's composition will vary by custom among school districts. What is most critical is that the bargaining team possess expertise particularly in the areas of "industrial relations, negotiations, labor law, school law, education, [and] school finance."[17] Generally, the bargaining unit is represented by a spokesperson who may be an attorney, a paid association official, or other such person. Each school district will be different in the culture of negotiations. As a broad generalization, most negotiating sessions follow the custom that only spokespersons may speak, that written initial nonexpandable proposals must be formally exchanged, that meetings are closed to the public, and that each team records its own notes. Generally, caucuses may be unlimited unless agreed otherwise. Each state varies in statutory guidelines and in local school district custom. For example, in some states sessions may not be closed to the public. The scope of a sample state negotiations law is provided in Figure 8.4.

FIGURE 8.4 Sample scope of negotiations law

SOURCE: K.S.A. 72-5413 *et seq* as amended.

Mandatorily Negotiable*

1. Salary
2. Wages
3. Pay under supplemental contracts
4. Hours of work procedure
5. Amounts of work
6. Vacation allowance
7. Holiday leave
8. Sick leave
9. Extended leave
10. Sabbatical leaves
11. "Other" leaves
12. Number of holidays
13. Retirement
14. Jury duty
15. Grievance procedure
16. Binding arbitration
17. Disciplinary
18. Resignations
19. Contract termination
20. Contract nonrenewal
21. Reemployment
22. Contract terms
23. Contract form
24. Probationary period
25. Evaluation
26. Insurance benefits
27. Overtime pay

In addition, the following items are rights of the bargaining agent (association). These items are mandatorily negotiable. The statute sets the following as absolute minimum, i.e., the list is specifically unlimited.

1. Voluntary payroll deductions
2. Use of school facilities for association meetings
3. Dissemination of negotiations information through direct contact
4. Use of bulletin boards
5. Use of school mail
6. Leaves of absence for members for union activities.

Permissibly Negotiable*

1. Academic and personal freedom (except constitutional)
2. Assignment and transfer of personnel
3. Association rights (in excess of those in statute)
4. Class size
5. Classroom management
6. School library hours
7. Teacher copyrights
8. Facilities, equipment, materials, supplies
9. Grading frequency
10. Security
11. Substitutes
12. Teacher aides

Non negotiable*

1. Number of days or total hours of school
2. Nondiscrimination
3. Special education placement procedures
4. Teacher discipline if constitutional issue
5. First Amendment issues
6. Affirmative action
7. Student discipline if constitutional issue
8. Federal programs

*Negotiations items cited herein are taken from one state's statutes. No inference to all states can be made.

Unfortunately despite best intentions, negotiations do sometimes fail to reach agreement and go to impasse. Under most states' laws, school districts are required to recognize impasse and to engage in fact-finding, followed either by binding arbitration or unilateral board contracts. Generally, impasse and fact-finding occur when the parties cannot reach agreement on terms and conditions of a new contract by some date specified by law. For both the personnel and finance functions, failure to successfully negotiate a contract is a stressful event that introduces much uncertainty and tension into employer-employee relations that are difficult to overcome.

When contract negotiations reach impasse, most states' statutes invoke a time line calling for an individual to be appointed to review the last best proposals from both sides and to determine the facts and issue a report (see Figure 8.5). This person, depending on individual state laws, may be a state employee of the employment relations board or a person approved by some other state agency. Generally, fact-finding in most states is not binding, but is persuasive to the parties. If the parties still cannot

FIGURE 8.5   Sample negotiation law time line

Date	Time Lapse	
Feb. 1		Exchange notices to negotiate or proposals.
	no limit	Commence long, hard negotiation sessions.
	no limit	A petition may be filed by either party or jointly with the Secretary for declaration of impasse.
June 1		Parties shall jointly file notice of existence of impasse with Secretary.
	five days	Excluding Saturdays, Sundays and holidays. Conferences, consultations and/or discussions to be held by Secretary as needed. If hearing is necessary it shall be held immediately.
	no limit	Secretary either: 1. Finds no impasse exists, issues findings and rulings to that effect and orders parties to continue negotiation; or 2. Finds an impasse exists and commences the impasse procedures.
	Forthwith	The Secretary appoints a mediator.
	seven days	Anytime after the seven day period either party or both may report to the Secretary that mediation has failed and within ten days of such notification request the appointment of a fact-finding board.
	Forthwith	The Secretary shall immediately notify the other party. Within three days thereafter each of the parties shall present to the Secretary a written description of the impasse issues and the party's final position on each. The Secretary shall appoint a fact-finding board of not more than three members and shall supply each party's memorandum on issues to the other.
	ten days	The fact-finding board shall submit privately to the parties and the Secretary findings and recommendations. Either the board of education or the association may release the report upon receipt.
	seven days	The parties may agree to an extension not to exceed seven days for the fact-finding board to report.
	ten days	Parties must meet at least once after receipt of the report in an effort to reach agreement.
	ten days	The Secretary shall make the report public ten days after receipt.
	seven days	The board of education and the association may agree to extend the confidentiality of the fact finder's report an additional seven days.
	Not specified	The board of education shall take such action as it deems in the interest of the public and the professional employees.

reach agreement after fact-finding, however, several states require mediation and/or binding arbitration. In theory, mediation always precedes arbitration. In practice, however, each state's statutes are somewhat unique. In several states, binding arbitration is immediately invoked so that an impartial panel issues a report and both sides must by law comply with the decision of the report. Short of charging illegal behavior, such a ruling cannot be challenged in court unless it can be successfully argued that the arbitrator exceeded legal authority under the state statutes. In other states, however, the process simply calls for impasse, fact-finding, mediation by some approved person such as a federal mediator, and the issuance of unilateral contracts by the board of education if agreement still cannot be reached. In both instances, a statutory time line strictly applies.

In states where binding arbitration exists, the finance and personnel functions are prevented from issuing contracts, setting budgets, and a host of other important activities until negotiations are finally settled. Such procedure is uncomfortable for both sides, who often continue to work side-by-side, particularly in states where public employee strikes are prohibited. Even more complex, however, is the total subjection of the district to the will of the arbitrator, who may make a decision that is financially difficult for the district to obey. In states with no binding arbitration, issues are just as tense, but the personnel and finance functions can usually resume operations at an earlier date, and salary costs in unilateral contract states are obviously in greater control.

Depending on the state, these negotiations processes are repeated in some degree of formality with each employee group. But when contracts are finally settled through negotiations, a major role of the personnel and finance functions is complete and these divisions are able to resume a cooperative employer-employee relationship in which the new contract must be administered on a daily basis.

OTHER ISSUES OF PERSONNEL AND FINANCE

Although the most intensive interaction of the personnel and finance functions in a school district occurs through contract negotiations, there are many other important instances of collaboration. For administrators, three particular broad areas of mutual interest are important because they may impact heavily on compensation structures and liability for court financial awards for some time into the future. These areas are proposals for merit pay for teachers, reduction in force and other staff dismissals, and due process concerns.

Merit Pay

The concept of merit pay for instructional and noninstructional staff has been in public education for a very long time. Numerous school districts have experimented with merit pay plans for many years, with merit pay for classroom teachers making its first formal appearance in 1908 in Newton, Massachusetts.[18] During the 1920s interest in merit pay grew, with the greatest interest peaking in the 1950s.[19] Although interest has followed cycles that alternately peak and wane according to various societal pressures, the concept of merit pay has never either completely died out or been adopted on a wide scale. Presently, however, merit pay plans seem to be receiving renewed interest as education accountability and antitax movements have recently gained momentum in the United States.

Merit pay plans are not designed to simply award employees additional compensation for additional duties. Such an approach is better described as a career ladder, which is designed to encourage outstanding teachers to stay in classroom teaching by increasing their responsibilities with an increase in pay.[20] In contrast, merit pay is designed to reward employee performance toward schoolwide or districtwide goals.[21] The basis for merit pay has thus been initially sensible, but its application has been both reasonable and highly illogical. Some of the call for merit pay has been laudable, such as Cubberley's view in 1916 that a merit pay plan would provide a better distribution of financial rewards and reverse the 25%–50% staff turnover then common in the teaching profession.[22] More recently *Nation at Risk* called for evaluation systems designed to facilitate reward for superior classroom teaching in response to declining achievement scores. On the illogical side, however, have been the persistent cries of critics of education who angrily condemn schools for poor performance, calling for dismantling the education system as the only solution to a poor investment.

Current proposals for merit pay vary greatly in their conceptual frameworks. Generally, present merit pay plans seem to have arisen from renewed interest in educational accountability among state legislators who are receiving pressure for reform from among their constituents. These plans are frequently offered in response to crises of a current moment and are not often accompanied by long-term financing plans.[23] Consequently, the structure of most current merit pay plans is based on a one-time award for meritorious performance which does not extend beyond the year of the award, although an outstanding employee may be rewarded in merit pay in unlimited consecutive years based on annual performance evaluations. The problem is not so much that legislators have not wanted to engage in long-term merit pay plans, but rather that funding merit pay can be costly. Additionally, there is some belief that merit is best evaluated on an annual basis because single salary schedules reward persons in perpetuity—a condition inimical to meritorious service and merit pay concepts.

Despite the call for merit pay, there has been only limited trial and success with such proposals. In fact, merit pay plans have consistently been implemented and abandoned over the course of American public education. In 1949, Ball determined that merit pay plans had failed due to the "difficulty [of] objectively measuring good teaching," as well as dissension among teachers.[24] In 1966, the California Teachers Association reported the reasons that merit pay plans were abandoned, again noting dissension among staff and difficulty in administering the plan. Other potential problems of merit pay have been identified in at least one case study in the areas of endangering the cooperative environment, subjective observation techniques, invalid evaluation instruments, lack of agreement on goals, and little agreement on the components of effective teaching.[25] Additionally, critics have questioned the problems of administering merit pay plans within public school districts, particularly implementation and maintenance, and the nonflexibility of most school finance distribution plans, which are believed to siphon money away from base salary schedules when merit pay is implemented. As early as 1940, concerns were expressed regarding the judgment of school administrators in merit pay plans.[26] The broader research literature has thus documented a variety of reasons for abandonment of merit pay plans, including administrative, personnel, collective bargaining, and financial concerns.[27]

Yet despite unenthusiastic reception, merit pay forms a part of current staff compensation plans in several states and continues to occupy a large role in the thinking of many state legislatures. In most instances, however, existing plans are not true merit pay plans because the majority simply provide more pay for more duties or rewards for professional growth. Research has indicated that nationally merit pay plans are relatively small in number due to the fact that many school districts do not have significant monies to implement such plans. Only in states where such plans are state funded (e.g., Iowa), does the research indicate that they are widespread within a given state.

It is very difficult to receive uncontradicted guidance on the wisdom of engaging in merit pay plans in a school district. From one perspective, it is very reasonable to believe that historic interest will continue and that districts should inform themselves about the benefits and problems of merit pay, if for no other reason than that sustained legislative interest may have a long-term effect of slowing revenue growth for schools if the educational enterprise is too resistant in accepting merit pay. Additionally, as states suffer from stagnant economies and as the demographic changes described in Chapter 1 continue to occur with negative achievement impacts on schools, powerful private sector interests may bring great pressure on legislatures to "clean up" schools through merit pay. On the other hand, there is a vast literature[28] suggesting limited empirical encouragement on the effectiveness of merit pay plans and encouraging other forms of professionalizing the field of education for the purpose of true reform. While clear data are not yet available, the personnel and finance functions in school districts continue to be confronted by both sides on the issue of merit pay, giving rise to the need for administrators to be informed.

For administrators directly involved with personnel and finance functions, two vital concerns about merit pay plans need to be briefly developed here. The first concern relates to whether merit pay plans can be forced on education employees. Under private sector guidelines, issues that affect wages and working conditions are normally considered the subject of the collective bargaining process.[29] This reasoning arises from regulations of the National Labor Relations Act (NLRA) that make it "an unfair labor practice to refuse to bargain with respect to wages, hours, and other terms and conditions of employment."[30] Thus by logic, forcing merit pay would require consent through negotiations, and alternatively a request by an employee group to institute merit pay would have to be honored by the employer. Such would not seem true, however, because the NLRA does not apply to public school districts. In fact, at least in one instance, a court has reasoned that a school district does not have to negotiate a merit pay plan. The court stated:

> In municipal employment relations the bargaining table is not the appropriate forum for the formulation or management of public policy. Where a decision is essentially concerned with public policy choices, no group should act as an exclusive representative; discussion should be open; and public policy should be shaped in the regular political process. Essential control over the management of the school district's affairs must be left with the school board, the body elected to be responsible for those affairs under state law.[31]

In other states, however, state legislatures have intentionally created statutes requiring merit pay consideration by both employers and employees. For example, massive recent education reform in Oklahoma resulted in passage in 1990 of House Bill 1017, which contained drastic changes in how schools are to be operated. Among the provisions of House Bill 1017 was a requirement that beginning in 1991–1992, all districts will be required to "adopt and implement an academically based, district incentive pay plan for any school year following receipt by the school district board of education of a petition signed by 20% of the classroom teachers employed in the district which calls for adoption of an incentive pay plan for the district."[32] Under these conditions, the opinion of the court cited earlier is obviously not binding in other jurisdictions; but equally as important, a state legislature whose task is the creation of public policy can apparently send the development of public policy to the negotiations table. As with many other points of law, forcing merit pay is highly dependent on state statutes and subsequent legal validation of such statutes.

The second concern relates to the wisdom of forcing merit pay plans. There appears to have been little enthusiasm even from the earliest days, and the amount of resentment surrounding merit pay is formidable. While there can be little doubt about the accuracy of points made by critics regarding single salary schedules providing poor motivation for superior performance, there is apparently good reason to believe that abandonment of structures that promote apathy will only create structures that promote resentment. Additionally, with little legal precedent for boards and legislatures bent on elimination or dilution of single salary schedules, the potential seems great for significant disruption of the personnel and finance functions of a school district if a merit plan is instituted and challenged. A better path might be through the research literature suggesting alternatives to true merit pay—such as job redesign and job enhancement—all of which hold greater compatibility with the norms of autonomy, equality, and civility that have long been entrenched in education.[33] All that may be confidently said is that great care should be taken before merit plans are implemented due to the potential to violate applicable collective bargaining statutes and agreements, and the negative impact on district morale that seems to follow merit pay.

Reduction in Force and Other Dismissals

The second area of general concern for the personnel and finance functions of a district revolves around reduction in force and other types of dismissals. Reduction in force (RIF), or the suspension of a tenured or nontenured classroom teacher for reasons unrelated to performance,[34] occurs when districts find themselves with more teachers or other personnel than can be justified. Other dismissals occur for a variety of reasons including poor performance or uncooperative behavior. In both instances, it is necessary for the finance and personnel functions to work together to minimize the damage and to estimate and justify the impact on the district.

In contrast to merit pay proposals where more money is proposed for certain behaviors, RIF proposes reducing the amount of money in a district's instructional or operations budget. In some instances merit pay and RIF may be joined together, but the basic concept behind staff reduction is reducing expenditures, often in response to student enrollment declines that have been common over the past decade. Because in many of these school districts this precipitous decline will continue for several years, some districts have had to brace themselves for reducing personnel because state aid formulas are always enrollment-driven, making it impossible for boards of education to retain excess staff and programs.

If a teacher's classroom performance has led to programmatic enrollment decline, such dismissal or nonrenewal may still be treated within the RIF realm.[35] Generally, the major reason for engaging in RIF is fiscal insolvency. When fiscal insolvency is claimed by a local board of education, counterclaims by the teachers' association are certain to center on the validity of the school board's fiscal data.[36] The local board of education must be able to substantiate its actions based on empirical evidence.[37] In this arena, the need for clear and precise data is paramount and demands cooperation between the personnel and finance divisions of a district.[38] When these data are clear, local boards of education will be supported by the court.[39]

Whenever RIF procedures are used, employee rights to seniority and "bumping" come into play along with state statutes and applicable local collective bargaining agreements. The vast majority of court decisions have ruled that teachers are to be treated alike, regardless of programmatic issues. From this issue, seniority and bumping are concepts that must be kept in mind when personnel and finance divisions collaborate to decide which teachers will be nonrenewed under RIFs.[40] Administrators should keep in mind that courts have extended certain rights to nontenured teachers in these instances.[41] Other courts, however, have ruled that nontenured teachers do not possess any seniority rights.[42] Within certification areas, teachers may in fact bump those teachers who possess less seniority.[43] Again, it must be understood that these issues are often dependent on state statutes and local collective bargaining agreements.[44] The courts have also ruled that once RIF is declared, the school district must complete the task and not create additional positions to avoid the full effects of RIF.[45] Thus, the educational leaders throughout the school district must be familiar with the collective bargaining agreement as well as appropriate statutory requirements for such drastic fiscal actions.

In addition to RIFs, other dismissals sometimes occur in school districts. Although it is commonly believed, for example, that a teaching job in the public schools is a lifelong appointment, reality suggests that both tenured and nontenured teachers are dismissed. There should be no misperception about the local board's power in personnel matters. Boards of education and appropriate supervisors within school districts have the authority to evaluate and dismiss public school employees, by virtue of the state legislature's having granted them implied and delegated authority to maintain and operate the public schools.[46]

Even though boards have dismissal powers, termination of employees under either RIF or other adverse conditions is not to be undertaken carelessly. In all instances, the law must be carefully observed because in the vast majority of states, significant differences exist between dismissal procedures for nontenured faculty and those for tenured employees. Tenured employees are generally granted a permanent or continuing contract and are thus entitled to rigorous due process procedures in the dismissal act. In contrast, nontenured teachers are typically provided only a term contract under whatever employment and/or dismissal procedures are accorded them under contract law.[47] This does not imply, however, that nontenured employees have no rights or protections, because no one can be denied their constitutional rights.[48] Under such conditions, nontenured employees may have cause to demand the full due process procedure if allegations are made that constitutional rights such as freedom of speech have been violated by the employer. In addition, statutes in each state govern other rights that may accrue to nontenured persons, making it mandatory for the administrator to understand the state's contract law, the process of termination, and the terms of the actual employment contract. The courts have addressed the issues of giving reasons, as well as a hearing, for nontenured employees.[49]

Although the preceding discussion accurately gives the impression that it is much easier to dismiss nontenured staff, and despite common beliefs that tenure is a lifelong employment contract, there are many instances where tenured faculty have also been successfully dismissed.[50] The procedure, however, is much more difficult because generally state statutes provide the specific reasons for permissible termination of tenured employees, lacking which no dismissal can occur. Statutory examples of permissible reasons for dismissal include *incompetence, immorality, insubordination, incapacity, neglect of duty, unprofessional conduct*, and *conviction of a felony*. Within limits of seniority and bumping, it can also be seen that fiscal exigency is a permissible reason for tenured dismissal. When any of these reasons is invoked, the right of termination falls to the employer, provided that claims can be substantiated. The penalty for failure to substantiate such serious charges, however, may result in numerous charges filed against the district and ensuing liability for various types of compensation and restitution. As a result, great care should be taken in choosing the reason for dismissal, as discussed next.

Successful dismissal for incompetence is dependent on the statutory definition as provided in the individual states. However, courts have often allowed broadening of the definition of *incompetence,* or the "lack of ability, legal qualification, or fitness to discharge the required duty."[51] Generally, the proof of incompetence will be measured against other individuals performing the same or similar duties. Incompetence may also be demonstrated by proof of any one of the following criteria or some combination thereof:

1. Lack of a proper teaching certificate;
2. Lack of knowledge of subject matter;
3. Lack of ability to establish reasonable discipline in class;
4. Deficiency in teaching methodology; and
5. Emotional instability that demonstrates an inability to effectively teach students.[52]

Both nontenured and tenured employees may be dismissed for any of the above reasons. In dismissing tenured employees, however, great care must be taken to maintain clear and precise documentation to substantiate any potential charges in hearings that may ensue. Additionally, in nearly all states there is an obligation for a remediation process before dismissal actually occurs. Remediation efforts must also be carefully and completely documented[53] and should include a variety of activities that will attempt to bring the employee in question up to at least an adequate level of performance. Remediation activities should help the employee toward success in the specific job, define the activities and responsibilities of all parties, and demonstrate a good faith effort on the part of the school district to salvage the contractual interest of the employee. Administrators should be cautioned that documentation of the employee's failure to respond to remediation must be entirely thorough because the first defense will be a challenge to prove that the employee in question is the worst employee in the district. It can easily be seen that the district can incur heavy liability for hasty dismissals.

Staff may also be dismissed for immorality. In the modern context, immorality is not merely confined to sexual misconduct. In a court proceeding, immorality is generally defined by the prevailing community standard in which the test is that the act must be deemed "inimical to public welfare."[54] Actions such as corruption or indecency may in fact constitute immorality in that the standards of immorality have been defined as "course of conduct as offends the morals of the community and is a bad example to the youth whose ideals a teacher is supposed to foster and to elevate."[55]

Although immorality is broadly defined, care must be taken not to expose the district to liability for misapplication of the immorality criterion. For example, one of the areas that has been a significant concern to many public school administrators is unwed pregnant school teachers. Generally, the courts have not supported claims of immorality in dismissing such persons because of a lack of "irrefutable proof" of immorality.[56] This simply means that it is difficult to prove in the vast majority of communities that such pregnancy results in damage to students in the learning process or that the teacher's respect in the community has been adversely affected.[57] The task is made more difficult because in 1978 Congress passed the Pregnancy Discrimination Act[58] amending Title VII in terms of the definition of sex. As a result, administrators should be careful of great liability in dismissing such an individual in order not to violate Title VII, which now states:

> Because of or on the basis of pregnancy, childbirth, or related medical conditions; and women affected by pregnancy, childbirth, or related medical conditions shall be treated the same for all employment-related purposes, including the receipt of benefits under fringe benefit programs, as other persons not so affected but similar in their ability or inability to work.[59]

Administrators have been more successful, however, in dismissal without liability for insubordinate employees. The willful disregard of or refusal to obey reasonable directives can constitute insubordination.[60] As always, however, the courts place the burden of proof on the district, particularly with tenured staff because of property rights inherent in a contractual relationship. A quick decision to charge insubordination can be devastating to a district, since insubordination as the cause for dismissal has *not* been upheld when:

1. The alleged misconduct could not be proved;
2. Existence of a pertinent school rule or a superior's order was not proven;
3. The teacher's motive for violating the rule or order was admirable;
4. The rule or order was unreasonable;
5. The rule or order was invalid as beyond the authority of the maker;
6. The enforcement of the rule or order revealed possible bias or discrimination against the teacher; or,
7. The enforcement of the rule or order violated constitutional rights.[61]

Thus, if the employee can show that one of these reasons led to the action, the courts will not generally support the school district in employee dismissal based on such charges because directives must be reasonable and rational. Insubordination and willful neglect must be proved and not merely assumed.[62] Administrators must therefore take great care in dismissing for insubordination because under an adverse ruling by a court, significant liability can follow.

Finally, employees may be discharged without liability under conditions of neglect of duty. In practice, neglect of duty may be part of a larger claim of incompetence. For example, neglect of duty may include such issues as failure to follow curricular guidelines, lack of discipline, failure to follow prescribed teaching lessons, and other similar actions or inactions.[63] Neglect of duty is distinct from insubordination, however, where an employee blatantly disregards directives. Generally, to withstand judicial challenge, charges of neglect of duty or insubordination must reflect prior notice and established policy or directive.[64] Finally, other dismissals for acts such as arrest on felony charges will likely be upheld because such arrest may have an impact on performance and standing of a teacher in the overall community.[65] In many states, statutes declare that conviction of a felony is evidence of "unfitness to teach."[66] As always, however, lack of care in substantiating dismissals for due process purposes may result in great harm to the district in many ways.

Due Process Requirements

The seriousness of the above discussion is evident when it is finally recognized that districts are multiply liable before a court of law for their actions. Liability of districts for unfair dismissal places a heavy burden on the personnel and finance functions of the district because improper dismissal impacts both personnel policy and the financial welfare of the district under claims for reinstatement, back pay, and potential damages for violating the rights and reputation of exonerated individuals. These modern realities place a grave duty on all boards and administrators to discharge their duties fairly and properly and to assure all employees of procedural and substantive due process as required by law. Procedural due process ensures that "parties whose rights are to be affected are entitled to be heard, and in order that they may enjoy that right, they must be notified."[67] Substantive due process is broadly defined as a "constitutional guarantee that no person shall be arbitrarily deprived of his life, liberty or property" and shall be protected "from arbitrary and unreasonable action."[68] As both of these concepts always apply to tenured employees and may apply at other times to nontenured personnel, administrators must exercise care in observing due process of law requirements.

The personnel division should have responsibility for developing due process guidelines consistent with the requirements of law that are written, reviewed by all administrative divisions including the finance function, approved by the board of education, and made known to all relevant persons. Generally, due process consists of at least four elements that also apply to dismissal.[69] First, based on applicable statute, the employee must receive written notification and the specific stated reasons in order to establish a valid notification of an action such as dismissal. This notification process must be in conformance with all state statutes as to timing and method of delivery. Second, a fair and impartial hearing is required for the employee to have an opportunity to hear, examine, and refute any evidence. Third, the employee must have an opportunity to challenge these statements and to call witnesses. Fourth, fair hearings must occur at several levels within the school district, beginning with the immediate supervisor and ending administratively with the local board of education. This process assures that the employee has multiple opportunities to be heard and to challenge the actions of the school district at each level.[70] Failure to provide all of these proceedings is almost certain to result in severe consequences.

Determination of whether due process has been accorded is a function of the external mechanics of proceedings and closer scrutiny of the total process. The administration and board of education must be careful to deal objectively with the factual situation and to procedurally follow the appropriate due process steps.[71] This is absolutely critical for tenured employees because such persons have property rights to a reasonable expectation of future employment,[72] and procedural and substantive due process must be accorded in that such property rights may not be removed arbitrarily. Responsibility on the district in such matters is grave, as the U.S. Supreme

Court has ruled that such interests of employees are "broad and majestic."[73] Yet administrators should not be afraid to dismiss poor employees because, notwithstanding the serious implications of violating rights and due process, failure to correct poor employment decisions also causes great harm to children over time. All that is required is that dismissal be reasonable, that reasons are not arbitrary or capricious, that documentation exists, and that procedural and substantive due process are followed when appropriate. While courts will be severe, they are also perceptive in that dismissal may stand even when constitutional infractions were merely "incidental."[74]

The concept of human capital described in Chapter 1 is an appropriate capstone to the discussion of personnel and finance in this chapter. Although all areas of school district leadership and management are vital to total successful operation, human capital in a school district is the single largest *cost* and the single most effective *investment* a district can make. With school budgets largely consisting of personnel salaries and fringe benefits, public schools are the best chance to invest money and the greatest risk of losing it. Efficient utilization of human resources can yield quite cost-effective returns, but the potential for waste is enormous. Administrators should guard vigilantly to assure the best investment of district resources, and it bears repetition that the personnel and finance functions overlap greatly in this arena. Both personnel and finance should collaborate, neither should act on poor reasons, and continual communication should occur because acts by each function have serious consequences and potential liabilities for the financial and overall welfare of the entire district. Consequently, the overlap of personnel and finance is a critical concern to administrators, boards, taxpayers, and children.

Recruitment, selection, and retainment of quality personnel is extremely complex and demands that leaders in school districts be extraordinarily competent and skilled. The future will only reflect greater complexity, as evidenced by other topics covered in this text, such as school site based management, differentiated staffing, and the ever-expanding scope of negotiations. For administrators, these are the realities of the contemporary public school operation in America. Under these conditions, we turn in Chapter 9 to another topic fraught with opportunities for legal liability by examining the complex area of purchasing.

Review Points

THE PERSONNEL FUNCTION

The importance of the personnel function is confirmed when it is recognized that well over 75% of all budgets for schools goes to personnel costs.

Personnel costs are also investments, with returns in educational product and with reinvestment in the economy through consumer purchases by educational employees.

While teachers make up the vast majority of educational personnel, the scope of education employment is actually much greater.

Selection, employment, and retention of quality people are *the* keys to cost-effective educational organizations.

The success of the personnel function will be severely damaged without recognition of the need for close cooperation and coordination with the finance function.

While the personnel function is quite broad, the most critical financial aspects relate to determining staffing needs; recruitment and selection of quality staff; employment compensation policies; and liabilities of districts for personnel's acts or errors.

Good personnel practices require linking the personnel and finance functions in determining all the above.

Various methods of determining staffing needs exist, and are often driven by state-specific requirements.

Recruitment and selection of personnel may also be tied to state requirements, but districts should develop standardized and well-designed selection procedures within the limits of resources and law.

PERSONNEL COMPENSATION POLICIES AND PROCEDURES

Personnel compensation is broad-based, taking in more than salaries and related fringe costs.

The personnel and finance functions should work together to develop standardized policies and procedures relating to compensation.

The overlap between the personnel and finance functions is particularly apparent in the negotiation process, where both offices must work jointly to project needs and costs.

While extraordinarily difficult, the negotiation process should be approached by both sides with the intent of win-win strategies.

Salary schedule negotiations need to be approached carefully by both the personnel and finance functions, as changes to these delicately balanced structures can create unexpected ramifications and costs.

Despite some conventional wisdom, administrators at all levels in a district should take a close interest in the negotiations process, as contract administration will apply in all instances, including people who should have taken an active interest.

Administrators in all positions must be well informed of state laws and local labor agreements governing all personnel and compensation to avoid serious trouble over contract violation.

OTHER ISSUES OF PERSONNEL AND FINANCE

The scope of personnel and finance functions are so broad as to take in almost all relationships in a district—particularly those relating to present practices and future liabilities.

The persistent interest in merit pay requires administrators to stay current on practices around the nation and to be able to respond knowledgeably to proposals to implement merit systems.

Although much research questions the value of merit pay plans, legislative and local board interest makes it imperative that administrators check state laws and court decisions closely before enforcing a merit scheme.

Reduction in force (RIF) is a current major concern for districts, given budget problems in many states.

Since the purpose of RIF is budget reduction via personnel, legal procedures must be carefully observed.

In RIF situations, administrators must be extremely careful not to violate locally negotiated contracts.

Because of extreme liability risk, the finance and personnel functions must also work cooperatively when considering other dismissals, such as those for incompetence, immorality, insubordination, incapacity, neglect of duty, unprofessional conduct, and felonious conviction.

While administrators must be concerned in dismissals with cost and ethics, districts must also follow all due process requirements to avoid liability.

In the final analysis, the personnel and finance functions combine to deal with the human capital of a school district—the largest and most effective educational investment a district can make.

Case Study

Formerly an experienced and successful secondary building principal, you recently completed your doctoral degree from the most prestigious university in your state, concentrating your studies in the discipline of personnel. In fact, your dissertation was a comparative analysis of collective negotiations laws in the 50 states. Upon completion of your degree, you accepted the position of assistant superintendent for personnel in a school district in a neighboring state.

During your first week on the job, you learned several disturbing facts. First, there are no job descriptions for any position in the district. Second, the support staffs have been working under an old contract for the past three years because of refusal to accept a unilateral contract following impasse and have not received a pay raise as a result. Third, the teachers association has been relatively successful at the bargaining table, primarily because the state legislature passed a binding arbitration law affecting only certified (teaching) employees three years ago. Fourth, the school board president has been serving as chief board negotiator, and an interim superintendent has just been named to replace the superintendent who resigned under a contract buy-out. Fifth, while you were at a negotiations conference, the school nurses delivered a petition under the state collective bargaining act demanding formal recognition, following the lead of the custodians the previous week. Sixth and finally, your secretary tells you that the senior building principal of the school district wants to schedule an appointment with you on behalf of all principals to discuss why their raises have not been commensurate with those for teachers.

As you contemplate your situation, you realize that you must respond quickly and effectively. Using the following sets of questions to launch your class discussion, what do you think you will choose as your plan of action?

Directed Discussion Questions

1. Using your own experience in education and your formal learning here and in other settings about personnel practices, what do you identify as the major

problems confronting you in this case study? In your estimation, how likely is such a situation to occur in the real world of administration? In your experience, have there been similar instances? If so, how was the situation handled? What was the result?

2. As you contemplate the need for action, where is the best place to begin? What needs to be done in this district? Where have errors been made? In correcting this situation, what must be resolved, and in what order? Who must be involved? What should your role be as the "lead" administrator? How effectively can you address these problems? What will you do, and how will you do it?

3. Could this situation occur in your own school district? Have there been instances in which similar tense moments have occurred? If so, what were the circumstances? How was the problem resolved? Compared to the recommendations of this chapter, how are personnel issues handled in your present setting? Are the essential elements of good personnel administration in place? What conscious method of coordination between the finance and personnel functions exists in your district? If you were in an authority role in your present district, what changes would you make?

4. In this case study, what assessment do you make of your chances of success? What will be your final plan of action?

NOTES

1. National Center for Education Statistics, *Digest of Education Statistics 1991* (Washington, D.C.: National Center for Education Statistics, 1991); National Center for Education Statistics, *The Condition of Education 1990* (Washington, D.C.: National Center for Education Statistics, 1990); and National Education Association, *Rankings of the States* (Washington, D.C.: National Education Association, 1991).

2. Adapted from Donald L. Robson, "The Personnel Function: Practitioners, Practices, and Participants," in *Principles of School Business Management,* ed. R. Craig Wood (Reston, Va.: Association of School Business Officials, 1986), 290.

3. Chapter 6 of this textbook explores how population projections are made.

4. David C. Thompson, *Preliminary Analysis and Recommendations Regarding the Closing of Select Rural Schools in West Virginia* (Manhattan, Kans.: University Council for Educational Administration Center for Education Finance, 1990).

5. David C. Thompson, R. Craig Wood, and David S. Honeyman, *Adequacy of Educational Revenues in Oklahoma School Districts: Expert Analysis on Behalf of Plaintiff in Fair School Finance Council, Inc., v. State of Oklahoma* (Manhattan, Kans.: Wood, Thompson & Associates, 1992).

6. Robson, "The Personnel Function," 298–299.

7. See Wilbert E. Scheer, *People Policies: Successful Personnel Management* (Chicago: Pluribus Press, 1984), 143.

8. National Education Association, *Teacher Salaries and Salary Trends in 1923* (Washington, D.C.: National Education Association, Research Division, 1923).

9. See National Education Association, *The Single Salary Schedule* (Washington, D.C.: National Education Association, 1985), 19.

10. Bruce M. Venter and JoAnn Ramsey, "Improving Relations: Labor Management Committees in School Districts," *School Business Affairs* 56:2 (1990), 21–23.

11. See for example John L. Grogan, "The Salary and Fringe Benefit Package," *School Business Affairs* 45:1 (1979), 22–23, 36.

12. See John W. Frombach, "Negotiations: Are You Prepared?" *School Business Affairs* 57:2 (1991), 15.

13. Robert H. Decker, "Helping the School Board and Negotiating Team Understand Their Roles," *School Business Affairs* 57:2 (1991), 8.

14. Ibid.

15. Ibid., 8–9.

16. Sandi Cloyd, "Involving School Board Members in Negotiations," *School Business Affairs* 56:2 (1990), 24–25.

17. Edward E. Eiler, "When Collective Bargaining Isn't Working," *School Business Affairs* 57:2 (1991), 21.

18. Gayle T. Schneider, "Schools and Merit: An Empirical Study of Attitudes of School Board Members, Administrators, and Teachers Toward Merit Systems," *Planning and Changing* 15:2 (1984), 89–105.

19. Jerry B. Mitchell, "Merit Rating: Past, Present, and Perhaps," *Phi Delta Kappan* 42:4 (1961), 139–142.

20. Susan M. Johnson, *Pros and Cons of Merit Pay* (Bloomington, Ind.: Phi Delta Kappa Educational Foundation, 1985), 16.

21. Committee on Education and Labor, *Merit Pay Task Force Report,* CEL Rep. No. 98-25-4440 (Washington, D.C.: U.S. Government Printing Office, 1983), 3.

22. John C. Almack, *Modern School Administration: Its Problems and Progress* (Boston: Houghton Mifflin, 1933), 17.

23. R. Craig Wood and Grover H. Baldwin, "Legal Challenges to Merit Pay Programs," *Journal of Education Finance* (Summer 1989), 135–155.

24. Lester B. Ball, "An Evaluation of Teacher Merit Rating Salary Schedules in the Public Schools" (Ph.D. diss., Northwestern University, 1949), 67.

25. E. M. Rotz, "A Study of Attitudes Toward Merit Pay in the Penn Manor School District and the School District of Lancaster" (Ph.D. diss., Temple University, 1961), 73.

26. Arthur B. Moehlman, *School Administration: Its Development, Principles, and Future in the United States* (Boston: Houghton Mifflin, 1940).

27. See for example Johnson, *Pros and Cons of Merit Pay;* see also F. S. Calhoun and N. J. Protheroe, *Merit Pay Plans for Teachers: Status and Descriptions,* Educational Research Service Rept. No. 219-21684 (Arlington, Va.: Education Research Service, 1983); Glen E. Robinson, *Paying Teachers for Performance and Productivity: Learning from Experience,* Educational Research Service Rpt. No. 226-00001 (Arlington, Va: Educational Research Service.

28. See for example Kern Alexander and David Monk, eds., *Attracting and Compensating America's Teachers,* 8th Annual Yearbook of the American Education Finance Association (Cambridge: Ballinger, 1987).

29. For a discussion of the persuasiveness of the NLRA to public school districts, see R. Craig Wood, "The Change of Union Affiliation in Public School Districts: Analysis and Implications of National Labor Relations Board Decisions," *Journal of Collective Negotiations in the Public Sector* 14:3 (1985), 213–230.

30. Wood and Baldwin, "Legal Challenges to Merit Pay Programs," 140, citing 29 U.S.C. 158(d).

31. Unified School Dist. v. WERC, 81 Wis.2d 89, 259 N.W.2d at 730–31 (1977). In public education, specific litigation on the obligation of the local board of education to bargain merit pay is somewhat limited and is highly state-specific. Great care should be taken before such plans are implemented due to the potential to affect the applicable collective bargaining statutes and agreements. See for example Charles City Educ. Ass'n v. Public Employee Relations, 291 N.W.2d 663 (Iowa 1980), Wygant v. Victor Valley, 214 Cal. Rptr. 205 (Cal. App.

4 Dist. 1985, School Board v. Levy County Educ. Ass'n, 492 So.2d 1140 (Fla. App. 1 Dist 1986).

32. Thompson, Wood, and Honeyman, *Adequacy of Educational Revenues in Oklahoma School Districts,* quoting at 12 and paraphrasing HB1017 Sec. 50-C.

33. Betty Malen, Michael Murphy, and Ann Weaver Hart, "Restructuring Teacher Compensation Systems: An Analysis of Three Incentive Strategies," in *Attracting and Compensating America's Teachers,* ed. Alexander and Monk, 91–142.

34. For a discussion of reduction in force and related issues, see R. Craig Wood, "Reduction In Force," in *Principles of School Business Management,* ed. R. Craig Wood (Reston, Va.: Association of School Business Officials, 1986), 537–557; see also R. Craig Wood, "Financial Exigencies and the Dismissal of Public School Teachers: A Legal Perspective," *Government Union Review* 7:3 (1982), 262–276; and R. Craig Wood, "Chapter Nine of the Federal Bankruptcy Act: A Fiscal Alternative for School Districts," *Journal of Education Finance* (Summer 1985), 56–68.

35. In re Gaetjens, 485 A.2d 1057 (N.H. 1984).

36. See for example Frimel v. Humphrey, 555 S.W.2d 350 (Mo. 1977); California School Employees Ass'n v. Pasadena Unif. School Dist., 139 Cal. Rptr. 633 (Ct. App. 1977).

37. Gross v. Board of Educ. of Elmsford, 577 N.Y.S.2d 200 (Ct. App. 1991).

38. See for example Unified School District v. Epperson, 583 F.2d 1118 (10th Cir. 1978); Bradford v. Renton School District, 577 P.2d 147 (Wash. 1978); Cigardski v. Lake Lehman School District, 407 A.2d 4609 (Pa. 1979); Baston v. Ricci, 391 A.2d 161 (1978); Freiberg v. Board of Education of Big Bay De Noc, 283 N.W.2d 775 (Mich. 1979).

39. See for example Britten v. South Bend Community School Corporation, 819 F.2d 766 (7th Cir. 1987), *cert. den.* 108 S.Ct. 288 (1987).

40. Heruth v. Independent School Dist., 434 N.W.2d 470 (Minn. Ct. App. 1989).

41. Alexander v. Delano Joint Union High School Dist., 188 Cal. Rptr. 705 (Ct. App. 1983); Bohmann v. Board of Educ. of West Clermont, 443 N.E.2d 176 (Ohio 1983); Carmody v. Board of Directors, 453 A.2d 965 (Pa. 1982).

42. See for example Lezette v. Board of Educ., 319 N.E.2d 189 (N.Y. 1974); Hill v. Dayton School Dist., 532 P.2d 1154 (Wash. 1975).

43. See for example McKeesport Area School Dist. v. Cicogna, 558 A.2d 116 (Pa. Commw Ct. 1989).

44. Fort Sumner Municipal School Board v. Parsons, 405 P.2d 366 (N.M. 1971); Penasco Indep. School Dist. No. 4 v. Lucero, 526 P.2d 825 (N.M. 1974); Karback v. Board of Educ. of Comm. Unit School Dist. No. 303, 428 N.E.2d 1126 (Ill. 1981).

45. See O'Hair v. Board of Educ., 805 P.2d 40 (Kan. Ct. App. 1990).

46. Graham v. Special School Dist. 1, 462 N.W.2d 78 (Minn. Ct. App. 1990).

47. Clark v. Mann, 562 F.2d 1104 (8th Cir. 1977).

48. Harris v. Florence City Board of Educ., 568 So.2d 827 (Ala. Civ. App. 1990).

49. See for example Kharrubi v. Board of Educ. of City of New York, 519 N.Y.S.2d 671 (N.Y.App.Div., 2 1987): Caldwell v. Blytheville, Arkansas School Dist. No. 5, 746 S.W.2d 381 (Ark. App. 1988): Ford v. Caldwell Parish School Board, 541 So.2d 955 (La. Cir. Ct. App. 2 Cir. 1989): Bellflower v. Bellflower Unif. School Dist.,

50. School Dist. v. Gautier, 13 Okla 194, 73 P. 954 (Okla. 1903).

51. *Black's Law Dictionary,* 5th Ed. (St. Paul, Minn.: West, 1985), 688.

52. See, e.g., Busker v. Board of Educ. of Elk Point, 295 N.W.2d 1 (S.D. 1980).

53. Brown v. Wood County Board of Educ., 400 S.E.2d 213 (W.Va. 1990); and Selby v. North Calloway Board of Educ., 777 S.W.2d 275 (Mo. Ct. App. 1989).

54. Black's Law Dictionary, 885.

55. Horosko v. Mt Pleasant Twp. School Dist., 335 Pa. 369, 6 A.2d 866 (1939), cert. denied, 308 U.S. 553 (1939).

56. Avery v. Homewood City Board of Educ., 674 F.2d 337 Dist. Ct. App. (5th Cir. 1982), cert.

denied, 461 U.S. 943 (1983); Andrews v. Drew Municipal Separate School Dist., 507 F.2d 611 (5th Cir. 1975), cert. granted, 423 U.S. 820 (1975), cert. dismissed, 425 U.S. 559 (1976).

57. See generally, Acanfora v. Board of Educ. of Montgomery County, 491 F.2d 498 (4th Cir. 1974); New Mexico State Board of Educ. v. Stoudt, 571 P.2d 1186 (N.M. 1977).

58. This was done primarily as a response to General Electric Co. v. Gilbert, 429 US 125, 97 S.Ct 401 (1976).

59. 42 U.S.C. §2000e(k).

60. School Dist No. 8. Pinal County v. Superior Court, 102 Ariz. 478, 433 P.2d 28 (1967). See also, Alderstein v. Board of Educ. of New York City, 485 N.Y.S.2d 1 (N.Y. 1984).

61. 78 *A.L.R.*3d 83–87.

62. Cowdery v. Philadelphia Board of Educ., 531 A.2d 1186 (Pa. Commw. 1987): Mechley v. Kanawha County Board of Educ., 383 S.E.2d 839 (W.Va. 1989); Johnson v. School Board of Dade City, 578 So.2d 387 (Fla Dist. Ct. App. 1991).

63. See, e.g., Harvey v. Jefferson County School Dist No. R-1, 710 P.2d 1103 (Colo. 1985).

64. Cowdery, 531 A.2d 1186; Board of Educ. City of Gilmer v. Chaddock, 398 S.E.2d 120 (W.Va. 1990).

65. For the definition of a felony, see *Black's Law Dictionary,* 555.

66. See for example Bertrand v. New Mexico State Board of Educ., 544 P.2d 1176 (N.M. 1975); Skripchuk v. Austin, 379 A.2d 1142 (Del. Super. Ct. 1977).

67. Black's Law Dictionary, 1083.

68. Ibid., 1281.

69. Remember that in most states procedural due process applies only to tenured staff. Nontenured faculty should generally not be informed of reasons of dismissal, as such notice invokes cause into the dismissal process. Two exceptions may apply. As stated earlier, if constitutional violations are subsequently raised by the employee, different rules will govern the balance of the process. Also, each state's statutes must be carefully examined to ensure compliance with the law.

70. Belcourt v. Fort Totten Public School Dist., 454 N.W.2d 703 (N.D. 1990).

71. See Nelson v. Board of Educ. of Doland School Dist., 380 N.W.2d 665 (S.D. 1986) (state tenure statute creates a contractual obligation); see also State ex rel Anderson v. Brand, 303 U.S. 95 (1938).

72. For claims involving expectations by nontenured teachers, see Sullivan v. School Board of Penellas County, 773 F.2d. 1182 (11th Cir. 1985); Carmichael v. Chambers County Board of Educ., 581 F.2d 95 (5th Cir. 1978).

73. Board of Regents v. Roth, 408 U.S. 564 (1972).

74. Sheets v. Stanley Community School Dist. No. 2, 413 F.Supp. 350 (N.D. 1975).

ADDITIONAL READINGS

American Education Finance Association. *Attracting and Compensating America's Teachers.* Edited by Kern Alexander and David Monk, eds. 8th Annual Yearbook of the America Education Finance Association. Cambridge, Mass.: Ballinger, 1987.

Association of School Business Management, International. *Principles of School Business Management.* R. Craig Wood, ed. (Reston, Va.: Association of School Business Officials, 1986).

Castetter, William. *The Personnel Function in Educational Administration.* New York: Macmillan, 1986.

Duke, Daniel. *Teaching: The Imperiled Profession.* Albany: State University of New York Press, 1984.

Fleisher, B.M., and T.J. Kniesner. *Labor Economics: Theory, Evidence, and Policy.* Englewood Cliffs, N.J.: Prentice-Hall, 1980.

Goodlad, John. *A Place Called School: Prospects for the Future.* St. Louis: McGraw-Hill, 1983.

Klein, K. *Merit Pay and Evaluation.* Bloomington, Ind.: Phi Delta Kappa Educational Foundation, 1984.

McDonnell, L.M., and A. Pascal. *Teacher Unions and Educational Reform.* Santa Monica, Calif.: Rand Corporation, 1988.

Rothwell, William, and H.C. Kazanas. *Strategic Human Resources Planning and Management.* Englewood Cliffs, N.J.: Prentice-Hall, 1988.

Scheer, Wilbert. *People Policies: Successful Personnel Management.* Chicago: Pluribus Press, 1984.

Strauss, George, and Leonard Sayles. *Personnel: The Human Problems of Management.* Englewood Cliffs, N.J.: Prentice-Hall, 1980.

Stronge, James, and Virginia Helm. *Evaluating Professional Support Personnel in Education.* Newbury Park, Calif.: Sage, 1991.

Taylor, Frederick. *The Principles of Scientific Management.* New York: Harper & Row, 1911.

Wallace, M.J., and C.H. Fay. *Compensation Theory and Practice.* Boston: Kent, 1982.

CHAPTER 9

Planning for Purchasing, Inventory, Distribution, and Control

CHAPTER THEME

- Because administrators engage in considerable personal and professional risk-taking when they purchase and handle goods or services on behalf of school districts, it is critically important that administrators at all levels be cognizant of the limits of authority and knowledgeable about the principles of sound procurement practices.

CHAPTER OUTLINE

- An overview of the purchasing process in school districts
- The statutory basis for purchasing, including the nature of contracts, legal limits of purchasing authority, the ethics of purchasing, and laws relating to competitive bidding
- The act of purchasing, including requisitions, purchase orders, and the total purchasing cycle
- An introductory discussion of other important aspects of purchasing, including warehousing, inventory, and control

CHAPTER OBJECTIVE

- A greater understanding of the risks and responsibilities of administrators for ethical and legal behavior in the supply function

It is apparent from the law that schools and school districts have absolutely no inherent power to purchase. This is based on the principle that schools are creatures or arms of the state and the legislature, and their powers are endowed by the propagating source. All authority to purchase is thereby found in the statutes of a given state. Yet school districts should not be assumed incapable of purchasing to fulfill their educational missions. The power to purchase is an assigned one, and those states which possess purchasing statutes have typically provided general and broad delegations of power. These provisions are . . . very different in scope, length, content, authority, and limitations. This makes a general study of purchasing powers very difficult because the breadth and limit of such authority is highly uneven.

> *David C. Thompson,* The Law of Purchasing: A Guide for School Business Officials

This chapter's introductory quotation[1] regarding the purchasing function in school districts may cause some administrators to react with alarm either because they do not realize their authority is not secure or because they can ruefully identify with the statement. Many good administrators have entered into contracts to purchase items or services for their school districts, only to have the board of education refuse to ratify the agreement. Such situations are highly uncomfortable for administrators, who worry whether an unhappy vendor will challenge the board's decision in court. The situation is further complicated by whether the administrator is at fault under law, and the operation of various states' statutes controlling other aspects of purchasing, such as complex rules of competitive bid laws, make purchasing a serious affair. When these problems are added to the need to plan for inventory, distribution, and control of a district's material resources, we again find that good administrators must be knowledgeable and wary to effectively conduct the business of a school district while avoiding problems that would almost inevitably result in expensive legal fees.

Because the various aspects of purchasing, such as procurement, inventory, distribution, and control, are critical to the instructional and operational aspects of school districts, a sound working knowledge is needed of the issues in the broad arena of purchasing, as well as a good grasp of potential purchasing problems administrators may encounter. This chapter is intended to provide such an introduction to these issues. The chapter begins with an overview of the role of procurement, followed by the statutory basis for purchasing, including the nature of contracts, legal concerns for authority and limitations on district purchasing, the ethics of purchasing, and laws relating to competitive bidding. We then briefly discuss the act of purchasing, including the internal and external procedures of requisitions, purchase orders, and the overall purchasing cycle. The chapter concludes with a summative discussion of several other important items, such as warehousing, inventory, and control of purchased supplies and products, completing another link in our examination of the functions and tasks of fiscal school leadership.

THE ROLE OF PURCHASING

Education today is a very different creature from what it was in the early days of the nation when James Garfield, who in 1881 became the twentieth president of the United States, wrote, about his former teacher at Williams College: "Mark Hopkins, the teacher, sat on one end of a log and a farm boy sat on the other. . . ."[2] Today's schoolhouse has become much more than a rough-hewn log, and the role of procurement of materials, goods, and services has become a vital and necessary technical function for the educational process and orderly and efficient fiscal management. Without the performance of the procurement function in an efficient and timely manner, the educational process as it is known today would be so significantly damaged that it could not continue to exist.

Procurement, or the purchasing function as it will be called in this textbook, is a complex field driven by numerous aspects of economics and law. From an economic perspective, a district's ability and need to purchase are driven primarily by its budget and the enrollment of the district. This assumption is fundamentally correct, but the role of purchasing in a school district is far more complex than simply deciding on the desired quantity of an item and checking to see if enough money is on hand to make the purchase. A myriad of required acts is involved in purchasing, some of which are legal requirements while others are attempts to engage in sound purchasing practices based on research and business principles found to be effective over time in both the public and private sectors. But regardless of how complex laws and district policies may become, it is important to remember that "in general, the objective of purchasing is to buy materials, supplies and equipment of the right quality in the right quantity from the right source at the right price at the proper time."[3] Or, as the Bureau of Business Practices has described this essential function, the act of purchasing is the "result of the relationship between the price paid for a particular item and its utility in the function it fills."[4]

Basis of School District Purchasing

Because the purchasing function of school districts is so complex, it is helpful at the outset of an introductory discussion of purchasing first to acquire a broad view of the basis and operation of procurement to heighten appreciation of the extreme complexity of rules surrounding the purchasing act. This is because the total process is best seen before it becomes cluttered with the many technical aspects of law and good business practices. For the student of education finance, an overall view of procurement should actually begin long before purchasing actually takes place by establishing three important milestones in the purchasing process: first, an understanding of the overall concept of authority to establish a district's budget; second, a grasp of the set of activities that lead to establishment of the budget; and third, an understanding of how the two previous milestones permit a district to prepare for and engage in purchasing. From these perspectives, the student can understand how purchasing becomes possible, which in turn will later lead to examination of how the purchasing act occurs.[5]

The first milestone toward establishing the district's budget makes a logical beginning point from which to introduce the role of purchasing in schools. From extended discussion in earlier chapters on budgeting and the law, it should now be highly apparent that school districts have no inherent authority to lay and collect taxes or to establish budgets for educational purposes. As extensions of the state, school districts serve entirely at the pleasure of the legislature, although in reality wholesale abolishment of school districts is effectively impossible for political reasons. The concept of districts as statutory creations of the state, however, is fundamentally important to all aspects of school district operation because without statutory authority, districts themselves would obviously be illegitimate and attempts to collect school taxes would be illegal. Without legal existence of school districts, other revenue mechanisms would have to be created because school budgets would not exist. Without budgets, it is obvious that no money could be spent to educate children. Statutory authorization of both school districts and their power to collect revenues and establish budgets is thus the obvious genesis of the entire educational process, including the basis from which to expend public funds for the purchasing function.

The second milestone is the set of activities that lead to actual establishment and adoption of the budget. In nearly every school district across the nation, certain common processes and procedures are followed in setting a budget. Where there are differences, such deviations are often simply a function of various statutory dates and technical procedures, all of which yield the same end product in all states. As seen in Chapter 6, activities leading to establishment of a budget include a variety of acts centered on determining the proposed expenditures of the district, estimating the district's revenues, and deriving a balance between the revenue and expenditure sides of the budget. Determining expenditures was seen to be a function of estimating enrollment that in turn drove staffing determinations, identification of other purchased resources, and a description in fiscal terms of the resources needed to implement and carry out the educational program of the school district. Prerequisite to this process, however, were efforts to lobby the state legislature to put more money into education through the state aid formula, inservicing the community and local board of education on the needs of the district for the coming year, and holding a public hearing on the proposed budget according to statutory requirements. The second milestone thus notes that a school district budget is profoundly influenced by numerous forces, many of which are external to the schools and which in fact precede actual expenditures in the procurement process.

The series of smaller steps involved in actually determining line item amounts and making expenditures is the third milestone, marking how budgets are built "from the ground up." It is likely here that most people would have begun this discussion on purchasing because it is reasonable to think that a budget must be built from the sum of its individual parts; that is, each proposed line item expenditure must be known before a total budget can be derived and adopted. From the preceding discussion, however, it is now known that unless the first milestone of statutory authority to establish budgets is granted and unless the second milestone of larger activities successfully garnering resources and mechanisms for expenditures is accomplished, there is no legal or adequate operational basis on which boards and administrators can purchase requisite equipment, supplies, and services for carrying out the educational program. Only when these vital conditions have been legislatively and locally achieved can the educational function be undertaken by assigning purchase amounts to the appropriate categories in the actual budget. The third milestone thus results in the realization that budgets and purchasing decisions are actually determined in reverse order to common logic because allocation of money to budget lines is more accurately the last act, rather than the first, in the budget process.

Establishment and operation of budgets is therefore a multistep process greatly complicated by the involvement of at least two levels of state and local government.[6] It can now be seen that even though many acts lead to final decisions about the amounts of money assigned to each line in the budget, the act of assigning money would have no meaning or effect without prior legislative establishment of board authority to create and approve annual budgets and expenditures. These fundamental realities allow summation of the basis of purchasing in three tersely accurate concepts. First, school district powers to collect and spend money rest entirely in statute. Second, the larger processes that lead to availability of money for expenditures precede actual establishment of budgets and in effect powerfully condition the purchasing decisions of individual districts. Third, operationalization of the educational mission is prevented until these two prior events are firmly in place. Because statutory authorization and the political process thus effectively drive budget building and purchasing decisions, administrators must understand that purchasing is highly technical and dependent on variables beyond control of the local district.

General Overview of the Purchasing Function

Legally constituted school districts therefore have no inherent basis for purchasing goods and services. However, in every state the statutory basis needed to carry out educational functions has been legislatively established because all states have recognized that revenue must be available to school districts for the purpose of buying the goods and services necessary to fulfill the educational mandate. From this statutory basis, school districts are permitted to establish budgets wherein the concept of budgeting is to allocate money to each of the various operations of the educational enterprise for the purpose of purchasing goods and services. The result of allocating such monies across a budget is a legally authorized procurement plan for the district.

Establishment and codification of the legal basis for school district expenditures permits local planning and execution of the purchasing function. In the broadest sense, operationalizing the purchasing function demands three phases of operations planning. The first phase is a function of learning from experience about the needs of the district, forming much of the modern basis for planned expenditures. For example, if enrollment is increasing, it is reasonable to estimate that bulk copier paper purchases must also increase simply because more children will utilize the district's instructional services. This estimate is repeated for every purchase the district made in the prior year, essentially limited only by available funds and the ongoing review process that determines whether an expenditure will continue to be made. For example, if a district has just purchased an electronic Individualized Learning System (ILS) supporting the district's textbook series, the purchase of disposable workbooks will no longer be needed since students will be able to print worksheets directly from the ILS screen, but the purchase of additional textbooks and computers to support the ILS will have to be made because enrollment is increasing. From this perspective, the purchasing function can combine prior experience with future plans and demographic changes. Obviously, such planning requires careful recordkeeping and foresight to accurately estimate district needs. Such planning is an ongoing process for many districts.

The second phase of purchasing generally involves consideration of purchase requisition from the professionals directly involved in every aspect of instructional and support services. Obviously this phase overlaps greatly with the first phase in that prior expenditure experience is a direct reflection of previous years' purchase requisitions by these same people. The procurement process requires that at some point in time, however, the district must again ask all employees to estimate needs for continuing and new purchases based on previous experience and improvement plans for the following year. In most districts this is called the requisition cycle, wherein the district budget office estimates revenues, prepares building and/or departmental gross budgets, and issues invitations to staff to submit purchase requisitions for the coming year. In some instances, the process is slightly different in that requisitions precede the budget draft. The rationale behind each approach is both wise and problematic. In the first example, requests will generally be restricted to the predetermined budget amount, both encouraging frugality and discouraging innovation. In the second example, no guideposts for appropriate requests are evident, but there is likewise no attempt to curb new thinking. Regardless of approach, however, prior experience and the requisition process combine to comprise much of the purchasing operation.

The third phase of purchasing is both current and prospective, as the purchasing cycle is both completed for the current year and very often simultaneously begun for the following year. In many ways, all three phases of operations planning are inseparable because each phase informs all others and follows from the previous phase. In the third phase, however, prior experience combines with the requisition process to predict the district's upcoming needs wherein immediately after establishing the current year's budget, planning for the following year can begin based on a calendar procedure that takes into account prior experience and prospective planning by district professionals. For example, the budget and purchasing calendar in Figure 9.1 illustrates that planning for purchasing can be a year-round process beginning in September and ending the following August, followed by immediate resumption of intensive planning on September 1 of the following year.

The intensive nature of purchasing operations has led to a central role for procurement in school districts. Because of the complexity of purchasing, many districts have responded by creating formal purchasing structures for efficiency and ease of administration. Generally, a purchasing hierarchy is established by specific board policies, often calling for the assistant superintendent for finance to manage the overall purchasing operation with direct accountability to the superintendent and board of education. Because of the sheer impossibility of expertise in every need ranging from chemistry supplies to bulk gasoline, the purchasing director usually further delegates responsibility to building principals or division directors who feed data back through the purchasing hierarchy. Depending on the size of the district, the purchasing function may be so large that the assistant superintendent for finance has several subordinates working exclusively in purchasing or who share their time with other related tasks.

Under the complex conditions of a modern school operation, the person charged with purchasing must be apprised of every aspect of law relating to procurement. Every state has specific statutory guidelines concerning discretionary and mandatory purchasing procedures. In addition to statutory procedures and local policies, school districts are especially prone to purchasing errors because they often must also observe a myriad of city charters and ordinances, particularly if the district is fiscally dependent on other government bodies. In addition, this person must be knowledgeable about sound business practices, both from the perspective of wise consumer behavior and public relations. Purchasing in the public arena is significantly different from that in the private sector because the purchasing of goods and services must be done in public and in a manner that assures the best price for taxpayer benefit.[7] When this role is combined with other complex political sensitivities, such as working with local merchants who understandably want to share in the school's economy, the administrator must successfully balance legal obligations and openness with various community pressures.

The basis and general overview of purchasing lead to the conclusion that the

September 1 through October 31
- Process of evaluating building and site alteration and improvement needs for the next school year is begun by building principals. Such needs are to be submitted to the Plant Facilities Department for cost estimates and then prioritized by the Division Director of Elementary Education for elementary buildings, the Division Director of Secondary Education for secondary buildings, Division Director of Vocational and Continuing Education for vocational and continuing education buildings, and the Assistant Director of Plant Facilities for all other buildings.
- The administrative staff reviews the need to adjust per pupil allocation budget amounts for library media materials, instructional supplies, and instructional equipment for the current school year.

November
- The Board of Education considers and approves per pupil allocations, serving as the basis for the general education program and individual school budgets.
- Pertinent instructions and per pupil budget allocations are distributed to all schools.
- Material catalogs and order forms are delivered to the schools.
- By November 14, all principals must submit building alteration requests to the appropriate division director.

November through April
- Administrative budget hearings scheduled to hear requests and justifications for fiscal requests above.

December 1 through January 30
- Equipment needs are evaluated and budget request forms are completed by principals and teachers.
- Magazine needs are evaluated and budget request forms completed by principals and teachers.
- Supply, classroom supplemental book and varsity athletic needs are evaluated and budget request forms completed by teachers and principals.
- By January 30, principals submit equipment requests, magazine requests, supply, classroom supplemental book, and varsity athletic requests to the Purchasing Department for processing.

February 20
- Editing and verification report of all catalog orders are sent from the Purchasing Department to all principals, with one corrected copy due back to Purchasing by February 27.

March 6
- Program supervisors print equipment reports from data processing terminals to evaluate equipment needs in the budget. Final replies from supervisors are due back March 20 in order to be included in the final budget consideration process.

March 31
- All budget requests, including personnel requirements, are submitted by program area supervisors and division directors to the Budget Management Department for consolidation into a preliminary budget.

April 17
- An early discussion of budget concerns is held for board members, superintendent, assistant superintendent, and select administrators.

May 15
- Principals receive status report on book, supply, and equipment items recommended for budget approval.

May 28
- A prebudget workshop for board and senior administrators. The focus is on presentation of budget needs by administrators and discussion by the board.

June 22
- The proposed expenditure budget is presented by the Board of Education at a committee-of-the-whole meeting. Patrons are invited and may speak.

July 6
- The board reviews its proposed amended budget in a public meeting with opportunity for patron input.

July __–__
- Publication of the budget according to statutory guidelines giving notice of the final budget hearing.

August 25
- Principals and directors of all instructional and service units receive final reports on budget approvals and denials.

August 26
- The process begins anew.

FIGURE 9.1 Sample budget planning and purchasing calendar

purchasing function is a critical factor in the overall success of the educational mission of schools. In fact, it may be accurately said that the purchasing function is the operationalization of the budget, making possible procurement of all the goods and services necessary to the educational functions of schools. But although procurement is a difficult task, it must be carried out efficiently and effectively by school administrators who are both skilled and above reproach. Thus, administrators must be as fully informed as possible about the purchasing function.

STATUTORY ASPECTS OF PURCHASING

The purchasing act in school districts has become complex in recent years, primarily due to case law arising from disputes between vendors and school districts over the purchasing process and to increasing state regulation designed to assure neutral purchasing transactions that achieve the best economy for taxpayers. As a result, statutory procedures and legal requirements almost completely enwrap purchasing, making it important for administrators to understand the process thoroughly to avoid complex problems. Although the topic is too vast to cover in this chapter, several important issues merit discussion, including the nature of contracts and purchasing, supervision and ethics of purchasing, competitive bidding, purchasing and professional services, and the relationship of the Uniform Commercial Code to school purchasing.

Nature of Contracts and Purchasing

The modern complexity of schools has gone far beyond the expertise of local boards of education in terms of involvement in the daily administration of school districts. If it ever was the board's role to play a daily management function, historic development of the field of administration now logically preempts that behavior. This is patently true given legal mandates in many states that each district and building be governed by certified administrators under control of a local board of education, and given other statutes setting forth the power of boards to conduct business, including ratification of contracts entered into by the district's appointed agents. The concept of agents acting on behalf of the board of education in contractual matters is a troublesome point, however, and the nature of contracts and purchasing in the public sector demands that administrators and boards understand the limitations of agency.

The basis for establishing agents to act on behalf of a board of education generally lies in statute. There is little question that the board may appoint persons as its agents, but there are limits to the concept of agency. Although the legal interpretation of such limitations is quite complex, the administrator can best understand the scope of such limits by classifying all acts by boards of education into the two legal concepts of ministerial and discretionary duties. Ministerial duties are those responsibilities expected of a board but which it may choose not to perform for itself, such as the daily control of playground supervision. Despite delegation of its ministerial duties, the board still has complete and final responsibility. In contrast, discretionary duties are those responsibilities for which the board was elected as a body,[8] such as evaluation of the superintendent of schools. Discretionary duties may not be delegated. These distinctions apply directly to the act of agency in the purchasing function because purchasing involves the expenditure of funds, a power delegated by statute only to boards of education.

In practice, however, boards commonly appoint a purchasing officer whose task is to engage in procurement on behalf of the school district. While such appointments are a modern necessity, it is important for boards and administrators to understand the limitations and risks inherent in the role of the purchasing agent. The limitations arise from the power to spend funds resting only with the board, and the risk arises by appointing someone to enter into purchase agreements without either statutory power to purchase or the legal authority to create a valid contract. Many of the court challenges surrounding purchasing have arisen because boards failed to honor contracts entered into by agents or because agents exceeded their authority to bind the board of education.

It is well established that expenditure of funds is a discretionary act that may not be delegated by a board. The role of a purchasing agent, however, gives the clear impression that appointment empowers the agent to bind the board to contracts within the reasonable scope of those goods and services school purchasing should normally encompass. The nature of contracts, however, belies that impression because the act of agency in schools does not conform to the elements of law that comprise a valid contract. In general the elements of a valid contract are mutual assent, consideration, legally competent parties, legal subject matter, and agreement in form as required by law. These elements simply mean that to create a valid contract, both parties must be able to enter into agreement, must agree to be bound by the contract, and must comply with other conditions including the terms of exchange and other details relating to legal purpose and contract form. Purchasing, for example, is clearly a contract under this description. To legally purchase an item with school funds, the school and vendor must be represented by persons empowered to act for each party and must meet the other requirements of law. The problem is, however, that boards may not delegate authority to bind the district to a contract since the board is the sole agency through which the district may act.[9] Thus, purchasing agents of the board are not legally competent parties as they have no valid standing in the contract.

The reality is, however, that boards have neither expertise nor time to engage in the actual daily administration of the purchasing function in a modern school district. The problem is thus generally resolved by either of two circumlocutions which, although workable, still remain awkward or tenuous. One practice is to plan expenditures well in advance, bringing each item to a legally constituted board meeting for the purpose of express approval to purchase. While this may work well in many instances, there are other occasions where it proves impractical. A second practice is to provide the district's purchasing agent with express authorization in board policy to issue purchase orders, knowing that such purchase orders are still subject to board approval and ratification. Both practices are quite common and in the instance of issuance of purchase orders in advance of a board meeting, many districts have printed a statement on purchase orders informing vendors that such orders are cancelable under state statute if the board subsequently refuses to ratify the purchase agreement (see Figure 9.6, p. 463).

Under normal conditions, a board regularly ratifies contracts entered into by its agent. Notice of agency to vendors is important, however, because neither boards nor agents always know the law of contracts well enough to avoid problems. For example, in a few instances boards may not actually be able to ratify a contract entered into by agency, and in still other instances may choose for some reason not to ratify a particular agreement. The first instance is illustrated when it is restated that boards have only statutory rights to purchase, rather than inherent rights. This concept limits the contractual power of a board to only those authorized in statute. While such authorization admittedly may be broad, the board always risks invalidation of an *ultra vires* contract if challenge arises. Additionally, boards may be prevented from ratifying a contract if it is subsequently discovered that the contract was *void* or *fraudulent,* violating one or more of the contractual elements described earlier.[10] There are other instances wherein boards may choose not to ratify an agent's actions, such as when a dispute arises between the board and its agent over the appropriateness of an expenditure. Although such instances are not overly common, there is a body of case law where such disputes have been adjudicated by the courts where vendors have been caught between feuding parties within a district. The risk to agency is apparent, however, because a board may obviously choose to nullify contracts.[11]

The need to appoint board agents to serve in the complex field of purchasing has generally overridden concerns about the tenuous nature of ratification of acts by agency. Recognition of the problem, however, has led most school districts to develop written policies on purchasing procedures that are formally adopted into the official board policy manual. As seen in Figure 9.2, such policies are usually designed to address concerns about the limitations inherent in attempting to delegate a board's discretionary purchasing power to persons who technically cannot finally exercise such power. The figure enumerates many of the good business practices recommended in this chapter and contains several references to the tentative nature of contracts entered into by agents acting on orders of the board. The policy centralizes the hierarchy of the purchasing process, identifies responsible parties, informs vendors of the regular procedures of the district in extending opportunities to supply goods and services, and notes in four separate references that only the board has final authority to issue contracts and spend public monies. While such policies are obviously designed to redress an irremediable dilemma, they represent a far better choice than for boards to administratively attempt a technical function beyond their expertise.

Supervision and Ethics of Purchasing

The serious nature of purchasing and the potentially uncomfortable position of an appointed purchasing agent in a school district illustrate a great need for school districts and administrators to understand the importance of supervision and ethics in purchasing. Many problems of agency are unforeseeable, and the only comfort and exoneration is to have engaged in impeccable communication and behavior in discharging the purchasing function. Opportunity for problems also arises in many other ways, and many fine administrators have regretted failure to properly induct and supervise employees in the handling of purchasing procedures. While the vast majority of public school employees are honest, loyal, and hardworking, good business practice still requires a district to adopt policies and procedures designed to prevent and respond to problems that can arise any time a human element is involved. In addition to preventing actual dishonest acts, it is appropriate to engage in supervision of ethical behavior in that even the appearance of wrongdoing when none is actually present is devastating. Good administrators should therefore have a constant concern for supervision of purchasing procedures and policies governing ethical behavior.

Generally, school districts have extensive policies addressing possible problems in the area of ethics. The sample purchasing policy in Figure 9.2 typified such interests in its statement of philosophy and repeated those concerns at other points. The many key words in Figure 9.2 addressing ethical issues included competitive purchas-

Statement of Philosophy

The function of the purchasing office is to serve the educational program by providing the necessary supplies, equipment, and services needed to properly conduct the educational enterprise. The Board of Education declares its intention to purchase competitively without prejudice and to seek the maximum educational value for every dollar expended.

The acquisition of services, equipment, and supplies is centralized in the purchasing department, which functions under the supervision of a person designated as being responsible for purchasing by the Board of Education. All purchasing transactions are conducted through this office.

Purchasing Policy

(1) An assistant superintendent will be appointed by the Board of Education to serve as purchasing agent. This officer will be responsible for developing and administering the purchasing program of the school district.

(2) Appointment of a purchasing officer does not relieve the vendor of knowledge that in this state purchase orders are cancelable as authorized by statute in S.A. 10-1113.

(3) The purchasing agent is authorized to issue purchase orders without prior approval of the Board of Education where formal bidding procedures are not required by law, and when budget appropriations are adequate to cover such obligations. All such issuances are subject to final approval by the Board of Education in a duly constituted legal meeting of the same.

(4) All purchase contracts for materials, equipment, and supplies involving an annual expenditure over $1,000 and all public works contracts involving more than $5,000 shall be awarded on the basis of advertising and competitive bidding. The assistant superintendent is authorized to open bids and record the same pursuant to law.

(5) All contracts requiring public advertising and competitive bidding shall be awarded by resolution of the Board. Recommendations for the award of all such contracts shall be submitted to the Board by the central office administration.

(6) Residence or place of business of local bidders may be a consideration only in cases where identical bids have been submitted.

(7) Purchases shall be made through available state contracts whenever such purchases are in the best interest of the school district.

(8) Items common to the various schools shall be standardized when consistent with the goals of efficiency and economy.

(9) Petty cash funds shall be established annually in the amount of $_____ for each attendance center and the administrative center. Such funds shall only be used for payment of properly itemized bills of nominal amounts under conditions requiring immediate payment. Allowances, responsibility and accounting shall be in accordance with Board regulations and the state's statutes governing the same.

(10) Purchasing procedures of the district shall comply with all applicable laws and statutes of the state.

(11) A statement of "general conditions" as approved by the Board shall be included with all specifications submitted to suppliers for bids and imprinted on purchase orders. These general conditions shall be included by reference and implication in all contracts awarded.

(12) Opportunity shall be provided to all responsible suppliers to do business with the district. To this end the purchasing agent shall develop and maintain lists of potential bidders for various types of materials, supplies, and equipment. This list will constitute a mailing list for distributing specifications and invitations to bid.

(13) No board member, officer, or employee of this district shall be interested financially in any contract entered into by the Board. This precludes acceptance of any gratuity, financial or otherwise of any said person from any supplier of goods or services to the district.

FIGURE 9.2 Sample board policy on purchasing

SOURCE: Adapted and modified from the purchasing policy of the Great Bend (Kansas) Public School District.

ing without prejudice, and statements about conflict of interest by board members, administrators, and employees. In addition, the policy forbade gifts of any nature to employees of the district because any such act could be construed as seeking unfair favor in contract awards. Almost without exception, such policies have become omnipresent in school districts across the nation. While ethics in purchasing is not confined to simply conflicts of interest or improper gifts by vendors, these policies uniformly center on maintaining neutral objectivity toward all vendors to foster a well-balanced and competitive marketplace. Some differences in ethics policies exist, but deviations tend to be fairly minor. For example, the purchasing ethics policy from a district in another state reads almost identically to Figure 9.2, with only small differences relating to advertising gifts:

> No employee of the purchasing department shall be financially interested, or have any personal beneficial interest, directly or indirectly in any contract or purchase order for supplies, materials, equipment, or utility services used by or furnished to any department or agency of the school district; nor shall any employee accept or receive directly or indirectly from any person, firm or corporation to whom any contract or purchase order may be awarded, by rebate, gift or otherwise, any money or anything of value, or any promise, obligation or contract for future reward or compensation. A violation of this policy is a felony according to law. Inexpensive advertising items bearing the name of the firm, such as pens, pencils, paper weights, calendars, etc., are not considered articles of value or gifts in relation to this policy.[12]

In addition, many state and local policies governing ethics of school personnel are even broader than the examples quoted here. Many states have widely inclusive policies and statutes that guard strictly against either actual impropriety or the appearance of illegal behavior in the purchasing act. As a general rule, board policies have rather extensively developed sections governing behavior of employees to prevent the appearance of wrongdoing, and there is usually lengthy illustration of examples of improper acts. Because the opportunity for wrongdoing or misperception is so great, there is often specific enumeration of improper practices that have recurred in school settings. While such policies and examples are too lengthy to set forth here, their existence is worth noting, and it is further worth identifying that the following practices are often specifically forbidden under penalty of dismissal and other legal prosecution:

1. Using information available only to an employee by virtue of position for personal profit, gain or advantage;
2. Directly or indirectly furnishing to any prospective bidder information not equally available to all bidders;
3. Providing confidential information to persons to whom issuance of such information has not been authorized;
4. Providing or using the names of persons from records of the department for a mailing list that has not been authorized;
5. Accepting, taking, or converting to one's own use products of any kind in the course of or as the result of inspections of such products or the facilities of the owner or possessor;
6. Using a position or status in the department to solicit, directly or

indirectly, business of any kind or to purchase supplies or equipment at special discounts or upon special concessions for private use from any person who sells or solicits sales to the school district; and

7. Serving, either as an officer, employee, member of the board of directors, or in any capacity for consideration, the interests of any organization which transacts or attempts to transact business with the school district for profit when such employee holds a position of review or control—even though such business transactions are remote.[13]

From the exhaustive nature of the foregoing list and the thorough focus on propriety of the two sample policies cited earlier, it is easy to see that the procurement function encompasses the ethical conduct of each employee in a school district. Anyone who has worked for a number of years in education is aware of at least one person whose behavior has been less than exemplary—whether deliberately or unintentionally wrong. Examples of deliberate wrongdoing can be illustrated by school employees who have used the school's purchasing power to gain unfair advantage through discounts on items purchased for personal use or to purchase high-dollar items for personal use on school purchase orders to avoid paying state sales tax, or have stolen school-purchased items such as tires and tools. Examples of unintentional wrongdoing include pilfering of school supplies for home use and many other improper acts. The nature of ethical behavior is so serious that many boards of education require employees to make disclosures of possible conflicts and even reveal outside income. In many districts, avoidance of the appearance of impropriety is so important that the superintendent and senior staff are prohibited from outside employment, by either statute or local board rules. While such precautions may seem strange to persons uninitiated in the public policy arena, experienced school fiscal officers always suggest that if one must err, then do so in the most conservative fashion.

Supervision and ethics of purchasing thus require a vigilant attitude on the part of administrators and boards because the mere investigation of impropriety is often sufficient to do irreparable harm. Perhaps the best admonishment was given long ago by the Association for School Business Officials, International, when it stated that good fiscal officers "observe foolish law, but work for its revision."[14] The admonition seems highly appropriate for absolutely every person in a school district.

Competitive Bidding

The great need for propriety in school purchasing and the enormous pressure on government to secure the greatest good for each tax dollar have given rise to the concept of competitive bidding in the public domain, a practice that has been in use for many years. As the Mississippi Supreme Court in *Beall v. Board of Supervisors*[15] noted in 1941: "These [competitive bidding] statutes were born of experience . . ." with an objective toward preventing "private and secret machinations."[16]

The different environment of openness involved in public monies and the fear of government operating in secrecy have led every state to adopt a series of statutes governing the procurement of goods and services by public agencies to demand a strict accounting of public expenditures under *sunshine* laws that require all official business to be conducted in accordance with open meeting acts. Without exception, school districts are subject to such laws. Because of the large amount of money and intense feelings about local ownership of schools, educational organizations are even further subject to a high level of scrutiny in purchasing practices by vendors and taxpayers alike. Generally, school districts are included under the local governmental unit provisions of applicable state statutes. For school districts, this means that no public money can be spent except by formal approval by a legally constituted body in open meeting and in accord with statutory provisions. This obviously returns to the concept that only the board of education can spend money either by initiation or ratification of contracts recommended by its agent, and such expenditure must be for a permissible purpose and approved in a legally called open board meeting.

Statutory restrictions on expenditure of public monies also usually include competitive bidding requirements. Competitive bidding is designed to allow tax dollars to take advantage of the open marketplace wherein competition between suppliers of goods may result in economies and where the appearance of impropriety can be avoided through an impartial choice among available suppliers. Considerable wisdom in bid laws exists, however, as statutes demanding competitive bids do not usually apply if the amount of money is not substantial enough to warrant the trouble and expense of bidding or when vendors would not consider it worthwhile to bid. For example, bidding the purchase of one $60 bus battery or a $30 case of bar soap would be counterproductive in most instances.[17] But when the price increases to where large sums of money are at stake or the frequency of competitors is greatly reduced, states usually require competitive bidding because of economies and opportunities for impropriety. For example, football field irrigation systems are so costly and highly specialized that an unfair monopoly could evolve, and the opportunity for suppliers to attempt to corner a market could be tempting. Likewise, a school bus dealer might be tempted to charge more than if bid requests were sent to several bus dealers. To protect the public treasury in such instances, states have constructed stringent bid laws.

Bid laws are generally written to cover procurement of "materials" generally defined as the acquisition of supplies, goods, machinery and equipment of any kind. Professional services are generally excluded from the competitive bid process even though a high price may accompany such services. Although bid laws vary from state to state, they generally contain several common elements.[18] Although the student of education finance should closely consult the appropriate state statutory code, a typical bid law designed to ensure competitive and open public bidding of goods and services generally includes statements about threshold expenditure amounts, split bids, unfair bid restriction, method of bid opening, award or rejection of bids, bid bonds, and exceptions under emergency conditions. Threshold expenditure amounts are intended to trigger bid laws only when large purchases are involved. Bid statutes also usually prohibit splitting large purchases into two or more smaller amounts in the belief that some persons would seek to manipulate the law on threshold. Unfair bid restriction prohibits writing bid requests in such as manner as to exclude all vendors except a preferred one. Method of bid opening and bid award assures uniform procedures that are ethical and aboveboard. For example, such a law usually requires bids to be opened in public, that the lowest responsible bid be accepted, that reasons for rejecting all bids be stated, and that reasons for not accepting the absolutely lowest bid be given in writing. Emergency exceptions to bid laws simply recognize that legitimate reasons may arise where time is of the essence (e.g., boiler explosion). Finally, such laws usually require financial commitment by the bidder in the form of a bid bond in case of contract default.

Although the language of bid laws and some provisions may differ from state to state, the purpose and commonalities of bid laws are uniform and highly apparent. For example, the common bid law might read in part as follows:

1. When the total amount of any purchase does not exceed $15,000 or the total annual rental payments do not exceed $10,000 the purchasing unit may buy on the open market without the giving of notice or the receiving of bids, in one of two ways: (a) the purchasing unit may invite quotes from at least three persons known to deal in the classes of materials by mailing them a copy of the specifications for the materials not less than seven days before the time fixed for receiving quotes. If satisfactory quotes are received, the unit shall award the contract to the lowest responsible and responsive quoter for each class of materials required. The unit may reject all quotes and, if no valid quotes are received for an item, purchase or lease that item on the open market without further invitations for quotes, (b) under these conditions, the purchasing unit has the option of purchasing or leasing materials in the open market without inviting or receiving quotes.

2. The total purchases of similar materials by a purchasing unit, from one person, during a six month period under paragraph 1 may not exceed $15,000 and the total annual rental payments to one person under all leases for similar materials may not exceed $10,000.

3. When a purchase or lease exceeds the $15,000 or $10,000 respective amount, the purchasing or leasing unit shall prepare specifications describing the kind and quantity of the materials needed, but the purchaser shall avoid specifications that might unduly limit competition. Under certain conditions, specifications may be solicited by way of publishing a legal notice . . . When specifications have been completed, a notice of the time and place for receiving bids shall be given by publication . . . All meetings for receiving bids must be open to the public. All plans and specifications shall be kept in a place available for public inspections which shall be specified in the notice.

4. The bids shall be opened publicly and read aloud at the time and place designated in the notice.

5. After a satisfactory bid is received, the purchasing unit shall award a contract to the lowest responsible and responsive bidder for each class of materials required. If a contract is awarded, but not to the lowest bidder, the factors used to justify that award must be stated in writing at the time the award is made, and a copy of that statement must be kept available for public inspection.

6. The purchasing unit may reject all bids and ask for new bids. If no valid bids are received for an item, the unit may purchase or lease that item on the open market without further advertisement for bids.

7. A certified check shall be filed with each bid by a bidder not having his principal place of business in the state in the amount determined and specified by the purchasing unit in the notice of the letting. For the purpose of this statute, it is lawful to submit a draft, cashier's check or money order issued by a financial institution insured by an

agency of the United States in all cases where it is required that a certified check be submitted with a bid. A bond shall be filed with each bid by a bidder having his principal place of business in the state in the amount determined and specified by the purchasing unit in the notice of the letting. The amount of the bond or certified check may not be set at more than 10 percent of the contract price. This does not preclude the use of a performance bond in addition to the bid bond or certified check if the amount of the performance bond is listed in the specifications and in the notice of the letting.

8. The purchasing unit shall allow a bidder not having his principal place of business in the state to submit a bid bond if the bond is secured by a surety having his principal place of business in the state.

9. All checks of unsuccessful bidders shall be returned to them by the purchasing unit upon selection of successful bidders. Checks of successful bidders shall be held until delivery or until completion of the contract.

10. Each bid for a purchase or lease of materials must be executed on forms prescribed by the appropriate state agency.

11. As an alternative to advertising for new bids, a purchasing unit may extend beyond the contractual period, a contract let under the provisions of this law.

12. Within thirty days after the acceptance of a bid, quote, offer, estimate, or contract for the purchase or lease of materials, the purchasing unit shall issue an original purchase order to the successful bidder, retain a copy for the unit's records, and file a copy for public record.

13. A purchasing unit upon declaration of an emergency, may make any purchase or lease materials without giving notice or receiving bids if quotes are invited from two or more persons known to deal in the required materials. The declaration of emergency and names of those persons invited to quote must be recorded in the minutes.

14. Materials may be purchased or leased from an agency of the federal government without the giving of notice or receiving of bids.[19]

The sample bid law above makes evident the seriousness, complexity, and thoroughness of competitive bidding. Because these statutes are so tightly written, the requirements of law must be followed carefully by the school district to avoid challenge by unsuccessful bidders or other interested persons. While the law is usually easy to read, it is often very difficult to follow because a few aspects are fairly technical and thus demand close attention by school administrators. School districts are frankly at a disadvantage in these activities because their primary mission is the instruction of children, while the mission of vendors is product knowledge and marketplace survival. Under such conditions, schools often broadly attempt to follow bid laws in which they are not expert, while the bidders with whom they must deal are so narrowly focused that they can jealously know the nuances of competitive bid statutes. As a result, bid errors do occur with resultant challenge. Most often bid law problems among school districts generally fall into the areas of bid notice, writing bid specifications, and awarding bids.

Advertising for bids must strictly follow statutory requirements. The purpose of advertising is obvious, as potential bidders must be able to learn of the district's intent to purchase some material or service. From the governmental perspective, advertising casts the purchase act into the public eye and secures the lowest bid when all other things are equal. Generally, statutes demand that the call for bids must be made in a statutorily defined public document, usually defined as local newspapers. In some instances, advertising for bids may also be appropriate in government publications. Many school districts also choose to advertise in professional and trade publications whose readership consists primarily of those persons or organizations specializing in providing certain types of goods or services. Vendors who respond to requests for bids can therefore either gather the specifications from the advertisement directly or contact the appointed office for a full set of bid specifications. Generally bid specifications are too complex to publish, making it necessary to simply publish a bid notice with bidders obtaining a bid packet from the appropriate office. A sample bid notice in the form that would actually be published in a newspaper is seen in Figure 9.3.

The actual bid packet usually consists of a copy of the initial legal advertisement, the technical specifications, and references to applicable state statutes regarding bid bonds and so on, as well as the actual bid proposal documents and the manner and location of bid opening. School districts are well within their legal rights to include a request in the bid packet requiring bidders to submit detailed information concerning how long the firm has been doing business, the financial stability of the firm, listing of successful installations, nature and specifications of any applicable guarantees and/or service contracts, ongoing training provided for their employees, and the overall service capabilities of the firm.[20] From the district's perspective, such information may be crucial in helping reach a decision. Additionally, such information may also provide valuable legal protection if a decision is made to award the contract to a bidder who did not submit the absolutely lowest bid. As Figure 9.3 indicates, when projects require outside consultant assistance, such as engineering firms, the district has the added benefit of not dealing directly with bidders. In other instances, such as bus purchases, however, the district must be doubly expert as bids are normally prepared and evaluated by the district itself.

As a general rule, bidders on public contracts are expected to submit a financial guaranty at the same time as bid submission. Generally bid bonds or cashier's/certified checks satisfy this requirement. The reason for requiring financial security from the bidder in this manner is to protect the school district in that the bid bond or certified check ensures that if the successful bidder subsequently refuses to accept the contract award, the bond company or certified check pays the difference between the client's bid and the next lowest responsible bidder. In other words, good faith acceptance by the school district of a bid guarantees that it will usually pay no more for the product than the amount of the first bid, even if it must resort to another higher bid. The reason is that the defaulting bidder loses the amount guaranteed by the bid bond or certified check. In one sense, the bid bond is thus a form of liquidated damages in the event of contract default. It is important to note, however, that the actual award of a bid bond is almost always adjudicated.[21] As a result, administrators should be careful to observe state laws of financial guaranty, prepared to obtain the item in another way while the dispute is resolved, and aware that resolution to bid default may require costly litigation.

The actual bid specifications for purchased items represent a second difficult aspect of bid laws for school districts. As stated earlier, the problem for school districts is a lack of legal skills in writing bids and of expertise in product knowledge, which when combined can create a potentially disastrous situation. Even the most

Published in the Daily Globe July 5, 1992; subsequently published July 6 and 7, 1992. Sealed bids, subject to the conditions contained herein, will be received until 4:00 P.M. (CDT) Wednesday, July 22, 1992, and then publicly opened and read in the Board of Education Office, Anytown, USA for furnishing all labor and materials and performing all work for constructing a concrete entrance road including earthwork, drainage structures, concrete pavement, seeding and miscellaneous items of work at the Anytown High School in Anytown, USA.

Anytown High School
Improvements Entrance Road

The project will include the following approximate quantities of work:

BASE BID

Unclassified Excavation	100 C.Y.
Contractor Furnished Borrow	11,500 C.Y.
9″ P.C.C. Pavement	4,480 S.Y.
8″ P.C.C. Pavement	1,090 S.Y.
Double 6′ × 5′ RCB	88.5 L.F.
Type A-10 Inlet	1 ea
Type II Ditch Inlet	1 ea
23″ × 14″ HERCP	90 L.F.
Asphalt surfacing (3″)	233 Tons
Monolithic Curb and Gutter	1,118 L.F.
Seeding	2.5 Acres
Pavement Marking	Complete
Fencing	Complete

ALTERNATE A

Contractor Furnished Borrow	1,850 C.Y.
8″ P.C.C. Pavement	653 S.Y.
Type A-10 Curb Inlet	1 ea
Asphalt Surfacing (3″)	27 Tons
Monolithic Curb and Gutter	655 L.F.
Time Limit 65 working days	

Copies of the drawings, specifications, and other contract documents are on file and available for public inspection at the Business Office of the school district, 1000 School Street, Anytown, USA. Interested bidders may secure a set of drawings, specifications, and all other contract documents from AESA Engineers, P.A., 8001 Garden Lane, Anytown, USA upon payment of one hundred dollars ($100.00).

All persons awarded and/or entering into contracts with the school district shall be subject to and required to comply with all applicable city, state and federal provisions pertaining to nondiscrimination, equal employment opportunity and affirmative action on public contracts.

FIGURE 9.3   Sample notice to bidders

uninitiated person, however, can appreciate the fact that to engage in bidding requires that specifications for the goods or project be prepared so as to result in the proper outcome. Many horror stories abound regarding districts that prepared specifications improperly or paid for products discovered later to be unsatisfactory due to bid specification error. A classic example is the purchase of the wrong engine size for a school bus, resulting in vehicles unsuited for local mountainous terrain. If it can be shown that the district erred in bid specifications or accepted delivery by signature of the wrong vehicle, much dissatisfaction can follow. Thus great care and experience are needed to ensure maximum purchasing power for the school district, fair and equal opportunity for all vendors, and efficient use of taxpayer funds.

The purpose of writing bid specifications is to make very clear to vendors the exact product or service being sought. A second purpose is to provide written proof of correctness of the district's position in dispute resolution. For school districts, it is important to remember that there are different types of specifications, depending on the goods or services sought. In some situations, writing bid specifications may call for consultants or vendors themselves to react to the specifications document[22] to determine whether such a product is available and whether specifications are clear and unambiguous. The guiding rule is that vendors should not be able to claim error or offer product substitution on the grounds of vague bid specifications. One helpful realization is that in many instances purchased supplies and equipment are so ordinary that school districts can develop standardized product lists to which bidders may reply. For example, the many paper products in a district can be standardized, while items such as buses, copiers, and computers may require expert assistance with individual specifications written for each purchase.

Responsibility for actually writing bid specifications depends on the project at hand. As mentioned earlier, school districts are not technically competent to write engineering specifications such as those contained in Figure 9.3. Consequently, expert assistance by specialty firms is expected. On the other hand, responsibility for preparing specifications will fall to the district in other instances, such as purchasing supplies, commodities, and many types of equipment. For example, bid specifications for a new copier will invariably be prepared by the district, and skill needs to be demonstrated to inform vendors of the district's desires. As a general rule, bid specifications must include both general conditions with which bidders must comply and the product specifications. For example, in purchasing a copier the general conditions should include statements about freight and installation charges, length of time the board has in accepting or rejecting the bid price, method of bid submission, insurance on the item up to point of delivery and installation, and issues of legal conformity to statute and contract law. In addition, a copy of any state notices to vendors such as preferential bid laws giving special consideration to in-state bidders is normally attached to general conditions.[23] Specifications of the copier would include speed, cost per copy, maintenance agreement costs set out separately, and special features requested by the district (see Figure 9.4). Under these precise conditions and specifications, the bidder can determine interest and ability to respond to the district's request for bids.

The third and final area where districts encounter problems in the competitive bid process involves opening any bids according to strict legal requirements, and following statutory guidelines in awarding or rejecting any and all bids. Statutes generally require advance notice of the date of bid openings and that bids be opened in public with bid amounts and vendors announced aloud. Depending on the nature of the product and bid specifications, opening of bids may be accompanied by product samples. In all instances, each bid must be thoroughly examined for compliance with written bid specifications. Often, the purchasing manager may discover a product that is a better value but is not the lowest bid meeting the written minimum bid specifications. The literature has long recognized the unwiseness of proceeding with the purchase of an inferior product, and under such conditions it is consistently suggested that all bids be rejected and new specifications drawn and rebid.[24] It is also suggested that unsuccessful bidders be informed of reasons why their bid was re-

The Board of Education will receive bids on _____ Copier _____ in the Board of Education Office, _____ until ___10:50 A.M.,___ on ___Wednesday___ , ___June 15, 1993.___ These bids will be opened at _____ , the same date and place. Late bids will be returned unopened.

General Conditions

Please note that the following conditions and stipulations must apply to your company's bids.
1. All freight and transportation charges shall be paid by the vendor and not added to the invoice.
2. All bids must be priced, extended, and totaled.
3. The Board of Education reserves the right to increase or decrease the quantity of any item bid by up to 10% at the time of the awarding of the bid without change in the bid price.
4. Price quoted must remain firm for a period of forty-five (45) days after the awarding of the bids.
5. Bids are to be made in consideration of the tax-exempt status of unified school districts.
6. All bids are to be on the form enclosed and received in a sealed envelope marked ___BID NO. 88-009___ .
7. All items bid must be the best of their respective kinds and must be guaranteed from defects in material and workmanship. Items must be manufactured in compliance with all existing legal or government directives.
8. All items must be properly packed and/or crated to insure delivery in good condition. *Rejected items will be held at the seller's risk and expense.*
9. Payment of the seller's invoice is subject to adjustment of any shortage or to rejection of any item or items.
10. Contracts entered into on the basis of submitted specifications are revokable if contrary to law.
11. Date of receipt will be considered the effective date all goods and invoices are received.
12. All merchandise will be delivered to the Unified School District ___Central Office___ ,
13. **THE BOARD OF EDUCATION RESERVES THE RIGHT TO ACCEPT OR REJECT ALL OR ANY PART OF EACH BID.**

Unified School District _____ is requesting bids on one (1) copier.

Minimum Specifications	Specifications Bid
• Twenty (20) copies per minute	_____
• Editing (six different areas at one time, trim and mask)	_____
• Pre-set enlargement and reduction	_____
• Automatic page and cassette selection	_____
• Three (3) way paper feed system	_____
• Stack sheet bypass/40 sheets at one time	_____
• Automatic color change/dual color	_____
• Margin shift	_____
• Border erase	_____
• Split paging	_____
• Interrupt key	_____
• Dry toner copier/dual components	

Monthly volume suggested: _____

Cost per copy: $ _____

Annual maintenance agreement: $ _____

(Continued)

FIGURE 9.4 Sample bid specifications

Brand/model being quoted: _____

Length of machine warranty: _____

COST FOR ONE COPIER: $ _____

_____
Company

_____
Address

_____   _____
Signed by   Title

_____   _____
Date   Telephone

FIGURE 9.4 (*Continued*)

jected, as this builds confidence and goodwill for the future.[25] If a bid is awarded, the district obviously should insist on strict compliance with contract terms and be sure of satisfactory delivery and operation before full payment is made.

The objective of competitive bid laws and processes is exceedingly clear. The district needs to write specifications for products that actually exist, that meet their special needs exactly as envisioned, that keep them out of trouble with the law and in full view of the public, and that describe products for which competitive prices can be obtained. Vendors and suppliers need specifications that are clear, that conform to their product features, and that provide them the opportunity to bid in fair competition. When all these conditions are met, the purpose of competitive bidding to prevent private and secret machinations and to secure the best public economy for tax dollars is a very wise practice indeed.

Purchasing Professional Services

A complication in competitive bidding arises when considering the purchase of professional services. Competitive bid laws were constructed on the dual premises of assuring fair and equal treatment of vendors and protecting the public treasury. By logic, it would seem defensible to make any sizable purchase subject to competitive bid laws. However, purchasing professional services—that is, expertise in architectural, engineering, legal, financial, and certain other services—normally falls outside otherwise strict competitive bid statutes.

School districts are often confused by the complexity of bid laws generally, and especially as applied to professional services. For example, when a board debates a letter from a professional accounting firm wanting to bid on the district's financial services, it may wonder whether it must bid such services, particularly since there is often language in state statutes and regulations that broadly prescribes conditions and procedures for competitive bidding for "all work, labor, and materials purchased by governmental agencies." Obviously it is easy for a lay board of education to assume from such language that no aspect of large purchases is exempt from competitive bid laws. The question is long-standing, as one court in the early 1900s held that "services requiring a peculiar professional education and experience, which distinguished the person in the industrial, economic, and social environment of life from one possessed only of the capacity to furnish work and labor"[26] did not come within the scope of public bid statutes.

Fortunately, in some instances the law is not so unclear. Numerous cases have upheld employment of architects and engineers by governmental agencies without public bid requirements.[27] In an early case examining this issue, the court in *Houston v. Glover* ruled that the phrase "all work in public improvements" in the bid statute did not apply to architectural fees. The court stated that "it was manifestly impossible to make specifications" to meet such requirement.[28] Further, where services are "highly and technically skilled in a science or profession, it would be poor judgment to bid where the lowest bidder might also be the least capable and most inexperienced."[29] Additionally, much case law has ruled that technical expertise embraces broad discretion in factors other than dollars, including skill, experience, and financial responsibility.[30] In a similar vein, employment without bidding has been upheld for engineers, whose work is similar to that of architects. Generally, if the work is professional and personal, the courts have considered such services outside public bid statutes,[31] since the value of such contracts is based on an individual's skill or performance and hence no specifications may be written.[32] Thus, districts generally need not be concerned with bidding services of high professional expertise.

On the other hand, districts have a harder time interpreting competitive bid laws in relation to other work performed, such as contracted services in facility projects. The sample public bid notice in Figure 9.3 is evidence of bidding expectations on some work services. For states with specific statutes on which services should be bid, the question is clearer. For example, Texas law provides for competitive bidding for all school construction projects of $5,000 or more but excludes "professional services rendered, including but not limited to architects' fees, attorneys' fees, and fees for fiscal agents."[33] Alaska statutes exempt professional services from competitive bid requirements where professional services are defined as "professional, technical, or consultant's services," including activities classified as "analysis, evaluation, . . . planning or recommendation."[34] Oregon statute requires that all contracts be let via public bid procedures[35] with the only exception in contracts for personal services where government agencies may let contracts "for services performed as an independent contractor in the professional capacity, including but not limited to the services of an accountant, attorney, architectural or land use planning consultant. . . ."[36] Somewhat different is Arizona's statutory language calling for competitive bidding for all construction, including contractual services,[37] except that bidding is not required for employment of architects and engineers as these professions "are otherwise regulated by law."[38] Although the phrase "not limited to" can be cause for concern, where statutes exist a careful reading can deduce inclusive or exclusive language, and with good legal counsel a school district can be fairly confident in ascertaining which services must be bid.

This ascertainment is more difficult in states where no specific statutes exist. For example, determining whether a general contractor's work is so highly skilled as to be excluded from bid statutes can be a fine line. Unless specific statutes exist that define the type of work excepted under bid laws, fiscal officers and school attorneys must carefully examine whether a type of work is professional expertise or service. If it can be justified that it is professional expertise, then the school district is generally not required to advertise and accept bids. The distinction is difficult and long-standing, as evidenced by an 1858 case in which a New York court studied the language of bid statutes to determine what constituted work versus service. The court ruled that "work" included all labor, both mental and corporeal, but also qualified it to mean the various kinds of manual labor that could be the subject of general competition or that would be awarded to the low bidder. The court then stated that it would be mischievous construction of statute to include services that required in their proper performance scientific or professional expertise.[39] While such language is generally common in case law, the lack of statute in some states is exacerbated by exception set out in other states in defining quasi-professional work, such as that performed by general contractors or construction superintendents, because these jobs are neither common labor nor generally excluded from bid laws by courts or in other states' statutes.

Even after extended analysis, determination of bidding all work not specifically exempted as expertise has to be left to court interpretation when statutes are unclear or silent on the finer points of law.[40] The subtle nuances are apparent. For example, designing a facility or the furnishing of plans and specifications for a facility would constitute the practice of architecture and an architect's license would be necessary, but supervision of actual construction of a facility is not, of itself, the practice of architecture and hence no such license is required.[41] Yet many states require proof of licensure for contracting firms that wish to bid on facility projects. These questions and their fine distinctions deserve careful legal counsel, as the question of bid requirements for work and services can become quite complex.[42] As always, the best advice must be to seek good legal counsel to ensure the district's observance of the law. Under no circumstances should a district decide that its interpretation of law is sufficient to preserve and protect the public treasury.

THE ACT OF PURCHASING

When determination is made about whether a purchase must be bid, the act of purchasing begins. It should be noted, however, that bidding may occur even when it is not statutorily required. For example, it is quite common to purchase many supplies under a bid process that fall below state minimum dollar bid amounts. The choice to engage in such elective bidding is entirely a district option, and the act of purchasing is not materially affected except in the form a district may choose to follow. This section presumes resolution of all such considerations and concentrates on other mechanics and issues in the purchasing process, tracing the purchasing act to the point at which the purchase decision is transmitted to potential vendors and discussing issues of product warranty after delivery.

General Purchasing Procedures and Problems

The purchasing act has generally followed a traditional path starting at the lowest point in the hierarchy and progressing to the highest point. In most instances, the person initiating the request prepares a requisition identifying the item to be obtained. The department head in charge of that individual's unit within the organization then determines whether the item is already in stock. If no such item exists and if the item is recommended for purchase by the department head, that person establishes specifications for the item in cooperation with the purchasing department. Multiple copies of the requisition are prepared, one copy remaining with the person requesting the item and other copies going up the approval chain, which usually includes the building principal, the division director, and various central office levels. The requisition process still occurs even if the item is available in inventory because the purchasing department must decide if the item should be restocked.

The overall purchasing procedure typically flows through a number of steps that are both internal and external to the district. At the internal level, the first step is to determine need. A teacher, department chair, service director, or some other appointed individual determines a need that has in concept already been approved in the budget via a large amount of money for such items as instructional materials. The second step is to draw a requisition wherein the need is activated by executing a requisition (see Figure 9.5). A requisition is an internal document making a formal request to ship from the district warehouse or to start the purchasing process. As with all other paperwork in the purchasing process, multiple copies of requisitions are necessary to establish a paper trail, both for auditing purposes and for future purchasing cycles. The third step of the purchasing cycle is to forward the requisition to the purchasing department. The purchasing department considers the request and, if ap-

FIGURE 9.5   Sample purchase requisition

PURCHASE REQUISITION   No. **91804**

Community School

DATE_____

SCHOOL OR OFFICE_____

ACCOUNT NO._____
ACCOUNT NAME_____
ORDERED BY_____
AUTHORIZED BY_____
APPROVED BY_____
(CO-ORD)

ITEMS AND DESCRIPTION	QUANTITY	UNIT PRICE	AMOUNT

SUGGESTED
VENDOR NAME_____

STREET_____

No._____

CITY & STATE_____

proved, procures the item outright, seeks phone quotations, or engages in the bid process if required by law or district policy. If bids are necessary, the bid process is activated. The fourth step occurs when the purchasing department prepares the formal bid or purchase order (see Figure 9.6) for board approval. The fifth and final step follows quickly as the purchasing department moves the process to its external phase as the purchase order or contract is sent to the supplier for prompt delivery. As a final precaution, the purchase order is never transmitted to the vendor until the finance office has verified the legality of the purchase and has checked for adequate funds in the proper account to pay for the item.

Compared to the complexity of legal considerations surrounding the procurement function of school districts, the physical act of purchasing is thus quite simple and straightforward. The cyclical flow of purchasing should be noted because its progress must be continual to prevent interruption of the educational process. Graphic summation of the flow of the purchasing act can be seen in Figure 9.7, where after defining a particular need, the requisition seeks approval and begins the process of executing the purchase order. The purchase order as approved by the board, either in advance or by ratification, authorizes the vendor to deliver the item in an expeditious manner. When all these events are carried out properly by well-trained personnel acting under expert direction by good school administrators, the educational mission of schools is greatly aided.

Despite best efforts by school districts to engage in sound business practices and to secure the greatest quality, economy, and efficiency in purchasing, there are still instances when problems arise with products or suppliers. Under these conditions, it is important for administrators to have a general knowledge of their rights and responsibilities and to anticipate the issues they may encounter if attempts are made to remedy unsatisfactory situations. While the law defies easy simplification, a brief overview of product warranty and consumer satisfaction should be helpful.

In the private sector, individuals and businesses are protected by various consumer protection statutes that seek to remedy problems in product warranty and liability that arise in the course of marketplace transactions. Generally those same protections are available to school districts. But because school districts as government agencies typically engage in procurement of a variety of goods and services significantly more complex than the average firm or individual in the private sector, administrators need to exhibit special care to assure quality protection measures where the public treasury is concerned. As with other areas of law, resolution of such problems is generally well beyond the knowledge of the local district. As a result, the rule is to first consult legal counsel in search of applicable state statute for protections. As it sometimes happens, however, problems arise that are not specifically covered in statute. In the absence of applicable state statutes, administrators and their legal counsel should understand that other protections are available because public school districts are beneficiaries of the Uniform Commercial Code (UCC).[43]

The benefit of the UCC is that its latest version revised in 1987 has been adopted by all states,[44] thereby providing some degree of interstate consistency to interpretation and application of a maze of dissimilar statutes governing many aspects of business practice. Even though a few states also adopted a nonuniform amendment to the UCC, the value of interstate application of commercial law is enormous in that the 800-page UCC is highly persuasive to courts during adjudication. Whereas previously school districts and vendors were virtually at the mercy of individual state courts, which in turn made the question of competent jurisdiction a matter of vital concern

Purchase Order and Claim Voucher

ORDER 7 6680

BOARD OF EDUCATION

DATE_____ 2 _____

WHEN SHIP: _____

VENDOR NO:_____ 1 _____

TO: _____

— 3 _____

SHIP TO:
BILL:

UNIFIED SCHOOL DISTRICT NUMBER

% _____

VENDOR: THIS IS A CANCELABLE PURCHASE ORDER AS AUTHORIZED BY S.A. 10-1113

QUANTITY	CATALOG NO.	DESCRIPTION OF ARTICLE	UNIT PRICE	EST. PRICE	OFFICE USE ONLY
5		7	8		10
	6			9	
				TOTAL	12

JUSTIFICATION OF ABOVE REQUESTS:

11

_____ 14 _____

WARRANT NUMBER _____ 13 _____

DATE PAID _____ _____

VENDOR/CONTRACTOR:
"In accepting this Purchase Order, the vendor/contractor hereby abides by State Statute: S.A. 44-1030, Sections 1-5"
— Copy printed on back of white copy —

Requested By:_____

Approved By:_____
Department Coordinators

Approved By:_____ 15 _____
Building Principal

Approved By:_____
Assistant Superintendent—Curriculum

Approved By:_____
Assistant Superintendent—Clerk

	Teacher	Room No.	Attendance Center	Department	Acquisition Method	Estimated Life
(	) (	) (	) (	) (	) (	

INVESTMENT SOURCE	FUND NUMBER	AMOUNT
16	17	18
TOTAL		

PREPAY ALL TRANSPORTATION CHARGES

I hereby certify that the within itemized account is true and correct, and remains due and unpaid in the amount shown thereon.

FIRM:_____

BY:
(Sign Here): 19 _____

INSTRUCTIONS TO VENDORS:
1. Submit two copies of your itemized invoice to Clerk.
2. Signed claim voucher (white copy), for the correct amount due, must reach our business office later than the 20th of the month to receive payment in the following month.
3. No warrants will be issued until the white copy is in the hands of the district business office.
4. Each shipment must be covered by separate invoice.
5. If prices are different than listed, please list under Actual Cost Column.
6. If shipment cannot be made as requested, notify us at once.
7. All transportation charges, if any, are prepaid and added to invoice.
8. Show Purchase Order No. on invoice & on outside of each package and carton.

FIGURE 9.6 Sample purchase order

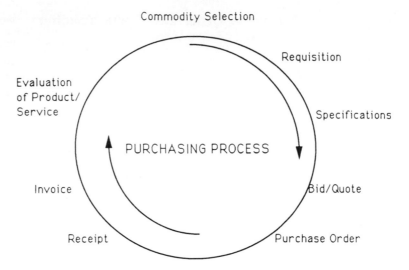

FIGURE 9.7   The purchasing cycle

to litigants, the UCC's ability to reach across state lines is invaluable because it provides some measure of predictable response in product disputes. As school districts quite often contract with out-of-state suppliers, such uniformity is invaluable because courts in the absence of state statutes specific to the situation will generally turn to the UCC. Such protection is particularly valuable for governmental entities operating in the political public arena.

Although technical knowledge of the UCC is most interesting to legal counsel, a general understanding of the coverage provided by the UCC is also helpful to the administrator. In many instances, the UCC may have its greatest application to school districts in their efforts to secure proper product warranties. For example, if problems with a product were to develop that were only sparsely addressed in state statutes, schools should be relieved to know that redress may still be available because the UCC contains interpretation of both expressed or implied warranties. Expressed warranties by manufacturers and suppliers are normally the easiest to enforce and highly valuable in dispute resolution because they speak specifically to standards for quality, fitness, and overall performance of the product in question. Manufacturers and suppliers, however, often attempt to escape liability under technical interpretation of warranty exceptions. The UCC may assist in such situations because it rules on an interstate scale that an expressed warranty is evidenced by more than the written warranty that normally accompanies a product. For example, the UCC states that an express warranty is evidenced by all of the following:

1. *An affirmation of fact,* i.e., the seller describes the item as consisting of a certain substance;
2. *Promise,* i.e., the goods must conform to all promises made by the seller as to the product's performance;
3. *Description,* i.e., the goods must conform to any description that the seller has supplied; and
4. *Sample,* i.e., the sample must be representative of the total goods in question.[45]

Examples may help the administrator understand the value of evidence of expressed warranty under the UCC. Most items carry a manufacturer's warranty. If the district cannot reach agreement with a supplier of a product under the terms of written warranty and if state statutes do not produce quick compliance, the UCC is available across state lines. Under the UCC, the supplier who has described a product as to substance must in fact supply such a product. A good example might be chainlink fence sold as heavyweight 12-gauge mesh but shipped as lightweight 14-gauge. The supplier under affirmation of fact would be held liable under the UCC. Similarly, if a supplier states that a high-speed copier will produce 20 duplex copies per minute, under promise the machine must perform at the guaranteed rate. Similarly, products cannot be substituted except by permission under description, and any samples shown must be of the same quality and nature as the goods received. The UCC thus provides extended protection to suppliers' warranties and covers some of the gaps in thoroughness that occur in individual state statutes.

In a few instances, school districts may fall into a trap wherein no expressed warranty can be construed. In absence of expressed warranty, the UCC provides that an implied warranty can be reasonably expected whereby the purchaser may expect the product to reasonably fit a general expectation for minimal performance standards. For example, under the UCC an implied warranty is evidenced by the following provisions:

1. *Ordinary usage:* the goods must meet or fit the ordinary purpose for which they were sold;[46]
2. *Reliance:* "When the buyer before entering into the contract has examined the goods or the sample or model as fully as he desired or has refused to examine the goods, there is no implied warranty with regard to defects which an examination ought in the circumstances to have revealed to him;"[47]
3. *Causation:* the buyer must demonstrate that a warranty of some description existed and that it was broken;
4. *Implied situations:* in certain areas certification as to the goods is a normal course of action (e.g., certification of breeding stock for agricultural courses); and
5. *Particular purpose:* the item in question must fit the particular purpose for which it is required as the buyer relies on the vendor's skills and knowledge in the selection and furnishing of suitable goods for the particular purpose for which it was purchased.[48]

Under these rules, an implied warranty is available to school districts for purchased products. An implied warranty is intended to subvert outright fraud wherein a product clearly is unable to meet the purpose for which it was sold, when the purchaser can demonstrate product dysfunction, when the buyer might reasonably expect certification of a product for actual performance not associated with fault of the purchaser, and whenever the purchaser has had to rely on the superior knowledge of a vendor. Additionally, the UCC dictates in highly specific language the responsibility of the vendor and purchaser as to the manner of transfer of ownership, responsibility for damages in shipment, and misrepresentation. It should be noted, however, that no such warranties may exist if the purchaser is negligent in taking reasonable care to understand and examine products for suitability and condition.

Because it is a complex system of outlining responsibilities of parties in various commercial transactions, the overall operation of the UCC is uninteresting to public school administrators. Nonetheless, the purchasing office should be reasonably familiar with its overall concepts and structure so as to minimize potential conflicts with vendors. Inasmuch as any purchase agreement entered into by the school district could conceivably be affected by the UCC, the chief purchasing officer and the attorney for the school district should take special care to become familiar with its complexities to protect the interests of the board and taxpayers.

WAREHOUSING, INVENTORY, AND CONTROL

Although the purchasing act may be complete when the goods are received and payment is made, the district's job is just beginning. Most school systems have become sufficiently sophisticated in discount buying that there is a concomitant need to arrange for warehousing, inventory, and control of purchased items. The range of materials and supplies kept in stock for distribution varies from district to district, but the effective purchasing and distribution of goods and supplies is tantamount to the efficient operation of the school district. In almost all instances the value of stored goods will run into many thousands of dollars, and in larger systems millions of dollars may be involved. For example, larger systems buy paper supplies by the trainload and store them in vast district-owned warehouses covering city blocks. Smaller districts have more choices, ranging from centralized storage areas to decentralized storage systems at individual buildings. The issue is complicated when smaller districts engage in cooperative purchasing with other districts to derive bulk discounts,[49] but encounter problems in warehousing, distribution, and control because they are not physically equipped for mass storage and distribution.

General Issues of Management

Regardless of a district's size, choices must be made about how to store, distribute, and control inventory. Some measure of choice is inherent in the size and complexity of the district in terms of the number of students served and in the number of school sites and geographic layout. For example, a large city system with 100 elementary schools, 30 middle schools, 6 high schools, and 2 alternative schools will almost necessarily require a centralized storage and distribution center. On the other hand, smaller districts may choose a central system if space in an existing facility is available, but construction of new space for warehousing is highly questionable in terms of efficiency. Similarly, a district with few students that covers a vast land area may choose several central points for warehousing, whereas districts with small land masses and large student populations may be able to choose between either centralized storage or some modification of decentralization. In other words, some choices are limited while others need to be made on the basis of intelligent processes.

Decisions about mechanisms for warehousing, distribution, and control should be made on the basis of one overriding principle: efficient and effective distribution of goods and materials for the uninterrupted educational operation of the school district. Materials should be delivered to each school site in a timely manner to assure no interruption of the instructional activities. For larger systems, the complexity of multiple school sites usually means a large centralized operation with regular deliveries to individual schools that in turn store and distribute much smaller amounts to end users. Centralized systems have many advantages, including:

1. Ample supplies are on hand to assure a continuous flow of needed materials to teachers and others for direct instructional and support purposes;
2. Larger and more economical purchases can be made based on supply and marketing conditions;
3. Central warehousing of large amounts of supplies frees up more expensive instructional space within the school district by utilizing less expensive dedicated warehousing space;
4. The necessity of peak purchasing and resultant negative cash flow can be minimized while assuring timely delivery to school buildings at later times;
5. In relatively larger and more complex school districts, a specialized staff can be utilized to inspect and handle the purchases and the computerized recordkeeping for nearly instantaneous information for future purchasing needs; and
6. Centralized storage avoids many of the complex problems of inventorying goods scattered across a school system.

Conversely, many school districts including some larger systems have found that decentralized storage and warehousing serves many useful purposes, based on the premise that receiving schools are best suited to ascertain whether specifications and quality have been met and can best determine the amounts to have on hand. This philosophy also argues that individual schools can best operate inventory reordering, as they are able to monitor supply usage on a daily basis. In other words, decentralized receiving and storage is predicated on each school site's ability to ascertain the quality and quantity of goods in an immediate time frame. Furthermore, with the advent of school site management in many districts, decentralized receiving and storage has gained new popularity throughout the country. Proponents of decentralized receiving and storage cite the following strengths to such a plan:

1. Smaller school districts have found that costs of building and maintaining storage facilities represent excessive costs in relationship to the instructional programs;
2. Districts can eliminate the personnel necessary for receiving, storing, and distributing to the various schools along with the associated space and handling of equipment;
3. More frequent purchasing results in less obsolescence and eliminates possible deterioration of certain supplies over time;
4. Smaller school districts can absorb associated costs within each school building as opposed to the overhead of another administrative organization within the school district; and
5. Funds tied up in massive inventories represent loss of interest earnings or utilization of funds for more immediate needs.

These differences in professional opinion make it impossible to identify a single best model for school districts. In general, however, it may be observed that decentralized purchasing forgoes a vast array of economies of scale and expertise, particularly in larger school districts,[50] while efficiency in purchasing, storing, and distributing is also necessarily a function of the size, complexity, and the geography of each school district. Thus, the decision must be determined on a district-by-district basis, given awareness of the benefits and drawbacks of each system.

Regardless of the warehousing system chosen, districts must always know the amount and condition of goods and materials on hand at any one time.[51] This is obviously important for the instructional and support functions of the district, and it is equally important because the chief fiscal officer must always be able to assure the board of education and the taxpayers that all goods and services are safe and secure from peril or mismanagement. Nearly every professional educator recognizes that some mismanagement occurs in educational inventories, ranging from careless spoilage to theft (see Chapter 10 for a discussion of risk management). As a result, districts must exert special care to inventory and control purchases.

Generally, school districts engage in either perpetual or periodic inventory management. Perpetual inventory procedures allow continuous updating of materials on hand, while taking into account those items on order and in the requisition process. With the advent of microcomputers and specific inventory software, such procedures are relatively easy to carry out, particularly if small quantities stored at individual school sites are also fed into the central data bank at remote computer terminals. The benefit to perpetual inventory, of course, is that absolute accurate information is available on a daily basis for decision making. In contrast, periodic inventory provides for recounting of all items in stock on a regular but more infrequent basis. In school districts utilizing periodic inventory, the accounting is generally made once a year, usually in conjunction with year-end purchasing. The choice between these inventory systems is not as simple as choosing a preferred method because the nature and size of the district may help dictate the choice. "Several factors generally influence the final choice of system, such as: (1) organization of the business office and adequacy of staff, (2) volume of stock and frequency of issue, (3) size of the central storage facilities, and (4) effectiveness of inter-office channels of communications."[52] Needless to say, an infinite range of modifications is possible, as in Figure 9.8 where this district has chosen to integrate the best features of perpetual and periodic inventory into its regular bulk purchasing calendar.

The choice of inventory method is only critical as it relates to efficiency in terms of materials on hand when needed and availability of cash supplies. Obviously, the more inventory a district has, the less idle cash can be on hand. The trade-off is the "just-in-time" purchasing system, whereby the district orders supplies just in time for use, running a risk of being short on needed items and forgoing significant bulk purchasing discounts. The goal is to strike the best possible balance given the nature of the district, making the purchasing, inventory, distribution, and control functions closely related and thoughtfully coordinated to assure smooth and continuous accomplishment of the educational mission.

The act of purchasing, inventory, control, and distribution is highly complex in modern schools. Yet the purpose is simple when it is realized that "the main economy of the purchas[ing] program comes from having materials in the hands of personnel when they are needed."[53] While simple to state, achieving this purpose is difficult, given that school district procurement procedures must conform to statutory provisions and board policies to avoid real traps and the appearance of wrongdoing. Although no one best model exists, there are models to choose from, and the plan initiated and carried out by the district should strictly follow written purchasing procedures for which one person is ultimately responsible. When these realities are combined with a purchase order system designed to ensure proper use of taxpayer funds to purchase the best goods and services at the best price in the public spotlight and a system for efficient distribution and control, the task is truly formidable. It is small wonder that ethical codes of behavior are important for persons charged with such

Item	Quantity Request To Staff	Quantity Request Due From Staff	To Vendor For Bid Prices	Due From Vendor	Final Quantities Due From Staff	Purchase Orders Mailed By	Merchandise Delivery Date	Warrant Issued
Art Supplies	Last Fri. in Jan.	Last Fri. in Feb.	3rd Fri. in Feb.	3rd Fri. in March	1st Fri. in April	3rd Fri. in April	After July 1	F.
Athletics			After Completion of Season		3rd Fri. in Jan.		60-days after order	I
Audio-Visual	2nd Fri. in Oct.	1st Fri. in Nov.	Last Fri. in Nov.	3rd Fri. in Dec.	3rd Fri. in Jan.	2nd Fri. in Feb.	After July 1	R
Classroom Furniture	1st Fri. in Oct.	Last Fri. in Oct.	3rd Fri. in Nov.	2nd Fri. in Dec.	2nd Fri. in Jan.	2nd Fri. in Feb.	After July 1	S
Custodial Supplies			Minimum Inventory Re-Order		3rd Fri. in April		30-days after order	T
Hardware			Minimum Inventory Re-Order		3rd Fri. in Jan.		30-days after order	
Home Economics	Last Fri. in Jan.	Last Fri. in Feb.	3rd Fri. in Feb.	3rd Fri. in March	1st Fri. in April	3rd Fri. in April	3rd Fri. in May	B.
Instructional Supplies	2nd Fri. in Feb.	1st Fri. in March	2nd Fri. in March	1st Fri. in April	3rd Fri. in April	1st Fri. in May	After July 1	O.
Library Furn. & Equip.	2nd Fri. in Feb.	1st Fri. in March	As Needed		3rd Fri. in April		60-days after order	E.
Library Supplies	1st Fri. in Nov.	3rd Fri. in Nov.	2nd Fri. in March	1st Fri. in April	3rd Fri. in April	1st Fri. in May	After July 1	
Light Bulbs			Minimum Inventory Re-Order		3rd Fri. in April		30-days after order	M
Mfg. Instruments			3rd Fri. in Dec.	3rd Fri. in Jan.	3rd Fri. in Jan.	3rd Fri. in Feb.	After July 1	T
Office Furniture			As Needed		3rd Fri. in April		60-days after order	G
Paper			Minimum Inventory Re-Order		3rd Fri. in April		30-days after order	
Physical Education	Last Fri. in Jan.	Last Fri. in Feb.	3rd Fri. in Feb.	3rd Fri. in March	1st Fri. in April	3rd Fri. in April	After July 1	A
Printing	Last Fri. in Feb.	Last Fri. in March	2nd Fri. in March	1st Fri. in April	3rd Fri. in April	1st Fri. in May	After July 1	F
Reading-Elementary	1st Fri. in Feb.	1st Fri. in March	2nd Fri. in March	1st Fri. in April	3rd Fri. in April	Last Fri. in April	After July 1	T
Science-Elementary	1st Fri. in Feb.	1st Fri. in March	2nd Fri. in March	1st Fri. in April	3rd Fri. in April	Last Fri. in April	After July 1	E
Vocational: Lumber	1st Fri. in Feb.	1st Fri. in March	3rd Fri. in March	1st Fri. in April	3rd Fri. in April	2nd Fri. in May	After July 1	R
Vocational: Materials and Proc. Equipment	1st Fri. in Feb.	1st Fri. in March	3rd Fri. in March	1st Fri. in April	3rd Fri. in April	2nd Fri. in May	After July 1	
Vocational: Materials and Proc. Supplies	1st Fri. in Feb.	1st Fri. in March	3rd Fri. in March	1st Fri. in April	3rd Fri. in April	2nd Fri. in May	After July 1	D
Vocational: Metals	1st Fri. in Feb.	1st Fri. in March	3rd Fri. in March	1st Fri. in April	3rd Fri. in April	2nd Fri. in May	After July 1	E
Vocational: Supplies & Equipment	1st Fri. in Feb.	1st Fri. in March	3rd Fri. in March	1st Fri. in April	3rd Fri. in April	2nd Fri. in May	After July 1	L
Vocational: Woods	1st Fri. in Feb.	1st Fri. in March	3rd Fri. in March	1st Fri. in April	3rd Fri. in April	2nd Fri. in May	After July 1	I
Vocational: World of Const.	1st Fri. in Feb.	1st Fri. in March	3rd Fri. in March	1st Fri. in April	3rd Fri. in April	2nd Fri. in May	After July 1	V
Vocational: World of Mfg.-Equipment	1st Fri. in Feb.	1st Fri. in March	3rd Fri. in March	1st Fri. in April	3rd Fri. in April	2nd Fri. in May	After July 1	E R
Vocational: World of Mfg.-Supplies	1st Fri. in Feb.	1st Fri. in March	3rd Fri. in March	1st Fri. in April	3rd Fri. in April	2nd Fri. in May	After July 1	Y

FIGURE 9.8 Sample inventory and purchasing calendar

SOURCE: Adapted and modified from the Great Bend (Kansas) Public School District.

serious duties. It is thus appropriate that in Chapter 10 we turn to a related topic of risk management: protecting the district's assets from multiple perils.

Review Points

THE ROLE OF PURCHASING

The educational enterprise has changed greatly since its inception in the United States, so that the act of securing goods and services and facilities has become a grave fiduciary and educational responsibility.

Education's delivery has become so sophisticated that it would be severely damaged without accurate and punctual purchasing procedures.

As a result of an increasingly complex society, purchasing has become fraught with legal and technical traps.

Purchasing is predicated on legal authority of districts to levy and collect revenues to be used as payments.

Establishing a district budget is only a first step in the fiscal responsibility of districts—a meaningless step until the act of purchasing personnel, supplies, equipment, and services is carried out.

Budgets are built from anticipated purchasing acts, wherein the educational plan of the district is set in motion.

STATUTORY ASPECTS OF PURCHASING

Since districts are statutorily created, their authority to purchase likewise rests in statute.

All states have created some legal framework for districts to engage in procurement for educational purposes.

Schools are subject to all laws of a general nature, making it important for administrators to understand the law generally and as it specifically applies in statute to schools.

Although the modern school environment demands appointment of purchasing agents, their power is limited.

Tenuousness of agency results from the board's lack of authority to delegate discretionary expenditure of funds.

In most instances, boards ratify contracts by agency, but only at their option.

The nature of agency virtually demands carefully crafted board policies on procurement procedures.

The need for good policy extends to the ethics and supervision of purchasing where the objective is to avoid even the *appearance* of impropriety with public funds.

The pressure to account blamelessly for public trust has aided adoption of competitive bid laws in many states.

Bid laws are generally state-specific, and usually result from severe sensitivities to gross errors in the past.

Bidding can be complex, making it difficult for administrators to comply and sometimes requiring technical assistance to observe the spirit of the law and to avoid serious product knowledge errors.

Purchasing professional services is especially error-prone, in that competitive bid laws may or may not apply, depending on the act to be performed and the intent of the individual state legislature in drafting a law.

Generally, bid laws are designed for economy, but in other instances courts have held against low bids when the wrong result could arise from false economy.

THE ACT OF PURCHASING

The act of purchasing should be described in policy, with specific assigned responsibilities to various staff.

The purchasing act begins with determination of need, followed by executing a requisition, obtaining internal approval, seeking prices and/or bids, preparing a purchase order, seeking board approval, and executing the purchase order to the vendor.

Despite careful policies, product problems needing resolution still arise. Generally, the district seeks vendor and/or manufacturer warranty, followed by legal action if appropriate.

Although complex, the public trust requires product dispute resolution. In serious cases, a lawsuit may follow wherein various laws, such as the Uniform Commercial Code, may be invoked.

When accepting an administrative position, administrators should confirm their policy roles and limitations.

WAREHOUSING, INVENTORY, AND CONTROL

The procurement function does not end with receipt of goods/services and payment, but also extends to warehousing, inventory, and control.

Warehousing may follow a centralized or decentralized model. Similarly, inventory may be perpetual or periodic, depending on the district's ability and needs.

Control decisions should maximize accountability, efficiency, and effectiveness.

The overriding principle in these functions should be efficient and effective distribution to assure an uninterrupted educational enterprise.

The fiduciary responsibility of administration demands high ethics and accountability in procurement and its extended functions.

Case Study

In the spring of this year, the superintendent of a small rural school district in the Midwest announced his retirement. The superintendent had been the district's senior executive for the last 20 years, following a popular career as building principal and basketball coach in the same community. By all accounts, he was well respected and numerous persons expressed regret and well wishes upon his retirement. In seeking a replacement, the board of education launched a search with the help of the state school board association and experts from state universities having doctoral programs in education administration. After a thorough search, including three rounds of interviews, you accepted an offer from the board to serve as the district's first new superintendent in nearly a quarter of a century. You felt very confident following the former superintendent, as your own experience included a doctorate from the leading state university, several years' experience as a successful teacher, principal, and small town superintendent of schools, and the belief that this district was stable and well managed.

On July 1, you assumed your new duties. As the district had only about 1,500 students, the central office staff consisted of yourself, a clerk, a secretary, and a bookkeeper. During the first week of employment you made a special point of visiting all the attendance centers to discuss at length the goals and vision of the district with each principal. During the second week on the job, you scheduled several days for a one-to-one conference with the bookkeeper to gain a firm picture of the fiscal health of the school district and to begin planning the fiscal goals of your tenure. Within the first 20 minutes of meeting with the bookkeeper, however, she revealed that she did not actually know the cash balances of each fund. The bookkeeper took you to the business office, where she opened a desk drawer containing a large pile of unpaid purchase orders dating as far back as three years. The bookkeeper explained that the state auditors had not audited the district in three straight years because of severe state budget cuts that reduced the state's available audit officers. She explained further that the former school superintendent told her not to process the purchase orders for payment because he had negotiated employee salary contracts greater than available funds and that these contracts were being funded by nonpayments to vendors. She finally informed you that he had instructed her to pay only local purchase orders on time and to pay other claims only after the vendors had threatened suit.

As the new superintendent, you face a real dilemma. Using the following sets of questions to help launch your class discussion, how will you resolve the problems you have inherited?

Directed Discussion Questions

1. Using your own experience in education wherein you have doubtlessly encountered delicate situations of some nature, what do you perceive to be the full scope of the problems you are facing in this case study? On a hypothetical continuum, what are the least of your concerns, and what are your greatest problems?

2. Who seems to be at fault? When (and if) this matter comes to light, who will likely be blamed? On a continuum from least to greatest, on whom do you place blame? What are the ramifications of bringing this issue to light? What options do you have? Do you think opening up this unfortunate situation is the proper thing to do? Why or why not? What are your legal responsibilities? What are your ethical responsibilities?

3. As you think about resolving this problem, you undoubtedly recognize that there is a political side to your dilemma. What political problems do you foresee? What are the outcomes that you can reasonably anticipate? How should

these problems be addressed to minimize damage? To whom (or to what) will damage potentially occur? What kinds of damage are likely to follow?

4. In your own experience or knowledge, has some type of similar problem (greater or smaller) ever occurred? If so, what were the circumstances? What was the initial outcome? What was eventually done? In your view, were the steps sufficient to redress or mollify the attendant consequences? What was done wrong, if anything? In that instance, what would you have done differently to improve the situation, both beforehand and after the fact?

5. As you consider resolving this problem, where do you believe you should start? What *several* initial steps should be taken? To whom will you turn? In thinking ahead to your own departure, how will you address concerns that some similar situation might occur in the district without your knowledge? How will you protect yourself against suspicion, innuendo, or actual error?

NOTES

1. David C. Thompson, *The Law of Purchasing: A Guide for School Business Officials* (Commissioned paper, Wichita, Kans., 1980), 1.

2. David C. Thompson and R. Craig Wood, *Educational Facility Equity and Adequacy: A Report on Behalf of Plaintiffs in Roosevelt Elementary School District No. 66 v. C. Diane Bishop et al.,* Petition and Affidavit filed in Maricopa County, Arizona (Manhattan, Kans.: Wood, Thompson & Associates, 1991), 3.

3. Joseph L. Natale, "School District Purchasing," in *Principles of School Business Management,* R. Craig Wood, ed. (Reston, Va.: Association of School Business Officials, 1986), 491.

4. Bureau of Business Practice, *Purchasing Agent's Desk Manual* (Waterford, Conn.: Bureau of Business Practice, 1984), 4.

5. Obviously, this presumes prior learning from Chapter 6 of this text on the principles and operation of school district budgets.

6. Remember from earlier discussion in Chapter 2 that in some states school districts are dependent on other governmental units such as cities and counties, making more than two levels of interaction possible.

7. As a general rule, this statement is entirely true and in keeping with appropriate school business practices. In a few instances, however, school districts are permitted to engage in confidential discussions. The best example is negotiating the purchase of land for a future building site, which in instance boards are allowed to discuss these matters in executive session to protect the public treasury. In other words, letting it be known that the school district intends to purchase land may result in raising prices or may cause land speculators to buy the property in advance for resale to the school district. Under these reasons of economy, secrecy is permitted. Once a deal is struck, however, the board must formalize its offer in a public board meeting where the actual purchase is said to take place in the public eye.

8. Thompson, *The Law of Purchasing,* 5.

9. Edmund Reutter and Robert Hamilton, *The Law of Public Education,* 2d ed. (New York: Foundation Press, 1976), 336.

10. An *ultra vires* contract exceeds the board's authority to contract; for example, an agreement to bond the district beyond its legal debt capacity. *Void* or *fraudulent* contracts are illegal because of defects in the contractual instrument itself or are out of compliance with the fundamental elements of contracts.

11. See for example Spradlin v. Board of Trustees, 515 So.2d 893 (Miss. 1987). See also Responsive Environments v. Pulaski County, 366 F.Supp. 241 (AK, 1973). In addition to such statutory construction by courts and various statutory requirements, local boards of education may have even more restrictive standards and policies regarding the purchasing of goods and services that may lead to disputes. Disregard of these policies may be grounds for dismissal of those responsible dependent on the circumstances. For example, if the local board of education were to have a policy that requires no single-source purchasing without specific board approval, any execution of a purchase order without this approval may be grounds for dismissal.

12. Purchasing Practices Forbidden by the Gary (Ind.) Community School Corporation, 1.

13. Adapted from the Gary (Ind.) Community School Corporation, which based its policy on the purchasing practices forbidden by the Minnesota Division of Procurement.

14. Association of School Business Officials of the United States and Canada, *Control Points in School Business Management* (Park Ridge, Ill: Association of School Business Officials, 1979), 3. The Association of School Business Officials, International (ASBO), has adopted a Code of Ethics and Standards of Conduct. The following portions of the code are specifically applicable to the purchasing arena: (1) conduct business honestly, openly, and with integrity, (2) avoid conflict of interest situations by not conducting business with a company or firm in which the official or any member of the official's family has a vested interest, (3) avoid preferential treatment of one outside interest group, company, or individual over another, (4) avoid using the position for personal gain, (5) never accept or offer illegal payment for services rendered, and (6) refrain from accepting gifts, free services, or anything of value for any act performed or withheld.

15. Beall v. Board of Supervisors, 191 Miss. 470, 3 So.2d 839 (1941).

16. Citing Beall in Reutter, *The Law of Public Education*, 321.

17. While technically this is true, a good administrator should not forget the value of public relations in the purchasing process. For example, the choice of a bus battery as an illustration is not by accident, as several instances are known to the authors where school districts in fact do call several resident auto parts stores to receive an informal quote on such a battery. The purpose is less for economy reasons than good public relations, as each supplier knows the wholesale price varies only fractionally, making this an artificial exercise. The merchants reportedly appreciate the opportunity, however, as they know they are personally in touch with the district. In a large district, the practice would need to be modified, perhaps by waiting to purchase several such batteries at one time.

18. For comparison purposes, a complete sample bid law from one state can be seen in Chapter 11 in Figure 11.5 in conjunction with discussion of transportation.

19. This section is based on Indiana Code 35-1-9.

20. See "Choosing a Telephone System for Your School District," *School Business Affairs* 50:12 (1984), 22; see also Caroll J. Pell, "Purchasing Guidelines: Can you Defend Your Best Buys?" *School Business Affairs* 51:12 (1985), 66–67.

21. The award is generally limited to the penalty of the bond, which is normally a percentage of the contract. Thus, not all losses may be recoverable even if judgment were entered on behalf of the school district. In such instances, the school district must demonstrate actual and significant harm—often difficult to do. For example, it is often argued by insurance firms that no harm resulted to the school district when in fact the second lowest responsible bidder was still below the budgeted amount for the project (See for example Boise Jr. College v. Mattefs Const. Co., 92 Idaho 757, 450 P2d 604 (1969). Generally, if the bidder can demonstrate an error without gross negligence and the district has not been significantly harmed, the courts are reluctant to enforce such penalties on behalf of the school district. Thus, in several states, the posting of cashier's/certified checks is allowed by statute to offer greater protection to the school district in such instances. In many states, it is

common practice for school districts to require cashier's/certified checks if the state statutes are silent on this issue.

22. See for example, Joseph P. Scellato, "Purchasing: The Vendor's Viewpoint," *School Business Affairs* 47:3 (1981), 8–9, 27.

23. Preferential bid laws are a point of contention among many suppliers. In states where such laws exist, out-of-state and out-of-district bidders are informed that to be considered, their bids must be discounted if the contractor's state of residence also has a preferential bid law. One state's preferential bid law reads: "To the extent permitted by federal law and regulations whenever the state of _____ or any agency, department, bureau or division thereof or any municipality of the state including, but not limited to, county, school district, improvement district or other public body lets bids for contracts for the erection, construction, alteration or repair of any public building or structure or any addition thereto or for any public work or improvement or for the purchase of any goods, merchandise, materials, supplies or equipment of any kind, the contractor domiciled outside the state of _____ , to be successful, shall submit a bid the same percent less than the lowest bid submitted by a responsible _____ contractor as would be required of the _____ domiciled contractor to succeed over the bidding contractor domiciled outside _____ on a like contract let in such contractor's domiciliary state" (Statute 75-3740a).

24. See George F. Smith, "Purchasing," in *School Business Administration*, Henry H. Linn, ed. (New York: Ronald Press, 1956), 272.

25. Smith, "Purchasing," 273.

26. Heston v. Atlantic City, 93 N.J.L. 317, 107 A. 820 (1919).

27. 15 *A.L.R.* ed 733.

28. 40 Tex. Civ. App. 177, 89 S.W. 425 (1905).

29. Cobb v. Pasadena City Bd of Educ., 134 Cal. App. 2d 93; 285 P.2d 41 (1955).

30. McNichols v. Denver, 1340 Colo. 202, 274 P.2d 317 (1954).

31. See for example Krohnerg v. Pass, 187 Minn. 73; 244 N.W. 329 (1932).

32. Vermeule v. Corning, 186 A.D. 206; 174 N.Y.S. 220 *aff'd,* 230 N.Y. 585, 130 N.E. 903 (1919); see also Hunter v. Whiteaker & Washington, 230 S.W. 1096 (1921).

33. Tex. Educ. Code Ann., Article 664.

34. Alaska Stat. § 35.05.230 (1)(c)(vi).

35. Or. Rev. Stat., § 127.10.010.

36. Ibid., § 127.10.092

37. Ariz. Rev. Stat. Ann. § 41-730(a)(b)(c).

38. Op. Att. Gen. 73-47-L.

39. People ex rel. Smith v. Flagg, 17 N.Y. 584, (1858); see Stratton v. Allegheny County, 245 Pa. 519, 91 A. 894 (1914); Gulf, 11 S.W.2d 305 (1928).

40. Steven M. Goldblatt and R. Craig Wood, "Construction Management for Education Facilities: Professional Services Procurement and Competitive Bid Statutes," *School Law Update, 1985* (Topeka, Kans.: National Organization on Legal Problems of Education, 1985), 37–53.

41. 82 A.L.R. 2d 1015.

42. School districts deserve much sympathy in this regard. For example, in Loewy v. Rosenthal (104 F. Supp. 496 [1952]) it was held that the defendant's supervision of construction, alteration, or repair of facilities was not the practice of architecture. In Walhlstrom v. Hill (213 Wis. 533, 252 N.W. 339 [1934]) the court stated that responsible supervision for the construction, enlargement, or alteration of the facilities was not the practice of architecture. The court noted that the plans and specifications had been made by a licensed architectural firm. Unless state statute specifically prohibits such arrangements, the general pattern of interpretation may be found in Gastaldi v. Reutermann (345 Ill. App. 510, 104 N.E.2d 115 [1952]) where the court stated: "Superintending the construction of a building

does not amount to architectural services where the licensing statute stipulates that nothing in the act shall prevent the employment of superintendents of construction . . . ."

43. *Uniform Commercial Code (UCC),* §1-10.

44. Louisiana adopted only Articles 1, 3, 4, 5, 7, and 8.

45. *UCC* § 2-313.

46. *UCC* § 2-314(2)(c).

47. *UCC* § 2-316(3)(b).

48. *UCC* § 2-315.

49. See for example, Dennis Murphy and Robert McKeen, "Cost-Saving Techniques That Work," *School Business Affairs* 57, 6 (June 1992), 22–25. Anecdotal testimony indicates that cost savings up to 20% may be achieved by cooperative purchasing.

50. Rex V. Call, "Purchasing in the Academic Institution," *Journal of Purchasing* 4 (May 1969), 70–77.

51. See generally Thomson M. Whitlin, *Theory of Inventory Management* (New York: McGraw-Hill, 1953).

52. Whitlin, *Theory of Inventory Management,* 15.

53. Arvid J. Burke, *Financing Public Schools in the United States* (New York: Harper & Brothers, 1956), 162.

ADDITIONAL READINGS

Alligan, George W., ed. *Purchasing Handbook.* New York: McGraw-Hill, 1982.

Ammer, Dean S. *Materials Management and Purchasing.* Homewood, Ill.: Richard D. Irwin, Inc., 1980.

Association of School Business Officials, International. *Cooperative Purchasing Guidelines.* Reston, Va.: Association of School Business Officials, 1979.

———. *Handbook for School Book and Supply Store Management.* Reston, Va.: Association of School Business Officials, 1977.

Barlow, C. Wayne. *Purchasing for the Newly Appointed Buyer.* New York: American Management Association, 1970.

Frohreich, Lloyd E., and Van Mueller, eds. *Managing Limited Resources: New Demands on Public School Management.* Cambridge: Ballinger, 1984.

Heinritz, Stuart, and P.V. Farrell. *Purchasing: Principles and Application.* Englewood Cliffs, N.J.: Prentice-Hall, 1960.

Leenders, Michael R., H. E. Fearin, and W. B. England. *Purchasing and Materials Management.* Homewood, Ill.: Richard D. Irwin, Inc., 1980.

Munsterman, Richard E. *Purchasing and Supply Management Handbook for School Business Officials.* Reston, Va.: Association of School Business Officials, International, 1978.

Page, H. R. *Public Purchasing and Materials Management.* Lexington, Mass.: D.C. Heath, 1980.

Wood, R. Craig, ed. *Principles of School Business Management.* Reston, Va.: Association of School Business Officials, International, 1986.

Zenz, Gary J. *Purchasing and Management of Materials.* New York: Wiley, 1981.

CHAPTER 10

Planning for Risk Management

CHAPTER THEME

- The risks assumed by people in everyday life are frightening when consciously confronted, and the burden of legal and ethical responsibility increases exponentially as organizations such as schools take temporary custody of children during the school day. But since risk is unavoidable, it is imperative that administrators recognize their liabilities and accept the responsibility of protecting their clients, the school district, and themselves against the financial and legal perils of modern existence.

CHAPTER OUTLINE

- General parameters of what risk management means to a modern school district
- The major types of insurance available to school districts
- The concept of legal liability, including discussion of torts and damages
- A brief discussion of alternatives to ordinary insurance contracts

CHAPTER OBJECTIVE

- A new awareness of the sobering responsibilities of districts and professional employees in safeguarding every person engaged in the educational enterprise

In 1990 alone, 93,500 persons died of accidental injuries and another 9 million suffered permanent impairments or temporary total disabilities. Statistics on principal types of accidental death were motor vehicle (46,300), falls (12,400), accidental poisoning (5,700), drowning (5,200), fires (4,300), choking (3,200), firearms (1,400), and poison gases (800). Of these accidental deaths, 10,500 occurred in the work place and another 19,000 occurred in public places. Disabling injuries totaled 9 million, of which 1.7 million were motor vehicle–related, another 1.7 million were work-related, and 2.4 million occurred in public places. Temporary total disabilities numbered 8.6 million, with 1.7 million occurring in a work setting and 2.3 million others occurring in public places. Total medical expenses, insurance administration, and wages lost due to death and injuries was $173.8 billion, of which $102.3 billion was related to work or public settings. Americans apparently take life-threatening existence in stride, but they are fairly sophisticated in taking financial precautions as existing life insurance policies totaling $9.4 trillion were in place in 1990. This amount does not even begin to include, however, the total of property and liability insurance purchased by various entities, ranging from private individuals to vast corporations.

World Almanac and Book of Facts

The data[1] on risks to the American public strikingly illustrate the peril we naturally assume every day of our lives. Living totally risk free is impossible, and it is likely true that few persons would choose to live the dreary existence that would be required if total physical security were even possible. Consequently, society has recognized the impossibility of risk avoidance and chosen the next best option, commonly known as risk management.

Because risk and litigation have become commonly associated at the end of the twentieth century, risk management has taken on greater importance than ever before, especially for schools, where the level of care expected for children is even greater than that required in protecting adults. Because schools are essentially full-service agencies charged with the care of children, the lengthy and complex statutory responsibilities required are extensive. No matter how careful schools are, however, public education will never be free of risk. For example, if public education were to be fully risk free, the schools would never open, classes would never be taught, and school buses would not transport students. Every school is at risk for accidental death or injury from vehicles, falls, poisonings, drowning, choking, firearms, and gases, and even such events as natural disasters. Because schools are in double jeopardy due to the high standard of care and large concentrated populations, it is necessary to establish policies and actions that reflect the best risk management practice to provide quality educational services and to protect both the public treasury and those persons engaged in the educational process.

Risk management for public school districts in America is thus a highly complex responsibility for local administrators and school boards, given the varied and multi-faceted tasks of public education. The purchase of insurance is a major component of risk management activities in a school district. However, insurance is not the *only* component. Other issues must be considered, and options may be available to help the district simultaneously reduce both risks and costs. Because risk is the administrator's constant companion, it is important that school professionals have a thorough grasp of the issues and best available solutions. In this chapter, we explore risk management from the view that if wisely structured, the district's risk management plan can serve patrons, taxpayers, staff, and children effectively and economically.

To help the administrator in this complex undertaking, this chapter first establishes some general parameters of what risk management means to a school district. We then expand discussion to include some basic principles of the most common form of risk management, the purchase of insurance, followed by the major types of insurance available to school districts, noting the need for adequate and comprehensive coverage. We then turn to examination of legal liability, including discussion of torts and damages for negligence. Finally, a brief discussion of alternatives to ordinary insurance contracts is provided. From this chapter, the administrator should gain a new awareness of the sobering responsibilities of districts and professional employees in safeguarding children and all other persons engaged in the educational enterprise.

THE CONCEPT AND ROLE OF RISK MANAGEMENT

From the outset, the student of school finance should note several important concepts. Risk management is the total overview of establishing the best possible manner of minimizing potential risks while protecting the public assets of the school district and the taxpayer. Equally important, the use of insurance is only one form of effective risk management. Further, insurance law precedes American jurisprudence by hundreds of years through English common law. Finally, insurance law and contracts are distinctive from other fields of law. These laws and contracts are interwoven within applicable state statutes, and in some instances within federal law, so as to present a complex overall picture of risk management. Based on the McCurran-Ferguson Act,[2] the insurance industry is regulated on a state-by-state basis. As a result, there are well over 1,000 insurance companies licensed to issue various types of insurance throughout the country.

Fundamental Concepts

Certain fundamental concepts of the nature of risk assessment must be fully understood before the school administrator can properly engage in any risk-related transactions. Randal has succinctly characterized these processes as follows:

1. *Identification and measurement;*
2. *Risk reduction or elimination;*
3. *Transfer of risks incapable of assumption;* and
4. *Assumption of remaining risks.*[3]

The first task of identifying and measuring risk is often difficult to operationalize. It is often suggested that parental committees and teachers be involved in identifying potential risks to both the risk management supervisor and the school district's risk management committee. In this manner, it is possible to first identify and then judge the potential risk of certain educational practices at each school and throughout the district.

Fortunately, the professional literature is quite informative as to attempting to minimize potential risks within school districts. Obviously, prevention has proved to be the *best* technique in a loss control program. *Systematic* prevention programs have proved to be the most cost-effective of all possible risk management programs. Preventive loss control varies from district to district, but in almost all instances would best be evidenced by such programs as:

1. *Pre-employment physical examinations* to assess in advance any identifiable risks;
2. *Job-related safety training programs* designed to prevent human error;
3. *Safety communications systems* to provide rapid response to emergencies;
4. *Accident investigation programs* designed to thoughtfully assess problems that do arise;
5. *Safety committees* whose primary task is to identify and prevent problems and to provide training;
6. *Safety inspections* designed to discover potential hazards;
7. *Safety materials, equipment and training;*
8. *Record-keeping systems* designed to help actuaries and planners predict risk variables; and
9. *Safety performance* as a part of employee evaluation procedures.

When risk reduction and elimination are ongoing activities engaged in by every school district on a constant basis, sound risk management practice may be structured well in advance of need.

The risk management literature identifies three criteria for judging potential risk: *probability, severity,* and *risk reduction.* Generally, the *probability* of risk can be divided into such areas as *none, low, moderate, high,* and *definite.*[4] Because only total avoidance of a given activity can fully eliminate potential risk—impractical in most situations except for those which should be forbidden—school activities should be classified into the categories of low to definite risk. The second measurement calls for examination of the potential *severity* of a probable event. Risk management professionals normally judge this to be the most critical element of the evaluation. Risk reduction is an ongoing effort to involve those who actually engage in these activities in minimizing the severity of potential risk through greater precaution and protection to reduce their liability whenever possible and practical. The third measurement, *risk reduction,* is most commonly accomplished by the purchase of insurance to protect the school district from potential financial losses. Insurance is available in many forms and may be purchased for a variety of hazards and other potential losses. The typical school district has between 6 and 12 different insurance policies covering a multitude of potential risks.[5] The risks facing schools are normally defined within the insurance industry as negligence (e.g., inadequate maintenance), malfeasance (e.g., theft), malpractice (e.g., personal wrongdoing), and other liabilities that may arise from error or omission. Some of these may be further classified as criminal acts or civil torts, depending on severity. Properties are also often insured, such as vehicles, buildings, and so forth, against acts of damage by persons or natural disaster. Thus, the purchase of insurance reduces risk by paying another party to assume the risk for a stated fee.

The terms of the insurance contract dictate the manner by which the risk is assumed in relation to the monies paid as premiums. The decisions on what to insure and for what amount of coverage must be weighed under the projections of probability, frequency, value, and liability. On occasion, the insurance company may reinsure the risk with another insurance firm so as to reduce its direct financial risk in the event of a major loss. Thus, risk management most often involves a level of internal efforts to minimize risks, accompanied by an insurance contract consisting of several parts:

1. *Legal names* of the insuror and the insured parties;
2. *Description of the type of insurance* issued and a legal description of what is to be insured;
3. *Type of coverage,* that is, the perils to be insured as well as the perils to be excluded;
4. *Amount of coverage,* as well as the manner of determining the value of the actual insurance coverage;
5. *Conditions* and manner of termination, expiration, and cancellation;
6. *Representation* and warranties;
7. *Waivers,* if any, that may be applicable and under what conditions;
8. *Reference to the manner of settlement* in the event of claim; and
9. *Subrogation,* that is, legal right to collect from third parties, primarily through countersuits between insurors.

PRINCIPLES OF INSURANCE AND RISK MANAGEMENT

The most fundamental principle of insurance is that insurance substitutes a known cost (i.e., insurance premiums) for the unknown hazard of a potential financial liability.[6] "Insurance amortizes the losses [and] . . . spreads the loss . . . equitably over others exposed to and insuring the same type of risk. By paying a definite known premium regularly, the individual district eliminates or reduces the possibility of a large, uncertain loss."[7]

The insurance contract is therefore the most basic tool by which insurance principles and sound risk management are carried out. The insurance contract is written by an insurance company, called a "carrier," under uniform insurance industry standards. This simply means, for example, that the basic policy for fire protection of a school building conforms to general and basic fire protection policies for commercial property and that all licensed companies must cover certain perils uniformly. As a result, the general language of a fire protection policy or an auto liability policy will be very similar from company to company.

Randal has succinctly described the responsibilities of school district leaders when working with insurance firms as follows:

1. *Prompt reporting* of claims and potential claims (failure may relieve the insuror of liability);
2. *Cooperation* with the defense of claims (this also applies to ordinary precautions after loss to prevent further loss);
3. *Employee education;*
4. *"Good Faith"* negotiations; and
5. *Ongoing contact.*[8]

These guidelines call for the insured—in this case the school district—to specifically engage in the notification of the insurer immediately after an accident to protect both parties against additional losses or legal claims, particularly negligence. The school district must promptly provide the insuror with complete and relevant information and all files and data regarding the claim and the activities of the school district and its employees. Representatives of the school district must also appear in court if requested to defend the interests of the insuror as well as the school district. The school district must constantly educate its employees to minimize the potential for claims.[9] The school district, in its discussions and negotiations at the time insurance is purchased, must reveal all prior and potential claims and liabilities known at the time so that the carrier may agree to accept these potential liabilities. Failure to do so generally cancels or voids coverage and risks additional legal troubles relating to insurance fraud. The school district risk manager must work closely with the insuror to minimize increased premiums and to be actively aware of areas where the insuror can suggest how to minimize potential financial loss.

Generally, one person is directly responsible for the task of managing all the risks of a school district, such as the assistant superintendent for finance, the finance director, or another knowledgeable and trained person. Frequently, this person works with a committee that recommends group consensus decisions to the district's superintendent and board of education regarding all insurance programs, including other forms of insurance, such as supplemental retirement plans.[10] The risk manager, who would normally be charged with actually carrying forward the formal recommendations of the committee, must thus possess certain basic skills.[11] Among the most important are:

1. *Ability to understand the entire risk management concept* in its full range of impacts;
2. *Some insurance experience,* either through insurance training or school business management training;
3. *Budgetary knowledge* to understand and coordinate insurance costs and payments;
4. *Knowledge of existing codes and statutes* applicable to the specific state;
5. *Knowledge of legal contracts;* and
6. *Knowledge of building design* requirements.

The school district risk manager is thus responsible to see that the school district does business only with insurance carriers that are rated at least *A+, AA, A,* or *AAAA* for most lines of coverage by the A. M. Best Company.[12] Overall, the school district risk manager must constantly seek to recommend the best course of action in providing the best cost-to-benefit ratio of every decision, not in simply purchasing an economical insurance policy.[13] The role of the risk manager is thus one of aggressive risk measurement in terms of probability and severity, taking numerous preplanned steps identifiable as risk reduction measures, and finally insuring the district against unavoidable perils. Because all school administrators are involved daily in risk factors and are liable for their actions relating to risk reduction in any court of law, we turn now to types of available insurance designed to protect the district, its employees, and its clients.

General Types of Insurance

There are almost an unlimited variety of standard or custom insurance coverages accompanied by almost unlimited ways in which insurance firms operate within the 50 states. Nevertheless, while a school district could perhaps purchase some form of insurance for almost any activity imaginable, the insurance that most school districts purchase is quite common and uniform. While the following is a thorough discussion of standard policies and coverages available and essential to schools, it is by no means exhaustive, for insurance contracts and liabilities are far too complex for administrators to act without proper state-specific counsel.

Property Insurance. The most common insurance for individuals as well as schools is property insurance. The school district risk manager must be aware of the various types of insurable property, such as buildings and contents, fixed and portable equipment that may vary from site to site, school district records, as well as highly specific software necessary for the school district's business and curricular programs to properly function. School district property is constantly exposed to various perils ranging from fire to theft to hurricanes. It may be surprising to learn that, according to insurance industry statistics, arson is currently the leading cause of loss of school buildings in America.

Broadly speaking, property can be classified as either *real* or *personal.* Generally, real property refers to buildings and the permanent fixtures therein. Personal property, also called contents, refers to those items that can be removed without changing the structure. Dependent upon the nature and type of insurance purchased, it may cover only the structure or the personal items in the structure, or it may cover both, with or without covering related property outside the structure. Generally, property insurance does not cover personal property, such as works of art, jewelry, precious metals, vehicles, and so on, unless specific policy extensions are purchased. The wide variety of policies available under basic or comprehensive coverages deserves close attention to ensure that the district understands any and all exclusions to the policy.

Property insurance is generally purchased for a specific period of time, *renewable at the option of the company.* Coverage for extensions of time may be written as often as necessary as the insuror's experience record changes. Many people mistake the purpose of insurance, believing that there will be no change in premium if a loss is incurred. Insurors are permitted under the law to adjust insurance rates on the basis of both actuarial probability and actual experience to accommodate such elements as loss of profit and increased overhead due to covering the loss of business property. The insuror cannot lose money or it will go out of business. In one way, a loss payment is no more than a loan recoverable in part by future premium increases. Consequently, insurees should not be angry when premiums increase, because insurance rates are a reflection of the actual claims of insurees against the insuror. Although it is a small comfort, increased premiums not only reflect misfortune, but also ensure that the policy is available and working properly.

Property insurance generally covers only named perils, which may include vandalism, theft, damage by lightning or wind, and so on. Generally, flood and earthquake insurance must be purchased separately. Other property insurance, however, may be purchased in most states on a named peril or an all-risk (extended coverage) basis. If a named peril policy is purchased, it should be extended beyond the named perils of the basic policy. Within the insurance industry, perils are normally defined as those events that cause losses, such as fire, windstorms, and so forth. Generally, an extended coverage policy will pay for all losses unless specifically excluded. This is even broader than just multiple hazard coverage. For example, a vehicle insured only for collision will not be covered for related damage such as glass breakage incurred from striking a utility pole *if* the first collision was with some other object. This is because a detailed insurance investigation will conclude that the glass loss was from a *proximate cause.* Comprehensive coverage, however, would repair glass and other damage, subject only to named exclusions and deductible amounts. While auto insurance is different from real property insurance, the example is a correct application of the principle of extended or comprehensive coverage. When extended coverage is purchased, it becomes the responsibility of the insuror to show that an exclusion does not allow for payment. In the named peril policy, however, responsibility resides with the school district to prove that the loss in question was due to a peril specifically named in the policy.

It is important that school district administrators understand that the basic purpose of property insurance is to reimburse for *catastrophic loss,* not to replace or repair worn or deteriorated infrastructures suffering from neglect and disrepair. These policies also do not cover theft, loss discovered through inventory, gradual deterioration, depletion, inherent vice, latent defect in construction or manufacture, or a host of other unrelated issues.[14] Special coverage is required for such items, just as any damage caused by steam or hot water pressure is generally covered separately under a "Boiler & Machinery" policy as discussed later this chapter. Although the insurance industry is strictly regulated, the buyer must be insurance-literate to avoid great errors of misconception about the extent of coverages, especially in basic or named peril policies.

Generally, property insurance is purchased on an actual cash value basis less deductible, which allows for financial payment on the replacement cost of the property. In some instances, depreciation at the time of the loss may also apply. While replacement cost policies are significantly more expensive, it is possible to purchase a full replacement cost policy that does not utilize either deductibles or depreciation. Most property insurance coverages allow only for the specific damages. If any undamaged property must be razed to repair the damage, such costs are not covered. This is often the case, as state or local codes regarding public facilities require that the entire facility to be brought up to the current code in force at the time of repair.[15] Such excess costs would not be included unless some form of demolition or increased cost of construction provisions are within or added to the basic property insurance policy. Because the policy will only reimburse to the value of the loss, however, excess insurance would only result in paying extra premiums without any visible benefit to the school district.

Most districts cannot afford to insure at full replacement cost without deductibles. In most states a school district may therefore insure property based on coinsurance, for which the premiums are less expensive. A coinsurance plan allows the school district to insure a set percentage of potential total loss, often specified in statute (e.g., 75%). Thus a coinsurance plan would operate as follows:

$$\frac{\text{Amount in Force}}{\text{Coinsurance}} \times \text{Actual Loss} = \text{Reimbursement}$$

Under principles of coinsurance, it would be possible for a school district to insure for more than the actual cash value of the property to receive the full loss through recovery, but the school district would not be able to receive any excess of the actual cash value of the property. For example, the school district might have a cash value of $1 million invested in a small school facility. The coinsurance recovery for a total constructive loss of the facility at $1 million would be 75%, or $750,000. If the school district were to insure the facility for $1.5 million, the recovery would then be 75% of $1.5 million, or $1.125 million. However, the school district could not receive an amount in excess of the value of the property. Thus, the school district's actual financial recovery would then be limited to the $1 million equaling the cash value of the property. In reality, however, the district might be better off financially to simply purchase an inflation rider at the highest level of coinsurance it can afford.

For most districts, coinsurance means the district is liable for some percentage of the loss. If the $1 million facility is insured at 80% coinsurance, or $800,000, then the district's liability is $200,000. Care must be exercised in coinsurance in two important areas. First, boards of education must fully understand the loss liability when insuring at less than 100%. Good administrators have lost their jobs over failure to confirm this understanding, and this decision must be reviewed frequently for old board members and immediately for new members. Second, state laws of insurance contracts govern the nondepreciable liability a district can assume. Often a minimum 80% coinsurance is statutorily required to avoid unexpectedly large losses due to depreciation. In other words, unless a minimum coinsurance is maintained, the district may suffer the difference between its policy limit and the full value of the property, compounded by severe depreciation of the property for failure to maintain the required minimum coinsurance ratio.

Claims made for damages to property must be carefully recorded by the school district's risk management office. Records must include the date of loss, the date reported, a copy of the report to the insuror, the cause of loss such as fire, wind, hail, and so on. Once settlement has occurred, records on the amount of the claim, recovered amounts and dates of payment, and verification of repairs, as well as additional information or pertinent remarks must be maintained. These records must be available for instant recall in future claims, as well as for verification of unpaid claims to various insurors. These data are crucial in ascertaining claims against the insurance carrier, as disputes *will end up* in court proceedings.

Because of the high cost of complete replacement coverage, deductibles are utilized by virtually every school district to help reduce insurance premiums. Deductibles may range as high as hundreds of thousands of dollars dependent upon the size and complexity of the school district. When deductible amounts are very high, the reality is that the school district is engaged in self-insuring to a certain amount, while at the same time commercially insuring against major losses that would be unfair to local taxpayers if uninsured. The administrator should remember the admonition earlier in this chapter that insurance is the substitution of a known, smaller ongoing cost in exchange for avoiding large losses that may arise from future conditions. Deductibles are an extension of that concept, making the purchase of insurance possible on a more economical scale because the insuror is insulated from the first dollar of loss up to the deductible amount. Of course, higher deductibles bring lower insurance premiums because the insuror's protection is increased, but the school district's risk obviously increases proportionately to the insuror's benefit.

School districts generally can purchase property insurance from several different types of insurors. States are one such provider through self-insurance programs and are discussed later in this chapter. The majority of school districts purchase property insurance from either a stock company or a mutual firm, which makes up the second major type of insurance supplier. The differences between stock and mutual companies, in reality, are quite minor in terms of premiums versus services for the vast majority of school districts. In a few states, however, school districts are statutorily prohibited from purchasing from a mutual firm, particularly if the school district is required to pay premiums several years in advance because these premiums themselves are not insured. Additionally, some states prohibit school purchases from mutual companies in the belief that because a mutual company is owned by policyholders who become "investors" in the organization, policyholders may experience higher costs because losses, as well as profits, are distributed across the group on an equal basis. These characteristics have led some states to conclude that such risk on the loss side is inappropriate for tax dollars.

In a few states, a third option for insurance coverage is cooperative agreements, which allow school districts to enter into what is often referred to as an interagency or pooling agreement. Interagency agreements allow school districts to pay into a centrally administered fund in an amount equal to a commercial insurance premium to cover losses by any of the pool's members. Generally, school districts under such conditions will enter into some form of joint powers agreement authorized by enabling legislation. While regulations vary from state to state,[16] typically each school district pays into the pool based on such things as the number of students, classroom teachers and other employees, school buses, the value of school facilities, payroll amounts, budgets, and the historical loss experience of each school district. In reality, a consortium of districts or the state is actually creating its own insurance company, with policyholders having a governmental interest in common. One advantage of these self-insurance agreements is that it may be possible to pay certain claims that would otherwise be financially prohibitive or uninsurable for schools (e.g., asbestos claims, pollution, and sexual molestation).[17] There is a great deal of evidence, however, to suggest that pools must not be established as a cost reduction plan, as the pool's costs may be higher than normal insurance due to the cost of transferring the enormous risk of these potential liabilities.[18]

Property insurance is complex and riddled with problems for the inexperienced administrator. While careful analysis is required to determine whether coverage is appropriate and affordable, no type of insurance is inherently more important than insuring a school district's single largest investment: its property. Wise management can effectively and economically provide the coverage needed by school districts in an increasingly complex and litigious society, but it is a task that must be undertaken with care and expert guidance.

Boiler and Machinery Insurance. While no single type of insurance policy covers every potential peril a school district may face, it is a common mistake to believe that property insurance is more inclusive than it actually may be. The potentially most devastating error regarding property insurance is to assume that buildings would be covered against damage and loss due to boiler and machinery problems. It is critically important for administrators to understand that boiler and machinery coverages are specific policies that must purchased as insurance against specific perils. Because great property damage and risk to humans can arise from boilers and machinery, no school district should be less than adequately protected.

Boilers and machinery under such policies are usually broken down into four basic groups, with numerous other subgroups for each classification that are beyond the scope of this chapter. Specific insurance for these items must be purchased. The four major groups are:

1. *Boilers,* fired and unfired pressure vessels;
2. *Mechanical* equipment;

3. *Electrical* equipment; and
4. *Production* machinery (sometimes referred to as miscellaneous machines).[19]

It takes little imagination to understand the prevalence of these items in schools. Virtually every school in America has some form of heating system, ranging from gas-fired furnaces and hot water heaters to boilers that drive steam heating units dating on the average to the 1950s and sometimes as much as 70 years old. Even new hot water heaters can explode. Additionally, every school has mechanical and electrical equipment that can cause fires resulting in property damage and personal injury from smoke and inhalation. Further, most secondary schools and trade schools have large quantities of production machinery, with significant risks from malfunction or personal injury. For administrators, four cautions relate to boilers and machinery. First, basic property insurance policies do not cover either damage to such items nor problems stemming from malfunction of boilers and machinery. Second, the risk is sufficiently large that steam boilers must be inspected by state-licensed inspectors and often by the insurance company representatives. Third, no district should be without sufficient property and liability coverage to redress problems arising from boilers and machinery. Fourth, while such coverage can be expensive, it is quite cheap in contrast to the losses incurred from false economy if a serious problem arises.

Property Appraisal.   Although not a type of insurance under the general heading of this section, property appraisal needs to be discussed along with basic and extended property insurance. Property appraisal applies to vehicles as well—in fact, where any valuable object is concerned, property appraisal is required. For districts to recover losses under an insurance policy, a system of property appraisal needs to be a conscious undertaking by the district.

The insurance company must be able to ascertain the actual value of losses claimed to process a claim for losses incurred by a school district. That is, the claimant must be able to back up its stated losses because the amount of monies received for an insured loss is entirely predicated on the proof of specific loss.[20] Where property insurance is concerned, an accurate inventory is required. In the instance of school buildings, the insurance company almost certainly conducted an inventory of the property at the time it issued the policy, basing the face value on its estimate of value. That estimate is also known as a property appraisal. The appraisal should have included such items as the value of the building and its permanent fixtures. Because the amount of money invested in schools is so large and because tax dollars are at stake, the school district should also have a professional appraisal rather than relying solely on the appraisal conducted by the insurance carrier.[21]

A good property appraisal is a complex undertaking. Efforts to conduct property appraisal in-house by local school personnel are highly discouraged, both from legal liability perspectives and because training is needed to accurately conduct the appraisal. Although some cost is involved, a professional appraisal avoids much dispute over losses, as it must be remembered that insurance companies will hire investigators in the event of a large loss to ascertain whether the exclusions or exceptions to the policy should be applied. While insurance companies want to please their clients, they are also greatly inclined to avoid payment where a possibility of impropriety or negligence on the part of the insured exists. This is entirely reasonable, as both the insuror and the insuree agreed to such conditions at the time the policy was issued.

Insurors cannot be expected to overlook careless behavior or wrongdoing, as their continued existence is at stake in very large claims. Consequently, independent appraisal by school districts is a wise precaution.

A major purpose of property appraisal is the current assessment of worth of the facilities. "The professional insurance appraisal report will set forth the total building reproduction values and subtract the allowable exclusions giving the client the reproduction cost insurable. Actual cash value is also provided and by definition is [defined as the] reproduction cost new, less an allowance for accrued depreciation, resulting from its age and condition."[22] It must be remembered, however, that items such as excavation, foundations below the surface, sewer systems, and wiring are not included under normal policies for appraisal purposes. Thus, it is common practice for many school districts to contract with private specialty engineering firms in addition to independent insurance appraisers to conduct complete and thorough appraisals of all school district property on a timely basis, thereby protecting the school district's interests more fully. Because the buildings and related property in school districts represent the single largest capital investment the district will ever make, wise property insurance management is not only recommended as an economy, it is vital to the security and safety of children, staff, and community patrons.

Automobile Insurance.   Another form of property insurance is automobile and vehicle insurance, which must be recognized as distinctly different from other forms of insurance because of the risks associated with moving objects, standard of care, and the amount of damage that can be actively inflicted on property and persons. For schools, this liability is especially heightened because children are transported on school buses in the custodial care of the district. Although specifically dependent on individual state statutes, it is generally true that the school district may be sued regarding the usage of its vehicles. The use of private autos may also create special problems regarding liability.[23]

While buildings and contents pose the largest single investment for a school district and thus require sufficient insurance, the operation of vehicles and school buses constitutes the largest potential risk exposure. Although all school vehicles are at risk, those transporting children have the greatest liability. Obviously, this places school buses at the top of the risk list because they carry large numbers of children. For this reason, vehicle insurance and related programs are of paramount importance to school district risk management.

State statutes regarding transportation may be classified into three broad categories of exposure for school vehicle liability. A few states have tried to maintain sovereign immunity as discussed later in this chapter. Another group of states has written into state statutes a set of limitations on liability. A third group has voided sovereign immunity with no limitations on financial awards assigned by courts through lawsuits over district liability. Although state statutes differ, wise risk management demands high levels of insurance to ward off financial losses if liability falls to the district. Generally, purchasing vehicle insurance for schools means providing coverage for bodily injury and property damage as defined within the insurance policy. Generally, these policies are written with limits on bodily injury and property damage, and the district may select higher limits for an additional premium. Liability limits in some states may be expressed as a separate amount of coverage for each of these areas, while in others a "Combined Single Limit" coverage is available. The administrator should note, however, that as with basic property insurance versus extended coverage policies, simply buying vehicle insurance does not cover all potential losses. For example, worker's compensation claims are outside the confines of the school vehicle insurance policy.

Automobile insurance is available on two general levels, with special variations based on purchased options. The first level is liability for damages to property or persons arising from operation of a vehicle. For school buses or other vehicles transporting children, liability coverage would protect the district up to the state liability limits for damage or injury caused by the driver while in the employ of the school district. Obviously, if the district is negligent in assuring the driver's qualifications, a whole new arena of litigation can arise in the event of an accident, even including criminal liabilities. This is especially true as the standard of care required for minors is greater than for adults who have reached legal age. The second level is insurance to protect the district against its own property losses arising from damage to or loss of vehicles in the event of an accident. Again, various refinements apply, such as coverage for collision only, comprehensive and collision coverage, and various deductible amounts. Under these circumstances, the best advice is to insure for both liability and property loss, to keep low deductibles and high liability limits, and to give total attention to reducing civil and criminal liabilities by assuring the qualifications of drivers charged with the care of children.

No two districts' vehicle insurance costs will be exactly the same because the cost of insuring the school bus fleet, as well as autos and trucks, is based on a variety of factors. Like other property insurance, these factors may include the loss record of the school district, number of children transported, distances traveled, replacement value of vehicles, and even the nature of the maintenance garage operation. A good insuror will even gather evidence about the school district's safety procedures and operations on the assumption that preventive training and maintenance will be favorably reflected in actuarial experience. As a result, risk reduction procedures in a district, such as driver safety training, frequent fleet inspections, ongoing maintenance records, accident-free experience, and even use of late model year vehicles may in fact result in reduced premiums. Insurance companies want to insure good risks—they *and* their clients are foolhardy if any other relationship is allowed to evolve.

Vehicle insurance is fully as complex as property insurance, and the liabilities arising from negligence are even greater because of civil and/or criminal lawsuits. But as in other forms of insurance, the school district must keep careful and detailed records regarding any accidents or claims. The typical information that must be kept includes date of loss, date the loss was reported to the insuror, and type of claim (e.g., comprehensive, collision, bodily injury, medical, and so forth). Additionally, strict records must be kept including the name of the driver, the claimant, persons present and/or involved, and recovery amounts and dates. The wisely managed district will have extensive training for transportation personnel and will require the transportation department to maintain exact records on bus routes and trips, mileage, departure and arrival times, maintenance schedules, and so forth. These records should be kept for all vehicles because evidence of prior care may be helpful if an accident ever occurs. Finally, each accident should include a complete folder with this information, as well as a copy of police accident reports and correspondence with any parties, including the insurance firm.

Risk management for vehicles is serious business, and includes both property and liability considerations. Wise administrators never neglect this aspect of school finance—for moral reasons if for no other.

Workers' Compensation and On-the-Job Safety Insurance. One of the increasingly important types of insurance for schools is workers' compensation insurance and on-the-job safety coverage. Every state has statutes providing a system of workers' compensation laws in an attempt to make restitution and rehabilitation available to an employee who has been injured in a job-related activity. The specific purpose for such laws is to compensate the person for medical costs and lost wages not otherwise covered by insurance. Generally, workers' compensation laws substitute for all other common law rights and liabilities. That is, the employee generally cannot sue the employer for negligence if recovery is available from the workers' compensation fund. "The employer loses the standard common law defense, but its liability is limited. An employee is generally entitled to benefits even if the accident was his own fault."[24] Obviously, severe negligence on the part of the employer does not prevent claims arising from other civil or criminal proceedings, but the existence of workers' compensation insurance has the benefit of first claim and further benefits workers who otherwise would not be likely to privately purchase coverage. Additionally, some theory suggests that employers will exercise greater care against employee injury since the premiums for workers' compensation insurance are paid by employers into the workers' compensation fund.

School districts are required by law in most states to provide workers' compensation insurance on their employees. As with other forms of insurance, the district must keep detailed records regarding workers' compensation claims, including such information as date of injury, date reported to the insuror, employee information, nature of the injury, starting and concluding dates of disability, and any loss of employee time incurred by the school district. Additionally, every state requires the school district to report workers' compensation claims to a given state agency, typically on a prescribed form requiring certain detailed information from all parties involved in any work-related injury falling under a potential workers' compensation claim. Every school district must establish an effective management information system capable of identifying accidents and the immediate supervisor, as well as having the school district safety committee periodically review every accident that occurs for future safety recommendations.[25] Liability from this arena is again large, requiring that the district report all injuries to appropriate supervisory personnel immediately, provide written explanations on late reports, and report only observable facts and statements made by the employee.[26]

Workers' compensation insurance is a complex arena requiring much attention. Over the course of the twentieth century, Congress has become vitally interested in public health and safety and has coordinated that interest with other concerns about general welfare and economic stability and employment. Although employers are required to pay workers' compensation premiums to support this system, those dollars are by no means sufficient to fully finance the disability funding available on the national level. Numerous federal dollars help support this program and are intermingled with other federal support for disabled workers through such huge programs as Social Security benefits, where money for disabled workers and survivor benefits find their way into the special funds set up to pay these costs from such programs as the Hospital Insurance Trust Fund, the Supplementary Medical Insurance Trust Fund, and the Supplemental Security Income Fund.

For school administrators, the arena of workers' compensation insurance takes on three prominent aspects. First, employers have an ongoing cost through required premiums resulting from mandatory participation. Second, some reduced employer liability results from the first aspect. Third, administrators must be careful to provide a reasonable standard of care for adults in the work setting. In schools, this is perhaps more natural than in other business and industry because of the high standards required for the custodial care of children. The district must not only be careful to meet all local, state, and national codes for facilities, equipment, and grounds, but must also be cognizant of basic safety requirements established for all job sites by the federal Occupational Safety and Health Administration (OSHA), whose standards are enforced through civil and criminal penalties against employers. School districts, as well as all other agencies, are required to post OSHA requirements and to maintain an annual log of job-related injuries. Citations for violations of safety regulations must be publicly posted as well. Meeting all applicable OSHA standards must be part of the overall safety program within a school district.

OSHA standards, as well as other aspects of the overall safety inspection system, are part of the ongoing risk management program of a school district. In addition, the education of all personnel for accident prevention is integral to any loss control program. Every employee must be actively engaged in accident prevention. Because of so many safety regulations creating liability for everything from asbestos to machinery and boilers, it is recommended that safety meetings be held at least annually in each school[27] to involve all employees in the accident prevention process.[28] As with all other types of insurance and risk management, the total system is generally directed by the risk management director because risk management is an overall plan, rather than scattered responsibilities of several people working independently of one another. Reverse gravity applies, as liability rises until it finally settles at the top.

Health Insurance.   The purchase of health insurance for employees has become for many school districts in America the single largest employee expense other than salaries. Public education is a labor-intensive industry, and the resultant health costs are a complex problem. The costs of medical care have skyrocketed in recent years, with most school districts presently spending well in excess of 75% of general fund budgets for salaries and fringe benefits, including the cost of medical insurance premiums.

Although costs are high and still rising, there is little that schools can do to aggressively reverse the basic trend. This is not to say that risk reduction does not apply to health insurance, because it obviously does. It is to say, however, that schools cannot choose to reduce their costs unilaterally because health care coverage is a mandated part of collective negotiations in most states. With health benefits paid on a pretax basis, these payments become more important to employees each year. Consequently, school districts are locked into negotiating health coverage and can only reduce their costs through other risk management practices related to wellness. Wellness has gained importance in recent years as more comprehensive laws relating to medical leave have been passed by Congress and insurors have canceled the group policies of schools whose experience record indicates poor wellness awareness among employees.

Medical care is, of course, the primary area of health insurance. Health maintenance organizations (HMOs) and indemnity plans constitute the major options for health coverage for employees of school districts, which are required by federal law to offer membership in HMOs to employees if requested by a federally chartered HMO. Thus, it is not sufficient for a district to provide only minimal health coverage, as the school district must offer its employees a choice of plans.

Indemnity plans are health insurance offerings by both for-profit insurance carriers and "nonprofit" organizations like Blue Cross and Blue Shield. Insurance rates for either an HMO or an indemnity plan are a function of loss ratios of premiums to claims. As claims rise, companies generally seek to increase premiums, reduce coverage, raise the first dollar deductible paid by employees, or cancel the group's policy entirely. In other words, like other types of insurance, claim payments are basically a loan against future increased premiums spread across a large group that will eventually have to repay the insurance company for its losses. With soaring health costs, increased premiums have recently become the most desirable of a poor selection of choices, as many employee groups have had the bitter experience of insurance cancellation with no other insuror willing to assume the risks.

Because of group cancellations, rising deductibles, and reduced coverages, some creative strategies have emerged, including a national health insurance plan provided to every American. Arguments against such a system are that there would be no incentive to hold down costs and that the government has poorly managed other programs, offering little promise for better success with national health insurance. A second plan more warmly received by the public has been preferred provider organizations, which effectively prepay medical costs to physicians through a preventive health care philosophy. Arguments against such a plan include incentive losses for good competitive health care, socialization of still another aspect of life, and lack of adaptability to the costs associated with major catastrophic illnesses and short- and long-term hospitalization.

Although hospitalization and primary care physician costs make up the large dollars involved in health care, school districts also need to be concerned with providing, coordinating, and managing other health care coverage, including dental, vision, long-term disability, and group and individual life insurance. Each of these areas has certain specific features and costs that are unique, requiring much care in selecting insurance coverage that offers the best plan to all eligible employees at the best cost. Although some of these coverages are employer options, stringent legal interest through collective negotiations has forced school districts to make such plans available, resulting in increased assumption of costs by districts as employee groups have successfully negotiated employer-aided coverages.

Although health costs are seemingly out of control, experienced school districts have begun to learn that one of the most cost-effective health care programs is risk prevention, that is, development of employee wellness programs. Although quantification is difficult, offering such programs "demonstrates to employees that the employer is concerned about employee well-being and is interested in helping employees [begin] a longer, healthier life."[29] In light of escalating costs and few choices open to school districts to hold their costs down, interest in wellness may be the wave of the future.

In recent years, the health care package provided by school districts has been further complicated by continuation of the employer-employee relationship after separation. In 1985 Congress passed the Consolidated Omnibus Reconciliation Act (COBRA), requiring school districts and other public agencies to offer continued group health plan coverage to employees and their dependents even after the employee is no longer in the hire of the school district. Specifically, school districts that offer group health insurance must continue benefits to qualified employees and their dependents, although the employee must pay 100% of the applicable premium if qualified to participate. The qualifying circumstances include the following:

1. The employee is terminated (voluntarily or involuntarily), including layoff or nonrenewal but not dismissal for gross misconduct;
2. The employee suffers a reduction in working hours requiring a loss of benefits;
3. The covered employee dies;
4. The covered employee is divorced or legally separated;
5. The covered employee becomes entitled to Medicare benefits; or
6. A dependent child ceases to be a dependent as defined by the plan.[30]

Under COBRA, the school district or other public agency is required to offer health insurance benefits to former employees for a period of up to 18 months after separation but may not charge a premium that exceeds 102% of the applicable premium paid by current public employees. Applicable premium is defined as the same cost of the plan for the same period of coverage as provided to all other participants of the same plan. A reasonable estimate of the cost by the school district will suffice for self-insuring school districts. The insurance may cease during the coverage period only if one of five events occurs:

1. The qualified beneficiary acquires coverage through another health plan;
2. The qualified beneficiary becomes entitled to Medicare;
3. The spouse remarries or acquires coverage under a new plan;
4. The premium is not paid; or
5. The employer terminates the plan.[31]

The likelihood that a district will entirely abolish a health care plan is remote given collective negotiations. But districts are seeking ways to replace or amend existing health plans in an effort to keep costs down. Under COBRA, this attempt to control costs is made more difficult because the qualified beneficiaries are also entitled to acquire the benefits of any new or amended plan. Thus, COBRA mandates continued health coverage for former employees and their qualified dependents under the specified conditions—which obviously can force district costs upward.

Greater health care costs, more sophisticated medical interventions that increase longevity at higher costs, and other features such as collective negotiations have made health insurance the second largest employee cost to school districts. That cost under COBRA obviously now even includes former employees no longer with the district but whose medical experience continues to affect costs paid by continuing employees. With 15.7% of all Americans not covered by health insurance[32] in 1989, concern over medical care will continue to rise, making risk management at the school district level an even greater daily problem. While no answers to these grave problems are apparent, the importance of health insurance to the overall risk management program cannot be overstated, because health care affects the district's budget through direct costs, negotiations, lost worker productivity, and countless other areas, including basic morality.

Crime Loss Insurance.   Unfortunately, natural and accidental perils are not the only losses against which school districts must protect themselves. Always an historically potential risk for any employer, employee dishonesty in modern society has found increased opportunities because so many jobs now require trustworthy employees. In contrast to labor-intensive jobs common in agricultural and industrial economies that made theft difficult, jobs in the information- and service-driven economy of today often involve handling cash and other stealable property. School districts are no less vulnerable to employee theft than the private sector and are particularly prone to embezzlement or misappropriation of funds and goods. Although the probability of cash theft is relatively minimal due to the manner in which school districts collect and disburse funds, schools must be concerned for this protection as well. Problems such as forgery and other alteration of documents have also increased in recent years. When internal dishonesty is added to the perpetual threat of burglary and robbery, schools face yet another peril.

Burglary and robbery are normally covered by the various property insurances ordinarily carried by districts, but to guard against losses stemming from employee dishonesty, school districts must purchase fidelity bonds. Typically, fidelity bonds cover actual losses, as well as other loss discoveries made during the time period covered by the bond. Some states allow for the purchase of a comprehensive Public Employees Blanket Bond. This type of bond covers all employees of the school district automatically, simply by virtue of their employment in the district. Other types of fidelity bonds only cover employees based on their actual contracted positions within the school district. For example, a fidelity bond in such instances would certainly be purchased to cover the school district treasurer, but cooks and custodians would not automatically be covered under such a bond. Additionally, certain states allow for purchase of Faithful Performance Bonds, which cover employees who may have created a loss resulting from failure to perform their duties or to account properly for funds or property by virtue of their positions.[33] Other forms of insurance include money and securities insurance covering loss of currency or checks and forgeries. Limitations and exclusions common to these insurance policies include losses due to specific acts of dishonesty, provable direct losses not covered by other required bonds or insurance, notification to the carrier in a timely manner, and restrictions on time limitations.[34]

No school district should be without such insurance. Although employees of the educational enterprise are usually the finest citizens willingly engaged in a noble profession, protection against employee-based losses is nonetheless required when handling public monies and properties in a fiduciary capacity. Although it may be disturbing to "distrust" education employees, the purchase of such insurance stems only partly from lack of trust. Other dishonest people may enter a school and steal cash or securities, leaving the person officially responsible in the awkward position of proving innocence. Loss of such items must also be covered in the event of destruction by fire or other disaster, and the district must be able to quickly recover its losses without having to wait for a full investigation and recovery of properties. The purpose of bonding employees is thus both for honesty concerns and for recovering losses regardless of cause. If the administrator considers that the purpose of bonding is to protect the public treasury, such coverage makes good sense indeed.

Other Types of Insurance

Still other types of insurance are available to school districts. The need for such insurance depends on several factors, including the size of a district, its financial readiness to assume uninsured losses, and its willingness to assume some risk as the trade-off for not paying insurance premiums. Normally, as the size of the district grows, these choices become more conscious because the district will control larger amounts of money, making consideration of these options more realistic. Depending upon the needs of the school district, insurance can be purchased for a variety of activities, including accounts receivable (coverage against the loss of income as a result of loss of financial records), valuable papers coverage for such items as computer tapes, blue-prints, and other such documents, and floater policies for equipment and other items excluded under property and contents coverage. The two most common and necessary policies are general liability coverage and errors and omissions policies.

Liability Insurance.   Although one kind of liability coverage was discussed previously under vehicle insurance, another very important type of liability insurance is known as general liability. General liability is a form of insurance that usually covers most types of liability not involving autos or employee injuries[35] or fiduciary matters. McComb has described the typical general liability claim as the "slip and fall-type," in which the incident happens away from school, such as on a field trip.[36] Basic coverage for such problems may be provided under the Comprehensive General Liability policy that is standard in many states, which contains a number of exclusions and conditions and may also contain a number of extended coverages. The overall pricing structure of such policies is largely dictated by the loss experience record of the school district, as well as the exposures of the school district determined under the risk assessment.

School districts commonly purchase a broad comprehensive policy known as umbrella liability coverage. The Commercial Umbrella Liability Policy serves two important purposes in that it can provide additional limits in excess of existing policies, including comprehensive general, auto, school board, and employers' liability, and it covers many liability exposures not provided by the primary liability policies.[37] Uniform umbrella policies vary from insuror to insuror but typically include personal injury protection, liability for property damage, and advertising liability. Personal injury "includes bodily injury in addition to personal injury 'offenses' of false arrest, detention, malicious prosecution, wrongful entry or eviction, libel or slander."[38] Some forms may also include coverage for "mental anguish, shock, disease, and discrimination. The advertising liability includes infringement of copyright, unfair competition and other advertising acts."[39]

Under commercial general liability insurance coverage, claims arising during the time of the policy are covered unless specifically excluded. Generally, not only must the claim be made during the time of the policy, but the incident that led to the claim must have also happened during this specific coverage period. Additionally, under these policies the costs of legal defense are considered part of the overall coverage.[40]

The overall concept of an umbrella policy is to protect from catastrophic loss. Thus, the insurance carrier may require that other policies (e.g., auto or other types of liability insurance) be in place as a precondition to issuance of an umbrella policy.[41] School administrators must understand that the complexity of liability requires external legal counsel to assure appropriate protection, that various liability policies are designed to cover different occurrences, and that multiple liability policies are necessary to fully protect the district.

Errors and Omissions.   A second type of special liability policy is based on a concept often misunderstood or forgotten by school administrators. While most people think of liability insurance as protection for themselves or their employers against their own acts that may result in claims for negligence or intentional harm, another type of liability insurance districts should have protects the district against errors and omissions, primarily by covering school board members in their official acts. Depending on state statute and insurance regulations, these policies may be called either board of education liability or school board professional liability policies.

The goal of such insurance policies is to protect school board members from liability arising from the discharge of their legal duties. School boards are charged with the responsibility of administering state policies and exercising discretion in fulfilling a variety of education goals while staying within budgetary constraints. But given the volatility of these decisions, school board members can be sued for a variety of activities. School board members possess a fiduciary duty to the school district.[42] For example, when a school board member has been judged by an appropriate court to have breached a fiduciary responsibility, the board member may be personally held responsible. If such insurance were not available to protect school board members while engaging in their official acts, no lay person would accept the duties and obligations of board service, and the benefits of having lay control over public education would be thwarted. In the past, board members have been individually and collectively sued for a variety of activities including employment termination and tenure decisions, administrative errors, personal injuries, discrimination, educational malpractice, and a host of other issues.[43]

Generally, similar coverage is available for all employees of the school district in exchange for a greater premium payment. Such policies normally provide clauses stating that the insuror will "pay on behalf of" (pay directly to the claimant) or "indemnify" (reimburse) the insured for losses. Generally, it is preferred to have a policy that indemnifies as it allows the insured school district to control the hiring of legal counsel and to conduct the defense rather than leaving such decisions to the insurance carrier.[44] While the distinction may seem small, insurance companies are driven by settling for the least amount of damages while school districts may be more interested in protesting the actual issues in dispute.

While such insurance policies are far reaching in nature, there are nonetheless common exclusions of which administrators must be aware. No coverage will be provided if any insured has to refund any remuneration that a court has ruled illegal, any insured gained any illegal personal profit, or subsequent investigation determines acts of fraud or dishonesty.[45] Additionally, coverage duplicated under other board policies is not allowed, nor is coverage for damages relating to any contractual obligations, salary/back pay or employment discrimination issues, desegregation issues (enrollment, busing, or student activities), tax matters, or nuclear energy incidents.[46] As with other insurance, restoring the claimant to prior status is the objective without profit, and exclusions are designed to protect the insuror against unwinnable or antisocial claims.

From this discussion, several important concluding points should be made. First, errors and omissions insurance for board of education members, as well as school board employees including the superintendent and staff, offers individual and collective protection subject to the general limitations discussed here. Second, this type of protection should be purchased in addition to other liability policies because errors and omissions insurance form the basis for preventing financial losses not otherwise covered in general liability policies. Third, unless such protection is available, no thinking person will serve in the pro bono board role. Fourth and most importantly, administrators and others needing this coverage should not develop a sense of false security from errors and omissions insurance or other types of liability coverage because no policy is designed to recompense and protect persons from acts of criminal omission or commission. Insurance still demands responsible behavior and protects those who behave responsibly.

Sovereign Immunity and Legal Liability

To protect districts from excessive losses arising from their high visibility through the public treasury, states have either statutorily ascribed to the doctrine of sovereign immunity or have placed statutory caps on damages that can be recovered from the public treasury in liability disputes. Because sovereign immunity is so highly state-specific, an analysis directly applicable to each state is prohibitive in this textbook. Of benefit to the administrator, however, is a general discussion of the conditions giving rise to liability, examples of limitations to liability, and common defenses. Because some liability is still unavoidable even in states that have attempted restrictions, the risk manager must still arrange for liability coverage and be very familiar with the applicable state code.

Because of various acts by state legislatures affecting liability laws, the potential liability of school districts varies greatly from state to state. However, there are general principles applicable to all states that have long been recognized in the literature. As presently structured, liability in our society follows from a series of events. Liability is typically a tort claim where a tort is a civil wrong independent of a contract. In American jurisprudence, a tort claim arises when an injured party seeks compensation for harm suffered as a result of the actions or inactions of the tortfeasor or negligent agent leading to the injury in question. Liability is then partially determined by a search for negligence through the legal concept of the "reasonable man theory." Negligence is defined as "the omission to do something which a reasonable man would do, or the doing of something which a reasonable and prudent man would not do."[47] Generally, the injured party or survivor enters into a lawsuit against an individual or entity such as a school district. Both individuals and school districts may be sued in many states because the district is also responsible for torts committed by its employees when engaged in their official responsibilities under the concept of *respondeat superior*.

Whether applied to individuals or entities, there are four basic standards from which to establish a claim of negligence, all of which must be present to establish liability: duty, breach of duty, proximate cause, and actual injury.[48] These standards are based on legal logic that requires responsible behavior on the part of the accused. The duty standard requires that the person or corporate body being sued has a legal duty to exercise care. The breach of duty standard creates the mythical reasonable person and what that person should have done in like or similar circumstances. The proximate cause standard examines whether the person's actions or inactions directly led to the injury in question. The last standard, actual injury, examines whether there was an actual loss.[49] Taken collectively, these standards conclude that where a person or entity has a duty to protect and where that duty has not been fulfilled, liability arises if an act or a failure to act in fact led to harm.

The defendant is likely to offer defenses for such liability claims, and almost without exception, liability defense falls into one or more of the following five broad categories, each designed to excuse or reduce the claims against the defendant:

1. *Contributory negligence;*
2. *Comparative negligence;*

3. *Assumption of risk;*
4. *Sovereign immunity;* and
5. *Acts of God.*

Each of these five defenses has a specific legal basis. *Contributory negligence* defenses center on an attempt to show that the injured party contributed to the problem by virtue of personal actions or inactions, that is, the injured party did not exercise the degree of care necessary for personal safety. In contributory negligence claims, such facts as the age of the person involved as well as the facts of the incident are important in establishing the proper standard of care. For schools, this is a critical issue as children are the likely recipients of harm. As a refinement of contributory negligence, most court jurisdictions also allow for defense of *comparative negligence,* which attempts to show that the defense was only partially responsible for the injury in relationship to all other potential parties. The *assumption of risk* defense argues that the injured party knew of the risk, accepted the risk, and engaged in the activity knowing that a course of action and conduct could lead to predictable consequences. All three of these defenses are applicable in part or in full to school districts, depending especially on the age of the child, and in recent years have frequently been utilized in the arena of organized sports activities.

The *sovereign immunity* defense, available in approximately half of the states, is highly state statutory specific. This defense attempts to shield the school district by invoking any applicable laws that prevent parties from suing the school district, or doing so in a limited fashion, due to caps on potential awards from a public treasury. The historic basis for sovereign immunity was the inability to "sue the king" and developed in more modern society to include prohibition against suing the body corporate under the theory that one cannot sue oneself in that each citizen is a member of the public entity being sued. In many states, sovereign immunity has fallen, but efforts to statutorily limit recovery of damages have been successful in many instances. Generally, those states that still have sovereign immunity statutes protect school district employees acting within the scope of their employment, that is, engaged in an action determined to be a governmental activity in the discharge of official duties.[50] However, this does not excuse the school district from proper insurance for all of the employees, including insurance for liability claims.

The last defense, an *act of God,* simply argues that whatever happened was an unknowable accident. The incident could not have been prevented by the defendant because no amount of action or inaction could have changed the outcome. Such defenses are largely applied to matters of physical destruction relating to weather, rather than to other acts such as vehicular accidents.

To illustrate the complexity confronting each state, many states have sovereign immunity or "save harmless" statutes for school employees. For example, the Florida legislature has specifically authorized all political subdivisions, including school districts, to purchase liability insurance.[51] The state legislature also provides protection beyond a specified level to local school employees by not including punitive damages or interest in awards. Additionally, immunity is waived up to $100,000 per person, not to exceed $200,000. The Florida law reads in part:

> The state and its agencies and subdivisions shall be liable for tort claims in the same manner and to the same extent as a private individual under like circumstances, but liability shall not include punitive damages or interest for

the period before judgment. Neither the state nor its agencies or subdivisions shall be liable to pay a claim or a judgment by any one person which exceeds the sum of $100,000 or any claim or judgment, or portions thereof, which when totaled with all other claims or judgments paid by the state or its agencies or subdivisions arising out of the same incident or occurrence, exceeds the sum of $200,000. However, a judgment or judgments may be claimed and rendered in excess of these amounts and may be settled and paid pursuant to this act up to $100,000 or $200,000, as the case may be; and that portion of the judgment that exceeds these amounts may be reported to the Legislature, but may be paid in part or in whole only by further act of the Legislature . . .[52]

Further, Florida statute provides that all employees or officials are personally immune from a suit for ordinary negligence in the performance of governmental employment. Also, actions can be maintained only against governmental entities. However, it is important to note that a suit claiming that an employee or official who acted in a wanton, willful, or malicious manner (i.e., outside the scope of employment) or committed an act in bad faith can only be brought against the individual employee or official, as the governmental entity is not a proper party to such a cause of action. The statute reads in part:

No officer, employee, or agent of the state or of any of its subdivisions shall be held personally liable in tort or named as a party defendant in any action of any injury or damage suffered as a result of any act, event, or omission of action in the scope of his employment or function, unless such officer, employee, or agent acted in bad faith or with malicious purpose or in a manner exhibiting wanton and willful disregard of human rights, safety, or property.[53]

Administrators at all levels need to draw several conclusions from this discussion. First, the doctrine of sovereign immunity, where applicable, does not excuse any person from related claims outside the scope of employment interpretation. Second, even where applicable, sovereign immunity is a concept not regarded with great sympathy by courts. Third, in the event of lawsuits alleging legal liability against persons or schools, the defenses of contributory and comparative negligence, assumption of risk, sovereign immunity, and acts of God are weakened by the mere presence of children for whom a greater standard of care is required. Fourth, no sense of security should be held by residents of states with save-harmless laws, and the protection of liability insurance is equally advisable anywhere in the nation. Liability is a serious matter for schools, administrators, and staff members. A comprehensive risk management program is essential to reduce loss potential.

Constitutional Torts

Although a tremendous leap of optimism is required to find many bright spots in the liability aspect of school district operations, one of the few heartening realities is that criminal issues are far less frequent than civil liabilities. Still, great care must be taken to protect the district against constitutional tort claims because there is much legislation and legal precedent for awarding plaintiffs' claims against public entities for constitutional violations. With the ever-increasing allegations of constitutional rights violations, districts are well advised to provide risk management measures in this arena as well.

Potentially, the most apparent exposure to constitutional tort claims rests in the area of civil rights. The most comprehensive federal legislation exposing public school employees to liability is the Civil Rights Act of 1871,[54] which states in part:

> Every person who, under cover of any statute, ordinance, regulation, custom, or usage, of any State or Territory, subjects, or causes to be subjected, any citizen of the United States or other person within the jurisdiction thereof to the deprivation of any rights, privileges, or immunities secured by the Constitution and laws, shall be liable to the party injured in an action at law, suit in equity, or other proper proceeding for redress.[55]

Thus, for more than 120 years, individuals who believe they have been victims of impermissible constitutional violations have been able to file suit against public employees, as well as other public servants, such as board of education members. These laws have been strengthened over the years by other federal legislation. Additionally, federal courts have been fairly stern in their application of such matters, ruling that a Section 1983 claim is flexible in nature because individuals whose actions violate constitutional freedoms under color of official school board actions or policies are subject to challenge. The flexibility of a Section 1983 claim under the Civil Rights Act of 1871 is best illustrated by the California Supreme Court in 1980, which issued in part the following opinion:

> Section 1983 was enacted over a century ago in response to the patent inadequacy of state enforcement of constitutional guarantees. . . . Society has not yet reached the idyllic state in which all vestiges of racism, oppression, and malicious deprivations of constitutional rights have been eliminated. Accordingly, the purpose underlying Section 1983, *i.e.,* to serve as an antidote to discriminatory state laws, to protect federal rights where state processes are available in theory but not in practice, must still be served.[56]

The level of consternation over such laws has sent school districts and administrators into a frenzy of activities designed to reduce risk of such claims. No amount of legal qualification can justify laxness in this area of risk management, but administrators should also know that school officials do generally possess qualified immunity if it can be shown that they have acted in "good faith,"[57] the definition of which was established by the U.S. Supreme Court in *Wood v. Strickland* when the Court stated:

> The Official must . . . act . . . sincerely and with the belief that he is doing right, but an act violating . . . constitutional rights can be no more justified by ignorance or disregard of settled indisputed law . . . than the presence of actual malice. To be entitled to a special exemption from the categorical remedial language of Sec. 1983 . . . [one] . . . must be held to a standard of conduct based not only on permissible intentions, but also on knowledge of the basic unquestioned constitutional rights. . . .[58]

The language of Section 1983 implies that the intent of Congress was to punish individuals and agencies for denying constitutionally protected freedoms of individuals. Violation of these rights is a serious matter, and every district should take measure to reduce its risks from such claims. As with all other risks, the best procedure is to insure heavily against such claims. While persons may still be held individually liable, employers can protect the district because employees are at present normally covered for constitutional torts under the school district's errors and omissions or general liability policies. While this could change if successful claims proliferate causing heavy losses to insurors, to date only one court has addressed the issue of allowing insurance carriers to pay claims for a Section 1983 claim.[59] In *Williams v. Horvath,* the California Supreme Court "reasoned that an award could be paid by the school district's insurance carrier under a Section 1983 claim." The California court noted, however, that California statute specifically allowed for such coverage "against any claim or action."[60]

School administrators must realize that a constitutional tort by a school employee cannot be justified by the ignorance of any law.[61] The courts have always held school employees to a high standard, assuming that teachers are highly skilled individuals by virtue of training and experience. School administrators would obviously be held to an even higher level given their training and experience. Further, municipalities, and therefore school districts, cannot claim immunity for the actions of their employees[62] under any of the various defenses. If insurance against normal liabilities is wise, protection against constitutional claims seems even wiser. The best defense as always is to engage in preventive risk management on several levels.

Punitive Damages

Discussion of liability eventually leads beyond ordinary recompense for civil and criminal claims into the area of punitive damages, or punishment for improper acts by individuals or entities that is designed to provide such harsh penalties that recurrence is unlikely, either in the offending instance or by analogy to other potential transgressors. A distinct and unique area of insurance coverage,[63] punitive damages are perhaps the least understood of all forms of risk management, largely because insurance coverage varies greatly under individual states' statutes and because rapid recent increases in claims for punitive damages have made this area volatile and unpredictable as insurors seek to avoid payment of claims. Although all insurance claims have risen in the past decade, punitive damages claims have increased even more dramatically. "Legal defense costs as a percentage of loss of general liability insurance has risen from 12.5% in 1956 to approximately 35% in 1984. Juries rendering million dollar award verdicts for compensatory and punitive damages only awarded those fifty times in 1975, but awarded over 400 in 1984."[64]

Punitive damages, when allowed by statute, are tort claims that allege injury or harm, or otherwise seek relief. Depending on state statute, punitive damages may also be made without claim of malice. Thus, punitive damages may be claimed with the lesser standard of "wanton, willful or reckless disregard."[65] The broad sweep of such claims is problematic for school districts, which must seek to protect themselves, as lawsuits often pursue the "deep pockets theory" by suing both persons and entities for individual and collective acts. Because districts may be liable for employee acts, the school district has a legal right to insure its financial interests. The problem is twofold because if individuals are not protected by school district insurance policies, many persons will not work in such situations due to unlimited personal liability. The district suffers either way, as on one hand it would not be able to employ persons,

POLICY

It is the policy and objective of the school district, through the Department of Risk Management, to obtain any required commercial insurance at the lowest cost to the school district consistent with the most desirable required level of agent/broker service, with insurance companies of adequate financial status, expertise, and service potential.

The school district reserves the right to negotiate for any contract of insurance directly with an insurance company if such company ordinarily does not utilize the services of an independent agent/broker. Nothing contained in this policy shall be construed as in any way abrogating this right.

The purchase of insurance is unlike the purchase of tangible items or service requirements in general, but most nearly resembles the contracting for professional services, as in the use of consultants or attorneys, or the selection of an architect. Accordingly, a purely competitive price basis cannot be the criterion used, since other factors must be considered.

The school district insurance program requires a high degree of sophistication on the part of an agent/broker. He or she is involved with the marketing and selection of an insurance company to underwrite the particular program and is also expected to provide services in varying degrees over the term of the insurance contract. This normally will be a minimum of three years. Thus, both the cost of the insurance itself and the services of the agent/broker must be considered.

PROCEDURE

The school district will accept proposals or negotiate only with agents/brokers who have previously established their qualifications, based on an agent/broker questionnaire.

Qualification of an insurance company will be based on financial and management classifications as determined from standard and national ratings and its expertise and service ability in the particular field of insurance.

It is anticipated that proposals or negotiations of the school district insurance coverages will be in several separate items (e.g., primary liability, fidelity, umbrella or excess liability, errors and omissions, blanket property insurance, and worker's compensation and group benefit coverages). These categories may be expanded or combined as conditions dictate.

SELECTION: AGENT/BROKER AND/OR INSURANCE COMPANY

1. Where there is a wide market availability for the particular coverage or group of coverages to be procured, proposals on the basis of total cost inclusive of fees or commissions will be entertained from those prequalified agents/brokers expressing interest. Specifications will be provided by the school district. In such instances, each interested agent/broker will be limited to one or more specific companies or markets, of his or her own choice whenever possible. If two or more agents/brokers indicate a desire to quote in the same company or market, selection of the agent/broker for that company or market will be by lot to avoid the complications present when two or more agents/brokers approach the same market.

2. Where there is a limited market availability for a particular coverage or group of coverages, those prequalified agents/brokers expressing interest will be requested to submit a proposal representing the fee for exploring all available markets to obtain insurance coverage at the lowest net cost to the school district, exclusive of fee or commission. Such fee will also include the provision of necessary services over the term of the insurance contract.

3. Where a particular coverage or group of coverages can only be provided by the use of a number of companies or markets, the procedure of Paragraph 1 shall be used, except that the cost of coverage through a particular company or market will indicate the capacity of that company or market as a percentage of the total requirement, as in property insurance.

4. When situations arise requiring insurance coverage where time is of the essence, or where estimated cost of coverage is less than $_____ , the coverage may be negotiated through the agent/broker currently handling other school district insurance most like that to be obtained.

FIGURE 10.1 A sample district insurance procurement policy

SOURCE: Based on City of Madison, Wisconsin, insurance procurement policy. This overall policy is provided as a guide for consideration. Under no circumstances should any board of education policy be adopted without appropriate legal counsel and verification of compliance with applicable state statutes and regulations.

5. It is anticipated that all contracts of insurance will be based on a term of three years, although annual payment of premium or adjustment may be required or permitted. If costs and level of service are satisfactory, a second term of three years may be negotiated with the current agent/broker thus providing stabilization of markets, continuity of service, and familiarity with the school district requirements.

6. The school district reserves the right to reject any or all proposals, or to accept any proposal deemed to be in the best interest of the school district.

7. Preferences will be given to school district domiciled agents/brokers.

8. Successful negotiation will result in presentation by the School District Risk Management Director to the Board of Education for final school district acceptance.

INSURANCE PROCUREMENT

Minimum Qualification of Agent/Broker

In view of the premium volume in each major category and the possible complexity of the program, the following minimum requirements must be met by any agent/broker for qualification as to a particular coverage.

A. General

1. Five years in business as a firm.

2. Premium volume: Over $_____, excluding Personal Lines, Life, and Accident and Sickness.

3. Two qualified principals or account persons (minimum of 10 years' experience each in commercial lines, or CPCU or RM designation).

B. Specific Categories

1. Primary Liability: At least two accounts, each with premiums of $_____ or more;

2. Umbrella Liability: at least two accounts, each with premiums of $_____ or more;

3. Property: at least two accounts, each having _____ or more locations and minimum insurance of $_____; and

4. All other: Indicated experience in the particular field of insurance.

C. Qualifying the Agent/Broker

Qualifying an agent/broker will be by the risk management committee appointed by the board of education chaired by the director of risk management and consisting of two risk or insurance managers from the private sector who have no financial interest in any potential purchase. The committee's responsibility will be to examine the qualifying questionnaire regarding its subjective elements.

Any agent/broker handling school district insurance as of the date of adoption of these procedures shall be deemed qualified as to the particular coverage handled.

FIGURE 10.1   *(Continued)*

while on the other hand districts must pay higher premiums resulting in higher school taxes in one form or another. An unfortunate aspect of insurance and risk management is that "school districts do not benefit from liability coverage, only claimants."[66] Thus, the potential for punitive damages presents school districts with another financially devastating risk.

In conclusion, state statutes either fully or partially protect school districts from punitive damage claims or are silent on the issue. While one might be tempted to work only in protected states, laws can change and juries could become unresponsive to such matters. The middle ground is represented by increasing sentiment to cap potential claims in the same manner as recent efforts to limit medical malpractice suits. Considerable risk is involved in "open game" states, however, as juries have historically awarded some very large awards in response to plaintiffs' arguments. Regardless of the state of residence, good school administrators will know the law in their states, and the risk management plan for the district (see Figure 10.1) will include both internal precautions against acts leading to punitive damages and insurance designed to pay when the district is unsuccessful in defending a lawsuit on these grounds. Clearly, no aspect of risk should go unaddressed—a stern warning to develop orderly evaluation of the district's insurance needs.

ALTERNATIVES TO ORDINARY INSURANCE CONTRACTS

Given the high cost of insurance and the general uncertainty of risk management, efforts have been made to develop alternatives to traditional insurance protection. The heading of this section of the textbook may be somewhat misleading, however, because the search for relief from the high costs of risk management has not produced many alternatives to ordinary insurance contracts. While some creativity is available, the choices are extremely limited, particularly when unwise choices are eliminated. Whether there are alternatives or not depends in large part on state statutes and on the relative wisdom of the school district in the management of its funds and activities. Generally, the only viable options may be described as variations on risk assumption by the local district.

Given the concept of risk pooling and other cost reduction strategies, such as increasing deductibles, and given the inherent foolhardiness of not purchasing insurance at all, the only remaining alternative to ordinary insurance is self-insurance. The term *self-insurance* is somewhat misleading because it can serve as a euphemism for unprotected risk. However, given recent premium increases in school districts, many states have enacted statutes allowing districts to set aside funds to pay potential claims in certain areas. Often, self-insuring school districts also utilize other types of insurance to pay for catastrophic losses, and many such districts also employ an independent claims administration agency to handle the more sophisticated aspects of insurance administration. Generally, there is therefore a continuum ranging from cash reserves analogous to large deductibles in ordinary insurance policies to full self-insurance where the district assumes all the risk of operations.

The business of risk management should stand as a caution to overeager administrators seeking quick cost reductions in the district, for *risk* management is not carelessly titled. It is very possible to experience no losses for a few years and then confront massive disaster. While no amount of cash hoarding could cover a district's potential liability because revenues are inadequate, self-insurance may make good sense in some areas if the potential for catastrophic loss is minimal or at least acceptable. Proponents argue that self-insurance provides incentives for efficiency that protect the taxpayers of the school district.[67] Whether self-insurance is wise depends on the specific situation. For example, a school district may decide to insure its buildings for claims only above $10,000. That is, any one claim above that amount would be insured. Thus, all claims less than this figure would essentially be the responsibility of the school district, which would set aside monies to repair and bring the property back to its intended educational purposes. While this system is essentially no different from accepting a large deductible, the district has for all intents created a modified self-insurance plan based on its internal analysis of historical loss experience data. In a straight self-insurance plan, the school district negotiates the type of coverage and the amount of contributions from individual employees in the area of health insurance, thus becoming the paying agent and assuming all risk beyond the premiums. Generally, such plans are unwise, and most self-insurance plans in the health care area are a modified type with commercial insurance for claims above a specified loss.

In several states the legislature self-insures against perils to property. In this manner, it may be argued that no public building is insured due to the fact that the state legislature will pass an appropriation to repair or rebuild the facility out of general state revenues. Although several states began such programs in the early 1930s,[68] the plan has not been applied with wide frequency either across the nation generally or to schools specifically. Some slowness is no doubt in response to lobbying by the insurance industry because if a state legislature were able to assume such risk for a variety of perils, then theoretically insurance with private firms would not be a necessity. The realities of such an eventuality are rather slim due to the nature of most state legislatures—both politically and because of the high cost and risk assumed by the state under such a plan.

Risk management is one of the school district administrator's most important tasks of fiscal leadership, requiring various levels of knowledge and expertise. Failure to ascertain and manage risks could lead to catastrophic fiscal losses to school districts, and thus to the taxpayers and even the state as a whole. Well-informed decisions must be made in terms of the risks the school district is willing to assume versus the cost of transferring the risk to an insurance carrier. Only through complete evaluation of insurance needs can local school administrators decide the total acceptable risk and costs associated with the entire risk management program and thus decide which risks can be assumed, which risks should be transferred to another party for a premium, and which risks can be reduced.

The remaining chapters in this section are very clearly interrelated with risk management. We turn now to food service and transportation, with all their inherent relationships to fiscal and risk management in a school district.

Review Points

THE CONCEPT AND ROLE OF RISK MANAGEMENT

At its most basic level, risk management is the total overview of establishing the best possible manner of minimizing potential risks while protecting the assets of the school district and the taxpayer.

Effective risk management requires a systematic program of identifying and measuring risk; reducing and/or eliminating risk; transferring risks that cannot be accepted internally; and deliberately assuming all other risk.

Risks are identifiable by their probability; these may be grouped into *none, low, moderate, high,* and *definite.* These risks then fall into management strategies on the basis of *probability, severity,* and *risk reduction.*

Systematic prevention is the *best* technique of managing risk. Risks that cannot be prevented require reduction, which requires insurance.

PRINCIPLES OF INSURANCE AND RISK MANAGEMENT

The basis of insurance is substituting a known cost (premium) for an unknown cost (risk of loss) given occurrence of an actual peril.

Insuring the district, however, does not relieve further responsibility. The district must still report claims, cooperate in defense, engage in risk prevention education, and maintain up-to-date insurance reviews.

The district's risk management expert must be knowledgeable of the risk concept, have experience and/or training in risk management, and engage in constant review and monitoring of the district's risk management strategies.

Many types of insurance are available to schools, among which the most common are *property* insurance, *boiler and machinery* insurance, *automobile* insurance, *worker's compensation* insurance, *health* insurance, *crime loss* insurance, *liability* insurance, and *errors and omissions* insurance.

Property insurance covers either real or personal property as provided in the policy. It is important to recognize that insurance covers only named perils unless comprehensive coverage is purchased at an extra cost.

Boiler and machinery insurance is normally an additional purchase and not covered by ordinary property coverage.

Automobile insurance is purchased to cover either liability or property damage; both should be purchased.

Worker's compensation insurance protects the district from employment-related claims due to on-the-job accidents.

Health insurance plans represent one of the most complex and frustrating issues facing school risk management.

Crime loss insurance is mandatory, as problems may arise from within or outside the schools themselves.

Given that sovereign immunity seldom applies to schools, liability insurance and errors and omissions insurance are mandatory in modern society—a risk heightened by punitive damage claims.

To properly document losses, appraisals and accurate records are mandatory.

Insurance is not meant to permit profit by the insuree, as it is designed only to redress castastrophic loss.

Since insurors cannot continually pay out claims in excess of premiums, insurance policies are cancelable.

Since deductibles and depreciation are normal insurance practices, sufficient coinsurance must be maintained to minimize the insuree's loss.

Careful data of claims must be kept by the district to document events in case adjudication is required.

ALTERNATIVES TO ORDINARY INSURANCE CONTRACTS

Although insurance costs are rising, there are unfortunately few options for school districts facing high costs or cancellations of coverage.

Stock or mutual insurance companies provide the traditional means of insuring school districts; some states, however, have other alternatives available, such as self-insurance, state assumption, or pooling.

Self-insurance can be attractive, but it must be approached cautiously and wisely.

The issue is perhaps easiest in states that assume the role of insuror—these instances, however, are fairly rare, given political and fiscal realities.

Pooling represents an intermediate method that has proved attractive in some states.

Where legally possible, a mix of alternatives may provide some fiscal relief to districts; for example, districts may self-insure for small losses, pool with other districts on medium risks, and insure commercially for catastrophic losses.

The complexity of modern society demands that every activity in a school district be interpreted as a risk—a reality demanding wise and informed leadership by school administrators.

Case Study

You have recently been appointed by the board of education of a local school district as the new superintendent of schools. Previously, you were a successful building principal and later the assistant superintendent for curriculum in the same district. The retiring school superintendent enjoyed the financial aspects of the school district and made virtually all fiscal decisions alone. In executive session at last night's board meeting, however, one of the board members said pressure was mounting from a local insurance agent regarding past decisions about insurance contract placements. The board member confided that the outgoing superintendent had simply recommended policy placements to the board, and no one on the board really thought much about it. The board member further confided that several other board members have recently mentioned concerns, particularly in light of a successful claim against the school district three years ago and rising insurance premiums annually.

As the new school superintendent, the board has charged you with reorganizing the risk management program in a way that will alleviate the vaguely defined concerns of the board of education. The board has instructed you to report back with a complete risk management plan in three months. Because of your recent experience in the curriculum aspects of the district, it is your own desire to reduce administrative overhead and to concentrate limited funds on direct educational services to students. Using the following sets of questions to help launch your class discussion, what will be your plan of action?

Directed Discussion Questions
1. As you read this case study, what do you see as the serious issues that must be addressed? What factual concerns do you perceive? What perceptual and/or political issues are you confronting?

2. How do you interpret the social and administrative milieu in this district? What have been the historic practices (both good and bad) that have characterized this district? How do you see the climate of the district changing, and in what ways? In your estimation, how much of the present concerns are

related to the nature of modern society itself, and how much is related to improper leadership in the past?

3. As you assess the data in this case study, do you perceive any real risks that the district may be facing as a result of what you now know? How is it perhaps good that these data have come to light at this point? How might it be unfortunate that a closer eye has not been kept on these affairs in the past?

4. As you consider your plan of action, what information do you need to know? How does tightening up these practices in the district fit with your desire to enhance curriculum expenditures in the district? What trade-offs will you experience, and on what criteria will you base your decisions? What events and actions will you recommend?

5. Are there analogous events in your own personal experience as an educator—for example, a notable peril that occurred? If so, what was it? How was it handled? Was the district properly insured? Was there a risk management plan in the district larger than simply commercial insurance? In your present instance, how is risk management structured? What efforts at risk prevention/reduction occur systematically?

NOTES

1. *World Almanac and Book of Facts* (New York: Pharos Books, 1992).
2. Public Law 15.
3. L. Nathan Randal, "Risk Management," in *Principles of School Business Management,* R. Craig Wood, ed., (Reston, Va: Association of School Business Officials, 1986), 345.
4. Chester A. William, *Risk Management and Insurance* (New York: McGraw-Hill, 1971), 66.
5. Thomas E. Glass, "Developing a Risk Management Program," *School Business Affairs* 50:6 (1984), 17.
6. Frederick W. Hill and James W. Colmey, *School Business Administration in the Smaller Community* (Minneapolis: Denison & Co., 1964), 201.
7. Schuyler C. Joyner, "School Insurance," in *School Business Administration,* Henry H. Linn, ed. (New York: Ronald Press, 1956), 312.
8. Randal, "Risk Management," 351–352.
9. The overlap between loss prevention and the act of insuring is thus apparent: that is, risk management is, as stated earlier, more than just purchasing insurance.
10. See R. Craig Wood, "Further Evaluation of Tax Sheltered Annuities," *School Business Affairs* 46:7 (1980), 33.
11. Randal, "Risk Management," 349.
12. Glass, "Developing a Risk Management Program," 16.
13. Jack P. Gibson, "A Primer on Risk Management," *School Business Affairs* 48:13 (1982), 14.
14. Deborah L. Heiden, "Property and Consequential Loss," in *School District Insurance Handbook* (DeKalb: Illinois Association of School Business Officials, 1985), 4.
15. This issue is potentially very significant for school districts, especially given handicapped accessibility laws. These requirements increased again with passage in 1992 of the Americans with Disabilities Act (PL 101-336).
16. See Ronald Rakich, "Before You Jump into the Pool—Check the Water," *School Business Affairs* 51:12 (1985), 28–29, 72; and Darrell L. Holley, *School Business Affairs* 56:6 (1990), 28–31.
17. Thomas F. Maedke, "Cooperative Purchasing of Insurance and Risk Management Services," *School Business Affairs* 54:6 (1988), 36.

18. Samuel L. Rosenthal, "Self-Insurance Pools: Fantasy or Reality?" *School Business Affairs* 53:6 (1987), 28–30.

19. Heiden, "Property and Consequential Loss," 10.

20. Arnold MaRous, "Appraisals: Buildings and Content Values for Insurance Purposes," in *School District Insurance Handbook* (DeKalb: Illinois Association of School Business Officials, 1985), 18.

21. William C. Golz, "Minimize the Risk in Risk Management," *School Business Affairs* 45:5 (1980), 39.

22. MaRous, "Appraisals," 20.

23. For a discussion of negligence as it pertains to school transportation fleets, see R. Craig Wood and Robert W. Ruch, "Negligence in Transporting Students," *School Business Affairs* 52:11 (1986), 49–51.

24. Deborah S. Dean, "Workers' Compensation," in *School District Insurance Handbook* (DeKalb: Illinois Association of School Business Officials, 1985), 46.

25. Glenn Crowe, "Self-Insured Workers' Compensation: An Effective Alternative Designed to Reduce Loss Through Local Claims Administration, *School Business Affairs* 47:6 (1981), 28.

26. Crowe, "Self-Insured Workers' Compensation," 28.

27. This is required in California, by the California General Industry Safety Order 3203.

28. Daniel C. Pope, "A Brief for School Site Administrators on Liability Concerns," *School Business Affairs* 51:12 (1985), 26, 65,

29. Gilbert R. Martini, "Wellness Programs: Preventive Medicine to Reduce Health Care Costs," *School Business Affairs* 57:6 (1991), 10.

30. Joseph A. Falzon and R. Craig Wood, "COBRA: Anatomy and Physiology of the Consolidated Omnibus Reconciliation Act of 1985," *American School & University* 60:2 (1987), 53.

31. Falzon and Wood, "COBRA," 53–54.

32. *World Almanac and Book of Facts* (New York: Pharos Books, 1992), 950.

33. Ronald R. Boggs, "Crime," in *School District Insurance Handbook* (DeKalb: Illinois Association of School Business Officials, 1985), 26.

34. Boggs, "Crime," 28.

35. John F. McComb, "General Liability," in *School District Insurance Handbook* (DeKalb: Illinois Association of School Business Officials, 1985), 37.

36. McComb, "General Liability," 37.

37. John F. McComb, "Umbrella Liability," in *School District Insurance Handbook* (DeKalb: Illinois Association of School Business Officials, 1985), 54.

38. Ibid.

39. Ibid.

40. James G. McConnell, " 'Claims Made' Insurance Requires Thoughtful Consideration," *School Business Affairs* 52:6 (1986), 16–18.

41. McComb, "Umbrella Liability," 56–57.

42. Deborah S. Dean, "School Board Liability," in *School District Insurance Handbook* (DeKalb: Illinois Association of School Business, 1985), 58.

43. Ibid., 59.

44. Ibid., 61.

45. Ibid.

46. Ibid., 62.

47. *Black's Law Dictionary,* 5th ed. (St. Paul: West, 1979), 930.

48. William Prosser, *Handbook on the Law of Torts,* 4th ed. (St. Paul: West Publishing Co., 1971).

49. See for example, Julie Underwood, "Legal Liabilities of Administrators," in *Principles of School Business Management,* R. Craig Wood, ed. (Reston, Va.: Association of School Business Officials, 1986), 471–489.

50. See for example Chimerofsky v. School Dist. No. 63, 257 N.E.2d 480 (Ill. App. 1970); Smith v. Broken Arrow Public Schools, 665 P.2d 858 (Okl. App. 1983).
51. *Fla Stat.* 768.28(5).
52. *Fla. Stat.* 768.28(5).
53. *Fla. Stat.* 768.28(9)(a).
54. 42 *U.S.C.* Sec. 1983.
55. 42 *U.S.C.* Sec. 1983.
56. Owen v. City of Independence, 445 U.S. 662, 100 S. Ct. 1398 (1980).
57. See for example McLaughlin v. Tilendis, 398 F.2d 287 (7th Cir. 1968).
58. Wood v. Strickland, 420 U.S. 308, 95 S.Ct. 992 at 321 (1975).
59. Williams v. Horvath, 129 *Cal. Rptr.* 453 (Cal. 1976).
60. Ibid., at 459–460 citing *Cal. Gov't Code* sec. 815.2(a).
61. Ibid., at 322.
62. Owen.
63. For a fuller discussion of this area see R. Craig Wood, "Insuring Against Punitive Damages," *School Business Affairs* 52:6 (1986), 30–33; see also R. Craig Wood, "Risk Management of Personal Liability," *School Business Affairs* 50:6 (1984), 12, 14, 40–41.
64. Wood, "Insuring Against Punitive Damages," 31.
65. See Maniaci v. Marquette University, 184 N.W.2d 168 (Wisc. 1971).
66. Wood, "Insuring Against Punitive Damages," 32.
67. See for example Robert J. Cornelius, "Self-Insurance: Reviewing the Basics of a Creative Risk Management Technique," *School Business Affairs* 50:12 (1984), 68–69; Murton L. Munson, "Self-Insurance: A Haven for School Districts Facing Hostile Carriers," *School Business Affairs* 52:6 (1986), 20–21.
68. National Association of Public School Business Officials, *Insurance Practices and Experiences of City School Districts,* Bulletin No. 2 (1932), 49. Chicago, Ill.: National Association of Public School Business Officials.

ADDITIONAL READINGS

Allen, Charles A. *School Insurance Administration.* New York: Macmillan 1965.

American Education Finance Association. *Managing Limited Resources: New Demands on Public School Management.* 5th Annual Yearbook of the American Education Finance Association. L. Dean Webb and Van Mueller, eds. Cambridge, Mass.: Ballinger, 1984.

Association of School Business Officials, International. *Principles of School Business Management.* R. Craig Wood, ed. Reston, Va.: Association of School Business Officials, 1986.

Castle, Gray, and Robert Cushman. *The Business Insurance Handbook.* Homewood, Ill.: Dow Jones-Irwin, 1981.

Hadden, Susan. *Risk Analysis, Institutions, and Public Policy.* Port Washington, N.Y.: Associated Faculty Press, 1984.

Hill, Frederick, and James Colmey. *School Business Administration in the Smaller Community.* Minneapolis: Denison & Co., 1964.

Linn, Henry, and Joyner Schuyler. *Insurance Practices in School Administration.* New York: Ronald Press, 1952.

Rejda, George. *Principles of Insurance.* Glenview, Ill.: Scott, Foresman, 1986.

Vaughn, E. J. *Fundamentals of Risk and Insurance.* New York: John Wiley & Sons, 1982.

Williams, C. Arthur, and Richard Heins. *Risk Management and Insurance.* 5th ed. New York: McGraw-Hill, 1985.

CHAPTER 11

Planning for Transportation and Food Service

CHAPTER THEME

- Although there is a tendency to believe that the mission of schools is exclusively instructional, other areas that support instruction are of almost equal stature due to their ability to enable or impede effective learning. Two such critical areas are transportation and food service, because equal educational opportunity cannot exist if educational programs are inaccessible to some children due to lack of transportation, and it is painfully clear that hungry children are very poor learners. As a result, administrators need to exert much care and planning to organize and conduct effective and efficient systems for transporting and feeding children.

CHAPTER OUTLINE

- The origins and purposes of transportation services
- The law and state aid plans as they apply to transportation services
- A brief discussion of other important considerations, including decisions about internal bus systems or external contractors, modernizing transportation services, and laws and operations governing bus purchases
- An overview of modern school food service in light of federal, state, and local funds and sophisticated dietetic and operational planning
- A brief analysis of issues affecting food service, such as personnel, decisions about central and satellite facilities, and budgeting

CHAPTER OBJECTIVE

- A greater appreciation for the importance and complexity of transportation and food service operations that points the way to further learning about state-specific rules and regulations

Of the 25,678,015 students in average daily attendance in public schools in the United States in 1929, states and local school districts provided transportation at public expense for 1,902,826 students, or 7.4% of the eligible population, spending a total of $54,823,000, or an average of $29 per pupil. In 1989, the same governmental units transported 22,635,000 students, or 60.7% of total student population, spending $7,309,000,000, or an average of $323 per pupil, making transportation a major industry in its own right. Similarly, food service commands enormous budgets and human resources, particularly since food service now includes hot lunch and breakfast programs, free and reduced meals for economically disadvantaged children, excess commodity support programs to both aid children and bolster a sagging agricultural economy, federal and state lunch subsidies to make meal prices affordable, and many other facets of assuring children a better learning opportunity through good health and nutrition. "Even yet, children come to school hungry, and stay that way, even when federal and state programs exist to feed them."

Data excerpted from various publications of the National Center for Education Statistics and Regents Task Force, Building Hope: Creating Tomorrow in Education

While the above data[1] excerpted from various publications suggest that many school budget areas are considered mundane accounting exercises best assigned to persons without the training or compassion to be true educators, nothing could be further from the truth. There is a real propensity in modern society to believe that the mission of schools is exclusively instructional in nature, with the unfortunate result being that other more ancillary areas of importance are shuffled aside when in fact they should also be at the forefront of educational thought and practice. If it is true that every child should have a right to a good education without regard for socioeconomic status, it is equally true that every child should be able to get to school without hardship and to attend classes free from hunger or related disadvantage. Equal educational opportunity cannot exist if educational programs are inaccessible because of lack of transportation, and hungry children make poor learners indeed. It may be appropriate for the transportation and food service functions of a district to be managed by noneducators, but it takes much knowledge and care and planning to organize and conduct effective and efficient systems for transporting and feeding children.

The support areas of transportation and food service are thus essential to the orderly and efficient education of students in every school district in America. These vital operations are generally larger and more complex than most citizens and educators ever realize, even in small districts with lower enrollments. While urban districts often utilize these services in a manner different from that of small or rural districts because of the large numbers of students in urban settings, rural districts also often utilize relatively large numbers of facilities and personnel. For example, urban districts may use many buses to transport thousands of children only short distances, but rural districts may also use many buses due to sparsity of student population. Thus, not only are transportation costs similar, but both systems also face important problems of safety, insurance, and the like. Similarly, food service operations in rural and urban districts represent employment of many individuals, as urban districts employ hundreds of food service personnel and as rural districts also employ many people relative to their enrollment and sites served. The result is a distinct need for effective and efficient organization of these areas, which are important and central to the social and educational missions of schools.

Because ancillary services are integral to effective and efficient schools, this chapter summatively examines the transportation and food service functions of modern school districts. While these services are functionally too complex to fully explore in this introductory text, there are several excellent books devoted entirely to these topics. The purpose of this chapter, therefore, is to introduce the student to the complexity of transportation and food service operations, to cultivate a basic understanding of the broader issues, and to note some highlights that form the foundation for further study, thus giving the general knowledge required to understand these complex operations that provide vital support to the learning process. Each state has specific rules and regulations regarding these support services that need careful review by the administrator before a complete operational picture is gained and before actual administration can be undertaken.

SCHOOL TRANSPORTATION

Origins and Purposes

Although it is commonly believed that transporting children to school at public expense developed from the consolidation of schools early in the twentieth century, it has in fact been in existence since 1869, when Massachusetts became the first state to spend public monies for pupil transportation.[2] Although Massachusetts' law was the earliest of its kind, pupil transportation has had no choice but to grow as compulsory attendance, school consolidation, and the advent of motorized transportation have changed society. For example, it is estimated that between 1917 and 1922 alone approximately 20,000 small schools ceased to exist and 4,500 one-room schools were eliminated each year.[3]

Unlike some other aspects of fiscal support for schools, from the earliest days the American public has seemed receptive to expenditure of public money for transporting students to public schools. This support was most likely due to "the good business sense of the American People" (i.e., what many could do alone inefficiently, the community could do as a whole more efficiently) and "the faith of the American farmer that his children could be afforded the same educational opportunity as their wealthier urban counterparts."[4] In more recent years, however, public school transportation has taken on even more importance due to a myriad of court decisions regarding other transportation aspects of educational opportunity, including transportation of parochial school pupils and the needs of physically handicapped students. A major role for transportation has also developed as a result of court-ordered desegregation plans revolving around forced busing that have further added to the size and problems of transportation. Even more recently the advent of magnet schools, as well as year-round schools, has caused the complexity of pupil transportation to grow. When the size of transportation is added to increasing regulation and insurance costs, this ancillary service has experienced phenomenal growth since the turn of the twentieth century.

The purpose of student transportation is simple and obvious, but its application is extremely complex. As stated earlier, no student can have an equal educational opportunity if a lack of transportation makes the school physically inaccessible. States and local districts have therefore worked together to make the schoolhouse accessible to students who live beyond a reasonable distance for which parents can be expected to provide transportation. The result has been a multibillion-dollar undertaking ranging from employment for drivers to insurance for liability protection. Complicating these objectives are the concepts of efficiency and accountability, which are further complicated by competing public goals, such as a conflict of expectations between parents and the state and community. Transportation may require construction of new facilities, the movement of population centers within a community may create new transportation demands, racial integration may require reassignment of school attendance boundaries, and so on. Additionally, each state, as well as each school district, has features that compound the complexity of transportation costs. For example, no two states or school districts are exactly alike on such variables as population density, number of pupils to be transported, physical topography, road conditions, and length of routes affecting the size of buses placed on routes.[5] There are also a host of other decisions that must be made at the local level, such as whether bus services should be contracted out to privately owned companies or fully operated by the district. These local decisions are even affected by state reimbursement formulas, making transportation an extraordinarily complex district function in comparison to its basic purpose.

Although the origins of transportation services can be traced to one simple concept, the implications are so profound that most districts have ceased trying to maintain an equally simple transportation system. The result for most districts has been a decision to devote a full- or part-time salary to a trained transportation director who, under the leadership of a senior administrator (such as the assistant superintendent for finance), has responsibility for preparing and carrying out transportation management procedures, establishing controls, arranging bus driver training programs, and coordinating preventive maintenance services to keep the district's system operating as smoothly as possible. Most often the transportation director also has responsibility for planning efficient bus routes and preparing regular and special route schedules for students and transportation personnel.

Because the transportation function is so central to district operations, the job of the director of transportation is a big one. The person charged with this function in a given school district must possess a variety of talents and skills, including the ability to efficiently organize a large transportation fleet and to consistently demonstrate good human relations skills in working with numerous personnel issues and problems. Additionally, the director of transportation must be skilled in decision-making abilities to employ the latest effective management and leadership techniques. The director must also be personally familiar with a wide range of diverse but interdependent topics, including "computer routing, maintaining and controlling a budget, labor relations, . . . inventory control, . . . drug testing, underground storage tanks, [and] hazardous materials."[6] Because of the high-risk liability involved in transportation, the transportation director must demand adherence to the chain of command because the director, together with hierarchical superiors, is ultimately responsible for all activities associated with the transportation fleet. Because of the complexity of operations, all school districts benefit greatly from a cost-effective approach to hiring the transportation supervisor.[7]

While many persons are involved in transportation's successful operation, the director of transportation is the single person who makes possible the overall fulfillment of its purposes. These purposes, and the attendant procedures and responsibilities of achieving them, should be placed into a comprehensive transportation manual, which should be a well-written document widely available to patrons and staff, and in-service training should be conducted with all transportation personnel so that they clearly understand the goals, objectives, and policies of the district. The manual should include all pertinent policies and regulations as well as the evaluation process and staff recruitment plans, job descriptions, training information, and the objectives of each position, with special emphasis given to driver training, pupil discipline, energy conservation practices, transportation of the handicapped, public relations, bus routes, and schedules.[8] While such elaborate procedures and responsibilities have only a distant relationship to the origins of transporting children at public expense, the basic purpose has not changed because making a quality education available to all children without regard for residence still remains the sole function of a transportation system in public schools.

School Transportation Law

While all aspects of a transportation system in public schools are complex, none are more entangled or more serious than the broad arena of school transportation law. Over the many years that students have been transported for educational purposes, multiple problems have arisen that have resulted in litigation. A number of cases have focused on liability in transporting students,[9] and a large body of case law has concentrated on the issue of authorization to provide school transportation services.[10] Still other cases have focused on the issues of providing public funds for transporting students who attend private schools.[11] Additionally, several cases have addressed the issue of who is to be transported,[12] as well as authority to curtail transportation services.[13] Clearly there has also been much tort litigation relating to transportation services, and transportation for desegregation reasons has been heavily litigated.[14] While transportation litigation cannot be exhaustively reviewed here, a brief overview of major highlights is helpful in understanding the need to proceed in this arena with considerable caution.

The issue of accessibility to education through transportation services has been the focus of litigation at the U.S. Supreme Court level on numerous occasions. In a case seemingly unrelated to transportation, the Court ruled in *Cochran v. Louisiana State Board of Education*[15] in 1930 that public funds could be used to purchase secular textbooks for private school children, applying a test that became known as the "child benefit theory." Under child benefit theory, courts were permitted to more liberally interpret the prohibition against church-state entanglement under the establishment of religion clause in the U.S. Constitution[16] by determining whether the child is the prime beneficiary of a public expenditure in the private school setting. Because the child received the benefit of textbooks, the Court reasoned, the expenditure could be permitted without violating separation of church and state if other care was taken. *Cochran* later became the basis for a 1947 ruling actually affecting school transportation in *Everson v. Board of Education,*[17] when the Court ruled that reimbursing bus fares to parochial and private school children was permissible under the analogy that public and private interests are not crossed with the establishment of religion clause given the child benefit theory applied to transportation. The Court made the further analogy that transportation is much like police, fire, and other protections available to private or church organizations and further noted that to deny such benefit would make the state an adversary of the church. Although the Court ruled favorably under child benefit in both *Cochran* and *Everson,* related issues concerning commingling public funds with private or parochial interests have returned many times for further rulings.

Litigation regarding school transportation has been larger than just disputes involving parochial students. The whole arena of transportation is generally unsettled as illustrated by a more recent case involving questions of violating equal educational opportunity when poor people must pay bus transportation fees in order to ride to school. This complex issue was addressed by the Court in *Kadrmas v. Dickinson Public Schools.*[18] At the root of *Kadrmas* were efforts, including financial incentives, by the North Dakota legislature to encourage school consolidation. Although consolidation was encouraged, it was not mandated and the Dickinson school district chose not to consolidate. The local school board further decided that to help pay the high costs of a nonconsolidated district, it would institute charges for door-to-door school bus service for all school district patrons. Under the arrangement adopted by the board, parents were charged $97 per year for one child or $150 per year for two children for bus services, which on average amounted to about 11% of total transportation costs being assessed for each child.[19] For plaintiffs, this presented some economic hardship, as the family was at or near the official poverty level. The parents brought suit, claiming violation of an alleged constitutional right to a free and appropriate public education.

The Court in *Kadrmas,* however, held for defendants in apparent contradiction to its earlier sympathy for child benefit theory, stating that such a fee scheme was rational and that equal protection was not violated. While the Court's rationale was complex, there was consideration for the fact that the state's fiscal exigency was a rational basis for assessing fees, that transportation services in fact need not be provided at all, and that "purely economic legislation" must be upheld unless it is patently arbitrary. The Court could find no such arbitrary effect, leaving numerous unsettled issues, among which was whether education is a constitutionally protected right.[20] More settled, however, was a permissive explanation surrounding the principle of child benefit theory where if a state chooses to offer transportation it may do so, but it is neither required to nor proscribed from providing busing. It is thus clear that, based on *Kadrmas,* it is permissible under certain circumstances for school districts to charge user fees for services, including transportation, and that there is no inherent right to transportation. Thus, in general, schools may charge user fees for such services.[21] In an unfolding and incomplete legal world, child benefit theory and the right to an education seemingly stand in apparent contradiction.

Other transportation litigation has impacted on school districts and their financial operations. No one doubts that transportation of students is a high-risk activity due to the potential liability.[22] School districts generally serve as a common carrier rather than a private carrier, and thus have the utmost responsibility to ensure the safety of students, a responsibility heightened by standard of care as discussed in Chapter 10. Generally, when transporting students, the school district assumes many various forms of liability that are controlled by various state tort concepts and further affected by state statutes governing the transportation of students. In relation to all other educational activities, transporting students is the highest risk activity. Transportation involves coordinating, training, and administering a number of routine and complicated tasks. Because of the weight of this responsibility and the potential for human error, there has been important litigation surrounding liability for student transportation, reemphasizing the fact that because risk cannot be avoided, school districts must minimize their liability by engaging in sound risk management and training practices for the transportation staff.

As stated in Chapter 10, when a school district or an employee is charged with negligence, it is normally a tort claim, meaning that someone must have been injured and it must be shown that a reasonable person under similar characteristics could have foreseen the harmful results and prevented the injury from occurring. Although such prevention is difficult for transportation because an accident may involve the actions of more than one driver, the rules of determining negligence are nonetheless applied. For example, the transportation director, normally the person who selects school bus stop locations, may be liable if an accident occurs and it can be shown that proper care was not exercised in selecting a safe school bus stop.

Numerous lawsuits under similar or related circumstances have been brought against school districts over the issue of transportation liability with varying results. For example, in *Vogt v. Johnson*[23] a seven-year-old waiting for a school bus at the designated stop attempted to cross the highway and was killed by an oncoming car. The Supreme Court of Minnesota ruled that the driver of the bus, acting as an agent of the school district, was not liable at the time of the accident since the driver's custodial responsibility for and protection of the child had not yet arisen and there was no precaution that could have been taken to avoid the accident. In a similar lawsuit, a Michigan court of appeals ruled in *McNees v. Scholley*[24] that the school district was not liable because the school bus was not present at the time of the accident. Under similar logic, another school district was sued when a child was killed crossing a highway after disembarking from a school bus in *Cobb v. Fox.*[25] Although the case was decided for the plaintiff in the trial court, the court of appeals in *Cobb* reversed in favor of the district, noting that the school bus was not involved in the accident and there was no intentional negligence on the part of the district to cause an exception to the governmental immunity statute in force at that time. Finally, there have been at least two cases, *Sanderlin v. Central School District*[26] and *Price v. York,*[27] in which a court has ruled that a school district is not under obligation to deliver each child to the door or to an area where no street must be crossed. However, this does not diminish the level of responsibility for taking adequate and prudent safeguards in providing bus stop locations.

The decision in *Brooks v. Woods*[28] stands in sharp contrast to decisions relieving districts and district personnel of liability. In *Brooks* the school district was found negligent due to the placement of a school bus stop and the subsequent injury of a student. The bus stop had been established adjacent to a five-lane highway with a 45-mile-per-hour speed limit. The regularly scheduled arrival of the bus also coincided with rush hour traffic. While waiting for the school bus, a child was struck and injured by an automobile. Important in the ruling was that the child was known by school authorities to have physical and mental limitations. The appeal court ruled that the district's "legal duty to exercise responsible care extends to any activity of school bus transportation *that lies outside the control of parents*" (emphasis added).[29]

No doubt some of the difficulty of establishing liability relates to the reality that no fixed rules can be established for every potential situation that a school bus driver and school district may face. However, in a negligence case, the defendant must show that all actions were those of a reasonable and prudent person under the specific circumstances. In direct contrast to earlier discussion, the Supreme Court of Iowa has ruled that the custodial relationship between school bus drivers and passengers "continues not only during the ride but also if the pupil must cross the road to the opposite side. . . ."[30] In this particular instance, the school bus driver was found not to be negligent in the death of a child, as the driver had exhibited reasonable care in checking the mirrors and area around the bus before driving away. The critical test came in testimony by witnesses during the trial who noted that the child had left the bus, crossed safely to the opposite side of the road, but ran back to retrieve a paper when struck by the bus.

School districts, under certain circumstances, have also been held liable for improper supervision at school bus stops. Illustrating this are two cases involving student injuries while boarding buses. In *Raymond v. Paradise Unified School District*[31] the district was found to be negligent in not providing supervision for loading buses while on a school site. A seven-year-old at the high school site waiting for transportation to an elementary school was injured while running unsupervised alongside a bus. Even though the student had been previously warned about such behavior, the court ruled that the high school was not an isolated stop and that the district's failure to supervise and control the child constituted negligence. Similarly, district failure to supervise students was the finding in *School City of Gary v. Claudio.*[32] For administrators, it is particularly important to note that the accident occurred shortly after the new school term began and there was conflicting evidence as to whether the children had been given instruction or warnings regarding busing procedures. The court ruled that the school had a duty to maintain some level of supervision over students in its control while waiting for and boarding buses. Thus, the school's "total lack" of supervision constituted negligence. In another related case, the district was held liable when an 11-year-old slipped on an icy sidewalk and fell under the rear wheels of the bus. It was determined that the bus was driven negligently because the bus had stopped, waited for the approach of children, then pulled forward after another bus moved. Testimony revealed that the bus was not in its usual pickup spot and that normal supervision was not present.[33] This area represents a special concern for administrators as numerous cases have examined bus driver negligence when buses have struck children waiting to be picked up.[34]

Other cases illustrate negligent actions that potentially could have led to tragic consequences. In *Cross v. Board of Education*[35] a school bus left the road after failing to negotiate a curve. The driver claimed that the steering had malfunctioned; however, testimony revealed that the driver had previously stated he was sleepy, had asked students to talk to him, and that he had been seen rubbing his eyes and yawning. Although no tragedy occurred in this instance, in a few cases and under specific state statutes bus drivers have been judged partially negligent for such behavior. In one case, the driver was ruled partially negligent for failing to maintain a proper lookout for children.[36] This negligence, however, was not a substantial factor in causing the injury to the student. Such distinction in degrees of liability can in certain instances allow the school district to successfully argue that the child contributed to the problem. Age, maturity, and mental capacity of the child are determining factors in such arguments of contributory negligence.

Other cases attest to poor judgment or training (or both) on the part of school bus drivers. In *Machenheimer v. Falkner*[37] a school bus driver allowed students to disembark in the middle of an intersection. A child was injured by an automobile that failed to stop at the intersection, and the bus driver was held negligent under the circumstances. Other cases include injury to a student in which the bus was parked contrary to statutory requirements[38] and negligence where the driver moved a bus too quickly after discharging students and resulting in injuries to students by not allowing them to safely cross a street.[39]

Finally, although the period of actual bus transportation is relatively short, high potential for negligence exists. Two such cases involve injuries sustained from objects thrown on a bus. The New Jersey Supreme Court in *Jackson v. Hankinson*[40] reversed a lower court ruling, finding the board of education liable for damages in the plaintiff's loss of an eye because the district failed to provide adequate supervision on the bus. The student had been struck in the eye by an object thrown by a fellow student. In another case, *Blair v. Board of Education,*[41] the board was liable for injury to a student's eye where the duties of the driver were held to include proper order and discipline. According to the court, the bus driver could have foreseen the danger because unruly activity had been occurring for 15 minutes prior to the injury, and no action was taken by the driver. In contrast, in *Hatlee v. Owego-Appalachian School District*[42] parents sued the district and bus driver for improper supervision after their nine-year-old child became sick from chewing a piece of gum picked off the bus floor that was allegedly covered with a hallucinogen known as "angel dust." The court dismissed the suit regardless of facts presented, as there was neither foreseeability of sickness nor proximate cause of injury resulting from the failure to appropriately supervise the bus.

This overview of liability litigation illustrates that, depending on a variety of circumstances, school districts have often been held negligent in the area of student transportation. In establishing successful arguments against the school district and its employees, certain conditions have been present in each case. When the plaintiff prevailed, the evidence was able to show that the potential for injury was foreseeable and/or actions by the school board or its agents did not meet the standards of what a reasonable and prudent person should or would do under similar circumstances. While it is not unreasonable to expect school bus drivers and other personnel to exhibit high standards of care for students, quality control and evaluation of transportation systems and personnel must be implemented and maintained to meet this standard of care, because the school district employee has a grave duty to protect students from all harm. *Failure to protect students may become the causal factor leading to injury of the student, and the school district and its administrators may be held liable for failing to adequately protect the students in their charge.* Under these conditions, liability and transportation of students have become constant companions in the modern world.

State Aid Plans

As pointed out in the opening comments of this chapter, the truly phenomenal growth in transportation systems in the United States since the turn of the twentieth century has resulted in transportation of vast numbers of children in school vehicles at public expense. Incidentally, those data were not fully inclusive, as no single government agency keeps centralized records on the "other" transportation costs and programs of school districts that fall outside the state reporting requirements for regular school instructional programs. Thus, a vast amount of student transportation also occurs in extracurricular events, such as athletic competitions. Because many states exclude extracurricular programs from their transportation reimbursement formulas and consequently do not require reporting by districts to the state, estimation of the size of the transportation industry escapes measurement because little hard data exist on these additional mileages.

As of 1992, however, every state with the exception of New Hampshire provided some form of fiscal aid to local school districts for regular pupil transportation. Like other forms of state aid, pupil transportation aid varies greatly in amount and distribution method from state to state. The state aid formulas include a wide variety of features, with factors such as expenditures per pupil, population density, bus capacities, flat grants, or some combination thereof as common denominators.[43] The operation of these factors is sometimes complex. For example, many states have a density formula based on an index consisting of the number of students transported divided by the eligible bus route mileage.[44] Additionally, states generally have an "allowable per student cost," which is usually the actual expenses plus the cost of bus replacements divided by the number of eligible students in each district. This amount is then plotted against a population density ratio, yielding a permissible cost per pupil that can be claimed for transportation aid.

Beyond these generalizations, formulas differ significantly on a state-by-state basis. Some states provide a transportation allowance based on hazardous walking conditions so that students who may not live far from school can still be transported with the assistance of state aid. In other states, no such hazard allowance may exist. In some states, transportation aid is tied to the general fund formula so that there is a relationship between the philosophy of regular education funding and the financing of transportation services. In other states, however, there appears to be no reason why the state may equalize the general fund while supporting transportation through a system of unequalized flat grants. Once the similarities are identified, the only other commonality is that, in the vast majority of instances, state transportation aid almost never meets the entire cost of transporting students.

In all fairness, however, it is important to point out that the reason formulas never fully fund transportation is because they were never designed to do so. Like other school district funds, it has been the intent of state legislatures to require local taxpayers to shoulder a portion of the cost of transportation. While such a practice might be provoking to some in principle, the concept is far more innocuous than the actual practice because of other state law operations. For example, in most states school districts fund their local share through transfers of money from the general fund to the transportation fund. In other states, the local share is funded by a transportation levy against the tax base of the local district. While this might seem to be a paper accounting procedure that makes little difference, in reality it can make a great difference in taxpayer burden given state law operation. In the first instance, if a state has an equalization plan for its general fund, then the transfer of general fund monies to the transportation fund equates to a degree of transportation equalization. In the instance of a special tax levy for transportation, there is no equalization in the transportation fund unless transportation aid also varies by local wealth. Unfortunately, many states do not equalize transportation as effectively as they do general fund financing.

Although each state calculates aid for transportation according to its own formula, many states use a philosophy closely related to the formula shown in Figure 11.1. Even casual examination of the figure illustrates that the underlying philosophical support is density; that is, the ratio of pupils in the district to the geographic size of the district. State aid is determined by following each step in the formula, where an index of density is calculated. In this particular example, while the total head count is 581, yielding a density of 3.80 students per square mile (see the density table at the bottom of the figure), the effect is to weight these pupils higher for transportation aid purposes than in a district where the number of pupils is great enough to result in a density factor of 15.23 or greater per square mile. When the density factor is tied back to the general fund formula (see Line 7), the actual number of students claimed for state aid purposes is 581 plus 74.1 more students—in effect yielding extra aid for

General Fund Budget—Lines 1 through 13

1. Estimated 9-21-92 FTE enrollment   =   940.0

2. Estimated weighted enrollment for districts under 1,900 FTE. 9-21-92 FTE enrollment __940.0__ × __.350374__ factor (from Table I)   =   329.4

3. Estimated weighted bilingual education enrollment. 9-21-92 bilingual FTE(a) _____ × .2   =   0

4. Estimated weighted vocational education enrollment. 9-21-92 vocational education FTE(b) __8.0__ × .5   =   4.0

5. Estimated weighted at-risk student enrollment(c). Number of eligible students that qualify for free lunches as of 9-21-92 __141__ × .05   =   7.1

6. Estimated weighted FTE for new facilities. 9-21-92 enrollment of students attending a new facility(d) _____ × .25   =   0

7. Estimated weighted FTE for transportation. (Table II, Line 6)   =   74.1

8. Estimated 9-21-92 FTE weighted enrollment (Lines 1+2+3+4+5+6+7)   =   1354.6

9. Estimated 1992–93 operating budget. Line 8 __1354.6__ × $3,600   = $ 4,876,560

10. 1991–92 adjusted operating budget (from Table III)   = $ 4,430,467

11. Total maximum increase (from Table IV)   =   1.1108

12. Maximum general fund budget. Line 10 × Line 11   = $ 4,921,363

13. 1992–93 proposed general fund budget (lower of Line 9 or Line 12)   = $ 4,876,560

Table II

1. Area of district in square miles 9-21-92   =   153.0

2. All public pupils transported who reside in the district 2.5 miles or more or for whom transportation is being made available 9-21-92 (Estimated)   =   581.0

3. Index of density = Line 2 __581.0__ divided by Line 1 __153.0__   =   3.80

4. Using index of density (Line 3), determine amount from density table below   =   459

5. Weighted factor. Density cost per pupil (Line 4) __459__ divided by $3,600 (4 decimal places)   =   .1275

6. Estimated weighted FTE for transportation. 9-21-92 number of students over 2.5 miles __581.0__ × __.1275__ factor (Line 5) (to Line 7, Form 150)   =   74.1

Density Table
(Pupils Per Square Mile)

Less than .11 = 1125	.33 to .35 = 834	.57 to .59 = 733	1.13 to 1.23 = 617	5.23 to 6.23 = 420
.11 to .13 = 1076	.35 to .37 = 823	.59 to .61 = 727	1.23 to 1.33 = 605	6.23 to 7.23 = 404
.13 to .15 = 1036	.37 to .39 = 813	.61 to .63 = 721	1.33 to 1.43 = 594	7.23 to 8.23 = 390
.15 to .17 = 1003	.39 to .41 = 802	.63 to .65 = 716	1.43 to 1.53 = 583	8.23 to 9.23 = 379
.17 to .19 = 975	.41 to .43 = 793	.65 to .67 = 710	1.53 to 1.63 = 574	9.23 to 10.23 = 369
.19 to .21 = 950	.43 to .45 = 784	.67 to .69 = 705	1.63 to 1.73 = 566	10.23 to 11.23 = 363
.21 to .23 = 928	.45 to .47 = 776	.69 to .71 = 700	1.73 to 2.23 = 544	11.23 to 12.23 = 355
.23 to .25 = 909	.47 to .49 = 768	.71 to .73 = 695	2.23 to 2.73 = 515	12.23 to 13.23 = 348
.25 to .27 = 891	.49 to .51 = 760	.73 to .83 = 689	2.73 to 3.23 = 491	13.23 to 14.23 = 339
.27 to .29 = 875	.51 to .53 = 753	.83 to .93 = 662	3.23 to 3.73 = 474	14.23 to 15.23 = 333
.29 to .31 = 861	.53 to .55 = 746	.93 to 1.03 = 645	3.73 to 4.23 = 459	15.23 and over = 326
.31 to .33 = 847	.55 to .57 = 739	1.03 to 1.13 = 630	4.23 to 5.23 = 440	

FIGURE 11.1 Calculation of transportation aid based on Kansas state law

each of those mythical 74.1 students because the density index is linearly tied to miles traveled and children transported. If the effect of this weighting were analyzed, it would be seen that in this instance the density index provided an extra $266,760 in transportation aid that would *not* have been received if the formula had simply distributed a flat grant per pupil.[45]

Regardless of the state, transportation aid calculation is a product of several decisions made at the legislative level. The first decision is adoption of a transportation philosophy. If the state has a high commitment to this function, aid will be higher than in states where other educational priorities have been established. The second decision is adoption of a state aid formula reflecting that philosophy. The third decision is a product of the two former choices by deciding the amount of funding that will flow through the formula. The level of funding is further determined by both commitment and available resources. When these decisions are made, the available resources will almost always determine the amount of state aid distribution by "backing into the formula." This simply means that the formula will be fully funded in each year, even though full finding in a given year may actually be less than in the prior year. While such practice may said to be a game of semantics, it is the reality of an imperfect world in which there is intense public policy competition for limited tax revenues.

The state aid formula therefore channels money to each district in a state where a set of records has established the legal claim a district has for transportation aid. Qualification for state aid normally requires significant amounts of record-keeping to verify all claims for state transportation aid, and in most states such records are audited thoroughly because of potential abuses for "ghost riders." Although the 50 states vary in their record-keeping requirements, a common set of records for state aid reimbursement purposes includes the following:

1. Area maps and bus route information;
2. The address and regular route destination of all enrolled students claimed for transportation aid;
3. A list of students using more than one category of transportation (e.g., vocational and special education) with interim and ultimate destinations;
4. A list of nonpublic school students transported if claimed for aid reimbursement under state law;
5. Evidence of bus seating capacity for each child claimed for aid;
6. Evidence of bridge or road condemnation or construction if the most direct route from residence to attendance center is inaccessible;
7. Evidence of mileage driven on all routes by all buses and breakdown of mileage for multiuse (e.g., activity) buses;
8. Basis and work papers showing the calculation for any prorated pupil transportation costs;
9. Supporting summary and original source documents for all pupil transportation expenditures related to regular routes, special education, vocational education, activities, food service if applicable, or other eligible transportation;
10. Claim vouchers for mileage payments in lieu of transportation, including exact mileages, dates, rates, and total payments;
11. Evidence of insurance costs for pupil transportation vehicles;
12. Evidence of purchase price or remanufacture costs of new or

remanufactured buses and depreciation history or dates of service for each vehicle used in pupil transportation;

13. A list of leased or lease-purchase buses, dates of lease, and identification numbers of individual buses; and

14. Other records as required by state-specific statute.

If these records are not kept, many serious problems will arise, ranging from denial of state aid to liability for negligence or malfeasance in a civil or criminal action if investigation for either financial impropriety or physical injury ever has reason to occur. In keeping with the serious nature of the transportation and risk management functions, loss of state aid under formula technicalities may be the least of worries under adverse circumstances.

The concluding observations regarding state aid plans can be stated fairly succinctly. First, almost every state has become involved in the transportation of students for educational purposes (see Table 11.1).Second, state aid has become a major financial cost to states' treasuries under the belief that children must be able to get to school to receive the full measure of education due to them. Third, state aid plans are generally tied in some way to how densely or sparsely populated school attendance areas are. Fourth, there is usually some attempt to judge the financial capability of a district to support transportation, either through tying transportation aid to general fund state aid or funding transportation categorically at some level believed to help local districts meet their obligations. Fifth, transportation aid must almost always be locally supplemented, either for good or bad reasons. Sixth, to qualify for state aid, most states require significant paperwork. Seventh and finally, these intensive activities underscore the importance of sound and well-managed transportation systems, from both liability and financial perspectives.

Other Important Considerations

Several other important considerations should be briefly addressed beyond the discussion that has occurred thus far, including owning versus contracting, computerization of transportation activities, and school bus purchases and competitive bids.

Owning versus Contracting.   An ongoing debate is the merits and disadvantages of district ownership of the transportation fleet versus utilization of private contractors. While the different opinions and circumstances of nearly 16,000 school districts in the United States make it doubtful that the debate will ever be definitively resolved, administrators should recognize that the debate exists and know the reasons for differences in opinion and, most importantly, the basis on which school districts often make the decision to own or contract their transportation systems.

Those districts which maintain they have saved money and time through letting contracts for transportation services base their claim on a number of reasons. First, school districts with severe cash flow problems avoid the stressful capital costs involved in building a fleet of buses. The average rural district in America runs from 10 to 20 buses ranging from 15-passenger to 65-passenger units or more. The average urban district may run several hundred units. At an average cost of at least $35,000 per bus, the purchase of a bus fleet is a tremendous capital investment. Second, cash-strapped districts also benefit because they often cannot afford new buses and the high maintenance costs associated with older buses are not a direct monthly liability if

TABLE 11.1 Transportation in the 50 States

State	Description
Alabama	Allowable ADA cost through general aid
Alaska	Fully funded categorical
Arizona	Dollar amount per miles in each district
Arkansas	Per-pupil amount and sparsity factor
California	Prior year aid plus COLA
Colorado	Per-mile reimbursement up to 90%
Connecticut	Equalized between 10% and 60%
Delaware	Fully state funded within guidelines
Florida	Density index
Georgia	Combination of standard and variable costs
Hawaii	Full state funding
Idaho	85% of allowable costs through general aid
Illinois	Per-pupil amount and/or allowable costs
Indiana	Equalized with density factor
Iowa	Funded through general aid
Kansas	82% of actual cost on density index
Kentucky	Density and interschool cost comparisons
Louisiana	Funded through general aid
Maine	Funded through general aid based on base year
Maryland	100% reimbursement based on 1981–1982 amounts
Massachusetts	Reimbursement at legislative rate of 100% in 1.5 miles
Michigan	Formula based on costs averaging one third costs
Minnesota	Complex formula with equalized features
Mississippi	Density and fixed rate table averaging 53% costs
Missouri	80% reimbursed subject to efficiency audit
Montana	Statutory schedule of costs per bus mile
Nebraska	Weighted equalization formula
Nevada	General aid equaling 85% of allowable costs
New Hampshire	No aid to general transportation
New Jersey	90% equalized formula
New Mexico	Categorical with equalization features
New York	90% reimbursement
North Carolina	Pays bus, staff per pupil/mile on prior year
North Dakota	Mileage and per-pupil reimbursement
Ohio	Partially funded through general aid
Oklahoma	Density formula
Oregon	70% reimbursement
Pennsylvania	Equalization formula
Rhode Island	Reimbursed through general aid
South Carolina	Fully state funded and monitored
South Dakota	Reimbursed through general aid
Tennessee	60% per-pupil and density formula on prior year
Texas	Density formula through general aid
Utah	Linear regression formula
Vermont	Equalized categorical aid
Virginia	Formula on pupils, mileage, and bus counts
Washington	Reimbursement on bus fleet size
West Virginia	80% of costs
Wisconsin	Flat amount per pupil based on distance
Wyoming	75% through general aid formula

SOURCE: Excerpted from American Education Finance Association and Nelson A. Rockefeller Institute of Government, *School Finance Programs of the United States and Canada 1990–1991* ed. Steven Gold (Albany, N.Y.: Rockefeller Institute on Government, 1992).

the district does not own the fleet. Third, state laws on bus purchases vary greatly, but in most instances require cash financing rather than amortization over a debt repayment schedule. Such laws can be cost-prohibitive. For example, in some states expenditures can only be made from the capital outlay, transportation, or debt service funds, effectively placing the total cost on the local tax base unless these funds are highly equalized. In such instances, ingenious analysis of state laws might permit paying contracted costs from an equalized general fund at significant savings and benefit to taxpayers, where such ingenuity might not be possible under actual fleet ownership.

The many other arguments favoring contracting are based on the following advantages: capitalization costs are lowered; personnel and administration costs are reduced because the district is relieved of the need for a collective bargaining contract with transportation employees; administration of the transportation services handled by nondistrict employees relieves pressure on scarce human resources; overall central office staff and support services are reduced significantly, making for simpler managerial responsibilities; and more economical services are possible through efficient operations by contractors whose primary business and livelihood is transportation. Issues to be considered, however, include the need to assure a contractor's quality performance when the district effectively no longer controls the public relations aspect of the contractor's behavior, and the need to appropriately insure the district and employees against liability for acts of contractors, making careful legal analysis a prerequisite to final commitment.

On the other hand, there are sound arguments favoring district ownership of its own transportation fleet. Advocates claim that benefits include a much higher degree of flexibility, better daily control over the district's operations, easier rerouting of buses without renegotiating contracts, and more economical and flexible services through internally efficient operation. The transportation fleet may also be utilized for other purposes, and because bus drivers are employees of the school board, selection, training, and supervision can be district-controlled.[46] Given the advocacy of both sides, it may well be that there is no one best option, as the preferred choice may depend entirely on the district's financial position and the community's values. What must be clearly understood by all persons is that if contracting is chosen, the written agreements should specify that the contractor is an independent agent, not an agent or officer of the board of education or any state agency, and that the contractor is obligated to comply with all applicable state statutes, rules, and regulations. It must also be clearly determined by all parties within state regulations that the contractor will provide vehicle liability insurance for bodily injury, property damage, and personal injury protection and further recognized that the school district must insure itself as well.

Computerization of Pupil Transportation Services.   As school system size has grown and as new technology has become available, computerization of pupil transportation services has begun to take on more importance. Every year more and more school districts are utilizing computerized bus routing plans, including some relatively smaller districts. Such plans may prove to be highly cost-effective, their major benefit being the ability to offer mathematical applications of efficiency in both time and use of buses. For many school districts, particularly large ones with vast mazes of streets to travel, the cost of bus routing systems has been reduced over the past few years due to the use of sophisticated microcomputers and bus routing software. Research has indicated that computerized routing has saved approximately 15% of total transportation costs while completing "routes within 90 percent of minimum travel time."[47]

While computerizing district operations is discussed later in Chapter 13 and while intricate detailing of transportation software is beyond the scope of this text, the administrator should know that there are sophisticated software products to assist in this aspect of transportation management. For example, software is available to help sophisticated school district operations preplan transportation routes in undeveloped areas well in advance of actual population movement, and these techniques are combined with demographic forecasting that helps districts economically purchase building sites many years before actual construction begins. Additionally, many school transportation systems use a series of computer-aided techniques in developing routes, including maps, census data, local highway time delay studies, and other devices, along with "manual coded data supplied by demographic, cartographic, and geocoding personnel."[48] Although computerized routing systems are complex, they can be easily understood by recognizing that they function either from geocoding (i.e., manual entry of data) or a DIME system (i.e., a computerized filing system maintained via Standard Metropolitan Statistical Areas—SMSAs—as defined by the U.S. Census).

Such systems do not come without costs, however. Several of those costs are significant and require some cost benefit analysis to justify their purchase. For example, neither plan is free-standing, requiring additional information through an up-to-date mapping system that is relatively expensive.[49] Additionally, costly planning for such services is necessary. Such planning may take the form of determining the most efficient schedules, eliminating deadhead runs, "evaluating changes in the transportation policies with impact on costs (e.g., new eligibility criteria, modified walking distances, different maximum riding times, introduction of new transfer schemes),"[50] as well as even potentially changing school attendance boundaries. The benefit, however, is efficiency and the ability of the school transportation planner to electronically engage in "what if" scenarios under a variety of situations or combinations so as to best advise the administration and board of education on transportation planning.[51] As software capability increases, it may be possible to introduce technology into progressively smaller school systems, particularly because more school districts will likely embrace year-round education, impacting the planning of student transportation for efficiency purposes.

While high-tech routing systems may be best suited for the largest districts, which must plan migration even before it occurs, computerized fleet maintenance is becoming commonplace. Such programs generally incorporate garage operations, vehicle replacements, mechanical repairs and maintenance, as well as fuel consumption into an electronic database and can reveal the relationship between preventive maintenance and emergency repairs. Additionally, the number and type of repairs for each vehicle, cost per mile, and cost per vehicle and repair is tracked. Overall and specific costs can be accounted for instantly in such systems, allowing administrators to make the most efficient decisions as to maintenance and longevity.[52] For example, one school district determined that maintenance costs for one bus was $148 during the first year, while the same bus consumed $3,117 in its seventh year.[53] This information is then compared with labor costs to determine the true net cost of a new bus. State reports are often prepared utilizing such programs because the system is highly useful for maintaining and analyzing information concerning each bus, including the number of students to be transported, preventive maintenance records, fuel consumption, and repair records, as well as future inspection and maintenance schedules.[54] Examples of a pretrip inspection checklist, vehicle service record, and defect report in a typical school district are shown in Figures 11.2, 11.3, and 11.4. These records can easily be generated by an efficient electronic system, saving countless human hours compared to the cost of manual collation.

School Bus Purchases and Competitive Bids.   The discussion regarding owning or contracting for transportation illustrates the enormity of school bus costs for local school districts. The price for a standard bus may average about $35,000 but the experienced administrator will quickly recognize that this cost is not the extent of bus costs. For example, the purchase of the largest type of school bus with a wheelchair lift can easily exceed $70,000. Such an expenditure requires careful consideration to avoid unhappy surprises on delivery due to failure to appropriately prepare tight bid specifications or failure to follow state-specific laws for such purchases.

Purchases of such large ticket items as buses is generally done by the local school district under strict written specifications detailing the vehicle's features. Specifications are also usually based on state rules and guidelines. All purchases must meet or exceed state minimal regulations. In a few states, a state agency actually prepares the specifications, awards the bids, and provides buses to the district. This is not normal procedure, however, and districts must become skilled at these acts themselves. Purchasing buses is particularly complicated because they are normally purchased on separate chassis bid and body bids. That is, the local school district will bid these items separately, and the body manufacturer will provide a body to fit the appropriate chassis at the school bus body factory. Although complex, this procedure actually provides an economy of scale and specialization that can be utilized by both manufacturers because the school bus body manufacturer can mass-produce to fit one of approximately four standard school bus chassis. The type of motor—that is, diesel or gasoline and horsepower rating—can also be bid to make the bus meet local conditions and preferences.[55] Most school districts find that a mix of bus sizes serves them most efficiently and that larger buses are more versatile because they may be utilized for larger numbers of students, thereby reducing the number of buses and personnel costs. Smaller buses are generally used in sparsely inhabited areas; likewise, smaller buses are sometimes utilized in inner cities due to busy and crowded streets.

Of all the complex problems in the purchase of school buses and other district transportation, none is more prone to error than observing state laws for protecting the public treasury. Most states have competitive bidding laws that apply to large purchases, including buses. The purpose of competitive bid laws is to force marketplace competition between suppliers who vie for tax dollars. For example, because there are only a few bus manufacturers in the country, it is possible that lack of competition can drive prices up. Similarly, in the past some districts have had favorite suppliers, who were able to develop relationships that did not require them to compete with other suppliers to win lucrative contracts. Consequently, many states have passed competitive bid laws requiring districts to accept the "lowest responsible bid" for comparable products. The administrator should be thoroughly knowledgeable about bid laws under which purchases are expected to be made, as severe penalties

PRETRIP INSPECTION
TRANSPORTATION DEPARTMENT

✓ OK
✗ NEED REPAIR

BUS# _____   MILEAGE _____   DRIVER _____   WEEK BEGINNING _____

Item	Monday AM	Monday PM	Tuesday AM	Tuesday PM	Wednesday AM	Wednesday PM	Thursday AM	Thursday PM	Friday AM	Friday PM	Extra AM	Extra PM	Extra AM	Extra PM
BODY--DENTS AND SCRATCHES														
GLASS														
TIRES, LUGS														
EXHAUST SYSTEM														
UNDERNEATH --VANDALISM														
LIGHTS														
STOP ARMS														
FIRE EXTINGUISHER														
FIRST AID KIT														
REFLECTORS														
REGISTRATION, INS. CARD INSPECTION SCHEDULE														
COPY OF ROUTE														
EMERGENCY DOOR & WINDOWS														
CLEANLINESS														
UPHOLSTERY CONDITION														
MIRRORS														
FASTEN SEAT BELT														
GAUGES														
HORN, WINDSHIELD WIPERS														
EMERGENCY BRAKE														
REMARKS														

Form No. TRN 878.003
Revised Date: 11/16/89

FIGURE 11.2 Sample Pretrip Inspection Report

TRANSPORTATION DEPARTMENT

Tax Exempt #03-00019-06-11

VEHICLE SHOP SERVICE RECORD

T15965

Lubricate	☐
Change Oil	☐
Change Oil Filter Cart.	☐
Change Trans Oil	☐
Change Diff Oil	☐
Pack Front Wheel Brgs.	☐
Adjust Brakes	☐
X Tires	☐
Wash	☐

Vehicle Number

Make — Type or Model — Date — Year — Received — A.M. / P.M.

Serial No — Engine No

Speedometer — License No

Order Written By — Driver

INSTRUCTIONS

Code	Date			HRS

AMOUNT — Comments:

Gas *	
Gas *	
Oils *	
Oil *	
Lbs	
Grease *	

Total Labor
Total Parts
Total Accessories
Total Sublet Repairs
Total Gas, Oil, Grease
GRAND TOTAL

QUAN.	PARTS · NUMBER · DESCRIPTION	PRICE

Sublet Repairs

LABOR CHARGE

(A) **PARTS CERTIFICATION**
I hereby certify that the above listed parts, accessories or sublet repairs are correct and accurate.

X

(B) **LABOR CERTIFICATION**
I hereby certify that the listed labor instructions were performed using the listed parts and/or listed gas, oil, and grease as specified.

X

(C) **GAS, OIL AND GREASE CERTIFICATION**
I hereby certify that the listed gas, oil and/or greases are correct and accurate.

X

Form No. TRN 888.010   Revised Date: 10/19/90

FIGURE 11.3 Sample Bus Service Record

529

Vehicle Defect Report

Vehicle Number: _____   Odometer Reading: _____   Time: _____   Date: _____

Check Defects

1. Brakes	_____	14. Tires	_____
2. Lights	_____	15. Wheels	_____
3. Horn	_____	16. Fluid Leaks	_____
4. Wipers	_____	17. Air Leaks	_____
5. Gauges	_____	18. Fuel Odor	_____
6. Heaters	_____	19. Exhaust Fumes	_____
7. Defrosters	_____	20. Muffler	_____
8. Seats	_____	21. Tail Pipe	_____
9. Glass	_____	22. Inside Mirrors	_____
10. Emergency Door	_____	23. Body Dents	_____
11. Emergency Equipment	_____	24. Cross-View Mirror	_____
12. Emergency Door Buzzer	_____	25. Two-Way Radio	_____
13. Steering	_____	26. Other (Explain)	_____

Remarks: _____

_____

_____

_____

_____

Driver's Signature: _____

Shop Report:

Defect Corrected: _____ Yes   Date: _____

Mechanic's Signature: _____   Work Order Number: _____

Distribution: White — File
Canary — Bus Driver (Before Service)
Pink   — Bus Driver (After Service)

FIGURE 11.4   Sample Vehicle Defect Report

for failure to comply often follow. A sample bid law published by an actual state appears in Figure 11.5.

Transportation Summary

It should be obvious by this point that a successful transportation program for a school district is contingent on many important practices. In fact, the opportunities for sophisticated management are endless, making thorough description of this function impossible in a book of this nature. It is virtually impossible to close such a discus-

UNIFIED SCHOOL DISTRICTS
GUIDELINES FOR COMPETITIVE BIDDING

S.A. 1991 Supp. 72-6760:

(a) No expenditure involving an amount greater than $10,000 for construction, reconstruction, or remodeling or for the purchase of materials, goods, or wares shall be made by the board of education of any school district except upon sealed proposals, and to the lowest responsible bidder.

(b) The provisions of subsection (a) do not apply to expenditures by a board of education for the purchase of:

(1) services;

(2) products required to be purchased under the provisions of S.A. 75-3317 through 75-3322 and amendments thereto;

(3) educational materials directly related to curriculum and secured by copyright;

(4) motor fuels required to provide or furnish transportation;

(5) perishable foods and foodstuffs required for operations of a school lunch program;

(6) articles or products that are produced, manufactured, or provided by inmates under the prison-made goods act;

(7) materials, goods, or wares required for reconstructing, remodeling, repairing, or equipping buildings when such purchase has been necessitated by the occurrence of a loss against which the board of education has purchased property or casualty insurance; and

(8) materials, goods, or wares which are purchased:

(A) From vendors who have entered into contracts with the state director of purchases pursuant to state purchasing statutes for purchases by state agencies; and

(B) under the same pricing provisions established in the state contracts, subject to agreement of the vendor to honor the state contract prices.

(c) Whenever the board of education of any school district lets bids for the purchase of materials, goods, or wares and bids are submitted by bidders domiciled within the school district and by bidders domiciled outside the school district and the low bid is submitted by a bidder domiciled outside the school district, the school district domiciliary which submitted the lowest bid may be deemed the preferred bidder and awarded the bid if:

(1) the quality, suitability and usability of the materials, goods, or wares are equal;

(2) the amount of the bid of the school district domiciliary is not more than 1% greater than the amount of the low bid; and

(3) the school district domiciliary agrees to meet the low bid by filing a written agreement to that effect within 72 hours after receiving notification of being deemed the preferred bidder.

(d) The provisions of subsection (c) do not apply to expenditures for construction, reconstruction, or remodeling.

DEFINITIONS

The definitions of construction, purchase of materials, goods, and wares would include the following.

Construction

1. Something tangible being built or erected, such as remodeling, reconstruction, additions to, repair, and alterations of school facilities.

2. Installation of irrigation systems or landscaping of school grounds.

Materials, Goods, and Wares

1. Supplies (includes all expendable items such as uniforms, custodial materials, teaching materials, and all other consumable materials).

2. Equipment (an article that is nonexpendable and if damaged, or some parts lost or worn, would be more feasible to repair than replace).

3. Tangible personal property.   (*Continued*)

FIGURE 11.5 Sample Competitive Bid Law, excerpted from Kansas statute

COMPETITIVE BIDDING recommendation

1. Recommend boards of education consider fixing a lower dollar amount as a minimum when competitive bids are required. State law requires a minimum of $10,000. Some boards may desire to go to a lower dollar amount.
2. Write clear and concise bid specifications.
3. Publish bid solicitation in official school newspaper.
4. Allow adequate time for the bidders to submit sealed bids.
5. Set a time for bid opening.
6. Open bids publicly.
7. Involve at least two school personnel in the bid opening.
8. Avoid negotiation of bid specifications after bids have been accepted.
9. Correct and request new bids if bid specifications are inadequately written.
10. Return bids unopened and rebid the project if an error is discovered in the bid specifications prior to bid opening.
11. Any bids which are submitted beyond the due date should be returned unopened for noncompliance with the bid specifications.
12. The bid specifications should provide for inclusion within the bid of the company name, address, telephone number, name of contact person, as well as the bid itself.
13. Include a specific date, time, and location for the submittal of bids and specific date, time, and location for opening such bids in the bid specifications.
14. Document and retain records to ensure bidding procedures are followed. Documentation should be on file in the school district office if any bids are rejected because the bidder is considered "not responsible."
15. All bidders should receive a bid summary with a letter of acceptance or rejection on the board of education's decision.

Preferential Bidding

1. Accept the lowest responsible bidder as required by law. (Review the exceptions provided in S.A. 1991 Supp. 72-6760 as shown on page 1 of these guidelines.)
2. Do not grant preferential bids for construction, reconstruction, or remodeling of buildings to local contractors or businesses unless they are in compliance with S.A. 1991 Supp. 62-6760.

Construction

1. Ensure that all construction contractors provide a payment bond (sometimes referred to as a public works bond, a surety bond, a statutory bond, or a labor and materials bond) for construction, reconstruction, and remodeling projects which exceed $10,000 as required by S.A. 60-1111. The amount of the bond should be at least equal to the cost of the project. Contractors should file a payment bond with Clerk of District Court in the county where the project is to be constructed and furnish the school district with copies of the bond bearing written approval of Clerk of the District Court.
2. In the process of accepting bids on construction projects, make sure it is clear who will provide the builder's risk insurance and in what amount.
3. Ensure the amendments or addendums to original bid specifications be submitted in writing by the school district and acknowledged by each bidder.
4. Include a five percent bid bond in all construction contract bids.
5. Include a statement which requires contractors to comply with all local, state, and federal laws, ordinances, and regulations in all bids. For example, see S.A. 44-1030 and 44-201.

Miscellaneous

1. Ensure that all out-of-state bidders comply with preferential bid law (S.A. 75-3740a).

    "S.A. 75-3740a. State and Local Government Contracts; Bidders Domiciled in Other States. To the extent permitted by federal law and regulations, whenever the State of _____ or any agency, department, bureau, or division thereof or any municipality of the state including, but not limited to, county, school district, improvement district, or other public body lets bids for contracts for the erection, construction, alteration, or repair of any public building or structure or any addition thereto or for

FIGURE 11.5   *(Continued)*

any public work or improvement or for any purchases of any goods, merchandise, materials, supplies, or equipment of any kind, the contractor domiciled outside the State of _____, to be successful, shall submit a bid the same percentage less than the lowest bid submitted by a responsible _____ contractor as would be required of such _____ domiciled contractor to succeed over the bidding contractor domiciled outside _____ on a like contract let in such contractor's domiciliary state."

2. Purchase orders should not be spilt to get under the $10,000 limit for the purpose of circumventing the bidding law.
3. Review the *School Bond Guide* provided by the _____ State Board of Education prior to any major construction projects which require a vote of the patrons.
4. Require sealed bids and do not allow telephone quotes (S.A. 1991 Supp. 72-6760).
5. Ensure that the board of education reserves the right to reject any or all bids. In some cases, school district may not have sufficient funds to fund the project or may desire to delay the project.

FIGURE 11.5   (*Continued*)

sion because so many areas still need in-depth treatment. For example, driver training is a critically important function of a transportation system as new rules continue to be applied in this area. For example, all administrators should know that as of April 1, 1992, the Commercial Drivers License (CDL) was required for all school bus drivers by federal law,[56] requiring applicants to pass more thorough knowledge and skill tests. The many requirements for transportation systems must be carefully studied if school administrators are to understand the seriousness of this school responsibility.

The next decade will offer many challenging opportunities for educational leaders at all levels to utilize their skills and training. Just as transportation of students has grown since 1869 when Massachusetts became the first state to aid transportation, student transportation needs will continue to increase. Districts should make a concerted effort to provide safe, economical, and efficient transportation systems.

SCHOOL FOOD SERVICE

Like transportation, the food service function is integral to the effective and efficient operation of a school district. Although many people tend to assign these functions to relatively low status in the educational hierarchy because their role is less visibly related to the primary mission of schools through the instructional process, such assignment is in error because these functions are vital to ensuring that instruction can occur in a timely and productive manner. This is certainly true for the food service function because, while it may be appropriate for auxiliary services in a district to be managed on a daily basis by noneducators, it takes much knowledge and care to organize and conduct an effective and efficient system for tending to the nutritional needs of children on a long-term planning basis. As stated at the outset, it makes little sense to claim loyalty to equal educational opportunity if children must go to school hungry.

This section focuses on a fairly brief introduction to the food service function by explicating within general parameters how food service systems most often operate, how meal prices are determined under federal, state, and local requirements, and how the typical revenues and expenditures in food service budgets are allocated, thus providing a better appreciation of this vital function on which to base extended learning. Several excellent highly technical books on school food service operations are available.[57]

Food Service Overview

The importance of the school food service function cannot be overemphasized or restated too frequently. Neither should it be assumed that the food service function is simple or inexpensive. Additionally, the federal government has assumed an extended interest in school food service, both from the perspective of general welfare and from other wide federal interests in such seemingly unrelated programs as agricultural price supports. The importance of food service in the educational enterprise has increased to such an extent that many schools across the nation are voluntarily offering breakfast programs to enhance student learning through good nutrition, and many other states have mandated breakfast programs in recent years under the belief that many children are poorly nourished, with severe negative consequences for their educational accomplishments.

As noted in Chapter 2, the federal government has long encouraged good nutrition in schools. The first major federal legislation addressing this arena actually sprang from an interest in agriculture under the severe economic depression experienced in the early part of the twentieth century. In 1935 the Bankhead-Jones Act (PL 74-182) authorized grants to states for agricultural experiment stations, and in the same year Congress passed the Agricultural Adjustment Act (PL 74-320) authorizing 30% of the annual customs receipts to be used to encourage the exportation and domestic consumption of agricultural commodities. Commodities purchased under this authorization began to be used in school lunch programs in 1936, benefiting both agriculture and schools by combining a social welfare agenda with a ready market for commodities. In 1946, Congress passed the National School Lunch Act (PL 79-396) authorizing assistance through grants-in-aid and other means to states to assist in providing adequate foods and facilities for establishing, maintaining, operating, and expanding nonprofit school lunch programs. In 1954, Congress passed the School Milk Program Act (PL 83-597) providing funds for purchase of milk for school lunch programs. Congress has sustained its interest in this area, from time to time engaging in benevolent involvement designed to assist children in meeting nutritional needs, particularly among low income families. By 1991, federal assistance to the National School Lunch Program totaled $3.9 billion, provided another $683 million for School Breakfast Programs, provided $21 million for the Special Milk Program, and targeted millions of other dollars for smaller programs. When all outlays including food stamps to the general population are counted, federal interest in good nutrition for Americans amounted to $28.7 billion in 1991.[58]

From originally attempting to decrease surplus foods in federal warehouses, school food service operations have come to permeate nearly every school in America. Every study of nutrition and student achievement has supported the concept that children must receive sound nutrition to learn properly. Any reasonable person would thus assume that all else would stand secondary to this vital prerequisite to student achievement. But while massive fiscal outlays have in fact occurred, local school districts have had to deal with a multitude of food service problems, mostly relating to difficulties in providing high quality services under rising costs, in turn making it difficult to financially break even on food service operations.

Food Service Operation

These problems have led to cost analyses of how school districts can better manage their costs. Like transportation, there has been interest in whether to contract for food services or to handle food operations in-house. While choices vary depending on circumstances, there have been many school districts in the last decade that have decided to contract for food service operations. Generally, the leading reason behind this decision has been the perceived benefits stemming from financial and managerial efficiency. Many districts that have moved to food contracts have been quite pleased with their decisions, reporting benefits that include increased and expanded menus, elimination of financial deficits that have historically plagued food service operations, and improved communication due to the aggressive market responsiveness of vendors who must cater to clientele. The literature reports many instances of school districts that believe that such contracts for food service operations have proved more efficient and less costly than their experiences with in-house provision.[59]

Specifically, proponents of contracting have reported the following five major benefits to external food service operations:

1. School administrators have more time to spend on school curriculum in an age where many noninstructional responsibilities seriously reduce instructional contact;
2. Because districts are relieved of the personnel function, they have been able to reduce wage and benefits costs, disputes, and grievances;
3. Because contractors are professionals in a single field, districts have experienced improved menu planning and purchase prices;
4. Because the district is no longer performing the food function, there has been significant reduction of in-house record-keeping requirements; and
5. Because contractors are commercial suppliers, there is strong incentive for food services to become a profit center if the contractor is to survive financially.[60]

Although educators might dispute some of these benefits, others are undeniably true. For example, one of the more unpleasant roles of a building principal is food service supervision. Few would deny that a better role for the building principal is involvement in the teaching and learning process, evaluation of teachers, and overall curriculum leadership in a school. The same is true for central office administrators, who sometimes spend large amounts of time organizing and monitoring food operations. Although food service is important and should be supported by all levels of administration, the instructional side of education loses out to management when administrators are in close daily charge of auxiliary services. The second cost savings benefit seems reasonable as well, although moving from an in-house operation to a contract requires considerable forethought because in certain states, contracting food service for reasons of reducing labor costs could be construed as unfair labor practice. The third and fourth benefits also seem unarguable, as professionals in the food industry would reasonably have the best grasp of pricing, consumer preferences, and record management. The fifth benefit might be distasteful to some educators, however, by introducing profit to a function designed to support the curricular and humanitarian missions of schools. However, the incentive for efficiency must be recognized as greater for contractors.

For school districts that wish to contract for food services, the literature suggests certain actions that reflect wise choices and sound management. First, the school district should take great care to review its potential providers from a list of reputable and experienced firms. This can be done in a variety of ways, including attending trade conventions and reviewing the experience of other districts already contracting for services. It is further suggested that the district deliberately prepare a set of written goals and objectives for the system in advance of decision time. This will facilitate the development of bid specifications and assist the bidders in deciding whether to bid, as well as establishing the criteria for evaluating proposals by bidders. Careful evaluation of comparable proposals by knowledgeable administrators with the help of outside consultants may also be useful. Because a relationship is likely to last for some time and because much public damage can be wrought by hasty choices, careful pursuit of the best bid for contracts will serve the school district well for years.[61]

For districts choosing not to contract for food services, the only option is to provide this function in-house. While there are effectively only two choices, the task of in-house service is highly complex. Generally, schools must meet a variety of regulations, both for permission to operate and to receive federal and state food aid. For example, participation in the National School Lunch Child Nutrition program requires that the district meet the following standards:

1. *Operate a nonprofit program.* This means that only up to a three-month operating balance may be kept on hand and still be considered nonprofit. In contrast, management companies operating at a profit are obviously exempt.

2. *Serve meals that meet nutrition requirements.* This may be accomplished by one or more types of meals. An approved program can offer a "Type A" lunch (single menu), a "fast food" choice menu, or an "à la carte" menu. Each must be planned so as to meet minimum dietary recommendations.

3. *Price the meals as a unit.* This limitation does not prevent foods from being sold as separate items. To be counted as a reimbursable lunch, however, the meal must be priced as a unit. Sales of seconds will be additional income.

4. *Supply free and reduced-price meals* to eligible needy children. Uniform policy requirements must be carefully followed.

5. *Agree to avoid discrimination.* No child may be refused a meal under the program because of inability to pay or due to race, sex, color, or national origin.

6. *Keep accurate records of income and expenditures.* These records are subject to intensive state and federal audits and must be maintained for three prior school years plus the current year.

7. *Complete a formal reimbursement claim.* The written claim must be sent on a timely basis each month to the state.

8. *Distribute applications for free and reduced-price meals.* At the beginning of each school year, the district must actively inform each student enrolled in an eligible school and must receive any submitted applications to participate in the program.

9. *Review and act on free and reduced-price meal applications.* In accordance with state guidance materials, parents/guardians must be notified with respect to any action taken on their application.

10. *Develop and implement a verification procedure.* To confirm eligibility for free and reduced-price meals, a systematic method of verifying the accuracy of applications must be developed, disseminated, and followed.

11. *Maintain accurate participation records.* The district must establish a procedure for obtaining accurate meal counts by reimbursable category (paid, free, reduced, and adult meals on the serving line at the point of service).

12. *Establish and implement purchasing procedures.* Purchasing procedures must be in compliance with state and federal regulations.

13. *Utilize federally donated foods or commodities.* This includes the ability to store commodities properly without spoilage.[62]

If these requirements look formidable, it is because they in fact form a highly complex task for school food service personnel. There is generally so much reporting and supervising that school districts operating in-house food service functions generally must hire a full-time director of food services, who must be highly trained to assure the efficient and cost-effective operation of modern complex support services and who is also a trained and certified dietitian. This person works closely with building principals and the central business office, as well as having direct responsibility for supervising food service workers. The position has been described as one of "planning, doing, and comparing results"[63] because the role incumbent is often ultimately responsible for the full range of activities encompassing menu planning, food purchases, and hiring and dismissal of all workers in this operation.

A major concern for in-house providers is for improving efficiency and cost effectiveness. These concerns may call for decisions about on-site versus satellite food preparation, fixed versus free choice menus, and a host of other issues. Satelliting generally involves delivery of ready-prepared food while utilizing a finishing kitchen on-site. From a cost perspective, central kitchens have proved very cost-effective for many school districts under certain conditions because the major benefit is mass preparation and nonduplication of facilities. For example, in well-designed and managed central kitchens, productivity has been shown to increase 300%–400% compared to small stand-alone food preparation programs. Costs must be carefully watched in such operations, however, because of costs due to use of specialized vehicles required to transport meals to sites, finishing kitchen equipment, and the use of specialized freezers for storage. But proponents point out that when properly managed, capitalization costs are spread over a greater number of schools and students, thereby lowering the ultimate cost to the taxpayer. Such centralized operations are not without their flaws, however, as critics point out that effectiveness may be damaged because site control is lessened and rigidity, overstandardization, and nonresponsiveness may follow a large centralized operation.

A second major problem faced by the food service director is in the arena of food service personnel. School food service operations often suffer from employee turnover as well as high absenteeism, particularly since school food service operations usually face the twin dilemmas of low-end pay scales and high labor costs. This seeming contradiction occurs because many positions pay more for similar work, while at the same time labor costs contribute significantly to the total overhead of the school food service operation. Many school districts have learned that by improving the working conditions of food service employees through such things as free uniforms, insurance plans, basic skill training, and free meals as well as a professional approach toward these workers, positive results can occur over time.[64] Additionally, successful programs have developed manager training seminars to internally replace site managers when vacancies occur.

The third major problem facing in-house food service operations is complex budgeting. Unless the food service director is well trained, food service budgeting can become overwhelming due to the potential number of sites and types of programs involved. Generally, the food service manager in cooperation with the district financial services division must establish the receipts and disbursements for each school site as part of the budget process and must provide leadership in setting prices for meals. This requires information and organizational skills that include ability to analyze records and to forecast revenues and expenditures over time. Each school site must be evaluated as to the impact of any projected changes in enrollments, food and labor costs, menu, meal prices, and so forth. This is extremely difficult and precise work because school food service budgeting is generally a cash operation, making projection of revenues and expenditures significantly different from other budgeting processes. The director of food service operations must project a budget that takes into account a variety of factors including:

1. Historical data;
2. Demographic changes (school openings or closings);
3. Projected enrollments;
4. Effects of menu changes;
5. Changes in operating procedures;
6. Goals and plans;
7. Changes in food and labor costs;
8. Meal price changes; and
9. State and federal guidelines.[65]

The budgetary items are then reduced to segments or subcategories and finally to monthly projections. In this manner, the director can identify potential trouble spots and plan for the entire year.[66] As with every budget in the district, monthly projections are reassembled into an annual budget wherein the revenue and expenditure sides must balance (see sample budget in Figure 11.6). The food services budget then becomes an integral part of the overall school district budget deliberations, much like budgets for other support services. Most school districts begin the budget process for the following year in August or September with the directors of each division preparing preliminary budgets. The assistant superintendent for finance reviews each preliminary budget and recommends a refined budget to the superintendent in October. The superintendent generally reviews the requests for new resources and price increases. Generally, by January the superintendent releases the proposed final budget to the board, including a food service operations budget.[67]

Because food service budgets are cash-funded in most states, the revenue and expenditure estimation process is critically important, particularly because total program costs minus federal and state aid yields the cost per meal that must be charged or locally supplemented. Thus, the level of state and federal aid is critical to a major goal

FOOD SERVICE	Code 24 Line	12 mo. 1990–91 Actual (1)	12 mo. 1991–92 Actual (2)	12 mo. 1992–93 Budget (3)
UNENCUMBERED CASH BALANCE JULY 1	01	11,077	19,346	22,152
REVENUE:				
1000 LOCAL SOURCES				
1510 Interest on Idle Funds	05			
1600 Food Service				
1611 Student Sales (Lunch)	15	110,155	125,296	160,340
1612 Student Sls (Breakfast)	25			1,491
1613 Student Sls (Spec Milk)	35		960	960
1620 Adult & Student Sales (Non-Reimbursable Prog)	45	17,932	19,604	11,550
1990 Miscellaneous	55	1,652	2,368	
3000 STATE SOURCES				
3203 School Food Assistance	65	5,840	5,726	8,390
4000 FEDERAL SOURCES				
4550 Child Nutrition Programs	75	54,277	58,430	98,917
5000 Other				
5206 Transfer from General	85	15,000		
5208 Transfer from Supp Gen	90			
RESOURCES AVAILABLE	170	215,933	231,730	303,800
TOTAL EXPENDITURES & TRANSFERS	175	196,587	209,578	303,800
UNENCUMBERED CASH BAL JUNE 30	190	19,346	22,152	xxxxxxxxxxxx
2600 Operations & Maintenance				
100 Salaries				
120 Non-Certified	210			
200 Employee Benefits				
210 Insurance (Employee)	215			
220 Social Security	220			
290 Other	225			
400 Purchased Property Serv				
411 Water/Sewer	230			
490 Other	235			
500 Other Purchased Services	240	588	621	675
600 Supplies				
610 General Supplies	245			
620 Energy				
621 Heating	250			
622 Electricity	255			
626 Motor Fuel-not sch bus	260	805	914	1,000
629 Other	265			
680 Miscellaneous Supplies	270			1,000
700 Property (Equip & Furn)	275			
800 Other	280			
3000 Oper. of Non-Instr. Serv.				
3100 Food Service Operation				
100 Salaries				
110 Certified	285	4,687	10,500	11,340
120 Non-Certified	290	82,457	78,676	85,000

FIGURE 11.6 Sample food service budget sides

*Enter on Code 24, Line 175.

		12 mo.	12 mo.	12.mo
FOOD SERVICE	Code 24 Line	1990–91 Actual (1)	1991–92 Actual (2)	1992–93 Budget (3)
200 Employee Benefits				
210 Insurance	295			
220 Social Security	300	5,721	5,902	6,500
290 Other	305			
500 Other Purchased Services				
520 Insurance	310			
570 Food Service Management	315			
590 Other Purchased Services	320			
600 Supplies				
630 Food & Milk	325	92,881	95,948	125,000
680 Miscellaneous Supplies	330	6,937	4,639	5,500
700 Property (Equip & Furn)	335	2,511	4,730	59,285
800 Other	340		7,648	8,500
5200 TRANSFER TO:				
960 Risk Management Reserve	345			
TOTAL EXPENDITURES & TRANSFERS*	xxxx	196,587	209,578	303,800

*Enter on Code 24, Line 175.

FIGURE 11.6   (*Continued*)

of good food service operations—that is, keeping the price of meals down so that all children can eat without economic hardship. The process of estimating revenue is shown in Figure 11.7, where federal, state, and local funds are added together to find the revenue available under federal and state reimbursement amounts. For example, the district in Figure 11.7 serves 65,000 fully paid elementary meals, for which it receives 30¢ federal reimbursement and 5¢ state aid. The district is charging $1.10 per meal based on its costs, which the district may subsidize if it chooses. If when preparing a new budget it is believed that estimated costs will go up next year, the district must then decide whether it wishes to raise meal prices, contribute local tax dollars to the food service fund, or engage in efficiency measures, such as cost analysis of contracted versus in-house services. The interrelatedness and circularity of the total food service and budget process can thus be seen from this example.

Despite best efforts, meal prices continue to rise, economically hurting some children in the process. Fortunately, help is available in the form of free and reduced-price meals, which again entails federal and state aid. As seen in earlier sample documents, the budget of the district has specific mechanisms to account for these aids.

To receive federal reimbursement for meals, the district must first agree to participate in the national school breakfast/lunch program. Eligibility for federal aid is first a function of the 13 requirements stated earlier in the chapter. Eligibility for students to participate in free or reduced-price meals is then secondly based on family income and size of household as established by the federal government and adjusted annually. Students whose family income is at or below established federal guidelines are eligible to participate in free or reduced-price services, and the student may also qualify if the family receives food stamps. As seen in Figure 11.7, these federal lunch subsidy payments for free and reduced-price meals come to the district through a state agency as actual revenue into the food service fund. These funds are strictly audited annually for

Estimated Food Service Revenue 1992–1993

		Total Annual Meals	Rate	Federal Reimbursement	Rate	State Reimbursement	District Local Price	Revenue	TOTAL 7-1-92 to 6-30-93
Lunches									
Paid Elem.	1.	65,000	0.3000	19,500	0.0500	3,250	1.10	71,500	94,250
Jr. High	2.	36,000	0.3000	10,800	0.0500	1,800	1.20	43,200	55,800
Sr. High	3.	34,000	0.3000	10,200	0.0500	1,700	1.20	40,800	52,700
Free	4.	20,700	1.8025	37,312	0.0500	1,035			38,347
Reduced	5.	12,100	1.4025	16,970	0.0500	605	0.40	4,840	22,415
Adult	6.	7,700					1.50	11,550	11,550
Total	7.			94,782		8,390		171,890	275,062
Breakfast									
Paid	8.	6,000	0.1850	1,110			1.10	1,221	2,331
Free	9.	1,800	0.9275	1,670					1,670
Reduced	10.	900	0.6275	565			0.30	270	835
Adult	11.								
Total	12.			3,345				1,491	4,836
Kindergarten Milk									
Paid	13.	4,000	0.11	440			.24	960	1,400
Free	14.	1,000	Cost	350					350
Total	15.			790				960	1,750
Other Cash Sales/Income	16.								
12 Months Total Income	17.			98,917		8,390		174,341	281,648

FIGURE 11.7   Sample Food Service Reimbursement Form

compliance with rules and regulations. The set of guidelines for student eligibility in 1991–1992 are shown in Table 11.2.

The budgeting aspect of food service is particularly frustrating because districts have relatively few opportunities to reduce their costs beyond the limited choices of contract versus in-house services, central kitchens, and only a few other options, such as multidistrict cooperative purchasing for bulk rate savings and other interdistrict cooperative arrangements.[68] Particularly troublesome is that if costs rise, the district must absorb them or put the cost back on students—a very counterproductive measure. However, because the prime objective of a school food service operation is the satisfaction of the student's hunger to improve learning, the overall goal must therefore be to enhance student participation while operating as close as possible to a break-even financial condition. Although difficult, this is possible through good management techniques that include measurable objectives, sound short- and long-range plans, an operations manager who is visible and involved, and support of the total program by committed and knowledgeable school administrators.

This chapter has demonstrated that no area of school finance is unrelated to the primary goals and missions of the educational enterprise. The opportunity for significantly enhancing equality of educational opportunity and student achievement is greatly aided by the transportation and food service operations in a district. Alternatively, failure to apply appropriate care and skills to these areas is virtually certain to have negative, if not destructive, impacts on all district operations. It is thus critically

TABLE 11.2   Free and reduced meals

1991–1992 Free Meal Program Income Guidelines

Household Size	Annual Income	Monthly Income	Weekly Income
1	$ 8,606	$ 718	$ 166
2	11,544	962	222
3	14,482	1,207	279
4	17,420	1,452	335
5	20,358	1,697	392
6	23,296	1,942	448
7	26,234	2,187	505
8	29,172	2,431	561
Each additional family member, add	+$2,938	+$245	+$57

1991–1992 Reduced-Price Meal Program Income Guidelines

Household Size	Annual Income	Monthly Income	Weekly Income
1	$ 12,247	$ 1,021	$ 236
2	16,428	1,369	316
3	20,609	1,718	397
4	24,790	2,066	477
5	27,333	2,415	558
6	28,971	2,763	638
7	33,152	3,112	718
8	41,514	3,460	798
Each additional family member, add	+$4,181	+$349	+$81

important for administrators to provide sensitive attention to these arenas. This theme of equality of educational opportunity combined with wise fiscal leadership and management is carried into Chapter 12, as we examine the important topic of capital outlay and facility concerns.

Review Points

SCHOOL TRANSPORTATION

Although states have only recently become involved in many aspects of schooling, state aid to transportation dates back to the middle of the nineteenth century.

A major cause of increased state involvement has been the massive consolidation of schools.

Although consolidation has slowed, transportation assistance has increased due to inflation, desegregation, special education, and a host of other issues surrounding equal educational opportunity.

The transportation function has become highly complex, with financial, legal, and social ramifications.

Since early in this century, courts have been at least peripherally interested in pupil transportation under the child benefit theory.

Other litigation has focused on legal liability of districts in transporting students, with a very high standard of care applied to schools, given the age of children being transported.

Results of liability claims against districts have worked to make transportation an area of grave concern to administrators, wherein the greatest care in protecting children from harm must be clearly evidenced.

State aid plans for transportation services are available in nearly every state, with common denominators of expenditures per pupil, density, flat grants, or other combinations to determine actual costs.

Many other specialized factors unique to states' needs are attached to transportation aid formulas, such as hazardous walking conditions and so forth.

Transportation aid formulas almost never pay the full costs, requiring local districts to fund a portion of costs.

Aid formulas generally demand high levels of record-keeping for audit and reimbursement purposes.

Because uniform prescription is not possible due to differing needs of states and locales, cost-benefit analysis is needed to determine other issues, such as owning or contracting bus services.

Several useful technological advancements are available to aid transportation, such as route mapping and tracking maintenance schedules.

Administrators must be careful to observe all laws relating to bus purchases, including competitive bid laws.

Above all, transportation in school districts must be sufficiently insured, and conducted by competent personnel.

SCHOOL FOOD SERVICE

Like transportation, school food service is an essential element of equal opportunity due to the role of nutrition in student achievement.

The federal government has become extensively involved over many years in food service, ranging from commodity support programs to school lunch reimbursement.

Since food service is a business, care must be taken to run an efficient and cost-effective program that meets students' nutritional needs.

Efficiency and effectiveness may include decisions about in-house services, satellite services, contracted services, and so forth.

Efficient and effective food service programs range from personnel issues to complex budget requirements.

Good food service programs require administrative attention and training for food service personnel, including credentialing for the director of food services.

Since food service programs are on a cash basis, administrators may face difficult choices given increased costs of supplies and labor.

Case Study

The business manager in your school district has recently decided to undertake a complete analysis of the transportation and food service operations. Because your role as principal of the largest elementary school in town also places you in charge of a building containing a high percentage of free and reduced-price meal recipients, you were selected to assist the business manager in the analysis since you intimately work with a segment of the population vitally affected by low income conditions. In a meeting earlier today with the business manager, you were told that over the years the district had not done a good job of centralizing information. Based on that conversation, you are fairly certain that food service records are maintained in a separate computer database that is not presently linkable to the district's financial database, and you also know that the transportation department is not yet fully computer-automated and still has much of its data in paper files. In the past, these two divisions have simply submitted budget requests, which were manually fed into the district's overall financial planning process. Some of these issues were concerns mentioned by state auditors at the district's last audit cycle stemming from complaints to authorities about poor bus service and unresponsiveness to applications for free and reduced-price meals.

You have been assigned two primary tasks that must be completed within the next school year. First, you must assess what data on these functions actually exist and report on progress of accessibility and computerization. Second, you must recommend a plan for centralizing these operations that will coordinate and automate the data and daily operations of these services with the daily operation of the business office. Using the following sets of questions to help launch your class discussion, how will you accomplish your assignment?

Directed Discussion Questions

1. As you read this case study, what seem to be the major causes of concern? Why do you think the district is interested in centralizing these functions? Of what benefit and utility can such a centralized database be? What cannot be done now that could be done if these tasks were automated? Inasmuch as transportation and food service were apparently not dysfunctional as handled under the present structure, why is there a need to centralize these functions? Who will profit most by these improvements, and why?

2. Because of your location within the district, what particular contribution can you make? Of what importance is it to the tasks at hand that your school is heavily concentrated with disadvantaged children? What role will you be better able to serve than perhaps another principal in the district?

3. In the instance of your own district, what is the organizational structure of the transportation and food service operations? What types of information are presently centralized? How is information communicated? How are decisions made? What linkages have been created between the district's auxiliary services and the central administration? How are these linkages beneficial? What formal cost-benefit analyses, if any, have been performed by the district? What were the results, and what decisions were subsequently made? What changes, if any, are planned for the future?

NOTES

1. Data excerpted from various publications of the National Center for Education Statistics, and Regents Task Force, *Building Hope: Creating Tomorrow in Education,* A Report to the Governor and Citizens of the Regents Task Force on Education (Topeka, Kans.: Regents Task Force, 1992), 3.

2. Everette M. Latta, "It's Been Going for a Century," *American School Boards Journal* 57:2 (1969), 30.

3. Roe L. Johns, *State and Local Administration of School Transportation* (New York: Columbia University Teachers College, 1928), 71.

4. Ibid., as quoted in Patricia Anthony and Deborah Inman, "Public School Transportation: State Aid and Current Issues," in *Principles of School Business Management,* ed. R. Craig Wood (Reston, Va.: Association of School Business Officials, 1986), 415.

5. Brian K. Dawson, "A Model for the Distribution of Public Education Transportation Funds in Indiana" (Ph.D. diss., Purdue University, 1988), 2.

6. G. E. Davis, "Management Training, Yes! Excellence?" *School Business Affairs* 56:4 (1990), 30–31.

7. See for example the discussion in Ernest Farmer, "The Impact on Staffing on Program Efficiency," *School Business Affairs* 54:4 (1988), 31–32.

8. Dave Douglas, "Developing a Pupil Transportation Manual," *School Business Affairs* 53:4 (1987), 38–39.

9. See R. Craig Wood and Robert Ruch, "Negligence in Transporting Students," *School Business Affairs* 52:11 (1986), 48, 50–51.

10. See for example Raymond v. Paradise Unified School Dist., 31 Cal. Rptr. 847 (Cal. 1963); Nishna Valley Comm. School Dist. v. Malvern Comm. School Dist., 121 N.W.2d 646 (Iowa 1963); Brown v. Allen, 256 N.Y.S.2d 106 (N.Y.App.Div. 1965); Landerman v. Churchill Area School Dist., 200 A.2d 867 (Pa. 1967); Manjares v. Newton, 411 P.2d 901 (Cal. 1966); Board of Dir. v. Roberts, 320 A.2d 141 (Pa. 1974); Woodland Hills School Dist. v. Pennsylvania Dept. of Educ., 516 A.2d 875 (Pa. 1986.).

11. See for example Board of Educ. v. Antone, 384 P.2d 911 (Okla. 1963); Brown v. Allen, 256 N.Y.S.2d 106 (N.Y. 1964); Chaves v. School Comm., 211 A.2d 639 (R.I. 1965); Fox v. Board of Educ., 226 A.2d 471 (New Jersey 1967); Rhoades v. School Dist, 226 A.2d 53 (Pa. 1967); Spears v. Honda, 449 P.2d 130 (Haw. 1969); McCanna v. Sills, 247 A.2d 691 (N.J. 1968); Honohan v. Holt, 244 N.E.2d 537 (Ohio 1968); Alexander v. Bartlett, 165 N.W.2d 445 (Mich. 1969); Cartwright v. Sharpe, 162 N.W.2d 5 (Wis. 1968); State ex rel. Hughes v. Board of Educ., 174 S.E.2d 711 (W.V. 1970); Americans United Inc. v. Independent School Dist., 179 N.W.2d 146 (Minn. 1970) *cert. denied,* 403 U.S. 945 (1971); Wolman v. Essex, 417 F.Supp. 1113 (Ohio 1976); Janasiewicz v. Board of Educ., 299 S.E.2d 34 (W.V. 1982); Board of Educ. Hauppauge Union Free School District v. Ambach, 462 N.Y.S.2d 294 (N.Y. 1983); Members of Jamestown School Comm. v. Schmidt, 699 F.2d 1 (R.I. 1983); Reed v. Attorney General, 478 A.2d 788 (N.J. 1984); McCarthy v. Hornbeck, 590 F. Supp. 936 (Md. 1984); Pushay v. Walter, 481 N.E.2d 575 (Ohio 1985); Cumberland School Comm. v. Harnois, 499 A.2d 752 (R.I. 1985).

12. See for example Madison County Board of Educ. v. Brantham, 168 So.2d 515 (Miss. 1964); Studley v. Allen, 261 N.Y.S.2d 138 (N.Y. 1965); People v. School Dir., 208 N.E.2d 301 (Ill. 1965); People ex rel. Schuldt v. Schimanski, 266 N.E.2d 409 (Ill. 1971); Sands Point Academy v. Board of Education, 311 N.Y.S.2d 588 (N.Y. 1970).

13. See for example Shaffer v. Board of School Dir., 522 F.Supp. 1138 (Pa. 1981); Sutton v. Cadillac Area Public Schools, 323 N.W.2d 582 (Mich. 1982); Lintz v. Board of Educ., 325 N.W.2d 803 (Mich. 1982); Kansas v. Board of Educ., 647 P.2d 329 (Kan. 1982).

14. See for example United States v. Jefferson County Board of Educ., 372 F.2d 836 (Ala. and La.

1967); Franklin v. Barbour County Board of Educ., 259 F.Supp 545 (Ala. 1966); Turner v. Goolsby, 255 F.Supp. 724 (Ga. 1965), Kelly v. Altheimer School Dist., 378 F.2d 483 (Ark. 1968); Kemp v. Beasley, 389 F.2d 178 (Ark. 1967); Boomer v. Beaufort County Board of Educ., 294 F. Supp, 179 (N.C. 1968); Smuck v. Hobson, 408 F.2d 175 (D.C. 1969); United States v. School Dist., 404 F.2d 1125 (Ill. 1968); Lee v. Nyquist, 318 F.Supp. 710 (N.Y. 1970) *aff'd,* 402 U.S. 935 (1971); Swann v. Charlotte-Mecklenburg Board of Educ., 312 F.Supp. 503 (N.C. 1970) *aff'd,* 402 U.S. 43 (1971).

15. Cochran v. Louisiana State Board of Education, 281 U.S. 370, 50 S.Ct. 335 (1930).

16. The First Amendment to the U.S. Constitution reads: "Congress shall make no law respecting an establishment of religion, or prohibiting the free exercise thereof; or abridging the freedom of speech, or of the press; or the right of the people peaceably to assemble, and to petition the Government for redress." This has been interpreted to mean that "entanglement" of church and state could follow from involving public funds and private schools, and resulting in the so-called Lemon Test in Lemon v. Kurtzman (403 U.S. 602, 91 S.Ct. 2105 [1971] *rehg. denied*), a tripartite test to determine if a law (a) advances the cause of religion, (b) results in excessive entanglement, or (c) has a secular purpose. Opponents of "parochiaid" object on these grounds of the Lemon test.

17. Everson v. Board of Education, 330 U.S. 1, 67 S.Ct. 504 (1947), *rehg. denied.*

18. Kadrmas v. Dickinson Public Schools, 108 S.Ct. 2481 (1988).

19. R. Craig Wood, "Kadrmas v. Dickinson Public Schools: A Further Retreat from Equality of Educational Opportunity," *Journal of Education Finance* (Winter 1990), 429–436.

20. A fuller discussion occurred in Chapter 5 of this complex issue. For purposes of this discussion and qualified in Chapter 5, it is sufficient to state that a federal right to an education is not yet available, although scholars question the notion that the door is completely closed.

21. Arcadia Unif. School Dist. v. State Dept. of Educ., 280 Cal. Rptr. 463 (Ct. App. 1991).

22. Much of this discussion is adopted from Wood and Ruch, "Negligence in Transporting Students," 48–51; see also Chapter 10 on risk management for greater development of vehicular liability concerns.

23. Vogt v. Johnson, 153 N.W.2d 247 (Minn. 1967).

24. McNees v. Scholley, 208 N.W.2d 643 (Mich. Ct. App. 1973).

25. Cobb v. Fox, 317 N.W.2d 583 (Mich. Ct. App. 1982); see also Pratt v. Robinson, 349 N.E.2d 849 (1976) and Harrison v. Escambia County Sch. Bd., 434 So.2d 316 (Fla. 1983).

26. Sanderlin v. Central School District, 487 P.2d 1399 (Or. Ct. App. 1971).

27. Price v. York, 164 N.E.2d 671 (Ill. Ct. App. 1960).

28. Brooks v. Woods, 640 P.2d 1000 (Okla. Ct. App. 1981).

29. Ibid., at 1002.

30. Johnson v. Svoboda, 260 N.W.2d 530 (Iowa, 1977) at 534.

31. Raymond v. Paradise Unified School District, 31 Cal. Rptr. 847 (Cal. 1963).

32. School City of Gary v. Claudio, 413 N.E.2d 628 (Ind. App. Ct. 1980).

33. Mitchell v. Guilford County Bd. of Educ., 161 S.E.2d 645 (N.C. 1968).

34. See for example Crawford v. Wayne County Bd. of Educ., 164 S.E.2d 748 (N.C. 1968) and Taylor v. Cobb, 187 S.W.2d 648 (Tenn., 1945).

35. Cross v. Board of Education, 371 N.Y.S.2d 179 (N.Y. App. Div. 1975).

36. See for example Norris v. Am. Casualty Ins. Co 176 So.2d 677 (La., 1965); Powers v. Joint School Dist., 87 N.W.2d 275 (Wis. 1958); LeFleur v. State Farm Ins. 385 So.2d 564, (La. Ct. App., 1980).

37. Machenheimer v. Falkner, 255 P. 1031 (Wash. 1927).

38. Shannon v. Gaither Sch. Dist., 23 P.2d 769 (Cal. Ct. App. 1933).

39. Green v. Mitchell County Bd. of Educ., 75 S.E.2d 129 (N.C. 1953).

40. Jackson v. Hankinson, 238 A.2d 685 (N.J. 1968).

41. Blair v. Board of Educ., 448 N.Y.S.2d 566 (N.Y. App. Div., 1982).

42. Hatlee v. Owego-Appalachian School District, 420 N.Y.S.2d 448 (N.Y.App.Div. 1979).

43. Dawson, "A Model for Distribution," 3.

44. R. Craig Wood, David S. Honeyman, and Brian K. Dawson, "The Distribution of Educational Transportation Funds in Indiana: An Examination and Equity Analysis," *Planning and Changing* 21:1 (1990), 53-62.

45. Mathematically this is easy to illustrate. Note that Lines 1-13 of the general state aid calculation is the method for actually determining total general fund state aid. Line 7 weights enrollment by density. If we were to simply run the 581 head count actually transported through the formula, omitting the density weighting in Line 7, we would have a flat grant per pupil system. Mechanically, the product would be the sum of Lines 1-7 entered into Line 9, with the product subtracted to find the difference in permissible state aid. Mathematically: (1280.5 FTE × $3,600) = $4,609,800. When this value is subtracted from the $4,876,560 shown in Figure 11.1, it produces the difference of $266,760 aid received through weighting that is not available under a flat grant approach.

46. Howard A. Dawson, "Transportation of Students," in *Encyclopedia of Educational Research,* ed. Chester W. Harris (New York: Macmillan, 1960), 1545.

47. Dennis Garden and Jack Liebermann, "State of the Art in Routing and Scheduling," *School Business Affairs* 55:4 (1989), 47-50.

48. Ibid., 47-50.

49. Frederick L. Dembowski, "Transportation Routing and Scheduling: Alternatives and Innovations," *School Business Affairs* 54:4 (1988), 18-22.

50. Stephen H. Salmon, "The Potential of Computerized Pupil Transportation," *School Business Affairs* 57:4 (1991), 20-24.

51. Computerized plans require a commitment for successful use. Information must be entered concerning the location of schools, stops, interstop distances, travel times, street addresses, and street directories for the assignment of students to stops. Algorithms have been developed to minimize bus purchases and reduce the mileage of each fleet. Generally, the algorithm begins with the calculation of the polar coordinates of each pickup point relative to the school. The stops are ordered by angle and a radial arm sweep is made until the route is in excess of a ride time constraint. The other algorithm model begins with each pickup point conceptually serviced by a different vehicle originating at the school. Stops from various routes are combined to produce savings. The process is continued until the maximum savings are generated and the routes combined.

52. John J. Cataldo, "Computerized Fleet Maintenance," *School Business Affairs* 51:4 (1985), 48-49.

53. "Bus Repair Costs Soar as Mileage Increases," *School Business Affairs* 46:7 (1980), 12-13.

54. Dan Levin, "This Ingenious Computer Program Makes School Bus Maintenance Reliable and Cost-Effective," *The American School Board Journal* (October 1984), 36-37.

55. The issue of alternative fuels for school buses has been examined by local and state officials for many years. Alternative fuels must be examined in conjunction with the standards existing in the Clean Air Act of 1970 and the Clean Air Act Amendments of 1990. Fuels for school buses include diesel, gasoline, methanol, ethanol, propane, and natural gas, with the overwhelming majority of fuel usage being either diesel or gasoline. Evaluations should be made in terms of availability, price, safety, range, startability, costs of support services, and long-term effects and should take into account such variables as vehicle performance, staffing needs, infrastructure, operations, and the total costs. While diesel buses have proven highly cost effective as compared to gasoline buses, a number of school districts have experience with alternative fueled fleets and several with all natural gas fleets have experienced overall success. In the future, transportation directors will be examining such alternatives more frequently as alternative technologies prove to be more reliable and as traditional fuels may become less available.

56. Thomas J. Casey, "Special Education Transportation Update and Forecast," *School Business Affairs* 57:4 (1991), 8–11.

57. See for example Dorothy Van Egmond-Pannell, "Foodservices at School," in *Principles of School Business Management,* R. Craig Wood, ed. (Reston: Va.: Association of School Business Officials, 1986), 381–407.

58. *World Almanac and Book of Facts* (New York: Pharos Books, 1992), 138.

59. See for example Ronald Stainbrook, "Contract vs. District-Operated School Food Services: The Perspectives of Three Superintendents," *School Business Affairs* 56:6 (1990), 10–13.

60. Robert E. Sanders and Richard Howard, "For These Schools, Contract Food Service Hikes Quality, Cuts Costs, and Turns a Profit," *The Executive Educator* (May 1986), 14.

61. Mary B. Crimmins, "Food Service Management: Selecting the Right Company, *School Business Affairs* 46:11 (1980), 22–23.

62. Van Egmond-Pannell, "Foodservices at School," 383–384.

63. E. Lewis Bryan and G. Thomas Friedlob, "Management Accounting in School Food Service," *School Business Affairs* (Nov. 1982), 50.

64. See Dorothy Van Egmond-Pannell, "Coping With Turnovers in School Food Service," *School Business Affairs* 54:11 (1988), 35–38.

65. John P. Hess and Dorothy Van Egmond-Pannell, "Budgeting for Food Service Operations," *School Business Affairs* 53:11 (1987), 36.

66. Ibid.

67. Ibid., 37.

68. William D. Dodge, "How Nine Schools Combined Their Purchasing Power to Lower Food Bills," *The American School Boards Journal* (Aug. 1983), 27. Research suggests that the typical cooperative arrangements can save as much as 8%–10% of operating costs. In a few cases, school districts have reported savings as high as 40%.

ADDITIONAL READINGS

Association of School Business Officials, International. *School Business Affairs.* Annual Transportation Issue. Reston, Va.: Association of School Business Officials, April.

———. *School Business Affairs.* Annual Food Service Issue. Reston, Va.: Association of School Business Officials, November.

———. *Principles of School Business Management.* R. Craig Wood, ed. Reston, Va.: Association of School Business Officials, (1986).

Educational Facilities Laboratories. *Twenty Million for Lunch.* New York: EFL, 1968.

Farmer, Ernest. *Pupil Transportation: Essentials of Program Service.* Danville, Ill.: Interstate Publishers, 1975.

Featherston, Glenn, and D.P. Culp. *Pupil Transportation: State and Local Programs.* New York: Harper & Row, 1965.

Gold, Steven. *School Finance in the Fifty States.* American Education Finance Association and the National Center for Education Statistics, 1992.

National Conference of State Legislatures. *School Finance at a Glance.* Deborah Verstegen, ed. Denver: National Conference of State Legislatures, 1988.

Van Egmond-Pannell, Dorothy. *The Food Service Handbook: A Guide for School Administrators.* Reston, Va.: Association of School Business Officials, 1987.

———. *School Food Services.* 3d ed. Westport, Conn.: AVI Publishing Co., 1985.

CHAPTER 12

Planning for Capital Outlay, Maintenance, and Operations

CHAPTER THEME

- Although much financial and technical improvement in schools has occurred since the inception of modern education in the United States, resources have never been sufficient to meet every need to the fullest possible extent. As a consequence, trade-offs have had to be made, and school physical facilities have incurred considerable neglect as scarce dollars have often been put first to direct instructional costs. While such decisions are clearly defensible, the result has been slow decay of education's physical infrastructure, yielding a crisis of unmet needs at the close of the twentieth century. Because needs are great while resources are sparse, it is critical that administrators understand the capital facility problems of schools.

CHAPTER OUTLINE

- The nature and extent of school facility problems
- The historical and current methods of financing schools' capital expenditures in the 50 states
- The facility planning role and function in school districts, including facility planning, demographic and capital program planning, and other features related to building or altering school facilities
- Aspects of daily facility operations

CHAPTER OBJECTIVE

- A greater appreciation for the facility issues facing public schools and a better understanding of how school facilities are financed and maintained

The most exciting curriculum innovations in the world have great trouble succeeding in cold, dank, deteriorating classrooms. If the work environment is unattractive, uncomfortable or unsafe, school districts have difficulty competing with other sectors of the economy to woo talented teachers. . . . Students know the difference, too! When USA Today polled 72,000 students as to what they would do with more school funds, their "No. 1" priority was school building maintenance and construction. Teens responding to the survey called their buildings "filthy" and a "disgrace."

American Association of School Administrators, Schoolhouse in the Red:
A National Study of School Facilities and Energy Use

The opening quotation[1] for this chapter on capital outlay, maintenance, and operations heralds a formidable problem facing American schools at the end of the twentieth century. While much concerted attention has been devoted in recent years to reforming education, little concomitant financial support has been given to the need for effective physical environments to house the educational process. As the American Association of School Administrators (AASA) noted: "From every corner have come reports, articles, speeches and goal statements about student achievement, unmet needs and education reform . . . but all these pronouncements have been strangely silent about one essential ingredient . . . that affects every child's health, safety and ability to learn: *the classroom.*"

Although the popular press has centered on school failure in the context of curriculum reform, there is evidence indicating that education's physical infrastructure is also rapidly failing in ways that can impede the progress of such reform. Numerous reports have begun to chronicle the condition of educational facilities, and school leaders and policymakers have been warned about the need for new capital investment in education. Estimates run into the billions of dollars to repair and replace sagging school facilities, primarily because districts have responded to other budget pressures by delaying basic facility maintenance and deferring repairs. As noted in one state's legislative review of capital needs in schools: "Our schools are old and worn out, and it must be stated in the most serious terms that we are facing a very serious crisis. . . . We can no longer guarantee parents their children are safe when they are sent off to school."[2] Although nearly every preceding chapter has been overshadowed by the economic principle of unlimited needs and finite resources, the reality of forced choice is most evident in capital improvements and maintenance, as districts have had to choose between spending for programs and spending for facilities in which to house those programs.

The looming crisis in facilities underscores the importance of fiscal planning, particularly since school buildings represent the single largest investment in a school district. Under such conditions, it is critically important for administrators to have a good understanding of the issues and operation of educational facilities. Accordingly, this chapter is designed to assist administrators in understanding school facility concerns on two fundamental levels. The first level provides an overview of facility needs that apply generally to school districts throughout the United States, exploring the condition of school facilities in the nation, briefly illustrating the nature of this crisis, examining how schools' facility needs have historically been financed, and concluding with a brief examination of current methods of capital finance in the 50 states. The second level provides a general overview of facility planning and maintenance operations in modern school districts, examining the role of facility planning—including demographic, capital program, site, architectural, and construction planning—and describing the role of maintenance and operations in a modern school district. On completion of this chapter, the administrator should have a greater appreciation for the facility issues facing public schools and a better understanding of how school facilities are financed and maintained.

THE STRUCTURE OF SCHOOL FACILITY AND CAPITAL NEEDS

The nationwide crisis in school facility needs has been a long-standing problem and is increasing dramatically as intergovernmental competition for scarce tax resources continues to escalate and as pressure has been placed on school facilities through the continually expanding role and scope of modern education. Because the crisis has resulted largely from neglect, it must be recognized that how school facilities are constructed and maintained is a direct function of the larger policymaking environment that dictates how schools are financed generally. As a result, it is important first to examine the condition of school facilities and to relate the present crisis to both historic and current methods for financing school districts' capital expenditures.

The Condition of School Facilities

The problems of educational facilities and capital needs in American schools are not new and have long been lamented by education's critics. William A. Alcott, writing in 1831, made graphic the problems of school facilities when he stated:

> Few, indeed, of the numerous schoolhouses in this country are well-lighted. Fewer still are painted, even on the outside. Play-grounds for the common schools are scarcely known. There is much suffering from the alternation of heat and cold and from smoke. The feet of children have even sometimes been frozen. Too many pupils are confined to a single desk or bench where they are constantly jostling or otherwise disturbing each other. The construction of desks and benches is often bad. Little or no provision is made for free ventilation. Hundreds of rooms are so small that the pupils have not, upon the average, more than five or six square feet of surface each; and here they are obliged to sit, breathing impure air, on benches often not more than six or eight inches wide, and without backs.[3]

Fortunately, there have been enormous improvements in educational facilities since the primitive conditions endured by the early settlers in America. Students no longer sit on long narrow benches, various health regulations provide at least minimum standards for ventilation, and most schoolhouses today strive to provide tolerable light and thermal environments. In addition, numerous other standards for safe physical environments have been promulgated by various construction industry organizations to which virtually all new schools adhere and to which many existing school structures have likewise attempted to conform.[4] At the very least, virtually no public schools still in operation have escaped some regulatory scrutiny because school facilities must comply with fire protection, boiler inspection, and other governmental requirements, including those imposed by the Environmental Protection Agency (EPA) for hazards such as asbestos, radon, and lead in drinking water, those required by the Occupational Safety and Health Administration (OSHA), and those required by the Americans with Disabilities Act (ADA) for handicap accessibility. As a result of numerous efforts to provide a better learning environment for schoolchildren, the modern schoolhouse is in many ways far removed from the depressing conditions of earlier times.

Simply improving conditions and legislating standards, however, have not resulted in assurances of uniformity or high quality in educational facilities for children. As can be easily surmised, the interests of such rules and regulations have often narrowly focused on specific contemporary crises, such as asbestos or other gross physical dangers. Although physical environments in new schools are rather rigidly controlled in terms of both health and safety, in the larger and more enduring context school facilities have not been subjected to the same standardization. Consequently, existing school facilities remain the object of much concern because numerous national reports have concluded that education's physical infrastructure is in a state of emergency. Although numerous fine schools exist throughout the United States, these reports have argued that the majority are in a badly deteriorated physical condition, with many schools too old to safely function or too outdated to meet the demands of modern equal educational opportunity.

The condition of public school physical infrastructures is shown in part by the striking data seen in Table 12.1 (pp. 554–555), illustrating that of the 88,021 buildings existing in 1986–1987 in the 50 states, 14,259 (25%) were judged to be seriously inadequate on some basis. The breakdown of these data indicates that despite the vast improvements over earlier times and new environmental and safety laws, major problems still exist in many public schools. Overwhelmingly, these problems relate to overcrowding, unattended major repairs, functional obsolescence, physical unsoundness, and uncorrected environmental hazards. While these problems are serious and sometimes in violation of the law, they are equally difficult to resolve because of very high costs. For example, population growth in the latter half of the twentieth century has led to rapidly increasing school enrollments in some parts of the country, with insufficient classroom space reported as a major problem in 3,630 (25%) schools—a problem requiring much time and money. Similarly, the pressure of limited resources has caused neglect of school facilities, as the number of schools needing major repairs reached 8,671 (61%) and with structurally unsound schools totaling 1,913 (13%). Likewise, serious legal violations were found in 6,000 (42%) schools that reported uncorrected environmental hazards. Finally, 6,165 (43%) obsolete structures were reported. These data clearly suggest a backlog of deteriorated physical plant conditions that affect both safety and educational suitability.

The data in Table 12.1 are also consonant with other national reports indicating trouble in school physical infrastructures. As might be expected, the problems of population, economic vitality, and adequacy of school facilities are often tightly interwoven. While population in some parts of the nation has steadily grown despite an unhealthy economy, schools have continued to age without the funds for commensurate construction and renovation. The result has been increased demands for space that have not been met by new construction. In fact, fully 49% of all schools in the nation were built approximately 30 to 40 years ago, and it is thus not surprising that so many buildings are reported in poor condition because the typical public school building was constructed with a life expectancy of about 50 years. While many persons might object to such a short life span, experts hold that maintenance costs increase rapidly when a building reaches 30 to 40 years of age, with accelerated deterioration evident between 40 and 50 years of age, and that schools over 50 years old should be completely reconstructed or abandoned, due to their high maintenance costs and technological inadequacy for modern curricula. Additionally, 21% of the public schools now being utilized were built between 1900 and 1950.[5] Under these conditions, it is truly startling to recognize that almost half of all school buildings in the nation have only marginal future utility, and another 20%–30% are candidates for reconstruction or abandonment because they are more than 50 years old.[6]

When a rapidly aging cohort of buildings is viewed in an economic and population context, reasons for the current crisis are evident. But equally evident is the high cost of resolving such problems. Although facility neglect is the cumulative product of many years of inadequate funds, the costs seem to escalate disproportionately. The AASA estimated that the cost of deferring maintenance on school buildings is enormous, spiraling from only $30 million in 1983 to over $100 million in 1991, due primarily to inflation and accelerated deterioration within cohort groups.[7] Additionally, these costs are not the full extent of physical capital needs, as new construction and other expenditures normally made from capital budgets, such as equipment purchases, have suffered in recent economic times. For example, one national study reported that 28% of classroom teachers were without access to photocopiers for duplicating student learning aids. This same study asked teachers' views regarding the physical plant, with respondents telling of the need for more classrooms (20%), more storage space (18%), larger classrooms (16%), and need for teacher work space.[8] These data clearly indicate that enrollments grow, curricula become more complex, equipment fails, and buildings fall into accelerated degrees of disrepair and technological obsolescence. The ultimate impact, of course, is deterioration of the learning environment.

When deferred maintenance and new construction needs are joined, the total amount of money is truly staggering. According to the Education Writers Association, national totals for needed construction reached $84.65 billion in 1988, and deferred maintenance totaled another $41.34 billion. The combined total of $126 billion represented nearly 30% of an estimated $422 billion required to replace all public school facilities in the nation. While full-scale replacement is unnecessary, the need to repair or replace 30% of all school facilities in the nation is a very heavy burden to the taxpaying public. Even more importantly, these totals are the sum of widely varying needs among the individual states. For example, the Oklahoma State Department of Education estimated that more than $622 million in needs had gone unaddressed in the state and that, if all districts extended themselves to the legal debt limit, unmet needs would still exceed $125 million.[9] Similarly, North Carolina recently reported $3.2 billion in unmet needs, enacting legislation authorizing more than $793 million in new state monies.[10] Likewise, Texas has estimated more than $5.4 billion in facility needs.[11] The problem is not limited only to more populous states, as rural states have also estimated hundreds of millions in unmet facility needs. For example, the state of Wisconsin noted in 1989 that 25% of all schools constructed before 1930 had serious safety deficiencies; that 80% of all schools had one or more serious deficiencies including open stairwells, unsafe wiring, lack of smoke detectors, and extremely shabby maintenance; that many pre-1930 schools were in worse condition than Our Lady of the Angels school in Chicago, which burned in 1948 killing 90 persons; and that serious structural deficiencies were found in numerous buildings, with 59 schools having inadequate or nonexistent fire escapes.[12]

TABLE 12.1 State analysis of building needs

State	Total Number of Buildings, 1986–1987	Percentage in Inadequate Condition	Total Number in Inadequate Condition	Overcrowded Buildings Percentage	Overcrowded Buildings Number	Need Major Repair Maintenance Percentage	Need Major Repair Maintenance Number	Obsolete Percentage	Obsolete Number	Unsound Structures Percentage	Unsound Structures Number	Environmental Hazards Percentage	Environmental Hazards Number
Alabama	1,300												
Alaska	448												
Arizona	1,026												
Arkansas	1,117	5%	56	2%	1.1	1%	5.6	1%	5.6	1%	5.6		
California	7,125	55%	3919	60	2351	100	3919	90	3527	10	353	80%	3135
Colorado	1,324	10%	132	20	26	20	26	20	26	20	26	20	26
Connecticut	937	60%	562	75	422	90	506	40	225	10	56	60	337
Delaware	185	4%	7										
District of Columbia	182	50%	91										
Florida	2,791	20%	558			48	268	2	11			50	279
Georgia	1,750	20%	350	20	70	20	70	40	140	10	35	80	280
Hawaii	2,914												
Idaho	573												
Illinois	4,220	50%	2110	5	106	45	950	10	212	10	212	50	1055
Indiana	1,916												
Iowa	1,651												
Kansas	1,464	25%	366	20	73	15	55	15	55			50	183
Kentucky	1,380	30%	414	20	83	60	248	18	75			2	8
Louisiana	1,615	10%	162	10	16	10	16	10	16	10	16		
Maine	900	20%	180	10	18	5	9	5	9				
Maryland	1,190	3%	36			100	36						
Massachusetts	1,785	30%	534	20	107	50	267	10	53	1	5	55	294
Michigan	3,630												
Minnesota	1,500	25%	375	10	38	25	94	20	75	20	75	25	94
Mississippi	976	30%	293	60	176	100	293	30	88	5	15	50	147
Missouri	3,000	30%	641			10	64	20	128				
Montana	548												
Nebraska	1,397	30%	419	1	.3	40	168	10	42	2	8		
Nevada	304												
New Hampshire	438												

State													
New Jersey	2,251												
New Mexico	642												
New York	3,753												
North Carolina	5,594	24%	1343		1343	80	1074	100	1343	80	1074	99.5	
North Dakota	613												
Ohio	3,977	10%	398										
Oklahoma	1,911	12%	229	20	80	20	80	30	119	5	20	25	12
Oregon	1,222												
Pennsylvania	3,313	.5%	17										
Rhode Island	220	40%	88	40	47	40	47	5	6	5	6	10	
South Carolina	1,106												
South Dakota	788												
Tennessee	1,600	10%	160	10	16	10	16	2	3	2	3	30	
Texas	3,493	13%	389										48
Utah	729	5%	36					10	4				
Vermont	329					90	32						
Virginia	1,693												
Washington	1,700	25%	425			100	425						
West Virginia	1,101												
Wisconsin	2,000												
Wyoming	400	15%	60			5	3	5	3	5	3	5	3
Total	88,021	25% of reporting states	14259	25%	3630	61%	8671	43%	6165	13%	1913	42%	6000

SOURCE: Education Writers Association, *Wolves at the Schoolhouse Door* (Washington, D.C.: Education Writers Association, 1989), 50.

Poor facility conditions are thus a very real problem throughout the nation and represent an obvious burden to states, school districts, and children. Although the special mandates under EPA, OSHA, and ADA and construction industry standards have greatly improved conditions in many schools, such improvements have required great sums of money. Even though school districts have had to prepare compliance plans and have otherwise struggled to repair and replace deteriorating facilities, the slow process of enforcement and general budget crisis have mostly resulted in emergency plans that have not been sufficient to either fully redress inadequate conditions or to provide uniformly adequate facilities for all children in all circumstances. As a result, great inequality in school facilities has been the rule, forcing many districts to divert instructional funds to facility repairs or to allow deferred needs to steadily grow. For many districts, the only other solution has been to seek refuge in the courts through litigation designed to force states to accept responsibility for capital needs.[13] As a consequence of inadequate funding and lack of legislation standardizing school environments, the struggle to repair and replace school facilities has steadily moved toward the judicial arena.

Capital Needs Litigation

As seen in Chapter 5, fiscal equity has been litigated for many years, with numerous state supreme courts also taking an interest in how facilities are financed. As early as 1973, the court noted in *Shofstall v. Hollins*[14] that funds for capital improvements in Arizona were more closely tied to district wealth than funds for operating expenses and that the capacity of a school district to raise revenue by bond issue was a function of assessed valuation. In considerably harsher language, the New Jersey court noted only a few months earlier in *Robinson v. Cahill*[15] that the state's obligation to children also included capital expenditures without which required equal educational opportunity could not be provided. Provisions were also made in *Serrano II*[16] for deferred maintenance funds, with the court adopting language indicating its presumption that facilities were naturally integral to educational opportunity. In similarly harsh language, the court noted in *Board of Education of the City of Cincinnati v. Walter*[17] that a thorough and efficient system of schools would not exist if any schools were starved for funds, teachers, buildings, or equipment. The court also showed concern for facilities in *Diaz et al. v. Colorado State Board of Education*[18] when it stated that some districts were better able to provide facilities due to their greater wealth. Likewise, in *Lujan v. Colorado State Board of Education*[19] the court concluded that fiscal capacity of school districts to raise revenue for bond redemption and capital reserve was a function of property wealth. Although these early cases had only limited success in redressing facility inequity, they were highly instrumental in shaping the court's growing awareness of the need for a fuller definition of equal educational opportunity.

These early cases were followed by other lawsuits that have helped to expand the judicial definition of equality. For example, facilities were an important issue in *Helena Elementary School District No. 1 v. State of Montana,*[20] in which the Montana Supreme Court observed that the ability of districts to raise funds for capital outlay was dependent on local tax levies, noting that the absence of state aid to facilities created an unacceptable wealth dependency in Montana's school finance system. Similarly, in *Edgewood Independent School District v. Kirby,*[21] the Texas court ordered wide-ranging remedies to various school finance woes, including funds to redress school facility needs. The saga of school finance reform in New Jersey first brought in *Robinson* has continued to probe that state's funding system, with the court in *Abbott v. Burke*[22] noting at various times appalling educational needs in poor school districts, including vast facility disparities. Similarly, *Jenkins v. State of Missouri*[23] resulted in a court order to issue $150 million in capital improvement bonds to correct facility conditions described by the court as "literally rotted." Deplorable facility conditions were also at issue in *Tennessee Small Counties System v. McWherter.*[24] Similarly, the Kentucky Supreme Court in *Rose v. Council for Better Education*[25] noted that facility construction and maintenance were not to be excluded from the definition of equal educational opportunity. Likewise, a challenge to force the state to aid facilities in the name of equal opportunity was successful in several consolidated actions in Kansas.[26]

The West Virginia case of *Pauley v. Bailey,*[27] however, offers the best and most extensive analysis of the potential redefinition of judicial concern for financing school buildings. Originally filed as *Pauley v. Kelly,*[28] stating broad concerns for inaccessibility to a quality education, the focus in *Pauley* became for the first time in history a direct concern for equal opportunity as defined by adequate school facilities. Originally dismissed, the lower court's ruling was reversed by the West Virginia Supreme Court based on findings that education was a constitutional right, that such a right required high quality across the state, and that lack of quality must not be due to actions or inactions by the state. The high court saw a primary flaw in the state's finance scheme because the state permitted the local property tax to control the quality of education provided in each local school district. On remand for evidentiary development, the trial court extensively defined equal educational opportunity in operational terms, including a heavy focus on the role of quality school facilities as the right of every child.

The *Pauley* decision was especially significant on two historic levels. First, no court in any state had ever gone so far in stating its interest in capital funding mechanisms. As a result, the noticeably broadened judicial interpretation of equal educational opportunity broached in other states was deliberately propelled to the forefront by this court, which intentionally related educational facilities to equal educational opportunity. Second, the court made a historic move far beyond traditional judicial deference to legislative prerogative by ordering the state to create a master plan for school improvement that included broad facility mandates and specified in detail that each school would provide quality facilities for each area of the curriculum. The court noted that specific standards should be developed and strictly followed. For example, each elementary school should have an art room for each 350–500 pupils with at least 50 square feet per child; similarly, every secondary school of 500 students would need at least one art room with a minimum of 65 square feet per pupil. Even storage areas were detailed, and similar minute specifications were given for each academic and activity function at the elementary, middle, and high school levels.

Although no court since has gone as far as *Pauley* in defining equal opportunity, litigants have continued to press for reform as several other lawsuits presently before the courts are seeking to achieve a greater degree of equalization in facilities. For example, courts in Alabama, Arizona, Indiana, Louisiana, Montana, North Carolina, Oklahoma, South Dakota, West Virginia, and several others will soon decide whether current methods of financing capital needs are sufficient under the law.[29] Although the history of litigation surrounding capital needs has always been secondary to larger equity issues, and although the outcome has been only cautiously favorable to plaintiffs, lawsuits are increasingly arguing that facilities are an equitable concern, and it is evident that the condition of facilities is of growing interest to many courts. The logic employed by a Kansas court in favoring plaintiffs may well become a common response to such pleas, as a district court stated in reply to whether the state must participate in capital costs. "How can a school be 'established' unless some edifice to house the school be built, bought, rented, or otherwise acquired? . . . If the 'state' were not responsible for building schools—who or what would be?"[30]

While the present crisis in school facilities is overwhelming, it is in fact a function of extended neglect and fiscal inadequacy at the local level. Most disturbing is the inequality among children that flows from vast differences in local wealth—an inequality that is not permitted in virtually any other aspect of the modern educational enterprise, but which is most strikingly apparent in the ability of school districts to provide equal educational facilities. Thus, the solution to the present crisis can only come as the states themselves assume a central role in assuring equal opportunity through educational facilities.

Methods of Funding Capital Needs

The poor condition of school facilities and the ensuing interest of many courts have their roots in historic methods of financing school facilities, both of which can be seen to be a direct result of the striking difference between funding general education expenditures and school facilities and capital needs. In sharp contrast to the sophisticated formulas that have been developed for state aid to general fund budgets, special education budgets, transportation budgets, and other school services, facilities have been the object of fiscal neglect at both state and local governmental levels due to at least three major causes.

One major cause has been widespread reluctance to depart from firmly entrenched tradition. School facilities have long been a local affair, dating from an era when a smaller percentage of children attended school and building costs and programs were simpler. In addition, school buildings stood as symbols of local cooperation, often raised by hand with volunteer labor and donated materials and land. Obsolescence of facilities was nearly nonexistent, and in a largely rural nation the demands on local tax bases for other government services were minimal. Under these conditions, local communities became protective of "their schools" and generally rejected outside interference. The dawn of the twentieth century, however, marked the end of local tax base sufficiency, as movement of the nation from an agricultural to an industrial base found rapidly expanding cities and school populations. Yet despite growing needs of school districts for larger revenues and expanded tax bases, many states continued to follow a tradition of total local responsibility for funding facilities. While other state aids came into existence, capital needs remained largely dependent on local property wealth and subject to low statutory debt limitations, mill rate caps, and other generally outdated restrictions.

These new pressures on local tax bases gave rise to a related problem that formed the second major cause for facility neglect. As education expanded and took on new importance in the American life-style, students stayed in school longer and were joined by growing populations who required instruction, materials, and the other elements of a compulsory education. In the early part of the twentieth century, educational growth was accompanied by economic prosperity, but the stock market crash in 1929 halted education revenue growth and consequently much of the growth in education. School construction was almost nonexistent for nearly a decade. Following World War II, the backlog of needs was recognized, but was "resolved" by rapid construction of relatively cheap facilities that were never intended to be enduring. The result was a backlog of unmet facility needs followed by hasty construction and emerging educational technology that quickly made existing facilities obsolete. Thus, the second reason for fiscal neglect of facilities was growth in budget pressures that resulted in fierce competition between facilities and other needs that related closely to a history of cheap solutions to population and economic woes.

Still a third cause was that these problems were worsened by slowness on the part of states to become involved in financing capital needs. Although increased educational costs and demands for new programs severely taxed local revenue capacity, states were nonetheless reluctant to become involved in fiscally aiding facility needs, often claiming local control as justification. As needs grew, however, a few states began to provide aid, but frequently such aid was offered as an inducement to other behaviors. For example, in 1901 Alabama began providing assistance to local districts for capital outlay; the purpose, however, was to assist only rural schools and was not offered generally in recognition of any state responsibility for education. Other states followed similar concepts, with each state's plan varying greatly in reasons, amounts, and procedures. For example, in 1903 Delaware and South Carolina began offering capital assistance to schools for black children. Similarly, Rhode Island (1898), Minnesota (1911), Oklahoma (1911), Missouri (1913), Wisconsin (1913), Delaware, Pennsylvania and Tennessee (1919), Maine (1921), New York (1925), and Arkansas (1927) all began offering facility aid as an inducement to consolidate tiny school districts.[31] The result of such selective aid was that as late as World War II, only 12 states made *general* financial allocations for capital outlay and debt service to local school districts. Although many states claimed to offer aid, for the most part these were "crude and inequitable distribution systems in which the principles of equalization were neither recognized or applied."[32]

The various pressures from economic conditions, fierce competition for resources, politics of intergovernmental sovereignty, and parochialism have thus been causes of poor facility conditions. Despite recognition of needs, however, states have not moved quickly or uniformly to assist local districts in meeting the high cost of maintaining and improving educational facilities. Yet it must be recognized that states have become more aware of facility needs, particularly since courts have begun to draw analogies between capital needs and other areas of school finance. Although far from sufficient or uniform in their funding methods, a slight majority of states now provides some form of aid to facilities. Some states assume a majority of costs, while others provide only salutary acknowledgment of the high cost of school facilities. As a general rule, those states genuinely attempting to aid facilities do so using *full state funding* or *equalization grants,* while those states providing deferential acknowledgment do so using *percentage-matching grants, flat grants, state loans,* or *state* or *local authorities,* or by merely authorizing local districts to incur *bonded indebtedness.* Although operation of each plan is dependent on the unique strength of commitment by each state's legislature, such plans are usually based on the general fund state aid schemes from which they derive their names.[33] A summary of current state aid plans is seen in Table 12.2.

Full State Funding.   As the name implies, in full state funding the state assumes full responsibility for the costs of the local building program. As with general fund financing under the same concept, the critical feature is that the state recognizes its ultimate responsibility for the education of all children within the state. Under these

TABLE 12.2 Funding of construction in the 50 states

State	Funding Share (%)				Type of Funding	Funding Growth (in millions) — State			Funding Growth (in millions) — Local			How Else Are Districts Meeting School Needs?
	Local	State	Federal	Other		1985	1988	Percentage per Year	1985	1988	Percentage per Year	
Alabama	67	30	3		Equal/flat							Re-open closed schools
Alaska	50	49	1		Percent match							
Arizona	94	3	3		Equalized/grant							
Arkansas	100				Equalized/grant							
California	15	80	3	2	Full state assistance	$ 377	$ 800	37%	$95	$ 200	37%	Additions, portables
Colorado	100				None							
Connecticut		40/80			Equalized/grant	29.3	55	30				Portables
Delaware		60			Percent match	4.4	8.2	28	2.3	3.4	16	Additions, renovations
District of Columbia												Relocatables
Florida	66	28	1	5	Equalized/grant							Leasing
Georgia		74	1		% Match/flat/state authority	94	156	22	16	26	21	Renovation, portables
Hawaii		100			Full state support							
Idaho	100				None	0						Additions, renovation
Illinois	30/80	20/70			Equal/flat/local authority		200					Operating with what have
Indiana	100				Local authority							
Iowa	100				None							
Kansas	90			10	None				106	98	–4	Portables
Kentucky	36	64			Local authority							Renovation, portables
Louisiana	100				None	54	88	21				Additions, renovations, portables
Maine	32	68			Equalized/state authority							
Maryland	50/25	50/75			Equalized/state authority	34.6	60.3	25				Portables
Massachusetts	5	50/75			Equalized/local authority	5	16	73				Portables
Michigan	100				None							Portables
Minnesota	45	3	2	50	Loans				50	235	123	Interiors, co-op

State				Type of aid							Temporary measures
Mississippi	50	50		Flat	4			25	50	33	Renovations, additions
Missouri	100			None		10	50				Trailers, portables
Montana	95	5		None							
Nebraska	100			None							Abandon buildings
Nevada	100			None							
New Hampshire	40/70	30/55		Bond bank							
New Jersey	68	32		Equal/flat							
New Mexico			20	Equal							
New York	40	40		Equal/localized authority	255			152	350	43	Renting & leasing
North Carolina	100			Equalized/loans							Trailer & portable
North Dakota	80	20		Bond bank							Bond issue
Ohio	90	10		None	20	4	-27				
Oklahoma	95		5	None				185			Portables or barracks
Oregon	100			None							Double shifting, renting
Pennsylvania	60/80	20/40		Equalized/local/state authority	142	134	-2	81	291	86	Portables
Rhode Island	70	30		Equal	4	3	-1	14	11	-7	Modular building
South Carolina	78	21	1	Equalized/flat							
South Dakota	100			None							
Tennessee	100		1	Flat	11.9	11.9	0	74	120.5	21	Renovation
Texas	99		1	None							Portables
Utah	87	12	1	Equalized/grant	9.6	6.4	-11	153	70	-18	Year-round, portables
Vermont	70	30		Bond bank							
Virginia	100		10	Loans/state authority							Co-op program, lease
Washington	20/90	20/90		Equal							
West Virginia	50	28		Bond bank							
Wisconsin			12	Equalized/loans							Portables
Wyoming	90	10		Equalized/loans							Portables

SOURCE: Education Writers Association, *Wolves at the Schoolhouse Door* (Washington, D.C.: Education Writers Association, 1989) 27.

conditions, the state accepts the costs of school facility construction and maintenance, and in return generally expects to make many of the decisions that were previously made at the local level. For example, the process of acquiring new facilities generally involves various levels of bureaucracy wherein state resources are allocated first to those districts in greatest need.[34] Although such innovative thinking is consonant with principles of equity, full state funding of facilities is rare, as most states have not yet been able to abandon the parochial school facility funding practices that have historically characterized education. Even in those states where full state funding is conceptually adopted, actual practice usually more closely resembles a modified full state funding approach that still utilizes a local property tax levy rather than a single statewide tax for facilities.

Full state funding has several advantages that also apply to school facilities. As in general fund financing, full state support conceptually represents the fairest funding system, providing facilities based on the wealth of the entire state. Obviously, this provides the broadest tax base possible because the sum of all resources within a state are applied to school facility needs without regard to the wealth of each school district. As such, full state funding adheres to the fundamental principles of wealth neutrality that presently govern other areas of modern school finance. As with general fund financing, however, there are disadvantages in full state assumption of facility costs. The difficulty of identifying the full extent of needs almost always results in higher than anticipated costs to the state. Similarly, concerns about loss of local control that arise whenever centralized authority is imposed must be overcome in the various school districts. Further, there is a legitimate basis for concern about extravagance when local districts no longer need to be frugal in assessing facility needs. Conversely, there is also basis for fears about declining local tax initiative when schools are not seen as locally owned. Although several states have experimented with forms of full state support for facilities, presently only Hawaii and California provide sufficient revenue to facilities to be accurately described under this aid plan.

Equalization Grants.   As might be expected, equalization plans for funding school facilities closely resemble the equalization formulas found in general fund financing. As the name implies, equalization aid to facilities usually involves grants to local districts established on some method by which facility aid increases as ability to pay declines. As with general fund financing, numerous variations on equalizing grants have been devised in a number of states. For example, if power equalization principles are observed, the unique feature may be that a district can choose to increase the local contribution and thereby qualify for increased state aid. Inversely, equalization grants may assist districts up to a specified maximum amount based on district wealth and limited by state definition of an ''appropriate'' school facility. Unlimited variations of the basic theme are possible as states construct aid criteria within the constraints of legislative philosophy and fiscal realities.

Regardless of how a state chooses to structure equalization aid to facilities, the critical feature is the cost-share based on ability to pay. This feature is also its greatest advantage in that aid flows in inverse proportion to local wealth. Another advantage is often a greater degree of local control wherein a district can manipulate its tax effort, either to purchase better facilities or to provide local tax relief. Inversely, conceptual disadvantages are few, relating more to political problems, such as the difficulty in achieving power equalization as discussed earlier in Chapter 4. Similarly, fiscal constraints and the political temptation to aid all districts often serve as depressants on the amount of aid available to the neediest districts. Although many states have adopted forms of facility equalization grants, they have generally refused to participate in power equalization, preferring instead to cap eligible expenditures in a modified power equalization structure. Presently the states of Alabama, Arizona, Arkansas, Connecticut, Florida, Georgia, Illinois, Maine, Maryland, Massachusetts, New Jersey, New Mexico, New York, North Carolina, Pennsylvania, Rhode Island, South Carolina, Utah, Washington, Wisconsin, and Wyoming claim to provide facility aid under an equalization scheme.

Percentage-matching Grants.   In a few instances, states have chosen to provide aid to facilities using a percentage-matching grant structure. Originally designed to aid general fund budgets, the percentage-matching grant is an effort by states to recognize districts' needs while more "neutrally" aiding districts. In its most basic form, a percentage-matching scheme would provide aid to all districts by granting a legislatively determined percentage of total facility costs regardless of actual need. For example, the state might determine that it wishes to share in facility costs in a 40:60 ratio based on legislative philosophy and state treasury limitations wherein the state would provide 40% of total facility costs, with the local district supplying the remaining 60%. Under such conditions, percentage-matching plans are designed to satisfy three primary purposes. First, percentage-matching is a recognition of the need and political benefit of assisting local districts with capital projects. Second, percentage-matching is an attempt to provide such aid on a neutral basis, either from the perspective of not wishing to discriminate among districts or recognizing the political benefits to aiding all districts regardless of need. Third, the level of state aid under percentage-matching is controlled directly by the state wherein the state can choose its destiny.

Although politically attractive, the obvious disadvantage of wealth bias has prevented wide adoption of basic percentage-matching grants. A more realistic variation would link the state's desire to engage in percentage-matching, while incorporating wealth factors to create a percentage-equalizing grant structure. For example, the state might decide to provide 50% of total spending for facilities, with the added feature that the state's share would be distributed by an equalization formula based on districts' ability to pay. The general rule would be that the local percentage of spending in any district must bear the same relation to the average local percentage as the local tax base bears to the average local tax base per pupil; thus, within the general limitation of maximum 50% state assumption of all statewide debt, a district with one-third less tax base than the average district in the state would be expected to bear only one-third of its costs from local sources.[35] Thus, beyond the dubious political advantages, basic percentage-matching grants have little inherent value. Presently only the states of Alaska, Delaware, and Georgia utilize percentage-matching grants.

Flat Grants.   As discussed earlier in this text, flat grants have historically been used to provide general aid to school districts based on a set of conceptions related to both equity and politics. Under these provisions, states offered districts a set amount of money legislatively determined that took into consideration the number of school districts and the state's financial condition. The distribution formula was generally quite simple wherein districts were granted a flat amount of money on some basis, such as head count or number of classrooms. The result was that the district's costs were reduced by the state share, leaving the district free to relieve tax pressures or to supplement its programs by the amount of the grant.

The same principle of flat grants by states has also been applied to facility funding. Operation of flat grants to facilities has generally been identical to other areas where such funding has been offered. Under these conditions, all districts are eligible to receive at least some funds, and local wealth dependency is superficially reduced. Importantly, political realities are often aided, at least among those districts that would otherwise not qualify for aid due to adequate wealth. These advantages are also disadvantages, however, in that flat grants have seldom been sufficient to meet districts' needs, and it is clear that flat grants do not truly reduce local wealth dependency. Additionally, in many states the concept of openly courting wealthy districts by offering unneeded aid has been unacceptable. While flat grants are clearly superior to no state assistance, their value to modern school finance principles is negligible. Presently the states of Alabama, Illinois, Mississippi, New Jersey, South Carolina, and Tennessee utilize flat grant aid structures.

State Loans. Unlike the other traditional methods used by states in assisting school districts' capital needs, loan programs represent one of only two original facility funding inventions. Although all other forms of facility aid are state admission of the inadequacy of the local tax base to meet districts' capital needs, the creation of state loan programs is special recognition by states of the very high cost of facilities because state facility loans are exceptions to the fairly strict cash basis operation of schools throughout the United States. Under these conditions, a loan program fundamentally concedes that current revenues are inadequate to provide school facilities and permits districts to engage in deficit spending to provide and maintain housing for the instructional activities of the district. Thus, a loan program is precisely what its name implies: the state loans money to local districts for facility needs. As a general rule, such loans are made on a temporary basis with the expectation that the district will repay the loan under the terms and conditions prescribed by the state.

State loan programs have both advantages and disadvantages that are inherent to their nature and design within individual states. The advantages include favorable interest rates and strong security ratings for investors because the state itself either makes the loan or effectively guarantees the loan,[36] enabling districts to either borrow money at a lesser cost or buy more facilities for the same cost that would be incurred under traditional debt mechanisms that carry higher interest rates. Similarly, a loan program may provide a second advantage in that some states have structured loans to include forgiveness features if the district is unable to repay its debt. The disadvantages, however, are meaningful because wealth and ability to pay are unchecked wherein districts in greatest need may also be least able to afford the extra expense of borrowed money. This method has proved attractive, however, for obvious "no-cost" or "profit" reasons. Presently some form of loan mechanism is utilized in the states of Minnesota, New Hampshire, North Dakota, Vermont, Virginia, West Virginia, Wisconsin, and Wyoming.

State or Local Authorities. The second original facility funding invention operates in a highly analogous fashion to state loan programs. Typically, state or local building authorities are legislatively created mechanisms that seek to compromise the normal debt structure of bonding for capital needs wherein local districts are allowed to borrow capital project monies without traditional bonding against the wealth of the local district. Building authorities are thus often designed to permit and encourage the use of private capital to construct and lease or lease-purchase school buildings for several reasons. First, building authorities do not generally involve state monies. Second, the state has the political benefit of having liberalized facility acquisition procedures at virtually no cost. Third, debt limitations do not usually apply, making it easier for low wealth districts to obtain facilities. Fourth, no bond referendum is usually required, thereby overcoming a major obstacle of voter resistance to school spending. Thus, building authorities have been utilized by several states for a variety of reasons relating to inability to fulfill districts' capital needs.

The major advantages to building authorities lie in the unique ability to tap fiscal resources without legal debt limit constraints and in the ability to efficiently obtain needed facilities in a shorter time period. School bond elections have increasingly failed across the nation as voters continue to resist higher taxes, and the time lines discussed later under voter approval for bonding are generally shortened by the use of building authorities. Opponents of authorities, however, argue fervently against such legislative "subterfuge" by citing avoidance of referenda and greater eventual costs associated with the higher interest rates inherent in using private capital to care for districts' facility needs. Opponents see serious consequences to these structures because they perceive avoiding referenda as inimical to democratic principles and local control. Nonetheless, several states permit such structures, with statutory authorization for some type of building authority in the states of Georgia, Illinois, Indiana, Kentucky, Maine, Maryland, Massachusetts, New York, Pennsylvania, and Virginia.

Although nearly all states have at least minimally recognized the impracticality of funding capital needs entirely from the local tax base, 15 states presently provide no aid. When those states offering only loans and authorities are also defined as providing no meaningful aid, the total rises to 23 states that do not effectively assist capital projects in school districts. When those states offering only token assistance through nonequalizing grants or low percentages of aid are included, there is evidence that the majority of states does not do enough to assist districts with the enormous costs of school facilities. In an era that has witnessed rapidly rising educational costs, increased enrollments, and pressure to improve student achievement and expand curricula while at the same time seeing capital expenditures as a percentage of total costs decline from nearly 18% in 1959 to only approximately 6% in 1988, it is clear that the crisis in school facility needs is a product of competition for scarce resources and pressure from the role and scope of modern education. Equally clear is that school facilities are a product of the environment of how schools are financed generally wherein all other aspects of education are first served before facility needs are addressed. Thus, the condition of facilities represents an impending crisis for American taxpayers.

Providing School Facilities in the Modern Environment

Although state aid for capital outlay and debt service grew from $78 million in 1951 to over $2 billion in 1992, these sums do not begin to account for the vast costs of providing school facilities in a modern complex environment.[37] Although such aid has been welcomed by local schools, the vast majority of districts throughout the nation have had to finance the major portion of capital projects using revenues derived from local property taxes levied against the district's taxable assessed valuation. Although such funding arrangements are highly questionable in an equity context,[38] most states have continued to require local districts to meet their capital needs in precisely such a manner. Although resulting revenues are highly variable due to differences in the tax base of each individual school district, the bulk of capital project funds continues to be made up of local dollars. Generally, the local share is derived from some combination of three principal funding methods: *current revenues, sinking funds,* or *bonded indebtedness.*

Current Revenues.   Local school districts generally must supplement state aid in caring for their facility needs. Obviously, in states providing no financial assistance, total responsibility for capital projects rests with the local district. Although several methods of raising local money are available, financing capital needs by *current revenues* is the oldest method of local support to school facilities. As the name implies, the local share of capital projects is derived on an annual basis from taxes levied during the current year. For example, if a district has an assessed valuation of $500 million and a legally permissible tax rate for capital outlay of four mills, the district can generate $2 million in current revenues for facility purposes. Similarly, if a district has an assessed valuation of only $7 million and the same permissible tax rate, current revenues for capital projects will only raise $28,000. If in the same example the state were to have no limit on the tax rate available to local school districts, the poorer district would have to levy 286 mills to achieve the same revenues available to the wealthy district under 4 mills of tax effort. Under these conditions, current revenues funding has several strengths and weaknesses.

The benefits and limitations of providing local financing via current revenues are implicit in the illustration. The major advantage is clearly that current revenues is a cash basis method that avoids the heavy interest costs involved in borrowing money to satisfy capital needs. Also, districts are more likely to refrain from extravagance if revenues must be available prior to actual expenditure, and generations enjoying capital projects are those who must also actually pay for obtaining facilities. At the same time, however, serious drawbacks are evident. The most important disadvantage results from widely varying wealth of districts, in that districts with high wealth will have fine facilities while low wealth districts will not be able to afford the same educational opportunity. For example, most professional educators are keenly aware of exemplary school facilities in some districts, oftentimes bordering another district that is struggling just to keep its facilities in physical repair. It is precisely this wealth difference that has caused the facility crisis noted earlier in the chapter—a crisis fueled by lack of state equalization of educational opportunities as expressed by school facilities.

Obviously, few districts in the United States are able to effectively or exclusively utilize the current revenues method of funding the local share of school facility costs for several reasons. First, most local tax bases are woefully inadequate to raise sufficient revenue to fully fund local facility requirements. Second, most states limit the maximum millage that can be levied against the local tax base for capital projects. Third, even if states permitted unlimited local leeway, it would be politically impossible to levy the millage required to raise adequate funds in poor districts on a current revenues basis. Fourth, the usefulness of current revenues is in most instances confined to small projects and to annual maintenance and operations budgets. Although all states gladly authorize districts to fund their capital needs via current revenues, the realities of limited resources compared to expensive facility needs have prevented wide-scale adoption of this primitive funding method. As a result, states have had to invent other methods of funding local facility costs.

Sinking Funds.   Because current revenues are generally inadequate to meet facility costs, the concept of a *sinking fund* has historically been permitted in some states. In principle, a sinking fund can be thought of as simply a savings account that is allowed to accumulate until it is large enough to pay for some project with cash money. As sinking funds have generally operated, the school district is allowed to levy general or special taxes that can be placed into a reserve fund for future specific or general use. Assuming sufficient tax base to generate significant revenues, sinking funds can grow fairly rapidly because such monies are usually invested in interest-bearing accounts. For example, an annual tax levy of $100,000 per year invested at 10% simple annual interest will yield total principal and interest earnings of $609,410 in only five years.

The concept of the sinking fund has several advantages that make it attractive to both school districts and taxpayers. The most obvious benefit is that it encourages saving for public projects. In addition a sinking fund, as a type of current revenue, can be highly cost-effective because money is not borrowed, resulting in immediate and dramatic savings in interest costs. Finally, a sinking fund seems highly prudent, giving districts the leisure of long-range planning. Unfortunately, however, these advantages have seldom been realized in actual practice for several reasons. First, sinking funds are still dependent on the wealth of the local district. As a result, only wealthy districts can significantly benefit by saving. Second, inflation greatly reduces the value of money for rich and poor districts alike. For example, a modest inflation rate of 2% reduces the future value of $1 to only 67¢ after 20 years. Third, sinking funds unfortunately have a dismal history of mismanagement, primarily because school leaders have not been skilled in investment techniques. Fourth, the ability to gather large sums not earmarked for specific projects can actually be a disadvantage in that needs change over time so that voters who originally approved such levies might disapprove of their eventual use. Even if sinking funds are earmarked, needs may change by the time enough monies are gathered. In either event, opportunities for resentment and mismanagement are great; therefore, few states allow true sinking funds in the modern watchdog environment.[39]

Bonded Indebtedness.   Because current revenues and sinking funds are not feasible solutions to most school facility problems, most school districts must eventually fund their facility needs through the bond mechanism, by which school organizations are statutorily permitted to incur debt to acquire long-term fixed assets, such as school facilities. Although debt is generally prohibited under cash basis laws for current operations in many states, the broad exception to cash basis is for acquisition of facilities. As with other areas of school finance, methods by which school districts may incur bonded indebtedness depend entirely on the statutory provisions available in a given state. In most states, school districts are broadly authorized to incur bond debt for facility needs, subject only to statutes relating to referendum and debt limitations. In other states, however, there are differences relating primarily to whether districts are fiscally independent or dependent, and to whether the state actively controls bonding by a central state authority.

As discussed earlier in Chapter 6, school districts in approximately a dozen states are fiscally dependent on another unit of government, such as a county or city municipal agency. Such school districts do not generally levy or collect taxes, and thus have no independent authority either to acquire facilities or to bond for such purposes.

Instead, the school district generally presents warrants or vouchers to some government agency for approval and payment of school district expenses. For fiscally dependent school districts, this usually means that school facilities are obtained by a much more restrictive process than is true in other states. For example, school bonds are likely to be sold as a unit of the local government and may thus be grouped with other municipal bond sale projects. This process can be either helpful or detrimental to a local district. As a benefit, the district can often save administrative fees because the costs of a multiunit bond sale are proportionally less to each participating unit of government. Similarly, a better interest rate can sometimes be obtained because the school district's credit rating is intermingled with ratings of other governmental units. Conversely, dependence on another unit of government can slow the facility acquisition process due to bureaucracy, and approval of a school bond issue depends on outside parties. Additionally, the district must usually convince some other unit of government of its needs. Finally, the district's credit rating could be harmed by other units of government.

In several states, school bond sales are actually conducted by the state itself. Under such instances, local bond issues in the traditional sense do not apply because the state assumes this function. Several scenarios are thus possible. Local districts can petition the state to participate in a bond sale based on voter approval to seek a facility project, or the state can simply use its reputation to guarantee all local bond debt, as is the case in approximately a dozen states. Or local districts can be placed on a state-wide priority project list, with the state periodically holding a bond sale to raise money to meet approved capital projects. In the latter example the state has created a form of dependent school district wherein local districts must qualify their needs to the state, making the state the critical agency that may even help determine local needs. The benefits of state bonding are obvious, however, as the state is equipped to handle massive bond sales and can negotiate the best financial arrangements given its taxing power and credit rating. The drawbacks increase, however, as states impose controls on local districts.

Bonding Principles.   In most states, however, bonding for school facility needs is a highly local affair requiring special care and competence on the part of administrators. Although bonding is a form of borrowing money, it is different from traditional borrowing in several ways. When citizens or businesses want to borrow money for a capital project, they usually approach a mortgage lender seeking a mortgage loan. A mortgage is a debt instrument that uses property as collateral to secure the loan in case of default by the borrower, in which case the collateralized property can be foreclosed and seized by the lender. In contrast, governmental units do not operate by these same rules. Although bonds create a legal debt on the part of a governmental unit, the traditional mortgage is replaced by the bond mechanism, which has two overriding features. First, bonds are sold in an open marketplace to be purchased by many different investors instead of a single mortgage lender. Second, public properties purchased through bond sales cannot be foreclosed. Thus, a bond sale for school facility purposes creates neither a mortgage nor collateral. The only collateral is theoretical in that the full faith and credit of the government (i.e., the school district or other government unit, such as the state) is pledged to repay the debt.

The bond mechanism has several benefits. First, although traditional collateral does not exist for public works bonds, investors usually find these bonds to be highly attractive investments because the chance of default is virtually nonexistent in most instances. In traditional mortgages, a lender risks the amount of the loan on the assumption that the borrower's income is secure and that the property will not depreciate below loan value. Although loan-to-value ratios are not considered in a bonding relationship, it should be obvious that the "borrower's" income is the surest obtainable risk.[40] This is because the school district generally has taxing authority, and the "collateral" is future tax revenues, which are pledged as repayment. Second, the interest rate paid by schools on bonds is likely to be much lower than on commercial loans, due primarily to low risk of default and because bonds are generally tax-exempt. The tax-exempt status of interest earned on school bonds is highly attractive to investors because lower untaxed interest earnings may actually net more income than higher yield investments after taxes.

The favorable financial security of a bond issue is further enhanced by a third benefit known as a professional bond rating, a professionally prepared opinion by a bond rating firm on the credit-worthiness of the unit of government seeking to raise capital by a bond issue. Although there is no requirement that a bond rating be obtained, most bond issues do carry such an appraisal because without such rating, the quality of the bonds is presumed suspect. As a general rule, professional bond ratings are prepared by Moody's, Standard and Poor's, or Fitch, whose professional reputations are authoritative in the financial world. Although bond ratings are complex creatures, investors will usually consider the bond rating's evaluation, which takes into account such factors as the assessed valuation per pupil, the bond attorney's reputation, expenditure per student, ratio of debt to district wealth, percentage of state aid to the district, and the overall tax effort of the district. In addition, the quality of data presented in the bond prospectus and any insurance associated with the issue will be evaluated. Although a price must be paid to evaluate the attractiveness of a bond issue, the school district bond rating is "a prediction of long-term ability to pay, and the rating agency analysis will focus on what may evolve in the future as well as on current economic conditions."[41] As seen in Table 12.3, high bond ratings will command lower interest rates, significantly reducing costs to the district.

Bonding has several unique characteristics with which administrators should be familiar. The first characteristic is how districts decide to issue bonds. As stated earlier, schools do not approach a given lender in search of a loan. Instead, most states require a bond referendum when a school district decides to engage in a facility project that exceeds cash reserves or current revenues. A referendum is a request for approval of facility debt by placing the question on the ballot at a local election so that registered voters of the school district can express approval or rejection of the proposed project. The purpose of referendum is to assure that a district's constituents understand the need for the project and are willing to pay the additional taxes that will have to be levied to retire the debt. Although many administrators fear bond elections, such a procedure is a good protection because approved projects are an assurance of patron appreciation of the needs of the district. Although horror stories of bond election failures abound and while the deplorable condition of many school facilities is the result of shameful voter unwillingness to pay for good schools, the referendum is basic to the democratic process. In most states, a bond referendum can be held in conjunction with another election, such as a presidential or gubernatorial election, or the school bond question may be voted on by special election.

A second characteristic of bonding is that although voters must approve a bond issue, voters themselves are still not the lender. As stated earlier, no one lender issues a mortgage, and taxpayers are not obligated to loan the money to pay for a facility

TABLE 12.3   Bond ratings

Moody's ratings and Brief Descriptions	
Rating	**Brief Description**
Aaa	Best quality
Aa	High quality
A	Favorable investment
Baa	Medium grade obligation
Ba	Speculative elements
B	Lacks as desirable investment
Caa	Poor standing, may default
Ca	High degree of speculation
C	Poor investment prospects
Con	Needing completion of data

Standard and Poor's Ratings and Brief Descriptions	
Rating	**Brief Description**
AAA	Prime
AA	High grade
A	Upper medium grade
BBB	Medium grade
BB	Lower medium grade
B	Some degree of speculation
CCC	Greater degree of speculation
CC	Greatest degree of speculation
C,DDD,DD	Various degrees of default

project. Rather, voters agree to pay taxes over a period of time to repay many investors who emerge as willing buyers of the bonds that are offered for sale. The bonds themselves are much like promissory notes in that an investor buys one or more bonds on open sale at a specified value, often in denominations of $1,000 or $5,000.[42] The investor then expects to be repaid in the form of principal and interest over a specified period of time. The basic features of the bond issue and the repayment period are specified in a bond prospectus. For example, some bonds are sold at face value and yield periodic interest payments, with the principal amount returned on maturation of the bond. Other bonds are discounted from face value, yielding full face value on maturation. Other arrangements are also made, but the basic characteristic is that investors buy bonds with the proceeds from the sale going to the local district to be used for the facility project. The district, of course, then levies taxes that are deposited to special funds[43] from which to make regular semiannual or annual bond payments.

The Bonding Process.   When a district decides to initiate a bond sale, a series of common events is usually required. Obviously, determination of the project is the first step. As will be discussed in the next section under facility planning, this includes local determination of needs by discussion at board and community levels and working with an architect and consultant to describe needs and identify costs. As both a political and technical consideration, these processes generally take a considerable amount of time to ensure public interest and to develop desirable educational and technical specifications.

When the proposed project has been envisioned and estimated costs are known, the district determines whether it can afford the proposed project. This second step is critical because even though many states do not aid facilities, every state has established debt limitations for public agencies, including schools.[44] Generally, the debt limitation is expressed as a percentage of the assessed valuation of the school district. For example, if a school district were to have an assessed valuation of $500 million with a 10% debt ceiling, the school district would not be allowed to have outstanding debt exceeding $50 million. Typically, a district may have had several bond issues over a period of years, and all outstanding debt generally must be included in the total liabilities of the district. When the liabilities are known, the total can be compared to the district's assessed valuation to determine the remaining debt that a district can legally incur. For example, a district with $2 million in outstanding debt and an assessed valuation of $50 million under a 14% debt limitation will determine its bonding capacity to be an additional $5 million or 10% of total assessed valuation.[45]

When the project has been planned and costs are within legal debt limits, the usual third step is to schedule the bond referendum. State statutes are usually very specific regarding these procedures and must be followed to ensure that the proper parties are notified, such as a county election board, and that the bond election occurs in a timely and proper manner. The local district usually has little responsibility for such activities, but does normally make all decisions about the timing of a bond election and usually engages in extensive advance community public relations in an attempt to ensure passage of the bond issue. If the bond election is not successful, the district must seek to determine cause of failure in order to decide whether to seek resubmission of the bond question to the public or whether to abandon its plans. Normally, failed bond issues are the result of inadequate advance public relations or the result of other economic problems simultaneously affecting the local community. In most instances, however, districts seek a new election after having determined the cause of failure. Generally, resubmitting the question is accompanied by renewed public relations activities and may include a scaled-down proposal at a lesser cost in an attempt to negotiate passage with an unwilling electorate.[46]

If the bond election is successful, the district can promptly proceed to the fourth step, preparing for the actual bond sale. Obviously, at this point these activities are well beyond the competence of local school district personnel. These highly technical activities require competent legal counsel and financial counsel. Specialized legal counsel is normally required because the complexity of bond laws requires the skills of attorneys who work exclusively in this arena, and skilled financial bond counsel is required because the bond market where the bonds will be advertised and sold is also a highly complex and competitive field. By hiring competent counsel, the district will be assured of both legal compliance and expert management of the bond sale in a highly complex financial and legal world.

When counsel has prepared properly for the bond issue, an official advertisement of the proposed sale will be issued. The purpose of advertising is twofold. First, investors must be notified via formal channels of an impending sale.[47] Second and very importantly, school districts in all states are legally required to engage in full disclosure of details surrounding the sale to protect both investors and the district against unfair or fraudulent business practices. Consequently, advertisement of the bond issue usually occurs by at least two means: in widely read financial publications where bond investors may become informed about upcoming bond sales and by a more detailed advertisement known as a *bond prospectus.* Normally, the initial publication is designed to briefly inform the investment community of the upcoming sale and to invite bond buyers to request a prospectus containing additional detailed information about the terms and conditions of the bond sale. As a general rule, the bond prospectus will contain information in the following areas, many of which can be identified in the foregoing discussion:

Statement, summarizing and highlighting the bond issue;

Purpose, describing the bond issue in terms of what the school district intends to do with the bond proceeds;

Date, Type, Denomination, and *Maturity,* discussing the bond issue generally, and describing such features as whether bonds are callable,[48] the length of the loan, and maximum interest rate acceptable to the district;

Paying Agent, describing how the successful bidder may select the depository and the time lines;

Interest Payment Dates and *Rates,* discussing the method of computing the bids, the method of the bid (e.g., face value versus discount);

Delivery, defining deadlines and procedures;

Legal Opinion, summarizing bond counsel's opinion of the legality of the bond issue;

Types of Bids and *Award,* describing the type of bid pursuant to state statute, nature of bidders' checks, and so forth;

Debt Limitations, certifying that the school district has standing to incur the proposed debt;

Overlapping Debt, displaying additional debt the district may hold;

Taxes, displaying the tax structure of the school district and all information needed to understand the overall tax burden in the district;

Notes to Statements and Receipts and Disbursements, normally discussing the district's accounting policies, investment practices, and overall financial status;

Future Financing, discussing the anticipated issuance of bonds or financial notes, if any, within the near future for capital improvements;

Pending Litigation, revealing whether there is pending litigation that may affect the financial status of the district;

Certification Statement, certifying that the school district has not withheld material information detrimental to the bond sale;

General Information, usually presenting an economic and demographic portrayal of the school district; and

Sale of Issue, containing a schedule of the actual opening and the time of the awarding of the bid.

With the assistance of competent legal and financial counsel, the sale of the bonds is then completed and the district enters the fifth step of the bonding process by receiving the proceeds. Although counsel continues to be extremely important, the district must understand that many restrictions apply to the use and investment of bond proceeds. For example, while all districts should seek to maximize idle funds prior to disbursement, the very large sums of money involved in bond sales have caused federal statutes to severely restrict investment procedures. Federal guidelines must be carefully interpreted by qualified legal counsel in that arbitrage is strictly prohibited. Under these rules, the district must be careful to disburse bond proceeds in a reasonable and timely manner and to avoid taking excess profits from investment. For example, if the rate of return on investment of idle bond proceeds were greater than the rate of interest paid on the bonds, the district would have to rebate excess earnings to the federal government.[49] Additionally, federal guidelines are specific as to a construction bond exception and the percentages that must be expended by certain periods of time.[50] Specifically, federal law allows arbitrage if the proceeds are expended within six months of selling the bonds.[51] Districts must receive good counsel, however, as numerous other rules also apply, such as requirements to submit various forms to maintain the tax-exempt status of such securities.[52]

Although the bonding process is normally completed in these five steps, the total facility project is far from complete. In fact, bonding merely represents the process of preparing for a facilities project because the actual work proposed by the bond issue can begin only when the bonding process has been successfully carried out. Additionally, the facility project extends even beyond completion and physical occupancy because the district has committed to long-term repayment of bond debt. Obviously this requires reviewing the financial plan for accuracy annually, making tax levies and depositing bond payments into special debt funds until the proper time for disbursement, and maintaining and protecting the new assets of the district. As seen in earlier chapters on budgeting, accounting, and taxation, these processes are vitally important to the successful operation of a school district. But because so much money is at stake, facilities and bonding require that the administrator take extra care to disprove the age-old maxim: "The administrator who built this building used to work here."

FACILITY PLANNING AND MAINTENANCE OPERATIONS

Despite the vast investment represented by a district's physical plant assets, facilities have generally been neglected by states and districts alike in the desire to improve instructional programs. Unfortunately, this has been both necessary and improvident because resources have not been sufficient to fully care for every aspect of school district operation. But while instruction of children must always be the first priority of a school district, it is nonetheless false economy and neglect of child-based education to allow facility goals and maintenance to go untended. Planning for facilities and the operation and maintenance of school plants is a critical aspect of providing an effective educational experience.

The vast fiscal resources obtained by current revenues and bonding are clear evidence of the need for an effective and efficient physical plant program. Administrators must therefore have a good grasp of the role of facility planning and understand the role of maintenance and operations in a district. This last section explores facility planning and maintenance operations by looking at several important activities of each.

The Role of Facility Planning

Although public school districts engage in long-range planning in a number of areas, in many ways facility planning represents success or failure in other plans the district may make. An exhaustive curriculum built around the latest technology cannot succeed if the district's facilities are poorly designed or maintained, nor can an excellent curriculum carefully structured by the most highly skilled experts succeed in a new facility if the building is so poorly designed that it cannot support the curriculum. For example, an old building with inadequate electrical service and cramped spaces often cannot support sophisticated computer labs. Similarly, an old building without proper ventilation is an unsuitable and dangerous place for a chemistry program. Even a new building may be unsuitable if it is crowded for space or planned without proper consideration for the educational program it houses. Although a fine facility will not reverse the effects of poor teaching, facility planning is much more than just architectural design of a new facility—it is the total integration of the district's physical plant with the instructional and support functions.

The importance of facility planning has long been recognized in many circles and many school districts have given deserved emphasis to this important educational function. Wise administrators have recognized that poor educational facility planning is costly to school districts in terms of wasted scarce money, underutilization of facilities, lack of long-range flexibility, and the sheer ineffectiveness of poor decision making. As a result, in districts where facility planning has become a systematic activity, there is generally an established hierarchy to oversee the many aspects of plant planning and operations. For example, many larger school districts appoint an assistant superintendent for plant planning who is charged by the board of education and the superintendent with a variety of facility-related tasks. Often this person may have subordinates who perform smaller or more specialized functions. In smaller districts more of these activities are taken on by the chief school administrator, with a significant increase in contracted services by commercial firms. Although the size of a district generally dictates these arrangements, every district should assure that the individual in charge of facilities has a background in both education and facility management.

The increasing sophistication and cost of facilities has led many districts to allocate a full-time position to facility planning and operations. Many other districts have moved toward appointing at least a half-time person under the supervision of a central office administrator due to the great responsibility and scope of the school plant tasks to be performed. In larger districts, an office of plant planning is usually established wherein all operations relating to school facilities are housed, including maintenance and operations. As with all planning services, this office has as its major task the systematic study and analysis of the district's facility needs according to five fundamental goals: preparation and maintenance of a comprehensive analysis of existing facilities; assurance of a well-designed physical plant that enhances teaching and learning; assurance that all facilities remain useful over the entire life of the facility because outmoded facilities can be a retardant to teaching and learning; evaluation of facilities in relation to future educational programs that will assist in decisions to reconstruct or abandon buildings; and preservation of the maximum flexibility in every facility so that future generations will be effectively served. Thus, every school district should have formal facility plans built around the present and future needs of the district, reflecting careful thought about:

1. School-age population to be served;
2. Location and transportation of school-age population;
3. Programmatic offerings of the district and each school;
4. Overall long-range facility needs of the district;
5. Fiscal ability of the taxpayers of the district;
6. Overall organizational structure of the school system; and
7. Overall economic and demographic future of the district.

These factors make up the major functions of the office of facility planning and can be described in terms of formal operations. Earthman has described the overall functions of this office as:

1. Demographic planning;
2. Capital program planning;
3. Facility planning and programming;
4. Architectural review;
5. Site selection and acquisition; and
6. Construction.[53]

These factors deserve greater development because they form the basis of facility planning on which districts should make and justify a wide variety of decisions about the total educational program.

Demographic Planning.   One of the most serious mistakes that can be made by a district in facility planning is failure to carefully account for the demographics of the school district. Even the finest facilities constructed without debt would be diminished in importance if the schools were inaccessible or inappropriate to the location of children in the district. Demographic planning is thus the study of the district's fundamental profile, including social, economic, and population concerns. Thus, demographics drive facility planning because the purpose of a facility program is to serve the needs of a school district's clients.

Demographic planning varies greatly among districts in relation to their unique characteristics. For example, large districts with expanding populations need to anticipate housing developments before they are actually begun so that land can be purchased before prices rise. Small districts also need demographic planning to predict future facility needs in relation to stable or declining enrollments. A major task of demographic planning is therefore to develop an educational facilities survey that descriptively researches the district's profile and identifies future needs, analyzes the findings and synthesizes alternative solutions, and recommends a plan of action. Most districts thus prepare a comprehensive educational survey that describes the community's characteristics and educational needs, determines pupil population characteristics, describes the educational program, appraises existing facilities in relation to needs, develops a master plan, assesses fiscal resources available to meet the plan, and formulates specific recommendations. Because the survey is such a comprehensive product, the sum of these activities is a vital tool for the district, providing the basis for careful long-range educational facility planning.

Description of the community's characteristics and educational needs is the starting point in demographic planning. While the community analysis must be tailored to each district's needs, the survey should include inquiry into population characteristics and density patterns and population changes over time. Additionally, the survey should examine changes in land use wherein zoning and rezoning have occurred according to changes in population patterns. Further, the analysis should examine traffic ways to assess the development and utility of land under growth conditions to predict the eventual location of new schools or the continued viability of existing facilities. Socioeconomic status is another key factor that should be studied wherein economic stress may limit choices. Inversely, rapid population growth in professional communities may result in continual upward mobility that requires new elaborate schools. Additionally, other characteristics of the community should be considered, including vocational opportunities, parental expectations, and citizen attitudes toward schools and taxes in general. The community survey should therefore descriptively profile the demographics of the total community so that these realities can be included in long-range planning.

The most critical element of demographic planning, however, is the student enrollment study because sufficient and appropriate space must be provided for all students in the district.[54] To properly plan for student population, the district must be able to accurately project pupil enrollment into the future. As discussed in Chapter 6, population projections entail identifying the district's population trends, birthrates, historic and present student enrollments, and student retention. When these data are known, the district can estimate the number of children at each grade level in each school and make projections for each school and the district. The most common enrollment projection techniques include cohort survival and trend line analysis, although many large districts require sophisticated computer programs that utilize saturation analysis techniques to estimate the effect of housing developments. Obviously, these data are critical to long-range capital planning as well as many other aspects of district fiscal operations, including estimating total district revenues and expenditures.

Capital Program Planning.   Capital program planning, closely related to district demographic analysis, is, as the name implies, the orderly anticipation of the district's capital needs in relation to its demographic profile. Thus, its primary purpose is to analyze the district's financial status and characteristics to estimate both the limitations and capabilities of the district to pay for current and anticipated facility needs. Capital program planning for most districts generally involves bonding, aided in some instances by federal impact funds or state aids, making capital program planning a critical aspect of facility planning because needs and resources must be linked to generate viable and affordable solutions to the district's needs.

The normal result of capital program planning is creation of a capital improvement program (CIP). Earthman defines the CIP at the local level as a document that lists and projects all capital needs for the future, usually over a period of 5 to 20 years. The CIP additionally prioritizes the identified projects, primarily because district resources are seldom sufficient to retire all the facility needs at one point in time, especially if current revenues are expected to provide a significant part of the money. For example, roof replacement on all buildings more than five years old might be the highest priority in a district, with the CIP prioritizing the sequence of replacement by greatest immediate need. Obviously, more aggressive CIPs can occur when bonding is utilized, wherein a district might choose to replace all roofs and air movement systems in a single bond issue. When renovation or new construction is contemplated, the CIP must also extensively analyze and anticipate revenues over the full period of debt retirement. A major feature of a CIP is that its adoption is generally considered authorization to proceed with capital projects, requiring only specific board approval of expenditures according to statutory requirements. Finally, the CIP should be reviewed and amended as projects are completed or as needs and financial conditions change within a district.

Facility Planning and Programming.   The nature of facility planning does not allow for totally discrete operations within a capital improvement plan. For example, while the sequence of activities clearly calls for first establishing the population base to determine a district's facility needs, it is entirely reasonable and necessary to overlap demographic planning with capital program planning. Similarly, facility planning and programming is not entirely separate from all the other issues involved in this section—for example, facility planning and programming is heavily driven by both demographics and finances. Likewise, to envision a facility and its educational program requires knowledge of the financial options and demographic requirements of a district. Thus, facility planning and programming makes up still a third activity of the plant planning office in conjunction with the many other activities described in this section.

The primary purpose of facility planning and programming is to accurately identify the desires and constraints under which an educational facility will be expected to function. Generally, this activity involves consideration of the goals and objectives of the district and the individual school, and the activity also usually defines instructional and organizational plans. The overlapping nature of activities is evident in that numerous audiences are generally involved in facility planning and programming, including the community and staff as well as professional facility planners, such as architects and educational consultants as discussed later. Although facility programming and planning is both complex and unique to each district, the overall goals should include at least the following:

1. *Educational adequacy* to enhance the teaching and learning process;
2. *Educational suitability* to suitably provide and enhance the delivery of the educational program;
3. *Safety and welfare* to protect and enhance the safety and welfare of all the students in all the programs contained therein;
4. *Functional usefulness* to effectively and efficiently handle all of the educational programs available in a school;
5. *Aesthetics* to provide a pleasant and pleasing environment for students;
6. *Flexibility* to provide a high degree of flexibility that accommodates future changes in programs and populations; and
7. *Efficiency* to ensure both economical construction and maintenance over the entire life of the building.

These characteristics comprise the heart of facility planning and programming and are clearly related to both demographic and capital program planning activities. Additionally, these activities are not limited only to planning new facilities because the role of facility planning is to assure that all facilities in a district conform to these and other more extensive standards. Thus, demographic planning, facility survey tools, and capital program planning should be joined with facility planning and programming to ask about all existing facilities and all new or proposed capital projects a series of questions as posed by the Council of Educational Facility Planners, International (CEFPI), as follows:

1. Is the facility structurally sound?
2. Is it healthful and safe?
3. Is it efficient to operate?
4. Does it support the program?
5. Is it attractive and comfortable?
6. Is its location convenient for the users?
7. Is its space optimally used?
8. Is it the right size?
9. Can it be modified?[55]

The answers to these questions in conjunction with demographic and capital program data thus form the basis of the carefully constructed CIP. If all answers are affirmative, the district should continue its exemplary performance by carefully maintaining its investment and by regular review of the CIP. If, on the other hand, some questions are answered negatively, the district should take steps to correct the deficiencies. As will be seen next, in many instances additional sophisticated planning will be required to provide the educational opportunities to which all children are entitled.

Architectural Planning.   Districts with properly identified demographic, capital, and program needs generally recognize that they have reached the limits of their expertise and now require the professional services of a qualified architect, especially as concerns about health and safety have appeared in both litigation and legislation in many states. Consequently, architectural planning represents a fourth activity in the context of modern school plant planning.

Although most educators understand that a properly licensed architect or professional engineer must design new or totally reconstructed public school facilities, fewer realize that many states also require architectural services whenever a facility is modified, such as removing or adding an interior wall or making a facility accessible to the handicapped, to bring the facility into compliance with building codes. For example, addition of an elevator in a multistory building may invoke seemingly unrelated code requirements, such as enhancing fire protection, bringing all electrical service into code compliance, or fulfilling other similar requirements that bring the entire facility up to the latest code. Even the simple addition of an interior wall may require an entire facility to be made accessible to handicapped persons under state law. Few facility projects can be undertaken in-house or by simply calling a construction company because architectural services are pervasive in facility planning. Under these conditions, administrators should check state requirements carefully and anticipate that facility planning will include the services of a qualified architect.[56]

Selection of an architect for all projects where services are required by law is thus a critical element of successful facility planning. Generally, most districts utilize the services of one architect for most smaller projects, but engage in some form of design competition when larger projects are involved. For example, small remodeling jobs involving air handling systems and perhaps divider walls to redesign interior spaces are often noncompetitive, leading many districts to call an architectural firm that has previously worked in the district. In contrast, high dollar projects such as complete renovation, major expansion, or new school construction generally involve competition between architects for the award of the contract. Because extensive formal competition is cumbersome and costly, design competition is usually reduced to asking interested architects to submit portfolios detailing their experience, qualifications, previous examples of similar public school projects,[57] and rough estimates. The board of education, administrative staff, and consultants then make a judgment based on such issues as the overall quality, experience, and reputation of the firm and the budget. The board and administration must carefully follow all statutory requirements for awarding any contract.

Construction Planning.   As districts approach sizable facility projects, the wisdom of competent architectural services is apparent in two critical aspects of facility planning. The first aspect involves planning the total facility project and working with the district and its consultants in developing educational specifications for the proposed project. This is equally true for large and small projects because unless the district's goals and objectives are integrated into the facility project, the outcome is certain to result in program misalignment with the facility. The role of the architect is thus to work with various personnel within the physical and fiscal realities of the district to be sure the facility will achieve its intended purposes. The second aspect involves actual oversight of the facility project as it is completed. These two critical features are part of the architect's overall responsibility in construction planning. The legal liabilities and technical competencies involved in these tasks make architectural services an absolute requirement in the modern environment.

Construction planning thus represents still a fifth task of the office of plant planning by combining the services of architects, consultants, and school personnel in planning a facility project. Because architects are not educators, districts usually require the services of a consultant to create a set of educational specifications that communicate the district's vision to the architect. Educational specifications are usually first stated in general terms by local school administrators and communicated to the consultant, who reviews these statements and often examines existing facilities in the district. Depending on the nature and size of the project, the consultant may also work with a committee of educators and citizens to further define needs and expectations. Regardless of the process, the goal of the district is to have the consultant use the district's broad vision to create a highly specific formal document that leads the architectural firm to develop an architectural answer to the district's needs. For example, the educational specifications define the educational program by classroom and by instructional facility, including specific requirements for all of the specialized areas of the school (e.g., media center, cafeteria, auditorium, physical education and vocational facilities, and so on). CEFPI has described educational specifications as the "blueprint for the future."[58] As a result, the architect works with the district and the consultant in reviewing the educational specifications to understand:

1. Objectives;
2. Activities to be housed;
3. Persons to be accommodated;
4. Space requirements;

5. Spatial relationships;
6. Equipment to be housed; and
7. Special environmental treatment.[59]

The process of construction planning thus generally involves a series of important activities. If new construction is required, these activities may result in preliminary designs and drawings that are presented to the board of education. Once the preliminary plans are accepted, actual working drawings and specifications are developed by the architect. Although some cost is involved in making changes in these preliminary documents, it is important that all parties be in full agreement because of the high cost and dissatisfaction that may occur if modifications are made during the construction phase. All plans must be thoroughly examined to ensure that the design of the school facility is properly integrated with the curricular and instructional goals, and the district should assess whether the proposed project facilitates instruction that meets or exceeds all applicable standards. The educational facility should be designed to embrace the needs of the larger community and reflect the organizational plan of the district, such as team teaching or flexible grouping of pupils. It is thus critical to receive input from the instructional leadership team before leaving the design phase because failure will result in inefficiency, disappointment, and wasted fiscal resources.

When the design of a facility project is satisfactorily completed, the construction phase is finally undertaken. Although responsibility shifts to the architect in working with the various firms that will perform the actual physical work, the district's tasks in facility planning and programming are not yet completed. The major task of the office of plant planning during the construction phase is to be certain that the school district remains in close contact with the project for three reasons. First, lack of proper interest in the project could result in significant legal problems if it is later determined that the district should have kept itself better informed of problems that may arise. Second, the school board's official representative must communicate any concerns or changes to the project through official written change orders with all parties agreeing in writing to any additional costs. Third, periodic payments for work will be made during the construction phase, and the district must be satisfied before any funds are released to the architect or contractor. Thus, it is easy to see the benefit of expert architectural services wherein all such activities flow through the architect to the general contractor, as seen in Figure 12.1.

The construction phase also includes regular payments from the district's cash reserves or from bond sale proceeds to satisfy claims of the various firms that are participating in the facility project, including fees for architectural and construction services. Typically, the architectural fee is a percentage of the overall project, while contractor fees are established in advance by competitive bidding.[60] Often architect fees are paid in percentage lump sums based on formal phases of project completion.[61] Contractors may be scheduled on a monthly draw basis or paid at periodic intervals based on architect approval of work completed. The value of architectural services is clearly evident here because of technical competence in working with various construction firms to keep the project on schedule and to serve as official liaison and inspector to the project. Consequently, most school districts require architectural certification for all monies disbursed. When the project is completed, a percentage is typically held back by the board, pending final acceptance of the facility and proof that all bills, payrolls, and liens by all contractors, subcontractors, and ven-

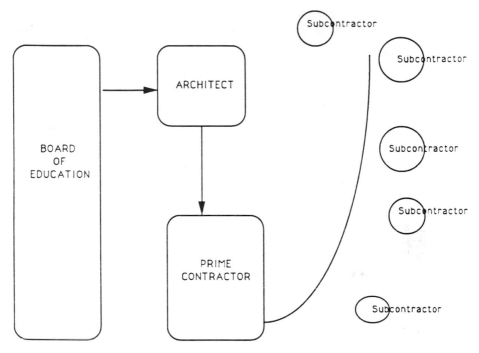

FIGURE 12.1 Facility planning relationships

dors have been fully met. Additionally, the board's attorney must review all records and satisfy applicable legal requirements to assure that the board will have clear title after full final payment.

The role of facility planning thus includes demographic planning, capital program planning, facility planning and programming, architectural planning, and various construction planning activities. These activities are equally applicable to alteration or expansion of existing facilities, and to construction of new facilities. Clearly, all such activities must be financed by legally permissible methods involving cash or debt, and in all instances competent counsel ranging from legal and financial services to architectural and construction firms must be acquired. Although no district should ever attempt to internally provide all such services, it is imperative that the district recognize that its primary role is to acquire and coordinate such services—a role that must be supported by sound educational and fiscal planning on the part of the district—thus enhancing the opportunity for an effective educational environment.

The Role of Maintenance and Operations Planning

The importance of facility planning has been heavily stressed in this chapter because the high cost of facilities and technological dependence of educational programs on appropriate facilities are enormous. A fine educational program will be unnecessarily hindered not only by poor facilities, but also by poor maintenance and operations. Thus, this chapter concludes with an examination of the role of maintenance and operations planning in preserving and protecting the district's physical plant investment because to do less will ultimately result in harmful and unwarranted tax increases.

The initial high cost of facilities and the natural proclivity of school buildings to deteriorate dictate that every school district must have a long-range maintenance and operations plan. Maintenance includes the tasks involved in keeping a building and equipment and grounds in near-new condition through repair and replacement of component parts. Operations includes the tasks of keeping a building open for use by its clientele. These important tasks form the basis for the following discussion, which examines organizing for maintenance and operations, determining maintenance needs, and conducting facility operations.

Organizing for Maintenance and Operations.   The plant service function in school districts is often organized under the direction of a central office administrator who has line authority over all physical plant activities and related personnel. Very often an assistant superintendent in charge of plant planning also oversees the operations and maintenance function of the school district. This type of structure greatly enhances the efficiency of a district because it places these related functions under one umbrella. Obviously the complexity of such an organizational structure depends on the size of the district, with very large districts often employing hundreds of plant service employees in both white-collar and blue-collar positions. In the macroperspective, a typical school district of medium-to-large size might resemble the organizational chart seen in Figure 12.2, wherein both diversification and economy of scale are evident. The hierarchy places ultimate responsibility with the board of education, which in turn delegates the daily operations to the superintendent. As the hierarchy expands downward, supervisory personnel usually function under the direction of the assistant superintendent for plant planning. This structure joins the related tasks of plant planning and operations and maintenance in a logical family where a senior administrator can integrate and coordinate their performance.

As district size increases, many school districts develop a centralized maintenance division that provides services to all schools in the district. Generally, these services are provided on an in-house basis similar to the make-or-buy decisions discussed earlier in Chapter 6, wherein the district assesses whether it is more cost-effective to employ full-time staff with specific skills or to contract with commercial firms. Figure 12.3 illustrates an actual school district of approximately 14,000 students and provides an example wherein the district has determined that it has enough work in each of these areas to justify the expense of hiring employees to perform one or more specialized tasks.[62] The hierarchy calls for an assistant superintendent for plant planning to oversee a general director of central services, who in turn oversees a director of maintenance and operations and the general supervisor of maintenance. These persons in turn direct the activities of a supervisor of operations and supervisors of four separate maintenance departments. Responsibilities are clearly identified, with the supervisor of operations in charge of custodial training and supervision and all energy management programs. Similarly, the various departments are grouped according to principal function, such as vehicles and grounds, building maintenance and repair, electrical systems, and other mechanical systems.[63] Obviously, as district size decreases the hierarchy will be reduced, although nearly identical tasks will still need to be performed.

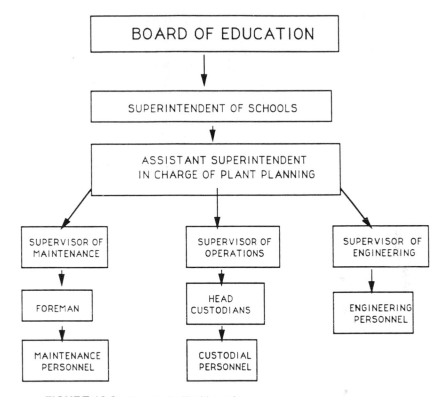

FIGURE 12.2 Sample facility hierarchy

Naturally, organizing for maintenance and operations involves assessing the entire district's ongoing facility needs from the perspective of repairing, replacing, and cleaning its capital investments. Thus, organizing for maintenance and operations includes determining the district's maintenance and operations needs, prioritizing those needs into both short- and long-term plans, and staffing maintenance and operations programs. Organizing for these tasks forms the basis of determining maintenance needs and conducting facility operations as discussed next.

Determining Maintenance Needs.   The maintenance function in school district facilities was defined earlier as the tasks involved in keeping buildings and equipment and grounds in near-new condition through repair and replacement of various component parts. As a general rule, proper maintenance in both old and new buildings alike requires regular skilled evaluation of the following component systems that make up all school buildings:

1. Footings, foundation structure, and basement;
2. Walls—both interior and exterior;
3. Roof and flashing structures;
4. Doors and windows and related frames;

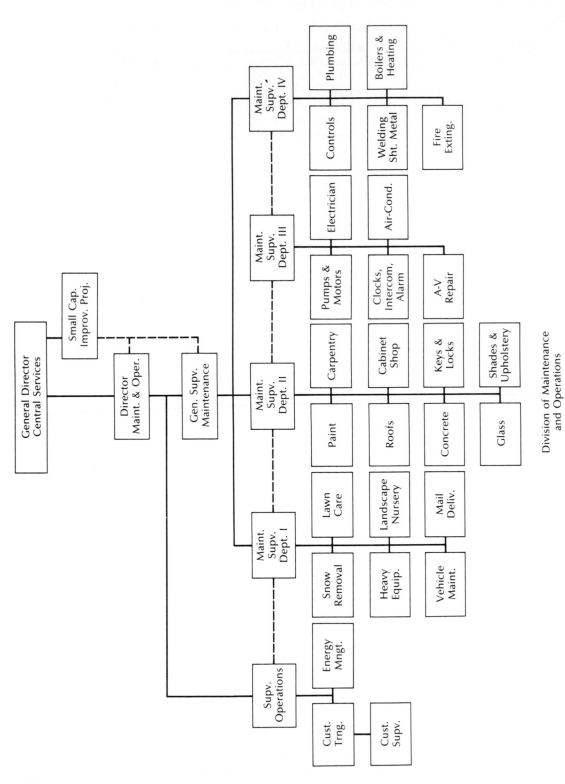

FIGURE 12.3 Sample detailed facility hierarchy

Division of Maintenance and Operations

584

5. Floors and ceilings;
6. Mechanical systems, including plumbing and air handling equipment;
7. Electrical systems, including lighting, electronics, and communications;
8. Aesthetics, equipment, and furnishings;
9. Grounds, including plantings, walks, drives, parking, and play areas; and
10. Energy conservation systems.

These systems require both skilled employees and contracted maintenance services. Foundations, footings, and basements should be regularly examined by employees for visible problems, and periodic evaluation by qualified engineers or architects should be scheduled, particularly for older buildings. Walls and roofs should be inspected regularly, with routine repairs, such as cosmetic cracks and light masonry repointing, completed by district personnel. Mechanical and electrical systems should also be routinely inspected by qualified technicians, and problems should be reported immediately. Evaluation of needs for aesthetic improvements and minor repairs can generally be accomplished by district staff, such as painting, refastening trim and moldings, cleaning traps, replacing washers in valves, adjusting doors, tightening fittings on doors and windows, replacing shades and rollers, replacing fluorescent lighting, and so on. The district's maintenance plan should include energy conservation assessment, including a formal energy audit and energy-saving plans, such as programs to involve staffs in conserving energy or modifying the school calendar to avoid extreme heat or cold periods. A good maintenance plan will thus yield the following basic facility profile:

1. *Site:* Grounds are neatly cared for; walks and drives are safe; ample parking free from mud and dust is available; play areas are safe for a variety of playground activities; and athletic areas are adequate for the outdoor sports they are designed to accommodate.
2. *Building exterior:* The roof should be free from leaks; rain gutters and downspouts should be in good condition; soffits should be solid and free from deterioration; mortar joints in brick or stone should be solid; window frames should be solid and neatly painted; doors should be in good working order; and windows and doors should be energy-efficient.
3. *Building interior:* The interior should be clean and neatly decorated, well illuminated, and comfortably heated and cooled and ventilated; floors should be clean, safe, and quiet; walls should be painted in light colors and free of cracks; ceilings should be made of fire-resistant acoustic materials; lighting should be by fixtures mounted flush to the ceiling and bare fluorescent tubes should not be used; and heating, ventilating, and air conditioning systems should provide at least two air changes per hour.[64]

The goal of determining maintenance needs is to identify existing problems and prevent new ones, and then to schedule repair or replacement by priority, with adequate financial commitment to assure that proper maintenance will be accomplished. As a general rule, districts should expect to spend at least 4% of the total general operating budget for the purpose of maintenance.[65] Unfortunately, the facility dilemma in the nation today is a result of failure not only by the district to systematically construct and follow a program of planned preventive maintenance, but also by society to provide sufficient revenues to protect this enormous investment. While facility operations as described next are an integral part of preventive maintenance, no amount of excellent facility operations can overcome the effects of failure to engage in proper maintenance of basic building systems. Thus, a critical aspect of modern school facility leadership rests in wise planning for maintenance and operations.

Conducting Facility Operations.   Although long-term facility maintenance is critical to the financial and instructional health of a school district, the daily operation of school facilities is equally necessary to ensure the health, safety, and welfare of the students assigned to the building. As stated in this chapter's epigraph, there is much evidence indicating that the physical condition of facilities has a powerful impact on the learning environment. For example, facilities that are dirty or sloppily maintained convey a message to students, staff, and patrons that school is not a high priority. While many educators complain that the quality of the educational program is generally judged by the shine of the floor, there is much research suggesting that students who attend school facilities that are clean and well-maintained will develop pride in their school that also extends to teaching and learning outcomes. Consequently, routine maintenance of the facility is vitally important and the contribution of a highly polished floor to student achievement should never be derided.

The maintenance function in school district facilities was defined earlier as the tasks involved in keeping a building open for use by its clientele. As a general rule, the most important operation is organization for assuring a clean school facility. Obviously, maintenance personnel must be organized for maximum efficiency within the constraints of costs, labor, and time. Every aspect of facility maintenance must be organized in such a manner that the custodian has responsibility and understands what must be done according to a timetable. These tasks can generally be broken down into the following areas:

1. Routine general vacuuming, sweeping, mopping, dusting, glass cleaning, emptying waste containers;
2. Scheduled steam-cleaning, buffing, or waxing of floors;
3. Cleaning chalkboards and trays;
4. Cleaning hall areas, including walls, water fountains, waste containers, and so on;
5. Collection and removal of trash in general areas; and
6. General notation of damage for maintenance repairs.

FIGURE 12.4   Daily custodial schedule

6:00–7:30 A.M.	Checks the proper operations of the boiler and the heating, ventilation, air conditioning system. Check the security of the building while unlocking all entrances and exits.
7:30–10:00 A.M.	Sweep hallways, entrances, and inspect the facility
10:00–12:00 A.M.	Cleaning assignments, restrooms, grounds, and hallways
12:00–2:00 P.M.	Lunch. General cleaning of the cafeteria after lunch periods
2:00–4:00 P.M.	General cleaning and care of grounds and buildings
4:00–6:00 P.M.	Cleaning of classrooms
6:00–6:30 P.M.	Dinner Break
6:30–12:00 P.M.	Cleaning of classrooms, periodic checks of sections of the building

These activities can be scheduled into standardized procedures within uniform schedules on a daily, weekly, monthly, quarterly, or yearly basis. Daily activities would include routine and standardized cleaning tasks, such as dry-mopping and vacuuming, with restroom cleaning occurring on a daily and weekly schedule. Component system evaluation by in-house staff can occur on a monthly or quarterly basis, with more extensive evaluation annually. Minor repairs, such as refastening trim or changing light bulbs, can be scheduled on an as-needed basis, while other tasks such as painting can be done by any appropriate schedule. Generally, daily tasks should be accomplished by custodians on staggered schedules based on a square footage/acreage concept or enrollment.[66] For example, formulas for custodial tasks using these methods of assignment might be calculated as follows:

Basic Plan A[67]

$$\frac{\text{Total Square Feet}}{\sim 15,000 \text{ sq. ft.}} + \text{Acreage [1 person per 10-acre site]}$$

or

Basic Plan B

Enrollment: [1 person per ~ 275 elementary students]

[1 person per ~ 200 secondary students]

On the basis of such a formula, we show an example of a typical custodial schedule for an elementary school in Figure 12.4. Obviously, the duration of the schedule presumes more than one custodian, with the tasks divided into staggered work shifts.

Although many activities not described here are necessary to assure a clean and healthful facility, no aspect is more important than proper training for custodial and maintenance staffs. Properly conducted training programs may result in increased efficiencies and improvements as evidenced by (1) higher standards of worker service, (2) fewer employees because of increased efficiency, (3) less waste of custodial materials, (4) greater efficiency in boiler operation with less waste of fuel, (5) less waste of electricity, gas, and water, (6) reduction of fire and accident hazards, (7) greater flexibility in shifting employees among buildings, (8) less deterioration of plant and equipment, (9) more minor repairs assumed by the custodial division, (10) a more professionalized spirit among employees, and (11) greater respect by the public for custodial service and workers.[68] To assist in these outcomes, the maintenance staff needs training on three levels: to understand daily routines, to communicate with various constituencies, and to develop a sense of ownership and pride in their work. Thus, training, evaluation, and praise are important to well-planned maintenance and operations.

Planning for capital outlay, maintenance, and operations is thus a highly complex function of modern school districts. While it is truly improvident that school facilities have been the object of neglect and underspending for many generations, unfortunately the age of cheapest construction and maintenance will continue to plague school districts because the nation has a long history of investing heavily in these false economies. As key policymakers, school administrators must recognize the vital importance of planning for capital outlay, maintenance, and operations, and the future will require much creative thinking to solve the facility crisis created during this century. As noted in one state's report to the legislature aptly titled *Children in Peril:*

> The bill is coming due on school repairs, and it will cost a lot. We have delayed our decisions to the point that repair in many buildings is no longer an option; costly reconstruction or new construction is the only alternative facing school policy makers. This bill will not go away and come back cheaper. By delay, the bill only grows larger and the danger grows greater.[69]

Review Points

THE STRUCTURE OF SCHOOL FACILITY AND CAPITAL NEEDS

Although much effort and money has been placed behind school reform in recent years, school facilities have continued to be neglected.

Facility needs have approached a crisis state, with many facilities in poor to dangerous condition.

The crisis has been worsened by other findings, such as radon, lead, asbestos, and so forth, straining tight resources even more.

Nationally and by individual state, the total dollars needed for repair and replacement are phenomenal.

Although there has been no concerted movement by courts to require facility equity, courts have nonetheless persistently noted the importance of school facilities in equal educational opportunity.

The major interest of courts is in the wealth-dependency inherent to most capital funding plans, wherein rich districts have better facilities.

Both as a result of court interest and political and moral obligations, states have begun to assume a more central role in providing educational facilities.

Historically, capital facility costs have been borne at the local level. Some states, however, broke early ground by providing capital aid to special projects such as rural schools, consolidation, and so forth.

State aid plans of some nature are present in most states today, but the structure and level of support varies greatly.

States genuinely offering substantial aid to facilities tend to adopt full state funding or equalization plans, while states making more token efforts tend to adopt less equalizing schemes with lower support levels.

State aid schemes currently operating in the United States include full state funding, equalization plans, flat grants, percentage-matching grants, state loans, and state and local building authorities.

Aside from state aid plans, local districts generally have only two options: current or sinking revenues, or bonding.

Due to the high cost of facilities, bonding represents the only viable choice for most districts.

Conducting a bond issue is highly complex, requiring special knowledge ranging from public relations to bond markets. In all instances, various kinds of legal and technical expertise must be provided by outside sources.

Bond elections are tightly controlled by highly state-specific laws, with severe penalties for error.

Although passage of a bond issue is a major accomplishment, it really signifies only the beginning of a long and arduous planning and operational task.

FACILITY PLANNING AND MAINTENANCE OPERATIONS

Preparing for any facility project, or simply maintaining existing facilities, demands long-range planning skills.

The importance of facilities is heightened by the potential for severe and costly impedance on educational programs if proper planning and maintenance do not occur.

The goals of facility planning and maintenance are to analyze existing needs; to assure compatibility between the educational program and the facility; to prevent facility obsolescence; to anticipate future facility needs based on a variety of factors, such as programs and enrollments; and to preserve flexibility of facilities in meeting future needs.

Whether established as a formal office or simply monitored by district personnel, a systematic planning system should be undertaken that considers demographics, capital programs, facility planning, architectural services, site concerns, and monitoring of existing or new construction.

Many districts profit greatly by preparing a capital improvements plan that projects future needs and revenues.

The complexity of facility planning and construction virtually prohibits exclusively in-house talent.

Whether building new facilities or preserving old ones, maintenance and operations is vital to the educational enterprise.

Regardless of district size, all school districts should organize for maintenance and operations, determine their maintenance needs, and conduct facility operations according to a preplanned agenda.

Depending on district size, either a central office administrator or a specially trained supervisor of plant services should assume responsibility for facility planning and maintenance operations.

Facility maintenance and operations should assure a comprehensive schedule of events designed to preserve and enhance the utility and life of each building.

At the heart of facility planning should be concern for the training and well-being of all staff engaged in facility operations.

Case Study

As the newly appointed assistant superintendent for finance and plant planning in a medium-size school district, you received a telephone call last evening from the local police department, informing you that a police officer during a routine security check noticed an odd cloud of dust emanating from a partially open window on the second floor of the high school building. Upon arriving at the high school, you discovered that a ceiling in an English classroom had fallen, covering the room with a thick blanket of powdery construction materials.

After surveying the damage and checking all the other rooms in the building, you called the superintendent to report the damage and to confer on emergency plans. To your surprise, the superintendent did not seem overly alarmed, and you were informed that the district has experienced numerous facility problems in the past 10 years. Among your findings were that the entire roof of the junior high school, built in 1908, has sagged eight inches and is presently being held up by heavy timbers; that Washington Elementary School, built in 1926, has buckling floors and support bars showing through concrete; that Adams Elementary School, built in 1918, has exposed asbestos in the basement walls and ceiling and that supports are wearing through the basement wall concrete; and that Lincoln High School, (where the ceiling fell) built in 1898, has also had problems with walls bulging outward and that the building has been braced with nine steel beams. In addition, you were informed that of the 12 schools in the district, all were built prior to World War II and that the district has been unable to pass a bond issue, even after the fire marshal condemned an elementary school two years ago. At the close of the conversation, the superintendent merely instructed you to make alternative plans for housing the affected students until the damage could be repaired.

Using the following sets of questions to help launch your class discussion, what are your options and what course of action will you choose?

Directed Discussion Questions

1. As you read this case study, what do you believe are the immediate issues that must be faced? What issues must be dealt with on an intermediate time line? Which issues can wait until an orderly long-range plan can be identified?

2. What is your reaction to the scenario's facts? As a new administrator to the district, what are your immediate impressions? Do you find the district's historic behavior reasonable? Why or why not? In your opinion, how serious are these problems? What is your reaction to the superintendent's instructions in this present instance? What steps will you take to comply with your orders? To whom will you turn in seeking alternative arrangements? What questions might you have asked the superintendent during your telephone conversation?

3. What are your extended obligations in this case study? Are you obliged to do anything more than respond to the superintendent's directives? If not, why not? If so, what must you do? If you see a need to take additional steps, what can you reasonably anticipate as possible consequences? Alternatively, if you do not act further, what potential consequences might arise if there are further problems? What questions do you need to explore, and with whom might you choose to communicate?

4. If you were the superintendent in this district, would you have acted differently? In considering plausible realities, what might lead this superintendent to react in this way?

5. In your own experience as an educator, have you knowingly worked in facilities in need of repair? If so, what were the circumstances? What corrective

plans, if any, were in place? If you have never worked in substandard facilities, what do you speculate were the reasons that buildings were in good repair? In either case, what were the demographics and fiscal profile of the district(s) in which you worked? What facility and operations planning was evident in the district? In your present district, are short/intermediate/long-range facility plans in place? If so, what are their critical elements? If none are in place, why not?

NOTES

1. American Association of School Administrators, *Schoolhouse in the Red: A National Study of School Facilities and Energy Use* (Arlington, Va.: American Association of School Administrators, 1991), 1.

2. State of Wisconsin, *Children in Peril: A Preliminary Report of the Senate Subcommittee on Aging Schools* (Madison: State of Wisconsin, 1989), 3.

3. William A. Alcott, *Essay on the Construction of School-Houses,* August 1831. Quoted in David C. Thompson, *Educational Facility Equity and Adequacy: A Report on Behalf of the Plaintiffs in Roosevelt v. Bishop* (Manhattan, Kans.: Wood, Thompson & Associates, 1991), 1.

4. A partial listing of such organizations includes the American Association for Health, Physical Education, and Recreation (AAHPER), American Association of School Administrators (AASA), American Concrete Institute (ACI), American Institute of Architects (AIA), American Institute of Electrical Engineers (AIEE), American Institute of Steel Construction (AISC), Association of Physical Plant Administrators (APPA), Association of School Business Officials (ASBO), American Society of Mechanical Engineers (ASME), American Society for Testing and Materials (ASTM), Architectural Woodwork Industry (AWI), American Welding Society Code (AWSC), Council of Educational Facility Planners, International (CEFPI), National Building Code (NBC), National Board of Fire Underwriters (NBFU), National Bureau of Standards (NBS), National Electric Code (NEC), National Fire Protection Association (NFPA), National Illuminating Engineering Society (NIES), National Plumbing Code (NPC), Uniform Building Code (UBC), and the Underwriters Laboratories, Inc. (UL).

5. The National Alliance for Business, "The Crumbling Infrastructure: Property, Plant, Equipment, and Technology," in *The Business Roundtable Participation Guide: A Primer for Business on Education* (Washington, D.C.: National Alliance for Business, 1990), 51.

6. Education Writers Association, *Wolves at the Schoolhouse Door: An Investigation of the Condition of Public School Buildings* (Washington, D.C.: Education Writers Association, 1989), 9.

7. AASA, *Schoolhouse in the Red,* 11.

8. Thomas B. Corcoran, Lisa J. Walker, and J. Lynne White, *Working in Urban Schools* (Washington, D.C.: Institute for Educational Leadership, 1989), 8.

9. Oklahoma State Department of Education, *State Capital Improvement Master Plan for Public Common Schools* (Oklahoma City: State Department of Education, 1987), iii.

10. North Carolina State Department of Public Instruction, *A Survey of Public School Facility Needs to Meet the Requirements of the Basic Education Program* (Raleigh: State Department of Public Instruction, 1986), 10.

11. Debra Haas and William Sparkman, "Financing School Facilities in Texas," *Journal of Education Finance* (Spring 1988), 413.

12. Wisconsin, *Children in Peril,* 3.

13. Because facilities have been heavily dependent on local tax capacity to fund capital expenditures, litigation has attempted to include facilities in the general school finance equity arguments discussed earlier in Chapter 5.

14. Shofstall v. Hollins, 515 P.2d 590 (Az. 1973).

15. Robinson v. Cahill, 289 A.2d 569 (N.J. Super. 1972).

16. Serrano v. Priest (Serrano II), 345 557 P.2d 929 (Cal. 1976).

17. Board of Education of the City of Cincinnati v. Walter, 390 N.E.2d 813 (Ohio 1979).

18. Diaz et al. v. Colorado State Board of Education, Superior Court of Colorado City and County of Denver, C-73688 (Colo. 1977).

19. Lujan v. Colorado State Board of Education, 649 P.2d 1005 (Colo. 1982).

20. Helena Elementary School District No. 1 v. State of Montana, 769 P.2d 684 (Mont. 1989).

21. Edgewood Independent School District v. Kirby, 777 S.W.2d 391 (Tex. 1989).

22. Later opinion is available. This citation is from Abbott v. Burke, OAL Docket EDU 5581-85, Agency Docket 307-8/85 (unpublished, 1988).

23. Jenkins v. State of Missouri, W.D. Mo. 639 F.Supp. 19, *aff. as mod.* 807 F.2d 657 (8th Cir. 1986), *cert. den.* 108 S.Ct. 70; and Kansas City (Missouri) School District v. Missouri, (W.D. Mo., 1985), 108 S.Ct. 70 (1987).

24. Tennessee Small Counties System v. McWherter, 88-1812-II (1991).

25. Rose v. Council for Better Education, 790 S.W.2d 186 (Ky. 1989).

26. Mock v. State of Kansas, 90-CV-0918; Hancock v. Stephan, 90-CV-1795; Newton Unified School District No. 373 et al. v. State of Kansas, 90-CF 2406; Unified School District No. 259 and Unified School District No. 202 et al., Intervenor, v. State of Kansas, 91-CV-1009. Facilities were not the sole focus of most of these lawsuits. In some instances, facilities were complained only peripherally but caught the attention of the court. In other instances, plaintiffs took a more aggressive line of attack. For greater development and analysis of capital fund mechanisms in expert testimony, see David C. Thompson, *Report to USD 259 on the Impacts of Hold-Harmless Aid to Select School Districts in Kansas: Consultant's Report in USD 259 v. State of Kansas* (Manhattan, Kans.: Wood, Thompson & Associates, 1991); see also David C. Thompson, R. Craig Wood, and David S. Honeyman, *Educational Fiscal Equality in Kansas Under the School District Equalization Act: Consultants' Analysis on Behalf of Newton USD 373 et al. v. State of Kansas* (Manhattan, Kans.: Wood, Thompson & Associates, 1991) and David C. Thompson, R. Craig Wood, and David S. Honeyman, *Fiscal Equity in Kansas Under the School District Equalization Act: Consultants' Analysis on Behalf of Turner USD 202 in Mock v. State of Kansas* (Manhattan, Kans.: Wood, Thompson & Associates, 1990).

27. Pauley v. Bailey, 324 S.E.2d 128 (W. Va. 1984).

28. Pauley v. Kelly, 255 S.E.2d 859 (W. Va. 1979).

29. For expert reports, see for example David C. Thompson, *Educational Facility Equity and Adequacy: A Report on Behalf of the Plaintiffs in Roosevelt Elementary School District No. 66 et al. v. C. Diane Bishop et al.* (Manhattan, Kans.: Wood, Thompson & Associates, 1991); see also various reports prepared by the same author in *West Virginians for Community Schools et al. v. Marockie et al.* (in press); David C. Thompson, R. Craig Wood, and M. David Miller, *Findings of Fact and Opinion on the Equity and Fiscal Neutrality of South Dakota's State Aid Formula to Public Schools: Expert Analysis on Behalf of the State in Bezdichek v. State of South Dakota.* (Manhattan, Kans.: Wood, Thompson & Associates, (1993); and others. See also David C. Thompson and R. Craig Wood, *Adequacy of Educational Revenues in Oklahoma School Districts: Expert Analysis on Behalf of Plaintiff in Fair School Finance Council, Inc., v. State of Oklahoma* (Manhattan, Kans.: Wood, Thompson & Associates (1992); R. Craig Wood et al., "Funding Education in Montana Based on the Concept of Cost of Living Indices" in *Montana Rural Education Association v. State* (Manhattan, Kans.: Wood, Thompson & Associates, 1992).

30. District Court of Shawnee County, *Opinion of the Court on Questions of Law Presented in Advance of Trial* (Topeka, Kans.: District Court of Shawnee County, Division 6, Oct. 14, 1991), 25.

31. Arvid J. Burke, *Financing Public Schools in the United States* (New York: Harper & Brothers, 1957), 594–595.

32. Gerald M. Weller, *State Equalization of Capital Outlays for Public School Buildings* (Los Angeles: University of Southern California Press, 1941), 5. For other capital outlay equalization studies of this time see for example Harlan Updegraff, *Financial Support Rural School Survey of New York State,* volume 3 (New York: Joint Committee on Rural Schools, 1922); Paul R. Mort, *State Support for Public Schools* (New York: Columbia University Teachers College, 1926); Jesse E. Adams, *A Study of the Equalization of Educational Opportunities in Kentucky* (University of Kentucky Press, 1928); Foster E. Grossnickle, *Capital Outlays in Relation to a State's Minimum Educational Program* (New York: Columbia University Teachers College, 1931); Erick L. Lindman, *Development of an Equalized Matching Formula for the Apportionment of State School Building Aid* (Seattle: University of Washington Press, 1948); and Wallace H. Strevell, *State Aid for Central School Building* (New York: Columbia University Teachers College, 1949).

33. The obvious exception is bonded indebtedness, which is discussed at length later in the chapter.

34. For a graphically descriptive narrative of the operation of one state's full state funding scheme that also includes educational facilities, see John A. Thompson, "Funding and Spending in Paradise: Notes on the Hawaii Model of Educational Finance," *Journal of Education Finance* (Fall 1986), 282–294.

35. Thomas H. Jones, *Introduction to School Finance: Technique and Social Policy* (New York: Macmillan, 1985), 122.

36. State loan structures have varied widely by individual state. For example, a state might choose to use tax revenues to make direct loans to districts, in which case the state can be said to impose taxation for the purpose of loaning those same proceeds back to residents on a profit basis because state loans usually involve interest payments. In contrast, the state could choose to guarantee private loans, in which case the state exercises great power at virtually no cost because no state money is required unless districts default on debts. Alternatively, the state could choose to sell debt instruments in the marketplace and then loan the proceeds to local districts, either at discount or for profit. While the options are complex, states possess great flexibility as long as no laws are violated.

37. For some districts, federal aid is available. As discussed in Chapter 2, aid to federally impacted areas is available under PL 815 and PL 874.

38. A fairly large body of literature exists about equity in capital outlay and facility finance. See for example *Journal of Education Finance,* David S. Honeyman, R. Craig Wood, and David C. Thompson, eds. (Winter and Spring 1988) for two issues devoted entirely to the topic of capital outlay finance in the 50 states; see also David C. Thompson and G. Kent Stewart, *Achievement of Equity in Capital Outlay Financing: A Policy Analysis for the States* (Charleston, W.Va.: ERIC Monograph Series, 1989); for technical reports, see for example David S. Honeyman et al., *A Technical Report on the Condition of School Buildings in Rural and Small School Districts,* funded by the Kansas State University Bureau of General Research and the National Rural Education Association (Manhattan, Kans.: Kansas State University Bureau of General Research, 1988). For specific state capital outlay analyses, David C. Thompson and William E. Camp, "Analysis of Equity in Capital Outlay Funding Mechanisms in Kansas," *Journal of Education Finance* (Winter 1988), 253–263; R. Craig Wood and Robert W. Ruch, "A Model for Distributing Capital Outlay Funds in Indiana," *Planning & Changing* (Fall 1986), 165–179; and R. Craig Wood and Robert W. Ruch, "A Reexamination of Capital Outlay Distribution in Indiana," *Journal of Education Finance* (Winter 1988), 240–252.

39. Although sinking funds as described here are not common, most states permit districts to accumulate monies in capital outlay funds. The difference rests in the conceptual distinc-

tion between a sinking fund and a capital outlay fund. A sinking fund is generally as nonspecific as suggested here. In contrast, a capital outlay fund is considered an operating fund for annual operation of the district. Thus, a sinking fund would more clearly intend to accumulate large sums of money for major projects, while a capital outlay fund is generally never large enough to pay for such projects. In practice, however, many districts are able to accumulate large capital outlay funds—for example, the authors are professionally acquainted with several small school districts with enrollments less than 300 students that have in excess of $5 million in capital outlay funds that are being used primarily to generate interest income. Thus, while sinking funds may not be legal in many states, school districts can often find ways to operate other funds in a manner highly similar to a true sinking fund.

40. According to one school of thought, there is no more sure risk than the full faith and credit of a government agency. For example, despite the huge national debt incurred by the United States, it is logical to believe that buying U.S. securities is wise because default can basically only occur by collapse of the entire government itself. Although the federal government is not backing local school bond issues, the same logic can be applied because the local school district can scarcely afford to default. Although such logic might be somewhat faulty to public policy critics, history has illustrated the strength of school bonds, because even during the Great Depression less than 2% of school district bonds actually defaulted.

41. David Hitchcock, "How School District Bonds Are Rated," *School Business Affairs* 58:2 (1992), 15–18.

42. It should be recognized that bonding is an entire professional field in itself and cannot be fully treated here in terms of both exhaustiveness or nuances. For example, small private investors do not usually participate in a direct bond sale where large units are purchased for resale. Instead, common citizens wishing to purchase school bonds usually do so through a broker, mutual bond fund, discount brokerage, or other investment counselor.

43. Chapter 7 describes the structure of debt retirement funds in greater detail.

44. Generally speaking, any debt in excess of the statutory and/or constitutional limitation is void. See for example Bradford v. San Francisco, 112 Cal. 537, 44 P.912 (1896) and Windsor v. Des Moines, 81 N.W. 476 (1900).

45. Defining legal debt capacity is highly state-specific. For example, one state defines assessed valuation for general fund purposes as the sum of all properties as appraised under a constitutionally mandated classification scheme wherein an assessment rate of 12% of market value is applied to residential property, 30% of use value for agricultural land, 30% of market value on commercial and industrial and utility properties, and 20% of value on commercial and industrial machinery and equipment. On the other hand, that state defines assessed valuation for bonding purposes as the assessed valuation as previously defined plus market value of all business aircraft and farm machinery within the district.

46. Anticipating the correct chemistry for passing a bond issue is one of two major responsibilities of the district. Resubmitting the question to voters is a common occurrence throughout the United States, but it must be remembered that each election costs many thousands of dollars. As a consequence, the value of expert planning cannot be overstressed. The other responsibility, of course, is correctly determining the district's needs.

47. Generally, investors may be investment companies that buy bonds for resale or individuals with the financial security to work in complex financial markets.

48. School districts, like other municipal agencies, routinely engage in advance refunding of bond issues. Callable bonds allow districts to refund (refinance) bonds before maturity if interest rates fall enough to warrant refunding.

49. I.R.C. § 148(f)(2) (1986).

50. I.R.C. § 148(f)(4)(C) (1986).

51. I.R.C. § 148(f)(4)(B) (II) (1986).

52. I.R.C. § 148(e) (1986).

53. Glen I. Earthman, "Facility Planning and Management," in *Principles of School Business Management,* R. Craig Wood, ed. (Reston, Va.: Association of School Business Officials, 1986), 612.

54. The mechanics of enrollment projection are discussed in Chapter 6.

55. Council of Educational Facility Planners, International, *Guide for Planning Educational Facilities* (Columbus, OH: CEFPI, 1976), 11.

56. It should be clearly stated that such requirements are protections rather than burdens. No administrator is qualified to design facility modifications, either from a knowledge or liability perspective. It should be remembered that paying for such services may be expensive, but it is always cheaper than paying for mistakes, which can at least ruin professional careers and at worst endanger lives. Like professional services such as accounting and auditing discussed in other chapters, the administrator should regard all such fees as a form of insurance.

57. For an overall discussion of state procedures in the selection of professional services, see R. Craig Wood, "Competitive Bidding of Architectural Services," *School Business Affairs* 51:7 (1985), 49–51.

58. CEFPI, *Guide for Planning Educational Facilities,* 48.

59. Ibid., 49.

60. See Chapter 9 for discussion of bidding on public works contracts and professional services and Chapter 10 for the topic of liability as applied in this discussion.

61. A normal contractual arrangement under the standard contract recommended by the American Institute of Architects (AIA) calls for payment of 5% on signing an agreement for services, with additional payments totaling 15% on completion of schematic design, 35% upon design development, 75% on completion of construction documents, 80% upon completion of bidding and negotiation, and 100% on construction. Other agreements can also be negotiated.

62. Reasons for in-house decisions have been discussed in earlier chapters. As such analysis applies to facilities, the logic of advantage argues (a) school employees wages are usually less than comparable wages in the private sector, (b) employees can be dispatched to needed locations quickly, (c) the nature and scope of work by maintenance employees requires a high degree of flexibility and skills, (d) school employees have loyalty and understanding of the educational process and its overall needs, and (e) many school districts are located in communities that do not have an abundance of competitive organizations to bid on such work contracts. The logic of disadvantage argues (a) to have certain skills on-hand, there may be a degree of idle time as these specialists are not likely to be utilized continuously, (b) in small school districts it is impractical to assume the overhead involved with having specialists in many areas, and (c) the work of persons who can do a little of everything may be significantly inferior to outside specialists.

63. Custodial operations are generally site-placed under general control of the building principal.

64. For a more extensive development of standards, see David C. Thompson, *Educational Facility Equity and Adequacy: Roosevelt.*

65. It should be emphasized that 4% is used in the context of ordinary maintenance and does not anticipate the existence of deferred maintenance problems. In other words, districts without significant problems should expect to spend at least 4% of their budgets to prevent problems from occurring. Obviously, districts with a backlog of unmet needs cannot realistically expect such a small amount to correct these problems. Similarly, districts with new facilities can expect to spend less—at least for a short while.

66. Numerous different formulas are available in the professional literature. See, for example, Frederick W. Hill and James W. Colmey, *School Business Administration in the Smaller Community* (Minneapolis: T. S. Denison & Co., 1964).

67. Based on Frederick W. Hill and James W. Colmey, *School Business Administration in the Smaller Community* (Minneapolis: T. S. Denison & Co., 1964), 377.

68. Henry H. Linn, "School Plant Operation and Maintenance," in *School Business Administration,* ed. Henry H. Linn (New York: Ronald Press, 1956), 401.

69. Wisconsin, *Children in Peril,* 4.

ADDITIONAL READINGS

American Education Finance Association. *Managing Limited Resources: New Demands on Public School Management.* L. Dean Webb and Van D Mueller, eds. 5th Annual Yearbook of the American Education Finance Association. Cambridge, Mass.: Ballinger, 1984.

American Institute of Architects. *State Requirements for School Construction.* Washington, D.C.: American Institute of Architects, 1987.

Association of School Business Officials, International. *Principles of School Business Management.* R. Craig Wood, ed. Reston, Va.: Association of School Business Officials, 1986.

Castaldi, Basil. *Educational Facilities: Planning, Remodeling, and Management.* Boston: Allyn & Bacon, 1977.

Council of Educational Facility Planners, International. *Guide For Planning Educational Facilities.* Columbus, Ohio: CEFPI, 1987.

Hawkins, Harold. *Appraisal Guide for School Facilities.* Midland, Mich.: Pendell Publishing, 1976.

Johnson, Robert. *Capital Budgeting.* Dubuque, Iowa: Kendall/Hunt Publishing, 1970.

Piele, Philip, and John Hall. *Budgets, Bonds, and Ballots: Voting Behavior in School Finance.* Lexington, Mass.: Heath, 1973.

CHAPTER 13

Planning for Technology in Fiscal Decision Making

CHAPTER THEME

- Although education has seen much evolution, there are few instances where change has occurred so rapidly as in the development and application of electronic technology. Because schools must both use technology to meet demands for productivity and accountability, and assume leadership in preparing young people to live in a technological age, it is important for administrators to understand the increasing role of technology in the school setting.

CHAPTER OUTLINE

- An overview of enduring computer environments to help administrators see beyond the high cost of planned obsolescence

- An overview of school automation design criteria that can be used to describe information management systems networks and their relationship to modern school operations

- Applications of computer-based technology that relate to the accountability and productivity functions of modern schools

CHAPTER OBJECTIVE

- A broader perspective on technology planning, and a better understanding of how the finance and productivity functions of education must be linked in effective schools of the future

The spread of communications technology is creating an information-based economy structured differently than the current industrial economy. These two economies have a complex relationship that will become increasingly evident in the future. Among the more dramatic future events shaping society will be science and technology determining global economic leadership, greater use of information technology as a teaching and learning aid, rapid turnover rate in new technologies, further integration of video, audio, and data transmission into single fiber-optic systems, greater pervasiveness of expert systems and artificial intelligence, a wider line between technological haves and have-nots, and information overload resulting in degradation of the quality of information.

United Way, What Lies Ahead: Countdown to the 21st Century

Rapid change has become the single most obvious hallmark of American society on the threshold of the twenty-first century. While many changes are the result of new realities relating to economic and social and political evolution in an advanced society, few are as dramatic as the technological changes that have occurred in the last two decades. As the data opening this chapter reveal,[1] technology is now driving economic, social, and political realities, with an impact comparable to the meaning of basic literacy in an earlier era. By all accounts, participation in technology will be as crucial to future survival as learning to read was for earlier generations who witnessed the transition from an agrarian society to the present industrial age. While technology takes many forms, the most fundamental change is in the birth of the information age, in which knowledge is power.

Obviously, schools are profoundly affected by such technological change. Highly apparent is the reality that schools must be both leaders and followers in technology because schools prepare young citizens for survival in emerging economies, and schools are themselves consumers of technological advancement. Increasingly, educators at all levels are being asked to make decisions that require data from a variety of sources, and those decisions are inevitably involved in the finance arena because all decisions are ultimately fiscal that in turn impact the school's productivity. Whether it is a teacher serving on a school site council discussing effectiveness distribution patterns for instructional funds, a parent on the school advisory board evaluating requests for special money to support a project to improve the quality of reading programs, a building principal developing a site budget plan, or the fiscal officer analyzing the effect of next year's projected tax rate increase, this new and expanding information role requires that school professionals have access to data that is increasingly available only through sophisticated technology. While many technologies contribute to a school's productivity, the most fundamentally important is the ever-changing computer environment because of its ability to effectively and efficiently gather and analyze information critical to wise decision processes.

Future administrators therefore must be highly knowledgeable about the rapidly expanding development of information technology for successful operation of individual building sites and entire school districts. As the demand for school site management continues to increase, administrators will be faced with integrating classroom instruction management systems with administrative applications historically reserved only to central office operations. The combined effect of rapid technological change and new demands for accountability and improved school performance is thus almost certain to force schools into becoming both leaders and followers in technology because instructional productivity data is destined to drive financial decisions in schools. Unfortunately, most school districts are poorly prepared to engage in technological production models, making acquisition of such skills a prerequisite for survival.

Because information technology is power, this chapter presents an overview of major concerns important to administrators confronting technological change in their lives. Although technology is a vast field in itself, the chapter focuses on three areas that relate information technology to the instructional mission of schools through the support function of fiscal operations. Because administrators are generally far too dependent on sales personnel in applying technology to school settings, the chapter first presents an overview of enduring computer environments to help administrators see beyond the glitter of planned obsolescence. While such discussion may seem afield from ordinary interests of school finance, basic technological literacy is overdue because schools have repeatedly fallen prey to poor investment and overspending for technology. The chapter next presents an overview of school automation design criteria that can be used to describe information management systems networks and the resulting requirements for modern school operation. Finally, the chapter presents several examples of computer technology applications appropriate for use in various planning functions. Unlike traditional school finance texts, the focus of this chapter is on *integrating* finance and administrative functions with instructional requirements for effective decision making.

INFORMATION TECHNOLOGY ENVIRONMENTS

Historically, the development of administrative uses of computers in education has focused on school business and financial reporting needs and has followed the evolution of business and industrial uses of technology. Originally, information management systems were designed and developed as classical centralized computer operations. As such, information processing was characterized as access, control, processing, and data storage concentrated at one location under the control of top management. As schools began to recognize the need to organize and manipulate data, the centralized business and industry model was readily available as a natural template to be applied to education information systems. Because of their huge data needs, larger school districts were the first to experiment with such technology, adopting the business model wherein multiple users gained access to the main system by remote job entry devices or real-time terminals. Although such systems in which remote entry users had their jobs processed in a batch mode through time-sharing arrangements were awkward, the capacity of schools to handle information was dramatically expanded through technology.

With the development of smaller but more powerful machines and improved computer networks, schools moved a step away from centralized systems toward more decentralized information processing. The centralized data systems typified by huge computers filling entire rooms evolved into more decentralized configurations where storage and data control were still maintained at a central site but processing could be accomplished at individual locations. As user involvement and technical understanding increased, demands for quick access to data also grew rapidly as districts discovered that information creates uses for itself. Increased demand for data and processing capabilities, however, created challenges for the central storage philosophy that characterized both centralized and decentralized systems.[2] As a result, many centralized systems were converted to hybrid environments supporting a variety of machines and software, which allowed some sites to store and process data independently, while other sites continued traditional time-share and batch procedures. Applications of information technology were thus available either as centralized or decentralized computer information systems. As might be expected, however, problems inherent to both environments have developed.

Benefits and Problems with Centralized Environments

Although there has been movement toward decentralized information environments, the long-standing existence of centralized systems has resulted in most school districts following an arrangement such as the one illustrated in the upper half of Figure 13.1. In a centralized configuration, the main computer stores and processes all data with interactive or batch terminals at other strategic locations. Under these conditions the system usually requires either a mainframe or minicomputer, with considerable cost associated with such large and sophisticated equipment commonly justified by economies of scale in hardware, software, and personnel that are achieved by concentrating unduplicated data storage and operations in a central location. Control,

FIGURE 13.1   Centralized and decentralized environments

CENTRALIZED ENVIRONMENT

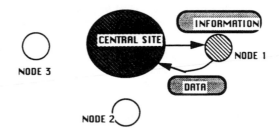

DECENTRALIZED ENVIRONMENT

THE ISSUE OF INCOMPATIBILITY

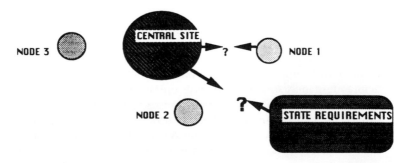

security, standards, availability, and data integrity are also more easily assured in a central computing system. These benefits are valid considerations, but there are at least three major concerns associated with centralization that must be considered by schools in initiating or redesigning school data structures.

First, centralized data services represent a very large investment in hardware. Although hardware prices have dropped in recent years, start-up costs are still prohibitive. A mainframe or minicomputer suitable for use in large centralized data applications can easily run many thousands of dollars at the initial purchase, and in some instances, several million dollars. Second, people costs are also great, because the price of technical talent required to maintain hardware has increased dramatically. People costs also include the price of writing and running sophisticated specialized software applications that are not available as prepackaged commercial products. The problems of hardware and software have been exacerbated by partial decentralization, in that many computing centers are using emulators to allow old expensive programs to run on newer machines because the programs were too expensive or too complex to rewrite. As a result, the costs of such sophistication and subvention have generally more than offset declines in hardware prices, and the success of subvention is highly questionable because such attempts are always efforts to artificially adjust for basic incompatibility, as seen in the bottom half of Figure 13.1.

A third concern relates to a self-fulfilling prophecy inherent to the nature of data itself. As data become available, the need for more data grows and users become dependent on data for daily decision processes. Additionally, as more tasks are automated the tasks themselves become linked together into complex interdependent data files. As the system grows and one user's data becomes the input to another program, modifications to the code in one application can adversely affect the operation of another application. At the extreme, such an interactive situation can bring the entire data operation to a halt. Additionally, expansion of a centralized computer system is finite and additional requirements may not be possible if the limits of the system's architecture have been reached. Eventually, demands on a system will exceed its capacity. In a centralized environment, failure of the information system results in both mechanical failure and high levels of dissatisfaction with data processing capabilities.

Centralized information systems are therefore highly finite despite their larger initial capacity. Because of high start-up costs, system limits, inherent flaws in quasi-decentralized environments, and development of lower cost technologies in the microcomputer arena, school districts have had to look beyond centralized data systems to satisfy their information requirements. The search has increasingly focused on efforts to more efficiently engage decentralization through technologies that attempt to overcome the inherent deficiencies of artificial emulation.

Benefits and Problems with Decentralized Environments

In time, all school districts face the problem of information system degradation. Degradation occurs when a system has grown too large, too cumbersome, or too slow and is no longer responsive to the needs of users. Because centralized environments are common and because the cost of replacing aging mainframe and minicomputers represents an enormous capital expense for most school districts, degradation has become a serious problem representing wasted money and lost opportunity by maintaining systems that have become archaic. Powerful inexpensive microcomputers that can be placed on desktops at numerous locations linked by high-speed communication devices, however, have enabled districts to take advantage of newer technologies designed to overcome the problems inherent to centralized information systems, thus allowing development of a new mode of decentralization known as distributed environments.

Although attempts at decentralization have often been made using a centralized system with remote terminals, true distributed environments using new microtechnology represent genuine advancement in information management systems. As shown in Figure 13.2, a distributed environment has computers in different locations that communicate and process data cooperatively. Obviously different from a centralized data system, a distributed environment is also vastly different from older conceptions of decentralization. Whereas decentralization was a limited attempt to distribute select operations of a centralized system across a small number of remote sites, a distributed environment is an effort to distribute information and functions across a much wide group of users. As will be seen in later discussion, the conceptual difference between centralized, decentralized, and distributed environments has the potential for enormous implications in the daily operation of school organizations.

The benefits associated with distributed environments significantly reduce the limitations of a centralized system. Start-up costs under current microtechnology are quite low by comparison to mainframe systems, and the availability of software in user-friendly shells has eliminated much of the human costs associated with programming special applications. Importantly, these systems are designed for decentralized interface with all other system components, eliminating the awkward attempts to overlay decentralization on systems never intended to function in such a mode. Most importantly, a distributed system has no finite limit on expansion because these systems are designed for expandability via the relatively low cost of adding computers and telecommunications devices and appropriate software. Actual decentralization is achieved by the synergistic effect of combining database management systems with data communications networks in efficient modes, making the current generation of

FIGURE 13.2   The distributed environment

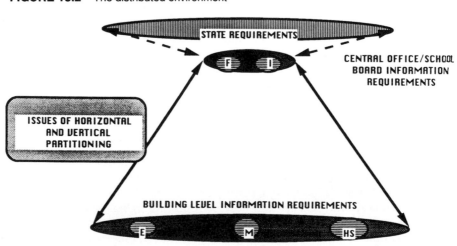

microtechnology a breakthrough in data manipulation for school districts because of reliability and resilience through replicated software applications, hardware environments, telecommunications modalities, and data.[3]

The benefits of decentralized systems are valid considerations for districts evaluating current structures or contemplating new information management systems. As with all management decisions, however, there are at least four major concerns associated with distributed data environments that school districts should consider before deciding to invest heavily in the requisite quantity of hardware, software, and training. These are *access* to data, *processing* of data, *security* and *control,* and the actual *distributing* of the data itself.

Access to Data.   The most fundamental characteristic of distributed systems rests in access to data. In sharp contrast to centralized systems where control of data is paramount, distributed systems presume wide usage by competent vested personnel. However, a conflict between data processing managers and users may occur when a decision to distribute operations is made. Data processing personnel in large district operations are often uncomfortable with the idea of offering other people or users free and open access to ''their'' data. Even in small district operations, users often perceive autonomous control by the central office as a restraint that prevents them from exploiting more advanced applications of information technology that would permit achievement of a desired level of internal productivity. To experiment with processing data for effective decision making, users must first have access to appropriate data to engage in such analytical behavior.

While anyone can appreciate the need for confidentiality of data, it is sometimes very difficult for key persons to gain wide access to information that in fact would be most useful in decision-making in schools. Although administrators are key players and usually have ready access to such data, the individuals most in need of information are classroom teachers who generally do not have wide access. This is particularly problematic since districts are beginning to demand that student performance data be used to improve learning outcomes. It is obvious, however, that teachers cannot make competent decisions if locked out of databases containing information on students. For example, teachers in school systems that have decided to design Instructional Information Systems (IISs)[4] are better positioned to make wise pedagogical choices because data housed in a variety of locations are made available to those persons most responsible for instruction of students. For example, data in IISs typically allow teachers to track and evaluate student and class performance and prescribe individualized instruction alternatives. Information in an IIS would usually include unit test results, homework, class participation, grades on final examinations, socioeconomic and home information, standardized test results, and more. Utilizing these data, however, requires an IIS and wide user access outside the central office domain — conditions most districts have neither the technology nor the authority structures to provide.

When combined with appropriate budget information, data available in IISs provide teachers with a sound basis for effective educational planning for the individual student, the school site, and the entire district. In fact, the examples of instructional productivity analysis seen later in this chapter assume access to both administrative and instructional data on students. However, to implement distributed systems of any type, fundamental conflicts over data access must be resolved at the outset. As it presently stands, districts face a long struggle in achieving such levels of technological sophistication because years of centralized systems have made data access a restricted area.[5]

Data Processing.   A second concern of distributed systems relates to intended and unintended data processing. One of the benefits of a centralized system is the ability to protect data from accidental loss or alteration. In contrast, a characteristic of distributed environments is the ability to manipulate data from virtually all locations, making control issues crucial to protect data integrity and accuracy of reports. Standards must be set and enforced to achieve integration of all parts of the system, because access to confidential records and the integrity and security of data are more difficult to control on microcomputers and telecommunications data due to hackers and viruses. While distributed systems are intended to make data available for appropriate processing, the danger lies in improper handling or loss of data in the absence of adequate safeguards.

Most often such safeguards involve system protections that allow access or downloading of data and individual site manipulation while preserving and protecting data integrity in the host computer. Entry generally requires access codes, and users responsible for running any processes that can directly access and alter data must be trained in correct use of the computer system and various application programs. While the benefits of distributed environments are well worth the precautions that must be taken, such preventive planning involves commitment by boards of education, administrators, managers, and all users to extensive training procedures.

Distributing Control.   A third concern of distributed environments relates to control of individual components of the system. In a centralized system, control of data entry and operations rests in one location and is carefully protected against unauthorized or inexpert entry. In contrast, a decentralized environment diffuses responsibility to those users responsible for data processing at each location using the component. For example, management at each node of a distributed environment would control data entry and operations, interaction with the system, program development, logistics, operating methods, and future system development. This does not imply that data processing will lose control over the system as a whole; rather, it does imply that under the direction of the central office, control is widely shared among authorized users of the system. The central office computer will become the official repository of archival, summary, and systemwide data with responsibility for processing reports required for systemwide operation. Data must eventually flow upward within an organization to give central office decision makers the best information available,[6] but it is a basic premise of distributed systems that control of data is no longer an exclusive central office function.

Distributing Data.   A fourth concern involves distribution of data from the perspectives of effectiveness and efficiency. Because decentralized environments obviously require data to be distributed, decisions must be made regarding distribution, centralization, and replication. Because data distribution in educational settings is intended to permit technical experts to make wise decisions that facilitate educational and support services, data should reside at the level most capable of using it to make decisions, assigned to the appropriate local nodes so that the local database management system (DBMS) appears transparent to the total system. Unlike remote access to centralized systems, transparency ensures that global queries, transactions, and updates written in the common user language with standard protocols can migrate to different local DBMSs to execute their tasks without encountering problems.[7] Unless such ability is carefully structured, degradation of data quality will result.

In general, data can be distributed according to use. Data used for retrieval at all nodes may be replicated at each node to reduce communication costs. Frequently updated data may be centralized or, if most of the references for certain parts of the database are made at a certain node, that part of the database can reside at that node.[8] One likely arrangement, referred to as horizontal and vertical partitioning of data, is determined by its functional description and the users that require access. A vertical partition is the separation of different but interdependent subsystems. Payroll, food service and transportation reporting, and site-specific (elementary or high school) grade reporting are examples of vertical partitioning. In these instances, vertical partitioning would result in distribution of programs and data only to the appropriate node.[9] In contrast, horizontal partitioning is the separation of compatible interchangeable subsystems, such as processing attendance by all school buildings, in which application programs and data are distributed to all nodes performing the attendance function. Because partitioning not only improves distribution efficiency but also reduces accidental and improper access and treatment of data, appropriate system-wide availability is assured.

Although distributed environments present significant problems with access to data, processing of data, security and control, and distribution, they are no more problematic than archaic centralized data systems that consume vast amounts of resources through initial start-up and ongoing mechanical and human maintenance. Distributed environments seem more reasonable for schools in a technological era because the philosophical underpinning of providing information to experts in the field is consistent with the basic work of education. But because centralized systems are still prevalent and because attempts to meld centralized environments with data distribution concepts have had only awkward success, it may be argued that schools need to completely rethink and reimplement data management environments for a new era of school productivity. Because schools have not progressed very far in such directions, the next section revolves around preparing administrators to deal with school automation analysis in a distributed information environment.

SCHOOL AUTOMATION ANALYSIS

The use of a problem-solving technique called systems analysis has proved effective when dealing with the design of information systems for business and industry. Like many other advanced planning tools, however, systems analysis has been only infrequently applied to the complex data requirements of school systems. Schools are excellent candidates for systems analysis, however, because this planning technique calls for analyzing the data needs of an organization in relation to the tasks it performs. For example, systems analysis would consider data processing capabilities for schools including attendance monitoring, budgeting, scheduling, computer-assisted instruction (CAI) and tools required to analyze students' learning and career aptitudes. Unfortunately, few information systems currently in place in schools have used such a comprehensive method for integrating information throughout the school environment.

The lack of a systems approach to data management planning is not unique to schools, but given constraints of school budgets and the diverse and conflicting requirements of a school system, the absence of such planning is complex and can negatively affect students. As stated at the outset of the chapter, lack of systems analysis has led to much overspending for technology in school districts primarily because administrators have been too dependent on sales personnel to perform the district's needs assessment. Consequently, the remainder of this chapter uses a systems approach to school automation analysis, beginning with an analysis of the current status of information technology development in schools to better understand their position in the application of technology. Once the current status is identified, the second step is an overview of computer network options available for implementing an integrated distributed data system in the view that administrators cannot depend on anyone else to competently know their needs. Once understanding and options are in place, the third step allows for conceptualization of a model of school automation. Finally, the fourth step permits application of the model of school automation through examples of integration of the administrative and instructional functions in school productivity questions. The balance of the chapter is thus application of a systems approach to fully integrated data management in a modern complex school environment.

Information Technology Development in Schools

Unfortunately, school districts often "automate" administrative and instructional operations without a coherent long-range plan for integrating these two separate but very related information systems. When these functions are automated using microcomputers, two manufacturers or system types with different software and growth commitments are usually considered. Typically, schools favor the IBM platform for administrative information management purposes, and the instructional side generally favors the Apple-Macintosh product line. Because unduplicated information useful to instructional productivity generally resides in both administrative and instruction databases, teachers and other professionals frequently do not have easy access to information that may be important to the wide range of capabilities and motivation encountered among students. While part of the lack of availability is appropriate access to data as discussed earlier, another significant part is due to lack of understanding that the basic incompatibility of these rival computer families will inhibit full integration of the multiple functions of school districts.

Failure to understand full integration of district functions is partly a result of lack of accountability structures and partly a product of the process by which schools become sophisticated in technological issues. As with other types of learning, it can be expected that knowledge and use will progress from an entry level to more highly sophisticated needs. As stated earlier, a remarkable phenomenon of data services is that data creates its own uses limited only by availability and ease of access. As a result, the growth and development of computer acceptance and implementation in organizations commonly follows a set pattern called a growth curve. First described by Nolan,[10] a growth curve represents the extent of user interaction as data systems proliferate over time. As seen in Figure 13.3, the shape of the curve indicates four stages of growth encompassing *initiation, expansion, formalization,* and *maturity,* with each stage characterized by identifiable behaviors and leading to the next stage. For schools, these stages are poignantly descriptive of information technology development, and as will be seen later, unplanned progression through these stages has significantly impeded development of accountability structures in schools.

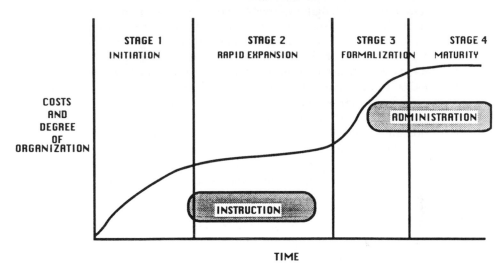

FIGURE 13.3 Maturation of information systems

The *initiation stage* of the growth curve is marked by recognition of the need for automation, followed by introduction of one or more computers to the district usually to serve the needs of one person, a single function, or a single department, thus reflecting little extended planning activity. If a data processing department exists in the organization, there is high probability that the department may not even be consulted in computer purchases at this stage. Very often, there is no consideration given to maintenance planning, compatibility with other internal or external data systems, or extensibility of future functions. If the initiation stage continues over a period of time, the result is high expenditures, incompatible equipment and software, and inadequate support for each system. All too frequently, school districts exhibit a long period of initiation wherein classrooms become cluttered with low-end computers never intended to be compatible with other administrative units in the district that contain information vital to instructional improvement. While most districts in the nation have moved beyond the initiation stage, many of these characteristics are still highly visible in a very large number of districts.

While the second stage, *rapid expansion,* may overlap with the initiation phase in many ways, it is noteworthy because of the proliferation of data processors that follows after the first introduction. Once a few computers are in place and several persons have become comfortable with the equipment, the expansion stage usually continues the path of little formal planning coupled with the purchase of many computers and a wide variety of software. The expansion stage is further marked by little forethought for integration of the various parts into a systemwide problem-solving tool. This stage is further characterized by rapidly increasing hardware and software expenditures and the first realization that proliferation is out of control. Frustration is highly evident in this stage as users are faced with too many software packages, each with a different set of commands, too little hardware training, incompatible hardware utilizing different operating platforms, and unrealistic expectations of the data system's capabilities. As the expansion stage continues, management is plagued with increasing maintenance costs for equipment from multiple vendors. The result of failure to use a systems approach to data management is most often equipment and software that may be impossible to integrate, resulting in additional purchases to either replace dysfunctional systems or to further attempt bridging incompatible environments. All too often, this stage ultimately results in higher costs and lower equipment usage. Unfortunately, the vast majority of districts today are still deeply engaged in the rapid expansion stage.

The third stage, *formalization,* is evident when the need to integrate information functions is belatedly realized. At this point, data processing and systems analysts must be brought together to integrate hardware and software, to standardize applications, and to set workable policies for information system purchasing and utilization. The formalization stage is often highly stressful for an organization as service is disrupted while applications are integrated, a moratorium on purchases of new equipment is enforced, and standards and policies are set. Once the organization has successfully integrated its information functions, however, a fourth stage, *maturity,* is entered that is marked by planned growth and mature system use in an environment structured around uniform standards and policies. Although many school systems are beginning to move to the formalization stage, few have truly begun to bring all the pieces together, and only a few school systems have actually moved into the maturity stage.

Information technology development in schools remains at a fairly low level of sophistication, not only because of lingering centralized systems, failed attempts at decentralization, and lack of knowledge among district leaders about technological options, but more importantly because of failure to understand the power of information systems that integrate the administrative and instructional functions of school districts. For school automation analysis to make teachers more effective, data on students must be available in a format that accesses all relevant segments of the information system in the district. For example, the natural intersection of student records and attendance data requires communication between the administrative and instruction functions, just as the computers on which CAI resides and the computers on which related administrative records exist must be able to easily communicate with each other. Because little such interaction now occurs, the time is ripe for redesign and progress. The key to such an interfaced distributed environment rests in redesigning school district information systems to include computer networks that facilitate such communication, thus administrators must be knowledgeable about network options.

Computer Network Options

Part of the problem identified earlier is that administrators have been captive to the recommendations of sales consultants who understandably promote their product configuration as the best market option available. While schools will always depend to some extent on sales staff in comparing available products, such dependency needs to be reduced through technological literacy that identifies benefits and drawbacks to various options. As a result, administrators need to understand the concept of networking and to be knowledgeable of strengths and limitations inherent to the most common network options under current microtechnology. From this discussion, it will be possible later to develop a conceptual framework for school district automation.

The Network Concept.   The concept of a computer network is to distribute information across legitimate users who share common needs for information. Several types of computer networks exist, but all are intended to provide prompt and reliable data to appropriate users.[11] At the highest conceptual level, a Wide Area Network (WAN) is a communication system extending over large distances, such as an entire school district. Mechanically, these networks often employ multiple communication link technologies, such as copper wire cables, coaxial cables, fiber-optic links, digital switched circuits, and microwave and satellite links. They can also integrate multiple school districts and educational agencies and consortiums at the state and federal levels. A Local Area Network (LAN) communicates over shorter distances, such as within a single setting or a city, and employs many of the same technologies as a WAN. Typically, a WAN uses leased lines or communications owned by a public carrier or communication provider, while a LAN is usually owned and administered by a single agency, such as a school district. Uses for both WANs and LANs are enormous, ranging from internal communication and data planning to external communication on topics such as electronically submitting prepared budget documents to state agencies for state aid reimbursement purposes.

Presently, there are three types of public digital service computer communication networks available.[12] In *circuit switching,* a complete route of connected links from the source host computer to the receiving host computer is established prior to initiation of data transmission. These connected links remain "intact" and dedicated to this transmission until released by both the source and the receiver. As with a telephone network for voice communication, the data route is established by a special signaling message that finds its way through the network from the source to receiver, seizing channel links along the route as it proceeds. Once the route is completed, a return signal is sent to the source to indicate successful transmission of the image data. During the entire transmission, the source and receiver have a continuous connecting circuit.[13] When the transmission is completed, signaling on the network disconnects the link.

The same general concept governs *message switching* (also called "store-and-forward" switching) wherein differences relate to method of data transfer. In the previous mode of circuit switching, communications consist of bursts of high data rates followed by no data transmission. This implies that average use of such communication paths is low because of the extremely high rate of speed when transmission is occurring. In message switching, a different transmission method is present because there is no complete path established prior to actual transmission. Rather, the sending host computer transmits a message to a switching center where the message is temporarily stored in a buffer. The stored message is kept in the buffer until the line to another switching center is available. When this line becomes available, the stored message is forwarded. This process is continued until the data arrives at the receiving host computer. The advantage of this technique is that link utilization is high because one link may be involved in sending data to many host computers. The disadvantage is that long messages require large buffers. A further disadvantage may be that even if a link becomes available, a switching computer will not begin transmission until the message has been completely received.

A third network type called *packet switching* subdivides messages into small packets, typically 1,024 bits, with messages transmitted packet by packet.[14] Packet switching is a store-and-forward system where each packet is stored in buffers at the nodes on the network and then forwarded. Packets may follow different routes on the network and may arrive at the receiving host computer out of sequence. For this reason, all packets are numbered so that they can be reassembled into the original message. Packet switching for messages of varying length provides the advantage of dynamic and fair allocation of the WAN's available bandwidth. The end-to-end transmission delay is smaller than that of message switching due to the division of the message into many smaller packets and transmission over multiple path lengths. Packet switching also requires smaller storage at each node on the network compared to message switching. Each packet includes information bits as well as additional bits known as overhead information, which are used to identify the destination of the packet, the source of the packet, user identification for billing purposes, synchronization bits, and numbering bits for proper reassembly of packets at the receiving host computer. Packet switching has several disadvantages in that packet switching requires larger transmissions due to information bits and overhead bits, and hardware must be highly sophisticated to complete the packeting/depacketing process.

Regardless of the complexity of technologies involved in transmitting data, the network concept is invaluable to school districts because it is designed to share data among various legitimate users. The underlying technologies of transfer method are important to school administrators in that costs vary according to sophistication and in that some technologies are more common and enduring than others. With networking conceptually established, we can now look at several different types of networks that have significant differences along these lines.

Integrated Services Digital Network (ISDN).   Telephone networks are the oldest form of networking and were developed as an analog-voice-transmission system. The analog system was subsequently replaced by a digital system that was broadened to also include data and images in addition to voice transmission. The advent of digital signal processing technology and computer systems, digital switches, and digital transmission has gradually replaced electromechanical switches and the analog facilities used to support them. Advantages are sizable in that mechanical failure is less frequent, and speed and efficiency of service is increased severalfold.

Despite the fact that ISDN service is among the older technologies, it is expected that ISDN will provide a wide range of applications in a public end-to-end digital communications network in the future. For example, an ISDN socket in the home, classroom, or office of a school principal or superintendent would allow connection of telephones, microcomputers, display stations, and other ordinary devices well known to most people. The major benefit of such technology is its proven reliability, its availability, and its familiarity to most individuals. Given applicability to virtually any environment in which telephone lines are available, networks utilizing ISDN may increasingly provide an economical and pervasive medium for convenient information exchange.

Fiber-Optic Networks.   A current buzzword in educational circles is fiber-optic networks. Although talk about fiber optics is far greater than actual utilization, in all likelihood fiber optics will become as commonly used as ordinary telephone lines, if for no other reason than that communications utility companies are rapidly converting their service lines to fiber-optic cables in most parts of the country. As a consequence, school administrators will likely hear much about various devices employing fiber optics as such products become widely available on the market in the near future.

The primary reasons for conversion of communications services to fiber-optic transmission are economy, speed, and efficiency. Optical transmission has extended the available bandwidth in that space available for data transmission is increased. This has naturally resulted in increasing transmission speed and volume, with current systems' signaling rates operating between two and four gigabits/second.[15] The result of this higher transmission rate is that broad bandwidth services required for large-scale applications are now available, and the cost of using switched circuits is significantly reduced because equipment can more efficiently handle increased traffic at higher rates of speed. For school districts, widespread deployment of fiber-optic links has served to increase expectations for additional services that include a wider range of applications previously too expensive or unavailable by conventional transmission methods. At present, the greatest applications appear to be in the reduced costs of sustained data exchange across distances and the added ability to transmit multimedia images.

Local Area Networks.   While the foregoing discussion presumes that school districts need to transmit data across considerable distances, other network technology is available for shorter and more ordinary transmission purposes. Schools are increasingly looking for educational telecommunications systems that can serve sites within the same building, campus, or even the same city. Local area networks (LANs) are the most promising source of such communication and have the particular potential of economically supplying connectivity at very reasonable prices.

LANs supply a means for dedicated exchange in a data communications system and represent a particularly viable method for such connectivity since the transmission media is usually owned and administered by the agency implementing the system.[16] For example, using a LAN for telecommunications within a school district or a single building can provide interactive access to classrooms, workrooms, laboratories, and offices. LANs are capable of vastly improving teaching activities, such as retrieval of instructional materials from local or distant electronic databases and transmitting digital images for multimedia presentations, including simultaneous viewing at multiple sites. Because LANs can use supporting technologies such as ISDNs and fiber optics, the technical requirements for implementation are commonly available, and because they are the best current available technology for connectivity in a distributed environment that includes integration of all school district administrative and instructional operations, administrators should become familiar with the types of LANs that exist and the potential they hold for increased school productivity.

Types of Local Area Networks.   The importance of LANs in planning for distributed environments creates a further need for administrators to understand the most common system configurations commercially available. The three most commonly used configurations are the *star, bus,* and *ring* topologies, as shown in Figure 13.4. As will be briefly discussed later, combinations of these three principal designs can be used to build network configurations of almost infinite "shapes" based on the unique needs of a particular information-sharing system. Each design, however, has strengths and drawbacks that may affect the choices a district makes when considering the purchase of a communications network.

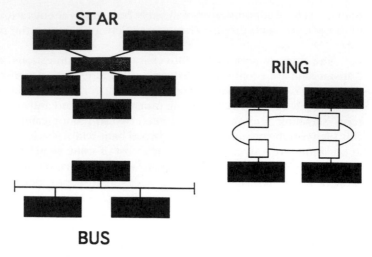

FIGURE 13.4   Local area network arrangements

Star Topology.   The star topology is the least commonly used design in information networks. Functionally, the center computer in the star topology usually performs the function of circuit switching. When two computers on different legs of the
star need to communicate, the center computer reserves a dedicated communication
line until the connection is broken. Although this configuration is less used in LANs
for a variety of efficiency reasons in the event of component failure, the star topology
is convenient when a controlling computer routes messages to slave terminals (not a
true network). Because the star configuration is less frequently used in networking,
administrators might want to carefully examine the needs their data systems will be
expected to serve to determine whether a star topology will appropriately meet their
system loads.

Bus Topology.   The bus topology, currently the most common type of LAN, is a
multipoint, packet-switched network with only one station at a time able to transmit a
packet containing the address of a destination. Each packet is broadcast to all stations
on the network and kept by the destination. Since multiple stations share a common
data link, a method of obtaining access to the medium for transmission must be established. When a station wishes to transmit a packet, it samples the carrier for usage. If
the carrier is not busy, it transmits the packet, but continues to sample the carrier for
possible collisions. If a collision is sensed, the station immediately stops transmission
and issues a jamming packet, while the other station, which has also attempted transmission, will also sense the collision. Both stations back off, wait a random amount of
time, and try again. Propagation delay is defined as the time it takes for the beginning
of a message to travel the greatest distance between two stations on the bus. Since it
is important for a station to detect a collision before the end of the transmission of a
packet, the time for transmission of a packet should be at least twice the propagation
delay.

The primary benefit of a bus configuration is that the bus currently represents
the most common type of network in the marketplace. The administrator can thus

expect that there are engineering preferences related to bus technology, and it is therefore also easier to compare product values. The primary drawback to the bus topology is that it suffers from undetermined waits for access to the station and is limited by its speed, usually two megabits per second (2Mbps). Unless an information management system is so sophisticated that such waits become noticeable, the bus topology represents an affordable state-of-the-art configuration.

Ring Topology.   As the name suggests, in a ring topology computers are connected in a circle with unidirectional communication. To function, each computer must have a repeater connected to two other repeaters forming the ring. The most common LAN ring control technique is the Token Ring first proposed in 1969. A message representing a "token" is placed on the ring. A station wishing to send a packet to another station must wait until it captures the token before transmitting. After transmission, the station reissues the token, allowing the next station to capture the ring if desired.

The main advantage to a token ring is the potential of providing fair access to all stations on the distributed system. Additionally, token rings can operate at either 4Mbps or 16Mbps and are thus two to four times faster than bus topologies. The principal drawback to token ring networks, however, is that they are costly to implement, require complicated token administration techniques, and result in loss of the entire network if one repeater fails.

Other Configurations.   In addition to the three most common network structures, two other configurations should be mentioned. The *Fiber Distributed Data Interface* (FDDI) deserves comment because it may become viable in the next generation of network connectivity. Although the FDDI protocol is still new, it shows promise for faster transmission using fiber-optic cable. This protocol still includes a ring topology, but can take advantage of the higher bandwidth of fiber-optic cable in transmission speeds of 100Mbps. The main disadvantage at this time is cost. Recent estimates put the cost of connecting computers with FDDI at $10,000 per individual unit. Costs may decline, however, as fiber-optic installations become more commonplace. At the present time, however, efforts to sell systems depending on FDDI should probably be viewed conservatively.

The second configuration that deserves mention is a combination of two earlier methods and is called a *star-ring* topology. This hybrid seeks to overcome one of the disadvantages of a ring topology related to system failure if a repeater fails. If there are many stations on the ring, locating a bad repeater may be a long and tedious job. The star-ring configuration uses a concentrator at a central location connecting multiple rings or subnets, each with fewer stations. The concentrator can include a built-in bridge/router between rings which can filter messages, sorting them into local and nonlocal traffic, and routing nonlocal packets to the correct subnet. The stations on a single ring have the advantage of deterministic waits to send, and the network administrator can isolate a nonfunctioning subnet in case of failure. School districts might still want to hesitate before adopting a star-ring topology, simply because the prevalence of bus topology in the marketplace should indicate to wise consumers that there will likely be fewer problems and more solutions in predominant topology. Perhaps good advice in technology is to never be the first or last to adopt an innovation.

The discussion to this point offers several conclusions that are vitally important to school districts. First, information management systems are a complex issue wherein it must be recognized that school productivity will increasingly require interfacing data between instruction and administrative functions. Second, it would appear that centralized environments have already served their best utility, and a decision to invest in a distributed environment would be more consistent with the work of schools wherein information is best lodged in the hands of experts in the trenches. Third, a distributed environment in a network configuration would appear to be the best option because of connectivity and ability to replace and expand parts of the system without total disruption. Fourth, emerging technologies such as fiber optics promise even greater efficiencies yet to be developed, and it is reassuring that these technologies are interfaceable with present networks without disruption or total obsolescence. Fifth, network topologies come in a variety of designs, and administrators are well advised to at least be able to ask intelligent questions to avoid premature costly purchases of incompatible or nonexpandable equipment. Sixth and finally, the decision to invest in technology should not be undertaken lightly. In sum, a systems analysis approach to technology that seeks a high level of integration of the various district functions is highly advisable.

A FRAMEWORK FOR INFORMATION MANAGEMENT

Given the rationale for adopting a systems approach to technology planning, our third step next requires construction of a conceptual model of an information management system that meets the requirements of school productivity analysis. The administrative and instructional functions are inherently indivisible, and productivity will eventually drive all decisions, including financial decisions, at some point in the future. Since school districts are already required to collect and report data such as budget detail and revenues and expenditures, financial and other administrative data are presently widely available to school decision makers. Data on instructional productivity, however, are generally less available and considerably more difficult to generate. Data to be collected, its form, and the proper sources are thus typical questions that must be addressed in designing an information system that will facilitate a system capable of competent instructional productivity analysis.

Professional computer systems analysts generally use one or more of a number of conceptual approaches to designing computer systems based on the specific needs of an organization. The three main analytical techniques currently in use are the *communications approach*, the *information and resource management approach*, and the *functional analysis approach*. In addition, a *sociotechnical approach* increasingly used in office automation is becoming widely accepted. While all approaches share the common goal of improving data structures, their differences are generally in terms of focus on various elements of the data system.

The communications approach views the organization as a communications system and treats integration and automation as a communication problem between sections of the system.[17] The objective of the analyst using this approach is to improve communications between persons using the system and to facilitate better communications between computers at various locations throughout the system. In the communications approach, the principal focus is on establishing effective and efficient communications paths. The analyst attempts to optimize communications paths to maximize the use of information in the organization. The information and resource management approach focuses on data storage, effective resource sharing, effective data presentation, and efficient data transfer between users.[18] The functional analysis approach to system design identifies and analyzes the functions performed in an organization to increase efficiency in the performance of each function.[19] While data is considered in this approach, efficiency of application programs is stressed. Finally, the sociotechnical approach views an organization as a social system within which jobs are performed. This approach considers the quality of work life as a primary factor in organizational success or failure, particularly in the introduction of automation to the workplace.

These methods of viewing organizational design are helpful in conceptualizing a data management system for education. Because this textbook maintains that information management system design needs to integrate administrative and instructional functions, the conceptual model for school automation can draw from all four approaches in that a system should take into account the communications, information, functional, and sociological operations of schools. This is particularly true given the nature and problems inherent to distributed data systems discussed earlier in this chapter. As a result, all these factors should be taken into account when designing a distributed environment in which people must come to accept data-based productivity as an unavoidable eventuality. Consequently, these aspects of system design are consciously implicit in the conceptual model described next.

A Conceptual Model for School Automation

On the threshold of the twenty-first century, the richly complex information and functional requirements of modern schools cannot be analyzed using only one approach. The different foci of various participants in the school setting indicate an urgent need to involve users in the development of the system. To achieve such participation, however, schools must actively conceptualize and internalize a complete model that reflects the many requirements of both administrative and instructional users according to their function within the total school system. As an initial vision, a model based on this view is presented in Figure 13.5.

The conceptual school model depicted in the figure is derived from organizational analysis based on the needs of information users.[20] The stakeholders are those persons with an interest in the system, who are also the primary drivers of the analysis and design process. In the educational setting, stakeholders are vested members of the educational community—administrators, teachers, students, and parents. Each stakeholder has goals and objectives, with each person and each goal or objective contributing to the overall organizational mission, as shown in the figure. The central importance of stakeholders is evident in each of the four main nodes of the model wherein the administrative and instructional operations are both visually and functionally linked. Linkage is established between classrooms, the collective teacher workroom, the principal's office, and the business office. The model is immediately seen to be a distributed system with expertise and data located at the appropriate site according to the stakeholder's function.

Operation of this model may be better understood in contrast to the model of a traditional classroom. Most school systems would like to engage in frequent monitoring and reporting of student progress. But because student monitoring through testing of curriculum objectives involves a series of detailed analyses of individual student progress for every objective, detailed tracking to the extent needed to continuously

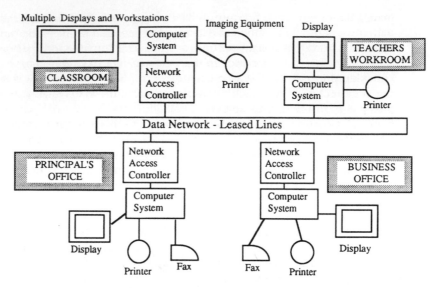

FIGURE 13.5 Four-node educational network

monitor progress is not readily feasible in a traditional classroom due to lack of time and analytical tools. Furthermore, other information needed to analyze student performance may not be available, and remedial resources may not be identifiable. Consequently, item analysis of percentages of students reaching curricular objectives is not performed. At best the teacher may make a scanned survey of questions missed, making an imprecise judgment about remediation. Because no historic data were ever compiled, there is no reference as to whether previous classes missed the same objectives. Under these typical conditions, it is easy to see how productivity cannot be measured because teachers cannot assess the progress of a class relative to an established time line. It is also very difficult to identify an individual student's progress in relation to the curricular objectives and in relation to total achievement of the class. In sum, *the traditional classroom described here is a poor opportunity to assess productivity.*

As demands for accountability increase, however, school decision makers at all levels must be in a position to evaluate the effectiveness of instructional programs and to make adjustments and justifications. An integral part of providing such analysis is an information management system that makes possible the impossible common-sense educational tasks described above. In sharp contrast to the traditional setting, there is compelling need for a data system that integrates currently discrete systems for test production, grade calculation, grade reporting, report card generation, and midterm progress reports with building level and district data. The ability to perform ad hoc queries on student progress at any point in time is needed to inform principals or teachers of potential problems at both individual or classwide levels. One must wonder why no such planning has occurred on a wide basis, and one must question even more closely how such a need can escape an industry that should be vitally concerned about its productivity.

The answer to these questions is generally only that schools are not sophisticated in production analysis because they have not conceptualized the relationship between all information functions of a district. Ability to perform such monitoring as described above, however, is not beyond district capabilities if proper data systems such as the one in Figure 13.5 are constructed. For example, large quantities of data are invariably generated during monitoring of student progress, even in highly traditional districts. However, such data are rarely available to teachers in a useful format. If properly processed, these data can be used to more clearly communicate to students, teachers, and parents the objectives that have been mastered and those that still need additional work. Any school that tests its students possesses the data necessary to perform a variety of sophisticated tracking analyses *if* the proper information management system is in place. The information network conceptualized in Figure 13.5 allows for collection and distribution of data necessary to engage in meaningful productivity analysis.

Implementing the Model.   Implementing an integrated distributed information system such as the one in Figure 13.5 would make it possible for schools to perform a wide variety of instructional productivity analyses. As conceptualized in the figure, schools should be empowered to perform the following:

1. *Test Production Function.* This function should allow teachers to design tests such that the relationship between test items and curricular objectives is easily specified to the computer system. The function should support test design utilizing variable formats, including the ability to incorporate pictures and graphs in the actual document. It should also be able to generate different versions of the same test. An extensive database of test questions and corresponding curriculum objectives should be available. The system should constantly monitor test item use, record the distribution of responses from each test, and over time refine the discrimination value of a given test item.

2. *Student Test Item Analysis Function.* This function should extensively summarize the results of a given test for each individual student in the class. It should indicate those objectives addressed by the test that have been mastered and those needing additional or alternative remediation.

3. *Class Test Item Analysis Function.* This application should summarize the performance of the entire class on a given examination with the analysis specific to the objectives tested. The report should indicate the percentage of the class demonstrating mastery of each objective and the distribution of responses. The report developed by the system would be useful to teachers in monitoring and improving teaching, and in planning for future instruction.

4. *Teacher Objective Analysis Function.* This function should generate a summary of data regarding performance of students assigned to a given teacher. It should list, by teacher, the percentage of all students demonstrating mastery of each objective. The report should also show the percentage of students assigned to a given teacher who have achieved target mastery goals (e.g., 10%, 20%, 100%) of the objectives for a course. Data for this report may come from an analysis of student performance as measured by term grades or curriculum-specific examinations designed to test mastery of course objectives. It should also be possible to correlate these data with other data generated by regular reporting processes in the course. This report would be useful to teachers in evaluating the performance of students over a longer period of time. It would

also be valuable to administrators in evaluating performance of individual teachers. Although potentially controversial, this report is a required tool if productivity in education is ever to be achieved.

5. *Student Resource Function.* Not all students progress at the same rate or master objectives by the same instructional methodology. This function of the data system should link success or failure on individual objectives to the teaching method used, and list alternative resources and activities available to students for those objectives needing additional work. The report should be available to teachers and parents seeking guidance on homework and alternative activities to assist students. This list would also form the basis for reinforcing or modifying teaching strategies employed by the teacher.

6. *Objective Mastery Time Line Function.* This unique function is designed to produce a time line indicating the point during the term when a given percentage of the class has demonstrated mastery of a set of objectives. The desired percentage can be changed by the user to allow analysis from various perspectives. For example, the report might show that by the fifth week of the term 80% of the students in a class have shown mastery of Items A, B, and C, while only 25% have mastered Item D. This report would be useful to teachers in assessing the progress of individuals relative to total class performance. The report could also be used by supervisors to analyze the effects of ability grouping, student achievement profiles, and so forth.

7. *Reports, Utilities, and Report Generators.* In addition to providing the above analysis and reporting functions, the system should be designed to provide monitoring of student progress in many other areas. Accordingly, the system should provide the teacher with a set of tools that makes the reporting task easier. Possible tools include:

   a. *Grade Calculation Utility.* This tool would assist the teacher in preparation of required periodic grades. The function must be flexible to permit grade calculation from a variety of sources, such as final examinations, homework, projects, and so forth. Given the results obtained from the Mastery Time Line, the system would generate a comparative numerical score. This would allow the teacher to assign a letter grade reflecting a more extensive view of a student's performance. The data generated from this utility should become part of the student's permanent record.

   b. *Student Progress Monitor.* This utility would generate summaries of the instructional objectives that the student has mastered at any point during the year. This mastery progress report could be generated daily, weekly, monthly, or as needed. In addition, the report could be available to parents at any time.

   c. *Grade Collecting Utility.* This function would facilitate rapid collection of grades from all teachers. While many methods for collecting grades could be designed, two required features of the system would be ease of use and accuracy of the process. Since grades would be determined by data generated in other utilities, the teacher would have to be able to "adjust" the machine grade according to one or several preestablished guidelines. This function would "automate" the administrative task of collecting and compiling grades for report cards.

   d. *Report Generators.* This function should facilitate actual production of periodic report cards or interim grades as needed. This application would permit the individual teacher to formulate reports monthly, weekly, or daily for an entire class or for individuals.

While the above functions are by no means an exhaustive list of the total set of tools that should be available in a distributed data environment, the system envisioned here effectively illustrates the powerful nature of a systems approach to engaging instructional functions of a school district in productivity analysis. To design and engage such a system, however, demands all the prerequisites previously discussed in this chapter. Data systems must be distributed, control must be released, quality and confidentiality of data must be maintained, and a systems approach to networking under assumptions of stakeholder expertise must be clearly conceptualized. Teachers need access to an information system that facilitates accurate analysis and reporting of data, and the model in Figure 13.5 envisions a highly interactive and distributed data environment that facilitates accountability and also targets resources toward production deficiencies as described in the next section. Until such information management designs are widely adopted, however, the traditional classroom will continue to plague education because integration of administrative and instructional operations is functionally impossible under historic conditions.

INTEGRATING ADMINISTRATIVE AND INSTRUCTIONAL TECHNOLOGY MODELS

The systems approach to information management virtually demands integration of the various functions of school districts. Examples of the exciting applications of data in the instructional setting represent a vast improvement over historic productivity measurement in schools, but much opportunity for school improvement would be lost if plans for utilizing data failed to integrate the administrative function of schools into the total information environment. Because all decisions are eventually fiscal concerns, integration of these two dimensions of schools will be an absolute requirement in the future.

We therefore turn in this last section to the fourth step of our systems approach by suggesting several possible integrated applications of data from the administrative and instructional sides of school district operations. However, when information management systems undertake integration of discrete functions such as administrative and instructional operations, opportunities for illustration become infinite. Consequently, we limit discussion to three examples of data applications. The first example mirrors a traditional data function at the district level by illustrating data management in projecting revenues and expenditures. The second example demonstrates that the same data analysis can be extended down to single school sites through building level revenue projections. The third example moves beyond historic data applications by offering a case study approach to instructional productivity measurement in a scenario that likely portrays common problem-solving applications in future school settings. While these examples admittedly only scratch the surface of the power of data analysis in an environment demanding high integration, they are sufficient to confirm that districts must prepare to face an inevitably vast array of integrated performance structures in schools of the future.

General Considerations

In any organization, data are constantly changing. For schools, revenue and expenditure patterns shift, available funds by budget category vary by amounts spent at any given time, and student test scores and grades change almost daily. Before any analysis leading to decision making can be made, the inconstancy of data must be recognized. Thus, *the basis of accurate decision making is knowing how much change has occurred in a given period of time.*

In order for school administrators, teachers, parents, and others concerned with the effective and efficient operation of schools to develop a model for sound decision making, they must understand three basic criteria that govern all assumptions on which decisions are eventually based:

1. Thorough understanding of the parameters influencing a decision must be stated and evidenced;
2. Detailed and accurate data must be available at the location where the decision or recommendation will be made; and
3. Participants in the decision-making process must understand the methods used in the analysis to accept the results and recognize any inherent limitations.

Thus, all factors that may potentially influence that decision must be considered. This is the foundation of the first criterion, which effectively states that the accuracy of a decision is directly dependent on the number of factors relevant to the problem that can be identified for consideration. For example, a district might require a decision about the distribution of instructional funds to individual school buildings wherein the factors affecting the decision are numerous. The decision process should raise such questions as: Does each program truly cost the same amount of money? Do high schools require funds not needed by middle schools? Should funds be distributed on a per-pupil basis, on a weighted pupil basis, or on a simple head-count basis? Do smaller schools require additional funds compared to their larger counterparts because of diseconomies of scale? The list of questions is endless, but these examples illustrate that asking many questions will reveal valuable insights on factors influencing the accuracy of a decision. Answers to these questions are obtainable only by integration of administrative and instructional operations in a district.

While information is important to the total decision-making process, decisions will only be as accurate as the data that led to the decision. This is the foundation of the second criterion, which effectively states that data is useless unless it is available, accurate, and timely. For example, a district might need to determine whether additional instructional funds distributed to various buildings in the district resulted in increased performance on teacher-made tests. Such an analysis would require accurate and up-to-date information from both administrative and instructional functions because it is useless to monitor a budget with data that has not been adjusted for recent expenditures and equally useless to make decisions about midyear student performance if the only data are last year's test scores. Data must be available to decision makers when they are making decisions, not several weeks later, and distributed in a way conducive to the proposed analysis.

Finally, anyone in a decision-making capacity must understand the methods used to arrive at the decision. Very often school administrators and other stakeholders do not understand how problem-solving models are created and simply trust the results.

This is the foundation of the third criterion of effective decision making in that if thorough definition of the problem and accuracy of data are not addressed, the model can be flawed and can indicate erroneous conclusions. In addition, the decision will be better implemented if it is understood by stakeholders because they will have ownership and trust in the results.

In distributed decision-making environments, the criteria of problem definition, data accuracy, and conceptual understanding can be difficult. While there is no substitute for extended planning and study to reveal the conceptual underpinnings of a data analysis, the process should be aided by information management structures that simplify data handling. On this basis, the electronic spreadsheet is probably the most popular software package for decision modeling because people can better see and understand this format. Regardless of equipment used to manipulate the program, spreadsheet software offers school personnel a simple method for addressing complex and detailed problems. Although spreadsheets are simple and intuitive, their capabilities are extensively complex because they allow for assumptions and handling of large amounts of data. For example, a district might be concerned about inflation rates for the next three years as it relates to interest paid on debt service, the cost of medical care for employees during the next biannual budget cycle, or student performance data in relation to budget expenditures. Because such software is both powerful and user-friendly in an environment that allows importation from other relational databases, it aids problem definition, data accuracy, and conceptual understanding.

The changing nature of data and demands for accurate and intuitive data handling techniques are paramount in effective problem-solving by educational stakeholders. The ability of an integrated distributed data environment to achieve these ends is illustrated below, using simple spreadsheet software in the three examples of district and building level budget analysis and instructional productivity.

District Revenue and Expenditure Projection Analysis. A common administrative function in school districts is projecting revenues and expenditures over a future time period. While such activities preceded electronic information management systems, the ability of a school district to engage in various scenarios has been vastly facilitated by instantaneous recalculation based on ability to experiment with different assumptions. In the example provided here, the district's financial database maintained for accounting and auditing purposes is combined with district concerns about effectively managing fiscal resources while simultaneously increasing staff salaries by an unprecedented amount. The goal of this analysis is therefore to determine the fiscal feasibility of remaining financially solvent while increasing teacher salaries.

Figure 13.6 shows a spreadsheet of revenue projections for a hypothetical school district, constructed so that revenue projections could be calculated from historic data electronically imported from the district's accounting database. Each revenue entry was summarized from audited reports and included information on beginning cash balance, mill rate, assessed valuation, and amounts received from each of the district's revenue sources. These data were provided for two prior years and the current year to provide the historic basis for assumptions about future trends. Calculation of a percentage of total amounts by years provided the user a quick reference in determining trends across time and identifying problem areas where special concerns might arise. For example, it can be seen that special education revenue will drop from the previous year's level as a percentage of total (current 1.11% is projected next year at 1.02%). Such a trend may indicate reduced state or federal revenue sources, and

	Historic Information					Current Year			Projected Information		
SCHOOL YEAR	PREVIOUS YEAR		LAST YEAR			CURRENT YEAR			NEXT YEAR		
		% TOTAL		% TOTAL	%CHANGE		% TOTAL	%CHANGE		%TOTAL	%CHANGE
BEGINNING CASH BALANCE	$ 1,368,312		$ 1,499,369			$ 1,822,825			$ 1,979,207.81		
MILLAGE	50.21		50.36			51.00			50.99		
DOLLARS PER MILL	$ 90,000		$ 95,000			$ 100,000			$ 101,000		
ASSESSED VALUATION	$90,000,000		$95,000,000			$100,000,000			$101,000,000.00		
GENERAL FUND											
REVENUES											
6000-LOCAL SOURCES		% TOTAL		% TOTAL	%CHANGE		% TOTAL	%CHANGE		%TOTAL	%CHANGE
REAL ESTATE TAX	$ 4,518,693	47.34 %	$ 4,784,085	46.72 %	5.87 %	$ 5,100,000	47.72 %	6.60 %	$ 5,150,000	43.67 %	0.96 %
PUBLIC UTILITY TAX	$ 72,141	0.76 %	$ 73,353	0.72 %	1.68 %	$ 79,645	0.75 %	8.58 %	$ 80,000	0.68 %	0.45 %
REAL ESTATE TRANSFERS	$ 121,485	1.27 %	$ 190,622	1.86 %	56.91 %	$ 228,198	2.14 %	19.71 %	$ 229,000	1.94 %	0.35 %
DELIQUENT TAX COLLECTION	$ 222,274	2.33 %	$ 236,008	2.31 %	6.18 %	$ 204,279	1.91 %	−13.44 %	$ 201,000	1.70 %	+1.61 %
EARNED INCOME	$ 856,791	8.98 %	$ 874,727	8.54 %	2.09 %	$ 951,116	8.90 %	8.73 %	$ 900,000	7.63 %	+5.37 %
INVESTMENT EARNINGS	$ 324,935	3.40 %	$ 303,245	2.96 %	−6.68 %	$ 399,597	3.74 %	31.77 %	$ 250,000	2.12 %	−37.44 %
OTHER LOCAL REVENUE	$ 68,438	0.72 %	$ 84,877	0.83 %	24.02 %	$ 88,328	0.83 %	4.07 %	$ 89,777	0.76 %	1.64 %
7000-STATE SOURCES											
BASIC STATE AID	$ 2,527,350	26.48 %	$ 2,755,916	26.92 %	9.04 %	$ 2,798,703	26.18 %	1.55 %	$ 2,854,131	24.20 %	1.98 %
TRANSPORTATION	$ 508,988	5.33 %	$ 509,868	4.98 %	0.17 %	$ 521,106	4.88 %	2.20 %	$ 510,000	4.32 %	−2.13 %
RENT/SINKING FUNDS	$ 67,252	0.70 %	$ 59,192	0.58 %	−11.98 %	$ 61,359	0.57 %	3.66 %	$ 137,411	1.17 %	123.94 %
VOCATIONAL EDUCATION	$ 34,139	0.36 %	$ 8,752	0.09 %	−74.36 %	$ 12,178	0.11 %	39.14 %	$ 14,200	0.12 %	16.61 %
SPECIAL EDUCATION	$ 112,258	1.18 %	$ 227,514	2.22 %	102.67 %	$ 118,137	1.11 %	−48.07 %	$ 120,120	1.02 %	1.68 %
OTHER STATE REVENUE	$ 31,018	0.32 %	$ 30,559	0.30 %	−1.48 %	$ 29,354	0.27 %	−3.94 %	$ 1,127,903	9.56 %	3742.35 %
FEDERAL SOURCES	$ 80,262	0.84 %	$ 100,212	0.98 %	24.86 %	$ 96,304	0.90 %	−3.90 %	$ 130,000	1.10 %	34.99 %
TOTAL REVENUE	$ 9,546,023.02	100.00 %	$10,238,929.34	100.00 %	7.26 %	$ 10,688,303.98	100.00 %	4.39 %	$ 11,793,542.00	100.00 %	10.34 %

FIGURE 13.6   Revenue projection for sample school district

questions of continued service delivery at the current level would need to be investigated. Many other questions could also be raised, and various revenue scenarios could be constructed, limited only by their probability of occurrence.

Because revenues directly affect expenditures, Figure 13.7 was constructed to illustrate the considerations that must enter into a district's fiscal planning. Again accuracy and availability of data must be stressed, and it is equally important to observe that such analysis is possible only through effective data systems that provide accurate and convenient information. The obvious relationship of the structure of revenue and expenditure projections should also be noted, wherein revenue and expenditure analyses require the same set of governing assumptions to assure a relevant basis for comparison. For example, major expenditure categories consuming the bulk of educational budgets are built into expenditure projections, including instruction and support services, salaries, and transportation and facility costs. Similarly, the same three years of data form the basis for expenditure projections, noting increases and declines by individual expenditure series. For example, nonsalaried support services are expected to decline next year (−60.67%), while facility needs are expected to increase dramatically (e.g., debt service +184.14%) noting the difference between revenues and expenditures. In the present instance, the data show growing positive year-end cash balances.

In addition to observing general trends and changes in relationships between revenue and expenditures, the format used in construction of the model was intended to allow the user to test for the effect of certain expenditures on cash balances maintained at the end of each year. High cash balances were carried over into each following year, and in this scenario it was accepted as good fiscal management to preserve cash balances while holding the mill rate to a slow steady increase. To achieve this goal, the spreadsheet was designed to allow the user to manipulate variables and assumptions. For example, data on future district property values, salary requirements, instructional needs, and anticipated levels of revenue from all sources (federal, state, and local) could be manipulated to model the effect of changes in these variables on ending cash balances and mill rates. The projected results, contained in the shaded area of Figure 13.7, would change instantaneously if any of the manipulable variables were altered.

The combined revenue and expenditure projections allow for various district planning strategies. First, revenue analysis provides a firm basis for planning expenditures. Second, expenditure analysis provides a clear understanding of ongoing costs that must be funded, and subtraction of those costs from total revenues reveals the district's discretionary funds. Third, manipulating both the revenue and expenditure sides reveals the future impact of choices the district may make. For example, there were two reasons for performing these revenue and expenditure analyses. The first reason was obviously to gain a clearer picture of what the district can anticipate in the following year. The second reason, however, was that the district was trying to offer a 30% raise to teaching staff (see Figure 13.7), up from a total $5.15 million in the current year to a projected $6.8 million. Under current revenue projections, the district could decide to approve this plan because of steady growth in cash balances and consistent increases in property valuation. Because the model indicates that future cash balances will grow slightly and the mill rate will stay stable, the anticipated salary raise could be negotiated.[21]

The revenue and expenditure analysis in this example illustrates the effectiveness of a current database in pursuit of traditional administrative functions. Obviously,

SCHOOL YEAR GENERAL FUND EXPENDITURES	Historic Information					Projected Information					
	PREVIOUS YEAR		LAST YEAR			CURRENT YEAR			NEXT YEAR		
1000 (INSTRUCTION) NON-SALARIES	$ 966,566.48	10.27%	$ 940,616.90	9.49%	-2.68%	$ 995,304.92	9.45%	5.81%	$ 1,144,090	9.94%	14.95%
2000 (SUPPORT SERVICES) NON-SALARIES	$2,524,221.26	26.81%	$2,431,923.73	24.53%	-3.66%	$ 2,686,485.13	25.51%	10.47%	$ 1,056,541	9.18%	-60.67%
00 (OPERATING NON-INSTRUCTION) SALARIES	$ 80,491.24	0.85%	$ 81,076.66	0.82%	0.73%	$ 94,442.99	0.90%	16.49%	$ 104,349	0.91%	10.49%
4000 (BUILDING IMPROVMENTS)	$ 138.06	0.00%	$ 12,836.25	0.13%	9198 %	$ 10,513.00	0.10%	-18.10%	$ 28,897	0.25%	174.87%
5000 (OTHER)	$ 74,944.21	0.80%	$ 205,119.51	2.07%	173.70%	$ 74,437.85	0.71%	-63.71%	$ 196,148	1.70%	163.51%
BARGAINING UNIT-SALARIES 1000(100/200)	$4,423,960.39	46.99%	$4,793,926.58	48.35%	8.36%	$ 5,151,758.13	48.92%	7.46%	$ 6,800,000	59.07%	
2000(100/200)	$ 468,990.25	4.98%	$ 526,803.79	5.31%	12.33%	$ 564,437.28	5.36%	7.14%	$ 750,000	6.52%	
3000(100/200)	$ 113,137.01	1.20%	$ 120,124.82	1.21%	6.18%	$ 134,817.12	1.28%	12.23%	$ 245,000	2.13%	
2700 (TRANSPORTATION COSTS)	$ 596,517.40	6.34%	$ 642,044.37	6.48%	7.63%	$ 648,725.20	6.16%	1.04%	$ 700,878	6.09%	8.04%
5000 (DEBT SERVICE)	$ 166,000.00	1.76%	$ 161,000.00	1.62%	-3.01%	$ 171,000.00	1.62%	6.21%	$ 485,887	4.22%	184.14%
TOTAL	$9,414,966.30	100.00%	$9,915,472.61	100.00%	5.32%	$10,531,921.62	100.00%	6.22%	$11,511,790.00	100.00%	9.30%
DIFFERENCE	$ 131,056.72		$ 323,456.73			$ 156,382.36			$ 281,752.00		
REVENUE-EXPENDITURE											

FIGURE 13.7 Expenditure projection for sample school district

the same results could have been obtained by hand, but the process would be much more laborious, and it is highly unlikely that as many alternative scenarios would be constructed due to labor and time restraints. Not only does data create its own uses, but decisions are also improved on the basis of adequate data. While no automation will ever replace the human element in the process of deciding for or against the salary increase, the opportunity to make wise decisions on the basis of data is vastly improved by convenient and comprehensive information systems.

Building Level Revenue Projection Analysis.   Just as models can be developed for district revenue and expenditure patterns, data relative to such patterns at the building level can also provide valuable information for site level decision making. While the central office as the representative of the school board must still control all funds used in the operation of the school district, processes used to allocate resources to individual buildings can follow a variety of formats. Some districts distribute money to buildings by category of expenditure, such as instruction, library, science laboratories, art, and music, while other districts use different procedures, such as a lump sum to be divided by the individual staff according to building objectives. In either instance, these funds are usually allocated by the number of students. This allocation process can use head count, the number of students in average daily membership (ADM) or average daily attendance (ADA), full-time equivalency (FTE) of students, or weighting the previous methods to derive allocations such as weighted average daily membership (WADM) or weighted average daily attendance (WADA). Regardless of method, however, the result should be based on well-thought-out decisions.

Figure 13.8 illustrates how data analysis can be extended down to the individual school site through building level revenue decisions. In this example, decisions have been made at the district level that all funds are distributed on the basis of the total number of pupils in average daily membership. The number of students has been calculated by enrollment projections for this building using an average survival ratio method.[22] The district office has further determined that the building budget will

FIGURE 13.8   Instructional allocation for sample school site

Site Instructional Allocation by Grade Elementary School A							
Anticipated Growth		5%					
	Last Year			This Year		Next Year	
Allocation per Pupil	$ 113.56			$120.50		$126.53	
		Percent Increase		6.11%			
Grade							
Kindergarten	212	$ 12,037.36		217	$ 13,074.25	222	$ 14,044.28
First	223	$ 25,323.88		192	$ 23,136.00	197	$ 24,925.43
Second	112	$ 12,718.72		201	$ 24,220.50	173	$ 21,888.83
Third	114	$ 12,945.84		107	$ 12,893.50	192	$ 24,292.80
Fourth	221	$ 25,096.76		106	$ 12,773.00	99	$ 12,525.98
Fifth	144	$ 16,352.64		228	$ 27,474.00	109	$ 13,791.23
Sixth	135	$ 15,330.60		149	$ 17,954.50	236	$ 29,859.90
Total	1161	$ 119,806		1200	$ 131,526	1228	$ 141,328

increase by 6.11% next year because the district's anticipated revenue growth will be 5% and growth in the school's enrollment is expected. The formula for allocating revenues can be expressed as:

$$\text{Percentage Change} = \frac{(\text{This Year's Allocation}) - (\text{Last Year's Allocation})}{\text{Last Year's Allocation}}$$

or

$$\text{Percentage Change} = \frac{(\$120.50) - (\$113.56)}{\$113.56} = 6.11\%$$

If allocation of funds can be expected to grow by 5% next year, the funds available at each grade level can be calculated. At such time as growth assumptions need to be adjusted, a new "Anticipated Growth" figure is entered and the new results are automatically derived. A similar situation would occur if changes in enrollment were anticipated. The model can be expanded to include other categories of revenue from parent organizations, fund-raising efforts, or extended day programs, and fees and more detail can be added to the allocation parameters to include special education and other high-cost children. Of course, once the funds are actually received by the building, another set of exhaustive decision-making processes may apply, as discussed in Chapter 6 under various budgeting models. The implication here, however, is that models for allocation of resources within a school site can easily be developed by administrators using technology to explore different revenue and expenditure scenarios.

The revenue analysis in this example illustrates that the district's information database should not be restricted to central office functions, and that central office applications should include opportunities to consider alternative expenditure scenarios for individual buildings. Building level analysis should not merely calculate percentage increases in funding by building, but should also include numerous considerations related to actual student achievement in the individual buildings. As will be seen in the next example, extension of district information management systems to the building and individual student levels is a major goal of an integrated system by engaging in instruction productivity analysis that rewards high achievement and remediates deficiencies.

Instructional Productivity Analysis.   The ability to evaluate performance in the educational program is the most important aspect of school operation. However, few schools actually engage in systematic and rigorous evaluation of instructional programs and even fewer ever utilize the results of evaluations to make changes that predictably improve student outcomes. The reason is that few administrators and members of site councils or parent advisory committees have access to performance data in a usable format. But if allocation of resources is to have meaning, it is important that stakeholders understand the effect that financial decisions have on educational productivity—that is *how* and *if* students are learning. The task for schools is thus to study the effectiveness of instructional programs to allocate resources to their best use, so that areas that are not performing satisfactorily can either receive additional resources (with results monitored) or be restructured. The following example is the third illustration of using data management systems to join the fiscal and instructional functions of a school district to produce one type of educational productivity analysis.

In this example, an elementary building principal and members of the school site council want to investigate student performance. Of particular interest is investigation into whether any relationship exists between course grades assigned by teachers and recorded changes in achievement test scores at each grade level. Regardless of the outcome, the council has been asked in advance by the school board to undertake an additional study upon completion of this investigation to examine resource allocations, either confirming current fiscal resource distributions or recommending changes targeted at performance deficiencies that may be discovered in the first analysis.

To conduct this analysis, the principal and school site council requested access to data on course grades and achievement test scores housed in the school's information management system. From these data, changes in achievement scores were calculated and the results were compared to course grades assigned by teachers. Results of this analysis are shown in Table 13.1, where a three-year array of grade point averages (GPAs) in grades 1–6 is laid alongside changes in achievement test scores for the same time period.

Although recognizing that the numerical results of the analysis were essential to extended study, the council wanted to make them easier to decipher and asked the

TABLE 13.1   Grade point average and achievement level comparisons for three years: performance measures for a school site (Building A)

Year 1	Grade Level	GPA	Percentage Change in Achievement
	1	2.7	0.78
	2	2.44	0.79
	3	2.21	0.67
	4	2.01	0.58
	5	2.13	0.66
	6	2.22	0.88
Average		2.29	0.73
Year 2			
	1	2.33	0.68
	2	2.38	0.72
	3	2.12	0.77
	4	2.11	0.59
	5	2.45	0.66
	6	2.88	0.77
Average		2.38	0.70
Year 3			
	1	2.74	0.65
	2	2.35	0.71
	3	2.66	0.65
	4	2.11	0.55
	5	2.31	0.74
	6	2.44	0.74
Average		2.35	0.67
Grand Average		2.35	0.70

information management system to visualize any relationships presented in the data table. The graph in Figure 13.9 was constructed, from which the council was able to ascertain that there was indeed an increasing trend in GPA accompanied by a negative trend in achievement test scores in some grades. The council was thus able to see both actual numerical results of the analysis and graphic depiction of relationships that were hidden in the data.

As a result of this analysis, the council become concerned that grading practices in the school were not reflective of student achievement. As one council member said, it was impossible to know whether instruction was inadequate to meet the demands of the testing program, or whether the testing program was inappropriate for the level of instruction occurring in the school. The council thus decided that one of its recommendations would be for the district to engage in an extended study of the curriculum. The council was also interested in further analysis of the existing data and requested additional investigation to determine whether the trend was generally evident across all grade levels or whether one group's performance had resulted in the appearance of an overall decline. The subsequent analysis by individual grade levels showed that for most grades the trend was not consistent, but that significant problems existed at the fourth grade level (see Figure 13.10).

The data indicated that additional investigation was needed to determine possible reasons for such relationships. The site council recognized that at least two potential explanations should be examined. The first explanation would require examination of achievement scores and academic profiles of students at each grade level to determine if there were good reasons why the fourth grade might score lower than all other grades. The second explanation would require a much harder analysis into why course grades were increasing while achievement was declining. Because the second possible explanation involved personnel matters assigned by law to the administrative staff of the district, the council decided to refer that aspect to appropriate channels and to pursue disaggregation of performance data by grade level to determine whether achievement could be improved.

Achievement test data at each grade level were collected and students were individually classified according to whether their test scores were at expected grade level.

FIGURE 13.9   Trends in grade point average compared to changes in achievement level

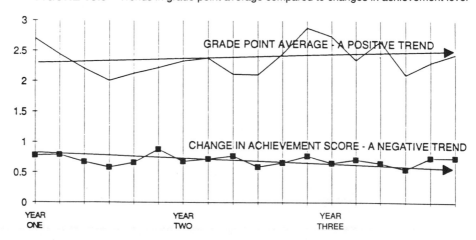

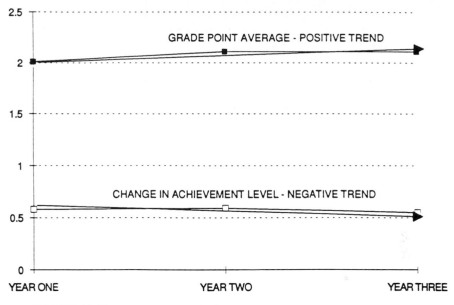

FIGURE 13.10   View of grade 4 for three years

Variances from grade level were plotted in decile percentages above or below respective grade level scores. The data were reaggregated for display in Table 13.2, where all six grade groupings could be compared. The council again requested graphic display of the results (Figure 13.11, p. 630). From this analysis, the council was able to draw several conclusions relating to achievement. First, the fourth grade in fact had the lowest percentage of students performing at grade level. Second, the fourth grade had the lowest percentage of students above grade level. Third, the fourth grade consistently had the highest percentage of students performing below grade level. Fourth, other data on student demographic characteristics in the administrative data base revealed that the fourth grade contained more at-risk students than any other grade level. Fifth, when these data were combined with administrative data on class size, numbers of instructional aides, percentages from low income homes, and instruction funds available to fourth grade teachers, it was determined that the fourth grade was consist-

TABLE 13.2   Achievement scores for a school site: Achievement groupings (Building A)

Grade	Reading Scores Profile: Percentage of Total Class Size					
	% At Level	10% Above	20% Above	10% Below	20% Below	30% Below
1	52	15	2	22	7	2
2	54	18	3	15	5	5
3	57	22	8	10	2	1
4	41	12	5	24	11	7
5	51	17	4	16	7	5
6	61	15	6	11	5	2

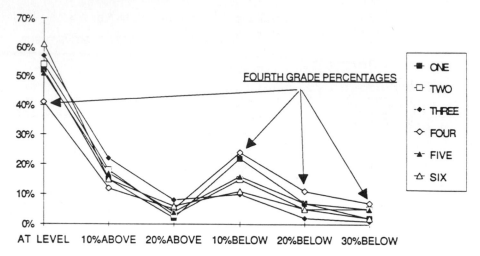

FIGURE 13.11   Percentage of students at, below, and above grade level

ently underfunded in comparison to other grade levels. From these data, the council decided to recommend channeling additional resources to the fourth grade program and to recommend continued monitoring of student performance to determine how much difference reallocation of resources might accomplish in the test score arena. Thus, analysis of a hypothesis was made possible by an integrated data system, resulting in important inquiries into achievement and personnel concerns.

Instruction productivity analysis thus holds significant promise for improving student performance. As illustrated in this scenario, however, isolation of factors that may lead to improved performance is a function of meaningful data in a usable format made available to stakeholders. Such analysis is possible only when timely data are distributed, when appropriate hardware and software tools are available, and when stakeholder are empowered to engage in meaningful analysis. Educators must realize that the ultimate goal of the successful educational environment is maximization of student performance. While opportunities for misuse of data are omnipresent, failure to enlist cooperation of the administrative and instructional functions of a district in appropriate productivity assessment ensures that any progress will be largely uninformed and accidental. In the context of a highly technological future, it is doubtful that traditions will be allowed to continue unchecked. It is on this rather tense note that we now turn to the final chapter in this text, which concludes our examination of the changing role of fiscal leadership in schools.

Review Points

INFORMATION TECHNOLOGY ENVIRONMENTS

Historically, schools have utilized information technology (i.e., computers) for data processing in a business environment.

Classic information environments were centralized under management control in mainframe systems.

With development of smaller processors, decentralization began to be evident, although the psychology of centralization has continued to be strong.

Centralized environments have several strengths, among which are economy, control, security, standards, availability, and data integrity.

Disadvantages of centralized environments include very large start-up costs for mainframes or minicomputers, very high technical costs for operations specialists, and the finiteness of the system, particularly when coupled with the potential for data degradation.

Decentralized environments have several benefits, including the primary intent to distribute data widely, lower start-up costs, user-friendly interface shells, and no limit on expansion.

Disadvantages of decentralization include appropriate access to data, standards in processing data, control of data, and barriers to efficient data distribution.

SCHOOL AUTOMATION ANALYSIS

Implementation of any large and costly goal requires systematic analysis; given the cost of technology and the complex aims of data distribution, schools must formally initiate automation analysis to determine goals and paths.

The lack of systems analysis in school automation has led to much wasted money on obsolete or inadequate technology.

Systems analysis considers the stages of the growth curve in learning about technology, that is, initiation, expansion, formalization, and maturity.

Initiation is marked by recognition of the need for automation; rapid expansion is often marked by growth without the needed formal planning; formalization is usually marked by belated recognition of the need for integration; and maturity begins to evidence planned growth and mature use based on uniform standards and policies.

Most schools have moved beyond the initiation stage, but a majority are still deeply involved in rapid expansion.

A major goal of automation analysis is designing a system for integrating data users' needs on a compatible platform.

The most typical vehicle to integration is one of several available computer network options.

While the technology of networking seems too technical to interest administrators, it is important that they understand the basic concepts to choose the enduring and expandable network configurations that will help avoid eventual obsolescence.

FRAMEWORK FOR INFORMATION MANAGEMENT

Professional analysts will work with districts to develop a coherent and comprehensive approach to information management.

The main analytical techniques are the *communications* approach, the *information and resource management* approach, and the *functional analysis* approach.

Regardless of the model, organizational analysis should be based on the needs of information users. In the context of modern schools, this should mean administrative, curricular, and evaluative processes that will permit linking all performance and fiscal data in the school into productivity analysis.

As information and productivity are the objects, the framework demands accessibility by all personnel involved.

INTEGRATING ADMINISTRATIVE AND INSTRUCTIONAL TECHNOLOGY MODELS

As the purpose of schooling is learning, the administrative and instructional dimensions of schools must be integrated to assess needs, allocate resources, and determine outcomes.

Potential model analyses include district revenue and expenditure projections; building level revenue projections; instructional productivity analysis; and so forth.

Because accountability and productivity are not mere fads and will increasingly drive financial decisions, administrators will need to become adept in integrating administrative and instructional technology for productivity.

Case Study

In recent years, the board of education in your district has become interested in cost-benefit analysis. As associate superintendent for financial services, you have been asked by your superintendent to analyze any cost factors that would be important in the district's annual transportation fleet eight-year replacement schedule. As the board has heard sales presentations from two bus dealers who made different recommendations regarding the purchase of gasoline versus diesel buses, the superintendent is particularly interested in knowing which choice represents the best overall economy. Because the board at its next meeting will authorize the purchase of 10 buses based on your analysis, you are especially concerned that your analysis be accurate in the long run.

In preparing your analysis, you know the following information and assumptions to be true. You will, however, need to make other assumptions and collect additional data.

1. Acquisition Costs

The purchase of buses is capitalized over the useful life of the bus. The annual cost is calculated as the difference between the purchase price and the salvage value, divided by the useful life of the vehicle. Since gasoline buses have a shorter useful life than diesel buses, an inflation factor is included for changes in the future cost of gasoline bus purchases. Specific assumptions are made as follows:

Purchase price	Diesel	$36,000
	Gasoline	$28,500
Inflation rates	Diesel equipment	6%
	Gasoline equipment	5%
Life expectancy	Diesel	12 years
	Gasoline	8 years

2. Fuel Costs

Calculation of fuel costs is influenced by a number of factors. These include cost per mile for miles actually driven and fuel consumption. Fuel consumption for gasoline buses increases at approximately four years of age. Specific assumptions are made as follows:

Fuel cost per gallon	Diesel	$1.25
	Gasoline	$1.20
Fuel inflation rate		4%
Total miles driven each year		16,000
Consumption	Diesel	6.8 miles/gallon
	Gasoline	5.8 miles/gallon (new)
		4.3 miles/gallon (old)

3. Repair Costs

Annual repair costs are based on the cost of repair per mile driven. Specific assumptions are made as follows:

Average repair costs	Diesel	$0.11/mile
	Gasoline	$0.10/mile
Total number of miles		16,000
Repair cost inflation per year		4%

Using the data in this case study and the following sets of questions to help guide your class discussion, what will you recommend?

Directed Discussion Questions

1. As you read this case study, what information can you identify that will be necessary to perform the cost-benefit analysis? What additional data not given will you need? In your own district, are such transportation analyses performed? If not, why not? If so, what process is used, and what data are included?

2. In your analysis, which of the following data are important to the outcome? Cost of fuel? Miles traveled? Life expectancy of the type of vehicle? Taxes on fuel? Ability to negotiate bid prices on fuel? Fuel consumption? Fuel consumption after four years? Repair costs? Start-up costs for "switching" garage services from one type of engine fuel to another? Insurance costs on different types of buses? Salvage value of buses after fully depreciated?

3. If you were *not* to perform a cost analysis in this instance, which type of bus would you be inclined to buy? After performing your analysis, was your choice the correct one? If not, why not? What type of buses does your present employing district buy? Why? What "proofs" does the district offer for its choices? Using your own district's data, what would be the result if you were to calculate a cost-benefit analysis?

4. What other cost-benefit analyses, if any, are performed in your present district? How are they carried out? Who is responsible? What major decisions are based on such analyses? Who is involved in those decisions? How widespread

is awareness of such analyses, and how well understood is the process? Has there been consideration of how cost-effective the cost-benefit analyses are?

NOTES

1. United Way, *What Lies Ahead: Countdown to the 21st Century* (Washington, D.C.: United Way, 1989).

2. Olin H. Bray, "Distributed Database Management: Concepts and Administration," *Journal of Telecommunications Networks* 2:3 (1983), 237–248.

3. Helen M. Wood, "Distributed Database Technology," *Journal of Telecommunication Networks* 2:3 (1983), 235–236.

4. Adrianne Bank and R. C. Williams, "An Agenda for Developing Instructional Information Systems," in *Information Systems and School Improvement,* Adrianne Bank and R. C. Williams, eds. (New York: Columbia University Teachers College Press, 1989), 225–234.

5. Because various laws protect against access to data by unqualified persons, making distributed environments a higher risk operation than is true for centralized systems, legal counsel should be sought. This discussion assumes appropriateness of teacher access to data and proper control measures relating to protection of confidentiality in a spirit of true professionalism.

6. J. R. Buchanan and R. G. Linowes, "Understanding Distributed Data Processing," *Harvard Business Review* 58:4 (1984), 143–154.

7. Virgil Gligor and Elizabeth Fong, "Distributed Database Management Systems: An Architectural Perspective, *Journal of Telecommunication Networks* 2:3 (1985), 249–270.

8. Bray, "Distributed Database Management."

9. S. Spaccapietra, "Heterogeneous Data Base Distribution," in *Distributed Data Bases,* I. W. Draffan and F. Poole, eds. (Cambridge: Cambridge University Press, 1980), 155–193.

10. C. F. Gibson and R. L. Nolan, "Managing the Four Stages of EDP Growth," *Harvard Business Review* 52:1 (1974), 76–88.

11. For an excellent discussion on networks, see Mark A. Miller, *Internetworking* (Red Wood, Calif.: M&T Publishing, 1991).

12. A. E. Joel, "What is Telecommunications Circuit Switching?" *Proceedings of the IEEE* 65:9 (1977), 1237–1253.

13. J. E. Bethold, "High Speed Integrated Electronics for Communication Systems," *Proceedings of the IEEE* 78:3 (1990), 486–511.

14. F. A. Tobagi, "Fast Packet Switch Architectures for Broadband Integrated Services Digital Networks," *Proceedings of the IEEE* 78:1 (1990), 133–167.

15. A. Hac and H. B. Mutlu, "Synchronous Optical Network and Broadband ISDN Protocols," *Computer* 22:11 (1989), 26–34.

16. William Stallings, *Data and Computer Communications* (New York: Macmillan, 1988), 79.

17. K. W. Deutch, "On Communication Models in Social Sciences," *Public Opinion Quarterly* 16 (1958), 356–380.

18. J. Martin, *Application Development Without Programmers* (London: Savant Research Studies, 1981), 4.

19. J. Martin, *Recommended Standards for Analysts and Programmers* (New Jersey: Prentice-Hall, 1987), 23.

20. D. Tapscott, *Office Automation: A User-Driven Method* (New York: Plenum Press, 1982), 93.

21. Beginning students of school finance should not assume any approval by the authors of the

scenario described here. These data are provided as illustration of the steps districts should initiate to study revenue and expenditures before committing funds to future projects. All too frequently, districts commit future funds without secure knowledge of trends in revenues and expenditures. In the present example, the authors would hesitate to negotiate such salary increases because of a variety of factors inherent in the data that suggest available resources may be tightly committed in future years.

22. See Chapter 6 in this text for discussion of enrollment projection methods.

ADDITIONAL READINGS

Association of School Business Officials, International. *Administrative Uses for Microcomputers*. Edited by Frederick L. Dembowski, ed. Reston, Va.: Association of School Business Officials, 1983.

Bank, Adrianne, and Richard Williams. *Information Systems and School Improvement: Inventing the Future*. New York: Teachers College Press, 1987.

Cronbach, Lee, and Associates. *Toward Reform in Program Evaluation*. San Francisco: Jossey-Bass, 1985.

Daft, Richard, and Richard Steers. *Organization: A Micro/Macro Approach*. Glenview, Ill.: Scott Foresman, 1986.

Graczyk, Sandra L., and J. H. Faux. *101 Ways to Make Your Job Easier with 101 Templates for School Business Administration for Use with Lotus® 1-2-3®*. Reston, Va.: Association of School Business Officials, 1990.

Hartman, William T. *School District Budgeting*. Englewood Cliffs, N.J.: Prentice-Hall, 1988.

Hentschke, Guilbert. *Management Operations in Education*. Berkeley: McCutchan, 1975.

———. *School Business Administration: A Comparative Perspective*. Berkeley: McCutchan, 1986.

Kazlauskas, E. J., and Larry O. Picus. *A Systems Analysis Approach to Selecting, Designing and Implementing Automated Systems*. Reston, Va.: Association of School Business Officials, 1990.

Kroenke, David. *Management Information Systems*. Santa Cruz, Calif.: Mitchell Publishing, 1989.

Levin, Henry. *Cost Effectiveness: A Primer*. Beverley Hills: Sage, 1980.

Lillie, David, Wallace Hannum, and Gary Stuck. *Computers and Effective Instruction*. New York: Longman, 1989.

Richards, Craig E. *Microcomputer Applications for Strategic Management in Education: A Case Study Approach*. New York: Longman, 1989.

Tanner, C., and C. Holmes. *Microcomputer Applications in Educational Planning and Decision Making*. New York: Teachers College Press, 1985.

Tufte, Edward. *Data Analysis for Politics and Policy*. Englewood Cliffs, N.J.: Prentice-Hall, 1974.

United Way. *What Lies Ahead: Countdown to the 21st Century*. Washington, D.C.: Author, 1989.

Wasik, John. *The Electronic Business Information Sourcebook*. New York: Wiley, 1987.

CHAPTER 14

Conclusion: Fiscal Leadership and the Future

CHAPTER THEME

- The message of this chapter and this textbook is that schools are facing a wide-ranging crisis, taking in a complex socioeconomic mosaic of American society in the late twentieth century. Because sociodemographics and economics combine to have a powerful impact on educational opportunity, school administrators must be keenly aware of the impact money has on children—conditions demanding strong fiscal leadership for the future.

CHAPTER OUTLINE

- Review of the lessons from history that have brought education to its present condition
- The influence of past and present on the future—both from the perspective of warnings about what can be avoided, and from the perspective of welcoming a new millenium after having come a very long way in financing quality education for every child

CHAPTER OBJECTIVE

- To reinforce lessons learned in earlier chapters, and to provide closure to our study of the exciting field of education finance

This book is not about things to come! It is not about the next century. Its thesis is that the next century is already here.

Peter Drucker, The New Realities

Although there have been many important lessons and messages in this textbook, few have equaled the intensity of the opening quotation for this chapter.[1] Clearly, the message is that schools are now facing an unprecedented crisis of wide-ranging problems involving a complex socioeconomic mosaic of society. In addition to the concerns addressed here, education faces other issues, such as school choice, and questions of basic values that, depending on one's viewpoint, represent either opportunity or repression. The problem is deceptively simple to state in that equal educational opportunities must be provided to every child, but the problem is vexatious in resolution because it requires agreement on diverse goals and enormous amounts of money to implement the many divergent expectations.

Although our study of school finance has embraced many concerns, much more could be said about this fluid and unstable environment. Although the field is so vast and complex that no single text can comprehensively examine every facet of school finance policy, we have gained sufficient knowledge to be able to draw closure to the parameters that frame this book. As this text is principally an analysis that has sought to draw from both principles and problems of practicing school finance in a policy context, it is fitting to conclude with some final reflections about school finance in a historic and prospective light. This short chapter therefore focuses on two central themes: a review of the lessons from history that have been highlighted in this text and the implications of these lessons for the future. The chapter thus reiterates the dilemma of modern school finance and concludes by considering the need for fiscal leadership in a dynamic and volatile future. Although entire careers are devoted to these complex concerns without reaching resolution, we draw closure by reinforcing their critical nature to a new generation of administrators to whom the future will be entrusted.

LESSONS FROM HISTORY

It should be highly evident by this point that this textbook has turned deeply to historical contexts in search of explanations for the successes and failures of modern public school finance, on the premise that almost nothing occurs vacuously. Indeed, nearly everything is a function of something else, if not by progeny, then by reaction. In the highly political context of public schools and public school finance, the lessons of history are indispensable to understanding and appreciating modern policy deliberations. Although there is far too little appreciation for the contribution of history to the present circumstance, it is only in this context that the roots of current issues can be seen—a necessary precondition to intelligent problem resolution. As such, these lessons serve a second major purpose: as they describe the past in nearly sequential causality, they may also help predict the future because present realities continually create the next generation of events. Summary and synthesis of the lessons from history are therefore vital to this chapter.

The social and economic context of education discussed in Chapter 1 found that schools are the source of both optimism and desperation in America. The chapter drew from the more than 30 national reports that called on the nation to rescue education from its "pending doom," commenting that American attitudes toward schooling have been a tangled web of hope and anger. Hope has been in large measure a function of faithful adherence to the power of education to provide social and economic mobility. That hope has been supported by evidence of self-fulfilling prophecy wherein the nation has repeatedly demonstrated the fruits of determination in the face of adversity, and further supported by hard data from economics and other disciplines that have analyzed the impact of education on opportunity. At the same time, however, anger has been a function of education's imperfect performance in that success has not come to all equally. Indeed, if hope has been preeminent, it has recently lost ground to despair as the dream has faded for the disadvantaged masses that have grown through demographic change. The lesson to be learned from this chapter is twofold. First, education has represented different realities to different people. Second, all people want a better life. Under these conditions, it is a fundamentally reasonable expectation that economic and social prosperity depend on education—a reality that finds it most difficult to justify failure to provide high quality education to every citizen.

The development of educational systems in a cultural context yielded a second lesson in Chapter 2 by casting a retrospective light on modern schools. The chapter developed the historical roots of common schools in America, noting the evolution of the federal-state-local triad of responsibility for education. Of special merit was recognition that the organization of schooling was mostly a function of deliberate intent, with only a small part attributable to inadvertent consequence of neglect. Under this reality, it can be observed that a strong federal role was deliberately precluded, leaving states and local communities to determine the proper respective roles for developing and maintaining educational systems. While critics may charge a lack of wisdom and foresight in the decisions that were made, they may less confidently charge that education has come to its present state by philosophic neglect. Indeed, the history of education dating from colonial times to the present day has placed it at the very center of American values—in truth, only the level of financial support and philosophic bases for dividing responsibility for educational systems can be honestly attacked. The lesson to be learned from this chapter is again that nothing is engendered vacuously, and that the present governance structure of education has been a function of intent rather than error.

Chapter 3's discussion of development of revenue sources for education noted in a historical context the causality of political phenomena wherein the intensely local/state nature of education is reflected in revenue systems. At the most basic level, it was noted that taxation has been a source of bitter contention throughout American history and that no other response can reasonably be expected, given human nature and the tradition of tax protest that has characterized the nation. Yet powerful tax systems have emerged by which schools derive vast revenues. Further, it was noted that while local responsibility for funding education has been intensely criticized for good reason, it is nonetheless irresponsible to fail to state that revenue systems' development has been consonant with assignment of responsibility for education. Likewise, the evolving nature of state responsibility for schools has been accompanied by state funding. Although these phenomena have not been precisely incremental, the data show revenue sources generally following assignment of responsibility. The lesson to be learned from this chapter is that while no perfect tax system can be constructed because it is the progeny of a political environment wherein insatiable needs compete for often poor revenues, there is much that can be done to provide the fairest tax system possible—a reality that can only flow from turning to revenue sources outside the local community for the support of schools.

The realities of problems in financing education were brought together in Chapter 4, which explored the dilemma of funding education in the 50 states. This discussion flowed intuitively from the previous chapter, where it was seen that absent a truly significant federal role, equal educational opportunity could not be provided without strong state partnership. As in prior chapters, it was again seen that present funding systems in the various states have their genesis in a political history that has generally struggled to keep pace with technological advancements in aid formulas designed to provide equitable distribution of finite resources. Although the aims of politics and technology have not maintained perfect alignment in a shifting and often ill-defined policy arena, the chapter nonetheless taught an important lesson by showing that there have been significant gains in equal educational opportunity as expressed by fiscal resources, despite adversity that can generally be attributed to lack of political readiness to adopt technologically superior funding schemes.

The culmination of these various chapters was found in Chapter 5, where a fifth harsh lesson was explored in the history of school finance litigation. As stated at the outset of that chapter, it is not surprising that the imperfect relationship of politics and equal opportunity has been the object of a bruising battle over how finite resources are distributed through state aid formulas. Although the analysis of litigation produced few incontrovertible victories, several truths emerged from decades of court struggles. Of paramount importance has been establishment of state responsibility for education. Of equal importance was the observation that state aid schemes are a product of litigation. Of final importance was the admission that litigation will continue, both because reform has not achieved all its ends and because it can never fully achieve a goal so elusive and ever-expansive as equal educational opportunity. The lesson to be finally learned is a cumulative one: that education is the key to socioeconomic mobility; that education's benefits are widely coveted in a capitalist society where success is defined by each person seeking to be more equal; and that the human condition naturally seeks to pay only the minimum price for any desirable commodity. The cumulation of these observations inevitably results in struggles for control of finite and precious resources. As a result, no perfect solution can be found, but the search for the best educational opportunity must be relentlessly pursued by all citizens, regardless of social or economic class.

The principles of school finance explored in the first five chapters provided the foundation on which to turn attention in Chapters 6–13 toward the more daily operationalization of school finance. Chapter 6, focusing on the concepts and practices that underlie budget planning, flowed naturally from the previous chapters and underscored their importance by identifying four basic concepts that govern school budget practices. First, without funds, there are no schools. Second, the purpose of a budget is to operationalize educational opportunity by converting raw dollars into programmatic priorities. Third, since budgets must be created, it is essential that administrators appreciate their own influence on achievement of equal opportunity through the budget process. Fourth, since money talks and because such communication occurs in a political arena, administrators and programs and budgets must be in continuous interface as no element may be severed without deleterious consequences. The lesson, then, was a powerful plea to administrators not to succumb to the temptation to view the budget as a mechanical accounting domain—rather, the budget is the principal planning system by which political and legal approval is secured for providing high quality education to all children.

Although the noble and moral dimensions of education have been stressed throughout this text, a seventh critical lesson was found in exploring the accounting and auditing function of school districts in Chapter 7. At stated at the outset of that chapter, good school administrators must first be good educators—but it is an equally important principle that effective education cannot occur without leaders who are highly skilled in fiscal management because without proper accounting, there is no control over the budget. As such, the chapter provided valuable lessons about the internal control functions of a district. Paramount in the discussion were two critical aspects of the accounting cycle: first, quality educational programs could never occur without wisely managed fiscal resources, and second, the educational process fundamentally depends on the fiduciary trust of administrators in this sensitive arena. In sum, the lesson to be learned was that even a technologically advanced aid scheme coupled with superior instructional programs would be utterly useless without technical and ethical competence in carrying out the educational and financial trust of the district—a trust that, as noted in the chapter and discussed in greater detail later, includes assessing the productivity of the district's educational mission.

Because education is extraordinarily labor-intensive, Chapter 8 examined the relationship of school finance and the personnel function of school districts. With school districts in a financial crisis and facing prohibitive costs in the future that will also demand more teachers to cope with the problems of disadvantaged populations, it is especially critical for administrators to be knowledgeable about the personnel function, which generally consumes about 80% of the average school district's budget. The chapter thus examined two seemingly opposing sets of skills. The first set explored the growth dimension of education wherein ever-increasing resources will need to be captured if education is to survive and succeed in an intensely competitive public tax marketplace. The second set of skills explored concomitant shrinkage that may occur—that is, problems in personnel compensation and other contemporary issues, such as merit pay, staff reduction, and due process concerns. The lesson of the chapter was thus twofold. First, administrators must be highly skilled on the human dimension, both ethically and legally. Second, administrators must have high skills relating to management of fiscal resources inasmuch as most district revenues are eventually converted into personnel services.

Chapter 9 explored the purchasing function of school districts beyond the commonly held view of purchasing as a clerical role. The modern sophistication of schools demands a myriad of purchased resources, and the complexity of the law is forbidding. The combination of these realities creates a grave responsibility for administrators at all levels wherein pitfalls are both subtle and devastating. As such, the chapter provided a valuable lesson in the legal basis of purchasing, the procedural aspects of the procurement process, and the operational aspects of purchasing, distribution, and control.

The critical nature of fiduciary responsibility was carried into a tenth lesson on risk management in Chapter 10. The chapter noted that education lawsuits are by no means limited to constitutional litigation over state aid formulas, as schools and administrators have come to operate in a high-stakes environment that literally sustains a segment of the legal profession. The chapter stressed that administrators are highly vulnerable in a maze of legal requirements and proscriptions and that all such liability ultimately carries fiscal implications through attorneys' fees and potential damages.

Because it is impossible to totally avoid risk, the lesson of the chapter was of paramount importance by carrying forward two messages. First, administrators must understand managing risks through awareness of vulnerability. Second, administrators must be knowledgeable about how to reduce and spread risks. In the context of an increasingly litigious society, these lessons must not be lost on a generation of new administrators who will face even greater risk for their acts of commission and omission.

A related lesson followed in Chapter 11, which examined the transportation and food service operations of school districts. Although many persons wrongly impute dullness to these functions, transportation and food service are vital fiscal operations of modern school districts. The point emphasized was that while the instructional mission of the school receives all deserved attention, instruction will be impaired if children are hungry or deprived of the means by which to travel to school. Relatedly, there is legal liability for these aspects of district operation. Neither transportation nor food service could operate except by wise fiscal management that purchases both goods and services. Thus, the lesson of this chapter should be clear: that schools are multifaceted complex fiscal organizations made up of interrelated parts that aid or hinder the central instructional mission. As such, all administrators benefit and survive by their working knowledge and skills in these and other operations.

The interrelationship of all facets of school district operation was carried into a twelfth lesson on capital outlay in Chapter 12. Although the nation has recently awakened to the crumbling physical infrastructure of education, the problems have reached epidemic proportions that will eventually require many billions of dollars to reconstruct America's school plant investment. Of critical perception to this chapter was the interrelationship of school facilities and equal educational opportunity—as one national organization stated: "From every corner have come reports, articles, speeches and goal statements about student achievement, unmet needs and education reform, . . . but all these pronouncements have been strangely silent about one essential ingredient . . . that affects every child's health, safety and ability to learn: the classroom."[2] In addition to these concerns, the increasingly complex maze of laws and instructional needs of children make a forbidding task of school plant planning and management. As such, the lesson of the chapter was threefold. First, facility planning and maintenance were viewed in a modern environment. Second, technical skills for demographic, capital program, and facility planning were provided. Third, some attention was provided to the maintenance and operation of facilities on a daily basis. The result, of course, is that all parts must work together to provide an effective learning environment for carrying out the instructional mission.

Technology was discussed in Chapter 13, This chapter was a fitting closure to the instructional purpose of this text—not because technology is the central focus of the book, but because it pointedly returns us to the single recognition that the purpose of schooling is productivity. While this does not deny a humane or social role for schools, it is to say that every structure discussed in the various chapters of this book eventually has only one purpose: improving educational outcomes for every child. While some reformers might argue otherwise, they must eventually be silenced by the simple question: *Of what good are schools if they make no difference?* Thus the chapter on technology returns us to the productivity model, which is in fact the basis for the discipline of school finance. The lesson to be learned from this chapter is therefore twofold. First, administrators must be knowledgeable about the ever-changing electronic environment of schools. Second and most importantly, administrators

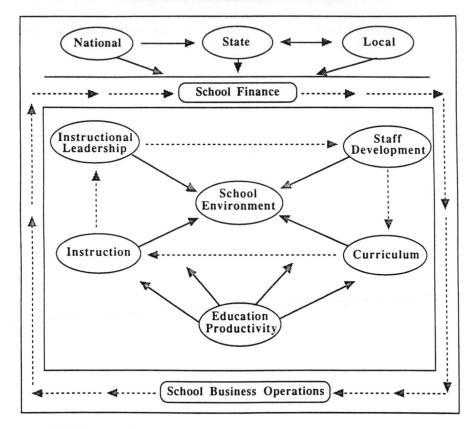

FIGURE 14.1   Education fiscal policy context

must be prepared to direct the power of technology toward enhancing educational productivity. Again the question is raised, of what good are schools if they make no difference? From an administrative perspective, while technology appears to offer a useful path in causing schools to effect genuine change, such technology will never be cost-free.

The final lesson of this text melds the lessons of every chapter into a unified whole. The predominant theme has been that school finance must be exorcised of its sterile preconceptions and that administrators must be invigorated by beliefs in the power of money and equipped with the skills needed to effect change through fiscal resource allocation. As may now be judged from the title of this textbook, school finance is *the* vital organ that supplies the essential nutrient (money) to an integrated and interdependent organism called schooling. The title rejects the historically dull view of school finance, calling instead for visionary leaders who will accept the challenge of financing schools in an intensely competitive (and sometimes adverse) climate. As such, this text is a call for fiscal leadership and a rejection of the impoverished view that school finance and school business management are best left to those who are ill-equipped to carry out the instructional mission of schools. While education is fortunate to have so many dedicated teaching professionals who give selflessly to children as tomorrow's best hope, altruism is not a sufficient condition to provide truly equal educational opportunity. As such, fiscal leadership must be entrusted only to those persons who see the fiscal dimensions of schooling as the enabling tool to unlocking every child's best future.

The importance of school finance and school business operations cannot be overestimated in either historical or future contexts. The successes of education are at root a direct function of improvement in resource allocation, and the failures of education are equally attributable to the imperfection of resource distribution design. If schools are to provide equal opportunity, school finance and fiscal operations must work in high coordination and sensitivity to concerns for equality and excellence—a goal that requires taking children where they are and recognizing that schools have failed when the instructional mission is not fulfilled for every child. There is no escape from the conclusion that money matters—a reality seen in Figure 14.1, in which the cycle is continuous and based in feedback loops that always return the focus to the global and local school finance/fiscal management policy arena. As stated in Chapter 5, if money is inadequate to improve education, its failure should be allowed to apply to all children equally. In the context of the productivity mission of schools, nothing less will suffice.

IMPLICATIONS FOR THE FUTURE

That nothing less than productivity can suffice is at once a frightening and heartening reality. When there are no longer any excuses, the failure of schools becomes starkly real in a nation that has become increasingly dependent on the educational engine to drive basic socioeconomic opportunity. Yet productivity as the central purpose of schooling is heartening because it is truth that defies the scoffing of those who argue that money makes no difference, and it is especially heartening that money can make a further difference if it is searchingly directed by strong demands for productivity. While productivity is difficult and ominously final when taken seriously, it is encouraging that the naysayers at the end of the twentieth century can be contradicted. Yet to do so requires courage uncommon to education. Although educators lament the demands of a focus on productivity, these demands represent unequaled opportunity and challenge. The future is ripe because the United States is approaching a new millennium while simultaneously engaged in a profound revolution that is reshaping its economic and social institutions. At least seven change drivers herald the new era and predict that schools will be more profoundly affected than any other institution, with enormous fiscal implications.[3]

The first change driver is found in the maturation of America. As seen in earlier chapters, America is simultaneously aging and growing younger. It is especially important to note how these trends act and react on schools of the future. First, the nation is predictably aging as more and more citizens with money move into retirement years. Second, however, America is dramatically aging as the baby boom generation moves into prime family- and asset-formation years. Third, the nation is growing younger—but as seen earlier, youth is vested in those without money and without historic majority backgrounds. The dichotomy is remarkable—the haves are retiring, the new haves have enjoyed a phenomenal standard of living, and a rapidly expanding generation of have-nots have become vocal about their inability to achieve the same standard of living. The combination is an older generation remembering an earlier America, a demanding present generation, and an emerging generation without the roots of advantaged economic lineage. Yet it is the latter group on which the economy will eventually depend. As such, schools are the vanguard of the future and the best opportunity for investing in continued national and individual prosperity.

A second change driver is seen in the new majority that can be called a mosaic society. As America matures, the countenance of the nation is changing so rapidly that it will never again resemble its historic self. Immigrants are increasingly populating American classrooms, giving rise to the need for a new educational system that will equip them to assume the weight of the future. Among the waves of change are alternative school configurations such as year-round schools, magnet schools, and multicultural and bilingual educational delivery systems. As stressed throughout this text, these needs are synonymous with the growth of an urban minority underclass. These realities have strong social and economic implications, as the fabric of society becomes more mosaic by forcing schools to train a labor force that likely cannot be taught by conventional methods. As such, schools are again the vanguard or the nemesis of America by their willingness and ability to constructively challenge the future headlong, where success can be defined as extensive investment in training these people to take their predestined place in society. Although quality education has never been truly cheap, it is painfully clear that the price of preserving a bright future will be very high in a society where difference—rather than similarity—is the major unifying theme.

A third change driver is found in the redefinition of individual and societal roles. Although the nation has long been a rich tapestry of nationalities that left their respective cultural mainstreams to pursue the American dream, individual and social roles have begun to blur even more as dense masses of people are thrust into close proximity in a finite landmass that no longer permits cloistering around communal mores. Although "the poor have always been with us," several phenomena have concentrated attention on this reality. First, it has become politically incorrect to argue against spending on social problems. Second, there has however been a shift in the last two decades toward more laissez-faire government wherein the private sector has begun to carry out contracts for services previously provided by government. Third, the states therefore have begun to take up some of this responsibility as the federal government has faded into a lesser role. The result is an odd mixture that portends heavily for schools in that since social problems must be addressed, schools are the best vehicle given their socioeconomic impact. In this strange scenario, momentum toward solution is both fragmented and focused on schools in a society that is being forced to abandon its fiercely rugged individualism. Again the price will be high as schools become the major tool by which factionalism and opportunity are redressed.

A fourth change driver that works in unison with all the foregoing is the increasing globalization of the nation. No longer able to engage in introspection, America is facing a future where movement of products, capital, and information is the new economic exchange. Beyond this apparent truth are still other indicators of globalization, as foreign ownership of America's industrial base is increasing at the same time that American firms are being moved offshore in search of cheap and efficient labor. Additionally, the economic power of America is no longer unchallenged as other nations develop mature economies and as cultural exchange and travel become more attractive. The implications for schools are powerful in that the nature of curricula and instructional delivery systems need to be redesigned and redirected—a reality that demands retraining and new faces to meet the future confidently. In a nation that must redefine itself internally to survive in the new world order, there is every reason to believe that the time for investing in education is now, and every sign indicates that investment must reach unprecedented heights if it is to effectively serve its anticipated outcome.

A fifth change driver can be found in the amalgamation of all the foregoing and in a trend that has merit of its own. While America is being profoundly reshaped by the overlay of other cultures on the family and home, these institutions are also being transformed from within. When cultural differences are added to the new family structure in which family members with divergent interests engage in unprecedented acts of autonomy, the results impact heavily on the custodial role of schools. This trend has been occurring for the last 20 years and appears to be accelerating rapidly into the foreseeable future, driven by low socioeconomic status of increasing numbers of nuclear and nontraditional families who derive basic financial maintenance from multiple employment. The implications for schools are great in that far more sweeping services and increased costs are looming, both in terms of sheer volume of clients and in terms of more expansive services that deal with both enrichment and response to dysfunctional and nontraditional families. In sum, the changes are leading to an increased custodial role for schools, and it is certain that the costs of family redefinition will ultimately be assigned in large part to the institution of education.

A sixth change driver is found in the shift from an industrial to an information-based economy. If it is a concern that working class people or economically and socially disadvantaged populations can only marginally function in an industrial economy, it must be of even greater concern to envision the new world order that is replacing the blue-collar system. The information economy fuels special concern about scientific literacy when it is recognized that global leadership in science and technology is quickly coming to determine economic superiority. For education, the implications are enormous for both pedagogy and preparing citizens for economic survival. The rapid increases in technological breakthroughs are expected to continue, wherein functional literacy will be redefined by telecommunications gateways based in video, audio, and data transmission. Traditional job skills will be of little use in a world that increasingly automates and that values only information processing skills. Indeed, learning itself will become the new instrument of commerce, leading to greater stratification of technological haves and have-nots. The implications for education are not complete until it is recognized that schooling will become a lifelong experience, both for learning and relearning in an age where obsolescence is the only permanent reality. The bottom line, then, is that this change-driver predicts that schooling will assume a lifelong parental/social/economic role.

Finally, a seventh change driver, known as the rebirth of social activism, is dramatically impacting education. While the integral thread of this book has been the value of education, there has been a parallel theme of the cyclical resurgence of social activism in the educational context. This reality is not born of political inclination, but rather from observations about modern life. As this book has focused much attention on history, it has shown that change follows political conception wherein freedom and opportunity have given rise to perpetual hopes and dreams. At the same time, it has been shown that hope never ceases to rise and that the search for the American dream is incessant. While the seemingly slow pace of political change is never satisfying to those who live at a particular moment, it has been equally evident that each era has achieved improbable dreams. But social opportunity for many has particularly been a phenomenon of the last 50 years. The result has been intense social activism on issues such as poverty and race and the environment, interspersed with eras of economic revitalization or entrenchment. Although change may be slow, freedom once tasted never dies, and education is the key to mobility. The outcome of this century's advances is social activism centered on education that will not be abandoned so that further change involving education is inevitable.

SUMMARY

On the threshold of a new millennium, the United States is poised for renewed greatness or bleak disintegration. Given history and the massive change drivers propelling the nation, bleakness will clearly follow if the difficult economic and social problems outlined in this text are not constructively resolved through equal educational opportunity. Greatness awaits, however, if the shining hope of America can be offered to every child. While the solutions will be complex, the alternative is deadly, making the question no longer whether there should be government intervention, but the extent to which government must go to achieve these goals. In a world in which democracy is so temporal and change is so permanent, the question must be answered *first* and *now,* because the future is here and the wrong solutions may lead to no future at all. In the end, the future depends on whether an appropriate education for every child is funded in such a manner as to provide an equal educational opportunity. To answer this call is the dilemma of modern school finance, where wise and strong fiscal leadership is the solution to a dynamic and volatile future.

Review Points

LESSONS FROM HISTORY

Education has represented different realities to different people, making the social and economic value of education highly differential in the population.

Despite these realities, education remains the key to a better life, both socially and economically.

The federal-state-local triad of responsibility for education developed largely by intent. As a result, critics may allege poor judgment, but must falter when claiming that lack of a central federal role was an oversight.

Administrators may expect reluctant payment of taxes, since the nation was founded in part on tax dissent; yet tax systems that are as fair as humanly possible will result in more willing compliance.

Inadequacy of local communities to fund quality schools has made external (state) support a modern inevitability. Although there is still room for improvement, modern state aid formulas represent significant equity gains.

Although much improvement is apparent, school finance will continue to be a source of strife and litigation—by virtue of seeking either improvement, perfection, or satisfaction of the politics of envy.

Educational opportunities are operationalized through school budgets, wherein the educational philosophies of local districts are ultimately made known in fiscal terms.

Accounting and auditing provide controls and protections of budgets and administrators, making it possible to secure the public trust and to guide and manage the educational goals of a district.

The impact of money on educational opportunity is seen most powerfully in purchasing personnel resources, making the finance/personnel relationship of paramount importance to administrators.

The vast legal and fiscal dimensions of the supply function require strong and skilled administrators.

Increasing litigation for liability also demands aggressive and sure leadership to protect the resources and reputations of districts and personnel.

The interrelatedness of all instructional and support functions in the educational mission of schools becomes evident when considering auxiliary services such as transportation and food services.

A similar interrelationship is found in financing capital needs of districts, where equal opportunities are conditioned in part by the nature and quality of school facilities.

On the threshold of the twenty-first century, technology for accountability and productivity can be expected to increasingly consume more energy and time.

IMPLICATIONS FOR THE FUTURE

Administrators must always finally recognize that the real purpose of schools is to make a difference in student outcomes—a difference that will have to be achieved in a different milieu than has historically been the reality.

As America matures, developing the new generation's skills will be increasingly important to economic stability.

America's new mosaic will increasingly demand new educational strategies to bring people into the economic and social mainstreams.

As society is redefined, schools may be the best vehicle for coordinating change, since they are the main source for transmitting socioeconomic status.

With increasing globalization, America is being challenged to maintain economic and cultural superiority.

Given rapid growth in underclasses, America's schools may need to encompass social and economic redress even more.

Schools must lead the way in preparing children to move from an industrial to an information-based economy.

Signs of resurging social activism may herald a new round of intense social and economic goals for schools.

Given the importance of education and the impact of money on educational opportunity, administrators must commit to wise and strong fiscal leadership if the nation is to survive and prosper in a changing and volatile future.

NOTES

1. Peter Drucker, *The New Realities* (New York: Harper & Row, 1989), ix.
2. American Association of School Administrators, *Schoolhouse in the Red: A National Study of School Facilities and Energy Use* (Arlington, Va.: American Association of School Administrators, 1991).
3. The change drivers discussed here are taken in part from several sources. See for example Alvin Toffler, *Power Shift: Knowledge, Wealth, and Violence at the Edge of the 21st Century* (New York: Bantam, 1990); Michael Wolf et al., *Where We Stand: Can America Make It in the Global Race for Wealth, Health, and Happiness?* (New York: Bantam, 1992).

ADDITIONAL READINGS

Drucker, Peter. *The New Realities.* New York: Harper & Row, 1989.

Toffler, Alvin. *Power Shift: Knowledge, Wealth, and Violence at the Edge of the 21st Century.* New York: Bantam, 1990.

Wolf, Michael, et al. *Where We Stand: Can America Make It in the Global Race for Wealth, Health, and Happiness?* New York: Bantam, 1992.

Index